Fourth Workshop on Arabic Natural Language Processing (WANLP 2019)

Florence, Italy
1 August 2019

ISBN: 978-1-5108-9112-8

ACL 2019

**The Fourth Arabic Natural Language Processing Workshop
WANLP 2019**

Proceedings of the Workshop

August 1, 2019
Florence, Italy

Preface

Assalamu 3alaykum, benvenuti a tutti! Welcome to the The Fourth Arabic Natural Language Processing Workshop (WANLP 2019) held at ACL 2019 in Florence, Italy.

A number of Arabic NLP (or Arabic NLP-related) workshops and conferences have taken place in the last few years, both in the Arab World and in association with international conferences. The Arabic NLP workshop at ACL 2019 follows in the footsteps of these previous efforts to provide a forum for researchers to share and discuss their ongoing work. This particular workshop is the fourth in a series, following the First Arabic NLP workshop held at EMNLP 2014 in Doha, Qatar; the Second Arabic NLP workshop held at ACL 2015 in Beijing, China; the Third Arabic NLP workshop held at EACL 2017 in Valencia, Spain. This workshop included a shared task on Arabic dialect identification. As opposed to previous shared tasks which focused on regional level dialect labeling, this shared task is the first to target a large set of dialect labels at the city and country levels.

We received 49 main workshop submissions, out of which 22 were accepted, 23 were rejected, and 4 were withdrawn. All main workshop submissions were reviewed by at least three reviewers. The shared task was also a success with 17 teams participating. The shared task system descriptions (short) papers were reviewed by two reviewers each and will be included in the proceedings and presented during the workshop as posters. A long paper describing the shared task was submitted as part of the main workshop and got accepted for publication.

The acceptance rate of 49% in the main workshop, the quantity of the main workshop submissions (highest number of submissions in this workshop series), the shared task success, and the high quality of all contributions are strong indicators that there is a continued need for this kind of dedicated Arabic NLP workshop.

We would like to acknowledge all the hard work of the submitting authors and thank the reviewers for the valuable feedback they provided. We hope these proceedings will serve as a valuable reference for researchers and practitioners in the field of Arabic NLP and NLP in general.

Wassim El-Hajj, General Chair, on behalf of the organizers of the workshop.

Organizers

General chair

Wassim El-Hajj, American University of Beirut, Lebanon

Program Chairs

Lamia Hadrich Belguith, Sfax University, Tunisia
Fethi Bougares, University of Le Mans, France
Walid Magdy, University of Edinburgh, Scotland
Imed Zitouni, Microsoft

Publication Chairs

Nadi Tomeh, LIPN, Université Paris 13, Sorbonne Paris Cité
Mahmoud El-Haj, Lancaster University, England

Publicity Chair

Wajdi Zaghouani, Hamad Bin Khalifa University, Qatar

Ex-General Chair / Advisor

Nizar Habash, New York University Abu Dhabi, UAE

Advisory Committee

Hend Al-Khalifa, King Saud University, KSA
Houda Bouamor, Fortia Financial Solutions, France
Fethi Bougares, University of Le Mans, France
Kareem Darwish, Qatar Computing Research Institute, Qatar
Mona Diab, The George Washington University, USA
Mahmoud El-Haj, Lancaster University, England
Wassim El-Hajj, American University of Beirut, Lebanon
Nizar Habash, New York University Abu Dhabi, UAE
Nadi Tomeh, LIPN, Université Paris 13, Sorbonne Paris Cité
Wajdi Zaghouani, Hamad Bin Khalifa University , Qatar

Invited Keynote Speaker

Ahmed Ali, Qatar Computing Research Institute (QCRI)

Program Committee

Abdelali Ahmed, Qatar Computing Research Institute, Qatar
Abdul-Mageed, Muhammad , UBC, Canada
Afli Haithem, Cork Institute of Technology, Ireland
Al Sallab Ahmad, Faculty of Enginneeing, Cairo university
Ali Ahmed, Qatar Computing Research Institute, Qatar
Alkhalifa Hend, King Saud University, Saudi Arabia
Alowsiheq Areeb, Imam University, KSA
Al-Twairesh Nora, King Saud University, Saudi Arabia
Alzahrani Salha, Taif University, Saudi Arabia
Aransa Walid, University du Maine, Le Mans, France
Attia Mohammed, George Washington University
B. Al-Said Almoataz, Cairo University, Egypt
Badaro Gilbert, American University of Beirut
Barrón-Cedeño Alberto, Qatar Computing Research Institute, Qatar
Ben-Hamadou Abdelmajid, University of Sfax, Tunisia
Bouamor Houda, Fortia Financial Solutions, France
Bougares Fethi, Le Mans University, France
Bouzoubaa Karim, Mohammad V University, Morocco
Buckwalter Tim, University of Maryland, USA
Cavalli-Sforza Violetta, Al Akhawayn University, Morocco
Chafik Aloulou, Univeristé de Sfax, Tunisia
Choukri Khalid, ELDA, European Language Resource Association, France
Darwish Kareem, Qatar Computing Research Institute, Qatar
Dayel Abeer, King Saud University, Saudi Arabia
Diab Mona, George Washington University, USA
Dichy Joseph, Université Lyon 2 , France
El-Haj Mahmoud, Lancaster University, UK
El-Hajj Wassim, American University of Beirut, Lebanon
Elbassuoni Shady, American University of Beirut
Elkahky Ali, Google AI
Ellouze Mariem, University of Sfax, Tunisia
Elmadany AbdelRahim, Jazan Univeristy
Elmahdy Mohamed, Qatar University, Qatar
Elsayed Tamer, Qatar University, Qatar
Emam Ossama, IBM, USA
Eskander Ramy, Columbia University, USA
Fahmy Aly, Cairo University, Egypt
Farghaly Ali, Monterey Peninsula College, USA
Gargouri Bilel, University of Sfax, Tunisia
Ghannay Sahar, LIUM Laboratory, France
Ghneim Nada, Higher Institute for Applied Sciences and Technology, Syria
Habash Nizar, New York University Abu Dhabi, UAE

Haddad Bassam, University of Petra, Jordan
Hadrich Belguith Lamia, University of Sfax, Tunisia
Hajj Hazem, American University of Beirut, Lebanon
Hamada Salwa, Cairo University, Egypt
Hasanain Maram, Qatar University
Jarrar Mustafa, Bir Zeit University, Palestine
Khadivi Shahram, Tehran Polytechnic, Iran
Maamouri Mohamed, Linguistic Data Consortium, USA
Magdy Walid, University of Edinburgh, Scotland
Mazroui Azzeddine, University Mohamed I, Morocco
Mechti Seif, University of Sfax, Tunisia
Medhaffar salima, Le Mans University, France
Megerdoomian Karine, The MITRE Corporation, USA
Mohamed Emad, Suez Canal University, Egypt
Mourad Ghassan, Lebanese University, Lebanon
Mubarak Hamdy, Qatar Computing Research Institute, Qatar
Nakov Preslav, Qatar Computing Research Institute, Qatar
Nasr Alexis, University of Marseille, France
Nwesri Abdelsalam, University of Tripoli, Libya
Oflazer Kemal, Carnegie Mellon University Qatar, Qatar
Rafea Ahmed, The American University in Cairo, Egypt
Rambow Owen, Columbia University, USA
Rashwan Mohsen, RDI, Egypt
Refaee Eshrag, Jazan University, Saudi Arabia
Salameh Mohammad, Carnegie Mellon University, Qatar
Sawaf Hassan, eBay Inc., USA
Shaalan Khaled, The British University in Dubai, UAE
Shaban Khaled, Qatar University, Qatar
Smrž Otakar, ÚFAL, Czech Republic
Suwaileh Reem, Qatar University, Qatar
Tomeh Nadi, University Paris 13, France
Trigui Omar, University of Sousse, Tunisia
Vogel Stephan, Qatar Computing Research Institute, Qatar
Wray Samantha, Qatar Computing Research Institute, Qatar
Zaghouani Wajdi, Hamad Bin Khalifa University, Qatar
Zerrouki Taha, University of Bouira, Algeria
Zitouni Imed, Microsoft Research, USA
Zribi Ines, Sfax University, Tunisia

Table of Contents

Conference Program

Thursday, August 1, 2019

8:30–8:40   *Opening Remarks*
Wassim El-Hajj

8:40–9:30   *Invited Keynote*
Ahmed Ali

9:30–10:20   Session 1: Machine Translation

9:30–9:55   *Incremental Domain Adaptation for Neural Machine Translation in Low-Resource Settings*
Marimuthu Kalimuthu, Michael Barz and Daniel Sonntag

9:55–10:20   *Morphology-aware Word-Segmentation in Dialectal Arabic Adaptation of Neural Machine Translation*
Ahmed Tawfik, Mahitab Emam, Khaled Essam, Robert Nabil and Hany Hassan

10:20–10:30   The MADAR Shared Task Overview

The MADAR Shared Task on Arabic Fine-Grained Dialect Identification
Houda Bouamor, Sabit Hassan and Nizar Habash

10:30–11:00   Coffee Break

11:00–12:40   Session 2: Selected Topics

11:00–11:25   *POS Tagging for Improving Code-Switching Identification in Arabic*
Mohammed Attia, Younes Samih, Ali Elkahky, Hamdy Mubarak, Ahmed Abdelali and Kareem Darwish

11:25–11:50   *Syntax-Ignorant N-gram Embeddings for Sentiment Analysis of Arabic Dialects*
Hala Mulki, Hatem Haddad, Mourad Gridach and Ismail Babaoğlu

11:50–12:15   *ArbEngVec : Arabic-English Cross-Lingual Word Embedding Model*
Raki Lachraf, El Moatez Billah Nagoudi, Youcef Ayachi, Ahmed Abdelali and Didier Schwab

12:15–12:40   *Homograph Disambiguation through Selective Diacritic Restoration*
Sawsan Alqahtani, Hanan Aldarmaki and Mona Diab

12:40–14:00   *Lunch*

14:00–14:50   **Session 3: Applications**

14:00–14:25   *Arabic Named Entity Recognition: What Works and What's Next*
Liyuan Liu, Jingbo Shang and Jiawei Han

14:25–14:50   *hULMonA: The Universal Language Model in Arabic*
Obeida ElJundi, Wissam Antoun, Nour El Droubi, Hazem Hajj, Wassim El-Hajj
and Khaled Shaban

14:50–15:30   *Workshop Poster Boaster*
2.5 minutes per poster

15:30–16:00   *Coffee Break*

16:00–18:00   **Poster Session**

+   ***Posters: Main Workshop Papers***

Neural Arabic Question Answering
Hussein Mozannar, Elie Maamary, Karl El Hajal and Hazem Hajj

Neural Models for Detecting Binary Semantic Textual Similarity for Algerian and MSA
Wafia Adouane, Jean-Philippe Bernardy and Simon Dobnik

Constrained Sequence-to-sequence Semitic Root Extraction for Enriching Word Embeddings
Ahmed El-Kishky, Xingyu Fu, Aseel Addawood, Nahil Sobh, Clare Voss and Jiawei Han

En-Ar Bilingual Word Embeddings without Word Alignment: Factors Effects
Taghreed Alqaisi and Simon O'Keefe

Segmentation for Domain Adaptation in Arabic
Mohammed Attia and Ali Elkahky

Assessing Arabic Weblog Credibility via Deep Co-learning
Chadi Helwe, Shady Elbassuoni, Ayman Al Zaatari and Wassim El-Hajj

Incremental Domain Adaptation for Neural Machine Translation in Low-Resource Settings

Marimuthu Kalimuthu   **Michael Barz**   **Daniel Sonntag**
German Research Center for Artificial Intelligence (DFKI),
Saarland Informatics Campus D3_2, 66123 Saarbrücken
{marimuthu.kalimuthu,michael.barz,daniel.sonntag}@dfki.de

Abstract

We study the problem of *incremental domain adaptation* of a generic neural machine translation model with limited resources (e.g., budget and time) for human translations or model training. In this paper, we propose a novel query strategy for selecting "unlabeled" samples from a new domain based on *sentence embeddings* for Arabic. We accelerate the fine-tuning process of the generic model to the target domain. Specifically, our approach estimates the informativeness of instances from the target domain by comparing the distance of their sentence embeddings to embeddings from the generic domain. We perform machine translation experiments (Ar-to-En direction) for comparing a *random sampling* baseline with our new approach, similar to active learning, using two small update sets for simulating the work of human translators. For the prescribed setting we can save more than 50% of the annotation costs without loss in quality, demonstrating the effectiveness of our approach.

1 Introduction

Neural Machine Translation (NMT) is the task of translating text from one language (source) to another (target) using, most commonly, Recurrent Neural Networks (RNN), specifically the Encoder-Decoder or Sequence-to-Sequence models (Sutskever et al., 2014; Cho et al., 2014). Recently, NMT has become a quite popular and effective alternative to traditional Phrase-Based Statistical Machine Translation (PBSMT) (Koehn et al., 2003). Major problems that arise include very high cost of training NMT models for new domains and that abundant parallel corpora are required for this task: the standard encoder-decoder models with attention have been shown to perform poorly in low-resource settings (Koehn and Knowles, 2017). Sufficient data might not be available for all languages due to resource restrictions, particularly for resource-poor languages. Hence, we are in need of cost-effective adaptation techniques that transfer existing knowledge to new domains as much as possible.

A recently proposed approach for domain adaptation filters generic corpora based on sentence embeddings of a potentially low amount of in-domain samples to train domain-specific models from scratch (Wang et al., 2017). However, the problem of time- and resource-consuming training still remains which is unsuitable for incremental model updates.

Fine-tuning can accelerate the training process because it transfers knowledge from a pre-trained *generic* model to a new domain and, hence, requires less parallel training samples. However, respective differences in contents and writing style can reduce machine translation quality, if they are not properly addressed.

Recent approaches include fine-tuning with mixed batches containing in- and out-of-domain samples (Chu et al., 2017) and with different regularization methods for differing amounts of new samples for English → German and English → Russian (Barone et al., 2017). The findings of Barone et al. (2017) suggest that there is an "approximately logarithmic relation between the size of in-domain training set and improvement in BLEU score". We want to find out whether incremental model training can be accelerated using an advanced query strategy for sample selection. Previous works on incremental machine translation include cache-based computer aided translation tools (Nepveu et al., 2004), active learning techniques for interactive statistical machine translation (González-Rubio et al., 2012), interactive visualizations for understanding and manipulating attention weights and beam search parameters in NMT (Lee et al., 2017), and domain adap-

Proceedings of the Fourth Arabic Natural Language Processing Workshop, pages 1–10
Florence, Italy, August 1, 2019. ©2019 Association for Computational Linguistics

tation through user interactions (Peris and Casacuberta, 2018).

In this work, we implement a new query strategy for selecting "unlabeled" instances from a target domain and investigate its effect on fine-tuning a generic NMT model. We borrow techniques and terms from the active learning domain (Settles, 2010): a *query strategy* is a method for selecting instances from a pool of unlabeled data that lead to a high information gain when used for training the machine learning model under consideration. Selected instances are labeled by an oracle which can be a human. Iteratively including the most informative instances, labeled on demand, has been shown to increase the model performance while using the same amount of training data. Our proposed methods for domain adaptation in NMT include query strategies that consider untranslated sentences as unlabeled instances. We simulate a human oracle by using parallel corpora in the evaluation, but we do not consider incremental updates for the query strategy. This is of interest for crowd-based domain-adaptation with limited resources as described in (Barz et al., 2018b), in particular, because our method only requires monolingual data for filtering (see Figure 1).

We compare random sampling as a naïve baseline strategy with our novel method based on distances between sentence embeddings. We estimate the informativeness of instances from the target domain by comparing the distances of their sentence embeddings to the embeddings of the generic domain. For computing the sentence embeddings, we present AraSIF: we adapted the methodology presented by Arora et al. (2017), which is known to capture the semantics of sentences well, to work with Arabic. In our experiments, we use existing parallel corpora for simulating human workers: The MEDAR[1] and GlobalVoices dataset (Tiedemann, 2012) are considered as new target domains which mainly concern the domain of *climate change* and *politics*, respectively. The LDC Newswire parallel corpus is used as the dataset for training *generic* domain model. We fine-tune this *generic* NMT model using different amounts of samples from a new domain and varying training epoch settings while observing the BLEU score (Papineni et al., 2002) on a held-out in-domain test set. Our hypothesis is that the proposed novel query strategy can effec-

tively reduce the number of fine-tuning samples required without hampering the translation quality when compared to the baseline.

The remainder of this paper is organized as follows: Section 2 provides an overview on related works, section 3 describes the NMT system and considered query strategies. In section 4, we describe our experiment, and we report the results in section 5. The results are discussed in section 6 and we conclude our work in section 7.

2 Related Work

Almahairi et al. (2016) presented their first result on AR–EN bidirectional NMT, showing that NMT models outperform traditional PBSMT models when they are tested on out-of-domain test data. This result motivates us to study domain adaptation of NMT models rather than PBSMT models.

Several approaches are proposed for domain adaptation in the context of statistical and neural machine translation. Wang et al. (2017) show a way to adapt existing corpora to new domains using learned sentence embeddings for the source language of an NMT model to identify training samples that are close to the new domain. This method allows us to train NMT models for new domains without requiring a parallel corpus in that domain, but models need to be trained from scratch. Chu et al. (2017) present a method called *"mixed fine-tuning"* where fine-tuning is performed with mini-batches composed of a mix of in- and out-of-domain parallel samples to address the problem of overfitting to the new domain. Barone et al. (2017) investigate regularization methods for domain adaptation in NMT. Their findings indicate that BLEU scores increase logarithmically with an increasing amount of in-domain training data. Peris and Casacuberta (2018) implement an online domain adaptation method based on user interactions on the sub-word level. In an experiment, simulating such interactions with available public corpora, they could show that their online learning approach successfully improves word error rates for EN-to-DE and EN-to-FR translations.

González-Rubio et al. (2012) present different active learning techniques that shall reduce human workload in interactive statistical machine translation. They consider three query strategies for selecting the most informative sentences for being translated by humans: a random sampling base-

---

[1] http://medar.info

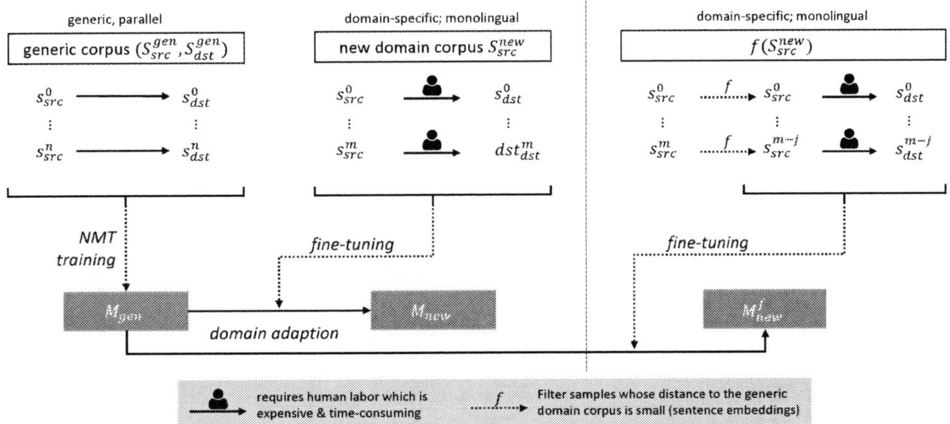

Figure 1: We focus on domain adaptation of a generic NMT model M_{gen} with humans-in-the-loop that translate monolingual data of the new domain with limited resources. We simulate crowd-translated content using two parallel corpora S^{new} representing data of new domains for training the adapted model M_{new}. We propose an advanced query strategy for selecting sentences from S^{new} that need to be translated by their similarity to the generic corpus.

line, rare n-gram sampling, and a sampling based on word confidences. In a recent work, Lam et al. (2018) suggest to incorporate human judgments on partial translations as reinforcement signal for improving NMT models and evaluate it in a simulation experiment with existing parallel corpora. For reducing human workload, they suggest an entropy-based method to trigger human judgments similar to active learning approaches with human oracles.

We focus on a query strategy for domain adaptation of NMT models based on active learning. We consider settings in which human workers provide new training data (Barz et al., 2018b,a; Green et al., 2015) for domains with no or only little parallel corpora due to, for instance, budget constraints. Our experiment includes random sampling as a baseline similar to González-Rubio et al. (2012) and an advanced sentence selection strategy based on distances between sentence embeddings that also encode the semantics of a sentence (Arora et al., 2017), adapted for Arabic.

3 Method

We implement a baseline query strategy (random sampling) and an advanced query strategy (see 3.3) for selecting training samples which are used for fine-tuning a generic NMT model. In this section, we describe the applied NMT model and the generic training process, as well as the two query strategies used in the domain adaptation process.

3.1 Model Architecture and Training

We use the TensorFlow implementation of NMT[2] (Luong et al., 2017) configured as an 8-layered bidirectional RNN with standard LSTM cells in each layer and residual connections between the layers. We use the same architecture for both, generic model training and fine-tuning tasks. The model is trained[3] with vanilla SGD for $350k$ iterations with a batch size of 50 and a dropout rate of 0.2. The initial learning rate is set to 1.0 and a decay factor of 0.5 is applied after every $1k$ iterations starting from $170k$ iterations. We use the standard hyperparameters provided in the NMT framework and set the vocabulary size to $32k$ for both Arabic and English. We train the generic model (M_{gen}) for one week using the LDC corpus (S^{gen}) (see Figure 1) and use the resulting checkpoint for all of our fine-tuning experiments.

3.2 Datasets and Preprocessing

In our experiment, we use the LDC Newswire corpus (Munteanu and Marcu, 2005) and two publicly available datasets, MEDAR and GlobalVoices. The corpus statistics are summarized in Table 1. The LDC Newswire parallel corpus (Ar-En) is used for training a *generic* model and the MEDAR and GlobalVoices datasets for *domain-specific* fine-tuning. We include datasets on two

---

[2]https://github.com/tensorflow/nmt

[3]All experiments were performed on an Ubuntu machine (Intel i7-5960X) with 8 cores and 2 GTX-1080 graphics cards

Corpus	Sentence Pairs	Domain	Usage
LDC Newswire	1.3M	Generic	Generic model training
MEDAR	0.5k	Climate Change	Domain specific fine-tuning
GlobalVoices	37k	Politics, Human Rights	Domain specific fine-tuning

Table 1: Details of datasets that we used in our experiments.

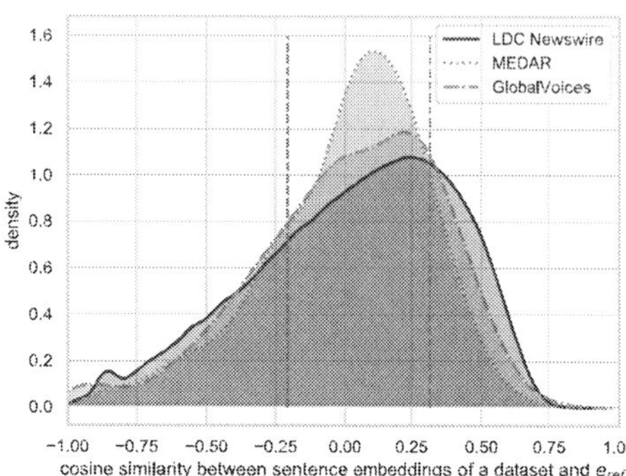

Figure 2: Kernel density estimates for the distributions of distances (cosine similarity) between sentence embeddings of each considered dataset and e_{ref}, the mean of sentence embeddings of the dataset used for training of the generic translation model. The gray dotted lines represent the 25% and the 75% percentile of the distance distribution for the generic model.

different genres to investigate whether our findings generalize irrespective of the domain of the fine-tuning set. To reduce noise in the data, we clean the datasets by discarding instances with mixed tokens (i.e. English sentences containing Arabic words or Arabic sentences containing English words). This step removes around 0.01%, 1.2%, and 10.14% of sentence pairs from LDC Newswire, MEDAR, and GlobalVoices datasets respectively. Further preprocessing steps of our system pipeline include normalization and tokenization[4] of the sentences and generation of *byte pair encodings* (BPE)[5] (Sennrich et al., 2016) for the tokenized sentences and the vocabulary.

3.3 Query Strategies for Sample Selection

For model adaptation in limited resource settings, it is desirable to reduce the number of samples from the target domain and, thus, the required time and cost for receiving human translations. Our goal is to develop a query strategy for selecting the most informative update samples, sim-

ilar to the active learning paradigm. We propose a method that estimates the informativeness of a sample based on its similarity to the generic corpus using sentence embeddings. We exclude semantically overlapping parts from the new corpus which reduces the amount of training samples that need to be translated by human labor and that need to be included in model training (see Figure 1). We refer to this method as fine-tuning with *advanced sampling*. In addition, we implement a baseline method which selects all samples from a new domain in random order (fine-tuning with *random sampling*).

For our advanced sampling method, we use *smooth inverse frequency* (SIF)-based sentence embeddings (Arora et al., 2017) extended for Arabic which we refer to as AraSIF (see Section 3.4). It encodes sentences from the source language $s \in S_{src}$ into a 300-dimensional vector e_s:

$$e_{sif} : S_{src} \to \mathbb{R}^{300}, s \mapsto e_s$$

Arora et al. (2017) show that SIF-based embeddings perform well for many semantic textual similarity tasks. This implies that the sentences which are close to each other in the embedding space can be considered to be semantically similar. We estimate the informativeness of a sample for domain adaptation based on the semantic similarity of two sentences. We use the cosine distance d between two sentence embeddings e_s and $e_{s'}$ as a proxy for semantic similarity:

$$d : \mathbb{R}^{300 \times 2} \to [-1, 1], (e_s, e_{s'}) \mapsto d_{s,s'}$$

Hereby, the mean of all sentence embeddings of the generic corpus $S_{src}^{gen} \subset S_{src}$ serves as the reference point e_{ref} in the sentence embedding space for comparing sentences from other corpora:

$$e_{ref} = mean(e_{sif}(S_{src}^{gen})), e_{ref} \in \mathbb{R}^{300}$$

Calculating the cosine similarity between all samples of a new domain $S_{src}^{new} \subset S_{src}$ and this

---

[4] https://github.com/moses-smt/mosesdecoder
[5] https://github.com/rsennrich/subword-nmt

reference point, results in a distribution of distances indicating the semantic similarity or dissimilarity of samples from the new domain to the generic domain. We show the distributions for all considered datasets in terms of a kernel density estimate in Figure 2: MEDAR and GlobalVoices as new domains and LDC Newswire as generic reference domain. Initially, we anticipated the target domain corpora to partially lie outside of the reference distribution, but the new corpora rather seem to be more specific subsets of the generic domain. Therefore, we select training samples for our fine-tuning process from the new domains that belong to the long-tail of the distance distribution of the generic domain corpus. We expect the informativeness of a new sample s to be high, if it is underrepresented in the generic domain dataset in terms of semantic similarity to e_{ref}, this is if $d_{s,e_{ref}}$ is high. The interval boundaries that frame the longtail are the only parameters that need to be defined for this approach. We use the 25% and 75% percentiles of the distance distribution of the generic domain to define these outer regions (see dotted vertical lines in Figure 2).

3.4 AraSIF: Arabic Sentence Embeddings

To obtain sentence embeddings for Arabic sentences we propose AraSIF. We use SIF[6] with AraVec[7] (Soliman et al., 2017), a Word2Vec pretrained model that is trained on 1.8M Arabic Wikipedia articles with a total vocabulary size of 662k. SIF is based on word weights for computing embeddings, for which we consider all tokens with a frequency count of at least 200. We preprocess the Wikipedia articles on which AraVec was trained on, for computing the word frequency. In addition, SIF expects the word embedding to be in GloVe embedding format. Hence, we convert the AraVec word embeddings from Word2Vec to GloVe format. The code for AraSIF is publicly available at *DFKI Interactive Machine Learning* repository on GitHub.

4 Experiment

We conduct a simulation experiment for investigating the effectiveness of our advanced query strategy in reducing the required amount of update samples for adapting an NMT model to a new domain. Our approach selects samples using mono-

[6]https://github.com/PrincetonML/SIF
[7]https://github.com/bakrianoo/aravec

epochs	1	5	10	20
n_t	T_{sgd}	T_{sgd}	T_{sgd}	T_{sgd}
50	1	5	10	20
100	2	10	20	40
150	3	15	30	60
200	4	20	40	80
250	5	25	50	100
300	6	30	60	120
350	7	35	70	140
400	8	40	80	160

Table 2: Considered combinations of update set sizes (n_t) and SGD updates or iterations (T_{sgd}) used for fine-tuning.

lingual information only, which can be assumed to be available without investing resources. For this, we compare the translation quality when fine-tuning a model with *random sampling* and when fine-tuning it with a reduced number of update samples resulting from our *advanced sampling*. Our generic NMT model M_{gen} is adapted to two new domains, represented by the GlobalVoices and the MEDAR datasets, using both query strategies. We include a varying number of epochs for identifying good training parameters. We hypothesize that our advanced query strategy for sample selection can effectively reduce the number of fine-tuning samples without hampering the translation quality when compared to the baseline.

5 Evaluation Procedure

We perform the simulation experiment with two new domain datasets and observe the impact of different parameters on domain adaptation of the generic NMT model using small amounts of new samples. These can be considered to stem from human workers, e.g., professional translators or crowdworkers. Considered parameters include the number of training samples in the update set n_t and the number of training epochs e. The number of epochs defines the number of training iterations: The number of Stochastic Gradient Descent (SGD) updates, denoted by T_{sgd}, is computed by:

$$T_{sgd} = \left\lceil \frac{n_t}{|S|} \right\rceil \cdot e$$

where $|S|$ is the mini-batch size which we set to 50 throughout our experiments, n_t is the number of sentence pairs in the *update set*, and e is the number of epochs. Table 2 provides an overview of all considered configurations.

The update sets used for model adaptation are generated from either MEDAR or GlobalVoices dataset, after excluding a static test set of 100 sentences for each. Both update sets are constrained to a maximum sample size of 400 to allow a fair comparison (this is the maximum size for MEDAR, see table 1). Further, we assume that the amount of data from the new domain might be small due to resource constraints or scarcity.

For the *random sampling* case, we select all 400 samples from each of the datasets in a random order and use it to adapt our generic model for all parameter configurations in Table 2. Samples 1 to 50 of the update set are used for training the $n_t = 50$ model for all epochs. The model fine-tuning is continued with samples 51 to 100 for the $n_t = 100$ model for all epochs, and so on. Considering the stochastic nature of SGD, we repeat the experiment 5 times and report the average scores on the respective test sets, instead of providing a point estimate. We observe the training times on the update set and the BLEU scores (Papineni et al., 2002) on the test set as a dependent variable.

For our *advanced sampling* strategy, we select a subset of all training samples for both datasets using the filter mechanism described above. We include a sentence s, if its cosine distance d to e_{ref} is smaller than the 25% percentile (-0.208) or larger than the 75% percentile (0.317) of the generic distance distribution (see Figure 2). This leaves us with 135 fine-tuning samples for MEDAR and 169 for GlobalVoices from the original 400 samples. We consider the same set of parameters than before with the difference that the size of the update set n_t is limited to the reduced number of samples.

5.1 Results

In this section, we present the results of our fine-tuning experiments for adapting the generic model with different sampling strategies. We use an increasing number of update samples (n_t), different epoch configurations (e) and two new domain datasets. The generic baseline model M_{gen} achieves a reference BLEU score of 18.6 for MEDAR and 13.4 for GlobalVoices. We used the same test set which we have used for evaluating the fine-tuned model.

Figure 3 summarizes the BLEU scores for all parameter settings and both new domains concerning the *random sampling* condition. For MEDAR, we can observe a monotonic improvement in BLEU score for increasing numbers of samples n_t in the update set for all epoch configurations. However, compared to the reference score of 18.6, only $e = 1$ and $e = 5$ achieve meaningful improvements: we can observe an improvement after fine-tuning with first two mini-batches. Higher numbers for e (10, 20) result in lower BLEU scores than the reference, also when including all samples ($n_t = 400$). Only for $e = 10$ and $n_t = [350, 400]$ we observe a BLEU score slightly better than the reference model. The best BLEU score on the MEDAR test set is achieved using $n_t = 400$ and $e = 5$ with a score of 19.39. Averaged over 5 repetitions of the experiment, the runtime ranges between $59s$ for $n_t = 50$ and $68s$ for $n_t = 400$ for $e = 1$. All other configurations require longer training times. For GlobalVoices, we observe a monotonic improvement with increasing number of samples n_t for $e \in \{1, 5\}$. Higher numbers for the epoch configuration result in a monotonic deterioration of BLEU score. In contrast to the models adapted to MEDAR, training with $e \in \{10, 20\}$ yields better results than the reference score of 13.4 for small n_t. Yet, due to the negative trend in BLEU scores, models with these epoch configurations fall below the reference score. The best BLEU score on the GlobalVoices test set is achieved using $n_t = 100$ and $e = 10$ with 14.36. Averaged over 5 trainings, the runtime ranges between $62s$ for $n_t = 50$ and $122s$ for $n_t = 400$. For $n_t \geq 200$, we observe better BLEU scores than the reference model for $e = 1$ and $e = 5$, where the training times for $e = 1$ grow considerably slower than for $e = 5$. Here, the training times range between $49s$ for $n_t = 50$ and $66s$ for $n_t = 400$.

Figure 4 summarizes the BLEU scores for all considered settings and domains for our *advanced sampling* condition. For MEDAR, we observe improvements in BLEU scores similar to the random sampling condition. All epoch configurations, except for $e = 1$, achieve scores higher than the reference (18.6) starting from the first update set. With the advanced sample selection, the best score of 19.34 is achieved using $n_t = 135$ and $e = 20$. Using $e = 1$ for varying number of samples (n_t) yields BLEU scores which are slightly lower than the reference BLEU score of 18.6. Averaged over 5 trainings, the runtime ranges between $54s$ and $58s$ for $e = 1$ and between $59s$

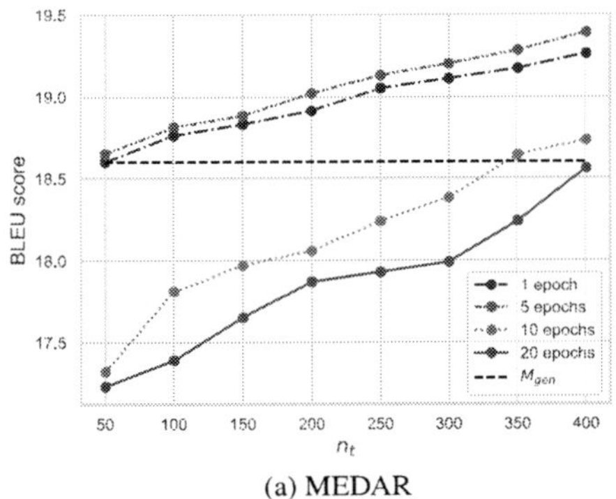
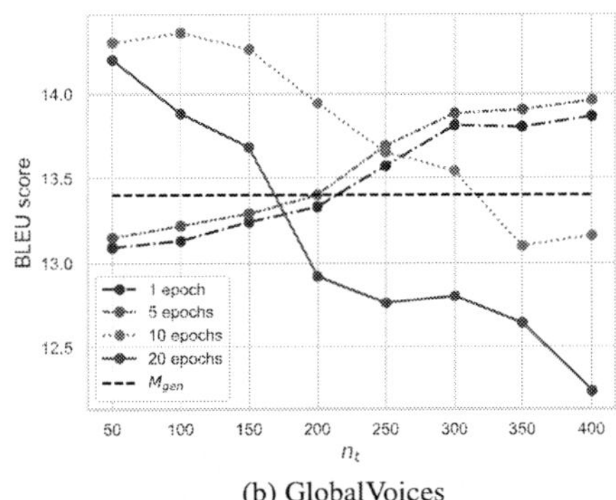

(a) MEDAR (b) GlobalVoices

Figure 3: BLEU scores of fine-tuned NMT models for MEDAR and GlobalVoices corpora with *random sampling* for varying sizes of the update set (n_t) and different number of training epochs (e).

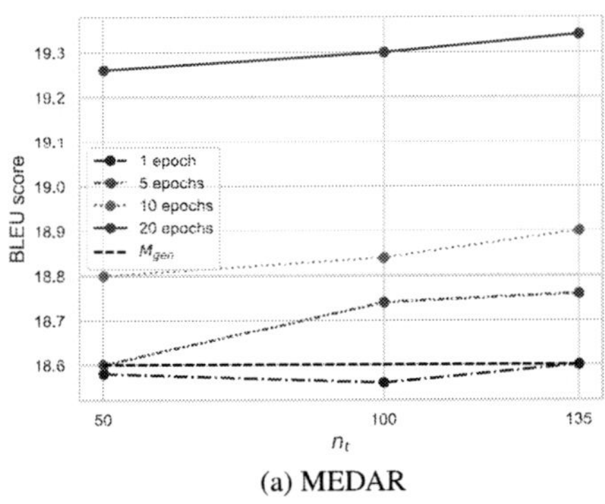
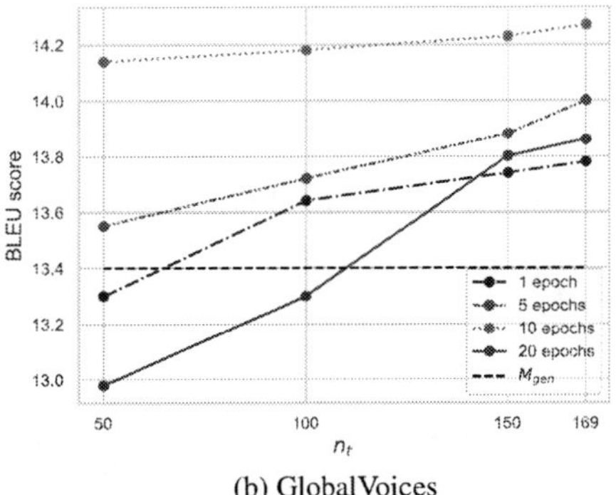

(a) MEDAR (b) GlobalVoices

Figure 4: BLEU scores of fine-tuned NMT models for MEDAR and GlobalVoices corpora with *advanced sampling* for varying sizes of the update set (n_t) and different number of training epochs (e).

and $70s$ for $e = 5$. For GlobalVoices, we obtain the best score of 14.27 with $e = 10$ which is comparable to $e = 10$ and $n_t = 100$ in the *random sampling* condition. For $e \in \{5, 10\}$, we observe better scores compared to the random sampling condition, for all update set sizes n_t. In addition, with our advanced sampling, we always observe a monotonic increase in BLEU score for all epoch configurations and increasing number of samples in the update set n_t, in contrast to the epoch configurations $e \in \{10, 20\}$ for the random sampling condition where we observe a decreasing trend in BLEU scores. The runtimes are similar to training times of MEDAR models.

6 Discussion

Our experiment shows that fine-tuning the generic model M_{gen} with *random sampling* for small up-

date sets can improve BLEU scores (see Figure 3). In particular, we observe improvements over the baseline with MEDAR data for $e = \{1, 5\}$ and with GlobalVoices data for $e = \{1, 5\}$ for update set sizes larger than 200 and for $e = \{10, 20\}$ with update set sizes less than 200. We did not find *log-like* relations similar to Barone et al. (2017). The reason for this could be because we included less data for the domain adaptation. For the random sampling condition, with MEDAR dataset, we can trade translation quality for faster training times since $e = 5$ training yields only slightly better BLEU scores when compared to $e = 1$ setting. Analogously, for GlobalVoices dataset, $e = 1, 5$ achieves similar performance and perform better than baseline model when $n_t > 200$, which allows to switch to a faster model training with $e = 1$ with a marginal loss in translation quality. Concerning larger values of e for both the new domains yield a slower gain in translation quality or even a loss in translation quality for $e \in \{10, 20\}$ (GlobalVoices) after an initial improvement over the baseline. This loss might be caused by overfitting to the training samples due to a high number of training iterations.

Using our *advanced* sampling for fine-tuning M_{gen} to a new domain, significantly reduces the amount of training samples without loss in translation quality compared to the commonly used fine-tuning with *random sampling*. This allows to dramatically reduce the amount of data that needs to be translated or post-edited by human labor, because the sampling of "unlabeled" instances is performed using monolingual data only. In case of MEDAR, our method reduces translation cost and time by 66.25% compared to random sampling. In addition, the BLEU scores improved overall: Except for $e = 1$ training setting, none of the scores is lower than the baseline score. An interesting observation when compared to the random sampling condition is that samples resulting from our advanced sampling need more epochs to achieve better BLEU scores. We believe this is due to the following two reasons: (i) Domain mismatch: the genre of samples of MEDAR dataset is significantly different from the domain of the samples observed in M_{gen} (Almahairi et al., 2016). (ii) Low amount of samples: our advanced sampling approach removes 66% of samples from the original 400. Both of these factors necessitates more training epochs to achieve the best BLEU score as with random sampling condition. In case of GlobalVoices, we can observe similar improvements in BLEU score for $e = \{5, 10\}$: we achieve a similar BLEU score as with random sampling baseline although we excluded 57.75% of the training data. All in all, we can confirm our hypothesis that our advanced sampling query strategy for sample selection effectively reduces the number of fine-tuning samples without degrading the translation quality compared to results of the baseline. A further advantage of our approach is that it supports continuous fine-tuning, in contrast to other methods which require a complete re-training of the model whenever new samples of the target domain become available (Wang et al., 2017).

Currently, there is one limitation in our work: The update sets in our evaluation are quite small. Hence, we want to investigate the performance of our method using all 36k samples of the GlobalVoices parallel corpus.

A promising direction for future work would be to investigate the impact of active learning in NMT using our advanced sentence sampling on translation time and quality of incremental model improvements. In settings with human workers that post-edit translation candidates, translations that improve over time might reduce this post-editing effort and, consequently reduce the overall time and budget required for model adaptation to a new domain. In addition, this technology can increase the efficiency of ubiquitous machine translation interfaces, e.g., for multimodal post-editing (Herbig et al., 2019; Oviatt et al., 2017), real-time translation systems in virtual reality (Toyama et al., 2014), or medical cross-language dialogue applications (Sonntag et al., 2009b,a) As a follow-up work, we would like to experiment with a *clustering-based sample selection* instead of using a single reference vector (e_{ref}) for the whole generic domain and observe the performance of domain-adapted sequence-to-sequence models based on the chosen samples.

7   Conclusion

We investigate the problem of incremental domain adaptation of a generic NMT model in a limited resources setting. Our NMT models improve BLEU score with only small amounts of data from a new domain. Hereby, sentences from the source language were randomly sampled for being used as parallel training data after human translations. We simulated the human translation task by using existing parallel corpora. Also, we introduced an *advanced sampling* strategy, based on semantic text similarity using a state-of-the-art technique, after extending it for computing sentence embeddings for Arabic (AraSIF). We found that our novel method achieves similar BLEU scores, compared to fine-tuning with random sampling, but using less than half of the initial training data. This enables more efficient domain adaptation of NMT models with humans-in-the-loop and with resource constraints.

Acknowledgments

This work is supported by EIT Digital (H2020).

References

Amjad Almahairi, Kyunghyun Cho, Nizar Habash, and Aaron C. Courville. 2016. First result on arabic neural machine translation. *CoRR*, abs/1606.02680.

Sanjeev Arora, Yingyu Liang, and Tengyu Ma. 2017. A simple but tough-to-beat baseline for sentence embeddings.

Antonio Valerio Miceli Barone, Barry Haddow, Ulrich Germann, and Rico Sennrich. 2017. Regularization techniques for fine-tuning in neural machine translation. In *Proceedings of the 2017 Conference on Empirical Methods in Natural Language Processing*, pages 1489–1494, Copenhagen, Denmark. Association for Computational Linguistics.

Michael Barz, Neslihan Büyükdemircioglu, Rikhu Prasad Surya, Tim Polzehl, and Daniel Sonntag. 2018a. Device-Type Influence in Crowd-based Natural Language Translation Tasks (short paper). In *Proceedings of the 1st Workshop on Subjectivity, Ambiguity and Disagreement in Crowdsourcing, and Short Paper Proceedings of the 1st Workshop on Disentangling the Relation Between Crowdsourcing and Bias Management (SAD 2018 and CrowdBias 2018) co-locate*, volume 2276 of *CEUR Workshop Proceedings*, pages 93–97. CEUR-WS.org.

Michael Barz, Tim Polzehl, and Daniel Sonntag. 2018b. Towards hybrid human-machine translation services. EasyChair Preprint no. 333.

Kyunghyun Cho, Bart van Merrienboer, Caglar Gulcehre, Dzmitry Bahdanau, Fethi Bougares, Holger Schwenk, and Yoshua Bengio. 2014. Learning phrase representations using rnn encoder–decoder for statistical machine translation. In *Proceedings of the 2014 Conference on Empirical Methods in Natural Language Processing (EMNLP)*, pages 1724–1734. Association for Computational Linguistics.

Chenhui Chu, Raj Dabre, and Sadao Kurohashi. 2017. An empirical comparison of domain adaptation methods for neural machine translation. In *Proceedings of the 55th Annual Meeting of the Association for Computational Linguistics (Short Papers)*, pages 385–391. Association for Computational Linguistics.

Jesús González-Rubio, Daniel Ortiz-Martínez, and Francisco Casacuberta. 2012. Active learning for interactive machine translation. In *Proceedings of the 13th Conference of the European Chapter of the Association for Computational Linguistics*, pages 245–254. Association for Computational Linguistics.

Spence Green, Jeffrey Heer, and Christopher D. Manning. 2015. Natural Language Translation at the Intersection of AI and HCI. *Queue*, 13(6):30.

Nico Herbig, Santanu Pal, Josef van Genabith, and Antonio Krüger. 2019. Multi-modal approaches for post-editing machine translation. In *Proceedings of the 2019 CHI Conference on Human Factors in Computing Systems*, CHI '19, pages 231:1–231:11, New York, NY, USA. ACM.

Philipp Koehn and Rebecca Knowles. 2017. Six challenges for neural machine translation. In *Proceedings of the First Workshop on Neural Machine Translation*, pages 28–39. Association for Computational Linguistics.

Philipp Koehn, Franz Josef Och, and Daniel Marcu. 2003. Statistical phrase-based translation. In *Proceedings of the 2003 Conference of the North American Chapter of the Association for Computational Linguistics on Human Language Technology - Volume 1*, NAACL '03, pages 48–54, Stroudsburg, PA, USA. Association for Computational Linguistics.

Tsz Kin Lam, Julia Kreutzer, and Stefan Riezler. 2018. A reinforcement learning approach to interactive-predictive neural machine translation. *CoRR*, abs/1805.01553.

Jaesong Lee, Joong-Hwi Shin, and Jun-Seok Kim. 2017. Interactive visualization and manipulation of attention-based neural machine translation. In *Proceedings of the 2017 Conference on Empirical Methods in Natural Language Processing: System Demonstrations*, pages 121–126. Association for Computational Linguistics.

Minh-Thang Luong, Eugene Brevdo, and Rui Zhao. 2017. Neural machine translation (seq2seq) tutorial. *https://github.com/tensorflow/nmt*.

Dragos Stefan Munteanu and Daniel Marcu. 2005. Improving machine translation performance by exploiting non-parallel corpora. *Comput. Linguist.*, 31(4):477–504.

Laurent Nepveu, Guy Lapalme, Philippe Langlais, and George Foster. 2004. Adaptive language and translation models for interactive machine translation. In *Proceedings of the 2004 Conference on Empirical Methods in Natural Language Processing*.

Sharon Oviatt, Björn Schuller, Philip R Cohen, Daniel Sonntag, Gerasimos Potamianos, and Antonio Krüger. 2017. Introduction: Scope, Trends, and Paradigm Shift in the Field of Computer Interfaces. In *The Handbook of Multimodal-Multisensor Interfaces*, pages 1–15. Association for Computing Machinery and Morgan & Claypool, New York, NY, USA.

Kishore Papineni, Salim Roukos, Todd Ward, and Wei-Jing Zhu. 2002. BLEU: a method for automatic evaluation of machine translation. In *Proceedings of the 40th Annual Meeting on Association for Computational Linguistics - ACL '02*, page 311, Morristown, NJ, USA. Association for Computational Linguistics.

Álvaro Peris and Francisco Casacuberta. 2018. Online learning for effort reduction in interactive neural machine translation. *CoRR*, abs/1802.03594.

Rico Sennrich, Barry Haddow, and Alexandra Birch. 2016. Neural machine translation of rare words with subword units. In *Proceedings of the 54th Annual Meeting of the Association for Computational Linguistics (Volume 1: Long Papers)*, pages 1715–1725. Association for Computational Linguistics.

Burr Settles. 2010. Active learning literature survey. Computer Sciences Technical Report 1648, University of Wisconsin–Madison.

Abu Bakr Soliman, Kareem Eissa, and Samhaa R. El-Beltagy. 2017. Aravec: A set of arabic word embedding models for use in arabic nlp. *Procedia Computer Science*, 117:256 – 265. Arabic Computational Linguistics.

Daniel Sonntag, Robert Nesselrath, Gerhard Sonnenberg, and Gerd Herzog. 2009a. Supporting a rapid dialogue system engineering process. *Proceedings of the 1st IWSDS*.

Daniel Sonntag, Pinar Wennerberg, Paul Buitelaar, and Sonja Zillner. 2009b. Pillars of ontology treatment in the medical domain. *J. Cases on Inf. Techn.*, 11(4):47–73.

Ilya Sutskever, Oriol Vinyals, and Quoc V. Le. 2014. Sequence to Sequence Learning with Neural Networks. In *Proceedings of the 27th International Conference on Neural Information Processing Systems*, pages 3104–3112. MIT Press.

Jörg Tiedemann. 2012. Parallel data, tools and interfaces in opus. In *Proceedings of the Eighth International Conference on Language Resources and Evaluation (LREC-2012)*. European Language Resources Association (ELRA).

Takumi Toyama, Daniel Sonntag, Andreas Dengel, Takahiro Matsuda, Masakazu Iwamura, and Koichi Kise. 2014. A mixed reality head-mounted text translation system using eye gaze input. In *Proceedings of the 19th international conference on Intelligent User Interfaces - IUI '14*, pages 329–334, New York, New York, USA. ACM Press.

Rui Wang, Andrew Finch, Masao Utiyama, and Eiichiro Sumita. 2017. Sentence embedding for neural machine translation domain adaptation. In *Proceedings of the 55th Annual Meeting of the Association for Computational Linguistics (Short Papers)*, pages 560–566. Association for Computational Linguistics.

Morphology-Aware Word-Segmentation in Dialectal Arabic Adaptation of Neural Machine Translation

Ahmed Y. Tawfik, Mahitab Emam, Khaled Essam
Robert Nabil and **Hany Hassan**
Microsoft
`atawfik|a-maemam|a-kessa|a-ronabi|hanyh@microsoft.com`

Abstract

Parallel corpora available for building machine translation (MT) models for dialectal Arabic (DA) are rather limited. The scarcity of resources has prompted the use of Modern Standard Arabic (MSA) abundant resources to complement the limited dialectal resource. However, clitics often differ between MSA and DA. This paper compares morphology-aware DA word segmentation to other word segmentation approaches like Byte Pair Encoding (BPE) and Sub-word Regularization (SR). A set of experiments conducted on Egyptian Arabic (EA), Levantine Arabic (LA), and Gulf Arabic (GA) show that a sufficiently accurate morphology-aware segmentation used in conjunction with BPE or SR outperforms the other word segmentation approaches.

1 Introduction

Building machine translation models for resource constrained languages can benefit from parallel corpora available in related languages. Vocabulary adaptation (Passban et al., 2017) has been used to train statistical and neural machine translation models for Azeri, a resource constrained language, leveraging its similarity to Turkish. Projection to a universal representation language (Gu et al., 2018) generates high quality machine translation model for a resource constrained language given a set of related resource-rich languages.

Research in dialectical Arabic translation tried to leverage the resources available in Modern Standard Arabic (MSA) using several techniques. Starting with statistical and rule-based methods for transforming DA to MSA (Al-Gaphari and Al-Yadoumi, 2012), and evolving to generating DA data from MSA parallel data using semantic projections (Hassan et al., 2017), and multi-task learning of part-of-speech tagging and machine translation to guide the translation model towards lever-

aging the grammatical roles in translation (Baniata et al., 2018). While earlier statistical and rule-based cross-dialectical techniques managed to leverage morphological word segmentation, more recent attempts have largely abandoned morphological segmentation in favor of language agnostic segmentation techniques like Byte Pair Encoding (BPE) (Sennrich et al., 2016) and Sub-word Regularization (SR) (Kudo, 2018). In fact, these learned language agnostic word segmentation have proved that they can rival morphological segmentation in neural MT. In a translation task from language D to language E, if language D (say an Arabic dialect) and language A (say modern standard Arabic) are two closely related languages such that a word W_A in language A is semantically equivalent to a word W_D in language D. Moreover, we assume that these two words share a common stem but have different clitics. So, the two words can be morphologically segmented as follows: $W_A = P_A R S_A$, and $W_D = P_D R S_D$ where P_A is a sequence of zero or more characters forming the prefix of W_A. Similarly, S_A is a sequence of characters forming the suffix of W_A, while P_D and S_D denote the prefix and suffix of W_D, and R is the shared root or stem.

Due to the limited training data for the language pair $\{D, E\}$, the root R is one that we hope to learn from the abundant data for the pair $\{A, E\}$. Intuitively, a morphology-aware word segmentation is more likely to produce the correct prefixes and suffixes, making it easier to learn the translation of R to E. As clitics tend to occur frequently, the MT model would have learned their translation from the scarce resources for the pair $\{D, E\}$; thus, successfully translation an out-of-vocabulary word for the $\{D, E\}$ pair. For illustration consider the example in Table 1 below. The dialectal Egyptian word ”هيقولوا“ [hayqwlwA] is segmented into four segments. Similarly, the correspond-

Proceedings of the Fourth Arabic Natural Language Processing Workshop, pages 11–17
Florence, Italy, August 1, 2019. ©2019 Association for Computational Linguistics

Segmented Dialectal Word	ﻫ#ﻱ#ﻗﻮﻝ#ﻭﺍ
	ha#y#qwl#wA
Segmented MSA Word	ﺱ#ﻱ#ﻗﻮﻝ#ﻭﻥ
	sa#ya#qwl#wn
English Translation	They will say
Alignment MSA-EN	0-1;2-2; 1,3-0
Alignment DA-EN	0-1;2-2; 1,3-0

Table 1: Illustrative word segmentation example

ing MSA word "ﺳﻴﻘﻮﻟﻮﻥ"[sayaqwlwn]. Both words share the same stem "ﻗﻮﻝ" [qwl], that can be learned from the resource rich MSA, while the dialectal future marking dialectal prefix "ﻫ#" [ha#] can be learned from other future tense verb in the training data. Similarly, the plural 3rd person markers can be learned from other verbs in the resource constrained parallel data. The alignments in the table are zero based word index alignment from Arabic to English.

The question that this paper aims to address is whether morphological word segmentation still has an advantage over language agnostic methods, in the context of leveraging parallel data in a resource-rich language to improve the MT of a related resource constrained one. This question is particularly interesting when we consider morphologically-rich languages like Arabic and its dialects. The remainder of this paper introduces the role of word segmentation in machine translation in Section 2. This section also reviews popular word segmentation techniques and introduces the morphology-aware segmentation approach that is used in our experiments. Section 3 reviews the neural machine translation approach that we use to train and adapt translation models for dialectal Arabic. Section 4 presents the experiments that we conducted along with their results. Section 5 reviews some related works. Finally, Section 6 summarizes the findings and concludes the paper.

2 Word Segmentation in NMT

The size of vocabulary found in a typical English dictionary is less than 100,000 words. A vocab around 16,000 words, provides 98% coverage for the Brown corpus. However, due to its agglutinative nature, the size necessary to achieve similar coverage for Arabic, whether standard or dialectal, is much larger. The size of the vocabulary extracted from the Arabic Gigaword corpus (Parker et al., 2009) exceeds 800,000 words.

Such vocab sizes are well beyond what current technology can handle efficiently. Therefore, it is common to use word segmentation for highly agglutinative languages like Arabic, or highly compounding languages like German (Huck et al., 2017), and more generally, for any large vocab NMT system. Two popular language agnostic word segmentation techniques are Byte-Pair-Encoding (BPE) (Sennrich et al., 2016) and Subword Regularization (SR) (Kudo, 2018).

2.1 Byte-Pair-Encoding (BPE)

Originally conceived as compression algorithm (Gage, 1994), BPE is a greedy technique often used to segment words into common subwords as a preprocessing step in a NMT training pipeline (Sennrich et al., 2016). BPE starts by splitting all the words in the training lexicon into individual characters, and proceeds by merging frequent character sequences until reaching a specified number of merge operations. Thus, by the end of the algorithm most frequent word segments would have been joined into a single symbol. The resulting trained segmenter is stored and applied to test and runtime inputs.

2.2 Subword Regularization (SR)

Subword Regularization (Kudo, 2018) generates probabilistic word segmentations to make the NMT training more robust. The probabilities of the segments are computed from a unigram language model defined over subword symbols. The intuition behind it is that if a sentence is represented by using multiple subword sequences it will produce some regularization during the training thus making the machine translation model more robust. The results achieved using SR, depends on the setting of three parameters: the vocab size, the size of n-best segmentation, and a smoothing parameter that controls the probabilistic sampling of segmentation.

2.3 Linguistically Motivated Segmenter

The problem with BPE and Subword Regularization is that they don't take into consideration any information about the language which might cause a loss of semantic and syntactic properties such as inflection and composition. These syntactic features are potentially useful in machine translation as semantic modifiers. The importance of using a linguistically motivated segmenter has been shown previously (Huck et al.,

2017) as they assist greatly in reduction of vocabulary size while helping improve the translation of unseen words (open vocabulary translation problem). The linguistically aware dialectal Arabic segmenter used in this work is a retrained version of the Unified Dialectal Arabic Segmenter (UDAS) (Samih et al., 2017). The unified segmentation model is based on a bidirectional Long Short-Term Memory (bi-LSTM) Recurrent Neural Network (RNN) that is coupled with Conditional Random Fields (CRF) sequence labeler trained to segment words from four different dialects namely Egyptian (EGY), Levantine (LEV), Gulf (GLF), and Maghrebi (MGR). The segmenter leverages the observation that different Arabic dialects do not only share vocabulary and some morphological properties with MSA, but they also share some commonalities amongst each other. Thus, a single model provides higher accuracy than a dialect specific model while eliminating the need for dialect identification before segmentation. This segmenter operates directly on raw text without requiring any preprocessing or word normalization while employing a lookup scheme that use segmentations that are seen in training directly during testing in order to improve the performance and the accuracy of segmenting a words into prefixes, stems and suffixes. To improve the segmentation model, we added to the training data, publicly available data from the LDC-Arabic Treebank (LDC2010T08, LDC2010T13, and LDC 2011T09), as well as dialectal Arabic treebanks (LDC2016T02, LDC2016T18, and LDC2018T23) to reach a total of 231,846 segmented sentences. Table 2 presents the accuracies of the segmentation for each dialect compared to the accuracy in the baseline model (Samih et al., 2017). To measure the accuracy, a 20% subset of the original UDAS training data is set aside as unseen testset. Despite some inconsitencies in segment labeling in the various datasets, the addition of data has resulted in improvements for all dialects. Like the original UDAS model, a lookup table has proved helpful in improving the trained model. We populated the lookup table with words found in the training data that the trained model fails to segment. The accuracy improvements were slightly higher for Egyptian which can be attributed to the fact that the added data had a large portion in that dialect (LDC2018T23).

	EGY	GLF	LEV	MGR
Retrained Model	99.4	98.9	96.2	96.1
Baseline	95.3	93.1	93.9	91.4

Table 2: Accuracy of the retrained unified dialectal segmenter compared to the baseline model (Samih et al., 2017).

3 NMT Training for Dialectal Arabic

To train Neural Machine Translation (NMT) for Arabic dialects, we use the now ubiquitous encoder-decoder structure. In these structures, the encoder maps a source language input to a dense internal vector representation, that the decoder maps to a corresponding target language output. Like other languages, a recurrent neural network (RNN-based) with attention (Bahdanau et al., 2015) or a feed-forward network with multi-attention (Transformer-based) (Vaswani et al., 2017), Sequence to Sequence architectures are used for the encoder and the decoder. Dialectical Arabic parallel resources are very scarce compared to the amount of data necessary to train general purpose NMT models. The parallel data publicly available for Arabic dialects used in this work are limited to:

- Crowd sourced translations for Levantine and Egyptian (LDC2012T09, (Zbib et al., 2012)),

- BOLT Egyptian Arabic parallel discussion forums data (LDC2019T01),

- Qatari Arabic Corpus that includes English translation for several hours of Qatari TV broadcast conversations.

- Dialectal contents extracted from the Arabic subtitles using a dialect ID trained fastText language ID type model (Joulin et al., 2017).

- Translation of the Egyptian Callhome (Kumar et al., 2014) a crowd-sourced translation of a conversational telephony dataset.

The total number of parallel sentences for each dialect ranges from tens of thousands for gulf to several hundreds of thousands for Egyptian and Levantine. These amounts are well below the minimum required for an adequate coverage for a language. Therefore, to leverage the abundant MSA resources, we train a base model using MSA data along with the limited amount of dialectal data. We use domain adaptation techniques to fine tune

Dialect	Training Set	DevTest
MSA	2.5 M sent.	-
Gulf	38 K sent.	2 K sent.
Levantine	219 K sent.	2 K sent.
Egyptian	502 K sent.	2 K Callhome.

Table 3: Training and test corpora sizes

the base model (Freitag and Al-Onaizan, 2016). Our methodology is different in that whereas they train the model on the out-of-domain data only and then adapt to the in-domain data, we train on the joint data to allow the model to learn dialect-specific vocab and then adapt using the in-domain data. Also, whereas they use an ensemble of the base model and the adapted model, we use an ensemble of two adapted models. Arabic dialects have some common words and idioms which overlap with MSA. So, when training a dialectical models it's beneficial to first train the model with the high-resourced MSA data jointly with the dialectical data with optional duplication so that the dialectical vocab is significant in the training data and doesn't get pruned or overwhelmed by the MSA vocab, and then adapting the model by training it for a few epochs with a small learning rate on the relatively small dialectical data to bias the model further to the dialect in the cases where the meaning in the dialect is different from the meaning in MSA.

4 Experiments and Results

Several experiments were conducted to examine the impact of the dialectical segmenter on the quality of the MT system built with it for a resource constrained languages, and how it compares to other segmentation techniques like BPE and SR. The experiments were carried out using Marian v1.7.6 (Junczys-Dowmunt et al., 2018) a public neural machine translation framework which supports sentence piece tokenization with its two variant BPE and SR (unigram language model) as well as word tokenization which is basically tokenizing the corpus on white spaces. Most parameters of Marian were the same as the defaults except for the validation set settings which were adapted to each dialect according to the size of its data.

Table 3 shows the distribution of the training and test data sizes used in the experiments. For the Gulf and Levantine dialects, 2000 sentences are set aside and equally divided into validation and test. For Egyptian, the callhome validation

Gulf – English Results		
Word Segmentation	**Base BLEU**	**Adapt BLEU**
Dialectal segmenter	12.36	12.64
BPE	13.19	13.36
SR	14.08	14.30
Dialectal segmenter + BPE	**14.58**	**14.58**
Dialectal segmenter + SR	14.18	14.18

Levantine – English Results		
Word Segmentation	**Base BLEU**	**Adapt BLEU**
Dialectal segmenter	19.41	19.98
BPE	20.83	21.56
SR	20.42	21.81
Dialectal segmenter + BPE	21.9	22.47
Dialectal segmenter + SR	**22.07**	**23.08**

Egyptian – English Results		
Word Segmentation	**Base BLEU**	**Adapt BLEU**
Dialectal segmenter	37.22	37.86
BPE	36.19	36.83
SR	36.79	37.76
Dialectal segmenter + BPE	36.93	**38.2**
Dialectal segmenter + SR	**37.44**	37.68

Table 4: The word segmentation technique, base model BLEU score, and adapted model BLEU score for each of the three dialects.

and test split is used after disfluency removal. The disfluency removal consists of removing incomplete words, filler words, and repeated words. This processing is necessary because we started with the speech transcripts (LDC97T19, LDC2002T38) which have full verbatim transcripts of the corresponding speech corpora. As described in Section 3, the base model training merges Arabic dialect sentences and MSA. Therefore, special care was needed to train the MT system for the Gulf dialect because it has far fewer sentences than MSA we needed to duplicate the Gulf data 10 times in order to make the sizes of the data of the Gulf dialect and other dialects comparable. The adaptation uses the dialect data only to fine-tune the base model trained for that dialect at a lower learning rate.

As summarized in Table 4, for each dialect, we evaluated five word segmentation approaches:

1. The dialectal segmenter as the only segmenter.

2. Byte-Pair Encoding (BPE) as the only segmenter.

3. Subword Regularization (SR) as the segmenter.

4. Byte-Pair Encoding applied to dialectically segmented corpora.

5. Subword Regularization applied to dialectically segmented copora.

In all cases, the vocab was kept at 40 K subwords. For the base models in all three dialects, the best performing word segmentation combined dialectal segmentation with either BPE or SR. This continued to be the case after adaptation. The gain attributable to dialectal segmentation[1] was 0.28 BLEU point for Gulf, 1.27 for Levantine, and 0.44 for Egyptian. It also worth noting that Subword Regularization has consistently outperformed BPE alone. The low scores for the Gulf dialect are due to the small size of the test set and the use of a highly dialectal spelling in the data that limited the model's ability to benefit from the MSA training. While Levantine and Egyptian training data are comparable in size, the BLEU scores reported for Egyptian are based on 4 reference translations, while Levantine scores use a single reference. To assess the similarity of word segmentation obtained by the various approach, we computed the Levenshtein edit distances between the segmented sentences for a random subset of 150 dialectal Arabic sentences. In this set, no two segmentation techniques produced the same word segmentation for all the words in any sentence. However, applying SR or BPE to a dialectically segmented sentences gives very similar segmentations with an average edit distance of 2.55 per sentence. The segmentations obtained by BPE and SR were also relatively similar with an average edit distance of 5.03.

Table 5 summarizes the average number of edits necessary to map a segmented sentence using one approach to the others. In the table, DS is the dialectal segmenter. The relatively large number of edits between the dialectal segmenter and both BPE and SR suggest that these language agnostic approaches have not fully captured the morphological aspects of Arabic dialects.

---

[1]Calculated as BLEU difference between the best adapted model with dialectal segmentation and the best adapted model without dialectal segmentation

5 Related Research

Translating Arabic dialects has been a focus with the machine translation community. In statistical machine translation (SMT), the use of morphology-aware word segmentation for Arabic has been studied (Lee et al., 2003),and (Habash, 2007). Sajjad et al. 2013 maps DA closer to MSA prior to translation. Sawaf 2010 also uses dialect normalizations and uses morphological for the dialects as well as MSA. This technique has significantly reduced the vocabulary size. However, the new vocab size restriction imposed by NMT and the advent of newer language independent word segmentation techniques like BPE and SR, as well as the advances in dialectal Arabic word segmentation prompted us to revisit the topic. Within the NMT context, Huck et al. 2017 studied the impact of linguistically-aware word segmentation on the translation from English to German. In their work, the linguistically aware techniques show some gains from combining linguistically-aware segmentation with BPE. In our work, we have observed similar gains from the combination with BPE, which suggests that such gains may be reproducible for other morphologically complex languages.

6 Conclusions and Future Work

Learning dialectal segmentation using a unified model (Samih et al., 2017) for the various dialects can achieve high accuracies provided sufficient training data. In our experiments, a segmentation accuracy of 99.4% was reached for Egyptian Arabic. Significant improvements were also achieved for other dialects. Our hypothesis has been that a high accuracy dialectal segmenter would maximize the transfer between the resource rich MSA machine translation and the resource restricted Arabic dialects. The experimental results seem to confirm that there is some advantage from using a high accuracy dialectal segmenter jointly with a language independent word segmentation technique like Byte-Pair Encoding or Subword Regularization. However, in using Subword Regularization in our experiments, we relied on the default values for the n-best size and smoothing as implemented in Marian. It would be interesting to see if our observations will continue to hold if these parameters are carefully tuned.

15

	BPE Only	BPE + DS	SR + DS	SR only
DS Only	11.47	10.91	11.51	9.71
BPE Only		15.10	16.37	5.03
BPE + DS			2.55	14.64
SR + DS				14.10

Table 5: Average Lenvenshtein Edit Distance between segmented sentences

References

Ghaleb Al-Gaphari and Mohammed Al-Yadoumi. 2012. A method to convert Sana'ani accent to modern standard arabic. *International Journal of Information Science and Management (IJISM)*, 8(1):39–49.

Dzmitry Bahdanau, Kyunghyun Cho, and Yoshua Bengio. 2015. Neural machine translation by jointly learning to align and translate. *Proc. International Conference on Learning Representations*.

Laith H. Baniata, Seyoung Park, and Seong-Bae Park. 2018. A multitask-based neural machine translation model with part-of-speech tags integration for arabic dialects. *Applied Sciences*, 8(12):2502.

Markus Freitag and Yaser Al-Onaizan. 2016. Fast domain adaptation for neural machine translation. *arXiv preprint arXiv:1612.06897*.

Philip Gage. 1994. A new algorithm for data compression. *The C Users Journal*, 12(2):23–38.

Jiatao Gu, Hany Hassan, Jacob Devlin, and Victor O.K. Li. 2018. Universal neural machine translation for extremely low resource languages. *Conference of the North American Chapter of the Association for Computational Linguistics on Human Language Technology*.

Nizar Habash. 2007. Syntactic preprocessing for statistical machine translation. *Proceedings of the 11th MT Summit*, 10.

Hany Hassan, Mostafa Elaraby, and Ahmed Y. Tawfik. 2017. Synthetic spoken data for neural machine translation. In *IWSLT*, pages 82–89.

Matthias Huck, Simon Riess, and Alexander Fraser. 2017. Target-side word segmentation strategies for neural machine translation. In *Proceedings of the Second Conference on Machine Translation*, pages 56–67.

Armand Joulin, Edouard Grave, Piotr Bojanowski, and Tomas Mikolov. 2017. Bag of tricks for efficient text classification. In *Proceedings of the 15th Conference of the European Chapter of the Association for Computational Linguistics: Volume 2, Short Papers*, pages 427–431. Association for Computational Linguistics.

Marcin Junczys-Dowmunt, Roman Grundkiewicz, Tomasz Dwojak, Hieu Hoang, Kenneth Heafield, Tom Neckermann, Frank Seide, Ulrich Germann, Alham Fikri Aji, Nikolay Bogoychev, André F. T. Martins, and Alexandra Birch. 2018. Marian: Fast neural machine translation in C++. In *Proceedings of ACL 2018, System Demonstrations*, pages 116–121, Melbourne, Australia. Association for Computational Linguistics.

Taku Kudo. 2018. Subword regularization: Improving neural network translation models with multiple subword candidates. *Proc. of ACL*.

Gaurav Kumar, Yuan Cao, Ryan Cotterell, Chris Callison-Burch, Daniel Povey, and Sanjeev Khudanpur. 2014. Translations of the callhome Egyptian Arabic corpus for conversational speech translation. In *Proceedings of International Workshop on Spoken Language Translation (IWSLT)*. Citeseer.

Young-Suk Lee, Kishore Papineni, Salim Roukos, Ossama Emam, and Hany Hassan. 2003. Language model based Arabic word segmentation. In *Proceedings of the 41st Annual Meeting on Association for Computational Linguistics-Volume 1*, pages 399–406. Association for Computational Linguistics.

Robert Parker, David Graff, Ke Chen, Junbo Kong, and Kazuaki Maeda. 2009. Arabic gigaword.

Peyman Passban, Qun Liu, and Andy Way. 2017. Translating low resource languages by vocabulary adaptation from close counterparts. *ACM Transactions on Asian and Low-Resource Language Information Processing (TALLIP)*, 16(4):29.

Hassan Sajjad, Kareem Darwish, and Yonatan Belinkov. 2013. Translating dialectal arabic to english. In *Proceedings of the 51st Annual Meeting of the Association for Computational Linguistics (Volume 2: Short Papers)*, volume 2, pages 1–6.

Younes Samih, Mohamed Eldesouki, Mohammed Attia, Kareem Darwish, Ahmed Abdelali, Hamdy Mubarak, and Laura Kallmeyer. 2017. Learning from relatives: unified dialectal Arabic segmentation. In *Proceedings of the 21st Conference on Computational Natural Language Learning (CoNLL 2017)*, pages 432–441.

Hassan Sawaf. 2010. Arabic dialect handling in hybrid machine translation. In *Proceedings of the conference of the association for machine translation in the americas (amta), denver, colorado*.

Rico Sennrich, Barry Haddow, and Alexandra Birch. 2016. Neural machine translation of rare words with subword units. *Proceedings of the 54th Annual Meeting of the Association for Computational Linguistics.*

Ashish Vaswani, Noam Shazeer, Niki Parmar, Jakob Uszkoreit, Llion Jones, Aidan N. Gomez, Łukasz Kaiser, and Illia Polosukhin. 2017. Attention is all you need. In *Advances in neural information processing systems*, pages 5998–6008.

Rabih Zbib, Erika Malchiodi, Jacob Devlin, David Stallard, Spyros Matsoukas, Richard Schwartz, John Makhoul, Omar F. Zaidan, and Chris Callison-Burch. 2012. Machine translation of Arabic dialects. In *Proceedings of the 2012 conference of the north american chapter of the association for computational linguistics: Human language technologies*, pages 49–59. Association for Computational Linguistics.

POS Tagging for Improving Code-Switching Identification in Arabic

Mohammed Attia[1]   Younes Samih[2]   Ali Elkahky[1]   Hamdy Mubarak[2]
Ahmed Abdelali[2]   Kareem Darwish[2]
[1]Google LLC, New York City, USA
[2]Qatar Computing Research Institute, HBKU Research Complex, Doha, Qatar
[1]{attia,alielkahky}@google.com
[2]{ysamih,hmubarak,aabdelali,kdarwish}@hbku.edu.qa

Abstract

When speakers code-switch between their native language and a second language or language variant, they follow a syntactic pattern where words and phrases from the embedded language are inserted into the matrix language. This paper explores the possibility of utilizing this pattern in improving code-switching identification between Modern Standard Arabic (MSA) and Egyptian Arabic (EA). We try to answer the question of how strong is the POS signal in word-level code-switching identification. We build a deep learning model enriched with linguistic features (including POS tags) that outperforms the state-of-the-art results by 1.9% on the development set and 1.0% on the test set. We also show that in intra-sentential code-switching, the selection of lexical items is constrained by POS categories, where function words tend to come more often from the dialectal language while the majority of content words come from the standard language.

1 Introduction

Code-switching (CS) is common in multilingual communities as well as diglossic ones, where the language of information and education is different from the language of speaking and daily interaction. With the increased level of education, mobility, globalization, multiculturalism, and multilingualism in modern societies, combined with the rise of social media, where people write in the way they speak, CS has become a pervasive phenomenon, particularly in user-generated data, and a major challenge for NLP systems dealing with that data.

CS is interesting for two reasons: first, there is a large population of bilingual and diglossic speakers, or at least speakers with some exposure to a foreign language, who tend to mix and blend two languages for various pragmatic, psycholinguistic

and sociolinguistic reasons. Second, existing theoretical and computational linguistic models are based on monolingual data and cannot adequately explain or deal with the influx of CS data whether spoken or written.

CS has been studied for over half a century from different perspectives, including theoretical linguistics (Muysken, 1995; Parkin, 1974), applied linguistics (Walsh, 1969; Boztepe, 2003; Setati, 1998), socio-linguistics (Barker, 1972; Heller, 2010), psycho-linguistics (Grosjean, 1989; Prior and Gollan, 2011; Kecskes, 2006), and more recently computational linguistics (Solorio and Liu, 2008a; Çetinoğlu et al., 2016; Adel et al., 2013b).

In this paper, we investigate the possibility of using POS tagging to improve word-level language identification for diglossic Arabic in a deep-learning system. We present some syntactic characterization of intra-sentential code-switching, and show that POS can be a powerful signal for code-switching identification. We also pay special attention to intra-sentential code-switching and examine the distribution of POS categories involved in this type of data.

The paper is organized as follows: in the remainder of this introduction we present challenges, definitions, and types of CS, and the particular aspects involved in Arabic CS. Section 2 gives an overview of related works. In Section 3, we describe and record our observations on the data used in our experiments. Section 4 presents a description of our system and the features used. Section 5 gives the details of our experiments and discusses the results, and finally we conclude in Section 6.

1.1 Why is CS Computationally Challenging?

When two languages are blended together in a single utterance, the traditional phonological and morphosyntactic rules are perturbed. When

Proceedings of the Fourth Arabic Natural Language Processing Workshop, pages 18–29
Florence, Italy, August 1, 2019. ©2019 Association for Computational Linguistics

judged by a standard monolingual model, these utterances can be deemed as ungrammatical or unnatural. Therefore, CS should generally be treated in its own terms and not to be conceived of as a peripheral phenomenon that can be understood by tweaking and twisting monolingual models and theories. When two languages come in contact, this implies the cross-fertilization and the emergence of structures that may be absent in either languages. When code-switching, speakers compromise the syntactic rules of the two languages involved, sometime adding in or leaving out a determiner, or applying a system of affixation from one language and not the other.

CS has conveniently been used as a cover term (Myers-Scotton, 1997; Çetinoğlu et al., 2016) for all operations where two languages are used simultaneously or alternately by the same speaker. When the user speaks one sentence in one language and another sentence in another language, this has been referred to as inter-sentential code-switching, while mixing elements from the two languages together in the same sentence has been termed intra-sentential. The language that provides the function words and grammatical structure is called the host (Bokamba, 1989) or matrix language, while the language being inserted is called the guest or embedded language.

While inter-sentential CS is relatively less challenging for computational analysis, as each sentence still follows a monolingual model, intra-sentential CS poses a bottleneck challenge. It needs a special amount of attention, because it is only this type that involves the lexical and syntactic integration and activation of two language models at the same time. NLP systems trained on monolingual data suffer significantly when trying to process this kind bilingual text or utterance.

CS has proved challenging for NLP technologies, not only because current tools are geared toward the processing of one language at a time (AlGhamdi et al., 2016), but also because code-switched data is typically associated with additional challenges such as the non-conventional orthography, non-canonicity (nonstandard or incomplete) of syntactic structures, and the large number of OOV-words (Çetinoğlu et al., 2016), which suggest the need for larger training data than what is typically used in monolingual models. Unfortunately, shortage of training data has usually been cited as the reason for the under-performance of computational models when dealing with CS data (Adel et al., 2015).

The study of CS does not only help downstream tasks (like ASR (automatic speech recognition), IR (information retrieval), parsing, etc.), but it is also crucial for language generation (e.g. TTS (text to speech), MT (machine translation), and automated responses by virtual assistants) in order to allow computational models to produce natural sentences that closely match how modern societies talk.

1.2 Definition and Defining Perspectives

The definition of CS has varied greatly depending on the different researchers' attitude and perspectives of the operation involved. While some viewed it as a process where two languages are actively interacting with each other (ultimately creating a new code), other viewed the operation just as two separate languages sitting side-by-side as isolated islands. Following the first perspective, Joshi (1982) defined code-switching as the situation when two languages systematically interact with each other in the production of sentences in a framework which consists of two grammatical systems and a mechanism for switching between the two. Following the second perspective, Muysken (1995) defined CS as "the alternative use by bilinguals of two or more languages in the same conversation", while other researchers (Auer, 1999; Nilep, 2006) defined it as the "juxtaposition" of elements from two different grammatical systems within the same speech.

The *juxtaposition* definition has been widely cited in the research on code-switching, advancing a monolingual view on the topic and promoting the idea that bilingual speech is the sum (or juxtaposition) of two monolingual utterances. The literal meaning suggests placing two heterogeneous and isolated pieces from different languages next to each other, but, in fact, foreign phrases are usually syntactically integrated and may often change phonologically, morphologically and pragmatically to fit homogeneously in the new position. The term also has a sense of randomness, which departs from the fact that CS is patterned and predictable.

The view we adopt is that when people code-switch, they interweave (Lipski, 2005) or blend two languages together, and the grammar of code-switching depends, to a large extent, on which languages are being interwoven, where, when, how, and by whom. The *where* and *when* relates to the sociolinguistic factors, such as the situation and power relations, and the *how* and *by whom* to the psycholinguistic factors, such as speakers' competence and proficiency in either or both languages. This is why we see a wide range of regular patterns as well as highly idiosyncratic behavior.

1.3   CS Types and Categories

A speaker can turn from one language to the other at the sentence level, or he/she can make the turn within the same sentence. Some researchers (Muysken et al., 2000) use the term "code-switching" to refer to the former case while reserving the term "code-mixing" to refer to the latter. However, these two types have more conventionally been termed as inter-sentential and intra-sentential code-switching, respectively, as explained above.

Intra-sentential CS has further been divided by Muysken et al. (2000) into three types: 1) insertion where words or phrases from one language are inserted into another, 2) alternation where there is a total shift from one language into the other, e.g. starting the sentence in one language and ending in another, and 3) congruent lexicalization similar to insertion, but with a high frequency, and found in typologically similar language pairs by fluent bilinguals.

Another classification is by looking at the nature of the language pairs, CS can be classified as diglossic, i.e. between varieties of the same language (e.g. Standard and Egyptian Arabic); typologically-related, i.e. between language pairs that belong to the same language family (e.g. English and Spanish); or typologically-distinct, i.e. between language pairs that come from different language families (e.g. Chinese and English). It has been suggested that CS between typologically similar languages is facilitated in ways that are different from (and not found in) those in typologically distinct languages (Lipski, 2005; Chan, 2009). By contrast, dialect/standard variation has been viewed by some as a form of style shifting (Trudgill, 1986) rather than proper CS, while others argue that style-shifting may serve the same kind of functions in conversation as CS (Boztepe, 2003), and that CS can happen between language varieties as well as different languages (Gardner-Chloros, 1991). It is to be noted however, that in diglossic code-switching, the shift is more likely to be lexical, morphological, and structural, rather than phonological, unlike the other two cases when we have two completely distinct language systems.

1.4   Peculiarities of Arabic CS

Arabic is a diglossic language, where the language of education is different from the language of speaking. Dialectal Arabic has traditionally not enjoyed the same prestige, socio-economic status, and official recognition as MSA. Dialects, by nature, diverge from the standard language, and, therefore, they can easily and freely draw from the larger repository of the standard language.

It has been suggested that CS most frequently happens from the subordinate language to the more superior one not vice versa (Lipski, 2005). This, however, might be true in general, but not in the absolute sense, as CS to the so-called subordinate language may be for the back-stage communicative purposes (e.g. establishing identity and friendliness or referencing a cultral meme).

Code-switching to MSA is used to establish authority and maintain credibility. Using the dialect (or mother tongue) on the other hand signifies a sense of belonging, community and solidarity, and attracts a higher level of attention and understandability. In other words, MSA is the intellectual language, while dialect is the emotive one.

The data used in the experiments in this paper comes from Twitter which are in the written modality, and this can significantly vary from the spoken interactions. Arabic speakers' competence in spoken MSA is remarkably lower than in the written one. While most Arabic speakers with some level of education can write in MSA, far fewer are able to utilize MSA in speaking. Spoken CS can be observed more with public speakers, like presenters, politicians and lecturers, and less often with ordinary people.

Moreover, there is a large number of lexical items which have shared orthography in EA (Egyptian) and MSA, though the pronunciation is different, e.g. متأكد muta>ak~id/mito>ak~id "sure", كاملة kamilap/kamolap "full", and قريب qariyb/quray~ib "near". This is generic to some extent, as the pattern mutaR$_1$aR$_2$~iR$_3$, for instance, is changed to mitoR$_1$aR$_2$~iR$_3$ where R stands for the root letter, or cardinal. As Twitter data is written without diacritization, there is no way to know precisely whether words are pronounced with dialectal or standard accent, though the context can give some clue, and we think that this kind of distinction was left to the annotators' best judgment.

Arabic, as a morphologically-rich language, has its peculiar behavior of merging morphemes and clitics from the matrix language to the embedded language. In diglossic mixed codes, standard verbs can show dialectal morphology, whether through affixes or templatic vowel shifting, e.g. هيرسلهالهم hayirosilhAlohum "will send it to them". For foreign words, they can receive agreement morphology هيكبيها haykabiyhA "he will copy it". This type of morpho-syntactic blending is stereotypical of CS when Arabic, or one if its dialects, is the matrix language.

2 Related Work

2.1 Computational Approaches

Research on computational approaches to CS has been mainly concentrated in four areas: predicting code-switching points, word-level language identification, POS tagging, and automatic speech recognition. However, some relatively recent research has tried to tackle CS in MT (Johnson et al., 2017), question answering (Raghavi et al., 2015), sentiment analysis (Vilares et al., 2015) and information retrieval (Chakma and Das, 2016).

The task of predicting code-switching points is significantly different from word-level code-switching identification, because in the former the classifier is allowed only to look at the past (previous) words and predict which language the coming word is going to be in, whereas in the latter, the classifier has the fuller context and evidently can achieve much higher accuracy. Moreover the former focuses on the elements or points after which you can make the switch, while the latter looks at the elements being switched themselves.

Solorio and Liu (2008a) pioneered the work on CS and developed an ML (machine learning) classifier to predict code-switching points in Spanish-English. The data they used was recorded conversations among three English-Spanish bilingual speakers. The conversations included 922 sentences and were manually transcribed and annotated with POS tags. They trained their Naive Bayes classifier on a number of features including language ID, lemma and POS tags and reported an f-score of 28%, with 1% positive variance gained through the POS feature.

In another effort, Solorio and Liu (2008b) tried POS tagging on Spanish-English CS data and concluded that feeding the output of two monolingual taggers to an ML algorithm yielded the best results.

Çetinoğlu et al. (2016) pointed out that POS tagging of CS data proved much harder than tagging monolingual texts, as models could reach 97% accuracy for the latter, but only around 77% for the former. They attribute the poor performance largely to the lack of CS annotated data, and the fact that many systems just devise methods to choose from the output of two monolingual POS taggers, e.g. the work of Solorio and Liu (2008b) and Sharma et al. (2016).

Similar to the work of (Solorio and Liu, 2008a), Adel et al. (2013b,a) tried to predict code-switching points for conversational speech in the Mandarin-English SEAME corpus to improve an ASR model. They used recurrent neural network language modeling relying on POS tags and using a factorized output layer. They noted that speakers most frequently switch to another language for nouns and object noun phrases. They also assumed that the switching attitude is speaker-dependent and clustered speakers into classes with similar switching attitude. They reported an accuracy of 43.31% and proved that POS tags have statistically significant role on improving the results. Adel et al. (2013b) tried to accommodate bilingual data by merging monolingual resources, such as the English and Mandarin Dictionaries, the output of two separate POS taggers, the Stanford POS tagger for Mandarin, and the Stanford tagger for English, and using two monolingual language models. Additionally they hard-coded some phonological rules to accommodate Singaporean English. They later extended their features to include Brown clusters, open class words and word embeddings (Adel et al., 2015) and found that Brown word clusters, part-of-speech tags and open-class words are the most effective at reducing the perplexity.

Fewer studies have focused on CS between related language varieties which is typically a diglossic kind of CS between a standard language and a dialect, e.g. Cypriot Greek and Standard Modern Greek (Tsiplakou, 2009).

CS research on Arabic included POS tagging and word-level language identification. AlGhamdi et al. (2016) explored different technique for the POS tagging of CS data and concluded that applying a machine learning framework as a voting mechanism on top of the output of two monolingual POS taggers achieves the best performance. Word-level CS identification for Arabic (along with Spanish–English) has been featured in a couple of shared tasks: the First Shared Task on Language Identification in Code-Switched Data (Solorio et al., 2014) and the Second Shared Task on Language Identification in Code-Switched Data (Molina et al., 2016), of which Samih et al. (2016) was the winning system, and against which we compare our results in this project.

Eskander et al. (2014) studied CS between EA written in Roman script (Arabizi) and English. Habash et al. (2008) created a standard annotation guidelines for CS between MSA and dialects.

CS has also been studied in Arabic as a predictor of social influence in the collaborative writing in Wikipedia discussion pages in (Yoder et al., 2017) and it was found that CS is positively associated with the editor's success in winning an argument.

We notice from the literature that in some instances POS tagging has been used to aid with the identification of code-switching points, and in some other instances language identification has been used as an indicator or a feature for POS tagging, showing what (Çetinoğlu et al., 2016) referred to as task inter-relatedness, or the cyclic nature of task dependencies. In our work, we use a POS tagger as a predictor of CS. The POS tagger used has been trained specifically on CS data.

3 Data Description

The organizers of the Second Shared Task on Language Identification in Code-Switched Data (Molina et al., 2016) provided the annotated dataset for the MSA–EA code-switched pairs. The data consists of 8,862 tweets (185,928 tokens) as training set, 1,117 tweets (20,688 tokens) as development set and 1,262 tweets (20,713 tokens) as final test set. The tagset statistics for the training set are shown in Table 1.

Furthermore, the training data contains 970 (11%) intra-sentential CS tweets, i.e. tweets with both $lang1$ (MSA) and $lang2$ (EA); 865 (10%) tweets with $lang2$ only; and the remaining tweets (79%) with $lang1$ only.

We analyze the POS distribution in the data us-

Labels	Token Count	Token Ratio %
ambiguous	1,186	0.64
unk	0	0.00
lang1	127,690	68.70
lang2	21,722	11.69
mixed	16	0.01
ne	21,567	11.60
other	13,691	7.37

Table 1: Tag count and ratio in the training set, where $lang1$ is MSA, $lang2$ is EA, and ne is a named entity.

ing the prediction of a specially designed POS tagger, described in 4.1, and notice that in those intra-sentential CS sentences, the majority of function words (particles, adverbs and pronouns) come from lang2 (dialect), while the majority of content words (adjectives, verbs and nouns) come from the $lang1$ (standard language). The distribution of $lang1$ and $lang2$ by POS is shown in Figure 1.

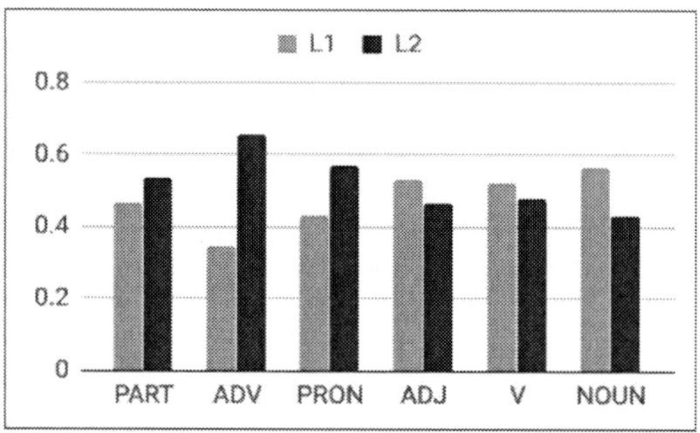

Figure 1: POS Distribution in CS data

Figure 2 shows CS behavior on a sample of users, and it indicates that the switching attitude is idiosyncratic and user-dependent.

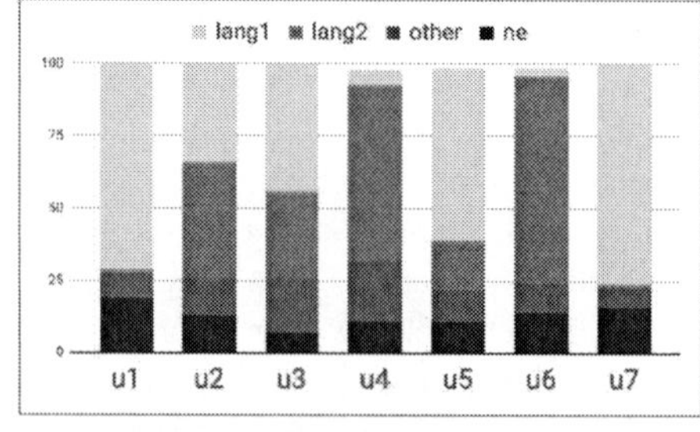

Figure 2: CS Distribution by Users

Data preprocessing: We transformed Arabic scripts to SafeBuckwalter (Roth et al., 2008), a character-to-character mapping that replaces Arabic UTF alphabet with Latin characters to reduce size and streamline processing. Also in order to reduce data sparsity, we converted all Persian numbers (e.g. ٢ و ١) to Arabic numbers (e.g. 1, 2), Arabic punctuation (e.g. '،' and '؛') to Latin punctuation (e.g. ',' and ';'), removed kashida (elongation character) and diacritics, and separated punctuation marks from words.

4 System Description

Deep learning and neural nets have been used extensively in the past decade and were shown to significantly outperform traditional (linear) ML models. The proclaimed advantage of deep learning is that it eliminates the need for feature engineering. Yet, there has been a growing interest recently to augment neural nets with more and more linguistic features, which has been shown to boost performance for many tasks.

We use a DNN (Deep Neural Network) model mainly suited for sequence tagging and is a variant of the bi-LSTM-CRF architecture (Ma and Hovy, 2016; Lample et al., 2016; Reimers and Gurevych, 2017; Huang et al., 2015). Our implementation is mostly inspired by the work of Reimers and Gurevych (2017). In its basic configuration, it combines a double representation of the input words by using word embeddings and a character-based representation with CNNs (convolutional Neural Networks). The input sequence is processed with bi-LSTMs, and the output layer is a linear chain CRF. We augment this model with various layers to accommodate the different features we want to incorporate. The features used in our model are explained below.

4.1 Dialectal POS Tagger

We develop a POS tagger using the data described in Darwish et al. (2018). The tagger used in this paper is developed using a deep neural network model, unlike Darwish et al. (2018) who use a linear model. Our model predicts POS tagging at the word level (not the token level), to suit how the CS data is structured. We experiment with two variants of the model, one that works with fine-grained POS tags and one that uses coarse-grained tags.

Basically, the difference between fine and coarse tags is that in fine tags we preserve and concatenate the POS representation of the affixes and clitics, while in coarse tags we eliminate affix rep-

Word	Translit. / Gloss	Fine Tag	Coarse Tag
بيحبك	byHbk likes+you	prog_part +v+pron	Verb
هيعبرنا	hyEbrnA will+ consider+us	fut_part +v+pron	Verb
والعمر	wAlEmr and+ the+life	conj+det +noun	Noun
قلبك	qlbk your+heart	noun+pron	Noun
طايقك	TAyqk standing+you	adj+pron	Adj
عالأقل	EAl>ql at+ the+least	prep+det +adj	Adj

Table 2: Examples of unsegmented words with fine and coarse POS tags.

resentation and keep the POS for stems only. The distinction between fine and coarse tags is illustrated further with some examples in Table 2.

Our system achieves 92.38% accuracy with the coarse tags and 88.43% using the fine tags. The gap in performance is mostly due to the size of the tagset. The number fine POS tags observed in the data is 218, while there are only 28 coarse tags. It is to be mentioned that the reported accuracy for segmented words by Darwish et al. (2018) is 92.9%.

4.2 Features Used

Here we describe the features used in our deep learning model.

POS tags. We include POS tags, as predicted by the specially developed model described in 4.1 above, as a layer in the neural network model.

Word-level embeddings allow the learning algorithms to use large unlabeled data to generalize beyond the seen training data. We explore randomly initialized embeddings based on the seen training data and pre-trained embedding.

For pre-trained embedding, we use FastText (Bojanowski et al., 2017) on a corpus that we crawled from the web with a total size of 383,261,475 words, consisting of user-generated texts from Facebook posts (8,241,244), Twitter tweets (2,813,016), user comments on the news (95,241,480), and MSA texts of news articles (from Al-Jazeera and Al-Ahram) of 276,965,735 words. After building the embeddings, we run the list of words in our dataset by the predictor in the word vector model to ensure that we get representations of all the words and reduce the number of OOVs (out of vocabulary words).

We find significant improvement using FastText embedding over the traditional word2vec representation (Mikolov et al., 2013). This is probably due to the utilization of sub-word (ex. prefixes or suffixes) information in the former.

Character-level CNNs. Although originally designed for image recognition, CNNs have proven effective for various NLP tasks due to their ability to encode character-level representations of words as well as extract sub-word information (Collobert et al., 2011; Chiu and Nichols, 2016; dos Santos and Guimarães, 2015).

Bi-LSTM Recurrent neural networks (RNN) are well suited for modeling sequential data, achieving ground-breaking results in many NLP tasks (e.g., machine translation). Bi-LSTMs (Hochreiter and Schmidhuber, 1997; Schuster and Paliwal, 1997) are capable of learning long-term dependencies and maintaining contextual features from both past and future states while avoiding the vanishing/exploding gradients problem. They consist of two separate bidirectional hidden layers that feed forward to the same output layer.

CRF is used jointly with bi-LSTMs to avoid the output label independence assumptions of bi-LSTMs and to impose sequence labeling constraints as in Lample et al. (2016). In our experiments with this task we find that CRF has a slight advantage over the softmax optimizer.

Brown clusters (BC). Brown clustering is an unsupervised learning method where words are grouped based on the contexts in which they appear (Brown et al., 1992). The assumption is that words that behave in similar ways tend to appear in similar contexts and hence belong to the same cluster. BCs can be learned from a large unlabeled corpus and have been shown to improve POS tagging as well as other sequence labelling tasks (Owoputi et al., 2013; Stratos and Collins, 2015). We test the effectiveness of using Brown clusters in the context of code-switching experimentation in a DNN model by training

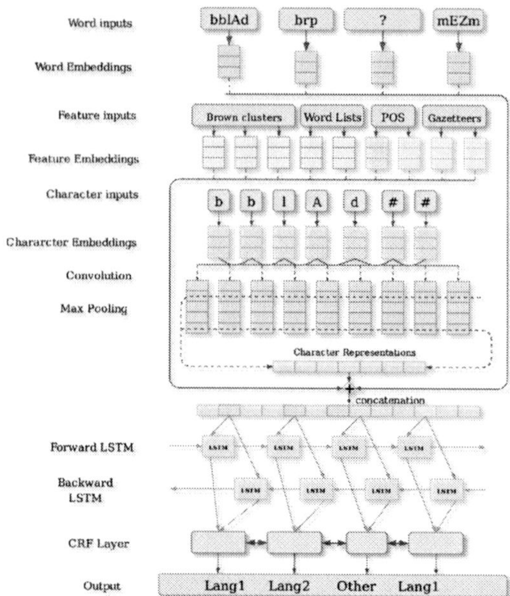

Figure 3: DNN Architecture.

BCs on our crawled code-switched corpus of 380 million words (mentioned above) with 100 Brown Clusters.

Named Entity Gazetteers We use a large collection of named entity gazetteers of 40,719 unique names from Attia et al. (2010), who collected named entities from the Arabic Wikipedia, and Benajiba et al. (2007), who annotated a corpus as part of a named entity recognition system. The assumption is that the gazetteer will enhance the system's recognition of NE's which constitutes between 11 and 14% of the tags in the datasets. The feature is used as a binary class, i.e. whether the word is present in the gazetteer list or not.

Spell Checking Word List Dialectal lexicon and inflection can vary significantly from the standard one. Based on this assumption we check for each word whether or not it exists in a large word list of fully inflected MSA words (Attia et al., 2012). The word list contains 9,196,215 and is obtained from the web as an open source resource [1].

The architecture of our model (with the best performance) is shown in Figure 3. For each word in the sequence, the CNN computes the character-level representation with character embeddings as inputs. Then the character-level rep-

---

[1] https://sourceforge.net/projects/arabic-wordlist/

resentation vector is concatenated with both word embeddings vector and feature embedding vectors (Brown Clusters, POS, and Gazetteers) to feed into the bi-LSTM layer. Finally, an affine transformation followed by a CRF is applied over the hidden representation of the bi-LSTM to obtain the probability distribution over all the code-switching labels. Training is performed using stochastic gradient descent with a momentum of 0.9 and batch size equal to 150. We employ dropout (Hinton et al., 2012) to mitigate over-fitting, and early-stopping (Caruana et al., 2000) (with patience of 35). We further use the hyper-parameters detailed in Table 3.

Layer	Hyper-Parameters	Value
Word Emb.	dimension	300
Characters Emb.	dimension	100
Characters CNN	window size	4
	number of filters	40
POS Emb.	dimension	166
Clustering Emb.	dimension	100
Gazetteer Emb.	dimension	2
Bi-LSTM	state size	100
Dropout	dropout rate	0.5
	batch size	150

Table 3: Parameter fine-tuning

5 Experiments and Results

We conduct a number experiments with different layers in the neural network model stacked on top of each other, making use of word and character representation, POS, FastText pre-trained embeddings, and other features. This allows us to see the significance of each feature and how it contributes to the overall performance of the system. The experiments are shown in Table 4.

The results in Table 4 are reported for the f-score measure on the validation set, except for the last row which gives the best model results on the test set. The results generally show that the DNN model is incrementally improving by adding more features and external resources. The best result is obtained with the aggregation of all features, excluding the SP (spell checking word list).

In the training data, $lang1$ (MSA) is the majority class representing 68.7% of the labels. We use majority voting as the baseline in order to detect if

#	Experiments	f-score	averaged f-score
1	Baseline (majority voting)	30.97	7.88
2	POS-coarse	66.19	40.57
3	POS-fine	72.99	45.28
4	Words	83.78	55.78
5	Words+POS-fine	84.68	57.06
6	Chars	84.02	56.52
7	Words+Chars	84.87	57.36
8	Words+Chars +POS-fine	86.47	58.15
9	Words+Chars +POS+BC	89.18	59.71
10	Words+Chars +POS+BC+GZ	89.21	59.63
11	Words+Chars +POS+BC+GZ +Embed	91.90	61.33
12	Words+Chars +POS+Embed +BC+GZ+SP	91.48	61.02
13	Words+Chars +POS+BC+GZ +Embed+PP	**91.92**	**61.35**
	Results on Test set	88.92	50.48

Table 4: DNN experiments and Results. Abbreviations: BC: Brown Clusters, GZ: named entity gazetteer, SP: Spelling word list, PP: post-processing

POS tags alone do send any positive signal to the model at all. We note that the baseline is very low which is due to the fact that the tag distribution in the training set is disproportionate with both the validation and the test set, where $lang1$ represents only 30.96% and 28.10% of the data respectively.

It is to be noted that we apply post-processing (PP) to the output of the prediction. The idea is that foreign words (words written in Latin script), punctuation marks, user names (words starting with the '@' sign), and hashtags (words starting with the '#' sign) should all be assigned the *other* tag. As these are deterministic cases, we develop a post-process procedure to correct errors in the predictions of the probabilistic model, and to make sure that they are assigned the right tag.

Our experiments show that POS tags do give a strong signal to the network that leads to a significant improvement over the baseline, from 30.97% to 66.19% using coarse-grained POS features and 72.99% using the fine-grained tags. We also no-

Labels	Token Count	Token Ratio %	Samih et al. (2016)	Current System
ambiguous	10	0.05	0.00	0.00
lang1	6,406	30.96	0.88	0.91
lang2	9,355	45.22	0.92	0.93
mixed	2	0.01	0.00	0.00
ne	3,024	14.62	0.84	0.86
other	1,891	9.14	0.97	0.98
Accuracy	–	–	0.900	0.919

Table 5: F1 score token level comparison between Samih et al. (2016) and the current system on the development dataset.

Labels	Token Count	Token Ratio %	Samih et al. (2016)	Current System
ambiguous	117	0.57	0.000	0.00
unk	26	0.13	0.000	0.00
lang1	5,804	28.10	0.854	0.860
lang2	9,630	46.62	0.904	0.913
mixed	1	0.00	0.000	0.000
ne	2,363	11.31	0.777	0.789
other	2,743	13.28	0.957	0.965
Accuracy	–	–	0.879	0.889

Table 6: F1 score token level comparison between Samih et al. (2016) and the current system on the test dataset.

	amb	ne	mixed	other	L1	L2
amb	0	0	0	0	1	9
ne	0	2507	0	14	277	226
mx	0	0	0	0	0	2
other	0	4	0	1844	7	36
L1	12	121	0	9	5931	333
L2	1	188	0	9	423	8734

Table 7: Confusion matrix for the development dataset.

tice that using the predicted fine-grained POS is significantly more helpful than using the predicted coarse-grained one (although the prediction accuracy for fine-grained tags is lower). This is probably because the fine-grained POS tags encode more lexical information (related to clitics and affixes) that can have distinctive combinations. Adel et al. (2015) claimed that part-of-speech (POS) tags can predict CS points more reliably than words themselves, but our results show that words still give a stronger signal than POS tags alone.

We also notice that Brown Clusters, named entity gazetteers and FastText pre-trained embeddings contribute to incrementally improve the performance of the system. Unfortunately adding information from the spelling word list did not show any improvement on the system, and this is why it is removed from the final system architecture.

Now we compare our best model to the state-of-the-art system of Samih et al. (2016), which won the 2016 Second Shared Task on Language Identification in Code-Switched Data (Molina et al., 2016) on the MSA–EA dataset. We compare the performance of the two systems in terms of f-score accuracy on both the development and test set, in Table 5 and Table 6 respectively. We also include the number of instances and the ratio percentage for each label. As the tables show, the category $lang2$ constitutes the majority class for both

the validation and test sets (45.22% and 46.62% respectively), contrary to the training set where $lang1$ makes up 68.70% of the labels.

For the development set our system outperforms that of Samih et al. (2016) by 1.9% absolute with significant gains for $lang1$ (3% absolute) and ne (2% absolute). For the test set our system again outperforms that of Samih et al. (2016) by 1.0% absolute with the gain spread almost evenly across all labels.

Table 7 presents the confusion matrix for the validation set, which shows that ne suffers the largest confusion as it gets mixed up as either $lang2$ (EA) or $lang1$ (MSA). This is due to the fact that many named entities in Arabic can also be used as ordinary words, and, unlike English, there is no case marking or other orthographic features that can superficially distinguish the two. For example, the word كريم krym, can mean either "Kareem" as an ne or "generous" as an adjective, and جمال jmAl can mean "Jamal" as an ne or "beauty" as a noun. The second largest confusion is between $lang1$ and $lang2$, where we find that a considerable amount of the mix-up coming from function words, such as و wa "and", أو >aw "or" and إلى <ilY "to", which can equally be used as either $lang1$ or $lang2$, depending on the context.

6 Conclusion

We have presented a neural network system for conducting word-level code-switching identification. Our system outperforms the current state-of-the-art, and we show that adding linguistic features can contribute to improving the performance of the deep learning models. We show that POS tagging gives a strong positive signal for code-switching prediction. We also examine the syntactic patterns in diglossic code-switching, and observe that dialects show a bias in the choice of word categories toward dialectal function words over content words.

References

Heike Adel, Ngoc Thang Vu, Katrin Kirchhoff, Dominic Telaar, and Tanja Schultz. 2015. Syntactic and semantic features for code-switching factored language models. *IEEE/ACM Transactions on Audio, Speech, and Language Processing*, 23(3):431–440.

Heike Adel, Ngoc Thang Vu, Franziska Kraus, Tim Schlippe, Haizhou Li, and Tanja Schultz. 2013a. Recurrent neural network language modeling for code switching conversational speech. In *2013 IEEE International Conference on Acoustics, Speech and Signal Processing*, pages 8411–8415. IEEE.

Heike Adel, Ngoc Thang Vu, and Tanja Schultz. 2013b. Combination of recurrent neural networks and factored language models for code-switching language modeling. In *Proceedings of the 51st Annual Meeting of the Association for Computational Linguistics (Volume 2: Short Papers)*, volume 2, pages 206–211.

Fahad AlGhamdi, Giovanni Molina, Mona Diab, Thamar Solorio, Abdelati Hawwari, Victor Soto, and Julia Hirschberg. 2016. Part of speech tagging for code switched data. In *Proceedings of the Second Workshop on Computational Approaches to Code Switching*, pages 98–107.

Mohammed Attia, Pavel Pecina, Younes Samih, Khaled Shaalan, and Josef Van Genabith. 2012. Improved spelling error detection and correction for arabic. *Proceedings of COLING 2012: Posters*, pages 103–112.

Mohammed Attia, Antonio Toral, Lamia Tounsi, Monica Monachini, and Josef van Genabith. 2010. An automatically built named entity lexicon for Arabic. In *Proceedings of the Seventh conference on International Language Resources and Evaluation (LREC'10)*, Valletta, Malta. European Languages Resources Association (ELRA).

Peter Auer. 1999. From codeswitching via language mixing to fused lects: Toward a dynamic typology of bilingual speech. *International journal of bilingualism*, 3(4):309–332.

George Carpenter Barker. 1972. *Social Functions of Language in a Mexican-American Community*, volume 22. University of Arizona Press.

Yassine Benajiba, Paolo Rosso, and José Miguel Benedíruiz. 2007. Anersys: An arabic named entity recognition system based on maximum entropy. In *International Conference on Intelligent Text Processing and Computational Linguistics*, pages 143–153. Springer.

Piotr Bojanowski, Edouard Grave, Armand Joulin, and Tomas Mikolov. 2017. Enriching word vectors with subword information. *Transactions of the Association for Computational Linguistics*, 5:135–146.

Eyamba G Bokamba. 1989. Are there syntactic constraints on code-mixing? *World Englishes*, 8(3):277–292.

Erman Boztepe. 2003. Issues in code-switching: Competing theories and models. *Columbia University Working Papers in TESOL and Applied Linguistics*.

Peter F Brown, Peter V Desouza, Robert L Mercer, Vincent J Della Pietra, and Jenifer C Lai. 1992. Class-based n-gram models of natural language. *Computational linguistics*, 18(4):467–479.

Rich Caruana, Steve Lawrence, and Lee Giles. 2000. Overfitting in neural nets: Backpropagation, conjugate gradient, and early stopping. In *NIPS*, pages 402–408.

Özlem Çetinoğlu, Sarah Schulz, and Ngoc Thang Vu. 2016. Challenges of computational processing of code-switching. In *Proceedings of the Second Workshop on Computational Approaches to Code Switching*, pages 1–11, Austin, TX.

Kunal Chakma and Amitava Das. 2016. Cmir: A corpus for evaluation of code mixed information retrieval of hindi-english tweets. *Computación y Sistemas*, 20(3):425–434.

Hok Shing Chan. 2009. Code-switching between typologically distinct languages. *The Cambridge handbook of linguistic code-switching*, pages 182–198.

Jason Chiu and Eric Nichols. 2016. Named entity recognition with bidirectional lstm-cnns. *Transactions of the Association for Computational Linguistics*, 4:357–370.

R. Collobert, J. Weston, L. Bottou, M. Karlen, K. Kavukcuoglu, and P. Kuksa. 2011. Natural language processing (almost) from scratch. *Journal of Machine Learning Research*, 12:2493–2537.

Kareem Darwish, Hamdy Mubarak, Ahmed Abdelali, Mohamed Eldesouki, Younes Samih, Randah Alharbi, Mohammed Attia, Walid Magdy, and Laura Kallmeyer. 2018. Multi-dialect arabic pos tagging: A crf approach. In *Proceedings of the Eleventh International Conference on Language Resources and Evaluation (LREC-2018)*, pages 93–98, Miyazaki, Japan.

Ramy Eskander, Mohamed Al-Badrashiny, Nizar Habash, and Owen Rambow. 2014. Foreign words and the automatic processing of arabic social media text written in roman script. In *Proceedings of The First Workshop on Computational Approaches to Code Switching*, pages 1–12.

Penelope Gardner-Chloros. 1991. *Language selection and switching in Strasbourg*. Oxford University Press.

François Grosjean. 1989. Neurolinguists, beware! the bilingual is not two monolinguals in one person. *Brain and language*, 36(1):3–15.

Nizar Habash, Owen Rambow, Mona Diab, and Reem Kanjawi-Faraj. 2008. Guidelines for annotation of arabic dialectness. In *Proceedings of the LREC*

Workshop on HLT & NLP within the Arabic world, pages 49–53.

Monica Heller. 2010. *Codeswitching: Anthropological and Sociolinguistic Perspectives*, volume 48. Walter de Gruyter.

Geoffrey E Hinton, Nitish Srivastava, Alex Krizhevsky, Ilya Sutskever, and Ruslan R Salakhutdinov. 2012. Improving neural networks by preventing co-adaptation of feature detectors. *arXiv preprint arXiv:1207.0580*.

Sepp Hochreiter and Jürgen Schmidhuber. 1997. Long short-term memory. *Neural computation*, 9(8):1735–1780.

Zhiheng Huang, Wei Xu, and Kai Yu. 2015. Bidirectional LSTM-CRF models for sequence tagging. *CoRR*, abs/1508.01991.

Melvin Johnson, Mike Schuster, Quoc V Le, Maxim Krikun, Yonghui Wu, Zhifeng Chen, Nikhil Thorat, Fernanda Viégas, Martin Wattenberg, Greg Corrado, et al. 2017. Google's multilingual neural machine translation system: Enabling zero-shot translation. *Transactions of the Association for Computational Linguistics*, 5:339–351.

Aravind K. Joshi. 1982. Processing of sentences with intra-sentential code-switching. In *Coling 1982: Proceedings of the Ninth International Conference on Computational Linguistics*.

Istvan Kecskes. 2006. The dual language model to explain code-switching: A cognitive-pragmatic approach. *Intercultural Pragmatics*, 3(3):257–283.

Guillaume Lample, Miguel Ballesteros, Sandeep Subramanian, Kazuya Kawakami, and Chris Dyer. 2016. Neural architectures for named entity recognition. *arXiv preprint arXiv:1603.01360*.

John M Lipski. 2005. Code-switching or borrowing? no sé so no puedo decir, you know. In *Selected proceedings of the second workshop on Spanish sociolinguistics*, pages 1–15. Cascadilla Proceedings Project Somerville, MA.

Xuezhe Ma and Eduard Hovy. 2016. End-to-end sequence labeling via bi-directional lstm-cnns-crf. In *Proceedings of the 54th Annual Meeting of the Association for Computational Linguistics (Volume 1: Long Papers)*, pages 1064–1074, Berlin, Germany. Association for Computational Linguistics.

Tomas Mikolov, Kai Chen, Greg Corrado, and Jeffrey Dean. 2013. Efficient estimation of word representations in vector space. *CoRR*, abs/1301.3781.

Giovanni Molina, Fahad AlGhamdi, Mahmoud Ghoneim, Abdelati Hawwari, Nicolas Rey-Villamizar, Mona Diab, and Thamar Solorio. 2016. Overview for the second shared task on language identification in code-switched data. In *Proceedings of the Second Workshop on Computational Approaches to Code Switching*, pages 40–49.

Pieter Muysken. 1995. *Code-switching and grammatical theory*, page 177–198. Cambridge University Press.

Pieter Muysken, Carmen Pena Díaz, Pieter Cornelis Muysken, et al. 2000. *Bilingual speech: A typology of code-mixing*, volume 11. Cambridge University Press.

Carol Myers-Scotton. 1997. *Duelling languages: Grammatical structure in codeswitching*. Oxford University Press.

Chad Nilep. 2006. "code switching" in sociocultural linguistics. *Colorado Research in Linguistics*, 19(1):1.

Olutobi Owoputi, Brendan O'Connor, Chris Dyer, Kevin Gimpel, Nathan Schneider, and Noah A Smith. 2013. Improved part-of-speech tagging for online conversational text with word clusters. In *Proceedings of NAACL-HLT 2013*, pages 380–390. Association for Computational Linguistics.

David J Parkin. 1974. Language switching in nairobi. *Language in Kenya*, pages 189–216.

Anat Prior and Tamar H Gollan. 2011. Good language-switchers are good task-switchers: Evidence from spanish–english and mandarin–english bilinguals. *Journal of the International Neuropsychological Society*, 17(4):682–691.

Khyathi Chandu Raghavi, Manoj Kumar Chinnakotla, and Manish Shrivastava. 2015. Answer ka type kya he?: Learning to classify questions in code-mixed language. In *Proceedings of the 24th International Conference on World Wide Web*, pages 853–858. ACM.

Nils Reimers and Iryna Gurevych. 2017. Reporting score distributions makes a difference: Performance study of lstm-networks for sequence tagging. In *Proceedings of the 2017 Conference on Empirical Methods in Natural Language Processing (EMNLP)*, pages 338–348, Copenhagen, Denmark.

Ryan Roth, Owen Rambow, Nizar Habash, Mona Diab, and Cynthia Rudin. 2008. Arabic morphological tagging, diacritization, and lemmatization using lexeme models and feature ranking. In *Proceedings of ACL-08: HLT, Short Papers*, pages 117–120, Columbus, Ohio. Association for Computational Linguistics.

Younes Samih, Suraj Maharjan, Mohammed Attia, Laura Kallmeyer, and Thamar Solorio. 2016. Multilingual code-switching identification via lstm recurrent neural networks. In *Proceedings of the Second Workshop on Computational Approaches to Code Switching*, pages 50–59.

Cicero dos Santos and Victor Guimarães. 2015. Boosting named entity recognition with neural character embeddings. In *Proceedings of the Fifth Named Entity Workshop*, pages 25–33, Beijing, China. Association for Computational Linguistics.

Mike Schuster and Kuldip K Paliwal. 1997. Bidirectional recurrent neural networks. *IEEE Transactions on Signal Processing*, 45(11):2673–2681.

Mamokgethi Setati. 1998. Code-switching in a senior primary class of second-language mathematics learners. *For the Learning of Mathematics*, 18(1):34–40.

Arnav Sharma, Sakshi Gupta, Raveesh Motlani, Piyush Bansal, Manish Srivastava, Radhika Mamidi, and Dipti M Sharma. 2016. Shallow parsing pipeline for hindi-english code-mixed social media text. *arXiv preprint arXiv:1604.03136*.

Thamar Solorio, Elizabeth Blair, Suraj Maharjan, Steven Bethard, Mona Diab, Mahmoud Ghoneim, Abdelati Hawwari, Fahad AlGhamdi, Julia Hirschberg, Alison Chang, et al. 2014. Overview for the first shared task on language identification in code-switched data. In *Proceedings of the First Workshop on Computational Approaches to Code Switching*, pages 62–72.

Thamar Solorio and Yang Liu. 2008a. Learning to predict code-switching points. In *Proceedings of the Conference on Empirical Methods in Natural Language Processing*, pages 973–981. Association for Computational Linguistics.

Thamar Solorio and Yang Liu. 2008b. Part-of-speech tagging for english-spanish code-switched text. In *Proceedings of the Conference on Empirical Methods in Natural Language Processing*, pages 1051–1060. Association for Computational Linguistics.

Karl Stratos and Michael Collins. 2015. Simple semisupervised pos tagging. In *VS@ HLT-NAACL*, pages 79–87.

Peter Trudgill. 1986. *Dialects in contact*. B. Blackwell.

Stavroula Tsiplakou. 2009. Code-switching and codemixing between related varieties: establishing the blueprint. *The International Journal of Humanities*, 6(12):49–66.

David Vilares, Miguel A Alonso, and Carlos Gómez-Rodríguez. 2015. Sentiment analysis on monolingual, multilingual and code-switching twitter corpora. In *Proceedings of the 6th Workshop on Computational Approaches to Subjectivity, Sentiment and Social Media Analysis*, pages 2–8.

Donald D Walsh. 1969. Bilingualism and bilingual education: a guest editorial. *Foreign Language Annals*, 2(3):298–303.

Michael Yoder, Shruti Rijhwani, Carolyn Rosé, and Lori Levin. 2017. Code-switching as a social act: The case of arabic wikipedia talk pages. In *Proceedings of the Second Workshop on NLP and Computational Social Science*, pages 73–82.

Syntax-Ignorant N-gram Embeddings for Sentiment Analysis of Arabic Dialects

Hala Mulki[*§], **Hatem Haddad**[†§], **Mourad Gridach**[**] and **Ismail Babaoğlu**[*]

[*]Department of Computer Engineering, Konya Technical University, Turkey
[†]RIADI Laboratory, National School of Computer Sciences, University of Manouba, Tunisia
[**]Computational Bioscience Program, University of Colorado, School of Medicine, USA
[§]iCompass Consulting, Tunisia
`halamulki@selcuk.edu.tr, haddad.Hatem@gmail.com`
`mourad.gridach@ucdenver.edu, ibabaoglu@selcuk.edu.tr`

Abstract

Arabic sentiment analysis models have employed compositional embedding features to represent the Arabic dialectal content. These embeddings are usually composed via ordered, syntax-aware composition functions and learned within deep neural frameworks. With the free word order and the varying syntax nature across the different Arabic dialects, a sentiment analysis system developed for one dialect might not be efficient for the others. Here we present syntax-ignorant n-gram embeddings to be used in sentiment analysis of several Arabic dialects. The proposed embeddings were composed and learned using an unordered composition function and a shallow neural model. Five datasets of different dialects were used to evaluate the produced embeddings in the sentiment analysis task. The obtained results revealed that, our syntax-ignorant embeddings could outperform word2vec model and doc2vec both variant models in addition to hand-crafted system baselines, while a competent performance was noticed towards baseline systems that adopted more complicated neural architectures.

1 Introduction

According to the used features, existing Arabic Sentiment Analysis (ASA) systems can be classified into: (a) hand-crafted-based systems (Abdulla et al., 2013; El-Beltagy et al., 2017) where linguistic/stylistic and lexical features are generated by morphological analyzers and semantic resources and (b) text embeddings-based systems that adopt word/sentence embeddings using one of the composition models (Gridach et al., 2017; Medhaffar et al., 2017). While the first type of ASA systems provide a comparable performance, the generation of hand-crafted features is considered a labor-intensive task that requires using language/dialect-specific NLP tools and techniques (Altowayan and

Tao, 2016). In contrast, text embeddings-based systems can use the raw unprocessed input content to generate expressive features to represent words or even longer pieces of text through using the composition models (Mikolov et al., 2013).

Composition models aim to construct a phrase/sentence embeddings based on its constituent word embeddings and structural information (Iyyer et al., 2015). Two main types of these models can be recognized: (a) Ordered models where the order and linguistic/grammatical structure of the input words do count while constructing the phrase/sentence vector and (b) Unordered models in which the word representations are combined irrespective of their order using algebraic operations (Sum of Word Embeddings (SOWE), average (Avg), mean and multiplication functions) (Mitchell and Lapata, 2010).

Context words along side their syntactic properties have been considered essential to build effective word embeddings able to infer the semantic/syntactic similarities among words, phrases or sentences. Consequently, most of the recently-developed SA systems adopted deep neural network architectures such as Convolutional Neural Networks (CNNs) and Recursive Neural Networks (RecNNs) where ordered composition models are employed to grasp the syntactic and linguistic relations between the words (Al Sallab et al., 2015; Dahou et al., 2016). These systems required more training time to learn words' order-aware embeddings due to the high computational complexity consumed at each layer of the model (Iyyer et al., 2015). However, such embeddings resulting from ordered compositionality might not form discriminating features for the Arabic dialects; especially that these dialects have a free word order and varying syntactic/grammatical rules (Brustad, 2000). For instance, the dialectal (Levantine) sentence in-

Proceedings of the Fourth Arabic Natural Language Processing Workshop, pages 30–39
Florence, Italy, August 1, 2019. ©2019 Association for Computational Linguistics

هالفكرة	انا	حبيتا
O	S	V
هالفكرة	حبيتا	انا
O	V	S
حبيتا	انا	هالفكرة
V	S	O
انا	حبيتا	هالفكرة
S	V	O

Table 1: Free word order of dialectal Arabic.

Dialect	Sentence	POS
Levantine	الوضع ماشي الحال The situation is **okay**	Adjective
Moroccan	نحن ماشي سعداء We are **not** happy	Negation
Egyptian	كنت ماشي فاتجاه البيت I was **walking** towards home	Verb

Table 2: Syntactic differences across the Arabic dialects.

vestigated in Table 1 meaning "I liked this idea" can be represented by several word orders: VSO, SVO, OSV and OVS and yet, implies the same meaning and sentiment.

On the other hand, the Arabic dialects show phonological, morphological, lexical, and syntactic differences such that the same word might infer different syntactic information across different dialects. To clarify that, Table 2 reviews how the word "ماشي" has several Part Of Speech (POS) tags, multiple meanings and different sentiments across three Arabic dialects.

Thus, to handle such informality of DA, we propose an unordered composition model to construct sentence/phrase embeddings regardless of the order and the syntax of the context's words. Nevertheless, when coming to the sentiment analysis task, sentence embeddings that are merely composed and learned based on the context words do not always infer the sentiment accurately. This is due to the fact that, some words of contradict sentiments might be mentioned within identical contexts which leads to map opposite words close to each other in the embedding space. To clarify that, both sentences in Example 1 and Example 2 contain the same context words organized in the same order; yet the first sentence is of positive polarity while the second has a negative sentiment since the words "ممتع" and "ممل" are antonyms that

mean "interesting" and "boring", respectively.

Example 1 هالفيلم ممتع بشكل ما بينوصف[1]

Example 2 هالفيلم ممل بشكل ما بينوصف[2]

One way to address this issue is to learn the embeddings from sentiment-annotated corpora such that the sentiment information is incorporated along with the contextual data within the composed embedding during the training phase. This was examined with the English language, as Tang et al. (2014) presented sentiment-specific word embeddings (SSWE) composed via unordered Min, Max and Avg composition models. Another pairing between Avg composition functions and supervised learning was introduced by (Iyyer et al., 2015) where a neural model of two hidden layers called Deep Averaging Neural network (DAN) was used to learn the embeddings together with sentiment, yielding a performance competent to much more complicated models such as Rec-NNs and CNNs-Multi Channel (CNN-MC).

While some of the recent ASA systems considered the syntactic information in the composed embeddings (Al Sallab et al., 2015), other models used pretrained or unsupervised unordered word/doc embeddings as features to mine the sentiment of MSA/DA content (Altowayan and Tao, 2016; Gridach et al., 2017). However, mining the sentiment of DA using syntax-aware ordered embeddings might be ineffective especially with the drastic differences between Eastern and Western Arabic dialects (Brustad, 2000). In addition, for the SA task, the embeddings learned from unlabeled data are not as discriminating as those learned with sentiment information integrated in the embedding vectors (Tang et al., 2014). This evokes the need to provide a sentiment-specific, dialect-independent embeddings with which the gap resulted from the differences among Arabic dialects can be bridged. Such embeddings would ignore the syntactic structure and focus on the semantic and sentiment information.

Inspired by (Iyyer et al., 2015; Tang et al., 2014), we hypothesize that representing a sentence by its constituent sentiment-specific, unordered and syntax-ignorant n-gram embeddings can handle the diversity of the Arabic dialects and provide better features for the dialectal Arabic SA task. In the current paper, we present a SA

---

[1] This movie is incredibly interesting.

[2] This movie is incredibly boring.

framework whose features are n-gram embeddings learned from labeled data (sentiment-specific) and composed via the additive unordered composition function (syntax-ignorant) known as SOWE. The embeddings composition and the sentiment learning processes were conducted within Tw-StAR framework which forms a shallow feed-forward neural network of single hidden layer. The contributions of this study can be briefly described as follows:

1. Based on the outperformance of SOWE composition function in sentence semantic similarity applications (White et al., 2015), we believe that SOWE can be an effective replacement of the Average (Avg) composition functions used in (Iyyer et al., 2015) and (Mikolov et al., 2013). Besides its low computation complexity as it conducts an element-wise sum over the word embedding vectors contained in a sentence, SOWE can capture and encode semantic and synonymous information in the resulting composed embeddings (White et al., 2015).

2. Given that, DA has a free word order and a varying syntactic nature, therefore, unlike (Tang et al., 2014) whose embeddings were generated using corrupted input n-grams from which the syntactic context nature are learned, we feed whole n-grams to our model as the training objective is to capture the semantic and sentiment relations regardless of the order and the syntax of the context words.

3. In contrast to previous studies, that composed unordered embeddings within deep neural models (Iyyer et al., 2015), the embeddings introduced here are generated and learned within a shallow feed-forward neural model as we are seeking to investigate whether SA of DA can be performed using less complicated neural architectures.

2 The Proposed Model (Tw-StAR)

As we are seeking to answer the question: To which extent a shallow neural model, trained with embeddings specifically formulated to target DA, can rival complicated neural architectures?, we chose to implement Tw-StAR as a feed-forward neural network in which sentiment-

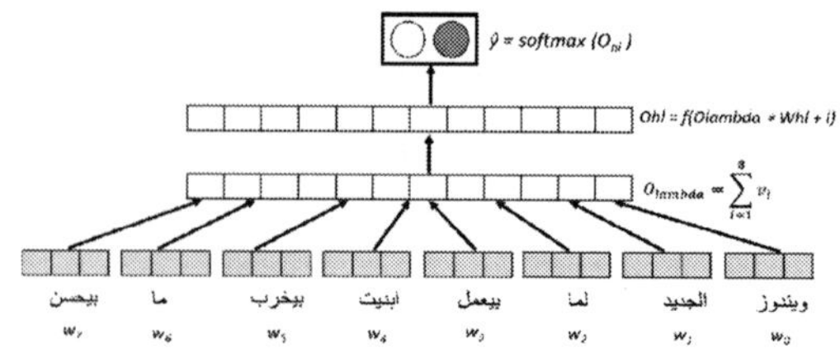

Figure 1: Tw-StAR neural sentiment analysis model.

specific, syntax-ignorant and semantic-enriched n-grams embeddings are composed using SOWE function and learned in a supervised manner. The generated n-gram embeddings were then employed as discriminative features to predict the positive/negative sentiment of the tackled input sentences. As it is shown in Figure 1, Tw-StAR model is a shallow feed-forward neural network composed of the following layers: the input or embeddings layer followed by lambda layer then a hidden layer and finally an output layer with softmax function applied for the classification into positive or negative sentiment.

2.1 Model Description

The embedding layer, in Tw-StAR, acts as a word lookup table, it is responsible of projecting words in the input into their corresponding dense vector representations. Given the input sentences, in order to handle their varying lengths, each sentence S of l words was formulated as a sequence of fixed-length n-grams generated using a sliding window of a specific size C. Instead of using corrupted input n-grams as in the SSWEu model provided in (Tang et al., 2014) and CBOW in (Mikolov et al., 2013), whole n-grams were fed to the embedding layer such that each n-gram is accompanied with the sentiment label of the sentence from which it was derived; where [1,0] and [0,1] vectors were used to represent the positive and negative polarities, respectively. Having the n-grams prepared, their constituent words are mapped into the corresponding embeddings using the weights matrix M $\in \mathrm{R}^{|V| \times d}$ of the embedding layer, where $|V|$ is the vocabulary size and d denotes the embedding dimension.

The weights of the embedding layer were initialized randomly using Glorot uniform initializer (Glorot and Bengio, 2010) then optimized while training the model. It should be noted that, we chose not to use pretrained word embeddings for initialization, as the available Arabic pretrained word embeddings from (Zahran et al., 2015) and (Al-Rfou et al., 2013) were generated based on MSA/Egyptian corpora. We assume that, this can lead to out-of-vocabulary (OOV) issues especially with the Tunisian and Moroccan content, used in this study, where less common words with MSA/Egyptian do exist. Thus, for a single fixed-length n-gram containing a sequence of words $\{w_i, w_{i+1}, w_{i+2}, ..., w_{i+C-1}\}$, each word w_i is represented by a unique integer index $i \in [0,V]$ and stored as a one-hot vector vec_i whose values are zero in all positions except at the i-th index. To obtain the embedding vector v_i of a word w_i, its one-hot vector vec_i is multiplied by the matrix M as in equation (1).

$$v_i = vec_i * M \in R^{1 \times d} \qquad (1)$$

As each row of the embedding matrix M denotes the dense embedding representation of a specific word in the vocabulary, multiplying the one-hot vector of each word in the input by the embedding matrix M, will essentially select one of M rows that corresponds to the embeddings of this word.

The resulting word embeddings were then combined using the compositional model SOWE which is applied by the next linear layer Lambda. In this layer, an element-wise sum is conducted over the word embedding vectors. Here we could refer to the fact that, although the n-gram scheme retains the local order of its constituent words, formulating the n-gram embeddings vector via the additive function SOWE, totally ignores the words' order since an identical embedding vector would be composed for any order of the words contained in an n-gram. Thus, the output of the lambda layer is a single embeddings vector $O_{lambda} \in R^{1 * |d|}$ resulted from summing the embeddings vectors produced by the embedding layer which correspond to the input words contained in a window of size C:

$$O_{lambda} = \sum_{i=1}^{C} v_i \in R^{1 \times d} \qquad (2)$$

In the subsequent hidden layer (hl), the output from the previous layer O_{lambda} is subjected to a linear transformation using the weights matrix $W_{hl} \in R^{d \times 2}$ and biases $b_{hl} \in R^{1 \times 2}$:

$$O_{hl} = f(O_{lambda} * W_{hl} + b_{hl}) \in R^{1 \times 2} \qquad (3)$$

Where W_{hl} and b_{hl} form the model's parameters that are learned and optimized during the training process and f refers to the activation function that introduces non-linear discriminative features to our model. Here, we used Hard sigmoid activation function (h_σ). Hard sigmoid is a piecewise function whose output are very similar to the traditional sigmoid, however, it is computationally cheaper which leads to a smarter model since it accelerates the learning process in each iteration (Gulcehre et al., 2016).

Finally, the output O_{hl} resulting from the hidden layer is forwarded into the output layer (Ol) where a softmax function is applied to induce the estimated probabilities for each output label (positive/negative) of a specific n-gram. Where each n-gram is accompanied with the predicted two dimensional label [1,0] denoting positive or [0,1] indicating negative.

$$\hat{y} = softmax(O_{hl}) \in R^{1 \times 2} \qquad (6)$$

Softmax selects the maximum score among the two predicted conditional probabilities to denote positive or negative polarity of an input n-gram where the distribution of the form [1,0] was assigned for positive while [0,1] distribution form was adopted for negative. Thus, if the gold sentiment polarity of an n-gram is positive, the predicted positive score should be higher than the negative score while if the gold sentiment polarity of a word sequence is negative, its positive score should be smaller than the negative score. To decide the polarity of the whole sentence, the predicted positive scores and negative scores of n-grams are summed then each of which is divided by the number of the n-grams contained in this sentence resulting two values representing the potential positive and negative scores of the input sentence. The final sentence polarity is, thus, decided according to the greater among these two values. Cross-entropy loss between gold sentiment distribution and predicted distribution was adopted such that the loss function of the model:

$$J(\theta) = - \sum_{k=\{0,1\}} y_k \log \hat{y}_k \qquad (7)$$

Where $y \in R^2$ is the gold sentiment value represented by a one-hot vector, $\hat{y}$ is the sentiment distribution predicted by the model while θ refers to the parameters (weights and biases) of the model to be learned and optimized during the training process.

Dataset	Train	Dev	Test	Voc.
ArTwitter	1,280	320	400	7,253
TEC	1,948	487	608	10,675
TSAC	4,680	1,170	1,516	17,741
MEC	6,561	1,641	2,051	37,888
MDT	2,747	687	860	16,450

Table 3: The statistics of the used datasets.

Data	C=6	C=7	C=8	C=9	C=10
ArTwitter	82.7	83.0	**83.3**	82.3	81.5
TEC	87.6	**87.9**	87.9	83.6	81.2
TSAC	86.1	85.9	**86.6**	86.5	86.3
MEC	63.9	**68.6**	68.6	67.1	66.5
MDT	73.4	73.4	**73.8**	73.3	72.5

Table 4: F-measure values (%) obtained with dev sets for different window sizes.

2.2 Training details and Model's Parameters

The key hyper parameters of the proposed model are the sliding window size C and the embeddings dimension d. We have selected both parameters' values empirically during the model tuning period.

To train the proposed neural network, the back-propagation algorithm with Adaptive Moment estimation (Adam) stochastic optimization method (Kingma and Ba, 2014) has been used. Adam optimizer combines the early optimization speed of Adagrad with the better later convergence of various other methods like Adadelta and RMSprop. This is done through calculating learning rates and storing momentum changes for each model parameter separately.

To deal with the overfitting issue, Dropout was used as a regularization mechanism. The value of the dropout parameter was selected empirically during the model's tuning period.

3 Experimental Study

3.1 Datasets

For the model evaluation, Tw-StAR was employed to predict the sentiment in five publicly available datasets (See Table 3). Four of them were written in Eastern (Jordanian) and Western (Tunisian, Moroccan) Arabic dialects, while the fifth combined Eastern, Western and Gulf Arabic dialects. They are as follows:

- Arabic Twitter Dataset (ArTwitter): combines 2,000 positive/negative tweets mostly written in the Jordanian dialect (Abdulla et al., 2013).

- Tunisian Election Corpus (TEC): refers to 3,043 tweets positive/negative combining MSA and Tunisian dialect where Tunisian tweets form the majority of the data (Sayadi et al., 2016).

- Tunisian Sentiment Analysis Corpus (TSAC): combines 7,366 positive/negative Facebook comments (Medhaffar et al., 2017).

- Moroccan Election Corpus (MEC): combines 10,253 positive/negative Facebook comments (Elouardighi et al., 2017).

- Mixed-Dialects Tweets (MDT) (Altowayan and Tao, 2016): forms a combination of 4,294 positive/negative tweets from three datasets of MSA and dialectal content including: (a) Jordanian: Artwitter (Abdulla et al., 2013), (b) Egyptian: ASTD (Nabil et al., 2015) and (c) Multiple dialects: QCRI (Mourad and Darwish, 2013).

3.2 Results and Discussion

The model's parameters (C, d, dropout) were assigned empirically. Among several window sizes ranging from 6 to 10, a window size value equals to 8 was adopted since it produced the best F-measure in all datasets as it is shown in Table 4. Consequently, each input sentence is represented by a set of 8-grams to be fed to the model. Similarly, upon examining three embedding dimensions values equal to 50, 100 and 150, and several dropout values ranging from 0.2 to 0.5, d=100 and dropout=0.2 were adopted for dimensions and dropout, respectively.

The efficiency of the proposed n-gram embeddings composed by SOWE were compared against word embeddings (word2vec) and document embeddings (doc2vec). Using a supervised learning strategy with sentiment labels included in the training corpora, and provided with the same parameters of Tw-StAR model in terms of window size and embedding dimensions, we trained word2vec (Mikolov et al., 2013) and doc2vec (PV-DBoW/PV-DM) (Le and Mikolov, 2014) algorithms on each of the tackled datasets to generate the proper embedding features. In the distributed bag of words (DBoW), the embeddings vector representing a sentence is composed with words' order ignored, whereas the distributed memory variant (DM) follows the CBOW mechanism as it considers the words order while learning the

Dataset	Model	P. (%)	R. (%)	F1 (%)	A. (%)
ArTwitter	Combined LSTMs (Al-Azani and El-Alfy, 2017)	**87.3**	**87.3**	**87.2**	**87.2**
	CNNs (Dahou et al., 2016)	-	-	-	85.0
	word2vec	72.0	71.9	71.9	72.0
	doc2vec (DM)	61.2	60.7	60.1	60.4
	doc2vec (DBoW)	63.1	60.6	58.2	59.9
	Tw-StAR	85.4	84.9	84.8	84.9
TEC	hand-crafted (Sayadi et al., 2016)	67.0	71.0	63.0	71.1
	word2vec	62.6	59.7	58.4	61.9
	doc2vec (DM)	65.6	59.3	56.4	62.2
	doc2vec (DBoW)	62.9	58.9	56.7	61.4
	Tw-StAR	**87.4**	**88.4**	**87.8**	**88.2**
TSAC	MLP (Medhaffar et al., 2017)	78.0	78.0	78.0	78.0
	word2vec	78.0	77.2	77.4	78.2
	doc2vec (DM)	61.0	58.3	57.2	61.7
	doc2vec (DBoW)	55.9	54.1	52.1	58.0
	Tw-StAR	**86.2**	**86.3**	**86.2**	**86.5**
MEC	hand-crafted (Elouardighi et al., 2017)	-	-	-	78.0
	word2vec	63.6	64.0	63.8	69.1
	doc2vec (DM)	74.7	65.0	66.4	76.6
	doc2vec (DBoW)	60.4	56.6	56.4	69.3
	Tw-StAR	**76.2**	**71.2**	**72.8**	**79.2**
MDT	Arabic word embeddings (Altowayan and Tao, 2016)	**83.0**	**76.5**	**79.6**	**80.2**
	word2vec	59.3	59.2	59.2	59.4
	doc2vec (DM)	58.5	57.9	57.4	58.4
	doc2vec (DBoW)	61.2	59.4	58.2	60.2
	Tw-StAR	75.8	74.3	74.3	74.8
Average	word2vec	67.1**	66.4*	66.1*	68.1**
	doc2vec (DM)	64.2*	60.2**	59.5**	63.8*
	doc2vec (DBoW)	60.1**	57.9**	56.3**	61.7**
	Tw-StAR	**82.2**	**81.0**	**81.2**	**82.7**

Table 5: Tw-StAR performances against baseline systems and word2vec/doc2vec for all datasets. (*,**,***) refers to a significant difference at P-value<0.05, <0.01, <0.001, respectively, compared to Tw-StAR.

composed sentence embeddings vector (Le and Mikolov, 2014). Having the word embeddings and document embeddings generated for each dataset by word2vec and doc2vec algorithms, they were used as features to train Tw-StAR neural model on recognizing the sentiment of the datasets in Table 3. This was done through replacing the embeddings layer in Tw-StAR by the embeddings produced by word2vec and both variants of doc2vec. It should be noted that, word2vec and both variants of doc2vec were trained in a supervised manner. Thus, their learned embeddings are sentiment informed as the polarity labels were associated with the input training instances. This enabled a fair comparison between word2vec/doc2vec variants and our sentiment-specific syntax-ignorant n-grams embeddings.

Table 5, reviews the sentiment classification performances achieved using n-grams by SOWE, word vectors by word2vec and sentence vectors by doc2vec (PV-DBoW/PV-DM) for all datasets. The obtained performances of Tw-StAR were further compared against the baseline systems that tack-led the same datasets and also listed in Table 5; where P., R., F1 and A. denote the achieved averaged precision, recall, F-measure and accuracy respectively. It should be mentioned that, due to the limited work in SA of under-represented dialects such as Tunisian and Moroccan, it wasn't possible to perform the comparison against text embeddings-based baselines for these dialects, as the provided models for MEC and TEC datasets used only hand-crafted features.

The results in Table 5 suggest the outperformance of the proposed embeddings over those generated by word2vec and doc2vec for most datasets. This was emphasized through the significance test (T-test), where the sentiment classification performance of Tw-StAR with n-grams embeddings used for training was proved to be significantly better than that produced with word2vec/doc2vec embedding features. For instance, the best achieved F-measure was in TEC dataset with a value of 87.7% compared to 58.4%, 56.4% and 56.7% scored by word2vec, doc2vec (PV-DM) and doc2vec (PV-DBoW), respectively.

This could be explained by the ability of SOWE to capture the semantic information along with the synonymous relations among words more accurately than the average function used by doc2vec variants (White et al., 2015). On the other hand, it can be seen from Table 5 that, for datasets having an MSA-dominated content such as MEC, doc2vec (PV-DM) performs better than word2vec and doc2vec (PV-DBoW). Indeed, the achieved accuracy for MEC dataset with the embeddings learned by doc2vec (PV-DM) was 76.6% compared to 69.1% and 69.3% scored by word2vec and doc2vec (PV-DBoW), respectively. This could be due to the fact that, doc2vec (PV-DM) is a syntax-aware embeddings learning method where it acts as a memory that remembers what is missing from the context to predict a (typically) center word (Le and Mikolov, 2014). Therefore, it can handle the MSA-dominated data where syntax does matter in indicating the sentiment.

Compared to the state-of-the-art applied on the tackled datasets, our results showed that Tw-StAR trained with the proposed embeddings could improve the performance over the baselines in most of the datasets. As we can see in Table 5, with Tw-StAR applied, the accuracy increased by 17.1%, 8.3% and 1.2% for TEC, TSAC and MEC datasets, respectively. On the other hand, the less accuracy increment was reported in MSA/Moroccan MEC dataset; This defines the proposed embeddings as expressive features of pure dialectal content more than they are of MSA. Since the free word order and varying syntactic structure of dialects can be be better handled by SOWE. Moreover, for ArTwitter dataset, a competent performance was achieved by Tw-StAR against complicated neural architectures such as CNNs adopted by (Dahou et al., 2016) and combined LSTMs used in (Al-Azani and El-Alfy, 2017), where the accuracy decreased by 0.1% and 2.3% compared to (Dahou et al., 2016) and (Al-Azani and El-Alfy, 2017), respectively. Hence, a shallow neural model such as Tw-StAR trained with embeddings specifically composed to target the DA content can rival much more complicated neural architectures. In addition, for MDT dataset that contains three different dialects, although Tw-StAR could not outperform the baseline system, a satisfying performance was achieved without the need for a huge training corpus used by (Altowayan and Tao, 2016).

Aiming to inspect the performance of the n-

Dataset	word2vec	doc2vec	Tw-StAR
ArTwitter			
TEC			
TSAC			
MEC			
MDT			

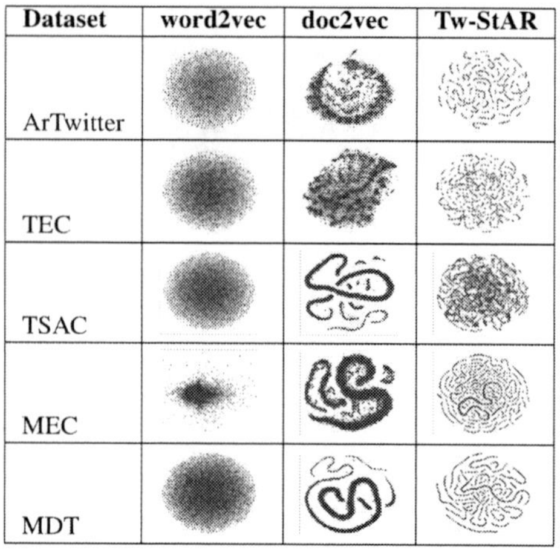

Figure 2: *t*-SNE visualization of word vectors learned by word2vec/doc2vec against word vectors learned by Tw-StAR.

gram embeddings more deeply, we visualized the embedding vectors learned by Tw-StAR against word vectors generated by word2vec and paragraph vectors learned via doc2vec (PV-DBoW). This is done by projecting the embedding vectors into a two dimensional space using the t-Distributed Stochastic Neighbour Embedding (t-SNE) technique (Maaten and Hinton, 2008).

Considering Figure 2, a clustering behavior of the words that compose n-grams or document embeddings could be observed in both doc2vec (PV-DBoW) and Tw-StAR models. In word2vec model, however, word vectors tend to spread sparsely in the embeddings space. This was reflected on the performance of the embeddings as discriminating features for the SA task. To clarify that, considering TSAC dataset, we have noticed that pure Tunisian dialectal words such "إنحبوك" and "باهي"[3] which bear positive sentiments were mapped by Tw-StAR model close to each other in the embeddings space. However, when looking to the representations created for the same dataset by doc2vec (PV-DBoW), we have come through the words "إنحبوك" and "هايلة"[4] which refer to a positive sentiment, yet they are mapped close to the negative words "ممسطها" and "خامج"[5] in the embeddings space.

---

[3]We love you and good.

[4]We love you and excellent.

[5]Dull and a dirty man.

4 Related works

In (Altowayan and Tao, 2016), Arabic word vectors were generated through training Continuous Bag of Words (CBOW) algorithm (Mikolov et al., 2013) using an Arabic corpus of 190 million words. To evaluate the generated embeddings, they were used to train several binary classifiers on recognition of the subjectivity and sentiment polarity in a combination of twitter datasets: ASTD (Nabil et al., 2015), ArTwitter (Abdulla et al., 2013) and QCRI (Mourad and Darwish, 2013) and MSA news articles. The model's performance was slightly better than (Mourad and Darwish, 2013) in subjectivity classification, while for the polarity classification of the twitter datasets, the best metric values were scored by the Nu-SVM with an accuracy of 80.21% and an F-measure of 79.62%.

A study by (Dahou et al., 2016) introduced a CNN-based deep learning SA model. The model was trained with word embeddings learned from a corpus of 3.4 billion Arabic words using CBOW and Skip-Gram (SG). Using CNN as a building unit, a neural model with one non-static channel and one convolutional layer was developed. Multiple filter window sizes were adopted to perform the convolutional operation while a max-overtime pooling layer was utilized to capture the most relevant global features (Collobert et al., 2011). The model was applied on several datasets such as ASTD (Nabil et al., 2015), ArTwitter (Abdulla et al., 2013). The results revealed that the performance of the presented model mostly outperformed all the state-of-the-art systems where for ArTwitter, the achieved accuracy was 85.0%.

The idea of including Arabic pre-trained word embeddings in a deep neural SA model was introduced by (Gridach et al., 2017). The authors used word embeddings provided by (Zahran et al., 2015) previously trained with MSA/dialectal corpora by Glove, SG and CBOW methods. These embeddings were used to initialize the input word embeddings with which their model CNN-ASAWR was trained. The proposed model was developed as a variant of (Collobert et al., 2011) system and customized to conduct SA on two MSA/dialectal datasets: ASTD (Nabil et al., 2015) and SemEval-2017 (El-Beltagy et al., 2017). Results showed that using pre-trained word embeddings led to better evaluation measures compared to the baseline systems. In ASTD dataset for instance, the best F-measure scored by CNN-ASAWR was 72.14% compared to 62.60% achieved by (Nabil et al., 2015) while for SemEval-2017, an F-measure of 63% was achieved against 61% scored by the system of (El-Beltagy et al., 2017).

As a first attempt to leverage document embeddings in ASA, doc2vec model was used in (Medhaffar et al., 2017) to generate training vectors for a Tunisian SA model. The presented model was evaluated using a combination of publicly available MSA/multi-dialectal datasets and a manually annotated Tunisian Sentiment Analysis Corpus (TSAC) obtained from Facebook comments about popular TV shows. The input data was represented by document vectors which were used later to train SVM, Bernoulli NB (BNB) and Multilayer Perceptron (MLP) classifiers. The best results were scored by a multi-layer perceptron (MLP) classifier when TSAC corpus was solely used as a training set where it achieved an accuracy equals to 78% and an F-measure value of 78%.

5 Conclusion

We introduced syntax-ignorant, n-gram embeddings as discriminating features in the context of sentiment analysis of Arabic dialects. The presented model Tw-StAR trained with these embeddings could classify the sentiment of several dialects better than most baseline systems. Being composed via SOWE function, our embeddings emphasized the efficiency of using unordered additive composition model in SA as the produced performances by n-gram embeddings were better than those learned via word2vec and doc2vec (PV-DM/PV-DBoW) models. Based on the visualization of the word embeddings learned by Tw-StAR, word2vec and doc2vec (PV-DBoW) models, it was possible to deduce that several words of close sentiments were better mapped using Tw-StAR model. Finally, it was revealed that, for Arabic dialects, a shallow neural model trained with unordered embeddings can address the varying syntactic structure and free word order issues yielding a competent performance with much more complicated deep learning architectures. A natural future step would involve using the proposed embeddings to represent the sentiment of other languages. Furthermore, a multi-dialectal lexicon would be constructed based on the distances among the word embedding vectors learned via Tw-StAR and visualized by *t*-SNE tool.

References

Nawaf A. Abdulla, Nizar A. Ahmed, Mohammed A. Shehab, and Mahmoud Al-Ayyoub. 2013. Arabic sentiment analysis: Lexicon-based and corpus-based. In *2013 IEEE Jordan Conference on Applied Electrical Engineering and Computing Technologies (AEECT)*, pages 1–6. IEEE.

Sadam Al-Azani and El-Sayed M. El-Alfy. 2017. Hybrid deep learning for sentiment polarity determination of arabic microblogs. In *International Conference on Neural Information Processing*, pages 491–500. Springer.

Rami Al-Rfou, Bryan Perozzi, and Steven Skiena. 2013. Polyglot: Distributed word representations for multilingual nlp. *arXiv preprint arXiv:1307.1662*.

Ahmad Al Sallab, Hazem Hajj, Gilbert Badaro, Ramy Baly, Wassim El Hajj, and Khaled Bashir Shaban. 2015. Deep learning models for sentiment analysis in arabic. In *Proceedings of the Second Workshop on Arabic Natural Language Processing*, pages 9–17.

Aziz A. Altowayan and Lixin Tao. 2016. Word embeddings for arabic sentiment analysis. In *2016 IEEE International Conference on Big Data (Big Data)*, pages 3820–3825. IEEE.

Kristen E. Brustad. 2000. *The Syntax of Spoken Arabic: A Comparative Study of Moroccan, Egyptian, Syrian, and Kuwaiti Dialects.* ERIC.

Ronan Collobert, Jason Weston, Léon Bottou, Michael Karlen, Koray Kavukcuoglu, and Pavel Kuksa. 2011. Natural language processing (almost) from scratch. *Journal of Machine Learning Research*, 12(Aug):2493–2537.

Abdelghani Dahou, Shengwu Xiong, Junwei Zhou, Mohamed Houcine Haddoud, and Pengfei Duan. 2016. Word embeddings and convolutional neural network for arabic sentiment classification. In *Proceedings of COLING 2016, the 26th International Conference on Computational Linguistics: Technical Papers*, pages 2418–2427.

Samhaa R. El-Beltagy, Mona El kalamawy, and Abu Bakr Soliman. 2017. Niletmrg at semeval-2017 task 4: Arabic sentiment analysis. In *Proceedings of the 11th International Workshop on Semantic Evaluation (SemEval-2017)*, pages 790–795. Association for Computational Linguistics.

Abdeljalil Elouardighi, Mohcine Maghfour, Hafdalla Hammia, and Fatima-zahra Aazi. 2017. A machine learning approach for sentiment analysis in the standard or dialectal arabic facebook comments. In *3rd International Conference of Cloud Computing Technologies and Applications (CloudTech)*, pages 1–8. IEEE.

Xavier Glorot and Yoshua Bengio. 2010. Understanding the difficulty of training deep feedforward neural networks. In *Proceedings of the Thirteenth International Conference on Artificial Intelligence and Statistics*, pages 249–256.

Mourad Gridach, Hatem Haddad, and Hala Mulki. 2017. Empirical evaluation of word representations on arabic sentiment analysis. In *International Conference on Arabic Language Processing (ICALP)*, pages 147–158. Springer.

Caglar Gulcehre, Marcin Moczulski, Misha Denil, and Yoshua Bengio. 2016. Noisy activation functions. In *International Conference on Machine Learning*, pages 3059–3068.

Mohit Iyyer, Varun Manjunatha, Jordan Boyd-Graber, and Hal Daumé III. 2015. Deep unordered composition rivals syntactic methods for text classification. In *Proceedings of the 53rd Annual Meeting of the Association for Computational Linguistics and the 7th International Joint Conference on Natural Language Processing (Volume 1: Long Papers)*, volume 1, pages 1681–1691.

Diederik P. Kingma and Jimmy Ba. 2014. Adam: A method for stochastic optimization. *CoRR*, abs/1412.6980.

Quoc Le and Tomas Mikolov. 2014. Distributed representations of sentences and documents. In *International Conference on Machine Learning*, pages 1188–1196.

Laurens van der Maaten and Geoffrey Hinton. 2008. Visualizing data using t-sne. *Journal of machine learning research*, 9(Nov):2579–2605.

Salima Medhaffar, Fethi Bougares, Yannick Esteve, and Lamia Hadrich-Belguith. 2017. Sentiment analysis of tunisian dialects: Linguistic ressources and experiments. In *Proceedings of the Third Arabic Natural Language Processing Workshop*, pages 55–61.

Tomas Mikolov, Ilya Sutskever, Kai Chen, Greg S. Corrado, and Jeff Dean. 2013. Distributed representations of words and phrases and their compositionality. In *Advances in neural information processing systems*, pages 3111–3119.

Jeff Mitchell and Mirella Lapata. 2010. Composition in distributional models of semantics. *Cognitive science*, 34(8):1388–1429.

Ahmed Mourad and Kareem Darwish. 2013. Subjectivity and sentiment analysis of modern standard arabic and arabic microblogs. In *Proceedings of the 4th workshop on computational approaches to subjectivity, sentiment and social media analysis*, pages 55–64.

Mahmoud Nabil, Mohamed Aly, and Amir Atiya. 2015. Astd: Arabic sentiment tweets dataset. In *Proceedings of the 2015 Conference on Empirical*

Methods in Natural Language Processing, pages 2515–2519.

Karim Sayadi, Marcus Liwicki, Rolf Ingold, and Marc Bui. 2016. Tunisian dialect and modern standard arabic dataset for sentiment analysis : Tunisian election context. In *To appear in the ACLing 2016 IEEE proceedings*. CICLING.

Duyu Tang, Furu Wei, Nan Yang, Ming Zhou, Ting Liu, and Bing Qin. 2014. Learning sentiment-specific word embedding for twitter sentiment classification. In *Proceedings of the 52nd Annual Meeting of the Association for Computational Linguistics (Volume 1: Long Papers)*, volume 1, pages 1555–1565.

Lyndon White, Roberto Togneri, Wei Liu, and Mohammed Bennamoun. 2015. How well sentence embeddings capture meaning. In *Proceedings of the 20th Australasian Document Computing Symposium*, page 9. ACM.

Mohamed A. Zahran, Ahmed Magooda, Ashraf Y. Mahgoub, Hazem Raafat, Mohsen Rashwan, and Amir Atyia. 2015. Word representations in vector space and their applications for arabic. In *International Conference on Intelligent Text Processing and Computational Linguistics*, pages 430–443. Springer.

ArbEngVec : Arabic-English Cross-Lingual Word Embedding Model

Raki Lachraf
Echahid Hamma Lakhdar University,
El Oued, Algeria
raki.lachraf@univ-eloued.dz

El Moatez Billah Nagoudi
Echahid Hamma Lakhdar University,
El Oued, Algeria
LIM laboratory, Laghouat
moatez-nagoudi@univ-eloued.dz

Youcef Ayachi
Echahid Hamma Lakhdar
University
El Oued, Algeria
youcef.ayachi@univ-eloued.dz

Ahmed Abdelali
Hamad Bin Khalifa University
Qatar Computing Research Institute
Doha, Qatar
aabdelali@qf.org.qa

Didier Schwab
LIG-GETALP
Univ. Grenoble Alpes,
France
didier.schwab@imag.fr

Abstract

Word Embeddings (WE) are getting increasingly popular and widely applied in many Natural Language Processing (NLP) applications due to their effectiveness in capturing semantic properties of words; Machine Translation (MT), Information Retrieval (IR) and Information Extraction (IE) are among such areas. In this paper, we propose an open source ArbEngVec which provides several Arabic-English cross-lingual word embedding models. To train our bilingual models, we use a large dataset with more than 93 million pairs of Arabic-English parallel sentences. In addition, we perform both extrinsic and intrinsic evaluations for the different word embedding model variants. The extrinsic evaluation assesses the performance of models on the cross-language Semantic Textual Similarity (STS), while the intrinsic evaluation is based on the Word Translation (WT) task.

1 Introduction

Distributed word representations in vector space (Word Embeddings) are one of the most successful applications in deep learning for capturing the semantic and syntactic properties of words. Lately, many NLP tasks have been enriched using tools based on Mono and Cross-Lingual word embedding models. For instance, Mono-Lingual Word Embeddings (MLWE) have been widely used in information retrieval (Vulić and Moens, 2015a), sentiment analysis (Tang et al., 2014; Nagoudi, 2018) text classification (Lai et al., 2015), semantic textual similarity (Kenter and De Rijke, 2015; Nagoudi and Schwab, 2017) and plagiarism detection (Nagoudi et al., 2018).

Cross-Lingual Word Embeddings (CLWE) is a more challenging task because the knowledge is transferred between two or more different languages (Doval et al., 2018). Recently, cross-lingual word embeddings was used to address several issues, e.g. machine translation (Zou et al., 2013), cross-language information retrieval (Vulić and Moens, 2015a; Zhou et al., 2012), cross-language semantic similarity (Ataman et al., 2016; Nagoudi et al., 2017b) and plagiarism detection across multiple languages (Ferrero et al., 2017; Barrón-Cedeño et al., 2013). Many cross-lingual word embedding models in natural language have been developed, particularly for English, but Arabic did not get that much of interest.

In this paper, we propose six Arabic-English cross-lingual word embedding models[1]. To train these models, we have used a large collection with more than 93 million pairs of parallel Arabic-English sentences.

The rest of this paper is organised as follows: in section 2 we provide a quick overview of work related to the cross-lingual word embedding models. We describe our dataset collection and the preprocessing process in Section 3. Section 4 presents our proposed cross-lingual models. Section 5 presents the evaluation results. Section 6 concludes the paper with our main findings and points to possible directions for future work.

2 Related works

While we focus on the cross-lingual word embedding models, the interested reader may refer to a number of research studies on the subject of mono-lingual word embeddings in general (Collobert and Weston, 2008), (Turian et al.,

---

[1]All models can be downloaded from :
https://github.com/Raki22/ArbEngVec.git

Proceedings of the Fourth Arabic Natural Language Processing Workshop, pages 40–48
Florence, Italy, August 1, 2019. ©2019 Association for Computational Linguistics

2010), (Mnih and Hinton, 2009), (Mikolov et al., 2013c,b) and (Peters et al., 2018).

In the cross-lingual context, several word embedding models are proposed. Blunsom and Hermann (2014) introduced a Bilingual Compositional Model (BiCVM). Leveraging from the fact that aligned sentences have the same meaning. BiCVM is based on a sentence-aligned corpus to learn the bilingual word embedding vectors.

Vulić and Moens (2015b) introduced a Bilingual Word Embedding Skip-Gram (BWESG), this model is constructed through three main steps: i) prepare a Skip-Gram Negative Sampling (Mikolov et al., 2013b) architecture that deals with document aligned comparable data, ii) provide bilingual document pairs, iii) shuffle each pair producing pseudo-bilingual document that serves as the architecture's input which is to be trained.

Luong et al. (2015) proposed a Bilingual Skip-Gram model (BiSKip). BiSKip uses the Skip-Gram of (Mikolov et al., 2013b) to train two different languages at the same time by manipulating the Skip-Gram architecture to obtain two pivots and two contexts and provide a training session for each combination. Choosing two Germanic languages (English and German) made it easier to predict target language's appropriate pivot and context for the ones from source language by simply aligning the target words at position $[i * T/S]$ with source words at position i where S and T are source and target sentence lengths respectively.

Chen et al. (2018) presented an Adversarial Deep Averaging Network (ADAN) for cross-lingual sentiment classification. In fact, they trained many bilingual WE models, one of them was trained using the United Nations (UN) English-Arabic parallel aligned corpus (Ziemski et al., 2016) and Bilingual Bag-of-Words without Alignments (BilBOWA) (Gouws et al., 2015). Additionally, ADAN replaces the softmax and regularization terms by a less costly alternatives.

Recently, Devlin et al. (2018) have proposed a deep learning method called Bidirectional Encoder Representations from Transformers (BERT) based on overcoming the limitations of *next* and *previous* token prediction procedures benefiting from Masked Language Modeling (MLM) (Taylor, 1953) by masking 15% of the sentence tokens fed into the architecture alongside the transformer encoder (Vaswani et al., 2017). Devlin et al. (2018) have extended their work by applying the same architecture in a Wikipedia corpora of 104 different languages, requiring not a single alignment signal and realising, if not outperforming, state-of-the-art score in many NLP tasks such as Part Of Speech Tagging and Named Entity Recognition. However, BERT demands significantly more machine effort (Wu and Dredze, 2019). Table 1 summarises the cross-language embedding models mentioned above according to the architecture and used corpus, the target languages and the evaluation methods.

3 Dataset Collection

3.1 Corpus Used

The main objective of this work is to provide an efficient Arabic-English cross-lingual word embedding models across different text domains. Indeed, we used a large dataset of parallel Arabic-English sentences mainly extracted from the Open Parallel Corpus Project[2] (OPUS) (Tiedemann, 2012). OPUS contains 90 languages, and more than 2.7 billion parallel sentences. This corpus consists of data from multiple domains and sources including: MultiUN Corpus (Daniel Tapias, 2010), OpenSubtitles (Creutz, 2018), Tanzil (Zarrabi-Zadeh, 2007), News-Commentary, United Nations (UN) (Ziemski et al., 2016), Wikipedia, TED 2013[3], GNOME[4], Tatoeba[5], Global Voices[6], KDE4[7] and Ubuntu[8] corpus. To train our models, we extract more than 93.9 million parallel sentences of Arabic-English from whole collection, this alignment contains more than 800 million Arabic tokens and 1 billion for English. More details about our dataset are given in Table 2.

3.2 Preprocessing and Normalization

Preprocessing is an important step in building any word embedding model as it can potentially significantly affect the end results. We first remove the punctuation marks, non letters, URLs, emojis and emoticons from the Arabic and English sentences. Additionally, we normalize Arabic sentences using the preprocessing suggested by Nagoudi et al.

---

[2]http://opus.nlpl.eu/
[3]http://www.casmacat.eu/corpus/ted2013.html
[4]https://l10n.gnome.org
[5]www.tatoeba.org
[6]https://globalvoices.org/
[7]http://i18n.kde.org
[8]https://translations.launchpad.net

CLWE Models	Corpus Used	Arch.	Languages	Evaluation
BiCVM (Hermann and Blunsom, 2014)	Europarl (Koehn, 2005), TED (Cettolo et al., 2012), RCV (Lewis et al., 2004)	CVM	English, German, French, Arabic, Spanish, Italian, Dutch, Brazilian	Cross-lingual classification
BiSKip (Luong et al., 2015)	UN corpus Koehn (2005)	Skip-Gram	English, German	Mono and bilingual word similarity, cross-lingual classification
BWESG (Vulić and Moens, 2015b)	UN corpus Koehn (2005)	Skip-Gram	English, Dutch	Mono and cross-lingual ad-hoc retrieval
BilBOWA (Gouws et al., 2015)	RCV (Lewis et al., 2004), WMT11 (2011)	CBOW	English, German, Spanish	Word translation, cross-lingual classification
ADAN (Chen et al., 2018)	UN corpus (Ziemski et al., 2016)	Skip-Gram	English, Arabic, Chinese	Domain Adaptation and Machine Translation
mBERT (Devlin et al., 2018)	Large Wikipedia Corpora	BERT	104 Languages (including Arabic)	POS Tagging and NER...etc

Table 1: Different cross-language word embedding models

(2017a):

1. The letters أ ، إ ، آ are replaced with ا while the letter ة is replaced with ه. Also, The letter ى followed by ء replaced with ئ.

2. We converted elongated words back to their original form, example : معاهدةﺍﺍﺍﺍﺍﺍﺍﺍﺍ, which means *treaty* in English, and الجزائـــــــــر, which means *Algeria* will be converted to الجزائر, معاهدة.

3. In addition, we remove the stop-words from Arabic and English sentences.

4 Building ArbEngVec Models

4.1 Used Architectures

In Mikolov et al. (2013a) all the word embedding models (Collobert and Weston, 2008), (Turian et al., 2010), (Mnih and Hinton, 2009), (Mikolov et al., 2010), (Mikolov et al., 2013c) and (Mikolov et al., 2013b) have been compared and evaluated, and they show that CBOW (Mikolov et al., 2013c) and Skip-Gram (Mikolov et al., 2013b) models are significantly faster to train with better accuracy. Accordingly, we used the CBOW and Skip-Gram to build our Arabic-English cross-lingual word embedding models.

The CBOW (Mikolov et al., 2013c) and Skip-Gram (Mikolov et al., 2013b) are two shallow neural network architectures with a single hidden layer that learns similar vector representations for words with similar distributional properties. The CBOW model, predicts a targeted word w_t according to the context in which w_t appears by using a window of contextual words. While the Skip-Gram model, predicts the words around the word w_t (Mikolov et al., 2013a), as illustrated in figure 1.

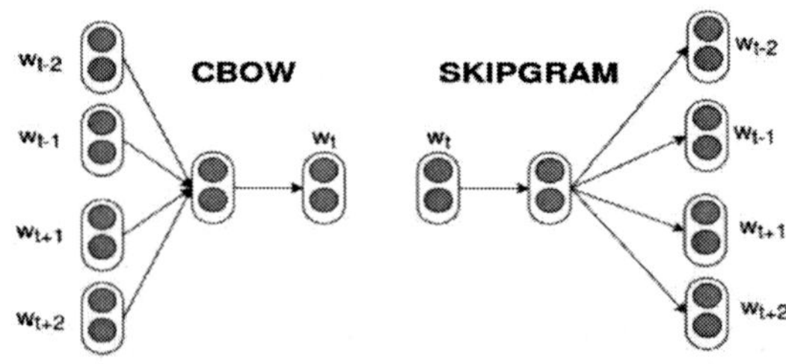

Figure 1: Architecture of CBOW and Skip-gram as described in (Mikolov et al., 2013b)

4.2 Proposed Models

In this section, we present our proposed ArbEngVec models. In order to learn our models, we have relied basically on shuffling the cor-

Corpus	Content	Documents	Sentences	Ar Words	En Words
MultiUN Corpus.	The official documents of the United Nations (UN)	67617	10.6M	263.1M	289.6M
OpenSubtitles.	A new collection of translated movie subtitles	104325	81.4M	501.5M	695.9M
Tanzil.	A collection of Quran translations	30 Quran Party	0.2M	7.9M	5.6M
News-Comment	A parallel corpus of News Commentaries provided by WMT for training Statistical Machine Translation (SMT)	7185	0.6M	15.4M	15.5M
UN.	A collection of translated documents from the United Nations originally	1	74.1k	3.3M	3.7M
Wikipedia.	A corpus of parallel sentences extracted from Wikipedia	1	0.2M	3.2M	3.5M
TED2013.	A parallel corpus of TED talk subtitles provided by CASMACAT	1	0.2M	2.4M	3.0M
GNOME.	A parallel corpus of GNOME localization files	1313	0.5M	2.4M	2.6M
Tatoeba.	A collection of translated sentences from Tatoeba	1	13.0k	90.1k	3.6M
GlobalVoices.	A parallel corpus of news stories from the web site Global Voices	7017	93.9k	2.1M	3.0M
KDE4.	A parallel corpus of KDE4 system messages	784	0.1M	0.7M	0.8M
Ubuntu.	A parallel corpus of the Ubuntu Dialogue Corpus	299	56.3M	0.2M	0.5M
EUbookshop.	Corpus of documents from the EU bookshop an online service and archive of publications from various European institutions	30	1.7k	80.0k	0.4M
Total	All the corpus used and extracted from OPUS	188606	93.9M	802.3M	1.0G

Table 2: Some statistics about the used dataset (Tiedemann, 2012)

	CBOW					Skip-Gram				
#Modes	Top1	Top2	Top3	Top5	Top10	Top1	Top2	Top3	Top5	Top10
Parallel	0.1%	0.5%	0.7%	1.2%	2.1%	2.8%	4.5%	6.1%	6.1%	9.3%
W. by W.	4.1%	11.3%	17.4%	25.3%	37.2%	60.6%	73.5%	78.3%	86.8%	92.4%
Random	57.7%	71.4%	79.2%	85.3%	90.5%	62.4%	74.2%	78.4%	87.5%	**93.8%**

Table 3: Intrinsic evaluation results of ArbEngVec models

pus as in Vulić and Moens (2015b), with one major difference choosing sentence-aligned parallel data rather than their comparable document-aligned choice. Indeed, we propose to use three methods for learning our models: *Parallel Mode*, *Word by Word Alignment Mode* and *Random Shuffling Mode*.

4.2.1 Parallel Mode

To make clear that shuffling methods adds cross-lingual improvements, we decided to train a model without any alignment. For example, let S_{ar} and S_{en} be Arabic and English sentences:

$$S_{ar} = \text{"الولدان الصغيران شقيقان".}$$

$$S_{en} = \text{" The young boys are brothers"}.$$

The pair (S_{ar}, S_{en}) were fed directly to the training as follows: "*young, boys, brothers*, الولدان, شقيقان الصغيران".

4.2.2 Word by Word Alignment Mode

The second method used on the same corpus type with aligning pairs *word by word* and paying attention to sentences length and start aligning with the longest (the short sentence words will be surrounded with those of the long sentence). This method supports using pairs with almost equal lengths. In this situation, stop-words removal pre-processing step is highly blessed. We shall continue with the sentences of the previous example, the input of the training is : "*young,* الولدان, *boys,* الصغيران, *brothers,* شقيقان".

4.2.3 Random Shuffling Mode

In this method, we put each pair of bilingual sentences as a list that contains their words and shuffle it **randomly** and separately from the rest of the corpus to have a list of combined English-Arabic tokens. As shown in our example : " *young,* الصغيران الولدان, *boys, brothers,* شقيقان".

4.3 Parameters and Training Environment

Training word embedding models require the choice of some parameters affecting the resulting vectors. For our CBOW models we have used recommended parameters values proposed by (Mikolov et al., 2013c). Thus, we set the *vector size* to 300, the *window* = 5, and *Frequency threshold* = 100. Regarding the Skip-gram models we have chosen Negative Sampling with *negative* = 5 instead of Hierarchical Softmax. Worth mentioning that all models were trained on 10 epochs with Řehůřek and Sojka (2011) GenSim tool.

Concerning the training environment, we have used *Google Colaboratory*[9] research project (also known as *Colab*) for training our model variants. It is a perfectly prepared developing environment with no requirements but a browser. This environment provides a free 12 GB of GPU, also access to *Google Drive* personal account for saving and loading files and there are many other services that can be plugged into it.

5 Evaluation

Usually multilingual models go against two aspects of evaluation methodology: maintain monolingual aspect and provide the other cross-lingual. Clearly for us, after creding on the shuffle we lost the former willingly to stick around the latter. Preserving the model's monolingual behaviour requires keeping words in a semantic meaningful order, which is exactly what happens with our first parallel (non-shuffling) model with completely skewed cross-lingual aspect. To clarify that, we have evaluated our models through Semantic Textual Similarity as extrinsic, and Word Translation as intrinsic.

5.1 Intrinsic Evaluation

In this step, we basically focused on word translation following (Gouws et al., 2015) evaluation procedure, so we generated a 1000 tuples starting with choosing random 1000 words from the model vocabulary. Then, we find their *k-closest* (*k* most similar) cross-lingual words based on the cosine similarity in our six ArbEngVec models. In fact, we have used five different values of *k* to generate the 1-*closest*, 2-*closest*, 3-*closest*, 5-*closest* and 10-*closest* words.

For example, Table 4 shows the 5-*closest* words of مالزيا and *weapons* in our *random Skip-Gram* model. Afterwards, we calculate the accuracy of each range, which has been calculated by giving a value 1 to each word couple that represents a translation, we make sure that the word provided by our model is a translation with comparing it to Google Translate API's bag of words, if this comparison comes negative we compare manually, if also manual comparison comes negative we give negative score 0. Eventually we count the average of the 1000 scores. Results of the six studied models are provided in Table 3.

Discussion. Parallel results were so dim bilingually as Table 3 shows, but monolingual aspect was preserved especially in CBOW variant. This fact is illustrated in Table 5, the same 5-*closest* words of مالزيا and *weapon* using Parallel CBOW model. Switching to *word by word* alignment method, both variants gave promising results and notably Skip-gram's by an average of 59.26% from CBOW, and these are a consequence of getting word translation pairs at the context window range but still since Arabic and English are structurally different this alignment method had its inconvenience. Arriving to *random shuffle* variants which have given the best results and again Skip-Gram with average of 2.44% better than CBOW.

5-closest (مالزيا)	5-closest (weapons)
malaysia, ‫قرغيزيستان,‬ ‫منغوريا ,تونغا ,كودت‬	‫الأسلحة ,الدمار ,أسلحة,‬ mass, indiscriminite

Table 4: A sample of 5-*closest* words of مالزيا and *weapons* in our Random Skip-Gram model

5-closest (مالزيا)	5-closest (weapons)
‫مدغشقر, المكسيك,‬ ‫ليسوتو ,نيجريا ,نيبال‬	arms, weaponry, warheads, missiles, arsenals

Table 5: A sample of 5-*closest* words of مالزيا and *weapons* in our Parallel CBOW model

---

[9]https://colab.research.google.com/

5.2 Extrinsic Evaluation

Extrinsic evaluating means surveilling the model performance under real-world Natural Language Processing tasks use. Our choice fell on Semantic Sentences Similarity (STS) task. To estimate the semantic similarity between the Arabic-English sentences, we have used the WE-based approach proposed by Nagoudi et al. (2017b) jointly with our ArbEngVec models. In fact, we have had STS2017-Eval[10] datasets drawn from the shared taskSemEval-2017 Task1: STS Cross-lingual Arabic-English (Cer et al., 2017). The sentence pairs of STS2017-Eval have been manually labelled by five annotators, and the similarity score is the average of the annotators judgments. Afterwards, in order to evaluate the performance of each model, we calculate Pearson correlation between our assigned semantic similarity scores and human judgement. Table 6 reports the results of the six studied models.

# Modes	CBOW	Skip-Gram
Parallel.	6.3%	18.1%
W. by W.	49.4%	73.6%
Random.	52.8%	**75.7%**

Table 6: Extrinsic evaluation results of ArbEngVec models

Discussion. These results indicate that when the *parallel* alignment is used the correlation rate gets very low in both architectures. This is due to the distance of every word and its translation in the parallel sentences pair shape. However, when applying the *word by word* alignment the correlation rate is clearly outperformed to 49.4% and 73.6% with the CBOW and Skip-Gram model respectively. Additionally, the observed results indicate that the *random shuffling* method with Skip-Gram model is the best performing method with a correlation rate of 75.7%.

5.3 Models Visualization

As part of the discussion, we have chosen to illustrate our models using *pyplot* scatters with Maaten and Hinton (2008) *t-SNE* algorithm. We provide these visualizations by choosing 20 arbitrary words from our vocabulary, run $4\text{-}closest$ similarity to each word and finally project all of them on the 2-dimensional plot. Starting with *parallel* mode models, charts show that distance between Arabic markers are distant from others of English comparing to those of the same language. Same thing can be said on the situation that concerns *word by word* method CBOW variant with less distant languages but still marker bags most often do not include translation pairs. Eventually, *random* variant charts make it clear that close markers include translation pairs alongside mono and cross-lingual similarities, six model charts are in figure 2. Especially for Skip-Gram variant, supposedly that t-SNE feature reduction procedure got rid of both language characteristics, as figure 3 shows, words and their translations most often appear next to each other.

6 Conclusion

In this paper, we have presented the open source project named ArbEngVec. This project provides several Arabic-English cross-lingual word embedding models. The embedding models are learned through a large dataset of parallel Arabic-English sentences. Additionally, we evaluated the ArbEngVec models via extrinsic and intrinsic evaluations. In the extrinsic evaluation, we used the cross-language semantic similarity task to test the capability of our models to capture the semantic and syntactic properties of words in two different languages. While in the intrinsic evaluations, we employed the embedding vectors to evaluate the word translation task.

As future work, we are going to use these models with those of other classical NLP techniques, including word sense disambiguation, named entity recognition to make more improvement in the Arabic-English cross-language semantic similarity and plagiarism detection. We also are going to aim on finding better word alignment methods to improve features capturing regarding the transfer between Semitic and Germanic languages.

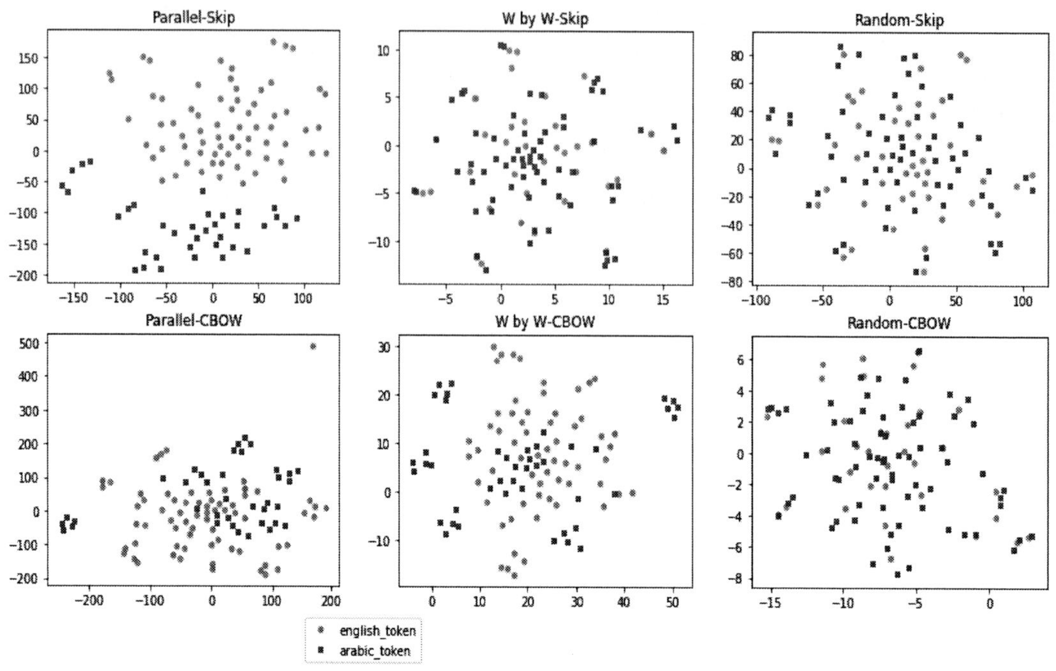

Figure 2: Charts of the model's six variants

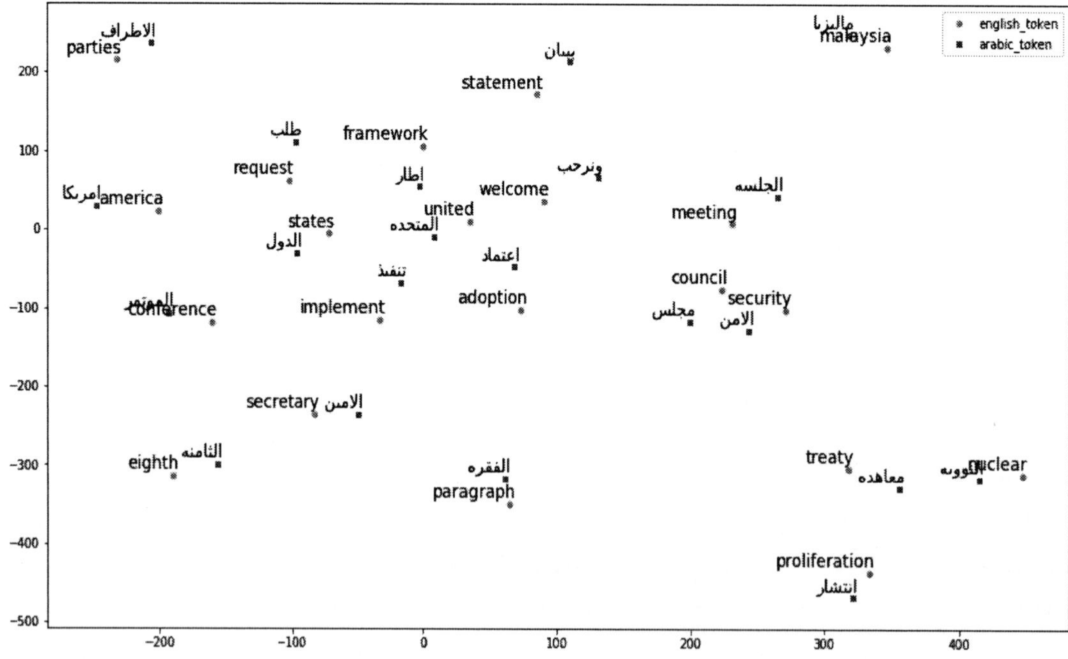

Figure 3: Chart of Random Skip-Gram model

References

Duygu Ataman, Jose GC De Souza, Marco Turchi, and Matteo Negri. 2016. Fbk hlt-mt at semeval-2016 task 1: Cross-lingual semantic similarity measurement using quality estimation features and compositional bilingual word embeddings. In *Proceedings of the 10th International Workshop on Semantic Evaluation (SemEval-2016)*, pages 570–576.

Alberto Barrón-Cedeño, Parth Gupta, and Paolo Rosso. 2013. Methods for cross-language plagiarism detection. *Knowledge-Based Systems*, 50:211–217.

Phil Blunsom and Karl Moritz Hermann. 2014. Multilingual models for compositional distributional semantics.

Daniel Cer, Mona Diab, Eneko Agirre, Inigo Lopez-Gazpio, and Lucia Specia. 2017. Semeval-2017 task 1: Semantic textual similarity multilingual and crosslingual focused evaluation. In *Proceedings of the 11th International Workshop on Semantic Evaluation (SemEval-2017)*, pages 1–14, Vancouver, Canada. ACL.

Mauro Cettolo, Christian Girardi, and Marcello Federico. 2012. Wit3: Web inventory of transcribed and translated talks. In *Conference of European Association for Machine Translation*, pages 261–268.

Xilun Chen, Yu Sun, Ben Athiwaratkun, Claire Cardie, and Kilian Weinberger. 2018. Adversarial deep averaging networks for cross-lingual sentiment classification. *Transactions of the Association for Computational Linguistics*, 6:557–570.

Ronan Collobert and Jason Weston. 2008. A unified architecture for natural language processing: Deep neural networks with multitask learning. In *Proceedings of the 25th international conference on Machine learning*, pages 160–167. ACM.

Mathias Creutz. 2018. Open subtitles paraphrase corpus for six languages. *arXiv preprint arXiv:1809.06142*.

Stelios Piperidis Jan Odjik Joseph Mariani Bente Maegaard Khalid Choukri Nicoletta Calzolari Daniel Tapias, Mike Rosner. 2010. Multiun: A multilingual corpus from united nation documents.

Jacob Devlin, Ming-Wei Chang, Kenton Lee, and Kristina Toutanova. 2018. Bert: Pre-training of deep bidirectional transformers for language understanding. *arXiv preprint arXiv:1810.04805*.

Yerai Doval, Jose Camacho-Collados, Luis Espinosa-Anke, and Steven Schockaert. 2018. Improving cross-lingual word embeddings by meeting in the middle. *arXiv preprint arXiv:1808.08780*.

Jérémy Ferrero, Frédéric Agnes, Laurent Besacier, and Didier Schwab. 2017. Using word embedding for cross-language plagiarism detection. *arXiv preprint arXiv:1702.03082*.

Stephan Gouws, Yoshua Bengio, and Greg Corrado. 2015. Bilbowa: Fast bilingual distributed representations without word alignments.

Karl Moritz Hermann and Phil Blunsom. 2014. Multilingual models for compositional distributed semantics. *arXiv preprint arXiv:1404.4641*.

Tom Kenter and Maarten De Rijke. 2015. Short text similarity with word embeddings. In *Proceedings of the 24th ACM international on conference on information and knowledge management*, pages 1411–1420. ACM.

Philipp Koehn. 2005. Europarl: A parallel corpus for statistical machine translation. In *MT summit*, volume 5, pages 79–86.

Siwei Lai, Liheng Xu, Kang Liu, and Jun Zhao. 2015. Recurrent convolutional neural networks for text classification. In *Twenty-ninth AAAI conference on artificial intelligence*.

David D Lewis, Yiming Yang, Tony G Rose, and Fan Li. 2004. Rcv1: A new benchmark collection for text categorization research. *Journal of machine learning research*, 5(Apr):361–397.

Thang Luong, Hieu Pham, and Christopher D Manning. 2015. Bilingual word representations with monolingual quality in mind. pages 151–159.

Laurens van der Maaten and Geoffrey Hinton. 2008. Visualizing data using t-sne. *Journal of machine learning research*, 9(Nov):2579–2605.

Tomas Mikolov, Kai Chen, Greg Corrado, and Jeffrey Dean. 2013a. Efficient estimation of word representations in vector space. In *In: ICLR: Proceeding of the International Conference on Learning Representations Workshop Track*, pages 1301–3781.

Tomas Mikolov, Martin Karafiát, Lukas Burget, Jan Cernockỳ, and Sanjeev Khudanpur. 2010. Recurrent neural network based language model. In *Interspeech*, volume 2, page 3.

Tomas Mikolov, Ilya Sutskever, Kai Chen, Greg S Corrado, and Jeff Dean. 2013b. Distributed representations of words and phrases and their compositionality. In *Advances in neural information processing systems*, pages 3111–3119.

Tomas Mikolov, Wen-tau Yih, and Geoffrey Zweig. 2013c. Linguistic regularities in continuous space word representations. In *Hlt-naacl*, volume 13, pages 746–751.

Andriy Mnih and Geoffrey E Hinton. 2009. A scalable hierarchical distributed language model. In D. Koller, D. Schuurmans, Y. Bengio, and L. Bottou, editors, *Advances in Neural Information Processing Systems 21*, pages 1081–1088. Curran Associates, Inc.

El Moatez Billah Nagoudi. 2018. Arb-sen at semeval-2018 task1: A new set of features for enhancing the sentiment intensity prediction in arabic tweets. In *SemEval@ NAACL-HLT*, pages 364–368.

El Moatez Billah Nagoudi, Jérémy Ferrero, and Didier Schwab. 2017a. Lim-lig at semeval-2017 task1: Enhancing the semantic similarity for arabic sentences with vectors weighting. In *Proceedings of the 11th International Workshop on Semantic Evaluation (SemEval-2017)*, pages 134–138.

El Moatez Billah Nagoudi, Jérémy Ferrero, Didier Schwab, Hadda Cherroun, et al. 2017b. Word embedding-based approaches for measuring semantic similarity of arabic-english sentences. In *International Conference on Arabic Language Processing*, pages 19–33. Springer.

El Moatez Billah Nagoudi, Ahmed Khorsi, Hadda Cherroun, and Didier Schwab. 2018. A two-level plagiarism detection system for arabic documents. *Cybernetics and Information Technologies*, 20.

El Moatez Billah Nagoudi and Didier Schwab. 2017. Semantic similarity of arabic sentences with word embeddings. In *Third Arabic Natural Language Processing Workshop*, pages 18–24.

Matthew E Peters, Mark Neumann, Mohit Iyyer, Matt Gardner, Christopher Clark, Kenton Lee, and Luke Zettlemoyer. 2018. Deep contextualized word representations. *arXiv preprint arXiv:1802.05365*.

Radim Řehřek and Petr Sojka. 2011. Gensimstatistical semantics in python. *statistical semantics; gensim; Python; LDA; SVD*.

Duyu Tang, Furu Wei, Nan Yang, Ming Zhou, Ting Liu, and Bing Qin. 2014. Learning sentiment-specific word embedding for twitter sentiment classification. In *Proceedings of the 52nd Annual Meeting of the Association for Computational Linguistics (Volume 1: Long Papers)*, volume 1, pages 1555–1565.

Wilson L Taylor. 1953. cloze procedure: A new tool for measuring readability. *Journalism Bulletin*, 30(4):415–433.

Jörg Tiedemann. 2012. Parallel data, tools and interfaces in opus. 2012:2214–2218.

Joseph Turian, Lev Ratinov, and Yoshua Bengio. 2010. Word representations: a simple and general method for semi-supervised learning. In *Proceedings of the 48th annual meeting of the association for computational linguistics*, pages 384–394. Association for Computational Linguistics.

Ashish Vaswani, Noam Shazeer, Niki Parmar, Jakob Uszkoreit, Llion Jones, Aidan N Gomez, ukasz Kaiser, and Illia Polosukhin. 2017. Attention is all you need. In *Advances in neural information processing systems*, pages 5998–6008.

Ivan Vulić and Marie-Francine Moens. 2015a. Monolingual and cross-lingual information retrieval models based on (bilingual) word embeddings. In *Proceedings of the 38th international ACM SIGIR conference on research and development in information retrieval*, pages 363–372. ACM.

Ivan Vulić and Marie-Francine Moens. 2015b. Monolingual and cross-lingual information retrieval models based on (bilingual) word embeddings. pages 363–372.

Shijie Wu and Mark Dredze. 2019. Beto, bentz, becas: The surprising cross-lingual effectiveness of bert. *arXiv preprint arXiv:1904.09077*.

Francisco Zamora-Martinez and Maria Jose Castro-Bleda. 2011. Ceu-upv english-spanish system for wmt11. In *Proceedings of the Sixth Workshop on Statistical Machine Translation*, pages 490–495. Association for Computational Linguistics.

Hamid Zarrabi-Zadeh. 2007. Tanzil project. *URL: http://tanzil. net/wiki/Tanzil_Project*.

Dong Zhou, Mark Truran, Tim Brailsford, Vincent Wade, and Helen Ashman. 2012. Translation techniques in cross-language information retrieval. *ACM Computing Surveys (CSUR)*, 45(1):1.

Michal Ziemski, Marcin Junczys-Dowmunt, and Bruno Pouliquen. 2016. The united nations parallel corpus v1. 0. In *Lrec*.

Will Y Zou, Richard Socher, Daniel Cer, and Christopher D Manning. 2013. Bilingual word embeddings for phrase-based machine translation. In *Proceedings of the 2013 Conference on Empirical Methods in Natural Language Processing*, pages 1393–1398.

Homograph Disambiguation Through Selective Diacritic Restoration

Sawsan Alqahtani,[1,2] Hanan Aldarmaki,[1] Mona Diab[1,3]
[1]The George Washington University
[2]Princess Nourah Bint Abdul Rahman University
[3]AWS, Amazon AI
sawsanq@gwu.edu, aldarmaki@gwu.edu, diabmona@amazon.com

Abstract

Lexical ambiguity, a challenging phenomenon in all natural languages, is particularly prevalent for languages with diacritics that tend to be omitted in writing, such as Arabic. Omitting diacritics leads to an increase in the number of homographs: different words with the same spelling. Diacritic restoration could theoretically help disambiguate these words, but in practice, the increase in overall sparsity leads to performance degradation in NLP applications. In this paper, we propose approaches for automatically marking a subset of words for diacritic restoration, which leads to selective homograph disambiguation. Compared to full or no diacritic restoration, these approaches yield selectively-diacritized datasets that balance sparsity and lexical disambiguation. We evaluate the various selection strategies extrinsically on several downstream applications: neural machine translation, part-of-speech tagging, and semantic textual similarity. Our experiments on Arabic show promising results, where our devised strategies on selective diacritization lead to a more balanced and consistent performance in downstream applications.

1 Introduction

Lexical ambiguity, an inherent phenomenon in natural languages, refers to words or phrases that can have multiple meanings. In written text, lexical ambiguity can be roughly characterized into two categories: polysemy and homonymy. A polysemous word has multiple senses that express different but related meanings (e.g. 'head' as an anatomical body part, or as a person in charge), whereas homonyms are different words that happen to have the same spelling (e.g. 'bass' as an instrument vs. a fish) (Löbner, 2013). Homographs are words that have the same spelling but may have different pronunciation and meaning.

A diacritic is a mark that is added above, below, or within letters to indicate pronunciation, vowels, or other functions. For languages that use diacritical marks, such as Arabic or Hebrew, the orthography is typically under-specified for such marks, i.e. the diacritics are omitted. This phenomenon exacerbates the lexical ambiguity problem since it increases the rate of homographs. For example, without considering context, the undiacritized Arabic word *ktb* may refer to any of the following diacritized variants:[1] *katab* كَتَب "wrote", *kutub* كُتُب "books", or *kutib* كُتِب "was written". As an illustrative analogy in English, dropping vowels in a word such as *pan* yields the under-specified token *pn* which can be mapped to *pin*, *pan*, *pun*, *pen*. It should be noted that even after fully specifying words with their relevant diacritics, homonyms such as "bass" are still ambiguous; likewise in Arabic, the fully-specified word *bayot* بَيْت can either mean "verse" or "house".

In this paper, we devise strategies to automatically identify and disambiguate a *subset* of homographs that result from omitting diacritics. While context is often sufficient for determining the meaning of ambiguous words, explicitly restoring missing diacritics should provide valuable additional information for homograph disambiguation. This process, diacritization, would render the resulting text comparable to that of languages whose words are orthographically fully specified such as English.

Past studies have focused on developing models for automatic diacritic restoration that can be used as a pre-processing step for various applications such as text-to-speech (Ungurean et al., 2008) and reading comprehension (Hermena et al., 2015). In theory, restoring all diacritics should also help improve the performance of NLP applications such as machine translation. However, in practice,

---

[1]We adopt Buckwalter Transliteration encoding into Latin script for rendering Arabic text http://www.qamus.org/transliteration.htm.

Proceedings of the Fourth Arabic Natural Language Processing Workshop, pages 49–59
Florence, Italy, August 1, 2019. ©2019 Association for Computational Linguistics

full diacritic restoration results in increased sparsity and out-of-vocabulary words, which leads to degradation in performance (Diab et al., 2007; Alqahtani et al., 2016). The main objective of this work is to find a sweet spot between zero and full diacritization in order to reduce lexical ambiguity without increasing sparsity. We propose selective diacritization, a process of restoring diacritics to a subset of the words in a sentence sufficient to disambiguate homographs without significantly increasing sparsity. Selective diacritization can be viewed as a relaxed variant of word sense disambiguation since only homographs that arise from missing diacritics are disambiguated.[2]

Intrinsically evaluating the quality of a devised selective diacritization scheme against a gold set is challenging since it is difficult to obtain a dataset that exhibits consistent selective diacritization with reliable inter-annotator agreement (Zaghouani et al., 2016b; Bouamor et al., 2015), thereby necessitating an empirical automatic investigation. Hence, in this work, we evaluate the proposed selective diacritization schemes extrinsically on various semantic and syntactic downstream NLP applications: Semantic Textual Similarity (STS), Neural Machine Translation (NMT), and Part-of-Speech (POS) tagging. We compare our selective strategies against two baselines full diacritization and zero diacritics applied on all the words in the text. We use Modern Standard Arabic (MSA) as a case-study.[3]

Our approach is summarized as follows: we start with full diacritic restoration of a large corpus, then apply different unsupervised methods to identify the words that are ambiguous when undiacritized. This results in a dictionary where each word is assigned an ambiguity label (ambiguous vs. unambiguous). Selectively-diacritized datasets can then be constructed by restoring the full diacritics only to the words that are identified as ambiguous.

The contribution of this paper is threefold:

1. We introduce automatic selective diacritization as a viable step in lexical disambiguation and provide an encouraging baseline for future developments towards optimal diacritization. Section 2 describes existing work towards optimal diacritization and how they differ from our approach;

2. We propose several unsupervised data-driven methods for the automatic identification of ambiguous words;

3. We evaluate and analyze the impact of partial sense disambiguation (i.e. selective diacritic restoration of identified homographs) in downstream applications for MSA.

2   Related Work

We are concerned mainly with studies that target word disambiguation through the use of diacritics/accents restoration. Homograph disambiguation through accents has been explored previously in several studies with the use of different rule-based and machine-learning approaches for languages such as Arabic, Spanish, Igbo, and Vietnamese (Ezeani et al., 2017; Nguyen et al., 2012; Nivre et al., 2017; Said et al., 2013; Tufiş and Chiţu, 1999).

Bouamor et al. (2015) conducted a pilot study where they asked human annotators to add the minimum number of diacritics sufficient to disambiguate homographs. However, attempts to provide human annotation for selective diacritization resulted in low inter-annotator agreement due to the annotators' subjectivity and different linguistic understanding of the words and contexts (Bouamor et al., 2015; Zaghouani et al., 2016b). To address this issue, Zaghouani et al. (2016b) used a morphological disambiguation tool, MADAMIRA (Pasha et al., 2014), to identify candidate words that may need disambiguation. A word was considered ambiguous if MADAMIRA generates multiple high-scoring diacritic alternatives, and human annotators were asked to select from these alternatives or manually edit the diacritics if none of the options was deemed correct. This resulted in a significant increase in inter-annotator agreement. Our work differs in two aspects: first, we develop automatic methods for ambiguity detection based on word usage. We then restore the diacritics for all occurrences of these ambiguous words, whereas in (Zaghouani et al., 2016b), the same word may be tagged as ambiguous in some cases but not ambiguous in other cases depending on

---

[2]Identifying empirically successful selective diacritization strategies can help discover optimal diacritization schemes; however, this direction is currently beyond the scope of this work.

[3]Proposed methodologies can be applied to other languages where diacritics are omitted.

context, which makes it harder to generalize to new datasets.

Yarowsky (1994) developed an accent restoration algorithm for Spanish and French that specifies the accent patterns for ambiguous words (i.e. multiple accent patterns). Our intuition is different than that of Yarowsky (1994) in two ways. First, they added diacritics to all words that have more than one diacritic pattern while we add the diacritics for only a subset of candidate words. Second, they used context for adding diacritics, while we use context to isolate words that require diacritics, for which we apply an off-the-shelf diacritic restoration model.

Rather than restoring all diacritics in the written text, the idea of adding diacritics sufficient to resolving lexical ambiguity was initially introduced in (Diab et al., 2007). They developed several linguistically-based partial schemes and evaluated their methods in Statistical Machine Translation. They found that fully diacritizing texts led to performance degradation due to sparseness while no diacritization increased the lexical ambiguity rate. Similar results have been found in (Alqahtani et al., 2016), where several other basic diacritic patterns were investigated. Although the impact of diacritics in machine translation was promising, the development of partial schemes does not show significant improvements over the non-diacritized and fully-diacritized baselines.

Alnefaie and Azmi (2017) introduced a partial diacritization scheme for MSA based on the output of a morphological analyzer in addition to WordNet (Black et al., 2006), and Alqahtani et al. (2018) created a lexical resource that assigned an ambiguity label for each word, where a word is considered ambiguous if it has more than one diacritic possibility, with and without considering its part-of-speech tag. However, both (Alnefaie and Azmi, 2017; Alqahtani et al., 2018) did not evaluate their methods empirically to demonstrate their effectiveness for NLP applications. Hanai and Glass (2014) similarly developed three linguistically-based partial diacritic schemes for automatic speech recognition and found statistically significant improvement over the baseline. However, their work is focused on improving word pronunciations whereas we focus on word sense disambiguation. Ezeani et al. (2017) discussed the impact of adding accents for each and every word in Igbo language, potentially increasing the performance for machine translation and word sense disambiguation.

All of the aforementioned approaches either apply full diacritics on all words whenever appropriate or derive partial diacritic schemes based on linguistic understanding; crucially these partial diacritic schemes are applied to *all* words in a sentence.[4] Our devised strategies differ in that we apply full diacritization to a *select* set of tokens in the text. Our work is related to these previous studies in the sense that we reduce the search space of candidate words that could benefit from full or partial diacritization without increasing sparsity. Furthermore, the novelty of this work lies in utilizing automatic unsupervised methods to identify such words.

3 Approach

3.1 Selective Diacritization

Selective diacritization is the process of restoring diacritics to a subset of words in a text corpus. Manually annotating words in a dataset with binary ambiguity labels (ambiguous vs. unambiguous) is challenging due to the difficulty in defining ambiguous words that would benefit from diacritics (Zaghouani et al., 2016b). Therefore, we propose several techniques to automatically identify ambiguous words for selective diacritization. Since it is common to use distributed word vector representations in downstream tasks, we define ambiguity in terms of distributional similarity among diacritized word variants. Our intuition is that variants with low distributional similarity are more likely to benefit from diacritization to disambiguate their meanings and tease apart their context variations. On the other hand, word variants with highly similar contexts tend to have very similar distributional representations, which results in unnecessary redundancy and sparsity if all variants are kept.

Based on this definition, we developed several context-based approaches to identify candidate ambiguous word types and generate a set of dictionaries with ambiguity labels (AmbigDict), where each word is marked as either ambiguous

---

[4]For instance, the undiacritized sentence *bEd ywm* بعد يوم "after a day" would be diacritized as *baEod yawom* بَغد يَؤم when fully diacritized, ***bEod ywom*** بغد يؤم ((Diab et al., 2007; Alqahtani et al., 2016)'s SUK scheme) when partially diacritized, ***baEod*** *ywm* بَغد يوم when selectively diacritized.

or unambiguous. The proposed approaches can be classified by the type of tokens used to create the AmbigDict: diacritized (AmbigDict-DIAC) or undiacritized (AmbigDict-UNDIAC). For example an entry in AmbigDict-UNDIAC would be "Elm" علم: ambiguous; "ktb" كتب: unambiguous, whereas in AmbigDict-DIAC would be "Ealam" عَلَم: ambiguous; "kutub" كُتُب: unambiguous.

3.2 AmbigDict-UNDIAC Generation

We explore two methods for creating ambiguity dictionaries from undiacritized text: using a morphological analyzer, and unsupervised sense induction.

Multiple Morphological Variants (MULTI): The number of diacritic alternatives for a word can be a clue to determine whether a word is ambiguous due to missing diacritics (Alqahtani et al., 2018). In this approach, context is not considered, but rather the output of a morphological analyzer applied to the text. We leverage the morphological analyzer component of MADAMIRA (Pasha et al., 2014) to generate all possible valid diacritic variants of a word whether these variants are present in the corpus or not. If an undiacritized word has more than one possible diacritic variant, we consider it ambiguous. We use this context-independent approach as a baseline.

Sense Induction Based Approach (SENSE): Selective diacritization is related to word sense disambiguation, however we only target disambiguation through diacritic restoration. Techniques used in automatic word sense induction can be used as a basis for identifying ambiguous words. Using undiacritized text, we apply an off-the-shelf system for word sense induction developed by Pelevina et al. (2017), which uses the Chinese Whispers algorithm (Biemann, 2006) to identify senses of a graph constructed by computing the word similarities (highest cosine similarities) through using word as well as context embeddings. We apply the first three steps described in Pelevina et al. (2017) but we do not use the generated sense-based embeddings; we only use the system to identify the words with multiplw senses. We set the three parameters as follows: the graph size N to 200, the inventory granularity n to 400, and the minimum number of clusters (senses) k to 5.[5] A word type is deemed ambiguous if it appears

in more than one cluster.

3.3 AmbigDict-DIAC Generation

We explore clustering and translation based methods to create ambiguity dictionaries from diacritized text.

Clustering-based Approaches (CL): Similar in spirit to SENSE, we apply unsupervised clustering to our corpora to induce AmbigDict. However, unlike SENSE, we apply clustering to diacritized data. Our intuition is that dissimilar words are likely to occur in different contexts, and therefore likely to be in different clusters. Therefore, we tag words as ambiguous if diacritized variants of the same underlying undiacritized form appear in different clusters.

As a preprocessing step, we apply a full contextualized diacritization tool to the underlying corpora. We leverage the MADAMIRA tool (Pasha et al., 2014) to produce fully diacritized text (for every token in the data) covering both types of diacritic restoration: lexical and syntactic. The latter covers syntactic case and mood diacritics. In this study, we are only concerned with lexical ambiguity; Moreover, MADAMIRA has a very high diacritic error rate in syntactic diacritic restoration (15%) compared to (3.5%) for lexical diacritic restoration. Hence, we drop the predicted word final syntactic diacritics resulting in a diacritization scheme similar to the partial scheme in (Diab et al., 2007; Alqahtani et al., 2016), namely, FULL-CM. In FULL-CM, every token is fully lexically diacritized (e.g. the fully diacritized words Ealama عَلَمَ and Ealamu عَلَمُ differ in their syntactic diacritics and are mapped to Ealam عَلَم "flag" in FULL-CM).

Given this diacritized corpus, we apply three different standard clustering approaches: Brown[6] (Brown et al., 1992) (CL-BR), K-means[7] (Kanungo et al., 2002) (CL-KM), and Gaussian Mixture via Expectation Maximization (CL-EM)[8] (Dempster et al., 1977). We tune the number of clusters for downstream tasks; in particular, we empirically investigate the performance on the de-

---

[5]We tuned these parameters empirically.

[6]https://github.com/percyliang/brown-cluster

[7]We use "sickit-learn" version 0.18.1. We use the value 1 for both random_state and n_init and the default values for the remaining parameters.

[8]We use "sickit-learn" version 0.18.1. with the following parameters: max_iter=1000, random_state=1, and covariance_type=spherical

velopment set in the downstream tasks for different number of clusters.

Translation-based Approaches (TR): Translation can be used as a basis for word sense induction (Diab and Resnik, 2002; Ng et al., 2003) since words across different languages tend to have disparate senses. Following a similar intuition, we use English translations from a parallel corpus as a trigger to divide the set of diacritic possibilities of a word into multiple subsets. The intuition here is that homographs worth disambiguating are those that are likely to be translated differently. We leverage an English MSA parallel corpus, where the MSA is diacritized in the Full-CM scheme using MADAMIRA (the same preprocessing step for CL described above). In this approach, diacritized variants that share the same English translations are considered unambiguous, whereas those that are typically translated to different English words are considered ambiguous. To that end, we first align the sentences at the token level and generate word translation probabilities using fast-align (Dyer et al., 2013), which is a log-linear reparameterization of IBM Model 2 (Brown et al., 1993). If a word shares any translation with its diacritized variant in the top N most likely translations, we consider it unambiguous (e.g. Ealam عَلَم 'flag' and Ealima عَلِم 'learned' are unambiguous since they do not share top translations). Otherwise, the word is tagged as ambiguous. We tune N to include 1, 5, 10, and all translations.

4 Evaluation

Once we have generated the two variants of AmbigDict (AmbigDict-UNDIAC and AmbigDict-DIAC), we evaluate their efficacy extrinsically on downstream applications. For all downstream applications, training and test data are preprocessed using MADAMIRA (Pasha et al., 2014) with the FULL-CM diacritization scheme where we only keep lexical diacritics.[9] Then the data is filtered based on the AmbigDict of choice; namely, only word tokens in the text deemed ambiguous according to each AmbigDict maintain their full diacritics (as generated by MADAMIRA) while the unambiguous words are kept undiacritized.

---

[9]Full diacritics are included except inflectional diacritics that reflect the syntactic positions of words within sentences but do not alter meaning.

4.1 Datasets

For MULTI, SENSE, CR, we use a combination of four Modern Standard Arabic (MSA) datasets that vary in genre and domain and add up to ~50M tokens: Gigaword 5th edition, distributed by Linguistic Data Consortium (LDC), Wikipedia dump 2016, Corpus of Contemporary Arabic (CCA) (Zaghouani et al., 2016a; Al-Sulaiti and Atwell, 2006), and LDC Arabic Tree Bank (ATB).[10] For TR, we use an Arabic-English parallel dataset which includes ~60M tokens and is created from 53 LDC catalogs. For data cleaning, we replace e-mails and URLs with a unified token and use SPLIT tool (Al-Badrashiny et al., 2016) to clean UTF8 characters (e.g. Latin and Chinese), remove diacritics in the original data, and separate punctuation, symbols, and numbers in the text, and replace them with separate unified tokens. We split long sentences (more than 150 words) by punctuation and then remove all sentences that are still longer than 150 words. We use D3 style (i.e. all affixes are separated) (Pasha et al., 2014) for Arabic tokenization without normalizing characters. For English, we lower case all characters and use TreeTagger (Schmid, 1999) for tokenization. We used SkipGram word embeddings (Mikolov et al., 2013), where applicable.

4.2 Extrinsic Evaluation

We evaluate the effectiveness of the proposed approaches using three applications: Semantic Textual Similarity (STS), Neural Machine Translation (NMT), and Part-of-Speech (POS) tagging. We used different significance testing methods appropriate for each application with $p = 0.05$.

4.2.1 Semantic Textual Similarity (STS)

STS is a benchmark evaluation task (Cer et al., 2017), where the objective is to predict the similarity score between a pair of sentences. Performance is typically evaluated using the Pearson correlation coefficient against human judgments. We used the William test (Graham and Baldwin, 2014) for significance testing. We experiment with an unsupervised system based on matrix factorization developed by (Guo and Diab, 2012; Guo et al., 2014), which generates sentence embeddings from a word-sentence co-occurrence matrix, then compare them using cosine similarity. We use a dimension size of 700. To train the model, we use the

---

[10]Parts 1, 2, 3, 5, 6, 7, 10, 11, and 12

Arabic dataset released for SemEval-2017 task 1 (Cer et al., 2017). Since the training dataset is small, we augment it by randomly selecting sentences from the dataset ($\sim$1,655,922) described in Section 4.1 where the chosen sentences have to satisfy the following conditions: the number of words lie between 5 and 150; and, the minimum frequency for each word is 2. We apply these conditions in the diacritized data since it suffers more from sparseness, and then use their undiacritized correspondents in the undiacritized setting.

4.2.2 Neural Machine Translation (NMT)

We build a BiLSTM-LSTM encoder-decoder machine translation system as described in (Bahdanau et al., 2014) using OpenNMT (Klein et al., 2014). We use 300 as input dimension for both source and target vectors, 500 as hidden units, and 0.3 for dropout. We initialize words with embeddings trained using FastText (Bojanowski et al., 2017) on the selectively-diacritized dataset described in Section 4.1. We train the model using SGD with max gradient norm of 1 and learning rate decay of 0.5. We use the Web Inventory of Transcribed and Translated Talks (WIT), which is made available for IWSLT 2016 (Mauro et al., 2012). We use BLEU (Papineni et al., 2002) for evaluation, and bootstrap re-sampling and approximate randomization for significance testing (Clark et al., 2011).

4.2.3 POS tagging

POS tagging is the task of determining the syntactic role of a word (i.e. part of speech) within a sentence. We use a BiLSTM-CRF architecture to train a POS tagger using the implementation provided by (Reimers and Gurevych, 2017), with 300 as dimension size, initialized using the same embeddings we use in NMT. We used ATB datasets parts 1,2, and 3 to train the models with Universal Dependencies POS tags, version 2 (Nivre et al., 2016). We use word-level accuracy for evaluation, and t-test (Fisher, 1935; Dror et al., 2018) for significance testing.

4.3 Automatic Diacritization

For generating the various AmbigDict approaches, we used either fully diacritized versions, without case and mood related diacritics,[11] or undiacritized versions of the datasets. Since it is ex-

---

[11]FULL-CM diacritization scheme, where we only keep lexical diacritics.

pensive to obtain enormous human-annotated diacritized datasets, we use the morphological analysis and disambiguation tool, MADAMIRA version 2016 2.1 (Pasha et al., 2014)

4.4 AmbigDict Statistics

Table 1 shows the number of identified ambiguous words using each approach. Note that the total vocabulary sizes vary due to either different datasets (e.g. for TR) or different preprocessing (e.g. MULTI is based on undiacritized text). For a given corpus, the number of ambiguous words identified by MULTI can be viewed as an estimate of the upper bound on ambiguous words due to diacritics. In MULTI, words that have no valid analysis generated by MADAMIRA are filtered; this resulted in significant drop of the number of types since the dataset includes noisy and infrequent instances.

Dictionary	Types	% Ambig Words
AmbigDict-UNDIAC		
MULTI	168,384	33.82
SENSE	467,953	8.50
AmbigDict-DIAC		
CL	497,222	8.70 - 8.98
TR	36,533	27.58

Table 1: Vocabulary size and percentage of ambiguous entries in AmbigDict-DIAC and AmbigDict-UNDIAC.

4.5 Results and Analysis

Dictionary	STS	NMT	POS
NONE	**0.608**	**27.1**	97.99%
FULL-CM	0.593	26.8	**98.06%**
AmbigDict-UNDIAC			
MULTI	0.591	27.0	**98.11%** *
SENSE	0.598	27.1	97.97%
AmbigDict-DIAC			
CL-BR	0.601	27.1	**98.09%**
CL-KM	0.608	**27.2**	98.05%
CL-EM	**0.617** *	27.1	98.05%
TR	**0.616** *	**27.3** *	97.94%

Table 2: Performance with selectively-diacritized datasets in downstream applications. **Bold** numbers indicate approaches with higher performance than the best performing baseline. * refers to approaches with statistically-significant performance gains against the best performing baseline.

Table 2 shows the performance of all strategies in downstream tasks. Comparing baselines NONE and FULL-CM, we observe that applications that require semantic understanding (STS and NMT) show better performance when the dataset is undiacritized, whereas POS tagging yields better performance with the fully diacritized dataset.

The differences in performance between the baselines are significant across all tasks. In all tasks, at least one of the selective diacritization schemes leads to performance gains compared to both baselines. However, the choice of best performing selective diacritization scheme varies across tasks. In general, AmbigDict-DIAC approaches provide more promising results on semantic related applications.

TR and CL-EM approaches yield the highest performance in two of the applications (STS and NMT), while MULTI and CL-BR achieved the highest performance in POS tagging. Incidentally, MULTI has the highest rate of ambiguous words, which leads to more disambiguation through diacritization. This is consistent with the observation that diacritization is useful for syntactic tasks like POS tagging, as observed through the baselines. In all other tasks, all selective diacritization schemes performed significantly higher than full diacritization.

Homograph Evaluation: We compared the performance of the various schemes on subsets of the test sets that include homographs, which are identified from the FULL-CM version of the training datasets. For STS and NMT evaluation, we kept only the test sentences that contain at least one homograph. For POS word-level evaluation, we only considered the homographs. Table 3 shows homograph performance across applications. The performance on these subsets follow the same trend as the overall results illustrated in Table 2 except for POS tagging, where FULL-CM achieved the comparable performance to the selective schemes. Note, however, that almost all schemes achieved higher POS tagging accuracy than NONE in these subsets, and almost all schemes achieved comparable or higher performance than FULL-CM in STS and NMT, with TR significantly outperforming the rest of the schemes as well as the baselines. This illustrates the usefulness of selective diacritization for balancing homograph disambiguation and sparsity compared to full or no diacritization.

Frequent POS Tag Performance: POS tagging labels each word in the sentence as opposed to

Dictionary	STS	NMT	POS
NONE	**0.590**	**27.4**	98.26%
FULL-CM	0.575	27	**98.70%**
AmbigDict-UNDIAC			
MULTI	0.574	27.2	98.65%
SENSE	0.581	27.3	98.37%
AmbigDict-DIAC			
CL-BR	0.584	27.4	98.59%
CL-KM	**0.591**	**27.5**	98.52%
CL-EM	**0.60***	27.4	98.47%
TR	**0.597***	**27.6***	98.22%

Table 3: Performance of selectively-diacritized datasets on homographs. **Bold** numbers indicate approaches with higher performance than the best performing baseline. * refers to approaches with statistically-significant performance gains against the best performing baseline.

NMT and STS which are evaluated at the sentence level. Thus, we compared the best performing scheme (MULTI) and the baselines in terms of their per tag performance on the four most frequent tags: verbs, nouns, adjectives, and adverbs. Table 4 shows the results of the baselines and MULTI. For verbs and nouns, MULTI has better performance than both baselines followed by FULL-CM. For adjectives and adverbs, NONE followed by MULTI have better performance than FULL-CM. While FULL-CM has overall higher accuracy, these results indicate that selective diacritization is a better approach for the most frequent tags, possibly due to reduced sparsity compared with FULL-CM.

OOV Performance: We measured the POS tagging performance on Out-of-Vocabulary (OOV) words to measure the effect of sparsity on performance. We consider a word OOV if it does not occur in the fully-diacritized training set. FULL-CM achieved 87.43% tag accuracy, while NONE achieved 87.56%. Using the MULTI scheme, the POS tagging accuracy on OOV words was 87.51%, which falls between the two baselines, as expected.

The results above indicate that using a selective diacritization scheme like MULTI can achieve a desirable balance between disambiguation and sparsity, such that better performance can be achieved in the frequent cases without increasing sparsity and OOV rates.

Scheme	Verb	Noun	Adj	Adv
MULTI	**95.98%**	97.63%	94.43%	97.05%
NONE	95.08%	97.45%	**94.71%**	**98.08%**
FULL-CM	95.87%	97.56%	94.40%	96.79%

Table 4: POS Tagging performance per most frequent tag. **Bold** scores indicate the highest score in a column.

Type	Example
part-of-speech	$ak شَك "doubt" (noun)
	$ak~ شَك "doubted" (verb)
action direction	>a*okur أَذْكُر "remember"
	>u*ak~ir أَذَكِّر "remind"
number	$uyuwEiy~ayon شُيُوعِيَّيْن "communists"
	$uyuwEiy~iyn شُيُوعِيِّين "communists"

Table 5: Examples of ambiguous word pairs detected by the clustering approaches.

Pattern Pair	Example
CaC~aC	Ear~aD عَرَّض "make wider"
CuCiC	EuriD عُرِض "has been shown"
CaCiCaCoC	ba$iEayon بَشِعَيْن "ugly" (dual)
CaCiCiCC	ba$iEiyn بَشِعِين "ugly" (plural)

Table 6: Examples of consistent diacritic patterns of ambiguous words between CL and TR approaches.

4.6 Properties of Ambiguity Dictionaries

Clustering-Based Ambiguity: While MULTI, TR, and SENSE approaches have intuitive justifications, the clustering approaches are based entirely on distributional features. We analyzed some of the results qualitatively to shed light on types of words that are deemed ambiguous through clustering. While the various clustering approaches resulted in different labeling, their overall statistics and patterns were highly similar. Using a random subset of words from these CL dictionaries, we extracted the examples shown in Table 5, which shows some of the most common types of ambiguity. Note that the detected words are either semantically ambiguous (e.g. derivations or distinct lemmas) or syntactically ambiguous (e.g. part-of-speech).

Diacritic Pattern Complexity: We investigated whether there are regular diacritic patterns among words that were considered ambiguous by CL and TR. Both approaches are data-driven, and we applied them on different corpora, so we investigated their degree of agreement. To do so, we abstracted the diacritic patterns for words in the vocabulary by converting all characters other than diacritics to a unified token "C", then we collected statistics of patterns of word pairs that are deemed ambiguous vs. unambiguous. For example, the ambiguous pair "katab" كَتَب and "kutib" كُتِب have the pattern CaCaC-CuCiC. For CL methods, the number of unique diacritic patterns of unambigu-

ous word pairs (i.e. falling in the same cluster) were between 197-219 patterns, whereas patterns of ambiguous pairs were between 813-872. The majority of patterns between unambiguous words also occurred between ambiguous words. For TR, while most patterns were labeled unambiguous, around 300 patterns were always labeled ambiguous. We did not find overarching semantic or syntactic rules that consistently explain ambiguity tags. However, a number of patterns ($\sim$ 20) were always tagged as ambiguous by both TR and CL approaches. Table 6 shows a sample of these patterns with examples.

5 Discussion & Conclusion

We investigated selective diacritization as a viable technique for reducing lexical ambiguity using Arabic as a case study. To our knowledge, this is the first work that shows encouraging results with automatic selective diacritization schemes in which the devised approaches evaluated on several downstream applications. Our findings demonstrate that partial diacritization achieves a balance between homograph disambiguation and sparsity effects; the performance using selective diacritization always approached the best of both extremes in each application, and sometimes surpassed the performance of both baselines, which is consistent with our intuition of balancing sparsity and disambiguation for improving overall performance.

While the increase in performance was not consistent across all tasks, the results provide an empirical evidence of the viability of automatic partial diacritization, especially since manual efforts in this vein had been rather challenging. We believe that the approaches described in this paper could help advance the efforts towards optimal diacritization schemes, which are currently mostly based on linguistic features. We analyzed some patterns that were recognized as ambiguous using our best-performing schemes, and showed some consistencies in the diacritic patterns, although the results were not conclusive. We believe that a deeper analysis of these patterns may help shed light on the lexical ambiguity phenomenon in addition to allowing further improvements in selective diacritization.

References

Mohamed Al-Badrashiny, Arfath Pasha, Mona Diab, Nizar Habash, Owen Rambow, Wael Salloum, and Ramy Eskander. 2016. SPLIT: Smart preprocessing (Quasi) language independent tool. In *International Conference on Language Resources and Evaluation (LREC)*.

Latifa Al-Sulaiti and Eric Atwell. 2006. The design of a corpus of contemporary Arabic. *International Journal of Corpus Linguistics*, 11(2):135–171.

Rehab Alnefaie and Aqil M. Azmi. 2017. Automatic minimal diacritization of Arabic texts. In *3rd International Conference on Arabic Computational Linguistics (ACLing)*.

Sawsan Alqahtani, Mona Diab, and Wajdi Zaghouani. 2018. ARLEX: A large scale comprehensive lexical inventory for Modern Standard Arabic. In *OSACT 3: The 3rd Workshop on Open-Source Arabic Corpora and Processing Tools*.

Sawsan Alqahtani, Mahmoud Ghoneim, and Mona Diab. 2016. Investigating the impact of various partial diacritization schemes on Arabic-English statistical machine translation. In *International Association for Machine Translation in the Americas (AMTA)*.

Dzmitry Bahdanau, Kyunghyun Cho, and Yoshua Bengio. 2014. Neural machine translation by jointly learning to align and translate. In *International Conference on Learning Representations*.

Chris Biemann. 2006. Chinese whispers: an efficient graph clustering algorithm and its application to natural language processing problems. In *Proceedings of the first workshop on graph based methods for natural language processing*. Association for Computational Linguistics.

William Black, Sabri Elkateb, Horacio Rodriguez, Musa Alkhalifa, Piek Vossen, Adam Pease, and Christiane Fellbaum. 2006. Introducing the Arabic WordNet project. In *Proceedings of the third international WordNet conference*.

Piotr Bojanowski, Edouard Grave, Armand Joulin, and Tomas Mikolov. 2017. Enriching word vectors with subword information. *Transactions of the Association for Computational Linguistics*.

Houda Bouamor, Wajdi Zaghouani, Mona Diab, Ossama Obeid, Kemal Oflazer, Mahmoud Ghoneim, and Abdelati Hawwari. 2015. A pilot study on Arabic multi-genre corpus diacritization. In *Proceedings of the Second Workshop on Arabic Natural Language Processing*.

Peter F Brown, Peter V Desouza, Robert L Mercer, Vincent J Della Pietra, and Jenifer C Lai. 1992. Class-based n-gram models of natural language. *Computational linguistics*, 18(4):467–479.

Peter F Brown, Vincent J Della Pietra, Stephen A Della Pietra, and Robert L Mercer. 1993. The mathematics of statistical machine translation: parameter estimation. *Computational linguistics*, 19(2):263–311.

Daniel Cer, Mona Diab, Eneko Agirre, Inigo Lopez-Gazpio, and Lucia Specia. 2017. Semeval-2017 task 1: Semantic textual similarity-multilingual and cross-lingual focused evaluation. In *SemEval workshop at ACL*.

Jonathan H Clark, Chris Dyer, Alon Lavie, and Noah A Smith. 2011. Better hypothesis testing for statistical machine translation: Controlling for optimizer instability. In *Proceedings of the 49th Annual Meeting of the Association for Computational Linguistics: Human Language Technologies*, pages 176–181.

Arthur P Dempster, Nan M Laird, and Donald B Rubin. 1977. Maximum likelihood from incomplete data via the EM algorithm. *Journal of the royal statistical society.*, 39:1–38.

Mona Diab, Mahmoud Ghoneim, and Nizar Habash. 2007. Arabic diacritization in the context of statistical machine translation. In *Proceedings of MT-Summit*.

Mona Diab and Philip Resnik. 2002. An unsupervised method for word sense tagging using parallel corpora. In *Proceedings of the 40th Annual Meeting on Association for Computational Linguistics*, pages 255–262.

Rotem Dror, Gili Baumer, Segev Shlomov, and Roi Reichart. 2018. The hitchhikers guide to testing statistical significance in natural language processing. In *Proceedings of the 56th Annual Meeting of the Association for Computational Linguistics*, volume 1, pages 1383–1392.

Chris Dyer, Victor Chahuneau, and Noah A Smith. 2013. A simple, fast, and effective reparameterization of ibm model 2. In *Proceedings of the 2013 Conference of the North American Chapter of the Association for Computational Linguistics: Human Language Technologies*, pages 644–648.

Ignatius Ezeani, Mark Hepple, and Ikechukwu Onyenwe. 2017. Lexical disambiguation of Igbo using diacritic restoration. In *Proceedings of the 1st Workshop on Sense, Concept and Entity Representations and their Applications*, pages 53–60.

Ronald Aylmer Fisher. 1935. *The design of experiments*. Oliver And Boyd.

Yvette Graham and Timothy Baldwin. 2014. Testing for significance of increased correlation with human judgment. In *Proceedings of the 2014 Conference on Empirical Methods in Natural Language Processing (EMNLP)*, pages 172–176.

Weiwei Guo and Mona Diab. 2012. Modeling sentences in the latent space. In *Proceedings of the 50th Annual Meeting of the Association for Computational Linguistics*, pages 864–872.

Weiwei Guo, Wei Liu, and Mona Diab. 2014. Fast tweet retrieval with compact binary codes. In *Proceedings of COLING 2014, the 25th International Conference on Computational Linguistics: Technical Papers*, pages 486–496.

Tuka Al Hanai and James R Glass. 2014. Lexical modeling for Arabic ASR: A systematic approach. In *Fifteenth Annual Conference of the International Speech Communication Association*.

Ehab W Hermena, Denis Drieghe, Sam Hellmuth, and Simon P Liversedge. 2015. Processing of Arabic diacritical marks: Phonological–syntactic disambiguation of homographic verbs and visual crowding effects. *Journal of Experimental Psychology: Human Perception and Performance*, 41(2).

Tapas Kanungo, David M Mount, Nathan S Netanyahu, Christine D Piatko, Ruth Silverman, and Angela Y Wu. 2002. An efficient k-means clustering algorithm: Analysis and implementation. *IEEE Transactions on Pattern Analysis & Machine Intelligence*, pages 881–892.

G. Klein, Y. Kim, Y. Deng, J. Senellart, and A. M. Rush. 2014. OpenNMT: Open-Source Toolkit for Neural Machine Translation. In *Proceedings of ACL 2017, System Demonstrations*.

Sebastian Löbner. 2013. *Understanding semantics*. Routledge.

Cettolo Mauro, Girardi Christian, and Federico Marcello. 2012. Wit3: Web inventory of transcribed and translated talks. In *Conference of European Association for Machine Translation*, pages 261–268.

Tomas Mikolov, Kai Chen, Greg Corrado, and Jeffrey Dean. 2013. Efficient estimation of word representations in vector space.

Hwee Tou Ng, Bin Wang, and Yee Seng Chan. 2003. Exploiting parallel texts for word sense disambiguation: an empirical study. In *Proceedings of the 41st Annual Meeting on Association for Computational Linguistics*, pages 455–462.

Minh Trung Nguyen, Quoc Nhan Nguyen, and Hong Phuong Nguyen. 2012. Vietnamese diacritics restoration as sequential tagging. In *IEEE RIVF International Conference on Computing Communication Technologies, Research, Innovation, and Vision for the Future*, pages 1–6.

Joakim Nivre, Marie-Catherine De Marneffe, Filip Ginter, Yoav Goldberg, Jan Hajič, Christopher D Manning, Ryan McDonald, Slav Petrov, Sampo Pyysalo, Natalia Silveira, Reut Tsarfaty, and Daniel Zeman. 2017. A Bambara tonalization system for word sense disambiguation using differential coding, segmentation and edit operation filtering. In *Proceedings of the Eighth International Joint Conference on Natural Language Processing*, volume 1, pages 694–703.

Joakim Nivre, Marie-Catherine De Marneffe, Filip Ginter, Yoav Goldberg, Jan Hajic, Christopher D Manning, Ryan T McDonald, Slav Petrov, Sampo Pyysalo, Natalia Silveira, et al. 2016. Universal dependencies v1: A multilingual treebank collection. In *Proceedings of the Tenth International Conference on Language Resources and Evaluation (LREC)*.

Kishore Papineni, Salim Roukos, Todd Ward, and Wei-Jing Zhu. 2002. BLEU: a method for automatic evaluation of machine translation. In *Proceedings of the 40th annual meeting on association for computational linguistics*, pages 311–318.

Arfath Pasha, Mohamed Al-Badrashiny, Mona T Diab, Ahmed El Kholy, Ramy Eskander, Nizar Habash, Manoj Pooleery, Owen Rambow, and Ryan Roth. 2014. MADAMIRA: A fast, comprehensive tool for morphological analysis and disambiguation of Arabic. In *LREC*, volume 14, pages 1094–1101.

Maria Pelevina, Nikolay Arefyev, Chris Biemann, and Alexander Panchenko. 2017. Making sense of word embeddings. In *Proceedings of the 1st Workshop on Representation Learning for NLP on Association for Computational Linguistics*.

Nils Reimers and Iryna Gurevych. 2017. Reporting score distributions makes a difference: performance study of LSTM-networks for sequence tagging. In *Proceedings of the 2017 Conference on Empirical Methods in Natural Language Processing (EMNLP)*, pages 338–348.

Ahmed Said, Mohamed El-Sharqwi, Achraf Chalabi, and Eslam Kamal. 2013. A hybrid approach for Arabic diacritization. In *International Conference on Application of Natural Language to Information Systems*, pages 53–64.

Helmut Schmid. 1999. Improvements in part-of-speech tagging with an application to German. In *Natural Language Processing Using Very Large Corpora*, pages 13–25.

Dan Tufiş and Adrian Chiţu. 1999. Automatic diacritics insertion in Romanian texts. In *Proceedings of the International Conference on Computational Lexicography COMPLEX*, volume 99, pages 185–194.

Cătălin Ungurean, Dragoş Burileanu, Vladimir Popescu, Cristian Negrescu, and Aurelian Dervis.

2008. Automatic diacritic restoration for a TTS-based e-mail reader application. *UPB Scientific Bulletin, Series C*, 70(4):3–12.

David Yarowsky. 1994. Decision lists for lexical ambiguity resolution: application to accent restoration in Spanish and French. In *Proceedings of the 32nd annual meeting on Association for Computational Linguistics*, pages 88–95.

Wajdi Zaghouani, Houda Bouamor, Abdelati Hawwari, Mona T Diab, Ossama Obeid, Mahmoud Ghoneim, Sawsan Alqahtani, and Kemal Oflazer. 2016a. Guidelines and framework for a large scale Arabic diacritized corpus. In *The Tenth International Conference on Language Resources and Evaluation (LREC)*, page 36373643.

Wajdi Zaghouani, Abdelati Hawwari, Sawsan Alqahtani, Houda Bouamor, Mahmoud Ghoneim, Mona Diab, and Kemal Oflazer. 2016b. Using ambiguity detection to streamline linguistic annotation. In *Proceedings of the Workshop on Computational Linguistics for Linguistic Complexity (CL4LC)*, pages 127–136.

Arabic Named Entity Recognition: What Works and What's Next

Liyuan Liu
University of Illinois
Urbana-Champaign
ll2@illinois.edu

Jingbo Shang
University of Illinois
Urbana-Champaign
shang7@illinois.edu

Jiawei Han
University of Illinois
Urbana-Champaign
hanj@illinois.edu

Abstract

This paper presents the winning solution to the Arabic Named Entity Recognition challenge run by Topcoder.com. The proposed model integrates various tailored techniques together, including representation learning, feature engineering, sequence labeling, and ensemble learning. The final model achieves a test F_1 score of 75.82% on the AQMAR dataset and outperforms baselines by a large margin. Detailed analyses are conducted to reveal both its strengths and limitations. Specifically, we observe that (1) representation learning modules can significantly boost the performance but requires a proper pre-processing and (2) the resulting embedding can be further enhanced with feature engineering due to the limited size of the training data. All implementations and pre-trained models are made public[1].

1 Introduction

Aiming to identify entities in natural language, named entity recognition (NER) serves as one of the fundamental steps in various applications. In many languages, the performance of NER has been significantly improved because of recent advances in representation learning (Peters et al., 2018; Akbik et al., 2018). To promote the development of Arabic NER, a challenge was hosted on Topcoder.com[2] based on the public Arabic NER benchmark dataset (i.e., the AQMAR dataset) (Mohit et al., 2012). Challenge submissions were required to only use annotations from the training set, and manual reviews on the submitted solutions were further conducted to prevent cheating.

Among 137 registrants competing in the challenge[3], we placed the first by tailoring various techniques and incorporating them all together. Intuitively, it is hard to only rely on feature engineering to capture textual signals, especially for morphologically rich languages like Arabic (Habash, 2010). At the same time, neural networks have demonstrated their great potentials to automate high-quality representation construction in an end-to-end manner. Therefore, we leverage embedding modules to represent words with pre-trained vectors for a better quality. Besides, we observe that handcrafted features can bring a considerable improvement. Consuming all these features, we train multiple LSTM-CRF models to construct the mapping from representations to predictions, and further aggregate their outputs with ensemble learning. Moreover, we incorporate a dictionary-based string matching model and observe that it can improve the recall at some cost of precision, which results in a marginal F_1-score improvement.

Our final ensemble model achieves a test F_1 score of 75.82%, outperforming all other participants as well as the previous state-of-the-arts by significant margins. We further conduct analyses on our solution to get deeper insights on the task: (1) the effectiveness of representation learning and (2) the role of feature engineering.

The rest of paper is organized as follow. The next section discusses related work. Section 3 introduces the problem setting and presents the data analysis. The proposed framework is presented in Section 4, including model ensemble and dictionary-based model. Tailored representations modules are introduced in Section 5. Finally, we discuss the experimental results in Section 6.

---

[1] https://github.com/LiyuanLucasLiu/ArabicNER

[2] https://www.topcoder.com/challenges/30087004

[3] 220 submissions from 30 participates are made in total.

Proceedings of the Fourth Arabic Natural Language Processing Workshop, pages 60–67
Florence, Italy, August 1, 2019. ©2019 Association for Computational Linguistics

2 Related Work

Typically, named entity recognition is conducted as a sequence labeling task. Before deep learning demonstrated its effectiveness, traditional methods rely on handcrafted features (e.g., features based on POS tags) and language-specific resources (e.g., gazetteers) to capture textual signals. Machine learning models like conditional random field (CRF) and hidden Markov model (HMM) are employed to capture the label dependency (Lafferty et al., 2001; Florian et al., 2003; Chieu and Ng, 2002). Many attempts have been made to reduce the reliance on feature engineering or other human endeavors, which makes the NER task be solved in an end-to-end manner (Lample et al., 2016; Ma and Hovy, 2016; Shang et al., 2018). Recent studies have revealed that language model is an effective representation module for NER (Peters et al., 2017, 2018; Liu et al., 2018b; Akbik et al., 2018; Liu et al., 2018a).

At the same time, many approaches have been proposed specifically to solve the NER task in Arabic. Traditional Arabic NER models are mostly rule-basedmodels (Shaalan, 2014). Recently, people have started to attach this task with machine learning methods (Helwe and Elbassuoni, 2017; Gridach, 2016). To further improve the performance, attempts have been made to combine both rule-based and learning-based approaches into a unified framework (Pasha et al., 2014; Abdelali et al., 2016). Besides, incorporating additional supervision from other domains or languages has been explored as well (Darwish, 2013).

3 Problem Setting

In this section, we first introduce the problem setting of sequence labeling. Then, we discuss the aforementioned Arabic NER challenge.

3.1 Sequence Labeling

In the sequence labeling framework, NER problems are usually annotated following the labeling schemes like BIO and IOBES. These labeling schemes help us encode the information about entities (Ratinov and Roth, 2009). For example, in the BIO scheme, when a token sequence is identified as a named entity, its starting token and middle/end tokens are labeled as B- and I- followed by the type; and all other words are labeled as

O. The IOBES scheme is similar to BIO but further use S- for singleton entity and E- for end-of-entity, respectively.

Using such labels, we define the input sequence as $X = \{x_1, x_2, \ldots, x_T\}$, where x_i is i-th token and its label is y_i. Moreover, we define the character-level input for X as $C = \{c_{1,1}, c_{1,2}, \cdots, c_{1,\_}, c_{2,1}, \cdots, c_{T,\_}\}$, where $\{c_{i,1}, \cdots, c_{i,\_}\}$ are the characters contained in the word x_i and $c_{i,\_}$ is the space character right after x_i. Then, the goal of NER becomes to predict the label y_i for each token x_i in the input sequence X.

3.2 Arabic NER Challenge

The Arabic NER challenge uses the public Arabic NER benchmark dataset (i.e., the AQMAR dataset) (Mohit et al., 2012). Its annotated entities are classified into four types (i.e., "Person", "Location", "Organization" and "Miscellaneous"). This dataset contains 28 hand-annotated Arabic Wikipedia articles, 14 articles are used as the training set, 7 articles are used as the development set, and 7 articles are used as the test set.

Data cleaning is further conducted on this dataset. Specifically, we observed that the label sequence is encoded in a noisy manner. For example, some entities are labelled as $\{$B-, O, I-$\}$, while the legit label sequence should be $\{$B-, I-, I-$\}$; Some entities are labelled as $\{$B-T$_0$, I-T$_1\}$ (here, T$_0$ and T$_1$ are two different entity types), while the legit label sequence should be $\{$B-T$_0$, B-T$_1\}$. In the pursuit of more powerful models and more meaningful comparisons, we conduct a label cleaning to regularize the label sequence. The resulting dataset is released for future study[4], and its statistics are summarized in Table ??. In the following sections, all comparisons are conducted on this cleaned dataset.

4 Model Framework

As visualized in Figure 1, we design a heterogeneous framework, which incorporates various techniques: (1) It employs representation learning and sequence labeling as the basic sequence labeling model; (2) It leverages ensemble learning to combine outputs from different NER models; and (3) It further incorporates a dictionary-based string matching model.

---

[4]https://github.com/LiyuanLucasLiu/ArabicNER

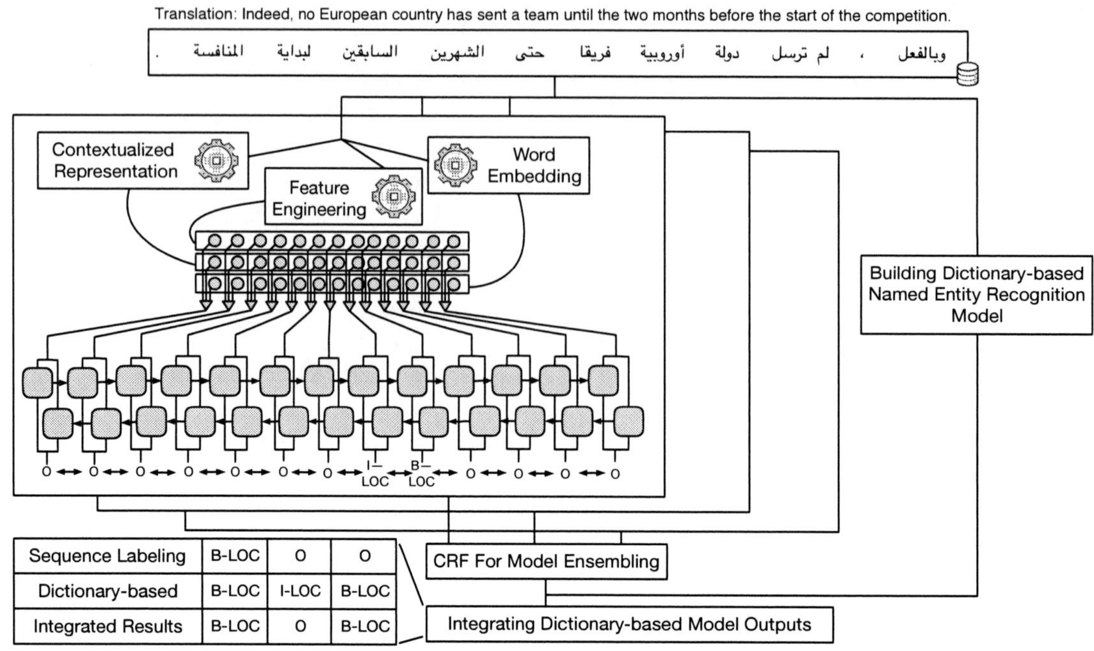

Figure 1: Our proposed framework for Arabic NER.

	Train	Dev	Test
# Sent	1,329	711	606
# Token	36,050	19,519	18,284
# Char	156,941	83,267	80,565
# PER	752	292	424
# LOC	971	146	326
# ORG	234	114	102
# MISC	1,092	660	722

Table 1: Dataset Statistics of the AQMAR dataset.

4.1 Sequence Labeling Model

As to the basic sequence labeling model, we assume there are n different representation modules, namely M_i ($1 \leq i \leq n$). Given the j-th token in the input sequence, the representation vector produced by module M_i is denoted as $\mathbf{f}_{i,j}$. In this paper, we concatenate the output from different modules as the representation (input of LSTM-CRF), i.e., $\mathbf{f}_j = [\mathbf{f}_{1,j}; \mathbf{f}_{2,j}; \cdots; \mathbf{f}_{n,j}]$. Given the input sequence X, we define its token representations as $\mathbf{F} = \{\mathbf{f}_1, \mathbf{f}_2, \cdots, \mathbf{f}_T\}$. Building upon representation modules, we use LSTM-CRF (Huang et al., 2015) to conduct entity extraction: we first feed $\mathbf{F}$ into Bi-LSTMs, whose outputs are marked as $\mathbf{Z} = \{\mathbf{z}_1, \mathbf{z}_2, \cdots, \mathbf{z}_T\}$. A linear-chain CRF is further leveraged to model the whole label sequence simultaneously. Specifically, for the input sequence $\mathbf{Z}$, CRF defines the conditional probability of $\mathbf{Y} = \{y_1, \cdots, y_T\}$ as

$$p(\mathbf{Y}|\mathbf{Z}) = \frac{\prod_{t=1}^{T} \phi(y_{t-1}, y_t, \mathbf{z}_t)}{\sum_{\hat{\mathbf{Y}} \in \mathbf{Y}(\mathbf{Z})} \prod_{t=1}^{T} \phi(\hat{y}_{t-1}, \hat{y}_t, \mathbf{z}_t)} \quad (1)$$

where $\hat{\mathbf{Y}} = \{\hat{y}_1, \cdots, \hat{y}_T\}$ is a possible label sequence, $\mathbf{Y}(\mathbf{Z})$ refers to the set of all possible label sequences for $\mathbf{Z}$, and $\phi(y_{t-1}, y_t, \mathbf{z}_t)$ is the potential function of the CRF. In this paper, we define the potential function as:

$$\phi(y_{t-1}, y_t, \mathbf{z}_t) = \exp(W_{y_t} \mathbf{z}_t + b_{y_{t-1}, y_t})$$

where W_{y_t} and b_{y_{t-1}, y_t} are the weight and bias.

During the model training, we use the negative log-likelihood of Equation 1 as the loss function. In the inference stage, the predicted label sequence for input X is the one maximizing the probability in Equation 1. Although the denominator in Equation 1 contains an exponential number of terms [5], due to the definition of the potential function, both training and inference can be efficiently conducted using dynamic programming.

---

[5]The number of terms is exponential to the sequence length T.

The dictionary-based NER model and representation learning modules would be introduced in the following sections.

4.2 Sequence Labeling Model Ensemble

To get better performance, we applied the ensemble learning on sequence labeling results. Specifically, as in Figure 1, multiple NER models are separately trained with the shared representation modules, and their results are combined as the final output.

Specifically, we refer the output of N models as $\{\hat{\mathbf{Y}}_1, \hat{\mathbf{Y}}_2, \cdots, \hat{\mathbf{Y}}_N\}$, where $\hat{\mathbf{Y}}_i = \{\hat{y}_{i,1}, \cdots, \hat{y}_{i,T}\}$. Following the previous work (Nguyen and Guo, 2007), we first construct a list of transition matrices $\{R_1, \cdots, R_{T-1}\}$, where $R_i(j,k) = |\{n|\hat{y}_{n,i} = j, \hat{y}_{n,i+1} = k\}|$ is the number of times that i-th and $i+1$-th tokens are labelled as j and k in $\{\hat{\mathbf{Y}}_n\}$. Also, we calculate $B_i(j) = |\{n|\hat{y}_{n,i} = j\}|$, which is the times of i-th token being labelled as j. Then the integrated label sequence is calculated with dynamic programming:

$$\hat{\mathbf{Y}} = \arg\max \sum_{t=1}^{T-1} R_t(\hat{y}_t, \hat{y}_{t+1}) + \sum_{t=1}^{T} B_t(\hat{y}_t)$$

where $\hat{\mathbf{Y}} = \{\hat{y}_1, \cdots, \hat{y}_T\}$ is the integrated label sequence.

4.3 Dictionary-based NER Model

Besides the sequence labeling ensemble model, we also incorporate a dictionary-based NER model. Specifically, we first build a dictionary to map surface names to their types from the training set, then apply this dictionary via string matching. We will add the dictionary-extracted entities into the final prediction, if and only if they do not conflict with the sequence labeling results. For example, in Figure 1, since the two-word entity (i.e., B-LOC I-LOC) detected by the dictionary-based model overlaps with the sequence labeling results, this entity is dropped; At the same time, because the one-word entity (i.e., the second B-LOC) detected by the dictionary-based model is not overlapped with any entities detected by the sequence labeling model, it is therefore integrated to the final results. In our experiments, we found this enrichment by the dictionary-based model improves the recall at a relatively smaller cost of the precision, thus improving the F_1 score.

5 Representation Learning Modules

In this section, we introduce the three representation learning modules: (1) word embedding, (2) contextualized representation, and (3) handcrafted features.

5.1 Word Embedding

Based on the distributional hypothesis (*i.e.*, "a word is characterized by the company it keeps" (Harris, 1954)), word embedding methods aim to learn the distributed representations by analyzing their contexts (Mikolov et al., 2013). Recent work shows that word embedding could uncover textual information of various levels (Artetxe et al., 2018). Hence, we leverage word embedding as a part of the word representation. Due to the limited size of the training set, we fix the pre-trained word embedding during the training of NER models. When the pre-trained embedding has a high dimension, we will add a linear projection to further project them to a relatively low dimension.

5.2 Contextualized Representation

Contextualized representations have been widely adopted in the state-of-the-art sequence labeling models. Typically, they rely on bidirectional neural language models to capture the local contextual information before and after a certain word. Such representations provide rich, supplementary information to the context-agnostic information contained in a word embedding. Specifically, character-level language models are first used to provide additional supervision (Liu et al., 2018b), and further exploration observes its effectiveness as the pre-training task to construct contextualized word representation (Akbik et al., 2018).

We present the details of character-level language modeling and integration as below.

Character-Level Language Modeling. A bidirectional character-level language model contains two character-level language models to capture information from two directions. Character-level language modeling aims to model the probability distribution of the character sequence. Typically, the probability of the sequence $\{c_1, \cdots, c_T\}$ is defined in a "forward" manner: $p(c_1, \cdots, c_T) = \prod_{t=1}^{T} p(c_t|c_1, \cdots, c_{t-1})$.

To calculate this conditional probability, we first map the input sequence C to a list of character embedding vectors and pass them into a recurrent neural network, whose output is referred to $\mathbf{h}_t$. Then, the probability $p(c_t|c_1, \cdots, c_{t-1})$ is calculated using the softmax function. The backward language model is the same as the forward language model, except that it decomposes the probability of the sequence $\{c_1, \cdots, c_T\}$ from the end to the front as $p(c_1, \cdots, c_T) = \prod_{t=1}^{T} p(c_t|c_{t+1}, \cdots, c_T)$. Its output for character c_t is denoted as $\mathbf{h}_t^r$. Both language models use negative log-likelihood as the training objective.

Language Model Integration. Using the bidirectional character-level language models, we construct contextualized representations for each word. Specifically, we feed the input character sequence C to language models, and then concatenate the hidden state of the forward language model at $c_{i,\_}$ and the hidden state of the backward language model at $c_{i-1,\_}$ as the representations for x_i. We refer these two hidden states as $\mathbf{h}_i$ and $\mathbf{h}_i^r$. Due to the complex nature of natural language, large dimensions of $\mathbf{h}_i$ and $\mathbf{h}_i^r$ are usually required in language models, which might lead to overfitting in the NER task. To avoid such cases, we add a linear transformation layer to project $\mathbf{h}_i$ and $\mathbf{h}_i^r$ to a lower dimension. In details, we use $\mathbf{r}_i = W_{cr} \cdot [\mathbf{h}_i, \mathbf{h}_i^r] + \mathbf{b}_{cr}$, where W_{cr} and $\mathbf{b}_{cr}$ are parameters to learn during the training of NER models. The output $\mathbf{r}_i$ is the contextualized representation for x_i.

5.3 Handcrafted Features

Due to the limited amount of available annotations, we further handcraft word shape features to help the model better capture the textual features. Specifically, all words are classified into three classes: (1) We mark all numbers as "num"; (2) For remaining words, if it contains English characters, it would be marked as "en"; (3) Otherwise, it would be marked as "ar". These three categories would be further mapped to three different vectors as the token representation.

Although these handcrafted features are quite simple, similar to existing work (Dozat, 2016), it results in a remarkable performance improvement in our experiments. More discussion on this feature engineering design is included in Section 6.

6 Experiments

In this section, we present the experimental results on the AQMAR dataset.

6.1 Implementation Detail

As to pre-trained language models, we conduct training on the Arabic Wikipedia texts with a vocabulary of 256 characters (out-of-vocabulary characters are mapped to a special <UNK> character). Since the resulting language model would be used to construct contextualized representations for the downstream task, whose input would be space separated, we conduct further preprocessing. Specifically, we first tokenize the text, then concatenate the token sequence by space. To demonstrate the importance of pre-processing, we trained two kinds of language models, one with pre-processing, and the other without.

For pre-trained word embedding, we adopt two sets of pre-trained embedding. One is trained with the word2vec model (Mikolov et al., 2013). It has 100 dimensions and is public available [6]. The other is trained with the Fasttext model (Bojanowski et al., 2017), which is released together with 156 other languages [7]. It has 300 dimensions and would be projected to 100 dimensions before concatenating with other vectors.

6.2 Hyper-parameter

For language model training, we use Nadam (Dozat, 2016) as the optimizer, set the learning rate as 0.002, clip the gradient at 1, set the batch size as 128 and limit the back propagation length to 256. As to the RNN, we use one-layer LSTMs with 2048 hidden states. We set its character embedding to be 128 dimensional and project its outputs to 50 dimension before concatenating with other vectors.

As to the sequence labeling task, we use LSTMs with 250 hidden states in the LSTM-CRF layer, and apply dropout with a ratio of 0.5, and use additional word dropout to each representation module with a ratio of 0.1. Following the previous work (Reimers and Gurevych, 2017), we use Nadam (Dozat, 2016) as the optimizer, set the learning rate as 0.002, clip the learning rate at 1 and set the batch size as 32.

6.3 Performance Comparison

As summarized in Table 2, our final model achieves a F_1 score of 75.82%. Further ablation study is conducted to analyze the effectiveness of each module.

---

[6]https://github.com/bakrianoo/aravec
[7]https://fasttext.cc/docs/en/crawl-vectors.html

Methods	Pre	Rec	F_1
Final Model	81.06	71.22	75.82
– Dict-based	81.27	70.84	75.70
– Ensemble	79.33	68.99	73.80
– Word shape	76.43	67.13	71.47
– Pre-process	71.60	61.33	66.07
– Language model	66.92	45.96	54.50

Table 2: Model Performance and Ablation Study for the AQMAR dataset.

Ablation Study Setting. In the ablation study, we first detach the dictionary-based NER from the resulting system and refer ensemble sequence labeling model as "– Dict-based". Then, we refer the basic sequence labeling model as "– Ensemble". After that, we detach hand-crafted features and mark the resulting model as "– Word shape". Pre-processing is further removed from language model training, which is marked as "– Pre-process". In the end, we remove language model which leads to a typical LSTM-CRF model (Huang et al., 2015) with pre-trained word embedding, we refer this model as "– Language model". Their results are summarized in Table 2.

Discussion. We find that the dictionary-based NER model[8] improves the recall at the cost of the precision and improves the F_1 score by a small margin. Also, we observe that the results demonstrate the effectiveness of ensemble learning. At the same time, we find the major F_1 improvements come from a better capturing of task-related signals. For example, by properly adding language models or designing handcrafted features, the F_1 boosts significantly. It verifies the effectiveness of contextualized representation. Also, it reveals the weakness of these techniques. Specifically, although the constructed character-level language model has the potential to capture the word shape signals, adding handcrafted features (i.e., word shape) can improve the F_1 from 71.47% to 73.80%. We conjugate this is caused by the limited size of training data with English entities, which limits the model from properly constructing task-related representations. Further comparison between these two models finds their major differences are the predictions for entities containing both Arabic and English and validates our intuition. Besides, we find the pre-processing used

in language model training is crucial for the performance, which has a big impact on the model performance (from 66.07% to 71.47%). The main reason is that although pre-trained language models are powerful, they are agnostic to the target task corpus and suffer from their differences.

7 Conclusion

In this paper, we introduce the winning solution to the Arabic Named Entity Recognition challenge. First of all, we give a detailed introduction on system design and the integrated technologies. We further conduct ablation study to reveal the effectiveness of each module and figure out all modules bring performance improvements. We observe that properly capturing the task-related features is crucial to the performance. We also noticed the current contextualized representation learning techniques, although effective, could be further enhanced by incorporating handcrafted features to better handle some corner cases.

Acknowledge

Research was sponsored in part by U.S. Army Research Lab. under Cooperative Agreement No. W911NF-09-2-0053 (NSCTA), DARPA under Agreement No. W911NF-17-C-0099, National Science Foundation IIS 16-18481, IIS 17-04532, and IIS-17-41317, DTRA HD-TRA11810026, and grant 1U54GM114838 awarded by NIGMS through funds provided by the trans-NIH Big Data to Knowledge (BD2K) initiative (www.bd2k.nih.gov). Any opinions, findings, and conclusions or recommendations expressed in this document are those of the author(s) and should not be interpreted as the views of any U.S. Government. The U.S. Government is authorized to reproduce and distribute reprints for Government purposes notwithstanding any copyright notation hereon. This research was supported by grant 1U54GM114838 awarded by NIGMS through funds provided by the trans-NIH Big Data to Knowledge (BD2K) initiative (www.bd2k.nih.gov). The views and conclusions contained in this paper are those of the authors and should not be interpreted as representing any funding agencies.

[8]The dictionary-based NER model achieves Pre: 64.35%, Rec: 8.83%, F_1: 15.53%.

References

Ahmed Abdelali, Kareem Darwish, Nadir Durrani, and Hamdy Mubarak. 2016. Farasa: A fast and furious segmenter for arabic. In *Proceedings of the 2016 Conference of the North American Chapter of the Association for Computational Linguistics: Demonstrations*, pages 11–16.

Alan Akbik, Duncan Blythe, and Roland Vollgraf. 2018. Contextual string embeddings for sequence labeling. In *Proceedings of the 27th International Conference on Computational Linguistics*, pages 1638–1649.

Mikel Artetxe, Gorka Labaka, Inigo Lopez-Gazpio, and Eneko Agirre. 2018. Uncovering divergent linguistic information in word embeddings with lessons for intrinsic and extrinsic evaluation. In *Proceedings of the 22nd Conference on Computational Natural Language Learning*, pages 282–291.

Piotr Bojanowski, Edouard Grave, Armand Joulin, and Tomas Mikolov. 2017. Enriching word vectors with subword information. *Transactions of the Association for Computational Linguistics*, 5:135–146.

Hai Leong Chieu and Hwee Tou Ng. 2002. Named entity recognition: a maximum entropy approach using global information. In *COLING*.

Kareem Darwish. 2013. Named entity recognition using cross-lingual resources: Arabic as an example. In *Proceedings of the 51st Annual Meeting of the Association for Computational Linguistics (Volume 1: Long Papers)*, volume 1, pages 1558–1567.

Timothy Dozat. 2016. Incorporating nesterov momentum into adam.

Radu Florian, Abe Ittycheriah, Hongyan Jing, and Tong Zhang. 2003. Named entity recognition through classifier combination. In *NAACL*.

Mourad Gridach. 2016. Character-aware neural networks for arabic named entity recognition for social media. In *Proceedings of the 6th workshop on South and Southeast Asian natural language processing (WSSANLP2016)*, pages 23–32.

Nizar Y Habash. 2010. Introduction to arabic natural language processing. *Synthesis Lectures on Human Language Technologies*.

Zellig S Harris. 1954. Distributional structure. *Word*, 10(2-3):146–162.

Chadi Helwe and Shady Elbassuoni. 2017. Arabic named entity recognition via deep co-learning. *Artificial Intelligence Review*, pages 1–19.

Zhiheng Huang, Wei Xu, and Kai Yu. 2015. Bidirectional lstm-crf models for sequence tagging. *arXiv preprint arXiv:1508.01991*.

John Lafferty, Andrew McCallum, and Fernando CN Pereira. 2001. Conditional random fields: Probabilistic models for segmenting and labeling sequence data. *ICML*.

Guillaume Lample, Miguel Ballesteros, Sandeep Subramanian, Kazuya Kawakami, and Chris Dyer. 2016. Neural architectures for named entity recognition. In *Proceedings of NAACL-HLT*, pages 260–270.

Liyuan Liu, Xiang Ren, Jingbo Shang, Xiaotao Gu, Jian Peng, and Jiawei Han. 2018a. Efficient contextualized representation: Language model pruning for sequence labeling. In *EMNLP*.

Liyuan Liu, Jingbo Shang, Xiang Ren, Frank Fangzheng Xu, Huan Gui, Jian Peng, and Jiawei Han. 2018b. Empower sequence labeling with task-aware neural language model. In *Thirty-Second AAAI Conference on Artificial Intelligence*.

Xuezhe Ma and Eduard Hovy. 2016. End-to-end sequence labeling via bi-directional lstm-cnns-crf. *arXiv preprint arXiv:1603.01354*.

Tomas Mikolov, Kai Chen, Greg Corrado, and Jeffrey Dean. 2013. Efficient estimation of word representations in vector space. *arXiv preprint arXiv:1301.3781*.

Behrang Mohit, Nathan Schneider, Rishav Bhowmick, Kemal Oflazer, and Noah A Smith. 2012. Recall-oriented learning of named entities in arabic wikipedia. In *EACL*.

Nam Nguyen and Yunsong Guo. 2007. Comparisons of sequence labeling algorithms and extensions. In *ICML*, pages 681–688. ACM.

Arfath Pasha, Mohamed Al-Badrashiny, Mona T Diab, Ahmed El Kholy, Ramy Eskander, Nizar Habash, Manoj Pooleery, Owen Rambow, and Ryan Roth. 2014. Madamira: A fast, comprehensive tool for morphological analysis and disambiguation of arabic. In *LREC*, volume 14, pages 1094–1101.

Matthew Peters, Waleed Ammar, Chandra Bhagavatula, and Russell Power. 2017. Semi-supervised sequence tagging with bidirectional language models. In *Proceedings of the ACL*, volume 1, pages 1756–1765.

Matthew Peters, Mark Neumann, Mohit Iyyer, Matt Gardner, Christopher Clark, Kenton Lee, and Luke Zettlemoyer. 2018. Deep contextualized word representations. In *Proceedings of NAACL-HLT*, volume 1, pages 2227–2237.

Lev Ratinov and Dan Roth. 2009. Design challenges and misconceptions in named entity recognition. In *Proceedings of the ACL*.

Nils Reimers and Iryna Gurevych. 2017. Optimal hyperparameters for deep lstm-networks for sequence labeling tasks. *arXiv preprint arXiv:1707.06799*.

Khaled Shaalan. 2014. A survey of arabic named entity recognition and classification. *Computational Linguistics*.

Jingbo Shang, Liyuan Liu, Xiaotao Gu, Xiang Ren, Teng Ren, and Jiawei Han. 2018. Learning named entity tagger using domain-specific dictionary. In *Proceedings of the 2018 Conference on Empirical Methods in Natural Language Processing*, pages 2054–2064.

hULMonA (حلمنا): The Universal Language Model in Arabic

Obeida ElJundi [1] **Wissam Antoun** [1] **Nour El Droubi** [1]
Hazem Hajj [1] **Wassim El-Hajj** [2] **Khaled Shaban** [3]
(1) American University of Beirut, Electrical and Computer Engineering Department
(2) American University of Beirut, Computer Science Department
Beirut, Lebanon
(3) Qatar University, Computer Science and Engineering Department, Doha, Qatar
{oae15;wfa07;ngd02;hh63;we07}@aub.edu.lb;khaled.shaban@qu.edu.qa

Abstract

Arabic is a complex language with limited resources which makes it challenging to produce accurate text classification tasks such as sentiment analysis. The utilization of transfer learning (TL) has recently shown promising results for advancing accuracy of text classification in English. TL models are pre-trained on large corpora, and then fine-tuned on task-specific datasets. In particular, universal language models (ULMs), such as recently developed BERT, have achieved state-of-the-art results in various NLP tasks in English. In this paper, we hypothesize that similar success can be achieved for Arabic. The work aims at supporting the hypothesis by developing the first Universal Language Model in Arabic (hULMonA - حلمنا meaning our dream), demonstrating its use for Arabic classifications tasks, and demonstrating how a pre-trained multilingual BERT can also be used for Arabic. We then conduct a benchmark study to evaluate both ULM successes with Arabic sentiment analysis. Experiment results show that the developed hULMonA and multi-lingual ULM are able to generalize well to multiple Arabic data sets and achieve new state of the art results in Arabic Sentiment Analysis for some of the tested sets.

1 Introduction

Transfer learning (TL) with universal language models (ULMs) have recently shown to achieve state of the art accuracy for several natural language processing (NLP) tasks (Devlin et al., 2018; Howard and Ruder, 2018; Radford et al., 2018). ULMs are trained unsupervised to provide an intrinsic representation of the language using large corpora that do not require annotations. These models can then be fine-tuned in a supervised mode with much smaller annotated training data to achieve a particular NLP task. The established success in English with limited data sets makes ULMs an attractive option for Arabic consideration since Arabic has limited amount of annotated resources. Early language models focused on vector embeddings for words and provided word-level vector representations (Mikolov et al., 2013; Pennington et al., 2014; Bojanowski et al., 2017), sentence embeddings (Cer et al., 2018), and paragraph embeddings (Le and Mikolov, 2014; Kiros et al., 2015). These early models were able to achieve success comparable to models that were trained only on specific tasks. More recently, the language model representation was extended to cover a broader representation for text. BERT (Devlin et al., 2018), ULMFiT (Howard and Ruder, 2018), and OpenAI GPT (Radford et al., 2018) are examples of such new pre-trained language models and which were able to achieve state of the art results in many NLP tasks.

However, in the field of Arabic NLP, such ULMs have not been explored yet. The use of transfer learning in Arabic has been mainly focused on word embedding models (Dahou et al., 2016; Soliman et al., 2017). Among the recently, developed ULM models, BERT (Devlin et al., 2018) built a multilingual language version using 104 languages including Arabic but this model has only been tested on Arabic "sentence contradiction" task. One advantage of the multi-lingual BERT is that it can be used for many languages. However, one important limitation is that it was constrained to parallel multi-lingual corpora and did not take advantage of much larger corpora set

Proceedings of the Fourth Arabic Natural Language Processing Workshop, pages 68–77
Florence, Italy, August 1, 2019. ©2019 Association for Computational Linguistics

available for Arabic, making its intrinsic representation limited for Arabic. As a result, there is an opportunity to further improve the potential for ULM success by developing an Arabic specific ULM.

In this paper, we aim at advancing performance and generalization capabilities of Arabic NLP tasks by developing new ULMs for Arabic. We develop the first Arabic specific ULM model, called hULMonA. Furthermore, we show how pre-trained multi-lingual BERT can be fine tuned and applied for Arabic classification tasks. We also conduct a benchmark study to evaluate the success potentials for the ULMs with Arabic sentiment analysis. We consider several datasets in the evaluation and show the superiority of the methods' generalization handling both MSA and dialects. The results show the superiority of the models compared to state of the art. We further show that even though the multi-lingual BERT was not trained for dialects, it still achieves state of the art for some of the dialect data sets.

In summary, our contributions are: 1. The development of hULMonA, the first Arabic specific ULM, 2. the fine tuning of multi-lingual BERT ULM for Araic sentiment analysis, and 3. the collection of a benchmark dataset for ULM evaluation with sentiment analysis

The rest of the paper is organized as follows: Section 2 provides a survey of previous work in language development for English and Arabic. Section 3 presents a description of the methodologies to develop the targeted ULMs and the description of the benchmark data set. Section 4 presents the experiment results. Finally, section 5 concludes the paper.

2 Related Work

This section describes the use of language models for NLP tasks. Historically, language models can be categorized into representations at word level and representation of larger units of text such as phrases, sentences, or documents. We will call the second sentence level representation.

2.1 Language Models for English

2.1.1 Word-level Models for English

The word-level language model is based on the use of pre-trained embedding vectors as additional features to the model. The most common embedding vectors used are word embeddings. With word embeddings, each word is linked to a vector representation in a way that captures semantic relationships (Mikolov et al., 2013). The most common word embeddings used in deep learning are word2vec (Mikolov et al., 2013), GloVe (Pennington et al., 2014), and FastText (Bojanowski et al., 2017). Other embedding vectors have been also proposed for longer texts such as vectors at the sentence level (Cer et al., 2018) and at the paragraph level (Le and Mikolov, 2014; Kiros et al., 2015). The use of these embedding vectors has shown significant improvement compared to training models from scratch (Turian et al., 2010). One of the recent feature-based approaches is ELMo (Peters et al., 2018) which is based on the use of bidirectional LSTM models. Unlike the traditional word embedding representations mentioned previously, ELMo word embeddings are functions of the whole sentence which enables capturing context-related meanings. The use of these word embeddings was shown to improve the state-of-the-are results in six NLP tasks such as sentiment analysis and question answering.

2.1.2 Sentence-level Language Models for English

In contrast to word-level representation, sentence level representation develops language model which can then be fine-tuned for a supervised downstream task (Devlin et al., 2018). The advantage of these pre-trained language models is that very few parameters have to be learned from scratch. The use of the pre-trained language models has shown to result in a better performance than the use of the feature-based approach (Howard and Ruder, 2018). Several pre-trained language models have been proposed recently that were able to achieve state-of-the-art results in many NLP tasks. One of these language models is OpenAI GPT (Radford et al., 2018) which uses the Transformer network (Vaswani et al., 2017) that enables them to capture a long range of linguistic information. This is in contrast with ELMo (Peters et al., 2018) which uses the short-range LSTM models. OpenAI GPT was able to achieve state-of-the-art results in several sentence-level NLP tasks from the GLUE benchmark (Wang et al., 2018) such as question-answering and textual entailment.

Another proposed pre-trained language model is ULMFiT (Howard and Ruder, 2018) which is based on a three-layer LSTM architecture, called

AWD-LSTM (Merity et al., 2017). This language model was able to achieve state-of-the-art results in six text classification tasks with just a few task-specific fine-tuning.

In addition to these language models, one of the most recent and innovative pre-trained language models is BERT (Devlin et al., 2018). BERT is based on the use of the recently introduced Transformer attention networks (Vaswani et al., 2017). BERT uses the bidirectional part of the Transformer architecture which is the encoder which enabled the language model to capture both left and right context. This innovation enabled BERT to achieve remarkable improvements compared to previous models and to achieve state-of-the-art results in eleven NLP tasks with the addition of just one output layer.

2.2 Language Models for Arabic

Some word embedding models were built using multiple languages such as Polyglot (Al-Rfou et al., 2013) which was built using 117 languages including the Arabic language. This model was then tested in multilingual NLP tasks. In addition to that, building on the word embedding methods developed for English, several approaches were done to build word embeddings for MSA and dialectal Arabic. The first approach is AraVec (Soliman et al., 2017) which was built using a large Arabic corpus collected from Twitter, Internet, and Wikipedia articles. Another model was proposed by Dahou et al. (Dahou et al., 2016) in which Arabic word embeddings were built using a 3.4 billion words corpus.

For sentence-level representations, there has been a development of multi-lingual models using parallel corpora. As an example, multilingual BERT (Devlin et al., 2018) was built using 104 languages including Arabic. However, there has not been any Arabic only language models. Moreover, Bert was experimented on several NLP tasks, but sentiment analysis was not one of them.

2.3 Arabic Sentiment Analysis

In (Abdul-Mageed and Diab, 2014), a large-scale, multi-genre, multi-dialect lexicon named SANA was built for the sentiment analysis of Arabic dialects. This lexicon covers the MSA, the Egyptian dialect, and the Levantine Arabic. SANA has several features which are the part of speech (POS) tagger and diacritics, number, gender, and rationality. Despite this lexicons coverage, it was still not complete, and many terms were not present. In (Abdul-Mageed and Diab, 2012), Abdul Majeed et al. worked on expanding a polarity lexicon which was built on MSA using existing English polarity lexica. The problems faced with this lexicon was that many terms that existed in social media were not found in the lexicon. Hence, the coverage of dialectical Arabic was poorly achieved using this lexicon.

In the work of Duwairi (Duwairi, 2015), sentiment analysis was done on tweets where dialectical Arabic words were present. This work used both the supervised and unsupervised approaches to build the model. To deal with dialectical words, a dialect lexicon was created in which two annotators mapped each dialectical word to its corresponding Modern Standard Arabic word. Two classifiers were used to train the model which are the Naive Bayes (NB) and the Support Vector Machines (SVM). The model was then tested using a dataset of 22,550 tweets written in Arabic and that contain dialectical Arabic words. Testing was done on the dataset when the dialect lexicon was used and when it was not used. Results showed some improvement on the Macro-Recall when the dialect lexicon was used on the NB classifier. However, the improvement was negligible on the SVM classifier and the precision and the recall were even negatively affected when classifying the negative and the Neutral classes using both classifiers.

Recently, deep learning models were the main focus of Arabic NLP researchers (Badaro et al., 2019). The first deep learning attempt was conducted by (Al Sallab et al., 2015) who explored four deep learning models, namely Deep Neural Network (DNN), Deep Believe Network (DBN), Deep Auto Encoder (DAE), and RAE. The sentiment lexicon ArSenL (Badaro et al., 2014) was utilized to represent the text vector space. In a follow up work, (Al-Sallab et al., 2017) proposed a recursive deep learning model for opinion mining in Arabic (AROMA) to address some limitations of using RAE for Arabic. To address the morphological richness and orthographic ambiguity of the Arabic language, (Baly et al., 2017) proposed the first Arabic Sentiment Treebank (ARSENTB) and trained RNTN to outperform AROMA. AraVec word embeddings (Soliman et al., 2017) were utilized by (Badaro et al., 2018) to win SemEval 2018 (Mohammad et al., 2018). (Dahou et al.,

2016) and (Dahou et al., 2019) investigated a CNN architecture similar to (Kim, 2014) trained on locally trained word embeddings to achieve significant results.

Despite all this emerging progress in Arabic sentiment analysis, transfer learning was utilized by only using a single layer of weights - usually the first layer - known as embeddings. However, typical neural network architecture consists of several layers, and utilizing transfer learning for only the first layer was clearly just scratching the surface of what is possible.

3 Methodology

In this section, we describe how we constructed hULMonA and how we then tuned both hULMonA and the multi-lingual BERT ULM for Arabic classification tasks.

The high-level architecture for using a ULM model is shown in Figure 1. The complete model consists of the combination of a pre-trained ULM model and additional task-specific layers for the desired tasks. Once a ULM model is developed, the learning process becomes limited to learning the parameters of the additional layers. This transfer learning process is referred to as fine-tuning with ULM and this is the main benefit of using ULMs.

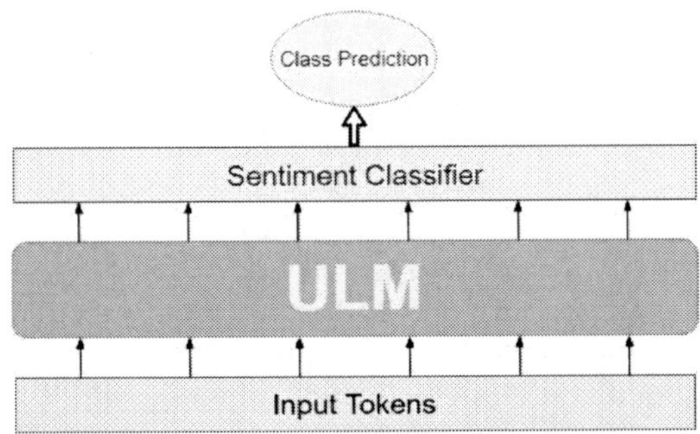

Figure 1: High Level Architecture for ULM Tranfer Learning

Below, we describe the data pre-processing step required for Arabic and the fine tuning process for the additional layers.

3.1 Arabic Specific ULM: hULMonA

Transfer Learning implies that training a model which already has some language knowledge performs better, converges faster, and requires less data for new task when comparing to training

from raw text. Language modeling is considered the ideal task to obtain general understanding of a particular language due to its ability of capturing many aspects of language relevant for downstream tasks, such as long-term dependencies (Linzen et al., 2016), hierarchical relations (Gulordava et al., 2018), and sentiment orientation (Radford et al., 2017).

Inspired by the Universal Language Model Fine-tuning (ULMFiT) (Howard and Ruder, 2018), we propose, develop, and make available for public[1], the first ULM in Arabic (hULMonA - حلمنا) that is trained on large general-domain Arabic corpus and can be fine-tuned on any target task to achieve significant results. hULMonA, illustrated in Figure 2, consists of three main stages: 1. pretraining the state-of-the-art language model AWD-LSTM (Merity et al., 2017) on a huge Wikipedia corpus (section 3.1.1), 2. fine-tuning the pretrained language model on a target dataset (section 3.1.2), 3. and adding a classification layer on top of the fine-tuned language model for the purpose of text classification (section 3.1.3).

3.1.1 General domain huLMonA pretraining

To capture the various properties of a language, we constructed a large scale Arabic language modeling dataset by extracting text from Arabic Wikipedia. The 600K Wikipedia articles were used to train a three layers of the start-of-the-art language model architecture, namely AWD-LSTM (Merity et al., 2017). The output of this stage is the model weights and the distributional representations of each word in the constructed corpus, also know as word embeddings. Although Wikipedia text is mainly in MSA, the resultant pretrained model can be fine-tuned later on different text text genres (e.g., tweets) and Arabic dialects to outperform training from scratch. Due to the huge amount of text and model parameters, especially at the last softmax layer which has as many neurons as the vocabulary size, the pretraining stage consumes much time and computational power. Fortunately, pretraining is done once, and the resultant model is made available to the community.

3.1.2 Target task huLMonA fine-tuning

Regardless of the diversity of the general-domain data, the target task data will likely come from

---

71

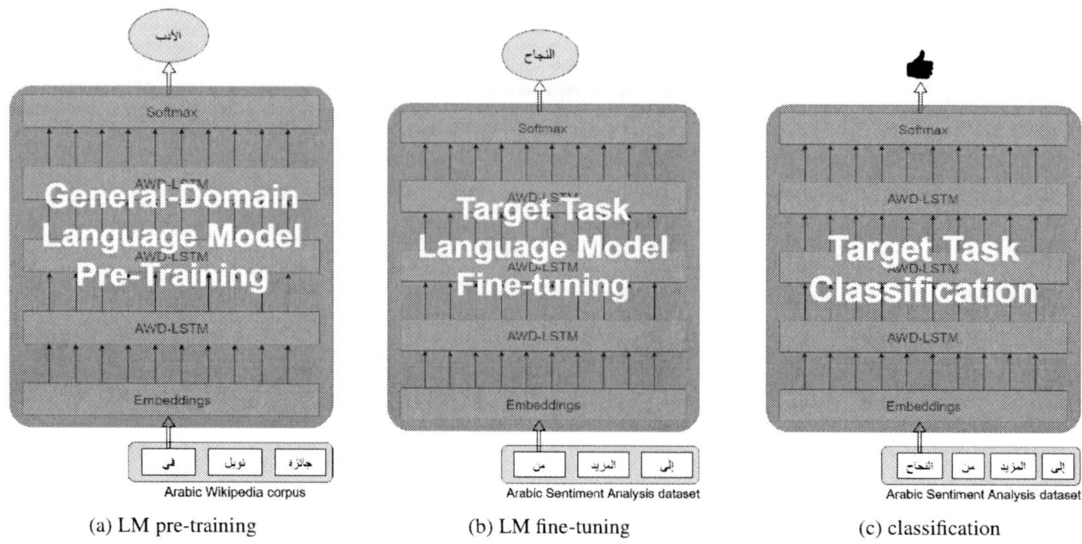

(a) LM pre-training   (b) LM fine-tuning   (c) classification

Figure 2: Three-step Process for Creating hULMonA

a different distribution. Although the general-domain LM is trained on MSA, most Arabic datasets and social media platforms contains dialects. Unlike MSA, dialects have no standard or codified form and are influenced by region specific slang. Thus, fine-tuning the pretrained general-domain LM on the target task data is necessary for the LM to adapt to the new textual properties. One difference though is that fine-tuning utilizes different learning rates for different layers, which is referred to as discriminative fine-tuning. This is crucial since different layers capture different types of information (Yosinski et al., 2014). Discriminative fine-tuning updates the model parameters as follows:

$$\theta_t^l = \theta_{t-1}^l - \eta^l \cdot \nabla_{\theta^l} J(\theta)$$

where θ^l is the model parameters of layer l, and η^l is the learning rate of layer l.

3.1.3 Augmenting hULMonA with target task classification layers

Finally, two fully connected layers are added to the LM for classification with ReLU and Softmax activations respectively. At first, the two fully connected layers are trained from scratch, while previous layers are frozen. After each epoch, the next lower frozen layer is unfrozen and fine-tuned until convergence. This is known as gradual unfreezing, and it is essential to avoid catastrophic forgetting of the information captured during language modeling.

3.2 Multi-lingual BERT ULM for Arabic tasks

3.2.1 Data Pre-processing

The ULM BERT model requires a special format for the data before feeding the model. A special token, called [CLS], is added at the beginning of every sentence and a special token, called [SEP] is added at the end of every sentence. For Arabic tokenization, we chose WordPiece(Wu et al., 2016) tokenizer as it was also used during the pretraining of BERT. Figure 3 presents a sentence before and after going through the BERT tokenizer.

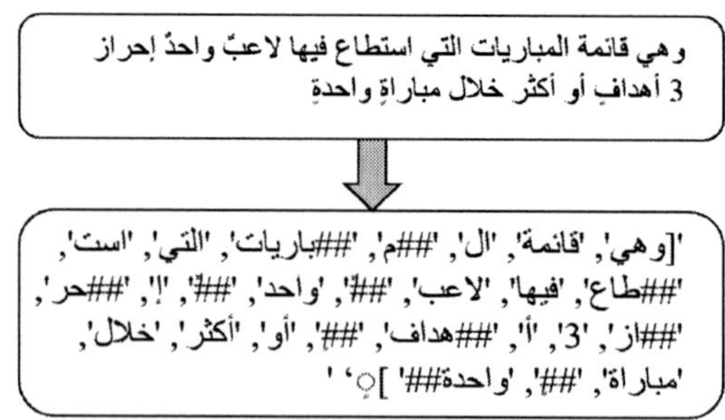

Figure 3: BERT Tokenizer Results

The tokenizer splits sentences into WordPiece tokens separated by ##. After tokenization, each word is mapped to an index using a 110k token vocabulary file that is provided by BERT for all the languages.

72

3.2.2 Model Fine Tuning

For sentiment analysis, or other Multi-label classification problems, a linear (fully-connected) layer with a standard softmax activation function is added to the last hidden state of the first token (the [CLS] token) as shown in Figure 4. With a hidden state vector $C \in R^H$ where H is the dimension of the hidden state and a fully-connected classification layer with weights $W \in R^{K \times H}$ where K is the number of classification labels, the label probability after applying the softmax function is then $P = softmax(CW^T)$.

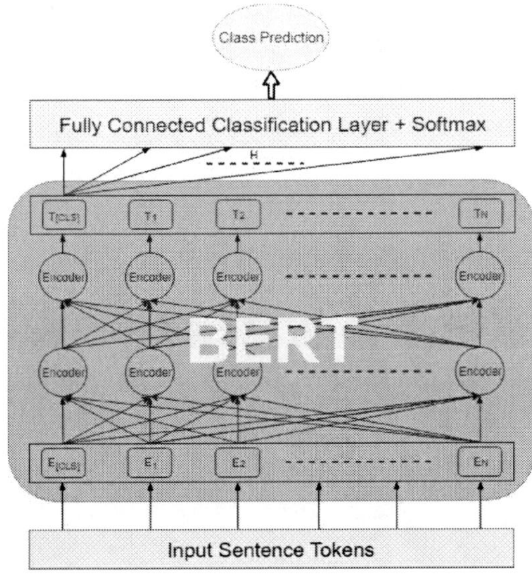

Figure 4: BERT Fine-Tuning Model Architecture

3.3 Benchmark Dataset for ULM Evaluation with Sentiment Analysis

To provide credible evaluation for the performance of the two ULM's, we catalog a benchmark dataset for Arabic which can also be used for future research benchmark evaluations. The data sets vary in size allowing us to demonstrate the ULM's abilities to fine tune with little data and achieve high performance. The benchmark data set is summarized in table 1 along with statistics on its content.

3.3.1 HARD data set

The Hotel Arabic Reviews Dataset (HARD) (Elnagar et al., 2018) is a dataset of hotel reviews written in Modern Standard Arabic and Arabic dialect classified into positive and negative. The dataset consists of a corpus of 93,700 hotel reviews which are equally divided into 46,850 positive reviews and 46.850 negative reviews. The dataset is structured in columns containing the number of the review, the name of the hotel, the rating given by the user, the type of the user, the type of the room, the number of nights stayed, and the review. Reviews have been classified into positive and negative according to the rating given by the user. A negative review is defined by a rating of 1 or 2 and a positive review is defined by a rating of 4 or 5. Neutral reviews of rating 3 were ignored in this dataset.

3.3.2 ASTD data set

The Arabic Sentiment Tweets Dataset (ASTD) (Nabil et al., 2015) is a corpus of 10,000 tweets written in MSA and Egyptian dialect. The unbalanced dataset has been manually annotated and structured in columns containing the tweet and its sentiment whether it is objective, neutral, positive, or negative. The dataset consists of 777 positive tweets, 1,642 negative tweets, 805 neutral tweets, and 6,466 objective tweets. A balanced version, called ASTD-B, is created as well taking into account positive and negative tweets only.

3.3.3 ArSenTD-Lev

(Baly et al., 2018) developed The Arabic Sentiment Twitter Dataset for LEVantine dialect (ArSenTD-Lev), a corpus of 4,000 tweets collected from Levantine countries (Palestine, Jordan, Syria, and Lebanon) and annotated for sentiment, topic, target, etc.

4 Experiments and Results

In this section, we discuss in detail the experiments that were conducted to evaluate the development of hULMonA, fine-tuning of hULMonA and BERT, and and testing the performance of the models with sentiment analysis. The benchmark data set was used to fine tune both models and provide different evaluations.

4.1 Experimental Setup

We evaluate our work on four widely-studied Arabic sentiment analysis datasets, with varying numbers of sentences and dialects. All used datasets are described in details in section 3.3, and datasets statistics are shown in table 1. Following previous works, 20% of the data was held out for testing for some datasets, while other datasets were tested on 10%.

Dataset	Resource	# samples	# classes	MSA ∥ Dialect
HARD (Elnagar et al., 2018)	Hotel reviews (www.booking.com)	93,700	2	MSA & Gulf
ASTD (Nabil et al., 2015)	Twitter	10,000	4	MSA & Egyptian
ASTD-B (Nabil et al., 2015)	Twitter	1,600	2	MSA & Egyptian
ArSenTD-Lev (Baly et al., 2018)	Twitter	4,000	5	Levantine Dialect

Table 1: Datasets statistics

Initial tokens	Generated sequence
الدكتور (Doctor)	الدكتور احمد الحسن ، كاتب وباحث سعودي ، ولد في يونيو (Doctor Ahmad Al Hassan is a Saudi writer and researcher. He was born in June)
لاعب كره قدم (football player)	لاعب كره قدم امريكي يلعب كلاعب وسط (American football player plays as midfield)
وتقع دوله (The country is located)	وتقع دوله الامارات العربيه المتحده في الشرق الاوسط (United Arab Emirates is located in the middle east)

Table 2: generating text using the pretrained Arabic language model

4.2 hULMonA Model Training

hULMonA was constructed by first extracting and preprocessing all Arabic Wikipedia articles up to March of 2019. Articles images, links, and HTML were removed using an online tool[2], and articles with less than 100 characters were excluded resulting in 600,559 Arabic articles consisting of 108M words, 4M of which were unique.

The large number of unique words requires more parameters to be learnt and is more prone to overfitting. This problem is called lexical sparsity, and it is a well-known challenge in Arabic NLP. Therefore, text was preprocessed by replacing numbers by a special token, normalizing Alif and Ta-marbota, separating punctuations from words by a white space, and removing diacritics and non-Arabic tokens. Moreover, MADAMIRA (Pasha et al., 2014), an Arabic morphological analyzer and disambiguator, was utilized to separate words prefixes, such as Al-taareef (the), and suffixes, such as possessive pronouns, resulting in words stems, thus, reducing lexical sparsity. Table 3 shows the number of unique words before and after preprocessing Arabic text using MADAMIRA. Finally, tokens that appeared less than 5 times were replaced by a special token.

The preprocessed text was then fed to train a

	Example	Unique tokens
Before	الماء مادةٌ شفافةٌ عديمة اللون والرائحة	4.1M
After	ال + ماء ماده شفافه عديمه ال + لون و + ال + راءحه	9.1K

Table 3: preprocessing reduces lexical sparsity

three layers AWD-LSTM for 4 epochs to predict next token given current sequence of tokens. Each epoch took around 200 minutes on an i7 CPU with 32 GB of RAM and Nvidia GTX 1080 GPU. We used a dropout of 0.1 with learning rate of 3e-3, and to account for GPU VRAM limitations, we were limited with batch sizes equal to 32. 10% of the data was held out for testing. Table 2 demonstrates the capabilities of the pretrained language model of generating Arabic sequence based on initial tokens. The Arabic language model dataset, code, and pre-trained weights are publicly available through the Opinion Mining for Arabic (OMA) website[3].

4.3 hULMonA Evaluation for Arabic Sentiment Analysis

To perform sentiment analysis, we fine-tuned the pretrained ULMs on a target dataset; meaning we

---

[2]https://github.com/attardi/wikiextractor

[3]http://www.oma-project.com/

Dataset	SOTA Results	hULMonA	BERT
HARD	93.1-93.2 (Elnagar et al., 2018)	**95.7-95.7**	**95.7-95.7**
ASTD	62.0-68.7 (Nabil et al., 2015)	**67.7-69.9**	67.0-77.1
ASTD-B	82.5-82.4 (Dahou et al., 2019)	**85.8-86.5**	80.0-80.1
ArSenTD-Lev	50.0-51.0 (Baly et al., 2018)	**51.1-52.4**	51.0-51.0

Table 4: Comparison of results (F1-Accuracy) obtained using hULMonA and other state-of-the-art models

resume training the language model to predict the next token but with a sentiment dataset instead of Wikipedia. Fine-tuning improved the model by adapting to new words (e.g., dialects) or words that may convey several meanings. Fine-tuning was done on each of the data sets in the aforementioned benchmark data separately and utilizing different learning rates for different layers, ranging from 2e-5 to 1e-3. Finally, after adding a classification layer, the network was trained by unfreezing one layer after each epoch, starting from the output layer. Results are reported in table 4. Note that hULMonA outperformed the state-of-the-art in four Arabic sentiment analysis datasets, demonstrating the benefit of transferring knowledge from a large corpus into small and dialectal datasets.

4.4 BERT ULM Model Fine Tuning for Arabic Sentiment Analysis

BERT was fine-tuned on the different datasets independently. The learning rate and number of epochs used for each dataset are shown in table 5. Batch size was also fixed for BERT at 32 due to our hardware memory limitations. Fine-tuning took 90 ~100 seconds for every 3000 data-point on Google's Colaboratory TensorFlow environment with GPU acceleration. BERT Base Multilingual Cased used as it is recommended in BERT's github repository[4] and the pre-trained weights were downloaded from TensorFLow's Hub[5].

Dataset	Learning Rate	# of Epochs
HARD	10^{-5}	3
ASTD	10^{-5}	5
ASTD-B	10^{-5}	5
AJGT	2×10^{-5}	6
ArSenTD-Lev	2×10^{-5}	5

Table 5: Learning rate and number of epochs used for training each dataset

[4] https://github.com/google-research/bert/blob/master/multilingual.md
[5] https://tfhub.dev/f/google

4.5 BERT ULM Evaluation for Arabic Sentiment Analysis

The results obtained are compared to state-of-the-art models and presented in Table 4. Eventhough BERT achieved state-of-the-art results on two benchmark datasets, during the evaluation, we noticed that the BERT multilingual tokenizer failed to tokenize Arabic sentences as seen in Figure 3. This tokenizer could have limited the model's accuracy and compromised the model's Arabic pre-training.

5 Conclusion

This works aims at utilizing transfer learning to develop the first Arabic universal language model, hULMonA, that can be fine-tuned for almost any Arabic text classification task. Language knowledge learnt unsupervisedly from general-domain dataset is transferred to target task to improve overall performance and generalization. We show that hULMonA outperforms several state-of-the-art Arabic sentiment analysis datasets, and we make hULMonA available for the community. In addition, we evaluate another ULM, BERT, and compare results.

As a future work, we aim at utilizing hULMonA to improve more Arabic NLP tasks such as emotion recognition, cyberbullying detection, question answering, etc. Moreover, we plan to develop Arabic specific BERT by improving its limited tokenizer and training on Arabic only instead of multiple languages at once.

References

Muhammad Abdul-Mageed and Mona Diab. 2012. Toward building a large-scale arabic sentiment lexicon. In *Proceedings of the 6th international global WordNet conference*, pages 18–22.

Muhammad Abdul-Mageed and Mona T Diab. 2014. Sana: A large scale multi-genre, multi-dialect lexicon for arabic subjectivity and sentiment analysis. In *LREC*, pages 1162–1169.

Rami Al-Rfou, Bryan Perozzi, and Steven Skiena. 2013. Polyglot: Distributed word representations for multilingual nlp. *arXiv preprint arXiv:1307.1662*.

Ahmad Al-Sallab, Ramy Baly, Hazem Hajj, Khaled Bashir Shaban, Wassim El-Hajj, and Gilbert Badaro. 2017. Aroma: A recursive deep learning model for opinion mining in arabic as a low resource language. *ACM Transactions on Asian and Low-Resource Language Information Processing (TALLIP)*, 16(4):25.

Ahmad Al Sallab, Hazem Hajj, Gilbert Badaro, Ramy Baly, Wassim El Hajj, and Khaled Bashir Shaban. 2015. Deep learning models for sentiment analysis in arabic. In *Proceedings of the second workshop on Arabic natural language processing*, pages 9–17.

Gilbert Badaro, Ramy Baly, Hazem Hajj, Wassim El-Hajj, Khaled Bashir Shaban, Nizar Habash, Ahmad Al-Sallab, and Ali Hamdi. 2019. A survey of opinion mining in arabic: A comprehensive system perspective covering challenges and advances in tools, resources, models, applications, and visualizations. *ACM Transactions on Asian and Low-Resource Language Information Processing (TALLIP)*, 18(3):27.

Gilbert Badaro, Ramy Baly, Hazem Hajj, Nizar Habash, and Wassim El-Hajj. 2014. A large scale arabic sentiment lexicon for arabic opinion mining. In *Proceedings of the EMNLP 2014 workshop on arabic natural language processing (ANLP)*, pages 165–173.

Gilbert Badaro, Obeida El Jundi, Alaa Khaddaj, Alaa Maarouf, Raslan Kain, Hazem Hajj, and Wassim El-Hajj. 2018. Ema at semeval-2018 task 1: Emotion mining for arabic. In *Proceedings of The 12th International Workshop on Semantic Evaluation*, pages 236–244.

Ramy Baly, Hazem Hajj, Nizar Habash, Khaled Bashir Shaban, and Wassim El-Hajj. 2017. A sentiment treebank and morphologically enriched recursive deep models for effective sentiment analysis in arabic. *ACM Transactions on Asian and Low-Resource Language Information Processing (TALLIP)*, 16(4):23.

Ramy Baly, Alaa Khaddaj, Hazem Hajj, Wassim El-Hajj, and Khaled Shaban. 2018. Arsentd-lev: A multi-topic corpus for target-based sentiment analysis in arabic levantine tweets. In *Proceedings of the Eleventh International Conference on Language Resources and Evaluation (LREC 2018)*, Paris, France. European Language Resources Association (ELRA).

Piotr Bojanowski, Edouard Grave, Armand Joulin, and Tomas Mikolov. 2017. Enriching word vectors with subword information. *Transactions of the Association for Computational Linguistics*, 5:135–146.

Daniel Cer, Yinfei Yang, Sheng-yi Kong, Nan Hua, Nicole Limtiaco, Rhomni St John, Noah Constant, Mario Guajardo-Cespedes, Steve Yuan, Chris Tar, et al. 2018. Universal sentence encoder. *arXiv preprint arXiv:1803.11175*.

Abdelghani Dahou, Mohamed Abd Elaziz, Junwei Zhou, and Shengwu Xiong. 2019. Arabic sentiment classification using convolutional neural network and differential evolution algorithm. *Computational Intelligence and Neuroscience*, 2019.

Abdelghani Dahou, Shengwu Xiong, Junwei Zhou, Mohamed Houcine Haddoud, and Pengfei Duan. 2016. Word embeddings and convolutional neural network for arabic sentiment classification. In *Proceedings of coling 2016, the 26th international conference on computational linguistics: Technical papers*, pages 2418–2427.

Jacob Devlin, Ming-Wei Chang, Kenton Lee, and Kristina Toutanova. 2018. Bert: Pre-training of deep bidirectional transformers for language understanding. *arXiv preprint arXiv:1810.04805*.

Rehab M Duwairi. 2015. Sentiment analysis for dialectical arabic. In *2015 6th International Conference on Information and Communication Systems (ICICS)*, pages 166–170. IEEE.

Ashraf Elnagar, Yasmin S Khalifa, and Anas Einea. 2018. Hotel arabic-reviews dataset construction for sentiment analysis applications. In *Intelligent Natural Language Processing: Trends and Applications*, pages 35–52. Springer.

Kristina Gulordava, Piotr Bojanowski, Edouard Grave, Tal Linzen, and Marco Baroni. 2018. Colorless green recurrent networks dream hierarchically. *arXiv preprint arXiv:1803.11138*.

Jeremy Howard and Sebastian Ruder. 2018. Universal language model fine-tuning for text classification. *arXiv preprint arXiv:1801.06146*.

Yoon Kim. 2014. Convolutional neural networks for sentence classification. In *Proceedings of the 2014 Conference on Empirical Methods in Natural Language Processing (EMNLP)*, pages 1746–1751, Doha, Qatar. Association for Computational Linguistics.

Ryan Kiros, Yukun Zhu, Ruslan R Salakhutdinov, Richard Zemel, Raquel Urtasun, Antonio Torralba, and Sanja Fidler. 2015. Skip-thought vectors. In *Advances in neural information processing systems*, pages 3294–3302.

Quoc Le and Tomas Mikolov. 2014. Distributed representations of sentences and documents. In *International conference on machine learning*, pages 1188–1196.

Tal Linzen, Emmanuel Dupoux, and Yoav Goldberg. 2016. Assessing the ability of lstms to learn syntax-sensitive dependencies. *Transactions of the Association for Computational Linguistics*, 4:521–535.

Stephen Merity, Nitish Shirish Keskar, and Richard Socher. 2017. Regularizing and optimizing lstm language models. *arXiv preprint arXiv:1708.02182.*

Tomas Mikolov, Ilya Sutskever, Kai Chen, Greg S Corrado, and Jeff Dean. 2013. Distributed representations of words and phrases and their compositionality. In *Advances in neural information processing systems*, pages 3111–3119.

Saif Mohammad, Felipe Bravo-Marquez, Mohammad Salameh, and Svetlana Kiritchenko. 2018. Semeval-2018 task 1: Affect in tweets. In *Proceedings of The 12th International Workshop on Semantic Evaluation*, pages 1–17.

Mahmoud Nabil, Mohamed Aly, and Amir Atiya. 2015. Astd: Arabic sentiment tweets dataset. In *Proceedings of the 2015 Conference on Empirical Methods in Natural Language Processing*, pages 2515–2519.

Arfath Pasha, Mohamed Al-Badrashiny, Mona T Diab, Ahmed El Kholy, Ramy Eskander, Nizar Habash, Manoj Pooleery, Owen Rambow, and Ryan Roth. 2014. Madamira: A fast, comprehensive tool for morphological analysis and disambiguation of arabic. In *LREC*, volume 14, pages 1094–1101.

Jeffrey Pennington, Richard Socher, and Christopher Manning. 2014. Glove: Global vectors for word representation. In *Proceedings of the 2014 conference on empirical methods in natural language processing (EMNLP)*, pages 1532–1543.

Matthew E Peters, Mark Neumann, Mohit Iyyer, Matt Gardner, Christopher Clark, Kenton Lee, and Luke Zettlemoyer. 2018. Deep contextualized word representations. *arXiv preprint arXiv:1802.05365.*

Alec Radford, Rafal Jozefowicz, and Ilya Sutskever. 2017. Learning to generate reviews and discovering sentiment. *arXiv preprint arXiv:1704.01444.*

Alec Radford, Karthik Narasimhan, Tim Salimans, and Ilya Sutskever. 2018. Improving language understanding by generative pre-training. *URL https://s3-us-west-2. amazonaws. com/openai-assets/research-covers/languageunsupervised/language understanding paper. pdf.*

Abu Bakr Soliman, Kareem Eissa, and Samhaa R El-Beltagy. 2017. Aravec: A set of arabic word embedding models for use in arabic nlp. *Procedia Computer Science*, 117:256–265.

Joseph Turian, Lev Ratinov, and Yoshua Bengio. 2010. Word representations: a simple and general method for semi-supervised learning. In *Proceedings of the 48th annual meeting of the association for computational linguistics*, pages 384–394. Association for Computational Linguistics.

Ashish Vaswani, Noam Shazeer, Niki Parmar, Jakob Uszkoreit, Llion Jones, Aidan N Gomez, ukasz Kaiser, and Illia Polosukhin. 2017. Attention is all you need. In *Advances in neural information processing systems*, pages 5998–6008.

Alex Wang, Amapreet Singh, Julian Michael, Felix Hill, Omer Levy, and Samuel R Bowman. 2018. Glue: A multi-task benchmark and analysis platform for natural language understanding. *arXiv preprint arXiv:1804.07461.*

Yonghui Wu, Mike Schuster, Zhifeng Chen, Quoc V Le, Mohammad Norouzi, Wolfgang Macherey, Maxim Krikun, Yuan Cao, Qin Gao, Klaus Macherey, et al. 2016. Google's neural machine translation system: Bridging the gap between human and machine translation. *arXiv preprint arXiv:1609.08144.*

Jason Yosinski, Jeff Clune, Yoshua Bengio, and Hod Lipson. 2014. How transferable are features in deep neural networks? In *Advances in neural information processing systems*, pages 3320–3328.

Neural Models for Detecting Binary Semantic Textual Similarity for Algerian and MSA

Wafia Adouane, Jean-Philippe Bernardy and Simon Dobnik
Department of Philosophy, Linguistics and Theory of Science (FLoV),
Centre for Linguistic Theory and Studies in Probability (CLASP), University of Gothenburg
{wafia.adouane, jean-philippe.bernardy, simon.dobnik}@gu.se

Abstract

We explore the extent to which neural networks can learn to identify semantically equivalent sentences from a small variable dataset using an end-to-end training. We collect a new noisy non-standardised user-generated Algerian (ALG) dataset and also translate it to Modern Standard Arabic (MSA) which serves as its regularised counterpart. We compare the performance of various models on both datasets and report the best performing configurations. The results show that relatively simple models composed of 2 LSTM layers outperform by far other more sophisticated attention-based architectures, for both ALG and MSA datasets.

1 Introduction

Detecting Semantic Textual Similarity (STS) aims to predict a relationship between a pair of sentences based on a semantic similarity score. It is a well-established problem (Agirre et al., 2012) which deals with text comprehension and which has been framed and tackled differently (Beltagy et al., 2013, 2014). In this work we focus on deep learning approach. For example, Baudis and Šedivý (2016) frame the problem as a sentence-pair scoring using binary or graded scores indicating the degree to which a pair of sentences are related.

Solutions to detecting semantic similarity benefit from the recent success of neural models applied to NLP and have achieved new state-of-the-art performance (Parikh et al., 2016; Chen et al., 2017). However, so far it has been explored only on fairly large well-edited labelled data in English. This paper explores a largely unexplored question which concerns the application of neural models to detect binary STS from small labelled datasets. We take the case of the language used in Algeria (ALG) which is an under-resourced language with several linguistic challenges. ALG is a collection of local colloquial varieties with a heavy use of code-switching between different languages and language varieties including Modern Standard Arabic (MSA), non-standardised local colloquial Arabic, and other languages like French and Berber, all written in Arabic script normally without the vowels.

ALG and MSA are two Arabic varieties which differ lexically, morphologically, syntactically, etc., and therefore represent different challenges for NLP. For instance, ALG and MSA share some morphological features, but at the same time the same morphological forms have different meanings. For instance, a verb in the 1st person singular in ALG is the same 1st person plural in MSA. The absence of morpho-syntactic analysers for ALG makes it challenging to analyse such texts, especially when ALG is mixed with MSA. Furthermore, this language is not documented, i.e., it does not have lexicons, standardised orthography, and written morpho-syntactic rules describing how words are formed and combined to form larger units. The nonexistence of lexicons to disambiguate the senses of a word based on its language or language variety makes resolving lexical ambiguity challenging for NLP because relying on exact word form matching is misleading.

(1) a. فوت ثمانة في دار مواليا كي وليت لقيت
وليدي دار حالة منداك نهار راجلي دار فرايو
ولا جاي أخليني نبات

    b. I spent one week at my parents' **house** and when I came back I found that my son **made** a big mess. After that my husband **changed** his opinion and never allowed me to stay over night (at my parents' house).

(2) a. حنا فلمولود نوجدو طعام لفطور ونتوما واش

Proceedings of the Fourth Arabic Natural Language Processing Workshop, pages 78–87
Florence, Italy, August 1, 2019. ©2019 Association for Computational Linguistics

غادي تديرو غدا

   b. In Mawlid we prepare Couscous for **lunch**, and you what will you prepare (for lunch)?

In many cases, while the same word form has several meanings depending on its context, different word forms have the same meaning. As an illustration, consider examples (1) and (2) which are user-generated texts taken from our corpus (Section 3.1.1). In (1), the same word form "دار" occurs three times with different meanings: "house", "made", and "changed" respectively. Whereas in (2), the different word forms "لفطور" and "غدا" mean both "lunch".

We mention these examples to provide a basic background for a better understanding of the challenges faced while processing this kind of real-world data using the current NLP approaches and systems that are designed and trained mainly on well-edited standardised monolingual corpora. We could, for instance, distinguish the meanings of "دار" in (1) if we knew that the 1st occurrence is a noun and the two others are verbs. Likewise, if we had a tool to distinguish between ALG and MSA, it were easier to detect the meaning of "غدا" as "lunch" in ALG rather than the MSA meaning "tomorrow".

Traditional models for detecting STS cannot be applied on such data because they require existing resources and tools, such as tokeniser, stemmer, PoS tagger, etc. to pre-process the data and extract useful features assuming that the data is correctly spelled (standardised orthography). Thus using deep neural networks (DNNs) is promising because representations can be learned in an unsupervised way. In particular, when trained end-to-end, inputs are mapped directly to the desired outputs without the need to handcraft features. Nevertheless, this learning approach based on pattern matching requires lot of data to learn useful patterns. Besides there are only a few cleaned and labelled textual corpora available for some languages and creating new ones is labour intensive.

Our contributions are as follows. (i) We introduce a newly built (small) ALG dataset for STS. (ii) We compare the performance of different DNN configurations on this dataset, namely: various combinations of Recurrent Neural Networks (RNNs), Convolutional Neural Networks (CNNs), pre-training of embeddings, including a replication of two new state-of-the art attention models. (iii) We test whether increasing the dataset size helps. (iv) We test whether language regularisation helps. For this purpose, we run the same experiments on a regularised and comparable MSA translation of the ALG dataset.

The paper is structured as follows. In Section 2, we briefly review some STS applications. In Section 3, we describe our experimental setup including data and models. In Section 4, we discuss the results and conclude with our future plans in Section 5.

2 Related Work

Diverse techniques and formalisms have been used to deal with various semantic-related tasks. Among others, machine learning has been applied to detect semantic textual relatedness such as Textual Entailment (TE) (Nielsen et al., 2009), STS (Agirrea et al., 2016), Paraphrase Identification (PI) (Liang et al., 2016), etc. Earlier systems use a combination of various handcrafted features and are trained on relatively small datasets. For example, Dey et al. (2016) uses Support Vector Machines with a set of lexical, syntactic, semantic and pragmatic features. As discussed earlier, these features are not available from our dataset.

These tasks have recently attracted more attention when DNNs became practical, mainly due to the availability of large labelled datasets such as the Stanford Natural Language Inference corpus (SNLI) containing 570K sentence pairs (Bowman et al., 2015), Sentences Involving Compositional Knowledge (SICK) containing about 10K sentence pairs (Marelli et al., 2014), the Microsoft Research WikiQA Corpus (WIKIQA) containing more than 23K sentence pairs (Yang et al., 2015), the Quora dataset released by Kaggle competition consisting of 400K potential question duplicate pairs[1], and the Microsoft Research Paraphrase (MSRP) consisting of more than 5K sentence pairs (Dolan and Brockett, 2005).

We follow the approach of Baudis and Šedivý (2016) who consider that several tasks dealing with detecting semantic relatedness are technically similar and can be formulated as sentence-pair

---

[1]Corpus webpage: `https://www.kaggle.com/quora/question-pairs-dataset`

scoring. They propose a generic framework for text comprehension for evaluating and comparing existing systems. Several DNN systems have been proposed. For instance, Mueller and Thyagarajan (2016) propose a siamese recurrent architecture using Manhattan LSTM (MaLSTM) for STS. They use word embeddings supplemented with synonymy information, LSTM and Manhattan distance to compose sentence representations.

Additionally, complex DNN systems with various attention mechanisms have been proposed to deal with more than one semantic similarity task at the same time. For instance, Yin et al. (2015) apply attention to represent mutual influence between the input sentence pairs. Similarly, Parikh et al. (2016) propose the Decomposable Attention Model (DecompAtten) which relies on alignment using neural attention to decompose the task of natural language inference into sub-tasks which are aggregated and used to predict the output. In the same direction, Chen et al. (2017) propose the Enhanced Sequential Inference Model (ESIM) composed of a bidirectional LSTM (BiLSTM) encoder, and a soft alignment which computes attention weights to determine the relevance between two input sentences. Then they use another BiLSTM layer to compose local inference information and aggregate the output by applying average and max pooling, and concatenating all in one vector.

All preceding models involve considerable sophistication of design and sometimes require specific dataset annotation. This is to say they are normally trained on large well-edited and labelled datasets that are available for English but are unavailable for most other languages. Unlike the previous work, we will compare the performance of two presumably best performing architectures to simpler architectures similar to MaLSTM but with different additional components on a small unedited dataset.

3 Experiment

3.1 Data

3.1.1 ALG STS data

To the best of our knowledge, there is no ready-to-use ALG data for any semantic similarity related task prior to this work. As a basis we use an extended version of the ALG unlabelled dataset (Adouane et al., 2018) which currently contains 408,832 unedited short colloquial texts (more than

6 million words) collected from online discussion forums. For the STS task we created a dataset of 3,000 sentence pairs as follows. We randomly selected 1,000 sentences from the ALG unlabelled data, including various topics and text lengths. We asked two ALG native speakers to produce for each given sentence two more sentences: one which is semantically equivalent and the other can be semantically similar but not equivalent, i.e., it could include the same words or could be about the same topic.

(3) a. . لالا ماشي باهية الروز قديم دوكا
الوردي ما عجبنيش ما هوش الامود .

  b. No, it is not beautiful, pink is outdated.
I do not like pink, it is not fashionable.

(4) a. . هديت ليما تارت تاع الشوكو
عجبتني لاتارت تاع الشوكو لي دارتها يما .

  b. I offered to my mother a chocolate pie.
I like the chocolate pie that my mother baked.

In (3), the two sentences are semantically equivalent but in (4) the two sentences are roughly about the same topic and include "chocolate pie", "mother" and "I" but some important information differs — like who did what.

The annotators were free to use whatever words as long as the produced sentences sounded natural to them and the above instructions were respected. We provided them with two examples of the desired sentences and explained the difference. We combined all the sentences and created 3,000 unique sentence pairs.

In the second part of dataset creation, we asked three different native speakers to provide a similarity score between 0–5 for each sentence pair following the guidelines used in the SemEval-2016 shared task (Agirrea et al., 2016). Finally, another annotator performed manual checking and majority voting of the annotations.

Because the annotators assigned scores according to their judgement, the resulting data is not balanced in terms of the number of instances per class (0–5) as shown in Table 1. The corpus contains

36,767 words, 7,074 unique words and sentence average length of 5.19 words or 34 characters.

Score	Interpretation	#Pairs
0	The two sentences are completely dissimilar.	1,550
1	The two sentences are not equivalent, but are on the same topic.	237
2	The two sentences are not equivalent, but share some details.	140
3	The two sentences are roughly equivalent, but some important information differs.	63
4	The two sentences are mostly equivalent, but some unimportant details differ.	16
5	The two sentences are completely equivalent, as they mean the same thing.	994

Table 1: Annotation guidelines and the number of instances in the ALG STS dataset.

We first tried to predict the graded six similarity scores as multi-class STS, but the systems (Section 3.2) only predicted the most frequent classes, namely scores 0 and 5. This behaviour suggests that given the size of the dataset and the number of instances for each class, the classes are not distinguishable enough. Therefore, we re-framed the task as a binary STS: either two sentences are semantically equivalent or not, rather than predicting their graded similarity (Agirre et al., 2015; Xu et al., 2015). To this end, we merged all scores which do not capture semantic equivalence (0 to 4) into a single class, and refer to them as non-equivalent. The remaining score of 5 stands on its own as completely equivalent. The resulting binary labelled data contains 994 equivalent sentence pairs and 2,006 non-equivalent sentence pairs.

3.1.2 MSA STS data

Contrary to ALG, MSA is a well-represented Arabic variety with standardised spelling. We use a large MSA Wikipedia corpus[2] consisting of more than 52 million tokens. We automatically removed all words written in non-Arabic script and punctuation. We refer to this corpus as MSA unlabelled data.

We also created a labelled STS corpus for MSA by commissioning another pair of ALG native speakers to faithfully translate the ALG STS dataset into MSA. They were instructed to keep the order of words and structures as close as possible to the ALG sentences without changing the

---

[2]The MSA corpus was downloaded from: `http://goo.gl/d7pxZb`.

meaning. We manually checked the quality of the translation, corrected some minor misspellings and checked the corresponding similarity scores (0–5). We proceeded in the same way as for ALG and created a binary MSA STS dataset including equivalent and non-equivalent sentence pairs.

Both binary and multi-class STS MSA datasets have the same number of sentence pairs as their ALG corresponding datasets. However, the MSA datasets have a smaller vocabulary, consisting of only 5,527 unique words from a total of 37,832 words. The average sentence length is 6.84 words or 33.26 characters. The difference in the vocabulary size is mainly due to misspellings and spelling variations in the ALG corpus: it is non-standardised language. Yet both ALG and MSA datasets have relatively short sentences and they are about the same topics since one is a translation of the other.

3.2 Models

All models have the same basic structure. They consist of two identical siamese networks, one for each input sentence as shown in Figure 1. The main differences between the models are in the embeddings, the sentence encoder, the distance measure, and the objective function for the final prediction.

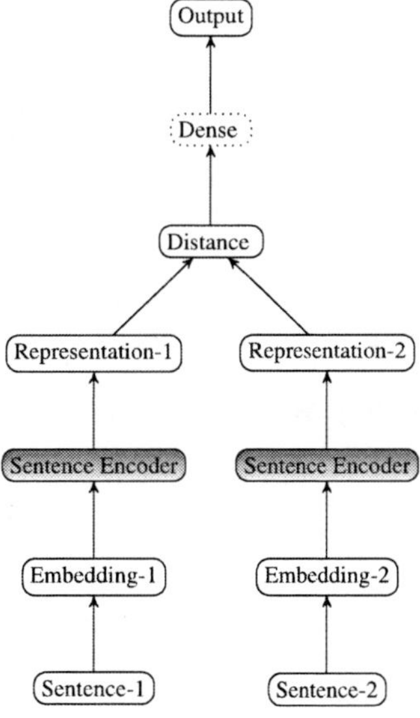

Figure 1: Siamese network architecture. The trained parameters are shared between the left (1) and right (2) part of the network.

3.2.1 Embeddings

We use two kinds of embedding layers. First, an embedding layer trained only on the training data based either on characters or words, initialised either with a uniform or a normal distribution. We refer to these embeddings as trainable as a contrast to pre-trained embeddings. Second, we pre-trained a word2vec and FastText embeddings on the larger unlabelled data mentioned in Section 3.1, using the Gensim (Řehůřek and Sojka, 2010) and FastText (Bojanowski et al., 2016) libraries. For word2vec embeddings, we used a context size of 5 words, minimum occurrence of 1 and dimension of 300. For FastText embeddings, we used dimension of 300, range of sub-characters between 3-5 characters, and a context size of 5 words, and training for 200 epochs. The goal of using pre-trained word embeddings is to test whether we can make use of the large unlabelled corpora.[3]

3.2.2 Sentence Encoders

We use either an RNN or a CNN with different configurations to encode each sentence and output a representation for each. The sentence encoders are identical for both sentences and share weights. Here are some of the encoders that we experimented with.

RNN-based encoder consisting of a stack of standard and/or bidirectional LSTM layers with 300 units and a dropout rate of 3%.

CNN-based encoder consisting of a stack of convolution layers with 60 filters of size 5, with a relu activation and a dropout rate of 10%, followed by max pooling with a pool size of 3, followed optionally by a global average pooling and global max pooling multiplied together.

CNN-RNN-based encoder A combination of RNN and CNN encoders where we stack a number of convolution layers with 60 filters of size 5, with a relu activation and a dropout rate of 10%, followed by max pooling with a pool size of 3 and a number of RNN layers (either standard or bidirectional LSTMs).

Attention-based encoder Roughly put, the idea of an attention mechanism is to attend to some

parts of an input/output when deriving its representation (Bahdanau et al., 2014). We implement the Decomposable Attention (DecompAtten) and Enhanced Sequential Inference Model (ESIM) models, as described in Section 2.

3.2.3 Distance

The distance component serves to compose the sentence representations. We use standard distances such as Euclidean distance, Manhattan distance, and Cosine similarity.

3.2.4 Dense

Instead of using a distance measure between the sentence representations, we compose the two sentence representations by multiplication (multp), subtraction (subtr), summation (sum), or concatenation (conct) as in the ESIM model. This operation is followed by a dense layer. We indicate that this layer is optional by using a dotted frame in Figure 1. When it is used, we use a sigmoid activation with a binary cross-entropy loss.

Except for the pre-trained embeddings, all models are trained end-to-end for 300 epochs using a batch size of 64 and Adam optimiser with a learning rate of 0.001.

4 Results and Discussion

We randomly selected from the binary ALG STS dataset 250 sentence pairs of each class (equivalent and non-equivalent) as the test set (500 in total), 200 sentence pairs as a development set, and the remaining 2,300 sentence pairs as a training set. Note that balancing the test set is not essential. Likewise, we split the binary MSA STS data by taking the corresponding translations for each instance in the ALG dataset.

The hyper-parameters reported in Section 3.2 were selected based on the reported common values in the literature for similar tasks and fine-tuned on the development set. Moreover, because of the stochastic nature of the neural models [4] where the results vary between each training run, we report the average performance on the test set over 10 training runs for the best performing models trained on both training and development data following (Baudis and Šedivý, 2016; Yin et al., 2015).

In order to increase the size of the training data and to boost the instances of the minority class

---

[3]The annotated data and the pre-trained embeddings are available from the 1st author.

[4]https://machinelearningmastery.com/randomness-in-machine-learning/

	Model	Emb	Encoder	Dist	ALG		MSA	
					Acc	Acc-aug	Acc	Acc-aug
1	char-RNN	trainable	2-LSTM	multp	55.78	61.84	59.65	67.80
2	char-RNN	trainable	2-LSTM	subtr	70.38	78.56	69.02	71.37
3	word-RNN	trainable	2-LSTM	multp	**85.06**	87.20	**85.19**	86.69
4	word-RNN	trainable	2-LSTM	subtr	73.73	**92.76**	68.90	88.20
5	word-RNN	word2vec	2-LSTM	subtr	71.40	92.51	67.86	**89.46**
6	word-RNN	FastText	2-LSTM	subtr	71.68	92.70	68.06	88.57
7	word-CNN	trainable	1-CNN	sum	50.00	50.00	50.00	50.00
8	DecompAtten	trainable	attention	sum	50.44	53.00	50.02	50.44
9	ESIM	trainable	attention	conct	52.34	52.80	50.34	50.39

Table 2: Average accuracy of the models (%). Acc is accuracy with non-augmented training data and Acc-aug with the augmented training data.

(equivalent sentence pairs), we duplicated equivalent sentence pairs by reversing their order so that each sentence pair appears only once in the same order. This is a standard data augmentation practice used to mitigate the limited availability of labelled training data (Yin et al., 2015; Mueller and Thyagarajan, 2016). The augmented training set contains 3,244 sentence pairs (1,488 equivalent and 1,756 non-equivalent pairs). Because there is no previous work reported for ALG on a similar task, we resort to the binary random guess, namely 50% as a baseline. We report the overall accuracy for the same models with and without the augmented training data, for both ALG and MSA separately. In Table 2, we only report the models that outperform the baseline.

4.1 Binary STS for ALG

Non-augmented data The results show that char-RNNs composed of 2 standard LSTM layers and trainable embedding layer with normal distribution (1) and (2) perform worse than their word-based counterparts (3) and (4). This result contradicts the conclusion that character models are better at modelling morphologically rich languages (Vylomova et al., 2017), and consequently they are better in dealing with misspellings and capturing spelling variations.

The best performance is achieved by a word-based 2-LSTM layer encoder and a trainable embedding layer (3), using multiplication as a distance with an accuracy of 85.06%. Nevertheless, char-RNN performs better with subtraction rather than multiplication as a distance (2). Adding pre-trained embeddings word2vec (5) and FastText (6) to the word-level RNN in (4) decreases the accuracy by 2.33 and 2.05 points respectively. This effect could be caused by the noise in the ALG unlabelled data on which the embeddings were trained.

A 1-layer CNN with no pre-trained embeddings and using summation of the sentence representations as a distance (7) performs the best compared to the other options with CNN encoder but overall it performs quite poorly. Likewise combining 1-CNN and 1-LSTM layers as encoder (not shown in Table 2) does not have an effect over using only 1-CNN layer. The models predict all the test sentence pairs as non-equivalent. In other words, the network could not learn enough to properly distinguish between the two classes.

These results contrast those reported by Kadlec et al. (2015), namely that CNN models perform better with little data compared to RNN models. However, it is hard to quantify what is considered to be small apart from the number of examples. In general, neural models learn useful features when they are trained on enough representative data. That is to say it is not just a question of data size, but it is more about the complexity of the features and the functions that they should learn. In our case, we suspect that the sparsity and the noise in the data is making learning harder for CNN models.

Regarding attention-based encoders, ESIM (9) outperform DecompAtten (8), and both perform slightly better than the baseline. The poor performance of these models with little noisy data could be related to the fact that attending to some parts of a sentence or focusing on surface form similarity is misleading since the same word form can have different meanings and different word forms can have the same meaning, especially that the data does not contain named entities or punctuation or digits which could help alignment.

Augmented data All models benefit from the augmented data, except word-CNN (7) for which the gain is not clear. The performance of the char-

	Model	Equivalent			Non-equivalent		
		Precision (%)	Recall (%)	F-score	Precision (%)	Recall (%)	F-score
1	char-RNN-multp	73.91	53.54	62.10	63.12	80.80	70.88
2	char-RNN-subtr	88.02	66.54	75.78	72.76	90.80	80.78
3	word-RNN-multp	86.96	88.00	87.48	87.85	86.80	87.32
4	word-RNN-subtr	89.67	97.20	93.28	96.94	88.80	92.69
5	word-RNN-word2vec	89.30	96.80	92.90	96.51	88.40	92.28
6	word-RNN-FastText	**90.84**	95.20	92.97	94.96	**90.40**	92.62

Table 3: Average performance of the models per class trained on the ALG augmented data.

RNN (2) shows 8.18 point improvement in accuracy. This result supports the hypothesis that the poor performance of the model trained on the non-augmented data is caused by the small size of the sparse noisy data which makes it hard for the char-RNN to learn useful patterns. Yet the significant improvement of the word-RNN (4) by 19.03 points, indicates that word-RNN suits better our case.

Models with subtraction as a distance benefit the most from the added data. Similar to their behaviour on non-augmented data, adding pre-trained embeddings slightly decreases the performance of the model compared to not adding them. Comparing embeddings, word2vec causes slightly more drop in the performance of word-RNN compared to FastText. Attention-based models benefit also from the added data, but the gain is larger for DecompAtten compared to ESIM.

Looking at the performance of the models for each class shown in Table 3, it is clear that the RNN models are doing quite well for both classes whereas CNN and Attention-based models, not included for space limits, are too biased to the non-equivalent class. Figures in bold are meant to highlight the gain due to pre-trained embeddings.

Error analysis of the word-RNN model (4) shows that 7 equivalent sentence pairs are misclassified as non-equivalent and 28 non-equivalent sentence pairs are misclassified as equivalent. We manually checked the errors and found that most of the non-equivalent pairs misclassified as equivalent have at least one word in common as in example (5) but the words have a different meaning depending on their context. However, distinguishing between word senses is hard because the context is not entirely sufficient. Example (6) is an equivalent pair misclassified as non-equivalent. The common pattern among the misclassified examples is that they have no exact words in overlap. This could explain why attention-based encoders, with some form of alignment, fail to generalise to

new instances. Probably there is a bias to the form with one meaning when senses are not sufficiently differentiated.

(5) a. . شفت حجا يبزار
   سي بيزار ما شفتوش .
   b. I saw a weird thing.
      It is weird that I did not see it.

(6) a. . راني نخمّ وقتاش تدخل لبورس
   يادرى هذيك المنحة وينتا تحي .
   b. I am thinking when the grant will be received.
      I wonder when the grant will be paid.

4.2 Binary STS for MSA

We now evaluate the performance of the same DNN configurations on parallel regularised MSA data using the same hyper-parameters as in Section 4.1. The results are reported in Table 2.

Non-augmented data Again, the word-RNN with multiplication (3) performs the best with an accuracy of 85.19%. The char-RNN (1) with the same settings achieves an accuracy of only 59.65%. Using subtraction, the char-RNN (2) slightly outperforms the word-RNN (4), with 69.02% and 68.90% accuracy respectively. Adding FastText (6) and word2vec (5) pre-trained embeddings causes the accuracy of the best word-RNN (4) of 68.90% to decrease slightly to 68.06% and 67.86% respectively. This could be due to the embeddings not distinguishing between the different senses of the same word, i.e., output one vector representation for each word form. Also the large MSA corpus on which the embeddings were trained can have different topical distribution than the MSA STS data. As with the ALG data, CNN (7) and attention-based encoders (8–9) behave the same.

Augmented data Trained on augmented data, models with subtraction yield the best performance compared to multiplication, and word-RNN (4) outperforms char-RNN (2) with 88.20%

		Equivalent			Non-equivalent		
	Model	Precision (%)	Recall (%)	F-score	Precision (%)	Recall (%)	F-score
1	char-RNN-multp	69.86	61.20	65.25	65.48	73.60	69.30
2	char-RNN-subtr	76.35	62.25	68.58	67.92	80.57	73.70
3	word-RNN-multp	87.04	86.00	86.52	86.17	87.20	86.68
4	word-RNN-subtr	85.77	91.60	88.59	90.99	84.80	87.78
5	word-RNN-word2vec	**87.17**	**92.77**	**89.88**	**92.21**	**86.23**	**89.12**
6	word-RNN-FastText	**86.97**	91.16	**89.02**	90.64	**86.23**	**88.38**

Table 4: Average performance of the models per class trained on the MSA augmented data.

and 71.37% accuracy respectively. Unlike when using the ALG data, pre-trained embeddings improve slightly the performance of (4) with 0.37 (6) and 1.26 (5) points gain in the error reduction respectively. The positive effect of the pre-trained models could be due to the fact that more regularities are captured. Training on augmented MSA data does not yield any significant gain over training on non-augmented data for CNN (7) and attention based models (8–9).

In Table 4 we report the performance of each model per class. Due to space limits, we do not include the CNN and attention-based models which are again struggling with the equivalent class and are biased towards the non-equivalent class. The gain from the pre-trained embedding is in bold. The models perform almost the same for both classes but slightly worse than with the ALG data.

Example (7) is a non-equivalent sentence pair misclassified as equivalent, and example (8) is an equivalent pair misclassified as non-equivalent by the word-RNN model (5).

(7) a. الكيكة أنا أيضا جربتها والله روعة وجدت
أولادي كلهم لعقوها .
جربتها كم من مرة كانت سامة وحاسدة .

b. I also tried the cake and it was great, I discovered that my kids finished it.
I tested her many times and she was jealous and envious.

(8) a. يا ليتهم يغيرون **الذيعة** هذه . .
يا ريت يغيرون لنا هذه **النشطة** .

b. Wish they change this presenter.
Hope they will replace this presenter.

It is hard to explain why these examples are misclassified, except that there is not enough context to discover the meaning of the words. For instance, in (8) the words in bold "منشطة" , "مذيعة" are synonyms in these two sentences, and the two sentences have two more word overlaps "هذه" and

"يغيرون" with the same meaning. This should help classifying the two sentences as equivalent, but it is not the case possibly because their contexts are different.

5 Conclusion and Future Work

We have presented a new STS dataset for ALG user-generated short texts and its MSA translation. We then described the neural network models trained end-to-end with different configurations and compared their performances on a binary STS task. The results show that relatively simple model architectures, composed of two word-based LSTM layers with subtraction as explicit similarity measure used in the training task, suit better our data compared to the other more sophisticated architectures which might require more data to achieve better performance.

We ran the same experiment on the MSA data, but the results were not really different from the ALG data. However, pre-training embeddings performed better with MSA, probably because the language is more regular and knowing some structure ahead helps. The performance improved with more data for the minority class (equivalent sentence pairs) for both ALG and MSA. However, surprisingly the gain of some models with ALG is greater than their gain with MSA. This is probably caused by the noisiness and the sparsity of the data, the linguistic differences between MSA and ALG, the data size, or all these factors together. Further and deeper experiments and analyses are needed for a better understanding of the results.

Overall, the results of the end-to-end training are promising and could be generalised to other related languages or language varieties with the same under-resource settings. As a future work, we want to explore ways to improve the learning capability of neural models from small noisy datasets without handcrafted features, for example by reducing the noise in the colloquial data (ALG) by normalising spelling variation.

Acknowledgement

The research reported in this paper was supported by a grant from the Swedish Research Council (VR project 2014-39) for the establishment of the Centre for Linguistic Theory and Studies in Probability (CLASP) at the University of Gothenburg.

References

Wafia Adouane, Jean-Philippe Bernardy, and Simon Dobnik. 2018. Improving Neural Network Performance by Injecting Background Knowledge: Detecting Code-switching and Borrowing in Algerian texts. In *Proceedings of the Third Workshop on Computational Approaches to Linguistic Code-Switching*, pages 20–28. Association for Computational Linguistics.

Eneko Agirre, Carmen Banea, Claire Cardie, Daniel Cer, Mona Diab, Aitor Gonzalez-Agirre, Weiwei Guo, Inigo Lopez-Gazpio, Montse Maritxalar, Rada Mihalcea, German Rigau, Larraitz Uria, and Janyce Wiebe. 2015. SemEval-2015 Task 2: Semantic Textual Similarity, English, Spanish and Pilot on Interpretability. In *Proceedings of the 9th International Workshop on Semantic Evaluation (SemEval 2015)*, pages 252–263. Association for Computational Linguistics.

Eneko Agirre, Daniel Cer, Mona Diab, and Aitor Gonzalez-Agirre. 2012. SemEval-2012 Task 6: A Pilot on Semantic Textual Similarity. In **SEM 2012: The First Joint Conference on Lexical and Computational Semantics – Volume 1: Proceedings of the main conference and the shared task, and Volume 2: Proceedings of the Sixth International Workshop on Semantic Evaluation (SemEval 2012)*, pages 385–393. Association for Computational Linguistics.

Eneko Agirrea, Carmen Baneab, Daniel Cerd, Mona Diabe, Aitor Gonzalez-Agirrea, Rada Mihalceab, German Rigaua, and Janyce Wiebef. 2016. Semeval-2016 task 1: Semantic textual similarity, monolingual and cross-lingual evaluation. In *Proceedings of SemEval-2016*, pages 497–511. Association for Computational Linguistics.

Dzmitry Bahdanau, Kyunghyun Cho, and Yoshua Bengio. 2014. *Neural Machine Translation by Jointly Learning to Align and Translate*. arXiv:1409.0473.

Petr Baudis and Jan Šedivý. 2016. *Sentence Pair Scoring: Towards Unified Framework for Text Comprehension*. arXiv:1603.06127v4.

Islam Beltagy, Cuong Chau, Gemma Boleda, Dan Garrette, Katrin Erk, and Raymond J. Mooney. 2013. Montague Meets Markov: Deep Semantics with Probabilistic Logical Form. In **SEM@NAACL-HLT*, pages 11–21. Association for Computational Linguistics.

Islam Beltagy, Katrin Erk, and Raymond J. Mooney. 2014. Probabilistic Soft Logic for Semantic Textual Similarity. In *Proceedings of the 52nd Annual Meeting of the Association for Computational Linguistics*, pages 1210–1219. Association for Computational Linguistics.

Piotr Bojanowski, Edouard Grave, Armand Joulin, and Tomas Mikolov. 2016. *Enriching Word Vectors with Subword Information*. arXiv:1607.04606v2.

Samuel R. Bowman, Gabor Angeli, Christopher Potts, and Christopher D. Manning. 2015. A Large Annotated Corpus for Learning Natural Language Inference. In *Proceedings of the 2015 Conference on Empirical Methods in Natural Language Processing (EMNLP)*. Association for Computational Linguistics.

Qian Chen, Xiaodan Zhu, Zhenhua Ling, Si Wei, Hui Jiang, and Diana Inkpen. 2017. Enhanced LSTM for Natural Language Inference. In *Proceedings of the 55th Annual Meeting of the Association for Computational Linguistics*.

Kuntal Dey, Ritvik Shrivastava, and Saroj Kaushik. 2016. A Paraphrase and Semantic Similarity Detection System for User Generated Short-Text Content on Microblogs. In *Proceedings of COLING 2016, the 26th International Conference on Computational Linguistics: Technical Papers*, pages 2880–2890. The COLING 2016 Organizing Committee.

William B. Dolan and Chris Brockett. 2005. Automatically Constructing a Corpus of Sentential Paraphrases. In *Proceedings of the Third International Workshop on Paraphrasing (IWP2005)*.

Rudolf Kadlec, Martin Schmid, and Jan Kleindienst. 2015. *Improved Deep Learning Baselines for Ubuntu Corpus Dialogs*. arXiv:1510.03753.

Chen Liang, Praveen Paritosh, Vinodh Rajendran, and Kenneth D. Forbus. 2016. Learning Paraphrase Identification with Structural Alignment. In *Proceedings of the Twenty-Fifth International Joint Conference on Artificial Intelligence*, IJCAI'16, pages 2859–2865. AAAI Press.

Marco Marelli, Stefano Menini, Marco Baroni, Luisa Bentivogli, Raffaella Bernardi, and Roberto Zamparelli. 2014. A SICK Cure for the Evaluation of Compositional Distributional Semantic Models. In *Proceedings of the Ninth International Conference on Language Resources and Evaluation (LREC-2014)*. European Language Resources Association (ELRA).

Jonas Mueller and Aditya Thyagarajan. 2016. Siamese Recurrent Architectures for Learning Sentence Similarity. In *AAAI*, pages 2786–2792. AAAI Press.

Rodney d. Nielsen, Wayne Ward, and James h. Martin. 2009. Recognizing Entailment in Intelligent Tutoring Systems*. *Nat. Lang. Eng.*, 15(4):479–501.

Ankur Parikh, Oscar Täckström, Dipanjan Das, and Jakob Uszkoreit. 2016. A Decomposable Attention Model for Natural Language Inference. In *Proceedings of the 2016 Conference on Empirical Methods in Natural Language Processing*, pages 2249–2255. Association for Computational Linguistics.

Radim Řehůřek and Petr Sojka. 2010. Software Framework for Topic Modelling with Large Corpora. In *Proceedings of the LREC 2010 Workshop on New Challenges for NLP Frameworks*, pages 45–50, Valletta, Malta. ELRA.

Ekaterina Vylomova, Trevor Cohn, Xuanli He, and Gholamreza Haffari. 2017. Word Representation Models for Morphologically Rich Languages in Neural Machine Translation. In *Proceedings of the First Workshop on Subword and Character Level Models in NLP*, pages 103–108. Association for Computational Linguistics.

Wei Xu, Chris Callison-Burch, and Bill Dolan. 2015. SemEval-2015 Task 1: Paraphrase and Semantic Similarity in Twitter (PIT). In *Proceedings of the 9th International Workshop on Semantic Evaluation (SemEval 2015)*, pages 1–11. Association for Computational Linguistics.

Yi Yang, Wen-tau Yih, and Christopher Meek. 2015. WikiQA: A Challenge Dataset for Open-Domain Question Answering. In *Proceedings of the 2015 Conference on Empirical Methods in Natural Language Processing*, pages 2013–2018. Association for Computational Linguistics.

Wenpeng Yin, Hinrich Schütze, Bing Xiang, and Bowen Zhou. 2015. ABCNN: Attention-Based Convolutional Neural Network for Modeling Sentence Pairs. *Transactions of the Association for Computational Linguistics*.

Constrained Sequence-to-sequence Semitic Root Extraction for Enriching Word Embeddings

Ahmed El-Kishky[†,*] **Xingyu Fu**[†,*] **Aseel Addawood**[†],
Nahil Sobh[†], **Clare Voss**[‡], **and Jiawei Han**[†]
[†]Department of Computer Science, The University of Illinois at Urbana Champaign
[‡]Computational & Information Sciences Directorate, Army Research Laboratory
[†]Urbana, IL, USA, [‡]Adelphi, MD, USA
`{elkishk2,xingyuf2,aaddaw2,sobh,hanj}@illinois.edu`
`clare.r.voss.civ@mail.mil`

Abstract

In this paper, we tackle the problem of "root extraction" from words in the Semitic language family. A challenge in applying natural language processing techniques to these languages is the data sparsity problem that arises from their rich internal morphology, where the substructure is inherently non-concatenative and morphemes are interdigitated in word formation. While previous automated methods have relied on human-curated rules or multi-class classification, they have not fully leveraged the various combinations of regular, sequential concatenative morphology within the words and the internal interleaving within templatic stems of roots and patterns. To address this, we propose a constrained sequence-to-sequence root extraction method. Experimental results show our constrained model outperforms a variety of methods at root extraction. Furthermore, by enriching word embeddings with resulting decompositions, we show improved results on word analogy, word similarity, and language modeling tasks.

1 Introduction

The Semitic languages are a language family commonly spoken throughout North Africa, the Horn of Africa, the Arabian peninsula, and the regions between. With approximately 500 million speakers, the proliferation of large online text collections of such news articles, social media, digitized literature, and web blogs has created a wealth of data offering challenges and opportunities for semantic understanding of Semitic texts. In these languages, a majority of words are derived from a small number of mostly triliteral consonantal roots, with some quadriliteral roots and a trace number of biliteral and quintliteral roots. It is estimated that two of the most prominent Semitic languages, Arabic and Hebrew, possess approximately 10,000 and 3,000 roots, respectively (Darwish, 2002; Daya et al., 2008). As such, root identification of a given Semitic word is often an important task in morphological analysis and the first step to morphological decomposition. Morphological analysis of Semitic languages poses a unique challenge to traditional NLP techniques due to the non-contiguous morphology inherent in these languages. This morphology is best described as the application of a *pattern* resulting in the interdigitation of morphemes within a single root to form derivative words (Habash, 2010). This fusional morphology allows for many surface form words derived from the same single root, but with different, yet abstractly-related semantic meanings depending on constituent morphemes. Because many surface words can be formed through this root and pattern word formation process, and the root's characters may not necessarily be contiguously situated within each resultant surface word, morpheme boundaries are often difficult to identify.

Unlike other fusional languages, the Semitic languages are unique in that the word formation process follows a highly-structured process of adding vowels and consonants to roots. This word formation process consists of a fixed number of slots for different morphemes, which are fixed in their position and order relative to each other. As such, these languages contain significant sequential (albeit not necessarily contiguous) substructure. In this work, we propose to leverage this sequential substructure to improve the root extraction process and morphological decomposition.

Morphological analysis is essential in working with Semitic languages as well as other highly-inflectional languages due to data sparsity. For instance, previous research has shown that many text corpora demonstrate long-tail distributions in

---

*Equal contribution

Proceedings of the Fourth Arabic Natural Language Processing Workshop, pages 88–96
Florence, Italy, August 1, 2019. ©2019 Association for Computational Linguistics

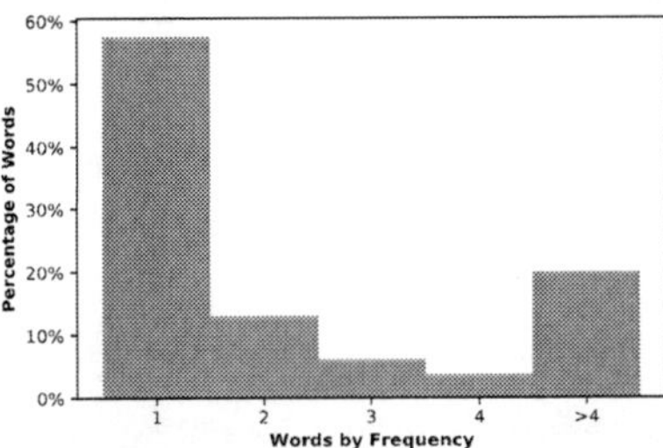

Figure 1: Word distribution in Arabic Wikipedia corpus.

relation to word frequency. This long-tail often results in corpora with many infrequent words, with $40\% - 60\%$ of words appearing just once (Kornai, 2007). We can verify this for Arabic in Figure 1, where, on a Wikipedia monolingual Arabic corpus (described in Section 5.1), approximately 80% of words occur fewer than five times and 60% occur once. To process such long-tailed corpora, it is necessary to exploit finer-granularity, highly-shared substructures between words that can be used to infer semantic meaning. In Table 1, we look at a selection of Arabic words sharing the common root – ك ت ب – (*transliteration K-T-B*), which means to *"write"*. These words are formed by appending different prefixes, suffixes, and other templatic interleavings of morphemes within the root. Despite the many surface words, the derivations share a semantic relationship based on the root, as well as other concatenative and interdigitated templatic morphemes. Additionally, as seen in the example, the root word's characters are not necessarily contiguous within the word; this is due to the non-concatenative templatic process whereby morphemes are inserted between characters of the root as part of the word formation process. Finally, not all characters in the root are necessarily found in the final surface-form of the word as some root characters can be dropped. Traditional concatenative morphological analyzers struggle to identify and extract roots precisely because root word characters are not necessarily contiguous or even present in the surface word.

To address these challenges, we present a supervised root extraction algorithm that, given a word, directly extracts the root with high accuracy. Given this root and the original word, we demonstrate how the templatic pattern-based word formation process that transforms the root to the original word can be used for further morphological decomposition. Our root extraction method differentiates itself from other methods in three

Word	Translit.	Meaning	Pref.	Suff.	R-1	R-2
كتبت	KTBT	she wrote	N/A	T	N/A	N/A
كاتب	KĀTB	writer	N/A	N/A	Ā	N/A
كتاب	KTĀB	book	N/A	N/A	N/A	Ā
الكتاب	ALKTĀB	the book	AL	N/A	N/A	Ā
مكتب	MKTB	desk	M	N/A	N/A	N/A
مكتبة	MKTBA	library	M	A	N/A	N/A

Table 1: Common Roots

ways: (1) It is fully data-driven, without any reliance on human-curated patterns; (2) it directly extracts word roots without stripping dictionary affixes, which can lead to incorrect roots when false affixes are stripped; and (3) by applying a novel sequence-to-sequence (seq2seq) model with a constrained decoding mechanism that leverages shared sequential semantics in the label (root) and input (word) space, it outperforms standard multi-class classification algorithms and achieves better generalization performance.

We demonstrate that our method outperforms unsupervised rule-based root extraction methods (Taghva et al., 2005; Khoja and Garside, 1999; Zerrouki, 2010) and our seq2seq classifier outperforms general multiclass classifiers (Kim, 2014; Chung et al., 2014). As a testament to the utility of root extraction, we demonstrate how one can leverage the root information alongside a simple slot-based morphological decomposition to improve upon word embedding representations as evaluated through word similarity, word analogy, and language modeling tasks.

2 Related Work

With the growth of the internet and the digitization of Arabic and other Semitic corpora, prior work has extensively studied root extractors with the goal of improving document retrieval (Larkey et al., 2002; Aljlayl and Frieder, 2002).

Early approaches to the problem of Arabic root extraction were predominantly unsupervised methods. Some researchers developed stemmers that remove some prefixes and suffixes while ignoring the templatic, interleaved morphemes within stems. A few of these methods relied on pattern matching and prefix/suffix pruning in order to extract roots (Taghva et al., 2005; Khoja and Garside, 1999). These methods may fail to identify the roots in many nouns and, like all prefix and suffix stripping algorithms, fail to correctly extract non-contiguous roots. Similar methods operate by removing not only prefixes and suffixes, but also "extra letters" until the triconsonantal roots remain (Momani and Faraj, 2007).

This method, however, may incorrectly remove many letters that are part of the root. Another of these models achieves high accuracy by incorporating sentence-level context and inferred syntactic categories into a parametric Bayesian model (Lee et al., 2011). Our model forgoes these context features as it attempts to identify the root solely on the word itself. Additionally, this method cannot model non-contiguous roots, of which Semitic languages have many. Other unsupervised methods utilize dictionaries to select the characters from within words (Darwish, 2002; Boudlal et al., 2011; Alhanini and Ab Aziz, 2011). Another line of research leverages the templatic nature for human-constructed rule-based constraints (Elghamry, 2005; Rodrigues and Cavar, 2007; Choueka, 1990). Finally, methods have been proposed that utilize both a root dictionary and rule-based templatic constraints (Yaseen and Hmeidi, 2014).

Supervised methods have been developed for identifying Hebrew roots by combining various multiclass classification models with Hebrew-specific linguistic constraints (Daya et al., 2004). This same technique was extended to extract both Arabic and Hebrew roots (Daya et al., 2008). While these supervised methods effectively address the non-contiguous nature of Semitic roots, they fail to leverage the sequential structure of the root label space. We show that such methods that forgo the sequential structure in the label space underperform on words with rare roots. Additionally, these methods are only applied to triconsonantal leaving out many biconsonantal and quadriliteral roots.

Sequence-to-sequence models have been utilized for learning to map sequences to other sequences and predominantly applied to machine translation (Sutskever et al., 2014), with later variations of these models enhanced with attention mechanisms (Luong et al., 2015). While LSTM variants have been dominant, previous work has shown that GRU-based models perform comparably to LSTM-based models with superior train time (Chung et al., 2014). More recent work has investigated character-level language models in order to handle the many out-of-vocabulary (OOV) words in morphologically rich languages (Gerz et al., 2018). Such methods have shown large improvements in language modeling across many morphologically rich languages. While such methods share the same character-level input space as does our own method, they ignore the sequential nature in the target class. Closely related to our model, constrained sequence-to-sequence models have been used for sentence simplification forcing the model to select simple words (Zhang et al., 2017). Similar approaches have been used for constrained image captioning (Anderson et al., 2017). Our model differs in that it constrains not only on specific vocabulary, but on specific sequences.

3 Root Extraction Framework

We introduce a framework for extracting the root from templatic words within the Semitic family. The proposed framework leverages the shared sequential semantics in both the word and root space to more accurately extract root morphemes.

3.1 Preliminaries

The input is a set of word-root pairs W, R, consisting of $|W|$ words and $|R|$ roots where $|W| = |R|$ and $W = w_1, \ldots, w_{|W|}$ and $R = r_1, \ldots, r_{|R|}$. In addition, the jth word w_j is a sequence of $|w_j|$ characters: $c_{w_j,i}, i = 1, \ldots, |w_j|$. For convenience we index all the unique characters that compose the input vocabulary with C characters and $c_{w,i} = x$, where $x \in \{1, \ldots, C\}$ means that the ith character in wth word is the xth character in the character vocabulary. Similarly the kth root, r_k corresponding to the jth word w_j is a sequence of $|r_k|$ characters: $c_{r_k,i}, i = 1, \ldots, |r_k|$. Given the input, the goal is to learn a function, $\mathcal{F} : W \to R$ that maps an input word onto its correct Semitic root.

3.2 Constrained Seq2Seq Root Extraction

Our main innovation and contribution is a unique way of extracting roots by utilizing seq2seq models for multiclass classification. While many methods traditionally approach root extraction through unsupervised application of templates or traditional supervised multiclass classification algorithms, we posit that the shared semantics between words and roots merits a different approach. As such, we apply a hybrid approach between multiclass classification and seq2seq models for root extraction. By constraining the outputs of the seq2seq models to the dictionary table of roots, the algorithm becomes a sequential multiclass classification model that implicitly leverages shared sequential substructure in both the input space and in the label space.

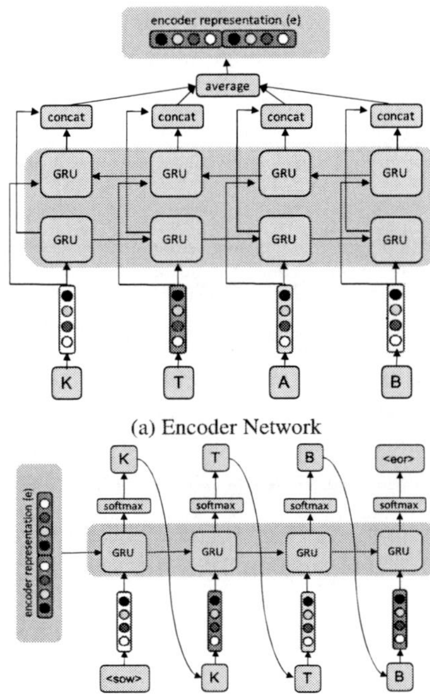

(a) Encoder Network

(b) Decoder Network

Figure 2: Sequence-to-sequence root extraction.

3.2.1 Encoder Network

As seen in Figure 2a, we begin with an encoder network that takes a word as input. Each of the input word's characters (from a total of C possible characters) is associated with a vector $c \in \mathbb{R}^d$. Using word, KTĀB from Table 1, the input becomes vector $[c_0, c_1, c_2, c_3] \in \mathbb{R}^{d \times 4}$. We then run this sequence of embedding vectors through both directions of a bi-directional GRU (BiGRU) and concatenate the resulting hidden vectors from each pass. Finally, we average the concatenated hidden vectors of the BiGRU across all time-steps. This serves as the encoder representation of the input word, which we denote as e. The encoding is then fed into a decoder network that attempts to generate the most likely root for the word.

3.2.2 Decoder Network

In Figure 2b, the decoder takes the encoder representation e that captures the input word and predicts a root word. This is done by feeding e and a special "start-of-word" character $\langle \text{sow} \rangle$ as the input. A GRU computes the next hidden state $h_0 \in \mathbb{R}^h$. A scoring function is then applied, resulting in an output the size of the character vocabulary, C. This function: $\mathbf{g} : \mathbb{R}^h \to \mathbb{R}^C$, is then softmaxed to obtain a valid probability distribution over characters for each hidden state. The decoding stops when the predicted root is terminated with a special "end-of-root" token $\langle \text{eor} \rangle$.

3.2.3 Constrained Beam Search

Traditional decoders select the best character at each step to feed into the next time step of the RNN. However, this decoding maps the input sequence into an infinite space of possible output sequences and, as such, may result in an *invalid root* that is not part of the dictionary set of roots. As such, we propose an alternative output that restricts the decoder, forcing the decoded sequence to map onto a root within the valid roots set.

We realize this constraint by modifying the decoding scheme itself. During decoding, a greedy approach is often used where the single best character output is selected and propagated to later time steps. This greedy approach may not only lead to suboptimal output sequences, but also result in invalid sequences (not corresponding to any class). This can be circumvented using a beam search decoding scheme. When decoding to obtain the predicted roots, instead of utilizing the character with the highest probability at each step, the top k characters are considered at each step. As such, at each new time-step, for each of the k hypotheses, there are C possible choices. The top k are then once again selected and this process is applied to each time step. Once all candidate roots reach their special $\langle \text{eor} \rangle$ token, the most probable root is selected. To tailor beam search to

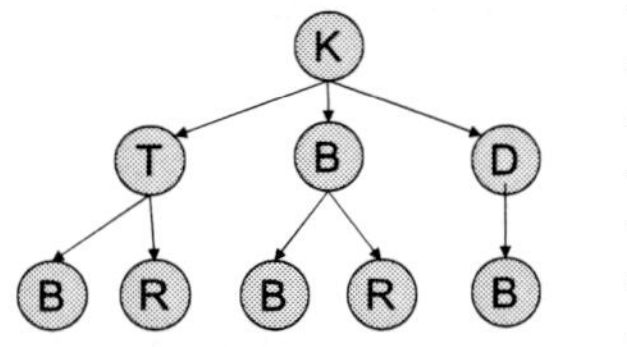
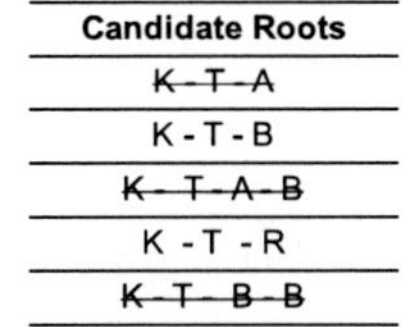

(a) Constraint Trie   (b) Candidate root pool.

Figure 3: Constrained beam search.

root extraction from a dictionary of roots, we seek to modify beam search by enforcing the linguistic sequential constraints present in the label root set. This leverages our classification tasks's relatively small and enumerable root label set, contrasted with an unbounded sequence as found in machine translation models. Simultaneously, by using a decoder, the model exploits the task's sequential structure by generating the target label character-by-character. We utilize the target roots as guidance for the decoding process in order to implement this sequential prediction. We demonstrate on a toy example in Figure 3a, where by storing all the possible target roots in a trie data structure (a.k.a a prefix tree), invalid roots can be pruned during the decoding process. For example, as seen in Figure 3b, during a typical beam-search process, the top k candidate characters are selected. By cross-referencing the current prefix of the root with the trie storing all valid roots, many invalid roots can be pruned. As such, we can enforce that the top-k selections all correspond to valid prefixes present in the target roots. This strictly improves overall extraction accuracy over traditional beam search.

4 Templatic Word Embeddings

As the Semitic languages are templatic, there exist fixed slots that can contain morphemes. Given the correct root for a word identified as described in Section 3, we introduce a simple slot-based template. We indicate how to identify these slots within a word utilizing the Semitic root. Finally, we demonstrate how the morphemes within these slots, along with the root, can be utilized to enrich distributed word representations.

4.1 Morphological Decomposition

We posit that each word possesses a fixed number of slots allocated to certain morphemes, whereby the slots are fixed in their position and order relative to each other. As demonstrated in Table 1, in addition to the root word, we propose a simplified template that consists of four slots – two concatenative (prefixes and suffixes) and two non-concatenative (morphemes interdigitated within the stem). While we demonstrate the simplicity of identifying these within Arabic, this same template-based structure can, without loss of generality, be trivially created for other members of the Semitic family.

Example 1 (Stem, Prefix, and Suffix Identification) *For the root K-T-B, we can identify the consecutive characters that encompass the full root.*

AL + [KTĀB] + EEN

ال + [كتاب] + ين

The characters grouped together by [] form the stem, the smallest consecutive set of characters containing the full root. Any characters not falling within the stem are, respectively, the prefixes and suffixes.

As seen in Example 1, given the root, the stem can be identified as the shortest contiguous substring containing the root in correct order. Once the stem is identified, the two concatenative slots containing prefix and suffix are trivially identified by selecting the remaining affixes after removing the stem. The non-concatenative slots can be found interdigitated within the word stem whose boundary is demarcated by the root. Given the

stem (as shown in square brackets in Example 1) and the root, these interdigitated slots can be identified as follows:

Example 2 (Interdigitated Slots) *Given a stem containing the core root K-T-B, the candidate slots are as follows.*

In stem, KĀTB, Ā occurs in the first slot.
In stem, KTĀB, Ā occurs in the second slot.

If a contiguous morpheme occurs after the first character in the root by before middle characters, it is a slot-1 addition. If after the middle character(s) of the root, it is slot-2.

Example 2 shows the identification of interdigitated slots within the stem. Once again, it is evident that correct extraction of the root is essential to correct identification of the slot positions within the word. In the next subsection we demonstrate how these extractions can be systematically leveraged to enrich distributed word representations in these templatic languages.

4.2 Morpheme-Enriched Embeddings

To demonstrate the utility of templatic subword extractions, we demonstrate how enriching word embeddings with these morphemes can improve word representations by providing parameter-sharing between words sharing common substructure. With this motivation, we propose TemplaticVec, an intuitive extension to FastText (Piotr Bojanowski and Mikolov, 2017), that utilizes the templatic decomposition of semantically-meaningful roots, affixes, and interdigitated morphemes for representation enrichment. By using these structures as embedding base units by and combining them to construct a word's distributed vector representation, the resultant word embeddings are robust to infrequent word-induced data-sparsity and can be constructed on many out-of-vocabulary (OOV) words. We begin with a brief review of FastText, and then demonstrate how one can naturally integrate roots as well as concatenative and templatic morphemes in place of FastText's standard naive subwords. FastText utilizes the skip-gram objective with negative sampling yielding the following objective (for simplicity, $\ell(x) = \log(1 + \exp(-x))$):

$$\sum_{x=1}^{|W|} \left[\sum_{c \in \mathcal{C}_x} \ell(s(w_x, w_c)) + \sum_{t \in \mathcal{N}_{x,c}} \ell(-s(w_x, t)) \right]$$

In the above equation, w_x is the xth word in the corpus, $\mathcal{C}_x$ denotes the set of context words within a predefined window of word w_x, and $\mathcal{N}_{x,c}$ denotes the set of negative examples sampled from outside the context window.

The scoring function is then adapted to incorporate subword information as follows:

$$s(w_x, w_c) = \sum_{m \in w_x} \mathbf{z}_m^\mathsf{T} \mathbf{v}_c$$

In the above equation, each $\mathbf{z}_m$ denotes a subword embedding vector, so that the scoring function equates to the inner product of the summation each over subword embedding vector with the context word vector. While FastText incorporates all contiguous substrings of lengths three to seven as morphemes in the scoring function, because Semitic roots are not necessarily contiguous, two words sharing the same root may not share the same subwords using FastText. Because this important semantic morpheme is not shared among words, we posit that FastText's indiscriminate enumeration of contiguous subwords does not capture the essential semantic substructure. We claim that directly incorporating the root embedding and each slot's morpheme embeddings that have been extracted for each word and summing over these embeddings results in higher quality distributed representations. As such, similar to the approach in (El-Kishky et al., 2018), we modify the scoring function to incorporate the extracted root and slot-based templatic information:

$$s(w_x, w_c) = (\mathbf{z}_r + \mathbf{z}_p + \mathbf{z}_s + \mathbf{z}_{r1} + \mathbf{z}_{r2})^\mathsf{T} \mathbf{v}_c$$

This modification yields a scoring function that is the inner product of the summation over the root word embedding ($\mathbf{z}_r$), prefix embedding ($\mathbf{z}_p$), suffix embedding ($\mathbf{z}_s$), as well as the two possible in-root interdigitated morphemes ($\mathbf{z}_{r1}$ and $\mathbf{z}_{r2}$).

5 Experiments

We introduce the datasets and methods for comparison used. We then describe evaluations for root extraction and embedding quality.

5.1 Datasets and comparison methods

We use the following datasets and ground-truth labels for evaluation purposes:

- **Arabic Word & Root Pairs**: 140K words along associated with 11K roots from dictionary (al Zabidi and Murthada, 1886).

- **Hebrew Word & Root Pairs**. 11.5K words associated with approximately 500 roots from Wiktionary[1] and human curation.

- **Arabic Wikipedia Corpora**. Wikipedia corpus with 274K articles and 62.5M tokens and 1.26M unique words.

<hr>

[1] wiktionary.org

For baseline methods to compare against our proposed constrained seq2seq (Constrain-S2S), we evaluate against three standard multiclass classification models: (1) a standard convolutional neural network, CNN-Class, (Kim, 2014), a GRU model, GRU-Class, and a bi-directional GRU model, BiGRU-Class. In addition, we compare against two unconstrained seq2seq models, encoder-decoder models using GRUs, GRU-S2S and bi-directional GRUs, BiGRU-S2S. Finally, for Arabic, we evaluate against three unsupervised Arabic root-extraction algorithms from the literature: Tashaphyne, ISRI, and Khoja. To evaluate on the quality of the resultant morphological decomposition, we compare against three variants of embeddings: (1) SkipGram (2) FastText (3) RootVec (Embedding enriched with solely the root) .

5.2 Root Extraction Accuracy

To evaluate the effectiveness of our proposed seq2seq extraction of roots, we perform five-fold cross-validation evaluation of our method compared to a variety of supervised and rule-based root-extraction methods. During each cross-validation, each supervised method is trained on four-fifth of the dictionary mappings of *word to root* pairs, and evaluated on a held-out 20%.

5.2.1 General Root Extraction

We first compare the performance of each supervised extraction method on extracting roots irrespective of root frequency. In Table 2, we re-

Method	Arabic		Hebrew	
	ACC.	SE	ACC.	SE
CNN-Class	.6753	±.0009	.9622	±.0019
GRU-Class	.7539	±.0023	.9591	±.0033
BiGRU-Class	.7548	±.0015	.9629	±.0009
GRU-S2S	.7596	±.0017	.9692	±.0013
BiGRU-S2S	.7854	±.0010	.9788	±.0016
Constrain-S2S	**.8324**	**±.0011**	**.9879**	**±.0008**
Tashaphyne	.2778	0	-	-
ISRI	.4508	0	-	-
Khoja	.4434	0	-	-

Table 2: Root Extraction Accuracy.

port the performance of each extractor at successfully identifying the ground-truth root in each held-out word in a five-fold cross-validation evaluation. It is apparent that the unsupervised methods under-perform at extracting the ground-truth root as compared to the supervised methods. This is likely due to errors from human-curated patterns which possess many exceptions as well as many Semitic roots being non-contiguously situated with the word due to interdigitated morphemes. Additionally, both the CNN-based and four RNN-based multiclass classification methods severely under-perform compared to our proposed constrained seq2seq model. This verifies our intuition that leveraging the shared semantic space between the words and the target roots is essential in extraction.

5.2.2 Rare Root Extraction

We claimed earlier that by decomposing root classification into seq2seq classification, sequential patterns within the roots can be leveraged for root extraction. This can be useful for identifying the correct root, even when the root is infrequent or even absent from the training data. To support this claim, we report the performance of each supervised extractor at successfully identifying the ground-truth of infrequent roots (appear three or fewer times in training) and a zero-shot case where the root is not present in the training data. As our Hebrew dataset consists of frequent roots, and performance is near perfect, we report results for the Arabic dataset.

Method	Infreq.		Zero-Shot	
	ACC.	SE	ACC.	SE
CNN-Class	.4823	±.0096	-	-
GRU-Class	.5697	±.0103	-	-
BiGRU-Class	.5706	±.0091	-	-
GRU-S2S	.6074	±.0166	.5389	±.0188
BiGRU-S2S	.6231	±.0191	.5532	±.0141
Constrain-S2S	**.6929**	**±.0164**	**.6292**	**±.0160**

Table 3: Arabic Rare Root Extraction Accuracy

As seen in Table 3, the seq2seq methods greatly outperform all multiclass methods with Constrain-S2S outperforming all methods on the infrequent roots. This effect is amplified in the zero-shot case, with only the seq2seq models handling unseen roots. This demonstrates the utility in jointly learning the sequential structure in semantically-shared label (root) and word space.

5.3 Word Analogy Evaluation

Given our comprehensive dataset of Arabic roots and human-curated evaluation set of Arabic word embeddings, we show the effectiveness of enriching Arabic word embeddings with their morphological decompositions via a word analogy task. The goal of said task is to identify the best value for D in analogies of the form "A is to B as C is to D". After training each embedding model on the Arabic Wikipedia dataset, we use an analogy dataset (Elrazzaz et al., 2017) curated for methodological evaluation of Arabic word embeddings.

We further differentiate the analogies into two categories: (1) morphemic analogies (e.g. plurals, tense or gender) where a derivational or inflectional morpheme is inserted, removed, or replaced while the root remains unchanged, and (2) semantic analogies where the root itself changes between the analogous pairs (e.g. bird is to fly as fish is to swim).

Embedding Model	Semantic	Morphemic
SkipGram	**19.1**	11.4
FastText	13.8	16.8
ISRI-RootVec	15.4	11.2
BiGRU-RootVec	14.2	11.9
S2S-RootVec	18.0	11.9
CS2S-RootVec	18.9	12.2
ISRI-TemplaticVec	15.3	14.5
Class-TemplaticVec	16.3	16.9
S2S-TemplaticVec	17.6	20.2
CS2S-TemplaticVec	18.8	**22.9**

Table 4: Word Analogies

As seen in Table 4, embeddings that utilize morphemes or subword-level features perform significantly better at morphemic analogies than do SkipGram word embeddings. This does not extend to semantic analogies where all methods appear to degrade with the use of morpheme and subword-level enrichment. This is not surprising since, under the vector algebra that is used to compute the word analogies, the summation of the morphemes used to enrich the embeddings captures morphemic relationships but not necessarily semantic ones. This can be seen in the performance gap between the morpheme-enriched embeddings and SkipGram. Unlike the other methods, Templatic embeddings based on constrained roots maintains comparable performance to SkipGram on the semantic analogies while demonstrating superior performance on the morphemic analogies.

5.4 Word Similarity

The next embedding evaluation we consider is a word similarity task. The ground truth data consists of pairs of words and a human-annotated similarity score averaged across all human evaluations from a translation of the WS-353 dataset (Freitas et al., 2016). The scores are computed via the cosine similarity between the vector representation of each word in a pair. Their results are quantified through Spearman and Pearson rank correlation coefficients.

As seen in Table 5, enriching the embedding vectors with the template-based extracted

Embedding Model	Pearson	Spearman
SkipGram	0.496	0.520
FastText	0.459	0.468
ISRI-RootVec	0.491	0.518
BiGRU-RootVec	0.492	0.510
S2S-RootVec	0.508	0.516
CS2S-RootVec	0.507	0.514
ISRI-TemplaticVec	0.482	0.501
Class-TemplaticVec	0.474	0.491
S2S-TemplaticVec	**0.514**	0.529
CS2S-TemplaticVec	0.512	**0.533**

Table 5: Word Similarity

Embedding Model	Perplexity	
	LM-One	LM-Two
SkipGram	1757	1075
FastText	1720	1069
ISRI-RootVec	1729	1072
BiGRU-RootVec	1731	1071
S2S-RootVec	1728	1071
CS2S-RootVec	1726	1071
ISRI-TemplaticVec	1728	1071
Class-TemplaticVec	1724	1070
S2S-TemplaticVec	1718	**1065**
CS2S-TemplaticVec	**1716**	**1065**

Table 6: Language Modeling

morphemes substantially improves embeddings in capturing word similarity. This is in contrast with lower correlation coefficients from FastText embedding vectors, likely due to the indiscriminate generation of subwords that may degrade the overall embedding. On this task, template-based decomposition using unconstrained and constrained root extraction appears to perform similarly, yet both greatly outperform the other baselines.

5.5 Language Modeling Perplexity

Finally, we evaluate the effect of utilizing the extracted root and templatic decomposition on a downstream language modeling task. On each language model, the model quality is evaluated by computing the perplexity on a held-out portion of the corpus. The model used for language modeling is an LSTM with three hidden layers, 600 hidden units per layer, regularized with 0.2 probability drop-out, unrolled for 35 steps with a batch of 20. Parameters are learned using Adagrad with a gradient clipping of 1. We evaluate on two subsets of the Wikipedia dataset: (1) LM-1, a small subset (2) LM-2, a larger subset. LM-1 consists of 3.3M tokens and a vocabulary of 260K words while LM-2 consists of 7.6M tokens and a vocabulary of 400K unique words. Each language model instance is trained for 5 epochs on the training data. Evaluation of perplexity was computed for each model on the independent test set consisting of 900K tokens where 62K tokens were OOV in LM-1 and 27K in LM-2. Evaluation is performed after selecting the best performing iteration of the model on a validation set. While the morpheme-enriched method can generate embedding vectors for many OOV tokens, for SkipGram and instances when they cannot, an unknown token with fixed embedding is used.

The results are summarized in Table 6. Al-
though perplexity is high, this is common for morphologically-rich languages such as Arabic as shown in (Gerz et al., 2018). It appears our constrained model's extracted roots yield a benefit over other baseline roots, yet utilizing the full decomposition outperforms all other methods, yielding lower held-out perplexity. The results also verify the intuition that morphemic decomposition is necessary to handle data-sparsity and OOV words when little training data is present, whereby perplexity is greatly reduced through the use of morpheme-based embeddings.

6 Conclusions

We proposed leveraging the shared semantic space between Semitic words and their roots for more effective root extraction. This was accomplished through a novel constrained sequence-to-sequence classifier. Experiments show a performance boost over unsupervised and supervised extraction models. We introduce a simple template-based morphological decomposition, and by enriching word embeddings with this decomposition, we show improved results on word analogy, word similarity, and language modeling tasks.

References

Yasir Alhanini and Mohd Juzaiddin Ab Aziz. 2011. The enhancement of arabic stemming by using light stemming and dictionary-based stemming. *JSEA*.

Mohammed Aljlayl and Ophir Frieder. 2002. On arabic search: improving the retrieval effectiveness via a light stemming approach. In *CIKM*.

Peter Anderson, Basura Fernando, Mark Johnson, and Stephen Gould. 2017. Guided open vocabulary image captioning with constrained beam search. In *EMNLP*.

Abderrahim Boudlal, Mohamed Ould Abdallahi Ould Bebah, Abdelhak Lakhouaja, Azzeddine Mazroui, and Abdelouafi Meziane. 2011. A markovian approach for arabic root extraction. *Int. Arab J. Inf. Technol.*

Yaacov Choueka. 1990. Mlim-a system for full, exact, on-line grammatical analysis of modern hebrew. In *ICCE*.

Junyoung Chung, Caglar Gulcehre, KyungHyun Cho, and Yoshua Bengio. 2014. Empirical evaluation of gated recurrent neural networks on sequence modeling. *arXiv preprint arXiv:1412.3555*.

Kareem Darwish. 2002. Building a shallow arabic morphological analyzer in one day. In *ACL-02 workshop on Computational approaches to semitic languages*.

Ezra Daya, Dan Roth, and Shuly Wintner. 2004. Learning hebrew roots: Machine learning with linguistic constraints. In *EMNLP*.

Ezra Daya, Dan Roth, and Shuly Wintner. 2008. Identifying semitic roots: Machine learning with linguistic constraints. *Computational Linguistics*.

Ahmed El-Kishky, Frank Xu, Aston Zhang, Stephen Macke, and Jiawei Han. 2018. Entropy-based subword mining with an application to word embeddings. In *SCLeM 2018*.

Khaled Elghamry. 2005. A constraint-based algorithm for the identification of arabic roots. In *Proceedings of the Midwest Computational Linguistics Colloquium. Indiana University. Bloomington, IN*.

Mohammed Elrazzaz, Shady Elbassuoni, Khaled Shaban, and Chadi Helwe. 2017. Methodical evaluation of arabic word embeddings. In *ACL*.

André Freitas, Siamak Barzegar, Juliano Efson Sales, Siegfried Handschuh, and Brian Davis. 2016. *Semantic Relatedness for All (Languages): A Comparative Analysis of Multilingual Semantic Relatedness Using Machine Translation*.

Daniela Gerz, Ivan Vulić, Edoardo Ponti, Jason Naradowsky, Roi Reichart, and Anna Korhonen. 2018. Language modeling for morphologically rich languages: Character-aware modeling for word-level prediction. *TACL*.

Nizar Y Habash. 2010. Introduction to arabic natural language processing. *Synthesis Lectures on Human Language Technologies*.

Shereen Khoja and Roger Garside. 1999. Stemming arabic text. *Lancaster, UK, Computing Department, Lancaster University*.

Yoon Kim. 2014. Convolutional neural networks for sentence classification. *arXiv preprint arXiv:1408.5882*.

Andras Kornai. 2007. *Mathematical linguistics.* Springer Science & Business Media.

Leah S Larkey, Lisa Ballesteros, and Margaret E Connell. 2002. Improving stemming for arabic information retrieval: light stemming and co-occurrence analysis. In *ACM SIGIR*.

Yoong Keok Lee, Aria Haghighi, and Regina Barzilay. 2011. Modeling syntactic context improves morphological segmentation. In *CoNLL*.

Minh-Thang Luong, Hieu Pham, and Christopher D Manning. 2015. Effective approaches to attention-based neural machine translation. *arXiv preprint arXiv:1508.04025*.

Mohanned Momani and Jamil Faraj. 2007. A novel algorithm to extract tri-literal arabic roots. In *Computer Systems and Applications, 2007. AICCSA'07*.

Armand Joulin Piotr Bojanowski, Edouard Grave and Tomas Mikolov. 2017. Enriching word vectors with subword information. *TACL*.

Paul Rodrigues and Damir Cavar. 2007. Learning arabic morphology using statistical constraint-satisfaction models. *Amsterdam studies in the theory and history of linguistic science. Series 4*.

Ilya Sutskever, Oriol Vinyals, and Quoc V Le. 2014. Sequence to sequence learning with neural networks. In *NIPS*.

Kazem Taghva, Rania Elkhoury, and Jeffrey Coombs. 2005. Arabic stemming without a root dictionary. In *Information Technology: Coding and Computing*.

Qussai Yaseen and Ismail Hmeidi. 2014. Extracting the roots of arabic words without removing affixes. *Journal of Information Science*.

Muhammad Murtada al Zabidi and Sayyid Muhammad Murthada. 1886. Taj al-'arus min jawahir al-qamus. *Dar al-Hidayah*.

Taha Zerrouki. 2010. Tashaphyne, arabic light stemmer/segment.

Yaoyuan Zhang, Zhenxu Ye, Yansong Feng, Dongyan Zhao, and Rui Yan. 2017. A constrained sequence-to-sequence neural model for sentence simplification. *arXiv preprint arXiv:1704.02312*.

En-Ar Bilingual word Embeddings without Word Alignment:
Factors Effects

Taghreed Alqaisi
University of York, UK
Taibah University, Saudi Arabia
`ta808@york.ac.uk`

Simon O'Keefe
University of York, UK
`simon.okeefe@york.ac.uk`

Abstract

This paper introduces the first attempt to investigate morphological segmentation on En-Ar bilingual word embeddings using bilingual word embeddings model without word alignment (BilBOWA). We investigate the effect of sentence length and embedding size on the learning process. Our experiment shows that using the D3 segmentation scheme improves the accuracy of learning bilingual word embeddings upto 10 percentage points comparing to the ATB and D0 schemes in all different training settings.

1 Introduction

In the last decade, neural networks (NN) have attracted many researchers attention and showed very promising results in many natural language processing (NLP) tasks. Many models have been introduced including: semantics and question answering (Bowman et al., 2015; Sukhbaatar et al., 2015; Hermann et al., 2015), Machine Translation (MT) (Sutskever et al., 2014; Bahdanau et al., 2015), parsing (Kong et al., 2015; Lewis et al., 2016) and many works in word embeddings have been reported. Word embedding is one of the most important NLP tasks due to its ability to capture the semantic similarities between words.

The main idea behind learning word embeddings is to transform words from discrete space into a continuous vector space of features that capture their syntactic and semantic information. In other words, words having similar meaning should have similar vectors. This similarity can be measured using different distance methods such as cosine similarity and Euclidean distance.

Now a days, many word embedding models have been introduced and show a significant improvement in different NLP tasks; language modelling (Mikolov et al., 2010; Mikolov and Zweig, 2012; Shi et al., 2013), MT (Cho et al., 2014; Bahdanau et al., 2015; Luong et al., 2015b), named entity recognition (Lample et al., 2016), document classification and sentiment analysis (dos Santos and Gatti, 2014; Kim, 2014; Severyn and Moschitti, 2015) etc. Word embeddings can be classified, based on the objective function that needs to be learnt, into two main categories. Firstly, Monolingual word embedding, which is the process of learning similar word representations for similar word meaning in the same language. Secondly, Bilingual/cross-lingual approaches, which is the process of learning similar words among languages.

In this paper, we investigate the effect of different Arabic segmentation schemes, sentence length and embedding sizes on learning Arabic-English (Ar-En) Bilingual word embeddings. The experiments show a noticeable accuracy change using different training settings. Firstly, we give an overview of some related recent works on bilingual word embeddings in Section 2. Section 3 gives a brief introduction to the Arabic language, and it describes the details of Arabic language morphological complex and preprocessing techniques. Next is the experiment section that contains a description of the model architecture, training dataset, preprocessing settings and training hyper-parameters. The evaluation section presents the evaluation methods used as well as discussing the trained models' evaluation results. Finally, we conclude this work outcomes in Section 6.

2 Related Work

Bilingual or cross-lingual word embedding is the process of learning the semantic similarity across two or more languages word embeddings using two or more corpora. Many successful models have been introduced and use different model

Proceedings of the Fourth Arabic Natural Language Processing Workshop, pages 97–107
Florence, Italy, August 1, 2019. ©2019 Association for Computational Linguistics

architectures and training corpora with different alignment levels to learn bilingual word embeddings.

Firstly, at word-level alignment, Luong et al. (2015a) extend the skip-gram model to learn efficient bilingual word embeddings. Also, at phrase-level, a bilingually-constrained phrase embeddings (BRAE) model learns source-target phrase embeddings by minimising the semantic distance between translation equivalents and maximising the semantic distance between non-translation equivalents (Zhang et al., 2014). Su et al. (2015) extend the BRAE model by introducing a "bilingual correspondence recursive autoencoder" (BCorrRAE) model, which incorporates word alignment to learn bilingual phrase embeddings by capturing different levels of their semantic relations. After that, Zhang et al. (2016) introduce a Bidimensional attention-based recursive autoencoder (BattRAE) model to learn bilingual phrase embeddings by integrating source-target interactions at different levels of granularity using attention-based models.

Using a sentence-aligned corpus, Gouws et al. (2015); Coulmance et al. (2015) introduce Bil-BOW and Trans-gram methods to learn and align word embeddings without word alignment. With a document level aligned corpus, Vulic and Moens (2015) present a model that learns bilingual word embeddings from non-parallel document-aligned data without using translation pairs. In addition, Mogadala and Rettinger (2016) introduce a Bilingual paRAgraph VEctors (BRAVE) model that learns bilingual embeddings from either a sentence-aligned parallel corpus or label-aligned non-parallel document corpus. Vulic and Moens (2015) introduce a model that learns multilingual (two or more languages) word embeddings using document-aligned comparable data.

In the literature we found three different bilingual embedding approaches: monolingual mapping, parallel corpus and joint optimisation approaches. In monolingual mapping, word representations are learnt separately for each language using large monolingual corpuses. Then, using word translation pairs, the model learns a transformation matrix that maps word representation from one language to the other (Ruder, 2017). Parallel corpus models require either word-level (Xiao and Guo, 2014) or sentence level alignments (Hermann and Blunsom, 2013; Lauly et al., 2014;

Gouws et al., 2015). These models aim to have same word/sentence representations for equivalence translations.

Finally, in the joint optimisation method, the monolingual and cross-lingual objectives are optimised jointly (Gouws et al., 2015; Coulmance et al., 2015). Gouws et al. (2015) propose a bilingual bag-of-words without word alignment model (BilBOWA) that uses a skip-gram model as the monolingual objective and jointly learns the bilingual embeddings by minimising the distance between aligned sentences, by assuming that each word in the source sentence is aligned to all words in the target sentence. This model shows success in translation and document classification tasks on ES-En and En-De languages pairs.

In the context of the Arabic language, no prior work has investigated learning bilingual word embeddings to such a morphologically complex language. Thus, in this work, due to the speed and success of BilBOWA models on learning bilingual words embeddings without word alignments, we train the model on a language with a different structure namely Arabic, in order to investigate the effects of complex language morphology in learning bilingual word embeddings.

3 Arabic language

The Arabic language still presents a challenge in MT as it is the official language of 22 countries from the Arabic Gulf to Morocco and varies between countries or regions in the same country. The Arabic language has many forms including: Classical Arabic, Modern Standard Arabic (MSA) and Arabic dialects. MSA, which is based on classical Arabic syntactically, morphologically and phonologically, is written and spoken in news broadcasts, while Arabic dialects are the true native language forms for daily communications (Habash., 2010). In this research we have focused on MSA as the most accessible form.

3.1 Arabic Morphology

The Arabic language is a complex language morphologically and syntactically (Monem et al., 2008). Much work has been done in Arabic NLP but the problems that are caused by the rich morphology of Arabic still exist. We discuss some of the complexity below.

3.1.1 Arabic Language Words

As with many languages, Arabic words can have affixations (prefix, suffix) and can turn the verb to a noun and vice versa. The prefix usually indicates the tense as well as gender, while the suffix indicates plural and the gender too (Khemakhem et al., 2010). So one Arabic word can translate into up to three English words. As a result, the meaning of an Arabic word can be changed when changing its affixation. There is a lot of affixation in the Arabic language and it has been considered as an issue in many NLP tasks, researchers have handled Arabic affixes using a morphological analysis to improve the Arabic NLP (Hatem et al., 2011).

Another issue is non- or short-vowelled Arabic words. The same word can have different meanings depending on its diacritisation and these diacritisations are not usually written. However, the state of the art tool MADAMIRA (See Subsection 3.2) can handle this issue by producing a diacritised corpus.

3.1.2 Arabic Language Sentence Structure

The Arabic language has two types of sentences: nominal (starts with a name) and verbal (starts with a verb). The Arabic and English languages are very different from a structural point of view. One of the main differences between Arabic and English is the order of words. As with other languages, Arabic sentences are built of verb, subject and object. And usually, an Arabic sentence is post-verbal (VSO) so the verb comes first and then the subject is followed by the object. However, it is possible to be pre-verbal (SVO) as the English language is, but it is not always preferred (Elming and Habash, 2009). In both cases, VSO or SVO, an Arabic sentence is flexible with its verb position. However, the subject needs to come before the object, except in passive sentences in which it can be either before its subject or without its subject. Secondly, in Arabic, the adjective always comes after its noun, which is not the case in English. So a reordering rule should move the object of an Arabic sentence to the right of the adjective. Finally, indicating possession and compounding in Arabic is called Idafa. Idafa consists of one or more nouns that have been defined by the following noun (Elming and Habash, 2009).

3.2 Arabic language Preprocessing

In pre-processing, lots of work has studied the impact of morphological pre-processing techniques on statistical machine translation (SMT) quality. Researchers agree on the importance of morphological and syntactic pre-processing in MT in terms of reducing both sparsity and the number of "out of vocabulary" words (OOV) (Khemakhem et al., 2010; El Kholy and Habash, 2012). At pre-processing level, current research focuses on two main pre-processing techniques: word segmentation and word pre-ordering. Many tools have been introduced: AMIRA (Soudi et al., 2007), MADA (Habash and Rambow, 2005), MADA+TOKAN (Habash et al., 2009), Farasa (Abdelali et al., 2016), AlKhalil Morpho (Boudchichea et al., 2017) and MADAMIRA (Pasha et al., 2014).

MADAMIRA is a tool for morphological analysis and the disambiguation of Arabic including normalisation, lemmatisation and tokenisation. It can tokenise the input text with 11 different tokenisation schemes and normalise Alif and Ya characters. MADAMIRA has been developed the same as MADA to accept two input forms: MSA and Egyptian Arabic (EGY). Pasha et al. (2014) have pointed out that MADAMIRA has outperformed both AMIRA and MADA and is the state of the art.

In this work, as word order and language modelling don't matter, we only applied segmentation and orthographic normalisation in the training datasets.

3.2.1 Word Segmentation

Word segmentation has been considered the same process as tokenisation in the Arabic language. It is one of many techniques that have been proposed to reduce morphological differences between languages such as Arabic and English (Akeel and B. Mishra, 2014). Many tokenisation schemes have been introduced for Arabic and have been successfully applied. Many researchers have studied the positive effect of morphological pre-processing on En-Ar SMT. El Kholy and Habash (2012) found that tokenisation and orthographic normalisation improves the performance on SMT, especially when translating from a rich into a poor morphological language. Their work also shows that lemma-based word alignment improves the translation quality in En-Ar SMT.

Many researchers have studied the effect of different segmentation schemes in MT quality on both En-Ar and Ar-En SMT. For example, Habash and Sadat (2006) show in their work that rule-based segmentation improves the translation quality for a medium-sized corpus but the benefit of word segmentation decreases when the corpus size is increased. Other researchers Al-Haj and Lavie (2012) believe that tokenisation schemes with more splitting lead to a decrease in the OOV rate. On the other hand, increasing the number of token types can affect word alignment, translation model and language model negatively as predicting these tokens correctly becomes more complex (El Kholy and Habash, 2012).

Researchers consider the Arabic tokenisation process one of the main solutions helping to decrease Arabic ambiguities in MT. Many researchers have introduced different rule-base segmentation schemes (See Table ??in Appendix). Some of these schemes are used in En-Ar SMT and they show the importance of word segmentation as a pre-processing step to minimise the differences between Arabic and English as well as its effects on SMT quality. The work of (Badr et al., 2008) shows a significant improvement in En-Ar SMT performance when combining segmentation with pre-processing and post-processing steps for small training data. Al-Haj and Lavie (2012); El Kholy and Habash (2012) have studied the effect of different segmentation schemes in En-Ar phrase-based machine translation (PBMT). Al-Haj and Lavie (2012), in contrast to the previous work, investigate the effect of different segmentation schemes on a very large amount of training data of at least 150M words. Their work shows that simple segmentation performs better than complex segmentation as the complex segmentation has a negative effect by increasing the size of the phrase table.

3.2.2 Orthographic Normalization

Orthographic normalisation is an important process at the pre-processing stage. (El Kholy and Habash, 2012) have introduced two schemes of orthographic normalisation: enriched Arabic (ENR) and reduced Arabic (RED). RED is used at the pre-processing level to convert all Hamzat-Alif forms to bare Alif (taking out Hamza) and Alif-Maqsura forms to Ya (add dots). ENR selects the correct Alif and Ya form in order to generate the correct Arabic form at the post-processing level.

4 Experiments

The aim of this set of experiments is to evaluate the effect of sentence length on the process of learning bilingual embeddings using different segmentation schemes.

4.1 Model Architecture

Bilingual Bag-of-Words without Alignment (Bil-BOWA): BilBOWA, introduced in (Gouws et al., 2015), is a simple efficient model to learn bilingual distributed word representations without word alignment. Instead, it assumes each word in the source language sentence is aligned to every word in the target language sentence and vice versa by using a sentence level aligned corpus. This feature is an advantage of this model as the word alignment process is very time consuming.

In the BilBOWA model, as has been mentioned, both monolingual and bilingual objective functions are learnt jointly. The monolingual words representations are obtained by training word2vec using a skip-gram model using negative sampling approach by (Mikolov et al., 2013b).The bilingual objective aims to minimise the distance between source and target sentences by minimising the means of word representations in each aligned sentences pair.

4.1.1 Monolingual Features

Instead of using Softmax, Gouws et al. (2015) implemented Word2vec model using a simplified version of a noise-contrastive approach: negative sampling training objective modified by (Mikolov et al., 2013a) as:

$$\log p(w|c) = \log \sigma(v_w^{'T} v_{cp}) +$$
$$\sum_{i=k}^{K} E_{w_i} \sim P_n(w)[\log \sigma(-v_w^{'T} v_{cn})] \tag{1}$$

Where v_w is word vector and v_{cp}, v_{cn} positive and negative context vectors respectively and K is the number of negative samples.

This approach learns high-quality monolingual features and speeds up the computation process in this model architecture by converting multinomial classification problem to a binary classification problem (Mikolov et al., 2013a; Gouws et al., 2015).

4.1.2 Bilingual/Cross-lingual Features

Gouws et al. (2015) believe that as with the importance of learning the relations between words in the same language, it is also very important to learn words representations that capture the relations among languages. Therefore, the BilBOWA model learns word representations by updating the shared embeddings jointly for both monolingual and bilingual objectives. With the cross-lingual objective, this model minimises the loss between sentence representation pairs computed as the mean of bag-of-words of the parallel corpus.

The bilingual objective is defined as:

$$\Omega = ||\frac{1}{m}\sum_{i=1}^{m} r_i - \frac{1}{n}\sum_{j=1}^{n} r_j||^2 \qquad (2)$$

Where m and n are the number of words in the source and target language , and r_i and r_j is a word representation for each language respectively.

4.2 Data

In this paper, we used WIT3, Web Inventory of Transcribed and Translated Talks, plain MSA Arabic and English language parallel corpus (WIT3, 2012). The dataset has been divided into a 50K monolingual-dataset and a 24K bilingual-dataset to train the monolingual and bilingual objectives. After preprocessing (See Section 4.3), two different bilingual training datasets have been extracted based on sentence length: 5-10 and 17-80 tokens sentence length. Giving the distribution of sentence length in the corpus, these sentence length (5-10 and 17-80 tokens) give us a reasonable size of dataset and distinction between short and long sentences. For the test dataset, similarly to (Gouws et al., 2015), we created a set of 3K words by extracting the most common words in the training datasets. Then, the extracted words have been translated word by word translation using Google translator (In line with common practice in the field) to create a word-based dictionary.

Datasets	5-10	17-80	Mono50K-data
Arabic ATB	195985	901013	902307
English ATB	153111	551508	554338
Arabic D3	187612	975221	1033188
English D3	132687	520190	553414
Arabic D0	190854	773826	771512
English D0	158577	557664	553414

Table 1: Number of tokens in training Datasets with different segmentations schemes. Note that preprocessing changes sentence length, and different methods therefore produce different datasets

4.3 Preprocessing

Both sides of the dataset (English and Arabic), are tokenised, cleaned, normalised and stop-words have been removed. For Arabic, a morphological segmentation process is applied in order to minimise the differences between each En and Ar language pair.

Literature shows many different segmentation schemes for Arabic language (See Table 2 for more details). We use MADAMIRA a state of the art Arabic morphological analyzer (Pasha et al., 2014) for Arabic tokenisation, segmentation and normalisation processes in this work. Three different training datasets with different segmentation schemes are generated: D0, ATB, And D3 (For example: See Table 3). For English, we used the Moses toolkit (Koehn et al., 2007) for tokenising the English dataset and cleaning both sides.

4.4 Training

After preprocessing, we train a BilBOWA model using six preprocessed datasets with different settings: two sentence-length (5-10 and 17-80) and three different segmentation schemes that give a range of amount of segmentations from no segmentation to more complex segmentation (D0, ATB and D3). The trained models produce different embedding sizes: (100D , 200D and 300D). As mentioned in (Gouws et al., 2015), the Asynchronous Stochastic Gradient Descent (ASGD) algorithm has been used to train the model and updating all parameters for each objective function (monolingual and bilingual threads) with a learning rate of 0.1 with linear decay. The number of negative samples is set to NS=5 for the skip-gram negative sampling objectives as we examined NS=15 and it didn't show an improvement in our language pair. All trained models has been trained on a machine that is equipped with four Quad-Core AMD Opteron processors running at 2.3 GHz and 128 GB of RAM. The training process takes up to 30 minutes depends on the model's embeddings size and sentence length.

5 Evaluation

As with word-level bilingual word embeddings (BWEs), similarly to (Gouws et al., 2015), the trained BWEs has been evaluated on a word translation task using *Edit Distance*, used by (Mikolov et al., 2013a). First, we extracted the most frequent 3K words from the Ar-En dataset

D0/UT	No tokenization.
D1	Separates the conjunction proclitics.
D2	D1 + Separates prepositional clitics and particles.
D3/S1	Separates all clitics including the definite article and the pronominal enclitics.
S0	Splitting off the conjunction proclitic w+.
S2	Same as S1 but all proclitics are put together in a single proclitics cluster.
ATB	The Arabic Treebank is splitting the word into affixes.
S3	Splits off all clitics from the (CONJ+) class and all suffixes form the (+PRON)class. In addition to splitting of all clitics of (PART+) class except s+ prefix.
S0PR	S0 + splitting off all sufixes from (+PRON) class.
S4	S3 + splitting off the s+ clitics.
S5	Splits off all possible clitics (CONJ, PART, DET and PRON) classes.
S4SF	S4 + the (+PRON) clitics.
S5SF	S5 + the (+PRON) clitics.
S5ST	S5 + prefixes concatenated into one prefix.
S3T	S3 + prefixes concatenated into one prefix.
DIAC	One of MADA features that add diactresation to Arabic text.

Table 2: Existing tokenisation schemes for Arabic (Al-Haj and Lavie, 2012)

D0	wtAvrt Tfwlty bAlryf ldrjp qd AEjz En $rHhA kmA tmyzt bAlfkr bmA yfwq twqEAtkm .
D3	wtAvrt Tfwlp +y b+ Al+ ryf l+ drjp qd AEjz En $rH +hA k+ mA tmyzt b+ Al+ fkr b+ mA yfwq twqEAt +km .
ATB	wtAvrt Tfwlp +y b+ Alryf l+ drjp qd AEjz En $rH +hA k+ mA tmyzt b+ Alfkr b+ mA yfwq twqEAt +km .

Table 3: The used Arabic tokenisation schemes examples

and preprocessed them similarly to the training dataset. Then, we translate the extracted words using Google translator to create a dictionary. After that, for Arabic as source and English as a target, we compute the distances between vectors in order to extract the embeddings of the k nearest neighbours for a given source word embedding in the target word embeddings.

After computing the similarity, the top k nearest neighbours (for k=1, 3, 5) have been selected to compute the accuracy among the test dataset, which consists of 3000 words and their translations. Then we computed the accuracy of 10 runs randomly selecting 500 source words and their k nearest neighbours as:

$$Acc = \frac{ct}{T} \qquad (3)$$

Where ct is the number of correct translations and T is the number of all test samples.

The accuracy is computed for all experiments with all different settings: sentence-length, embeddings size and segmentation schemes and the

results are discussed below. We also took into account the observed variance in considering significance of the observed differences in performance.

5.1 Results And Discussion

After computing each run accuracy, we computed the model final performance by computing the mean of the output values for each experiment as shown in Tables 4, 5 and 6. Based on the observed accuracies and using sample/population standard deviation (SSD and PSD) to indicate significant differences (See Tables 4, 5 and 6), our results cover three aspects of the problem:

- **Embeddings size:**
  Training the model on different embeddings sizes (100D, 200D and 300D) showed that, for more complex language pairs, increasing the vector size allowed the model to capture more information and lead to learn better Ar-En BWEs. Both Figures 1 and 2 show an increase in accuracy when the size of word representation is increased.

En-Ar 100D	k=1			k=3			k=5		
5-10	**Mean**	**SSD**	**PSD**	**Mean**	**SSD**	**PSD**	**Mean**	**SSD**	**PSD**
ATB	17.86	1.82	1.73	23.45	1.89	1.79	28.31	2.01	1.91
D0	15.32	0.97	0.92	18.82	3.85	3.65	20.99	2.44	2.31
D3	18.98	1.87	1.78	26.04	2.28	2.17	28.32	2.62	2.49
17-80	**Mean**	**SSD**	**PSD**	**Mean**	**SSD**	**PSD**	**Mean**	**SSD**	**PSD**
ATB	17.88	1.32	1.25	23.85	1.86	1.77	27.49	1.24	1.17
D0	16.14	1.76	1.67	19.99	1.74	1.65	21.94	2.37	2.25
D3	22.92	1.09	1.04	31.59	2.6	2.5	33.82	1.9	1.8

Table 4: 100D Models' Results

En-Ar 200D	k=1			k=3			k=5		
5-10	**Mean**	**SSD**	**PSD**	**Mean**	**SSD**	**PSD**	**Mean**	**SSD**	**PSD**
ATB	25.86	1.23	1.16	33.14	1.53	1.46	37.6	2.46	2.33
D0	21.19	1.65	1.56	27.71	2.12	2.01	30.28	1.81	1.72
D3	26.34	2.58	2.44	34.74	1.53	1.45	37.02	2.03	1.92
17-80	**Mean**	**SSD**	**PSD**	**Mean**	**SSD**	**PSD**	**Mean**	**SSD**	**PSD**
ATB	22.89	2.18	2.07	30.19	2.66	2.52	31.6	1.38	1.31
D0	22.22	2.17	2.06	28.87	1.67	1.58	31.32	1.55	1.47
D3	32.83	1.48	1.41	41.06	2.35	2.23	43.9	1.39	1.32

Table 5: 200D Models' Results

En-Ar 300D	k=1			k=3			k=5		
5-10	**Mean**	**SSD**	**PSD**	**Mean**	**SSD**	**PSD**	**Mean**	**SSD**	**PSD**
ATB	31.12	1.96	1.86	39.94	3.4	3.29	42.72	1.63	1.55
D0	26.88	1.65	1.56	33.99	1.10	1.04	37.67	2.63	2.50
D3	31.8	1.86	1.77	42.48	1.93	1.84	44.74	1.61	1.53
17-80	**Mean**	**SSD**	**PSD**	**Mean**	**SSD**	**PSD**	**Mean**	**SSD**	**PSD**
ATB	33.81	3.29	3.12	43.73	2.76	2.62	46.04	1.92	1.83
D0	30.38	2.09	1.98	37.09	1.73	1.64	40.39	1.98	1.88
D3	40.38	1.99	1.89	49.16	1.54	1.46	51.25	2.94	2.79

Table 6: 300D Models' Results

- **Sentence length:**
Comparing results from using short and long sentences, our results shows that long sentences (which increase the number of words "tokens") outperformed the short sentences in 300D embeddings size models using all three different segmentation schemes. While short sentences perform better only with 200D embeddings size and ATB segmentation scheme trained model. Thus, long sentences with 300D embeddings size allow trained models to capture more information and learn better bilingual word representations.

- **Segmentation schemes:**
Different segmentation schemes show different levels of learning BWEs. D3, which is more segmentation (breaking the word into more tokens: split all clitics), has a significant effect on the model learning process as it outperforms both D0 and ATB segmentation schemes (See Tables: 4, 5 and 6). In other words, increasing the number of tokens in training dataset using D3 segmentation scheme, as shown in Table 1, leads to better word alignment and consequently improve the model performance.

The main conclusion is that, for Arabic-English

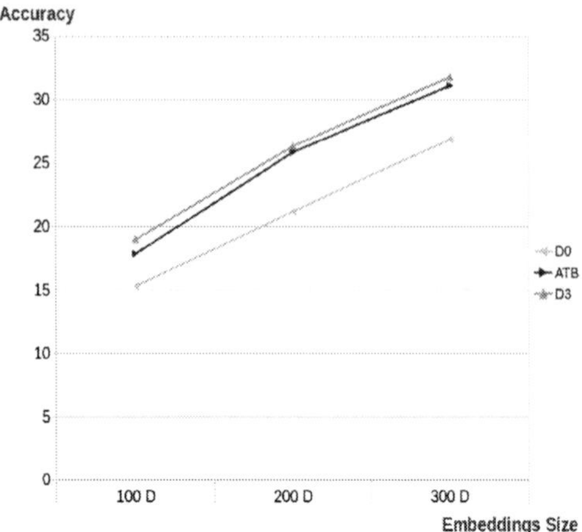

Figure 1: 5-10 sentence length training data results

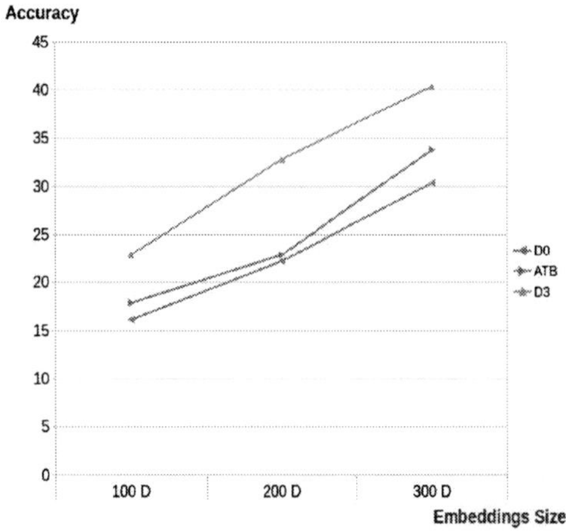

Figure 2: 17-80 sentence length training data results

in contrast to MT task, increasing embedding size, sentence length and more Arabic segmentation allow the model to capture more information and leads to learn better BWEs. See Figures 1 and 2. For Figure 1, short sentences training dataset shows that both segmented datasets: ATB and D3 give better results compared to D0 (No segmentation). D3 outperforms ATB slightly. In Figure 2, using the long sentence training dataset, D3 gives a much better performance compared to both other segmentation schemes, and increases the accuracy dramatically up to 10 %.

6   Conclusion

In this work, we have trained a BilBOWA model to investigate the effect of different morphological segmentations and different training settings (sentence-length and embeddings size) on learning BWE for Ar-En language pair. Our results show that increasing the word embedding size leads to improvement in the learning process of Arabic-English bilingual word embeddings.

For Arabic, as a morphological segmentation process is essential in many Arabic NLP tasks, segmentation also has a positive effect in this work as it leads to learning a better bilingual word embeddings. Going from D0 (full word form) to D3 (more segmentation, which increases the number of tokens in training dataset), decreases the distance between Ar-En pairs and increases the similarity more than 10 percentage points.

References

Ahmed Abdelali, Kareem Darwish, Nadir Durrani, and Hamdy Mubarak. 2016. Farasa: A fast and furious segmenter for Arabic. In *Proceedings of the 2016 Conference of the North American Chapter of the Association for Computational Linguistics: Demonstrations*, pages 11–16, San Diego, California. Association for Computational Linguistics.

Marwan Akeel and R. B. Mishra. 2014. A statistical method for english to arabic machine translation. *International Journal of Computer Applications*, 86(2):13–19.

Hassan Al-Haj and Alon Lavie. 2012. The impact of arabic morphological segmentation on broad-coverage english-to-arabic statistical machine translation. *Machine translation*, 26(1/2):3–24.

Ibrahim Badr, Rabih Zbib, and James Glass. 2008. Segmentation for english-to-arabic statistical machine translation. In *Proceedings of the 46th Annual Meeting of the Association for Computational Linguistics on Human Language Technologies: Short Papers*, number 4 in HLT-Short '08, pages 153–156, Stroudsburg, PA, USA.

Dzmitry Bahdanau, Kyunghyun Cho, and Yoshua Bengio. 2015. Neural machine translation by jointly learning to align and translate. In *3rd International Conference on Learning Representations, ICLR 2015, San Diego, CA, USA, May 7-9, 2015, Conference Track Proceedings*.

Mohamed Boudchichea, Azzeddine Mazrouia, Mohamed Ould Abdallahi Ould Bebahb, Abdelhak Lakhouajaa, and Abderrahim Boudlalc. 2017. Alkhalil morpho sys 2: A robust arabic morpho-syntactic analyzer. *Journal of King Saud University*

Computer and Information Sciences, 29(2):141–146.

Samuel R. Bowman, Christopher Potts, and Christopher D. Manning. 2015. Recursive neural networks can learn logical semantics. In *Proceedings of the 3rd Workshop on Continuous Vector Space Models and their Compositionality*, pages 12–21, Beijing, China. Association for Computational Linguistics.

Kyunghyun Cho, Bart van Merrienboer, Caglar Gulcehre, Dzmitry Bahdanau, Fethi Bougares, Holger Schwenk, and Yoshua Bengio. 2014. Learning phrase representations using RNN encoder–decoder for statistical machine translation. In *Proceedings of the 2014 Conference on Empirical Methods in Natural Language Processing (EMNLP)*, pages 1724–1734, Doha, Qatar. Association for Computational Linguistics.

Jocelyn Coulmance, Jean-Marc Marty, Guillaume Wenzek, and Amine Benhalloum. 2015. Transgram, fast cross-lingual word-embeddings. In *Proceedings of the 2015 Conference on Empirical Methods in Natural Language Processing*, pages 1109–1113, Lisbon, Portugal. Association for Computational Linguistics.

Ahmed El Kholy and Nizar Habash. 2012. Orthographic and morphological processing for english–arabic statistical machine translation. *Machine Translation*, 26(1-2):25–45.

Jakob Elming and Nizar Habash. 2009. Syntactic reordering for English-Arabic phrase-based machine translation. In *Proceedings of the EACL 2009 Workshop on Computational Approaches to Semitic Languages*, pages 69–77, Athens, Greece. Association for Computational Linguistics.

Stephan Gouws, Yoshua Bengio, and Greg Corrado. 2015. Bilbowa: Fast bilingual distributed representations without word alignments. In *Proceedings of the 32Nd International Conference on International Conference on Machine Learning - Volume 37*, ICML'15, pages 748–756. JMLR.org.

Nizar Habash. 2010. Introduction to arabic natural language processing. *Synthesis Lectures on Human Language Technologies*, 3(1):1–187.

Nizar Habash and Owen Rambow. 2005. Arabic tokenization, part-of-speech tagging and morphological disambiguation in one fell swoop. In *Proceedings of the 43rd Annual Meeting of the Association for Computational Linguistics (ACL'05)*, pages 573–580, Ann Arbor, Michigan. Association for Computational Linguistics.

Nizar Habash, Owen Rambow, and Ryan Roth. 2009. Mada+ tokan: A toolkit for arabic tokenization, diacritization, morphological disambiguation, pos tagging, stemming and lemmatization. In *Proceedings of the 2nd International Conference on Arabic Language Resources and Tools (MEDAR), Cairo, Egypt*.

Nizar Habash and Fatiha Sadat. 2006. Arabic preprocessing schemes for statistical machine translation. In *Proceedings of the Human Language Technology Conference of the NAACL, Companion Volume: Short Papers*, pages 49–52, New York City, USA. Association for Computational Linguistics.

Arwa Hatem, Nazlia Omar, and Khalid Shaker. 2011. Morphological analysis for rule based machine translation. In *International Conference on Semantic Technology and Information Retrieval (STAIR)*, pages 260–263.

Karl Moritz Hermann and Phil Blunsom. 2013. The role of syntax in vector space models of compositional semantics. In *Proceedings of the 51st Annual Meeting of the Association for Computational Linguistics (Volume 1: Long Papers)*, pages 894–904, Sofia, Bulgaria. Association for Computational Linguistics.

Karl Moritz Hermann, Tomas Kocisky, Edward Grefenstette, Lasse Espeholt, Will Kay, Mustafa Suleyman, and Phil Blunsom. 2015. Teaching machines to read and comprehend. *CoRR*, abs/1506.03340.

Ines Khemakhem, Salma Jamoussi, and Abdelmajid Ben Hamadou. 2010. The miracl arabic-english statistical machine translation system for iwslt 2010. In *Proceedings of IWSLT International Workshop on Spoken Language Translation*, pages 119–125.

Yoon. Kim. 2014. Convolutional neural networks for sentence classification. In *Proceedings of the 2014 Conference on Empirical Methods in Natural Language Processing (EMNLP)* ,, page 17461751, Doha, Qatar.

Philipp Koehn, Hieu Hoang, Alexandra Birch, Chris Callison-Burch, Marcello Federico, Nicola Bertoldi, Brooke Cowan, Wade Shen, Christine Moran, Richard Zens, Chris Dyer, Ondrej Bojar, Alexandra Constantin, and Evan Herbst. 2007. Moses: Open source toolkit for statistical machine translation. In *Proceedings of the 45th Annual Meeting of the Association for Computational Linguistics Companion Volume Proceedings of the Demo and Poster Sessions*, pages 177–180, Prague, Czech Republic. Association for Computational Linguistics.

Lingpeng Kong, Chris Dyer, and Noah A Smith. 2015. Segmental recurrent neural networks. In *ICLR*.

Guillaume Lample, Miguel Ballesteros, Sandeep Subramanian, Kazuya Kawakami, and Chris Dyer. 2016. Neural architectures for named entity recognition. *CoRR*, abs/1603.01360.

Stanislas Lauly, Alex Boulanger, and Hugo Larochelle. 2014. Learning multilingual word representations using a bag-of-words autoencoder. *CoRR*, abs/1401.1803.

Mike Lewis, Kenton Lee, and Luke Zettlemoyer. 2016. LSTM CCG parsing. In *Proceedings of the 2016 Conference of the North American Chapter of the Association for Computational Linguistics: Human Language Technologies*, pages 221–231, San Diego, California. Association for Computational Linguistics.

Thang Luong, Hieu Pham, and Christopher D. Manning. 2015a. Bilingual word representations with monolingual quality in mind. In *Proceedings of the 1st Workshop on Vector Space Modeling for Natural Language Processing*, pages 151–159, Denver, Colorado. Association for Computational Linguistics.

Thang Luong, Hieu Pham, and Christopher D. Manning. 2015b. Effective approaches to attention-based neural machine translation. In *Proceedings of the 2015 Conference on Empirical Methods in Natural Language Processing*, pages 1412–1421, Lisbon, Portugal. Association for Computational Linguistics.

Tomas Mikolov, Martin Karafit, Lukas Burget, Jan Cernock, and Sanjeev Khudanpur. 2010. Recurrent neural network based language model. In *Proceedings of the 11th Annual Conference of the International Speech Communication Association, INTERSPEECH*, volume 2, pages 1045–1048.

Tomas Mikolov, Quoc V. Le, and Ilya Sutskever. 2013a. Exploiting similarities among languages for machine translation. *CoRR*, abs/1309.4168.

Tomas Mikolov, Ilya Sutskever, Kai Chen, Greg Corrado, and Jeffrey Dean. 2013b. Distributed representations of words and phrases and their compositionality. In *Proceedings of the 26th International Conference on Neural Information Processing Systems*, volume 2 of *NIPS'13*, pages 3111–3119, USA. Curran Associates Inc.

Tomas Mikolov and Geoffrey Zweig. 2012. Context dependent recurrent neural network language model. *IEEE Workshop on Spoken Language Technology, SLT 2012 - Proceedings*.

Aditya Mogadala and Achim Rettinger. 2016. Bilingual word embeddings from parallel and non-parallel corpora for cross-language text classification. In *Proceedings of the 2016 Conference of the North American Chapter of the Association for Computational Linguistics: Human Language Technologies*, pages 692–702, San Diego, California. Association for Computational Linguistics.

Azza Abdel Monem, Khaled Shaalan, Ahmed Rafea, and Hoda Baraka. 2008. Generating arabic text in multilingual speech-to-speech machine translation framework. *Machine translation*, 22(4):205–258.

Arfath Pasha, Mohamed Al-Badrashiny, Mona Diab, Ahmed El Kholy, Ramy Eskander, Nizar Habash, Manoj Pooleery, Owen Rambow, and Ryan Roth. 2014. MADAMIRA: A fast, comprehensive tool for morphological analysis and disambiguation of Arabic. In *Proceedings of the Ninth International Conference on Language Resources and Evaluation (LREC'14)*, pages 1094–1101, Reykjavik, Iceland. European Language Resources Association (ELRA).

Sebastian Ruder. 2017. A survey of cross-lingual embedding models. *CoRR*, abs/1706.04902.

Cicero dos Santos and Maira Gatti. 2014. Deep convolutional neural networks for sentiment analysis of short texts. In *Proceedings of COLING 2014, the 25th International Conference on Computational Linguistics: Technical Papers*, pages 69–78, Dublin, Ireland. Dublin City University and Association for Computational Linguistics.

Aliaksei Severyn and Alessandro Moschitti. 2015. Twitter sentiment analysis with deep convolutional neural networks. In *Proceedings of the 38th International ACM SIGIR Conference on Research and Development in Information Retrieval*, SIGIR '15, pages 959–962, New York, NY, USA. ACM.

Yongzhe Shi, Wei-Qiang Zhang, Jia Liu, and Michael T. Johnson. 2013. RNN language model with word clustering and class-based output layer. *EURASIP Journal on Audio, Speech, and Music Processing*, 2013(1):22.

Abdelhadi Soudi, Günter Neumann, and Antal Van den Bosch. 2007. *Arabic computational morphology: knowledge-based and empirical methods*. Springer.

Jinsong Su, Deyi Xiong, Biao Zhang, Yang Liu, Junfeng Yao, and Min Zhang. 2015. Bilingual correspondence recursive autoencoder for statistical machine translation. In *Proceedings of the 2015 Conference on Empirical Methods in Natural Language Processing*, pages 1248–1258, Lisbon, Portugal. Association for Computational Linguistics.

Sainbayar Sukhbaatar, arthur szlam, Jason Weston, and Rob Fergus. 2015. End-to-End memory networks. In C. Cortes, N. D. Lawrence, D. D. Lee, M. Sugiyama, and R. Garnett, editors, *Advances in Neural Information Processing Systems 28*, pages 2440–2448. Curran Associates, Inc.

Ilya Sutskever, Oriol Vinyals, and Quoc V Le. 2014. Sequence to Sequence learning with neural networks. *CoRR*, abs/1409.3215.

Ivan Vulic and Marie-Francine Moens. 2015. Bilingual word embeddings from non-parallel document-aligned data applied to bilingual lexicon induction. In *Proceedings of the 53rd Annual Meeting of the Association for Computational Linguistics (ACL 2015)*, page 719725.

WIT3. 2012. Plain training and development sets for the mt track. https://wit3.fbk.eu/mt.php?release=2012-02-plain.

Min Xiao and Yuhong Guo. 2014. Distributed word representation learning for cross-lingual dependency parsing. In *CoNLL*, pages 119–129.

Biao Zhang, Deyi Xiong, and Jinsong Su. 2016. BattRAE: Bidimensional attention-based recursive autoencoders for learning bilingual phrase embeddings. *CoRR*, abs/1605.07874.

Jiajun Zhang, Shujie Liu, Mu Li, Ming Zhou, and Chengqing Zong. 2014. Bilingually-constrained phrase embeddings for machine translation. In *Proceedings of the 52nd Annual Meeting of the Association for Computational Linguistics (Volume 1: Long Papers)*, pages 111–121, Baltimore, Maryland. Association for Computational Linguistics.

Neural Arabic Question Answering

Hussein Mozannar, Karl El Hajal, Elie Maamary, Hazem Hajj
Department of Electrical and Computer Engineering
American University of Beirut
{hssein.mzannar,karlhajal,eliemaamary17}@gmail.com; hh63@aub.edu.lb

Abstract

This paper tackles the problem of open domain factual Arabic question answering (QA) using Wikipedia as our knowledge source. This constrains the answer of any question to be a span of text in Wikipedia. Open domain QA for Arabic entails three challenges: annotated QA datasets in Arabic, large scale efficient information retrieval and machine reading comprehension. To deal with the lack of Arabic QA datasets we present the Arabic Reading Comprehension Dataset (ARCD) composed of 1,395 questions posed by crowdworkers on Wikipedia articles, and a machine translation of the Stanford Question Answering Dataset (Arabic-SQuAD). Our system for open domain question answering in Arabic (SOQAL) is based on two components: (1) a document retriever using a hierarchical TF-IDF approach and (2) a neural reading comprehension model using the pre-trained bi-directional transformer BERT. Our experiments on ARCD indicate the effectiveness of our approach with our BERT-based reader achieving a 61.3 F1 score, and our open domain system SOQAL achieving a 27.6 F1 score.

1 Introduction

One of the goals in artificial intelligence (AI) is to build automated systems that can perform open-domain question answering (QA) through understanding natural language and gathering knowledge (Kwiatkowski et al., 2019). The driver behind progress in English QA has been the release of massive datasets including the Stanford Question Answering Dataset (SQuAD), WikiQA (Rajpurkar et al., 2016; Yang et al., 2015). The task in these datasets is to find the span of text in a document that answers a given question. On the other hand, progress in Arabic QA systems has lagged behind their English counterparts. While there has been a good body of work on methods for question

يلعب نادي نايفربول كل مبارياته الرسمية في ملعب الأنفيلد ، و الذي يتسع لحضور ٥٤٠٠٧٤ متفرج.
يعتبر نادي مانشستر يونايتد العدو اللدود لنادي ليفربول، فتلك المواجهات تعتبر من أهم المنافسات في كرة القدم الإنجليزية، حيث تجمع أكثر نادي تحقيقاً للألقاب، حيث حقق مانشستر يونايتد ٦٢، بينما حقق ليفربول ٥٩ بطولة .

كم من بطولة حققها نادي ليفربول؟

٥٩ بطولة

أين يلعب نادي ليفربول مبارياته ؟

ملعب الأنفيلد

Figure 1: Example data point from ARCD containing a paragraph with two accompanying questions

answering, they mostly have a common limitation of being tested on small amounts of data and relying on classical methods (Shaheen and Ezzeldin, 2014).

In this work, we tackle the problem of answering Arabic open-domain factual questions using Arabic Wikipedia as our knowledge source. The open-domain setting poses many challenges, from efficient large scale information retrieval, to highly accurate answer extraction modules, and this requires a sizable amount of data for training and testing.

First, to deal with the need of large Arabic reading comprehension datasets, we develop the following: (1) The Arabic Reading Comprehension Dataset (ARCD) composed of 1,395 crowd-sourced questions with accompanying text seg-

Proceedings of the Fourth Arabic Natural Language Processing Workshop, pages 108–118
Florence, Italy, August 1, 2019. ©2019 Association for Computational Linguistics

ments on Arabic Wikipedia as seen in figure 1, and (2) Arabic-SQuAD consisting of 48k paragraph-question-answer machine translated tuples from the SQuAD dataset.

Second, modern open-domain QA systems are generally composed of two parts: a retriever that obtains relevant segments of text, and a machine reading comprehension (MRC) model that extracts the answer from the text (Chen et al., 2017). For our retriever, we propose the use of a hierarchical TF-IDF retriever that is efficiently able to trade off between n-gram features and the number of documents retrieved. We chose raw Wikipedia text as our information source instead of knowledge bases (Lehmann et al., 2015) which are commonly used for open-ended QA as it enables our approach to tackle other domains and settings with little adaptation. Now there has been remarkable progress in designing neural MRC models that read and extract answers from short paragraphs; we selected two of the best performing models on the SQuAD dataset (Rajpurkar et al., 2016) as our document readers. The first is QANet (Yu et al., 2018), an efficient convolution and self-attention-based neural network, and the second is BERT (Devlin et al., 2018), a transformer-based pre-trained model. From the document retriever and reader we build an open domain QA system named SOQAL by combining confidence scores from each.

We evaluated our system components on the crowdsoured ARCD dataset: Our hierarchical TF-IDF retriever is competitive with Google Search, and our BERT reader is the current state-of-the-art for reading comprehension. Finally, our open domain system SOQAL achieves a respectable 27.6 F1 on ARCD.

To summarize, the contributions of the paper are:

- **Datasets for Arabic QA.** Crowdsourced Arabic Reading Comprehension Dataset (ARCD) of 1,395 questions, and translated Arabic-SQuAD: 48k translated questions from (Rajpurkar et al., 2016).
- **Neural Reading comprehension in Arabic.** State of the art MRC models for Arabic based on BERT (Devlin et al., 2018) and QANet (Yu et al., 2018).
- **Open domain Arabic QA system.** End-to-end system for open domain Arabic questions using a hierarchical TF-IDF retriever, BERT

Dataset	Source	Formulation	Size
Arabic-SQuAD	**Translated SQuAD**	**p,q,a**	**48,344**
ARCD	**Arabic Wikipedia**	**p,q,a**	**1,395**
ArabiQA (Benajiba Yassine, 2007)	Wikipedia	q,a	200
DefArabicQA (Trigui et al., 2010)	Wikipedia and Google search engine	q,a with documents	50
Translated TREC and CLEF (Abouenour Lahsen and Rosso, 2010)	Translated TREC and CLEF	q,a	2,264
QAM4MRE (Peas and Sporleder, 2011)	selected topics	document,q and multiple answers	160
DAWQUAS (Ismail and Homsi, 2018)	auto-generated from web scrape	q,a	3205
QArabPro (Akour et al., 2011)	Wikipedia	q,a	335

Table 1: Available question answering datasets in Arabic. p:paragraph, q:question and a:answer

and linear answer ranking.

All the data and system implementation is available at `https://github.com/husseinmozannar/SOQAL`.

2 Related Work

Open-domain Arabic question answering. The state of current Arabic QA systems is summarized in (Shaheen and Ezzeldin, 2014): research has focused mostly on open-ended QA using classical information retrieval (IR) methods, and there are no common datasets for comparisons. Consequently, progress has been slow. Furthermore, the Arabic language presents its own set of difficulties: given the highly intricate nature of the language, proper understanding can be difficult. For instance, فسيأكلونه means "so they will eat it", which demonstrates the complexity that can be presented by a single word. Moreover, Arabic words require diacritization for their meaning to be completely understood. For example, عَلَّم translates into "he taught", and عَلِم means "found out"; modifying one diacritic changes the meaning entirely.

We now review some of the methods and datasets used in the literature and compare them in table 1. Most of the datasets listed are of very limited size and do not include accompanying text segments so as to enable reading comprehension. Furthermore, all datasets with size bigger than

1000 questions are synthetically generated. Approaches have tackled specific types of questions and are heavily dependent on their nature focusing more on document retreival. In (Azmi and Alshenaifi, 2016), they attempt to answer "why" questions using classic IR methods and rhetorical structure theory, and their methods are evaluated on a set of 100 questions. On the other hand, DefArabicQA (Trigui et al., 2010) focuses on definition question and uses an answer ranking module based on word frequency. QArabPro (Akour et al., 2011) employs a rule-based question answering system and obtains an 84% accuracy on 335 questions based on Wikipedia. The SemEval task 3 in 2015, 2016, and 2017 (Nakov et al., 2017) tackled community question answering. It included a task in Arabic with each data point consisting of a paragraph, a question, and multiple answers, and the goal was to rank them in order of relevance. One of the strategies used to solve the 2015 edition was to train an SVM ranker by embedding the questions and answers using Word2vec (Belinkov et al., 2015). The type of data used is not constructive for training answer extraction systems but can be helpful for recognizing relevance.

QA Datasets. As previously mentioned, the driver behind progress in QA has been the release of large datasets in addition to advances in deep learning and language representation models (Devlin et al., 2018). The most popular benchmark for reading comprehension has been the Stanford Question Answering Dataset (Rajpurkar et al., 2016). Other notable datasets include: WikiQA (Yang et al., 2015), a sentence selection task using Wikipedia passages, and TriviaQA (Joshi et al., 2017), a dataset of trivia questions with provided evidence.

Reading comprehension and QA. Recently, machine reading comprehension has made significant progress using recurrent models and attention mechanisms to capture long term interactions (Seo et al., 2016), and this has prompted its use as part of open-domain QA. On the other hand, given that recurrent networks are slow in training and inference, QANet (Yu et al., 2018) proposes an approach based only on convolutions and self-attention that is able to achieve very competitive results on SQuAD while being 10x faster than recurrent based approaches such as Bidirectional Attention Flow (BiDAF) (Seo et al., 2016). For open-domain QA, (Chen et al., 2017) in-

Figure 2: Interface for the crowdworkers

vestigates the use of Wikipedia as a knowledge source and implements a two component system based on a TF-IDF retriever and a RNN reader achieving a 29.8% exact- match accuracy on open-SQuAD. Other approaches have attempted to build more sophisticated retrievers by formulating it as a reinforcement learning problem (Wang et al., 2018b,a), or as a supervised learning problem using distant supervision for data (Das et al., 2018; Lin et al., 2018).

In the following sections we will first describe the datasets collected, and then our proposed method for Arabic open-domain question answering.

3 Dataset Collection

3.1 Arabic Reading Comprehension Dataset

To properly evaluate our system, we must have questions written by proficient Arabic speakers, and thus we resort to crowdsourcing to develop our dataset.

Task Description. Each task presented to the crowdworkers consists of five articles taken from Arabic Wikipedia, from which we extracted the first three paragraphs with a length greater than 250 characters. The worker has to write three question-answer pairs for each paragraph in clear Modern Standard Arabic, where the answer to each question should be an exact span of text from the paragraph. The interface, shown in figure 2, consists of a paragraph along with two text boxes for each of the 3 question-answer pairs. Pasting is disabled in the question fields in order to encourage workers to use their own words, but it is enforced in the answer fields to guarantee that the answer is taken as-is from the paragraph. Before workers begin the task, they have to answer a reading comprehension question from a test set we created to make sure of their language proficiency. Only workers who succeeded in the test were accepted.

Article curation. The articles presented in the tasks were 155 articles randomly sampled from the 1000 most viewed articles on Wikipedia in 2018. We used MediaWiki's API[1] to retrieve the most viewed articles per month in 2018 for Arabic Wikipedia and aggregated the results. The articles covered a diverse set of topics including religious and historical figures, sports celebrities, countries, and companies. We additionally manually filtered out adult content.

Crowdsourcing. We resorted to Amazon Mechanical Turk for crowdsourcing. Crowdworkers were required to have a minimum HIT acceptance of 97%, and at least 100 HITs submitted. Moreover, our task description highlighted the need for good Arabic skills. Workers were advised to spend 3 to 4 minutes per paragraph and were paid close to 10 USD per hour. They were encouraged to ask difficult questions framed in such a way that they can be answered outside the scope of the paragraph. In total, we collected 1,395 questions based on 465 paragraphs from 155 articles based on the Amazon Turk HITs.

3.2 Arabic-SQuAD

Translating SQuAD. While the crowdsourcing of questions by proficient Arabic writers is essential to properly evaluate our systems, noisy data could well suffice for training. Indeed, backtranslation as a means for data augmentation has been effective in improving the performance of neural MRC (Yu et al., 2018), and this gives hope that translated data could be used to train our machine reading comprehension module. We chose to translate SQuAD version 1.1 (Rajpurkar et al., 2016). It is currently the most popular benchmark for MRC and was collected through crowdsourcing based on Wikipedia articles. SQuAD contains

107,785 paragraph-question-answer tuples on 536 articles, and we translated the first 231 articles of the SQuAD training set using the Google Translate neural machine translation (NMT) API (Wu et al., 2016). This resulted in 48,344 questions on 10,364 paragraphs.

4 Our System: SOQAL

We will now describe the architecture of our system for open domain question answering for the Arabic language (SOQAL). It is composed of three modules: (1) a document retriever that obtains relevant documents to the question, (2) a machine reading comprehension module that extracts answers from the documents retrieved, and an (3) answer ranking module that ranks the answers in order of relevance by taking in scores from both the document retriever and the reader. The inputs to the system are a question consisting of m tokens $q = \{q_1, \cdots, q_m\}$, and the entirety of Arabic Wikipedia, and its output is a small span of text extracted from Wikipedia which should answer the question. The pipeline is illustrated in figure 3.

4.1 Hierarchical TF-IDF Document Retriever

The goal of this module is to select the documents that are most relevant to the question, thus reducing the span of search of our reader. Arabic Wikipedia is made up of 664,768 indexed articles with an average of 3.4 paragraphs per article, totalling 2,683,743 paragraphs with an average of 233 characters per paragraph. We discard imagery, lists, and other structured information so that our approach could translate well to various knowledge sources.

There are two scopes on which we can search: either articles or paragraphs. We denote the set of documents searched over as $D = \{d_1, \cdots, d_n\}$, where for $1 \leq i \leq n$, d_i is a single document which can be either an article or a paragraph from an article.

Inspired by classical QA systems (Chen et al., 2017), we employ a term frequency-inverse document frequency (TF-IDF) based document retriever given its efficiency. Each document is first tokenized and stemmed using the NLTK (Bird, 2006) Arabic tokenizer where stopwords are removed. The TF-IDF matrix of weights of the document set, i.e. Arabic Wikipedia, is then constructed using n-gram counts to take into account

---

[1]Availabe at `https://en.wikipedia.org/w/api.php`

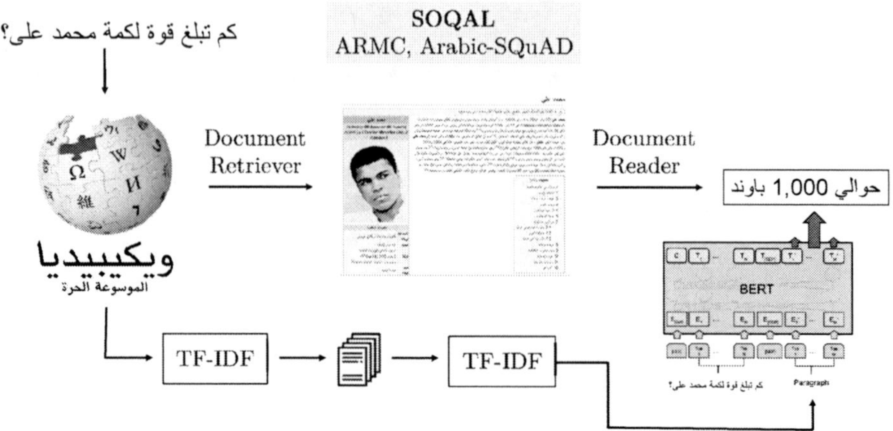

Figure 3: Architecture of our open domain question answering system SOQAL. BERT illustration is adapted from (Devlin et al., 2018)

local word order. As n increases, the retriever becomes more accurate, but the retrieval process becomes slower and more memory prohibitive. Each document's vector is normalized. Next, the TF-IDF vector weights of the question are computed based on the vocabulary of the document set. The score for each document is then computed as the cosine similarity between the question and the document vectors. We use a sparse matrix representation for the TF-IDF matrix to speed up computations. Finally, we return the top k documents with the highest similarity where $k \in \mathbb{N}$ is a hyperparameter. The higher k is, the more likely it is that the set of retrieved documents contains relevant documents, and the slower and more error-prone is the answer extraction process.

To obtain the benefits of using large n-gram features while keeping k small and being computationally efficient, we propose the following hierarchical TF-IDF retriever approach. The first step is to build a TF-IDF retriever on Arabic Wikipedia with bigram features and a very large k, say $\approx$ 1000, and obtain the set of retrieved documents for a given question, call it D'. Then, for each question, we construct a seperate TF-IDF retriever using as document set D' with 4-gram features and a small k, say ≈ 15. The second retriever does not sacrifice much in terms of the accuracy of the first retrieval step, as 4-gram features are highly informative and do not add significant computations.

4.2 BERT Document Reader

Our proposed reader is Bert (Devlin et al., 2018), a pre-trained language model that is currently the state of the art on the SQuAD leaderboard [2].

Its core model is a bi-directional Transformer (Vaswani et al., 2017). The input text is first tokenized using a shared Wordpiece (Wu et al., 2016) vocabulary of 104 languages, and it is then embedded; note that Arabic diacritics are removed. Each input point of question and paragraph pairs is represented as a single sentence separated by a special token. We need to learn two new vectors: start and end $S, E \in \mathbb{R}^H$ vectors indicating the position of the answer; H is the dimension of the last hidden layer outputs. For each token i in the paragraph, we take the final hidden state of the Transformer T_i and let the probability that i is the start or end of the answer be:

$$P_{start}(i) \propto \exp(S^T T_i)$$
$$P_{end}(i) \propto \exp(E^T T_i)$$

Note that we take the un-normalized exponential to be able to compare across documents. At inference time we predict the span (i, j) such that $i \leq j \leq i + 15$ that maximizes $P_{start}(i)P_{end}(j)$. The training objective is the sum of the log likelihood for each of the start and end positions.

4.3 Answer Ranking

Let us recall the operation of the end-to-end system. The question is first passed to the retriever

---

[2]SQuAD leaderboard `https://rajpurkar.github.io/SQuAD-explorer/`

and the top k documents are gathered; if a document unit is an article then we gather all of its paragraphs. Along with the documents' text, we obtain a score for each document denoted $DocScore(i)$ from the retriever; paragraphs have the same score as their document. For our hierarchical TF-IDF retriever, the scores are the cosine similarities between the document and the question.

The paragraphs obtained from the retriever are each then fed as input to the document reader to obtain candidate answers. We obtain a score for each candidate answer i denoted:

$$AnsScore(i) \propto P_{start}(i) \cdot P_{end}(i)$$

To make sure the answer and document scores are on the same scale, we normalize both individually by passing each through a softmax function. The final step to obtain the answer of the question is by combining the scores through a linear combination and pick the maximizing answer as follows:

$$\arg\max_{i \in [k]} \ \beta \cdot DocScore(i) + (1 - \beta) \cdot AnsScore(i)$$

Where $\beta \in [0, 1]$ is a hyperparameter chosen through a line search using a development set.

As a note, since articles can be very large, one can additionally use a TF-IDF retriever with $4-$gram features to obtain a smaller set of paragraphs, thus reducing the load on the reader. While this step was not performed for our experimental evaluation, it is crucial when deploying the QA system for usage.

5 Dataset Analysis

5.1 ARCD

In this section we analyze the properties of the Arabic Reading Comprehension Dataset. To better understand the difficulty of answering the questions, we randomly sampled 100 questions for the following analysis.

Answer diversity. We, the authors, manually categorized the answers by first separating the numerical and non-numerical answers. Numerical answers were either identified as dates by looking at the question, or were otherwise labeled as other numeric. For the non-numerical answers, we identify the type of phrase as either a verb, adjective, or noun phrase. If it is a noun phrase, we check using MADAMIRA (Pasha et al., 2014) for named entities, and then manually verify the outcome. The results are shown in table 2.

Answer type	Percentage	Example
Date	17%	١٠ مارس ١٩٧٦
Person	17%	الطبيب الشاعر سليم الضاهر
Location	10%	آسيا
Organization	9%	الاتحاد الإنجليزي لكرة القدم
Verb Phrase	7%	انقسمت الإمبراطورية
Adjective Phrase	4%	أقصى اتساع لها
Noun Phrase	12%	الوارد المنحدر
Other Numeric	15%	٢٥٠ كيلوغرام
Other Entity	9%	جائزة نوبل في الأدب

Table 2: Answer categories percentages in ARCD according to the categorization by (Rajpurkar et al., 2016)

Question Reasoning To better understand the reasoning required to answer the questions, we manually labeled the questions according to the following reasoning categories as in (Trischler et al., 2017; Rajpurkar et al., 2016):

- *Word matching (synonyms)*: question matches the same word pattern up to synonyms in the paragraph; simple pattern matching is required.
- *Word matching (world knowledge)*: question matches the pattern of the paragraph, however additional inference using world knowledge is required to answer.
- *Syntactic variation*: The question's syntactic dependency structure does not match that of the answer sentence.
- *Multiple sentence reasoning*: The question draws on knowledge from multiple sentences. Only after making necessary links across sentences can it be answered.
- *Ambiguous*: The question cannot be answered given the information in the paragraph or is unclear.

The results and examples are shown in table 3.

5.2 Arabic-SQuAD

We discuss some of the issues resulting from the machine translation of SQuAD and how we handled them.

We observed that translation performed well for paragraphs and questions and maintained their original meaning. The problem is, NMT is heavily context dependent, thus identical words and phrases have different translations if the context is varied. This led to an inconsistency between the translation of the answers and paragraphs with

Reasoning	Example	Percentage
Word matching (synonyms)	يلعب نادي ليفربول كل مبارياته الرسمية في ملعب الأنفيلد. يعتبر نادي مانشستر يونايتد العدو اللدود لنادي ليفربول ، حيث حقق مانشستر يونايتد ٦٢، بينما حقق ليفربول **٥٩ بطولة** . Q: كم من بطولة حققها نادي ليفربول؟	**59%**
Word matching (world knowledge)	نجيب محفوظ (١١ ديسمبر ١٩١١ – ٣٠ أغسطس ٢٠٠٦) روائي مصري، هو أول عربي حائز على **جائزة نوبل** في الأدب. كتب نجيب محفوظ منذ بداية الأربعينيات واستمر حتى ٢٠٠٤. Q: ما هي أهم جائزة عالمية حصل عليها نجيب محفوظ؟	**15%**
Syntactic variation	طرح عمر لطفي بك فكرة تأسيس النادي الأهلي في العقد الأول من القرن، لأنه اعتبر أن تأسيس نادي طلبة المدارس العليا سياسيًا بالدرجة الأولى، ووجد **أن هؤلاء الطلبة بحاجة إلى نادٍ رياضي يجمعهم لقضاء وقت الفراغ وممارسة الرياضة** . Q: لماذا أسس النادي للطلبة؟	**13%**
Multiple sentence reasoning	سليمان خان الأول بن سليم خان الأول ، عاشر السلاطين العثمانيين وخليفة المسلمين الثمانون، بلغت الدولة الإسلامية في عهده **أقصى اتساع لها** حتى أصبحت أقوى دولة في العالم في ذلك الوقت. Q: ماذا بلغت دولة سليمان خان تحت عهده؟	**10%**
Ambiguous	Q: متى رسمها؟	**3%**

Table 3: Examples of questions with their respective paragraph (trimmed to fit) and answer in bold from ARCD and the reasoning required to answer them.

25,490 answers not found in their respective paragraphs, almost 47.3% of the total questions. We remarked that the type of errors that caused the answers to not match in the paragraph mostly arised from two factors: (1) translation was unable to recognize named entities without context and thus transliterated them, and (2) minor typographic like errors from missing or added لام التعريف (the) and differing tenses. To fix this issue, we transliterated all the paragraphs and answers to Arabic and found the span of text of length at most 15 words with the least edit-distance with respect to the answer. To verify the efficacy of this approach, we randomly sampled 100 questions where the answer is not found in the paragraph and provided the correct answer. On this test set, the approach managed to exactly find 44% of the answers, and 64% of the proposed answers contained the correct answer and did not exceed more than twice its length.

6 System Experiments

We now showcase experiments for every component in our system and the end-to-end open domain system.

Datasets. Arabic-SQuAD is split 80-10-10% into three parts for training, development and testing: Arabic-SQuad-Test is composed of 2,966 questions on 24 articles; note that articles are distinct between the parts. Similarly, ARCD is split 50-50 into training and testing with ARCD-Test having 702 questions on 78 articles.

6.1 Retriever

Method	k	ARCD
Wikipedia API	15	34.8%
Google Search	10	**75.6%**
TF-IDF Unigram Article	15	41.7%
TF-IDF Bigram Article	15	47.7%
TF-IDF Bigram Article	350	73.5%
Hierarchical TF-IDF	15	**65.3%**
Embedding fastText Paragraph	50	27.0%

Table 4: Comparison of the different retrievers on ARCD. k: number of documents retrieved

We examine the performance of our different retriever modules on the full ARCD dataset. To compare the approaches we assign to each the ratio of questions for which the answer appears in any of the retrieved document over the total number of questions.

Method	Arabic-SQuAD Test			ARCD		
	EM	F1	SM	EM	F1	SM
Random Guess	0.23	4.34	23.5	0.07	8.13	51.0
Sliding Win. + Dist. (Richardson et al., 2013)	0.00	5.80	29.2	0.07	14.2	58.4
Embedding fastText	0.04	6.96	43.1	0.36	15.3	73.1
TF-IDF Reader	0.27	2.41	49.2	0.22	5.6	75.3
QANet fastText (Yu et al., 2018)	29.4	44.4	61.7	11.0	38.6	83.2
BERT (Devlin et al., 2018)	**34.1**	**48.6**	**66.8**	**19.6**	**51.3**	**91.4**

Table 5: Comparison of the different document reader modules on Arabic-SQuAD test set and all of ARCD. QANet and BERT were trained only on the training set of Arabic-SQuAD.

Baselines. We implement three baselines: the first is using Wikipedia's Search API [3], and the second is through Google Custom Search engine [4] restricted to the Arabic Wikipedia site. Furthermore, we implement an embedding based retriever using fastText embeddings 300 dimensional Wikipedia pre-trained word embeddings (Joulin et al., 2016) that computes for each paragraph a representation using the sum of its word embeddings. Other embedding models exist for Arabic but fastText is the most specialized to Wikipedia (Badaro et al., 2018; Al Sallab et al., 2015)

Results and Analysis Our results are reported in table 4. We find that even the simple TF-IDF unigram retriever is able to beat the Wikipedia API baseline. Google Search with $k = 10$ is the golden standard with 75.6%, TF-IDF using bigram features and $k = 350$ is able to come close with 73.5%. Using our hierarchical approach of adding a second 4-gram TF-IDF retriever to a bigram $k = 1000$ retriever achieves a respectable 65.3% improving on the single bigram by 17.6% and a reduction of 8.2% from the full $k = 350$ retriever. The embedding retriever using fastText (Joulin et al., 2016) performed badly in accordance with the results in (Chen et al., 2017).

It is important to note that since the questions in ARCD were written with a specific paragraph in mind, they might be ambiguous without their context, hence why it is hard to beat the Google Search baseline.

6.2 Reader

Metrics. We evaluate our different readers based on three metrics. The first is *exact match* (EM)

Method	ARCD-Test		
	EM	F1	SM
Reader:			
BERT (SQuAD)	23.8	53.0	**90.6**
BERT (ARCD)	23.9	50.1	88.0
BERT (SQuAD + ARCD)	**34.2**	**61.3**	90.0
Open-Domain:			
SOQAL (top-1)	12.8	27.6	29.8
SOQAL (top-3)	17.8	37.9	44.0
SOQAL (top-5)	20.7	42.5	51.7

Table 6: Results of BERT as a document reader on ARCD-Test under different data regimes and of our open domain system SOQAL when returning the top k answers

which measures the percentage of predictions that match the ground truth answer exactly, the second is a *(macro-averaged) F1 score* (Rajpurkar et al., 2016) that measures the average overlap between the prediction tokens and the ground truth answer tokens. Finally, we use a *sentence match* (SM) metric that measures the percentage of predictions that fall in the same sentence in the paragraph as the ground truth answer.

Baselines. We compare against three non-learning baselines. For all three methods, we generate candidate answers by considering every text span of length maximally 10 words in each sentence as a candidate. We implement the following baselines: the sliding window distance based algorithm of (Richardson et al., 2013), a TF-IDF reader based on 4-gram features which operates exactly like the retriever with $k = 1$, and finally an embedding approach where the candidate with the highest cosine similarity with respect to fastText embeddings is returned (Joulin et al., 2016; Belinkov et al., 2015). We also compare against QANet (Yu et al., 2018), a competitive MRC network that is especially fast for prediction.

---

[3] https://www.mediawiki.org/wiki/API:Search

[4] We use the official API https://developers.google.com/custom-search/

Implementation Details. For Bert, we follow the reference implementation for training on SQuAD[5]. We fine-tune from the BERT-Base unnormalized multilingual model which includes Arabic. The model has 12-layers with $H = 768$, 12-heads for self attention and inputs are padded to 384 tokens. We train on the training set of Arabic-SQuAD for 2 epochs with a learning rate of $3 \cdot 10^{-5}$. Similarly for QANet we modify the implementation of [6] and use fastText embeddings and train for a total of 4 epochs.

Results and Analysis We report all reader experiments in table 5. The non-learning baselines are unable to obtain a significant improvement over a random guess on the EM and F1 metrics. The embedding and TF-IDF readers reach a sentence match accuracy of almost 75%; this 75% accuracy in fact corresponds to the percentage of word matching questions as in table 3. On the other hand, BERT and QANet on the test set of Arabic-SQuAD reach 44.4 and 48.6 F1 scores respectively; as previously noted half of Arabic-SQuAD answers might be faulty as a result of NMT and this explains the relatively low results compared to the SQuAD leaderboard (Rajpurkar et al., 2016). Now without having been trained on ARCD, both neural MRC models are able to perform well transferring knowledge from Arabic-SQuAD with BERT reaching a remarkable 90.08 SM accuracy.

Transfer Learning. To evaluate the effectiveness of using translated data as training data on the ARCD test set we train BERT under the following data regimes: (a) Arabic-SQuAD only, (b) ARCD-Train only and (c) Arabic-SQuAD and ARCD-Train combined; results are reported in table 6. We remark that training under regimes (a) or (b) had very similar results, this gives strong evidence that Arabic-SQuAD could be in fact sufficient for obtaining powerful MRC models. When combining both datasets, we obtain an improvement of 8.3% on the F1 score with a total score of 61.3; the training on ARCD allowed the model to better adapt to its differing answer distribution.

6.3 Open Domain QA

We test our open domain approach SOQAL on ARCD-Test. For our retriever we combine our hierarchical TF-IDF retriever with the Google Custom Search Engine to make sure we have a total of 10 retrieved articles. We train BERT on Arabic-SQuAD for two epochs and then fine-tune on ARCD-Train for an epoch.

We report in table 6 the accuracy of our proposed system on ARCD-Test achieving a 27.6 F1 and a 29.8 SM. The close F1 and SM scores indicate that the system is able to correctly retrieve the answer when it selects the correct paragraph, the issue then lies with it not scoring highly enough the correct paragraph. We also report the accuracy when the system outputs the top 3 and top 5 results (choosing the best answer out of them).

7 Conclusion

To further the state of Arabic natural language understanding we proposed an approach for open domain Arabic QA and introduced the Arabic Reading Comprehension Dataset (ARCD) and Arabic-SQuAD: a machine translation of SQuAD (Devlin et al., 2018). Our approach consisted of a document retriever using hierarchical TF-IDF and a document reader using BERT (Devlin et al., 2018). We achieve a F1 score of 61.3 and a 90.0% sentence match on ARCD and a 27.6 F1 score on an open domain version of ARCD. We also showed the effectiveness of using translated data as a training resource for QA. Future work will aim to expand the size of ARCD and improve the end-to-end system by focusing on paragraph selection.

References

Karim Bouzouba Abouenour Lahsen and Paolo Rosso. 2010. An evaluated semantic query expansion and structure-based approach for enhancing arabic question/answering. In *International Journal on Information and Communication Technologies 3, no. 3*, pages 37–51.

Mohammed Akour, Sameer Abufardeh, Kenneth Magel, and Qasemm Al-Radaideh. 2011. Qarabpro: A rule based question answering system for reading comprehension tests in arabic. *American Journal of Applied Sciences*, 8(6):652.

Ahmad Al Sallab, Hazem Hajj, Gilbert Badaro, Ramy Baly, Wassim El Hajj, and Khaled Bashir Shaban. 2015. Deep learning models for sentiment analysis in arabic. In *Proceedings of the second workshop on Arabic natural language processing*, pages 9–17.

Aqil M Azmi and Nouf A Alshenaifi. 2016. Answering arabic why-questions: Baseline vs. rst-based approach. *ACM Transactions on Information Systems (TOIS)*, 35(1):6.

---

[5] https://github.com/google-research/bert

[6] https://github.com/NLPLearn/QANet

Gilbert Badaro, Obeida El Jundi, Alaa Khaddaj, Alaa Maarouf, Raslan Kain, Hazem Hajj, and Wassim El-Hajj. 2018. Ema at semeval-2018 task 1: Emotion mining for arabic. In *Proceedings of The 12th International Workshop on Semantic Evaluation*, pages 236–244.

Yonatan Belinkov, Alberto Barrón-Cedeño, and Hamdy Mubarak. 2015. Answer selection in arabic community question answering: A feature-rich approach. In *Proceedings of the Second Workshop on Arabic Natural Language Processing*, pages 183–190.

Abdelouahid Lyhyaoui Benajiba Yassine, Paolo Rosso. 2007. Implementation of the arabiqa question answering system's components. In *Proc. Workshop on Arabic Natural Language Processing, 2nd Information Communication Technologies Int. Symposium, ICTIS-2007, Fez, Morroco, April*, pages 3–5.

Steven Bird. 2006. Nltk: The natural language toolkit. In *COLING ACL 2006*, page 69.

Danqi Chen, Adam Fisch, Jason Weston, and Antoine Bordes. 2017. Reading wikipedia to answer open-domain questions. In *Proceedings of the 55th Annual Meeting of the Association for Computational Linguistics (Volume 1: Long Papers)*, volume 1, pages 1870–1879.

Rajarshi Das, Shehzaad Dhuliawala, Manzil Zaheer, and Andrew McCallum. 2018. Multi-step retriever-reader interaction for scalable open-domain question answering.

Jacob Devlin, Ming-Wei Chang, Kenton Lee, and Kristina Toutanova. 2018. Bert: Pre-training of deep bidirectional transformers for language understanding. *arXiv preprint arXiv:1810.04805*.

Walaa Saber Ismail and Masun Nabhan Homsi. 2018. Dawqas: A dataset for arabic why question answering system. In *Procedia computer science 142*, pages 123–131.

Mandar Joshi, Eunsol Choi, Daniel S Weld, and Luke Zettlemoyer. 2017. Triviaqa: A large scale distantly supervised challenge dataset for reading comprehension. *arXiv preprint arXiv:1705.03551*.

Armand Joulin, Edouard Grave, Piotr Bojanowski, Matthijs Douze, Hérve Jégou, and Tomas Mikolov. 2016. Fasttext.zip: Compressing text classification models. *arXiv preprint arXiv:1612.03651*.

Tom Kwiatkowski, Jennimaria Palomaki, Olivia Redfield, Michael Collins, Ankur Parikh, Chris Alberti, Danielle Epstein, Illia Polosukhin, Matthew Kelcey, Jacob Devlin, Kenton Lee, Kristina N. Toutanova, Llion Jones, Ming-Wei Chang, Andrew Dai, Jakob Uszkoreit, Quoc Le, and Slav Petrov. 2019. Natural questions: a benchmark for question answering research. *Transactions of the Association of Computational Linguistics*.

Jens Lehmann, Robert Isele, Max Jakob, Anja Jentzsch, Dimitris Kontokostas, Pablo N Mendes, Sebastian Hellmann, Mohamed Morsey, Patrick Van Kleef, Sören Auer, et al. 2015. Dbpedia–a large-scale, multilingual knowledge base extracted from wikipedia. *Semantic Web*, 6(2):167–195.

Yankai Lin, Haozhe Ji, Zhiyuan Liu, and Maosong Sun. 2018. Denoising distantly supervised open-domain question answering. In *Proceedings of the 56th Annual Meeting of the Association for Computational Linguistics (Volume 1: Long Papers)*, volume 1, pages 1736–1745.

Preslav Nakov, Doris Hoogeveen, Lluís Màrquez, Alessandro Moschitti, Hamdy Mubarak, Timothy Baldwin, and Karin Verspoor. 2017. Semeval-2017 task 3: Community question answering. In *Proceedings of the 11th International Workshop on Semantic Evaluation (SemEval-2017)*, pages 27–48.

Arfath Pasha, Mohamed Al-Badrashiny, Mona Diab, Ahmed El Kholy, Ramy Eskander, Nizar Habash, Manoj Pooleery, Owen Rambow, and Ryan Roth. 2014. Madamira: A fast, comprehensive tool for morphological analysis and disambiguation of arabic. In *Proceedings of the Ninth International Conference on Language Resources and Evaluation (LREC-2014)*.

Eduard H. Hovy Pamela Forner lvaro Rodrigo Richard FE Sutcliffe Corina Forascu Peas, Anselmo and Caroline Sporleder. 2011. Overview of qa4mre at clef 2011: Question answering for machine reading evaluation. In *CLEF (Notebook Papers/Labs/Workshop)*, pages 1–20.

Pranav Rajpurkar, Jian Zhang, Konstantin Lopyrev, and Percy Liang. 2016. Squad: 100,000+ questions for machine comprehension of text. *arXiv preprint arXiv:1606.05250*.

Matthew Richardson, Christopher JC Burges, and Erin Renshaw. 2013. Mctest: A challenge dataset for the open-domain machine comprehension of text. In *Proceedings of the 2013 Conference on Empirical Methods in Natural Language Processing*, pages 193–203.

Minjoon Seo, Aniruddha Kembhavi, Ali Farhadi, and Hannaneh Hajishirzi. 2016. Bidirectional attention flow for machine comprehension. *arXiv preprint arXiv:1611.01603*.

Mohamed Shaheen and Ahmed Magdy Ezzeldin. 2014. Arabic question answering: systems, resources, tools, and future trends. *Arabian Journal for Science and Engineering*, 39(6):4541–4564.

Omar Trigui, Lamia Hadrich Belguith, and Paolo Rosso. 2010. Defarabicqa: Arabic definition question answering system. In *Workshop on Language Resources and Human Language Technologies for Semitic Languages, 7th LREC, Valletta, Malta*, pages 40–45.

Adam Trischler, Tong Wang, Xingdi Yuan, Justin Harris, Alessandro Sordoni, Philip Bachman, and Kaheer Suleman. 2017. Newsqa: A machine comprehension dataset. *ACL 2017*, page 191.

Ashish Vaswani, Noam Shazeer, Niki Parmar, Jakob Uszkoreit, Llion Jones, Aidan N Gomez, ukasz Kaiser, and Illia Polosukhin. 2017. Attention is all you need. In *Advances in neural information processing systems*, pages 5998–6008.

Shuohang Wang, Mo Yu, Xiaoxiao Guo, Zhiguo Wang, Tim Klinger, Wei Zhang, Shiyu Chang, Gerry Tesauro, Bowen Zhou, and Jing Jiang. 2018a. R 3: Reinforced ranker-reader for open-domain question answering. In *Thirty-Second AAAI Conference on Artificial Intelligence*.

Zhen Wang, Jiachen Liu, Xinyan Xiao, Yajuan Lyu, and Tian Wu. 2018b. Joint training of candidate extraction and answer selection for reading comprehension. *arXiv preprint arXiv:1805.06145*.

Yonghui Wu, Mike Schuster, Zhifeng Chen, Quoc V Le, Mohammad Norouzi, Wolfgang Macherey, Maxim Krikun, Yuan Cao, Qin Gao, Klaus Macherey, et al. 2016. Google's neural machine translation system: Bridging the gap between human and machine translation. *arXiv preprint arXiv:1609.08144*.

Yi Yang, Wen-tau Yih, and Christopher Meek. 2015. Wikiqa: A challenge dataset for open-domain question answering. In *Proceedings of the 2015 Conference on Empirical Methods in Natural Language Processing*, pages 2013–2018.

Adams Wei Yu, David Dohan, Minh-Thang Luong, Rui Zhao, Kai Chen, Mohammad Norouzi, and Quoc V Le. 2018. Qanet: Combining local convolution with global self-attention for reading comprehension. *arXiv preprint arXiv:1804.09541*.

Segmentation for Domain Adaptation in Arabic

Mohammed Attia and **Ali Elkahky**
Google LLC
New York, USA
`{attia,alielkahky}@google.com`

Abstract

Segmentation serves as an integral part in many NLP applications including Machine Translation, Parsing, and Information Retrieval. When a model trained on the standard language is applied to dialects, the accuracy drops dramatically. However, there are more lexical items shared by the standard language and dialects than can be found by mere surface word matching. This shared lexicon is obscured by a lot of cliticization, gemination, and character repetition. In this paper, we prove that segmentation and base normalization of dialects can help in domain adaptation by reducing data sparseness. Segmentation will improve a system performance by reducing the number of OOVs, help isolate the differences and allow better utilization of the commonalities. We show that adding a small amount of dialectal segmentation training data reduced OOVs by 5% and remarkably improves POS tagging for dialects by 7.37% f-score, even though no dialect-specific POS training data is included.

1 Introduction

Processing of informal and dialectal data is increasingly becoming the focus of attention for many NLP tasks particularly due to the growing popularity of the various social media platforms and messaging apps which have transformed the way people interact and communicate with each other on daily basis and accelerated the pace of change of the language used on the web. Today, many people write in the language they speak, leading to the influx of informal and dialectal data with the huge challenges they pose, most prominently among them are the non-standard orthography (like repeated characters for emphasis), abbreviations, non-conventional syntactic structures, spelling variability as well as mispellings, and code-switching. These phenomena have been largely ignored in mainstream language processing models which mostly relied on (and also expected) standard, monolingual, clean, and edited texts.

Moreover, the emergence of intelligent personal assistant systems (such as Siri, Alexa, Cortana and Google Assistant) have created a paradigm shift in how people interact with smart devices. Instead of issuing key words searches and formal questions, they are now more tempted to speak casually with these systems using their everyday language, which lays a growing burden on virtual assistants to accommodate unconventional (and previously unseen) queries and requests.

In this paper we show how NLP applications can scale up their performance on dialectal data by integrating a basic and simple preprocessing step, i.e. segmentation. The process of segmentation is important for languages where the notion of word does not straightforwardly align with the common concept of a space-delimited string. Arabic is a clitic language, where syntactic units can attach to other lexemes, and segmentation means identifying and splitting these syntactic units from the main lexemes or from each others. This is not a deterministic process, as we need to tell, for example, whether the letter و wa is a conjunction as in وخالد wa-Khaled "and Khaled" or part of the internal word build-up as in وحيد wahid "Wahid".

This paper is structured as follows. Section 2 gives a brief account of the related research on standard and dialectal segmentation of Arabic. In Section 3 we introduce our segmentation annotation scheme, explaining the meaning of clitics and how different they are from affixes, and compare our annotation convention to other approaches. Section 4 gives the details of our work on dialectal data collection, explaining the challenges facing extraction, filtration and sampling. Section 5

119

Proceedings of the Fourth Arabic Natural Language Processing Workshop, pages 119–129
Florence, Italy, August 1, 2019. ©2019 Association for Computational Linguistics

spells out our hypothesis on how segmentation can help in domain adaptation and the approach we follow to test this hypothesis. In Section 6 we describe our parsing system and the features used. In Section 7 we explain our experimental setup and discuss the results, and finally Section 8 concludes.

2   Related Work

Segmentation of MSA has frequently been handled as part of a pipeline with multiple processes (including morphological analysis, and POS tagging). For example, MADA (Habash and Rambow, 2005; Habash et al., 2009) is a system that uses an SVM-based classifier to disambiguate the output of the Buckwalter morphological analyzer which conveniently also provided diacritization and English glosses. By contrast, AMIRA (Diab et al., 2004; Diab, 2009) is a lexicon-independent system for Arabic that conducts segmentation as well POS tagging and base-phrase chunking. Both systems are trained on the LDC's Arabic Treebank (ATB) data and both report an accuracy above 99%. The high accuracy is probably attributed to the high quality and low noise in this edited data.

Treating segmentation as a specialized task, Aliwy (2012) developed a hybrid system for Arabic segmentation trained on a manually-annotated dataset of 29k words extracted from the Al-Watan corpus and reports an accuracy score of 98.83%. Abdelali et al. (2016) developed a segmenter for their tool, Farasa, using SVM and trained on the ATB data with reported accuracy of 98.94%. Moreover, Mohamed (2018) developed a memory-based learning segmenter for Arabic religious texts trained on a manually annotated in-domain corpus of 27k words combined with the ATB data with reported accuracy of 95.70%.

Regarding Egyptian segmentation, Mohamed et al. (2012) developed a memory-based segmenter for Egyptian Arabic trained on manually-annotated user-generated data including 20k words combined with the ATB data and reported an accuracy of 91.90%. Habash et al. (2013) developed MADA-ARZ as an Egyptian extension to MADA, the MSA morphological processor. The approach they took was to replace the MSA analyzer SAMA with the ARZ analyzer CALIMA, and again disambiguate the output using an SVM classifier, and reported a segmentation adccuracy of 97.5%. Monroe et al. (2014) augment a pre-

viously developed character-level CRF-based segmenter for MSA with more features to accommodate Egyptian Arabic achieving an f-score of 92.09% on an Egyptian test data.

More recently Samih et al. (2017a) developed an Egyptian segmenter using neural architecture of Bi-LSTM with a CRF optimizer trained on a small dataset of 350 Egyptian tweets (8k words) and reported an f-score of 92.65%. They later extended their work to cover Gulf, Moroccan and Levantine Arabic (Samih et al., 2017b; Eldesouki et al., 2017).

3   Dialect Segmentation Convention

Clitics are prevalent and highly frequent in Arabic as they span a large class of function morphemes including conjunctions, negation, progressive and future particles, object and possessive pronouns, and the definite article. And these function morphemes attach to verbs (as in Table 1), nouns (as in Table 2), or other function words or morphemes.

3.1   Annotation Guidelines

Token	Sub-Type	Possible Values
Proclitic	Conj	و wa "and"
	Neg.	م ma "not" ⋆
	Compl.	ل li "to"
	Particle	ب bi "prog." ⋆
	Particle	ـس, sa, ـه ha ⋆ "will"
Stem		يحب yuhib "like"
Enclitic	Obj pron	ـه hu, و uw ⋆ "him"
	Post-Prep	ل li "to" ⋆
	PObj Pron	ـه hu, و uw "him" ⋆
	Post Neg	ش shi "not" ⋆

Table 1: clitics with a verb. Note that the progressive and future particles are in complementary distribution. ⋆ used in EG only.

The annotation guidelines are fairly straightforward. Here are the main instructions followed during annotation.

- Segment words in a way that would reflect the correct number of part of speech tags as in Tables 1 and 2 above.

- Words merged with other words should be separated, e.g. عبد+الله "Abdullah"

ما+شاء+ه+الله "God willing".

- When the post-preposition is fused with the last letter of the stem, the post-preposition should be retained at the expense of the stem, e.g. بـ+قو+لـ+ك "I am saying to you".

- Hashtags, emoticons and user names are treated as single units, e.g. #الحمد_لله "Thank_God", :-), and @mohamed_ali.

- Sometime letters are repeated for emphasis, in this case the token boundary is maintained, e.g. ووو+أخيييراااااا "annnnd finallllly".

- With spelling errors, we segment as if words are written correctly, e.g. رحلتـ+ه "his trip".

- Interrogative words and interjections are treated as one unit, e.g. مش "not" بلاش "don't" ليه "why".

- Some words are common, but nonetheless should be tokenized, e.g. م + حد+ش "no one", م + فيـ+ش "nothing".

- When vowels on prepositions are changed from short to long, the long vowel is considered as part of the preposition, e.g. معا+ه "with him", ليـ+هم "to them" بيـ+هم "by them".

Token	Sub-Type	Possible Values
Proclitic	Conj	و wa "and"
	Prep.	ل li "to"
	Det.	ال Al "the"
Stem		كتاب kitAb "book"
Enclitic	Poss pron	ـه hu "his"

Table 2: clitics with a noun. Note that the determiner and the possessive pronoun are in complementary distribution.

3.2 Clitics vs. Affixes

Clitics are different from affixes in that prefixes and suffixes are **morphological markers** that indicate tense, number, person, gender, case, etc., while clitics are **syntactic units** (like prepositions, conjunctions, pronouns and particles) with separate part of speech functions, but happen

to attached to other words. The difference is shown further by the example in the syntactic tree in Figure 1. Note how the verb retains the imperfective and plural markers, and the noun maintains the feminine marker.

Example: هيدفعوها للحكومة will-pay-it to-the-government (2 words = 6 token sentence)

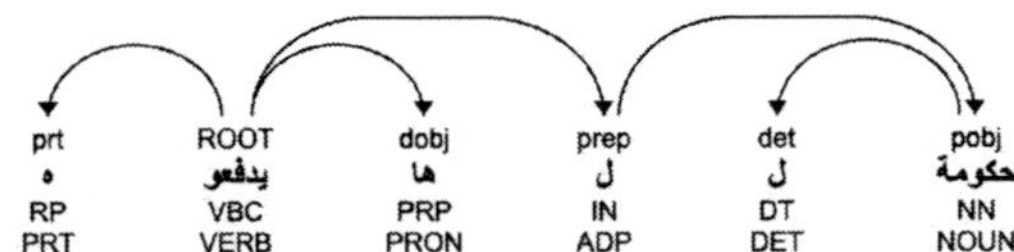

Figure 1: Clitics on a Syntactic Tree

Clitics can be challenging for intelligent virtual assistant applications dealing with Arabic in many areas. The problem is that without proper segmentation, it's impossible for the system to correctly identify the triggering phrase or the span of an argument, may it be a message, contact name, location, or artist name. Here are a few examples categorized by topic:

1. Planning:

   - فكرني بشراء اللبن fak~arni bi-$ira' Al-laban "Remind me to-buy milk".
     Type of attached argument: reminder subject

2. Communication:

   - اتصل بأحمد it~asil bi-Ahmed "Make a call to-Ahmed".
     Type of attached argument: contact name

3. Media:

   - أغنية لعمرو دياب >ugniyah li-Amr Diab "A song by-Amr Diab".
     Type of attached argument: artist

4. Device Control:

   - علي الصوت بأربع نقاط Eal~i al-Suwt bi->arbaE niqaT "Raise volume by-five points".
     Type of attached argument: numeric value

5. Local directions:

- المسافة بين البيت والعمل al-masafap bayn al-bayt wa-al-Eamal "distance between home and-work".

Type of attached argument: location

3.3 The definite article dilemma

Arabic has only one determiner, the definite article ال Al "the". However, different conventions conflicted on whether to consider it as a morphological marker or a syntactic unit (clitic). While all other clitics have some free-form counterparts of their own category, e.g. و wa "and" (a bound conjunction), ثم vum~a "then" (a free conjunction), ب bi "in" (a bound preposition), and في fiy "in" (a free preposition), the definite article is unique in its category. It constitutes one of two ways by which a noun can be definite, the other being through idafa or compounding in a genitive/possessive sense, such as كتاب الطالب kitAb Al-Talib "the student's book". Therefore, the definite article bears similarities to both morphological markers and clitics. In a parse tree it can be either separated from the noun and be represented as a determiner headed by the noun, or stay merged with the noun and a feature called "state" is marked as 'definite'.

In the LDC Arabic treebank, the definite article is treated as morphological marker (i.e. not considered as a separate token), and therefore, most NLP applications based on this data model reflect this convention. In most other research efforts, such as (Abdelali et al., 2016; Aliwy, 2012; Mohamed, 2018; Habash et al., 2012), it is considered as a clitic and is segmented away from the nouns and adjectives they attach to.

It is also observed that the affinity of the determiner to the modified element changes by the type of the noun or adjective it is attached to. While it is perfectly separable with common nouns, e.g. الكتاب Al-kitAp "the-book" and الطالب Al-TAlib "the-student", it becomes more rigid with proper nouns such as, البرادعي Al-Baradei and السيسي Al-Sisi. However, the boundaries are not always clear and the distinction become somewhat blurry when a proper name has a composition meaning, such as شارع الاستقلال $ariE Al-<isotiqolAl "Street of (the) Independence", or a homograph, such as الخنافس Al-xanAfis "The Beatles" or "the beatles". Even with proper nouns where the definite article seems frozen, it needs to be omitted in cerain cases, partcularly when the noun is preceded by a vocative particle, e.g. يا سيسي yA sisi "O, Sisi".

3.4 Comparison of Segmentation Conventions

Our segmentation convention matches with (Aliwy, 2012; Mohamed, 2018; Habash et al., 2012) where clitics are split from words and the of notion of clitics is aligned as the syntactic units that can be assigned a POS tag and can occupy a node on the syntactic tree. It is also similar to the Penn Arabic Treebank (ATB) (Maamouri et al., 2004) with the exception of the definite article where we consider it as a clitic while in the ATB it is taken as a definiteness marker.

However, the segmentation scheme adopted here is significantly different from that of Farasa (Abdelali et al., 2016; Samih et al., 2017a,b; El-desouki et al., 2017) in a number of ways. While Farasa segments all clitics as we do, they also split a number of additional morphemes as follows:

- The feminine marker is split from the noun, e.g. طالبة "student.fem" is split as طالب+ة. This convention, however, fails to recognize the fact that in Arabic the gender marker can indicate natural gender, as in the example above, or just a grammatical gender, such as ساعة "watch", حاجة "thing", and نسبة "ratio". Splitting the feminine marker in the later cases results in incomplete stems, or non-words.

- Dual and plural suffixes with nouns are split, such as كتاب+ين "book.dual", مدرس+ون "teacher.pl" and طالب+ات "student.fem+pl". The problem of oversegmentation shows again with the feminine plural with the grammatical gender, e.g. حاج+ات "things" and ساع+ات "watches". And while it normalizes stems for sound plurals, it leaves broken plurals unhandled, e.g. كتب kutub "books" the plural of كتاب kitAb "book".

- Number, gender, and person suffixes with verbs are split, such as ذهب+وا "went.pl" and ذهب+ت "went.fem". Farasa considers these suffixes as subject pronouns. However, this approach fails to acknowledge that Arabic is a pro-drop language, and the person, number, and gender affixes are just added to permit the dropping of the subject and allow for its semantic reconstruction.

- Case marker suffixes with nouns are split, such as كتابها "book.acc". This is clearly an affix, and splitting it causes a problem with frozen adverbs, such as أيضها "also" and طبعها "naturally".

Therefore, as illustrated above, the Farasa convention is a midway between a stemmer, and segmenter. It is to be noted that a stemmer aims to split all affixes and suffixes regardless of their nature, while a segmenter splits only bound morphemes that are syntactic units (or clitics) in nature.

4 Data Collection and Analysis

4.1 Challenges of Dialectal Data Collection

There are over 22 Arab countries with 22 national dialects and even larger number of sub-dialects. The population ranges from around 100m to less than 1m. Natural Language Understanding (NLU) systems that perform well on MSA are likely to face difficulties dealing with the various dialects. As dialects are becoming the main medium of the interaction between the Intelligent Personal Assistants and the Arabic speakers, it is important to have well-scaled NLP tools, with a good segmenter as a starting point. Here we develop a generic process for data collection and sampling that can be applied to one or more dialects.

With data collection, there are a number of challenges that need to be taken into consideration.

- Intra-sentential code switching: some user-generated data can contain a mix between MSA and dialects or dialect and a foreign language..

- Pan-Arab pages. Some web pages are popular across the Arab world and can attract audience from different regions, and therefore, it is not immediately obvious what dialect the comment is written in.

- Expatriates. Gulf states have a large number of expatriates. In Saudi Arabia, for instance, there are 2m Syrians, 1m Sudanese, and 1m Egyptians. For another example, only 17%

of residents in Dubai are Emiratis. Therefore, relying on the location of the user or the webpage alone can be misleading.

- Neighboring dialects. Within a particular region, dialects can be significantly similar. So, how can we separate Moroccan from Algerian, Saudi from Kuwaiti and Lebanese from Syrian?

4.2 Dialect Filtration

To handle the challenges mentioned above, our approach to dialectal data collection consists of a two-stage filtration process. We apply this process to four dialects (Egyptian, Saudi, Moroccan and Algerian). The reason for selecting these four dialects in particular is that we wanted to see how our method performs on dialects from discrete regions (Egyptian, Saudi and Moroccan) as well as dialects from neighboring countries (Moroccan and Algerian).

1. By locale. Detecting the location of the webpage and user who made the comment.

2. By seed-words. We construct dialect-specific word lists that contains high frequency, high confidence lexical items.

In the first filtration stage, we crawl data from local news websites as well as user-generated data (blogs, user comments, and social media posts) from the target countries: Egypt, Saudi Arabia, Morocco and Algeria.

We observe that user-generated data is outpacing edited data, and the makeup and structure of data on the web is rapidly changing. It seems that social media and sites allowing free comments and reviews are giving people unprecedented and mostly uncensored freedom and expressive power, which they seem to utilize effectively.

The second filtration stage is the development of dialect seed word. Lists of dialectal words available online are very limited in size, not well maintained, and have no information on frequency. Therefore, we extract our own wordlists from corpora. The assumption is that dialectal words will fail when matched against a standard lexicon. We randomly select 1m words from the data that we crawled, and we match them against an MSA lexicon primarily meant for spell checking (Attia et al., 2012).

We observe that the rate of unknown words in user-generated data ranges from 6% to 7%, and it can go up to as high as 20% with purely colloquial data, such as regional tales. We assume that the unknown words are most likely to be dialectal. To check the validity of this assumption, we select unknown words and order by frequency. We focus on top frequency words as these are assumed to contain function and common words that fit as good candidates for a seed list. Then we manually analyze the top 100 words for the Egyptian user-generated data. Figure 2 shows that over half of the words are actually dialectal, the remaining words are either spelling errors or names entities or standard words that happen not to be found in the spell checking wordlist.

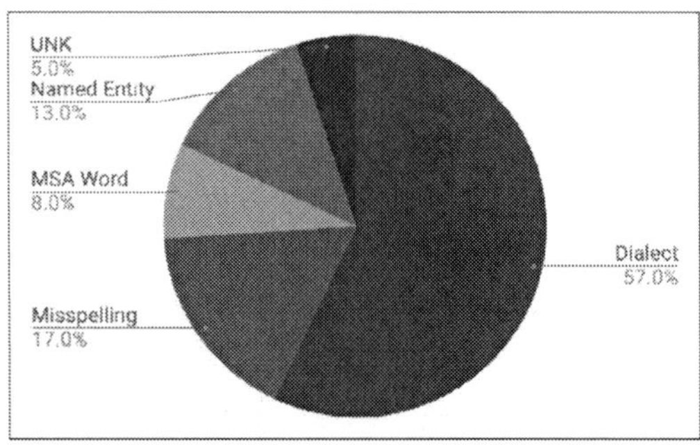

Figure 2: Analysis of Unknown Words in Corpora

4.3 Dialect Lexical Intersection

Having collected lists of potential seed words for the four target dialect and sorted them by frequency, now we try to evaluate how well can these seed words distinguish one dialect from the other. We test the distinctive nature of these lists by looking at the intersection between them with regards to the top 200 most frequent words. Figure 3 illustrates the results of the evaluation, where it shows two remarkable observations: 1) Dialects from different regions have lower intersection (below 20%), and 2) dialects from the same region have greater overlap (above 30%).

4.4 Data Sampling

Manual annotation of data is expensive and time consuming. Therefore, it is important to sample the data in such a way that we obtain the best possible coverage for the least possible amount of data. Data sampling is discussed in Active Learning as the need to strike the right balance between exploration and exploitation over the data space representation (Bouneffouf et al., 2014). The idea is that a system that only "exploits" will be too

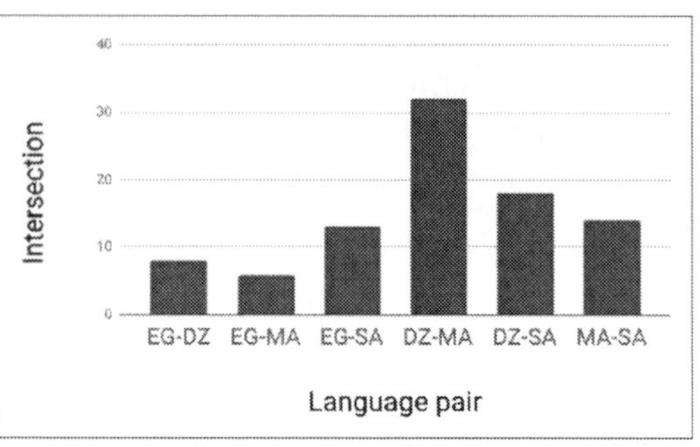

Figure 3: Lexical Overlap between Dialects. EG: Egyptian, DZ: Algerian, SA: Saudi, MA: Moroccan

specialized and unable to generalize, and a system that only "explores" does not improve its predictive power, and hence is the need to make the proper compromise between the two. In our sampling we try to select data that is representative, diverse, and lexically and syntactically varied. In order to achieve this goal, we rely on two criteria: sentence length and similarity matching.

1. Sentence Length. Different sentence lengths usually indicate different user fluency levels and represent different syntactic structures. We define 9 ranges for sentence length: 5–9, 10–14, 15–19, 20–24, 25–29, 30–34, 35–39, 40–44, 45–49. Then we extract an equal number of sentences from each length range. We excluded sentences shorter than 5 as they mostly included interjections and confirmation phrases, and longer than 49 as they include run-on sentences.

2. Similarity Matching. Exact repetitions, semi-repetitions, and similar sentences exist in any data collection, but they are particularly rampant in user-generated data. While it is straightforward to spot exact repetitions, or duplicates, and discard them, it is more challenging to identify similar sentences and to set out a threshold for this similarity, so that each sentence added to the annotation will ultimately carry an added-value to the system performance. There are mainly two paradigms for string matching: edit distance and longest common subsequence (LCS). Edit distance, as defined by Levenshtein (1966) tries to find one of three edit operations (insertion, deletion and substitution) when matching two strings. By contrast, the LCS (Wagner and Fischer, 1974) looks for

the longest subsequence that is common to two strings. To illustrate with an example, we evaluate these two stings using the two measures.

- "I saw the first episode." شاهدت الحلقة الأولى.
- "I saw the second episode." شاهدت الحلقة الثانية.

Using the edit distance, we obtain a similarity score[1] of 75.68% while with LCS, we get a score[2] of 81.08%, which means that LCS perceives the two sentences as more similar than the edit distance. By nature, the edit distance focuses on the differences, while LCS is more suited for finding similarities. Therefore we choose LCS (or SequenceMatcher) in our sampling method and set the threshold at 70%, so that any sentence that is similar to any existing sentence by this threshold or higher gets discarded.

5 Hypothesis and Approach

Dialects, by definition, are subsets of the standard language (or koiné) and they can easily, readily and freely draw from the larger repository. Therefore dialects should not be treated as separate and independent entities, but as a subtype that inherits from and extends a larger archetype. Dialects should be conceived of as the aggregate of the standard language and local variant.

Dialects diverge from the standard language and at the same time have a lot in common with this 'mother' language. Our hypothesis is that dialects can be accommodated fairly well without going through the lengthy and expensive acquisition of complete and new datasets, but through actively seeking and covering dialectal words, phrases and sentences as an add-on component that can be plugged in with the standard language.

Figure 4 demonstrates a prototype of our hypothesis showing the idea that if we inject specifically-targeted dialectal segmentation training data into the standard dataset and rebuild our model, we can achieve better support and coverage for dialects at a higher level of representation, namely POS tagging, by utilizing the shared lexi-

___
[1] edit distance / (len(substr1)+len(substr2)/2) * 100

[2] As implemented in the SequenceMatcher in the difflib library

con and reducing the number of OOV's and without having any dialectal POS training data.

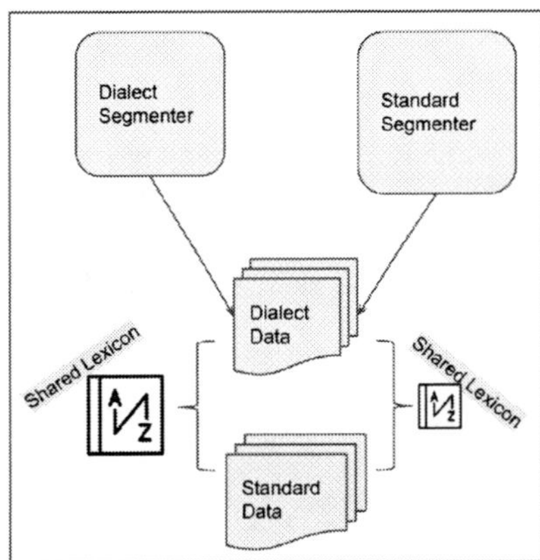

Figure 4: Anticipated Shared Lexicon Size

In order to test this hypothesis, we conduct the following three steps.

1. Manually annotate Egyptian dialectal segmentation data. After extracting and sampling the data, we manually annotate 1,058 sentences and split them into 739 sentences for training, 158 for validation and 157 for testing. Only the testing set is also annotated for POS tags besides segmentation.

2. Develop a segmentation model from the MSA data alone and another model from the combination of the MSA and dialectal data. The MSA data contains 9,717 sentences (399,774 tokens) and includes news articles (covering politics, sports, entertainment, business, health, sci-tech, arts), Wikipedia articles web articles (including blogs, forums, reviews).

3. Run the dialectal and standard segmenters on the dialect test set, evaluate how many words are shared with the dialect and MSA, and check the impact on the POS tagger. Hopefully the output of the model with dialectal data will have more shared lexicon with the Arabic standard dataset and improved POS tagging score.

6 System Description

In our experiments we use an arc-eager transition based dependency parser (Nivre, 2003) with a model trained using a linear SVM architecture similar to the one in Yamada and Matsumoto

(2003). When experimenting with morphological features, we add the morphological attributes for both stack-top and buffer-top tokens.

Features:

- A window of +/- 3 characters of uni-grams and bi-grams around the current position.

- A tri-gram of current character of previous two character

- A tri-gram of current character of next two character

- whether the current character is punctuation

- whether the current character is a digit

- Word length and position within a word

- First and last two characters of the current word

Our segmenter is part of a dependency tree parser for Arabic. Computational implementation within the Dependency Grammars framework has been realized in the creation of dependency tree-banks, such as the Prague Dependency Treebank (Hajič et al., 2001), the Stanford Dependencies (De Marneffe and Manning, 2008) and Universal Dependencies (Nivre et al., 2016; McDonald et al., 2013), and the development of dependency parsers, such as the Stanford parser (Chen and Manning, 2014), the inductive dependency parser (Nivre et al., 2004) and the MaltParser (Nivre et al., 2007).

A dependency parser complies with the Dependency Grammar formalisms. Within the Dependency Grammar, dependency relations can be represented either in a relational format or in a graph format. In a relational format, the representation is a triple which shows the relation between a pair of words. The head of the dependency relation is given as the first argument and the dependent as the second. This relationship is represented as follows:

```
relation(head, dependent)
```

For example, the sentence حضر الأولاد "the boys came" can be formulated as:

nsubj(حضر , أولاد) – det(أولاد, ال)

Similarly, in the graph representation the dependency arc points from the head category to the dependent category, and the relation (or grammatical function) is realized as a label on the arc as shown in Figure 5.

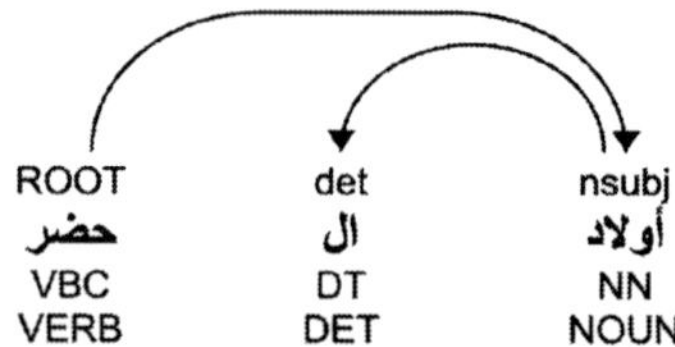

Figure 5: Sample Dependency Graphs

7 Experiments and Results

We have a high performance MSA segmenter, and when we adapt to the dialectal domain, we want to make sure that the performance on MSA data does not suffer from significant degradation. Therefore we build two models, one using the MSA data alone, and the other using MSA data combined with the Egyptian (EG) dialectal segmentation training data, and we evaluate both systems on the MSA and EG test sets.

| Model trained on | Segmentation Eval | |
segmentation data from	MSA	EG
MSA	97.91	82.56
MSA+EG	97.62	91.40

Table 3: Egyptian Segmentation Evaluation

As Table 3 shows, the model trained on MSA gives an F-1 score of 97.91% on the MSA test data and a remarkably lower score on the EG data (82.56%). For a task as basic as segmentation, this level of performance is not reliable to pass on to other downstream or upstream tasks such as IR or MT. When we train our model on the combined data of MSA+EG, there is a slight reduction in the performance on the MSA test set (about 0.3% absolute), while there a huge performance boost on the EG test set (8.84% absolute). The overall score on EG is 91.40%, which is not close to the performance on MSA data, but this is understandable given the small size of the training data, and it is still comparable to the scores reported in the literature: 91.90% by Mohamed et al. (2012), and 92.65% by Samih et al. (2017a). This also illustrates the need to invest in acquiring more annotated data for dialects.

Now we want to evaluate if this improvement on the EG segmentation will cascade up the processing pipeline and help the MSA POS tagger adapt to the dialectal domain. We run our POS tagger on three different segmentation inputs: predictions of the MSA segmenter, predictions of the MSA+EG segmenter, and gold segmentation. The reason we test on the gold segmentation is to see the headroom for improvement if we have a 'perfect' segmenter.

Model trained on segmentation data from	POS Eval	
	MSA	EG
MSA	94.36	66.70
MSA+EG	94.10	74.07
Gold data	96.66	81.33

Table 4: Egyptian POS Evaluation

Table 4 shows that the loss with MSA POS tagging from adding the new dialectal data is fractional (0.26% absolute). It also shows that using the MSA segmenter predictions as input, the POS tagger achieved only 66.70% f-1 measure on the EG test set. This has risen to 74.07% when using the MSA+EG segmenter predictions, a remarkable increase of 7.37% absolute. Improving the EG segmenter further can give a headroom up to 81.33%, which is another increase of 7.26% absolute. This is a significant improvement on the system performance that has been gained economically with few resources. This confirms our original hypothesis that segmentation can help with dialectal domain adaptation. One explanation of how the segmentation helps the POS tagging is that doing the right segmentation in EG data reduces the number of OOV tokens with respect to the POS tagging model, even when the POS tagger is trained with only MSA data. To verify that, we show , in Figure 7, the percentage OOV tokens for the POS tagger model when the data is segmented using the segmenter trained with MSA only, the MSA+EG segmenter or using the gold segmentation. MSA+EG segmeter reduced the OOV by 5% points absolute which is 25% relative reduction in OOV.

However, we observe that we cannot obtain POS tagging results for dialect comparable to MSA scores using segmentation alone. There will be a need for some in-domain POS training data, and we envision the optimal model of a parser training is to follow what we call a "data trape-

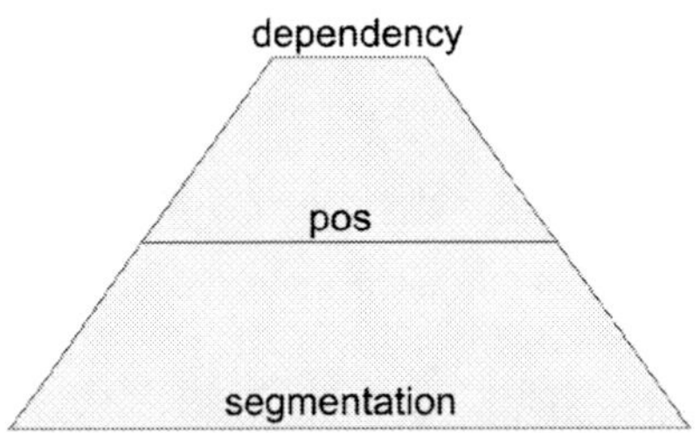

Figure 6: Data Trapezoid

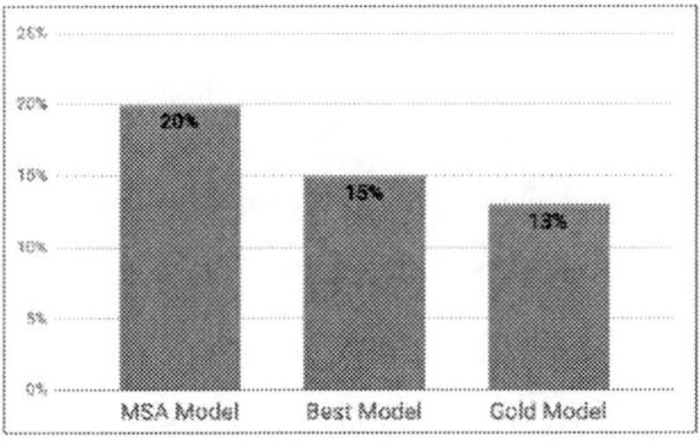

Figure 7: OOV percentage in POS Evaluation Data as segmented by different segmentation models

zoid", as shown in Figure 6. The data trapezoid has a wider base for segmentation training data, a medium base for POS tagging, and a narrower base for dependency annotation. As annotating data for POS and dependency is very costly and time-consuming, We believe that this model can achieve the right balance and compromise between resources to achieve reasonable system performance.

8 Conclusion

In this paper we have shown how segmentation helps in domain adaptation by scaling up the performance of a system trained on a standard language when it is applied to dialect. We showed how the injection of EG segmentation training data in a parser remarkably improves POS tagging despite the fact that no dialectal POS training data is included. From a few hundred dialectal segmentation sentences, we obtain a boost in POS tagging by 7.37% absolute. This does not per se eliminate the need for POS training data, but we suggest a data trapezoid model where there is a wide base of segmentation data, and a comparatively smaller amount of POS data and a yet smaller amount for dependency trees, a model that aligns with the time, effort and cost needed for each layer.

References

Ahmed Abdelali, Kareem Darwish, Nadir Durrani, and Hamdy Mubarak. 2016. Farasa: A fast and furious segmenter for arabic. In *Proceedings of the 2016 Conference of the North American Chapter of the Association for Computational Linguistics: Demonstrations*, pages 11–16.

Ahmed H. Aliwy. 2012. Tokenization as preprocessing for arabic tagging system. *International Journal of Information and Education Technology*, 2(4):348.

Mohammed Attia, Pavel Pecina, Younes Samih, Khaled Shaalan, and Josef Van Genabith. 2012. Improved spelling error detection and correction for arabic. *Proceedings of COLING 2012: Posters*, pages 103–112.

Djallel Bouneffouf, Romain Laroche, Tanguy Urvoy, Raphael Féraud, and Robin Allesiardo. 2014. Contextual bandit for active learning: Active thompson sampling. In *International Conference on Neural Information Processing*, pages 405–412. Springer.

Danqi Chen and Christopher Manning. 2014. A fast and accurate dependency parser using neural networks. In *Proceedings of the 2014 conference on empirical methods in natural language processing (EMNLP)*, pages 740–750.

Marie-Catherine De Marneffe and Christopher D. Manning. 2008. The stanford typed dependencies representation. In *COLING 2008: Proceedings of the Workshop on Cross-framework and Cross-domain Parser Evaluation*, pages 1–8. Association for Computational Linguistics.

Mona Diab. 2009. Second generation amira tools for arabic processing: Fast and robust tokenization, pos tagging, and base phrase chunking. In *2nd International Conference on Arabic Language Resources and Tools*, volume 110.

Mona Diab, Kadri Hacioglu, and Daniel Jurafsky. 2004. Automatic tagging of arabic text: From raw text to base phrase chunks. In *Proceedings of HLT-NAACL 2004: Short papers*, pages 149–152. Association for Computational Linguistics.

Mohamed Eldesouki, Younes Samih, Ahmed Abdelali, Mohammed Attia, Hamdy Mubarak, Kareem Darwish, and Kallmeyer Laura. 2017. Arabic multidialect segmentation: bi-lstm-crf vs. svm. *arXiv preprint arXiv:1708.05891*.

Nizar Habash, Ramy Eskander, and Abdelati Hawwari. 2012. A morphological analyzer for egyptian arabic. In *Proceedings of the twelfth meeting of the special interest group on computational morphology and phonology*, pages 1–9. Association for Computational Linguistics.

Nizar Habash and Owen Rambow. 2005. Arabic tokenization, part-of-speech tagging and morphological disambiguation in one fell swoop. In *Proceedings of the 43rd annual meeting of the association for computational linguistics (ACL'05)*, pages 573–580.

Nizar Habash, Owen Rambow, and Ryan Roth. 2009. MADA+TOKAN: A toolkit for arabic tokenization, diacritization, morphological disambiguation, pos tagging, stemming and lemmatization. In *Proceedings of the 2nd international conference on Arabic language resources and tools (MEDAR), Cairo, Egypt*, volume 41, page 62.

Nizar Habash, Ryan Roth, Owen Rambow, Ramy Eskander, and Nadi Tomeh. 2013. Morphological analysis and disambiguation for dialectal arabic. In *Hlt-Naacl*, pages 426–432.

Jan Hajič, Barbora Vidová-Hladká, and Petr Pajas. 2001. The prague dependency treebank: Annotation structure and support. In *Proceedings of the IRCS Workshop on Linguistic Databases*, pages 105–114.

Vladimir I. Levenshtein. 1966. Binary codes capable of correcting deletions, insertions, and reversals. In *Soviet physics doklady*, volume 10, pages 707–710.

Mohamed Maamouri, Ann Bies, Tim Buckwalter, and Wigdan Mekki. 2004. The penn arabic treebank: Building a large-scale annotated arabic corpus. In *NEMLAR conference on Arabic language resources and tools*, volume 27, pages 466–467. Cairo.

Ryan McDonald, Joakim Nivre, Yvonne Quirmbach-Brundage, Yoav Goldberg, Dipanjan Das, Kuzman Ganchev, Keith Hall, Slav Petrov, Hao Zhang, Oscar Täckström, Claudia Bedini, Núria Bertomeu Castelló, and Jungmee Lee. 2013. Universal dependency annotation for multilingual parsing. In *Proceedings of the 51st Annual Meeting of the Association for Computational Linguistics (Volume 2: Short Papers)*, pages 92–97, Sofia, Bulgaria. Association for Computational Linguistics.

Emad Mohamed. 2018. Morphological segmentation and part-of-speech tagging for the arabic heritage. *ACM Transactions on Asian and Low-Resource Language Information Processing (TALLIP)*, 17(3):22.

Emad Mohamed, Behrang Mohit, and Kemal Oflazer. 2012. Annotating and learning morphological segmentation of egyptian colloquial arabic. In *LREC*, pages 873–877.

Will Monroe, Spence Green, and Christopher D. Manning. 2014. Word segmentation of informal arabic with domain adaptation. In *Proceedings of the 52nd Annual Meeting of the Association for Computational Linguistics (Volume 2: Short Papers)*, volume 2, pages 206–211.

Joakim Nivre. 2003. An efficient algorithm for projective dependency parsing. In *Proceedings of the 8th International Workshop on Parsing Technologies (IWPT)*.

Joakim Nivre, Johan Hall, and Jens Nilsson. 2004. Memory-based dependency parsing. In *Proceedings of the Eighth Conference on Computational Natural Language Learning (CoNLL-2004) at HLT-NAACL 2004.*

Joakim Nivre, Johan Hall, Jens Nilsson, Atanas Chanev, Gülşen Eryigit, Sandra Kübler, Svetoslav Marinov, and Erwin Marsi. 2007. Maltparser: A language-independent system for data-driven dependency parsing. *Natural Language Engineering*, 13(2):95–135.

Joakim Nivre, Marie-Catherine de Marneffe, Filip Ginter, Yoav Goldberg, Jan Hajic, Christopher D. Manning, Ryan T. McDonald, Slav Petrov, Sampo Pyysalo, Natalia Silveira, et al. 2016. Universal dependencies v1: A multilingual treebank collection. In *International Conference on Language Resources and Evaluation (LREC 2016)*, pages 1659–1666, Portorož, Slovenia.

Younes Samih, Mohammed Attia, Mohamed Eldesouki, Ahmed Abdelali, Hamdy Mubarak, Laura Kallmeyer, and Kareem Darwish. 2017a. A neural architecture for dialectal arabic segmentation. In *Proceedings of the Third Arabic Natural Language Processing Workshop*, pages 46–54.

Younes Samih, Mohamed Eldesouki, Mohammed Attia, Kareem Darwish, Ahmed Abdelali, Hamdy Mubarak, and Laura Kallmeyer. 2017b. Learning from relatives: unified dialectal arabic segmentation. In *Proceedings of the 21st Conference on Computational Natural Language Learning (CoNLL 2017)*, pages 432–441.

Robert A. Wagner and Michael J. Fischer. 1974. The string-to-string correction problem. *Journal of the ACM (JACM)*, 21(1):168–173.

Hiroyasu Yamada and Yuji Matsumoto. 2003. Statistical dependency analysis with support vector machines. In *Proceedings of the 8th International Workshop on Parsing Technologies*, pages 195–206, Nancy, France.

Assessing Arabic Weblog Credibility via Deep Co-learning

Chadi Helwe , Shady Elbassuoni , Ayman Al Zaatari and Wassim El-Hajj

Computer Science Department
American University of Beirut
Beirut, Lebanon
`{cth05,se58,abz02,we07}@aub.edu.lb`

Abstract

Assessing the credibility of online content has garnered a lot of attention lately. We focus on one such type of online content, namely weblogs or blogs for short. Some recent work attempted the task of automatically assessing the credibility of blogs, typically via machine learning. However, in the case of Arabic blogs, there are hardly any datasets available that can be used to train robust machine learning models for this difficult task. To overcome the lack of sufficient training data, we propose *deep co-learning*, a semi-supervised end-to-end deep learning approach to assess the credibility of Arabic blogs. In deep co-learning, multiple weak deep neural network classifiers are trained using a small labeled dataset, and each using a different view of the data. Each one of these classifiers is then used to classify unlabeled data, and its prediction is used to train the other classifiers in a semi-supervised fashion. We evaluate our deep co-learning approach on an Arabic blogs dataset, and we report significant improvements in performance compared to many baselines including fully-supervised deep learning models as well as ensemble models.

1 Introduction

Weblogs, also known as blogs, are gaining popularity, as alternative sources of news and information. The size of the blogosphere is exponentially increasing. For instance, as of October 2018, the popular blogging website Tumblr estimates the total number of blogs on the website to be above 450 million blogs with over 167 billion blog posts[1]. With the surge in misinformation, disinformation and fake news on the Web, and their adverse effects on spreading rumors, tampering with election results and promoting propaganda, an important research question is how to assess the credibility of blog posts. This is particularly crucial in the case of the Arabic speaking world given its recent and constant turmoil.

There has been thus an increased interest in the machine learning and data mining communities to tackle the problem of fake news (Rubin et al., 2016; Wang, 2017; Ruchansky et al., 2017; Zhang et al., 2018; Wang et al., 2018) and the credibility of content in social media in general (Castillo et al., 2011; Gupta and Kumaraguru, 2012; Gupta et al., 2014; El Ballouli et al., 2017; Ma et al., 2016). Some works also focused on the credibility of blog posts (Kolari et al., 2006a,b; Salvetti and Nicolov, 2006; Lin et al., 2007). Most such approaches relied on careful feature-engineering. In this paper, we propose to utilize end-to-end deep learning to assess the credibility of Arabic blog posts. Deep Learning is a type of machine learning that uses deep neural networks to automatically learn features without spending an undue effort to engineer these features as is custom in traditional machine learning. It has been shown to perform significantly better than any other approaches for various NLP tasks. However, deep learning models require a large amount of training data. Assessing the credibility of blog posts is a difficult task and one that has not yet received enough attention from the research community. This has led to only scarce datasets of blogs that are labeled for credibility. This is again particularly true in the case of Arabic blogs, with hardly any such datasets available, with the exception of (Al Zaatari et al., 2016), which only consists of few hundreds of annotated blog posts.

To overcome the lack of sufficient training data, we propose a semi-supervised deep learning approach, which we refer to as *deep co-learning*. Deep co-learning is based on co-training, an approach first introduced by Blum and Mitchell (Blum and Mitchell, 1998) that utilizes multiple

---

[1] https://www.tumblr.com/about

Proceedings of the Fourth Arabic Natural Language Processing Workshop, pages 130–136
Florence, Italy, August 1, 2019. ©2019 Association for Computational Linguistics

classifiers that learn from each other using different views (i.e., features) of the data. In particular, the classifiers are all initially trained in a completely supervised manner using a small training dataset. Each trained classifier is then used to label some unlabeled data, and this automatically labeled data by each classifier is then used to re-train the other classifiers in a semi-supervised fashion.

In our approach, we use a small fully-labeled dataset to train two deep learning models for assessing the credibility of Arabic blog posts. The two classifiers are based on a convolutional neural network (CNN) architecture. The first model uses continuous bag of words (CBOW) word embeddings as features, while the second uses character-level embeddings. We then iteratively retrain our classifiers by applying each classifier on an unlabeled dataset of Arabic blog posts and use the output of each classifier to re-train the other classifier. We evaluate our approach on an Arabic blogs dataset (Al Zaatari et al., 2016) and compare it to various baselines.

Our contributions can be summarized as follows:

- We build an end-to-end deep learning model to assess the credibility of Arabic blog posts

- We utilize semi-supervised learning to train our model even in the lack of sufficient training data

- We evaluate our approach on an Arabic blogs dataset (Al Zaatari et al., 2016) and demonstrate its effectiveness compared to many baselines

The paper is organized as follows. We start by reviewing related work, then describe our deep co-learning approach for assessing the credibility of blog posts. We then present our experimental results where we evaluate our approach on a publicly available Arabic blogs dataset. Finally, we conclude and present future directions.

2   Related Work

Assessing information credibility on the Web is becoming a very hot area of research. Related work that addresses this general problem can be classified into a number of overlapping classes. One such class of works focuses on assessing credibility in social media such as tweets. Another family of works addresses the specific issue of fake news detection. Finally, there are some scarce works on the issue of blog credibility, in which our work also falls.

2.1   Credibility in Social Media

To date, several studies have developed approaches to assess the credibility in Social Media. Castillo et al. (Castillo et al., 2011) implemented automatic methods to predict the level of credibility of a given set of tweets, which was based on various types of features including message-based features, user-based features, topic-based features, and propagation-based features. Gupta and Kumaraguru (Gupta and Kumaraguru, 2012) developed a ranking algorithm to rank tweets, which occurred during high impact events, according to a credibility score. They first identified different features that were used to train a supervised learning model. Their approach is based on a rankSVM model and a relevance feedback method. In a follow-up study, Gupta et al. (Gupta et al., 2014) updated their method to run in a real-time system so that the machine learning model can be retrained from the feedback provided by the user. El Ballouli et al. (El Ballouli et al., 2017) proposed a decision-tree classification model to predict the credibility of Arabic tweets. They extracted different features from tweets and users. Other researches focused on detecting rumors in social media. Ma et al. (Ma et al., 2016) investigated a deep learning approach to detect rumors in microblog platforms such as Twitter and Weibo. They designed a neural network consisting of 2 Gated Recurrent Unit layers that outperformed different baselines.

2.2   Fake News Detection

One of the most important events in 2016 was the U.S presidential election. During this election, fake news began to emerge on social media to sway the votes of electors. Rubin et al. (Rubin et al., 2016) proposed an SVM approach to detect fake news. They used TF-IDF and other features such as absurdity, humor, grammar, negative affect and punctuation. Wang (Wang, 2017) created a benchmark dataset for fake news detection. The dataset consists of 12.8K labeled short political news statements with their meta data. He tested different deep learning models and his best model was a hybrid convolutional and recurrent neural network composed of a convolutional neural network (CNN) trained on the text and another consisting of a convolutional and a bidirectional long short term memory neural network (CNN-Bi-LSTM) that takes as input the meta data. The outputs of the two models were concatenated and passed to a fully connected layer. Ruchansky et al. (Ruchansky et al., 2017) proposed a hybrid deep learning model to detect fake news. Their model consisted of a recurrent neural network that captures the temporal aspects of articles and a feed-forward fully-connected one that takes as input user features. The output of both neural networks were concatenated and used for classification. Zhang et al. (Zhang et al., 2018) proposed a new deep learning architecture for fake news detection called deep diffusive network. This neural network is based on a gated diffusive unit, which takes as input multiple different sources simultaneously such as news articles, creators and subjects, and then is able to learn to fuse them and output a vector representation that is then used for classification. Finally, Wang et al. (Wang et al., 2018) investigated a deep learning method to detect fake news from newly emerged events.

2.3 Credibility of Weblogs

There is a relatively small body of literature that investigated the assessment of weblogs credibility. Kolari et al. (Kolari et al., 2006a) proposed a machine learning approach to detect spam blogs. They employed a linear support vector machines (SVM) approach that takes as input different features such as TF-Normalized features as well as binary features. Similarly, Salvetti and Nicolov (Salvetti and Nicolov, 2006) implemented a machine learning model to identify spam blogs. They segmented a blog URL into tokens, which were then passed to a Naive Bayes for classification. Lin et al. (Lin et al., 2007) extracted time-based and content-based features that were passed to an SVM classifier. Finally, Al Zaatari et al. (Al Zaatari et al., 2016) constructed a dataset of Arabic blogposts that were labeled for credibility using crowdsourcing. They also manually extracted a handful of features such as bias, sentiment, reasonability and objectivity, and they used these features to train various machine learning models such as Naive Bayes and Decision Tables. However none of these approaches employed end-to-end deep learning as we do in this paper.

3 Deep Co-learning Approach

An overview of our deep co-learning approach is depicted in Figure 1. We use a small fully-labeled dataset to train two deep learning models for assessing the credibility of blog posts. The two classifiers are based on a convolutional neural network (CNN) architecture. The first model uses continuous bag of words (CBOW) word embeddings as features, while the second one uses character-level embeddings. We then iteratively retrain our classifiers by applying each classifier on an unlabeled dataset of blog posts and use the output of each classifier to re-train the other classifier.

In our deep co-learning algorithm (Algorithm 1), we make use of three different datasets. The first dataset D^l, which is a small but *fully-annotated* dataset. This dataset is used to initially train our two CNN models M_1 and M_2 described above. Next, for each one of the two models M_1 and M_2, we pick m random instances from our *unlabeled* dataset D^{ul}. We then apply each of the models M_1 and M_2 on the corresponding m instances we picked for each model.

Next, we iteratively train each of the two co-learning models M_1 and M_2 as follows. We pick k instances out of the m instances on which one of the two models was applied and use them to train the other model. Our goal is to pick the k instances that have the highest accuracy. Once we have computed the score for each instance on which one of the co-learning models were applied, we pick the top-k highest scored instances that were tagged by one model and use it to train the other model and vice versa. Then we use an ensemble averaging of the two models and apply it on our third dataset D^{vl}, which is also a fully-annotated dataset that is used for validation. The validation score of the ensemble average of the two models M_1 and M_2 is stored in the variable $f1\_score$ in each iteration of the deep co-learning algorithm. We check if $f1\_score$ is higher than the current $best\_f1\_score$ and if it is higher, we update the models and augment their datasets with the top-k instances. Then, we set $best\_f1\_score$ to $f1\_score$. Note that the $best\_f1\_score$ is initially set to the validation score of an ensemble averaging of the initial models M_1 and M_2 that were trained using the fully-labeled dataset D^l. We keep repeating this whole process of retrain, apply and pick highest-scored instances for t iterations, which is a hyperparameter in our approach.

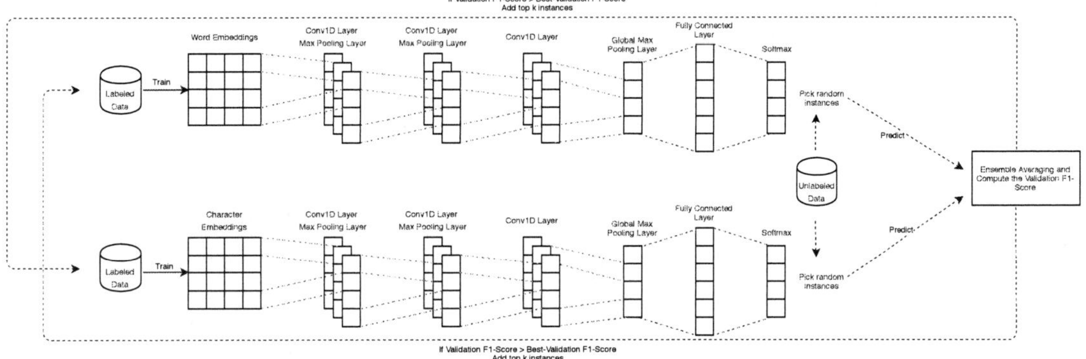

Figure 1: Overview of the Deep Co-Learning Approach

Our approach ends up returning two deep neural network models M_1 and M_2. To be able to use these two models on unseen data, we apply both models and then use ensemble averaging to finally predict the labels of the instances.

In our proposed deep co-learning approach, we utilize two convolutional neural network models. Both of them have the same architecture, except that the first layer of each network utilizes different embeddings. The first model uses pre-trained word-level embeddings that are not retrained in each iteration. However, the second model uses character-level embeddings that are retrained in each iteration. Each model consists of a two 1D convolution layers followed by a max pool layer, and then a 1D convolution layer followed by a global max pool layer. Each convolution layer is composed of 64, 128, and 256 filters, respectively, and a kernel size of 3 and a stride of 1. The max pool layer uses a pool size of 2 and a stride of 2. The output of the global max pool layer is passed to a fully connected layer of 150 neurons. The last layer is a softmax layer of dimension 3. In this architecture, all the hidden layers use RELU as an activation function. In addition, we regularize the neural networks using dropout, and we use a batch normalization layer between all the hidden layers. Figure 2 shows the architecture of the convolutional neural networks used by our deep co-learning approach.

4 Evaluation

To evaluate our deep co-learning approach, we use a dataset of Arabic blog posts constructed by Al Zaatari et al. (Al Zaatari et al., 2016). It consists of 268 Arabic blog posts. The collected blog posts were based on trendy topics at the time of construction, such as Lebanese parliament elections, FIFA world cup, Lebanese residential elections, the Gaza war, the Syrian war, and conflicts in Egypt. To annotate the blogs for credibility, the authors relied on crowdsourcing and the annotators had to label each blog post as credible, fairly credible, or not credible. Note that to the best of our knowledge, this is the only dataset that is publicly available and contains credibility assessment for Arabic blog posts.

We divided the dataset described above as follows: 60% training, 20% validation, and 20% testing. The data was split in a stratified fashion reserving the percentage of samples for each class. Our two deep learning models were bootstrapped using the fully-annotated training dataset, which was used to initially train the co-learning models in the first iteration of the deep co-learning algorithm. We then used the validation dataset to tune the different hyperparameters of our approach. These included the number of instances m we picked at each iteration of the deep co-learning algorithm and the number of instances k with the highest scores. It also included the low-level hyperparameters of the neural networks such as the number of neurons, epochs, and batch size.

In addition to the labeled dataset, we created a large corpus of unlabeled data, which was used to re-train our two deep learning models as described in the previous section. We developed a script to download a set of blog posts from Al Arabiya Blogs [2] and Al Hudood [3]. This dataset consists of 20392 blogs.

We compared our deep co-learning approach to various baselines. The first baseline is a lin-

---

[2] https://www.alarabiya.net/
[3] https://alhudood.net/

Data: Labeled Data D^l, Unlabeled Data D^{ul},
Validation Data D^{vl}, Iteration t

$D_1^l \leftarrow D^l$
$D_2^l \leftarrow D^l$
$M_1 \leftarrow train(D_1^l, WordLevelEmbeddings)$
$M_2 \leftarrow train(D_2^l, CharLevelEmbeddings)$
$best\_f1\_score \leftarrow Avg(M_1, M_2, D^{vl})$
repeat

  $D_1^{sl} \leftarrow$ Pick m random instances from D^{ul}

  $D_2^{sl} \leftarrow$ Pick m random instances from D^{ul}

  Apply $(M_1, D_1^{ul}, CBOW)$
  Apply $(M_2, D_2^{ul}, Skip - gram)$
  for $i = 1$ to m **do**

    Compute s_i for each instance $i \in D_1^{ul}$
    Compute s_i for each instance $i \in D_2^{ul}$

  end
  $TmpD_1^l \leftarrow D_1^l \cap top\text{-}k_2$
  $TmpD_2^l \leftarrow D_2^l \cap top\text{-}k_1$
  $TmpM_1 \leftarrow$
    $train(TmpD_1^l, WordLevelEmbeddings)$
  $TmpM_2 \leftarrow$
    $train(TmpD_2^l, CharLevelEmbeddings)$
  $f1\_score \leftarrow$
    $Avg(TmpM_1^l, TmpM_2^l, D^{vl})$
  if $f1\_score > best\_f1\_score$ **then**

    $top - k_1 \leftarrow$ Remove top-k instances
    with highest s_i from D_1^{ul}
    $top - k_2 \leftarrow$ Remove top-k instances
    with highest s_i from D_2^{ul}
    $D_1^l \leftarrow TmpD_1^l$
    $D_2^l \leftarrow TmpD_2^l$
    $M_1 \leftarrow TmpM_1$
    $M_2 \leftarrow TmpM_2$
    $best\_f1\_score \leftarrow f1\_score$

  end

until t *iterations*;
return M_1, M_2
Algorithm 1: Deep Co-learning Algorithm

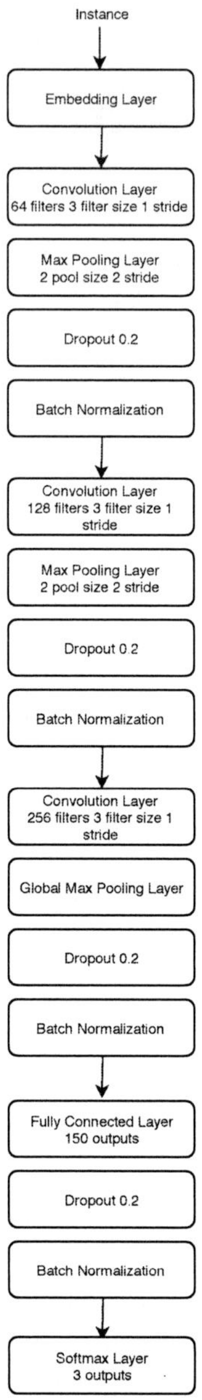

Figure 2: Convolutional Neural Network Architecture

ear SVM that is trained using the TF-IDF scores of the words in the blog posts, and we set the soft-margin weight C to 5 based on the validation set. This baseline is used to evaluate the effectiveness of a deep-learning approach such as ours compared to a more simple model such as SVM. The second and third baselines are word-level convolution neural networks (Word-CNN), and a character-level convolution neural networks (Char-CNN), respectively. The last baseline we

compared our deep co-learning approach to is an ensemble model of Word-CNN and Char-CNN (Ensemble CNN). All the model were trained on the same training dataset, and their hyperparemeters were tuned using the same validation set.

We trained all supervised models (i.e., the first two baselines and the initial models of the deep co-learning approaches) for 500 epochs with a batch size of 16, a dropout of 0.2 after each hidden layer, and we used Adagrad (Duchi et al., 2011) as

Model	F1-Score
SVM TF-IDF	0.57
Word-CNN	0.52
Char-CNN	0.54
Ensemble CNN	0.50
Deep Co-learning	**0.63**

Table 1: Evaluation Results

the optimization algorithm. All experiments were run on a Ubuntu machine with a 24 GB RAM, a CPU Intel Core I7 and a GPU NVIDIA GeForce GTX 1080 Ti 11GB. For the deep co-learning approaches, we repeated the process of co-learning for 50 times since retraining the models was taking significant time which is around 24 hours. In each iteration of the co-learning algorithm, we randomly picked 1000 sentences from the unlabeled data and used the top-50 scored sentences to retrain the other model. All the other parameters were adjusted using the validation set. Note that we also experimented with variations of the above, but we only report here the best performing ones based on validation data.

Table 1 shows the results of our deep co-learning approach and the baselines on the testing dataset. We observe that an SVM model trained with TF-IDF scores as features has an F1-score of 0.57, which is higher than all the fully supervised deep learning approaches. This can be mainly attributed to the small size of the training dataset, which makes it harder to train more complex models such as the fully-supervised deep learning models. Comparing the fully-supervised deep learning models to each other, we observe that the deep learning model trained on character-level representations has an F1-Score of 0.54, while the deep learning model trained on word-level representations has a lower F1-score of 0.52. The advantage of character-level models over word-level models is that they can learn misspellings, emoticons, and n-grams. Interestingly, the ensemble model of Word-CNN and Char-CNN (Ensemble CNN in Table 1) performs worse than all other models. This indicates that with the lack of enough training data, even ensemble models are not able of generalizing well. On the contrary, our deep co-learning approach, which combines the best of both worlds, the complexity of deep learning approaches and the ability to generalize well even when no sufficient training data is available through semi-supervision, significantly outperforms all the baselines with an F1-Measure of 0.63.

5 Conclusion and Future Work

In this paper, we proposed a deep learning approach to assess the credibility of Arabic blog posts. Our method, deep co-learning, is based on a semi-supervised learning algorithm known as co-training that we adopted to the realm of deep learning. To train our deep co-learning approach, we generated an unlabeled dataset that was then used to train our deep co-learning approach. We evaluated our approach on an Arabic blogs dataset and compared it to different baselines. Our deep co-learning approach significantly outperformed all other compared-to approaches including both deep and traditional machine learning models.

In future work, we plan to train the deep co-learning approach for a more extended period to improve its performance. We also plan to label some of our unlabelled blog posts that we used for training our deep co-learning approach using crowdsourcing and to make the labeled dataset publicly available to advance research in this area. Finally, we also plan to experiment with other neural network architectures and to incorporate more linguistic features in our models.

References

Ayman Al Zaatari, Rim El Ballouli, Shady Elbassuoni, Wassim El-Hajj, Hazem M. Hajj, Khaled B Shaban, Nizar Habash, and Emad Yahya. 2016. Arabic corpora for credibility analysis. In *LREC*.

Avrim Blum and Tom Mitchell. 1998. Combining labeled and unlabeled data with co-training. In *Proceedings of the eleventh annual conference on Computational learning theory*, pages 92–100. ACM.

Carlos Castillo, Marcelo Mendoza, and Barbara Poblete. 2011. Information credibility on twitter. In *Proceedings of the 20th international conference on World wide web*, pages 675–684. ACM.

John Duchi, Elad Hazan, and Yoram Singer. 2011. Adaptive subgradient methods for online learning and stochastic optimization. *Journal of Machine Learning Research*, 12(Jul):2121–2159.

Rim El Ballouli, Wassim El-Hajj, Ahmad Ghandour, Shady Elbassuoni, Hazem Hajj, and Khaled Shaban. 2017. Cat: Credibility analysis of arabic content on twitter. In *Proceedings of the Third Arabic Natural Language Processing Workshop*, pages 62–71.

Aditi Gupta and Ponnurangam Kumaraguru. 2012. Credibility ranking of tweets during high impact events. In *Proceedings of the 1st workshop on privacy and security in online social media*, page 2. ACM.

Aditi Gupta, Ponnurangam Kumaraguru, Carlos Castillo, and Patrick Meier. 2014. Tweetcred: Real-time credibility assessment of content on twitter. In *International Conference on Social Informatics*, pages 228–243. Springer.

Pranam Kolari, Tim Finin, Anupam Joshi, et al. 2006a. Svms for the blogosphere: Blog identification and splog detection. In *AAAI spring symposium on computational approaches to analysing weblogs*.

Pranam Kolari, Akshay Java, Tim Finin, Tim Oates, Anupam Joshi, et al. 2006b. Detecting spam blogs: A machine learning approach. In *Proceedings of the national conference on artificial intelligence*, volume 21, page 1351. Menlo Park, CA; Cambridge, MA; London; AAAI Press; MIT Press; 1999.

Yu-Ru Lin, Hari Sundaram, Yun Chi, Junichi Tatemura, and Belle L Tseng. 2007. Splog detection using self-similarity analysis on blog temporal dynamics. In *Proceedings of the 3rd international workshop on Adversarial information retrieval on the web*, pages 1–8. ACM.

Jing Ma, Wei Gao, Prasenjit Mitra, Sejeong Kwon, Bernard J Jansen, Kam-Fai Wong, and Meeyoung Cha. 2016. Detecting rumors from microblogs with recurrent neural networks. In *IJCAI*, pages 3818–3824.

Victoria Rubin, Niall Conroy, Yimin Chen, and Sarah Cornwell. 2016. Fake news or truth? using satirical cues to detect potentially misleading news. In *Proceedings of the Second Workshop on Computational Approaches to Deception Detection*, pages 7–17.

Natali Ruchansky, Sungyong Seo, and Yan Liu. 2017. Csi: A hybrid deep model for fake news detection. In *Proceedings of the 2017 ACM on Conference on Information and Knowledge Management*, pages 797–806. ACM.

Franco Salvetti and Nicolas Nicolov. 2006. Weblog classification for fast splog filtering: A url language model segmentation approach. In *Proceedings of the Human Language Technology Conference of the NAACL, Companion Volume: Short Papers*, pages 137–140. Association for Computational Linguistics.

William Yang Wang. 2017. " liar, liar pants on fire": A new benchmark dataset for fake news detection. *arXiv preprint arXiv:1705.00648*.

Yaqing Wang, Fenglong Ma, Zhiwei Jin, Ye Yuan, Guangxu Xun, Kishlay Jha, Lu Su, and Jing Gao. 2018. Eann: Event adversarial neural networks for multi-modal fake news detection. In *Proceedings of the 24th ACM SIGKDD International Conference on Knowledge Discovery & Data Mining*, pages 849–857. ACM.

Jiawei Zhang, Limeng Cui, Yanjie Fu, and Fisher B Gouza. 2018. Fake news detection with deep diffusive network model. *arXiv preprint arXiv:1805.08751*.

Morphologically Annotated Corpora for Seven Arabic Dialects: Taizi, Sanaani, Najdi, Jordanian, Syrian, Iraqi and Moroccan

Faisal Alshargi,* **Shahd Dibas,**‡ **Sakhar Alkhereyf,**† **Reem Faraj,**†
Basmah Abdulkareem,† **Sane Yagi,**‡ **Ouafaa Kacha,**‡ **Nizar Habash,*** **Owen Rambow**§
*Universität Leipzig, Germany   ‡University of Jordan, Jordan   †Columbia University, USA
*New York University Abu Dhabi, UAE   §Elemental Cognition, USA
`alshargi@informatik.uni-leipzig.de, shahddibas@hotmail.com, sakhar@cs.columbia.edu,`
`nizar.habash@nyu.edu, owen.rambow@gmail.com`

Abstract

We present a collection of morphologically annotated corpora for seven Arabic dialects: Taizi Yemeni, Sanaani Yemeni, Najdi, Jordanian, Syrian, Iraqi and Moroccan Arabic. The corpora collectively cover over 200,000 words, and are all manually annotated in a common set of standards for orthography, diacritized lemmas, tokenization, morphological units and English glosses. These corpora will be publicly available to serve as benchmarks for training and evaluating systems for Arabic dialect morphological analysis and disambiguation.

1 Introduction

As Arabic dialects (DA) become more widely written in social media, there is increased interest in the Arabic NLP community to have annotated corpora that will allow us to both study the dialects linguistically, and to create systems that can automatically process dialectal text. There have been important efforts to create relatively large corpora for Egyptian (Maamouri et al., 2014), Palestinian (Jarrar et al., 2014), and Emirati Arabic (Khalifa et al., 2018). While these resources are very helpful for single dialects, the problem is that there are many dialects, and in fact it is often unclear what to count as separate dialects (for example, the subdialects of Levantine). Therefore, we present a different approach in this paper: we annotate seven dialects, but with relatively smaller corpora (most around 30,000 words). Some of the dialects are closely related (Jordanian and Syrian), others are more distant (Moroccan). We use the same annotation methodology for all dialects: same guidelines, same processing steps, and same annotation file format. This makes our effort an ideal starting point for experimenting with using multidialectal resources to create and train NLP tools. The dialects we consider are Taizi Yemeni (YE.TZ)[1], Sanaani Yemeni (YE.SN), Saudi Najdi (SA.NJ), Jordanian (JOR), Syrian Damascene (SY.DM), Iraqi Baghdadi (IR.BG), and Moroccan Rabati (MA.RB) Arabic.

The paper is structured as follows. We start with a review of relevant literature (Section 2). We then summarize some linguistic facts about DA in general (Section 3) and subsequently present each of our seven dialects in Section 4, summarizing the corpora used and some interesting facts specific to each dialect. Section 5 then presents our annotation methodology. We then briefly discuss morphological analyzers, and conclude.

2 Related Work

Data Collections There have been several data collections centered on Arabic dialects, specifically spoken Arabic. A very useful resource is the Semitisches Tonarchiv at the University of Heidelberg in Germany.[2] We have included two Yemeni transcriptions from this resource in our YE.TZ and YE.SN corpora. Khalifa et al. (2016) is a large collection of over 100M words of a number of Arabic dialect, although the majority is from the Gulf. Bouamor et al. (2018) created a large corpus with parallel data text from 25 Arab cities. Further data collections include (Al-Amri, 2000) which has not yet been digitized for use in NLP research.

Annotated Corpora There are few annotated corpora for dialectal Arabic: the Levantine Arabic Treebank (specifically Jordanian) (Maamouri et al., 2006), the Egyptian Arabic Treebank (Maamouri et al., 2014), Curras, the Pales-

---

[1]The abbreviations we use intend to capture the country name and the city or region name when applicable.

[2]http://www.semarch.uni-hd.de

Proceedings of the Fourth Arabic Natural Language Processing Workshop, pages 137–147
Florence, Italy, August 1, 2019. ©2019 Association for Computational Linguistics

tinian Arabic annotated corpus (Jarrar et al., 2014), the Gulf Arabic Annotated corpus (Khalifa et al., 2018), Syrian, Jordanian dialectal corpora (Bouamor et al., 2014; Harrat et al., 2014), a small effort on Sanaani and Moroccan (AlShargi et al., 2016) (which this paper builds on), and SUAR (Al-Twairesh et al., 2018), a morphologically annotated corpus for Najdi and Hijazi which is semi-automatically annotated using the MADAMIRA tool (Pasha et al., 2014) and subsequently manually checked. Additionally, Voss et al. (2014) present a corpus of Moroccan dialect which has been annotated for language variety (code switching). Several of these efforts have followed the approach of Curras (Jarrar et al., 2014), which consists of around 70,000 words of a balanced genre corpus. The corpus was manually annotated using the DIWAN tool (Alshargi and Rambow, 2015), which we also use. The annotation in Curras is done by first using a morphological tagger for another Arabic dialect, namely MADAMIRA Egyptian (Pasha et al., 2014), to produce a base that was then corrected or accepted by a trained annotator.

Other NLP Resources for Dialectal Arabic The effort to annotate corpora in context is a central step in developing morphological analyzers and taggers (Eskander et al., 2013; Habash et al., 2013). However, other notable approaches and efforts that do not use annotated corpora have focused on developing specific resources manually or semi-automatically, e.g., the Egyptian Arabic morphological analyzer (Habash et al., 2012b) which is built upon the Egyptian Colloquial Arabic Lexicon (Kilany et al., 2002), the multi-dialectal dictionary Tharwa (Diab et al., 2014), or extending MSA analyzers and resources (Salloum and Habash, 2014; Harrat et al., 2014; Boujelbane et al., 2013).

Linguistic Studies There are many theoretical and descriptive linguistic studies for the dialects we work on: Yemeni dialects (Watson, 1993, 2002), Najdi (Ingham, 1994), Gulf Arabic dialect (Holes, 1990), Jordanian (Bani-Yasin and Owens, 1987), Moroccan (Harrell, 1962), Syrian (Cowell, 1964), and Iraqi (Erwin, 1963); not to mentions comparative studies across dialects and MSA (Holes, 2004; Brustad, 2000). We make extensive use of such studies as part of the design of our annotation guidelines.

3 Dialects: Linguistic Facts

In this section we present some general facts and phenomena shared across different dialects. In subsequent subsections, we present our dialects in more detail and commenting on the corpus sources.

Dialects and MSA Arabic dialects share many commonalities with Classical Arabic and Modern Standard Arabic (MSA). All variants of Arabic are morphologically complex as they include rich inflectional and derivational morphology that is expressed in two ways: namely, via templates and affixes. Furthermore, they contain several classes of attachable clitics. However, the dialects as a class differ in consistent ways from MSA, and they differ amongst each other. In fact, the differences between MSA and Dialectal Arabic (DA) have often been compared to those between Latin and the Romance languages (Chiang et al., 2006). The principal morpho-syntactic difference between DA and MSA is the loss of productive case marking, and nunation (*tanween*) on nouns, and mood on imperfective verbs.

Dialectal Variations Differences among the dialects are found on all levels of linguistic description, i.e., phonology, morphology, syntax, and the lexicon. We summarize three phonological and three morphological salient examples in Table 1 for our dialects: the pronunciation of MSA /q/ written ق q,[3] MSA /ʤ/ written ج j and MSA /k/ written ك k; and the various forms of the future, progressive and possessive particles.

From a lexical point of view, there are many words that have different meanings across dialects. For example, the word ماشي $mA\$y$ /maːʃi/ is 'no' in YE.SN and MA.RB, 'yes/ok' in SY.DM and JOR, and 'walking' in SA.NJ. Another example is the word صافي $SAfy$ /sˤaːfi/ which means 'enough' in MA.RB, but 'pure' in the other dialects and MSA. Some cases show subtle differences in meaning, e.g., خدام $xdAm$ /xaddaːm/ means 'employee' generically in MA.RB, but it has a more specific and negative connotation in YE.TZ and YE.SN, namely 'enslaved servant'. While the above cases are all homonyms (homophones and homographs), there are instances of

---

[3]We represent the Arabic words in Arabic script and in the Buckwalter transliteration (in italics) (Habash et al., 2007). When needed, we present the IPA (in /.../). The English gloss is added in single quotes.

Phenomenon	MSA	YE.TZ	YE.SN	SA.NJ	JOR	SY.DM	IR.BG	MA.RB
Pronunciation of ق *q*	/q/	/q/	/g/	/g/ or /dz/	/g/ or /ʔ/	/ʔ/	/g/	/q/ or /g/
Pronunciation of ج *j*	/ʤ/	/g/	/ʤ/	/ʤ/	/ʒ/	/ʒ/	/ʤ/	/ʤ/
Pronunciation of ك *k*	/k/	/k/	/k/	/k/ or /ts/	/k/ or /ʧ/	/k/	/k/ or /ʧ/	/k/
Future Particle	+س *s*+ سوف *swf*	+ش *$*+ اش *A$*	+ع *E*+ عد *Ed* +ش *$*+ +ي *y*+	+ب *b*+	+ح *H*+ رح *rH*	+ح *H*+ رح *rH*	+ح *H*+ رح *rH* راح *rAH*	+غ *g*+ غادي *gAdy*
Progressive Particle	φ	+ب *b*+	+ب *b*+	قاعد *qAEd* جالس *jAls*	+ب *b*+	+ب *b*+ عم *Em*	+د *d*+ قاعد *qAEd*	+ك *k*+ +ت *t*+
Possessive Particle	φ	تبع *tbE* حق *Hq*	تبع *tbE* حق *Hq*	حق *Hq*	تبع *tbE*	تبع *tbE* تاع *tAE*	مال *mAl*	+د *d*+ ديال *dyAl*

Table 1: Cross-dialectal and MSA variants in some phonological and morphological phenomena

homophones that have different meanings in different dialects. For example the utterance /fagr/ can mean 'morning' in YE.TZ (written as فجر *fjr*), or 'poverty in YE.SN (written as فقر *fqr*). The YE.SN pronunciation of فجر *fjr* is /faʒr/; and the YE.TZ pronunciation of فقر *fqr* is /faqr/.

There are also cases of the same meaning being expressed in different ways, e.g., 'spoon' is ملعقة *mlEqp* in MSA, metathesized معلقة *mElqp* in JOR and SY.DM, and خاشوقة *xA$wqp* in IR.BG.

Dialectal Orthography Since Arabic dialects do not have spelling standards, several previous efforts on Arabic dialect annotations (Maamouri et al., 2014; Jarrar et al., 2014; Khalifa et al., 2018) contributed to a movement that lead to the creation of a common Conventional Orthography for Dialectal Arabic (CODA) (Habash et al., 2012a; Zribi et al., 2014; Habash et al., 2018). We also follow this approach to map from any *spontaneous* orthography in our data to CODA. The spirit of CODA is to define a common and consistent approach to spelling DA words that acknowledges their etymological and historical relationship with MSA and CA, but also maintains their uniqueness and independence. For example, if a DA word has an MSA cognate containing ق *q*, then its CODA spelling will use ق *q* even if the dialectal pronunciation is different. In contrast, DA morphemes are spelled in a way to reflect their DA uniqueness. For example the SY.DM word حنفيق *Hnfyq* /ħanfiːʔ/ 'we will wake up' is a cognate of MSA سنفيق *snfyq* /sanafiːqu/: the future marker reflects the dialectal morphology and is not spelled as in MSA, but the stem is spelled as in MSA and thus the ق *q* does not reflect the dialectal pronunciation.

4 Dialect-Specific Corpora

Until recently, Arabic was mostly written in Modern Standard Arabic (MSA) and Classical Arabic, while written DA was rare. One early source of written dialectal Arabic are textbooks for learning an Arabic Dialect intended for non-Arabic speakers. Furthermore, sometimes spoken language has been recorded and transcribed. However, owing to the advent of the internet and its rapid growth among Arabic speaking populations, written materials in DA are now more accessible and easy to obtain than they were in the past. These written materials are typically informal written conversations among participant or traditional folk literature like short stories, poems, prose, thoughts and song. These texts can be found in online forums, blogs, and postings on social media networks. All of the our dialectal corpora consist of sources of various genres, collected from both online and print materials in order to cover many of the aspects of these dialects. Each of the YE.TZ, SA.NJ, IR.BG, JOR corpora has 30K words, while the YE.SN has 32K words, SY.DM has 35k words and MA.RB has 20k words. It should be noted that the data collected from the internet was written in Arabic characters, using "spontaneous" orthography since there are no orthographic standards for DA. The Roman alphabet sentence were transcribed from the textbooks into the Arabic alphabet using CODA. All examples presented in the rest of this section are in CODA except where specified otherwise.

4.1 Taizi Corpus (YE.TZ)

Sources The YE.TZ written data was collected manually from different resources such as forums, blogs, and social media networks. With reference to spoken data, half of the oral interviews were recorded and transcribed manually by the annotators, the remaining oral interview transcripts are taken from the Semitisches Tonarchiv (Section 2). The data includes wise anecdotes, proverbs, stories, poems, songs and dialogues.

Phonology and Orthography   A distinguishing feature of YE.TZ is that MSA ج *j* /ʤ/ is pronounced as /g/, e.g., جمل *jml* 'camel' /gamal/, and that MSA ق *q* /q/ retains its pronunciation. In that regard, CODA spellings were straightforward.

Morphology   Similar to a number of other dialects but unlike MSA, negation is expressed as an enclitic ش *\$* 'not', e.g., يدخلش *ydxl+\$* 'he does not enter'. The vocative particle is expressed as the proclitics يا *yA* 'Oh' and وا *wA* 'Oh', or as an the enclitic اه *Ah* as in أمّاه *AmAh* 'my mother'. The verbal proclitic قا *qA* 'already', which corresponds to MSA قد *qd*, frequently appears with past verbs, e.g., قا عملنا *qA EmlnA* 'we have already done that'.

Lexicon   There are many open-class words that make YE.TZ different from MSA and other dialects, e.g., زقوة *zqwp* 'shrewd', زكن *zkn* 'order', and قراع *qrAE* 'breakfast'. Some words have MSA meanings that differ from YE.TZ, e.g., شل *\$l* 'take' and بزّ *bz* 'take'. YE.TZ has a number of loanwords from English that underwent Arabization, e.g., سجارة *sjArp* 'cigarette', and كتلي *ktly* 'kettle'.

4.2   Sanaani Corpus (YE.SN)

Sources   The social texts were taken from a Sanaani Radio Station program called مسعد ومسعدة *msEd wmsEdp*, which addressed social issues and problems of the community. The oral interview transcripts were taken from the Semitisches Tonarchiv (Section 2). The interviews describe daily life, history and lifestyle in Sanaa. Folktales describing traditional stories handed down in Sanaa are taken from internet forums. Collections of wisdom sayings and tales of the famous wise man of Yemen, "Ali walad Zaid" are taken from internet websites. Other texts were taken from social media, and include political events in Yemen, Sanaani jokes, religious sermons and transcripts that discuss the Sanaani dialect in MSA.

Phonology and Orthography   MSA ق *q* /q/ is pronounced /g/ in YE.SN, including in religious contexts. For example, the word قمر *qmr* 'moon' is pronounced /gamar/. This variation is not unique to YE.SN and other dialects such as IR.BG and JOR have it as well. This /g/ is often spontaneously spelled as ق *q*, which is consistent with CODA guidelines. A particularly marking phenomenon in YE.SN is the devoicing and emphasis of some instances of word-medial /d/, e.g., غدوة *gdwp* 'tomorrow' is pronounced /ɣutˤwa/ and as a result may be written spontaneously as غطوة *gTwp*.

Morphology   As shown in Table 1, there are four future particles in YE.SN: +ع *E+*, عد *Ed*, +ش *\$+*, +ي *y+*. While +ع *E+* may be used with 1st, 2nd, or 3rd person conjugated verb, the rest are only used with 1st person singular conjugated verbs.

Lexicon   YE.SN has some distinguishing closed class words, such as prepositions قفى *qfY* 'behind' and شق *\$q* 'next', and numbers like ستات *stAt* 'six', and هطعش *hTE\$* 'eleven'. There are also some Turkish loanwords, e.g., ساني *sAny* 'direct' and كريك *kryk* 'shovel'.

4.3   Najdi Corpus (SA.NJ)

Sources   The SA.NJ corpus was collected from different sources that represent different genres: forums, poetry, jokes and tweets. We collected different posts from the Saudi web forum `eqla3.com`, including personal narratives (mainly sarcastic) and discussions. We also collected Najdi poems from the late twentieth century, mainly written by the contemporary Najdi poets Khalid AlFaisal, Mohammed bin Ahmed AlSudairy and Saad Bin Jadlan. We manually collected Najdi jokes from various online resources. And finally, on Twitter, we searched for distinctive Najdi keywords such as حنا *HnA* 'we', قروشة *qrw\$p* 'inconvenience', and منيب *mnyb* 'I'm not'.

Phonology and Orthography   As Table 1 shows, there are a number of phonological alternations in SA.NJ. The /dz/ variant of ق *q* /q/ and /ts/ variants of ك *k* /k/ are rather restricted in their usage. And unlike MSA, SA.NJ shows no distinction between the pronunciation of MSA etymological ض /dˤ/ and ظ /ðˤ/. These phenomena affect spontaneous orthography and had to be addressed in the CODA annotations.

Morphology   One marking morphological feature of SA.NJ (and other Gulf Arabic dialects) is the use of negation circumfix مـا + .. +ـب *mA+ .. +b*, as in مانيب *mAnyb* 'I am not' (spontaneously, often written as منيب *mnyb*). Similar constructions exist in other dialects but are more productive, e.g. Egyptian مـا + .. +ـش *mA+ .. +$* negates verbs in addition to pronouns. Unlike most DA and like MSA, SA.NJ retains some tanween (nunation). For example: أنا قايل لك >nA qAylK lk 'ʔana ga:ylin lak/ 'I said (active participle) to you'. However, as in MSA, the nunation is rarely written. Some morphological phenomena are becoming very rare, e.g., the use of تس *ts* for 2nd person singular feminine pronominal enclitic is dying out among younger people and merging with the masculine form لك *k*.

Lexicon SA.NJ has some distinguishing words such as أبخص *>bxS* 'more expert', كفو *kfw* 'good', and دافور *dAfwr* 'nerd' There are many borrowed words from English compared to borrowings from Turkish or Persian. For instance, the verb يفلم *yflm* is borrowed form English 'film' and means 'to act dramatically'.

4.4 Jordanian Corpus (JOR)

Sources The corpus includes written as well as spoken data. The written materials were drawn from internet sources, such as, forums, blogs, and social media. They include informal conversations among participant or traditional folk literature like short stories, poems, prose, memoirs, and songs. As for spoken data, oral interviews and observations were recorded and transcribed by the annotators. Nearly 20 informants were interviewed by the researchers. Older as well as uneducated people are included in order to ensure the authenticity of the data. The JOR data included a mix of sub-dialects that reflect the multiplicity of DA forms, including markedly Palestinian as well as Jordanian variants. For this reason, we refer to this corpus simply as JOR.

Phonology and Orthography In some JOR sub-dialects, as with IR.BG, MSA لك *k* is affricated to /tʃ/, e.g., كلب *klb* /tʃalb/ 'dog'. ق *q* also realizes in two forms as /g/ and /ʔ/. Some of these phenomena results in different spontaneous spellings that are then normalized during annotation.

Morphology JOR's 2nd person feminine singular pronominal clitic has two alternations depending on the sub-dialect: كي *ky* /ki/ and لك *k* /ik/. Examples include شفتكي *$ftky* or شفتك *$ftk* 'I saw

you'; however when following a vowel, both become كي *ky* /ki/, e.g. شافوكي *$Afwky* 'they saw you'. Negation is marked with the enclitic ش *$*; such as, باسويش *bAswy$* 'I do not do'.

Lexicon Some JOR words are from Syriac, e.g., شوب *$wb* 'hot', and بكير *bkyr* 'early in the morning'. Other words are borrowed from Turkish, e.g., دغري *dgry* 'straightforward' and درابزين *drAbzyn* 'ladder'. Some words that were borrowed from English underwent some morpho-phonological changes. For example, كوريدور *kwrydwr* 'corridor', فرمت *frmt* 'format', and بلك *blk* 'to block somebody'.

4.5 Syrian Corpus (SY.DM)

Sources The written data was collected manually from different online written resources such as forums, blogs, and social media networks. Among the data, there were anecdotes, proverbs, stories, some poems, songs and dialogues.

Phonology and Orthography SY.DM has a glottal stop phoneme /ʔ/ that is a cognate with either MSA Hamza (ء ئ إ أ ؤ & } > < ') or MSA Qaf ق *q*. In most spontaneous SY.DM orthography, the two forms are distinguished in a manner similar to CODA guidelines. A few exceptions include the word هلأ *hl>* 'now' which in CODA is written as هلق *hlq* highlighting its etymological link to هالوقت *hAlwqt* 'this time'. Less common spelling variations include the devoicing of ج *j* /ʒ/ to /ʃ/, which may be reflected in spontaneous orthography, e.g., نجتمع *njtmE* /niʒtmiʕ/ 'we meet' may appear as نشتمع *n$tmE* /niʃtmiʕ/.

Morphology A distinction of SY.DM (and North Levantine) compared to South Levantine and a number of other dialects is the absence of the negation enclitic ش *$*. SY.DM makes use of a number of future particles in free distribution (See Table 1). The progressive particle عم *Em* can only be used to indicate active progression at the moment, while the progressive proclitic بـ+ *b+* has a wider range from habitual to progressive.

Lexicon As with JOR, some SY.DM words were originally Syriac, e.g., شوب *$wb* 'hot', or براني *brAny* 'outer'. Other words are borrowed from Turkish, e.g., دغري *dgry* 'straightforward'. Some words encountered major semantic shifts, e.g., طز *Tz* comes from Turkish *tuz* 'salt', then shifting to mean 'something unimportant', and eventually 'good riddance'. Other words were found to be borrowed from French, e.g., ديكور *dykwr* 'decor' and جاتو *gAtw* 'gateaux', and from Persian like سرسري *srsry* 'bad man'. Markedly SY.DM expressions include حربوق *Hrbwq* /harbuːʔ/ 'shrewd'.

4.6 Iraqi corpus (IR.BG)

Sources The materials of the IR.BG corpus were obtained from social media websites, blogs and other online sources. The sources contain posts on political, social, and religious issues that touch upon the daily life of the Iraqi people. The sources include blogs, e.g., different sarcastic posts with a witty sense of humor gathered from the Iraqi blog شلش العراقي *l AlErAqy*, and short essays with commentary and views that sharply criticize loss in traditional values and morals in the Iraqi society after 2003. Proverbs, common sayings, and famous expressions were also collected from online blogs and forums.

Phonology and Orthography Some instances of MSA ك *k* appear as /tʃ/ in IR.BG, e.g., كانت *kAnt* 'she was' /tʃaːnat/. Some of these cases appear in spontaneous orthography as تش *t$* or even ج *J*/ج *j* (mostly due to Persian spelling influences). Some instances of MSA /q/ are pronounced as /g/, e.g., فوق *fwq* 'above' /foːg/. Some of these cases appear in spontaneous orthography as گ *G* or ك *k*, also due to Persian influences.

Morphology A strong marker of IR.BG is the progressive proctlitc +د *d+*, e.g., شدتسوق؟ *$dtswq?* 'what are you driving?'. IR.BG also has three future particles: راح *rAH*, رح *rH*, and +ح *H+*, which seem to be in free variation.

Lexicon The IR.BG lexicon has some distinguishing words such as أطوخ *>Twx* 'little darker', and آني *|ny* 'I'. IR.BG has many loanwords from Kurdish, Persian, and Russian, e.g., Kurdish كاكة *kAkh* 'mister', Persian قنداغ *qndAg* 'very weak tea or hot water and sugar', and Russian إستكان *<stkAn* 'a spindle-shaped tea cup'.

4.7 Moroccan Corpus (MA.RB)

Sources The corpus includes comments from the Moroccan news website `hespress.com` that have to do with sports, cinema, and education policy. The materials from forums include advice on social, religious, and economic issues. The oral interviews are transcriptions of people telling stories, most of which are events from their lives. The folktales come from a Moroccan website that reprinted stories originally published in an encyclopedia of traditional Moroccan folktales. The textbook examples include many basic greetings and expressions, as well as sample dialogues. The blog posts range in topic, but include relationship advice, recipes, and philosophical musings. The humor includes both short and long jokes from a few Facebook pages and one other website.

Phonology and Orthography Most MA.RB consonants are pronounced like their MSA equivalents; however, there are exceptions: dental consonants in MSA have become alveolar, so MSA ث *v* /θ/, ذ *** /ð/, and ظ *Z* /ðˤ/, are pronounced /t/, /d/, and /dˤ/, respectively in MA.RB. Such issues naturally interact with spontaneous orthography and are annotated as per CODA guidelines.

Morphology Among the set of dialects discussed here, MA.RB has the most distinct set of morphological features, such as its future, progressive and possessive particles (see Table 1). Like other North African dialects, and unlike MSA, MA.RB uses the prefix +ن *n+* for imperfect first person singular, and distinguishes first person plural by adding the plural suffix وا+ *+wA*. Interestingly the imperfect first person singular in MA.RB looks like the imperfect first person plural in MSA and numerous other dialects. Finally, the perfect second person singular masculine and feminine both use the suffix تي *ty*, which corresponds to the feminine suffix in other DA.

Lexicon MA.RB has a number of loanwords from Berber, French and Spanish; and many speakers code-switch between Moroccan and French or Spanish. Examples include French فورماج *fwrmAj* 'cheese', and بورتابل *bwrtAbl* 'mobile phone'; and Spanish سمانة *smAnp* 'week', and بابور *bAbwr* 'ship'.

5 Annotation Process

Process Overview To create new morphological annotated corpora, we follow (AlShargi et al., 2016)'s basic approach: we utilize the DIWAN tool (Alshargi and Rambow, 2015) to build and annotate the seven DA corpora discussed above. The project team consists of:

1. a project manager,

2. dialect leads for each dialect, and

Gloss		to him	and I will not go / and not going			this letter		I will write	
MSA	**Ortho**	إليه	أذهب		ولن	الرسالة	هذه	سأكتب	
	Lemma	<ilaY	*ahab		lan	risAlap	h`*A	katab	
	Morph	<lY +h	A+ *hb +φ		w+ ln	Al+ rsAl +p	h*h	s+>+ ktb +φ	
	Prefix	-	IV1S		CONJ	DET	-	FUT_PART+IV1S	
	Stem	PREP	IV		NEG_PART	NOUN	DEM_PRON_FS	IV	
	Suffix	PRON_3MS	IVSUFF_MOOD:S		-	NSUFF_FEM_SG+CASE_DEF_ACC		IVSUFF_MOOD:I	
YE.TZ	**Raw**	لو	شرحشي		وما	الجواب	أذ	شاكتب	
	CODA	له	شارحشي		وما	الجواب	اده	شاكتب	
	Lemma	li	saraH		mA	jawAb	Aa*ah	katab	
	Morph	l +h	$+A+ srH +φ+$		w+ mA	Al+ jwAb	A*h	$+A+ ktb +φ	
	Prefix	-	FUT_PART+IV1S		CONJ	DET	-	FUT_PART+IV1S	
	Stem	PREP	IV		NEG_PART	NOUN	DEM_PRON_MS	IV	
	Suffix	PRON_3MS	IVSUFF_SUBJ:1S+NEG_PART		-	NSUFF_FEM_SG	-	IVSUFF_SUBJ:1S	
YE.SN	**Raw**	له	شسيرش		وما	الرسالة	ته	عدكتب	
	CODA	له	شاسيرش		وما	الرسالة	ته	عد اكتب	
	Lemma	li	sAr		mA	risAlap	tayh	katab	
	Morph	l +h	$+A+ syr +φ+$		w+ mA	Al+ rsAl +p	tyh	Ed#+A+ ktb +φ	
	Prefix	-	FUT_PART+IV1S		CONJ	DET	-	FUT_PART#+IV1S	
	Stem	PREP	IV		NEG_PART	NOUN	DEM_PRON_FS	IV	
	Suffix	PRON_3MS	IVSUFF_SUBJ:1S+NEG_PART		-	NSUFF_FEM_SG	-	IVSUFF_SUBJ:1S	
SA.NJ	**Raw**	له	رايح		ومنيب	هارسالة		باكتب	
	CODA	له	رايج		ومانيب	هارسالة		باكتب	
	Lemma	li	rAyH		AnA	risAlap		katab	
	Morph	l +h	rAyH		w+m+ Any +b	h+Al+ rsAl +p		b+A+ ktb+φ	
	Prefix	-	-		CONJ+NEG_PART	DEM_PART+DET		FUT_PART+IV1S	
	Stem	PREP	ADJ		PRON_1S	NOUN		IV	
	Suffix	PRON_3MS	-		NEG_PART	NSUFF_FEM_SG		IVSUFF_SUBJ:1S	
JOR	**Raw**	ليه	رايح		ومنا	الرسالة	هاذي	كتب	رح
	CODA	ليه	رايج		ومنا	الرسالة	هاذي	اكتب	رح
	Lemma	li	rAH		mnA	risAlap	hA*iy	katab	raH
	Morph	l +h	rAyH		w+ mnA	Al+ rsAlp	hA*y	A+ ktb +φ	rH
	Prefix	-	-		CONJ	DET	-	IV1S	-
	Stem	PREP	ADJ		NEG_PART	NOUN	DEM_PRON_FS	IV	FUT_PART
	Suffix	PRON_3MS			-	NSUFF_FEM_SG	-	IVSUFF_SUBJ:1S	-
SY.DM	**Raw**	لعندو	روح	رح	وما	هارسالة		أكتب	رح
	CODA	لعنده	اروح	رح	وما	هارسالة		اكتب	رح
	Lemma	Eind	rAH	raH	mA	risAlap		katab	raH
	Morph	l+ End +h	A+ rwH +φ	rH	w+ mA	h+Al+ rsAl +p		A+ ktb +φ	rH
	Prefix	PREP	IV1S	-	CONJ	DEM_PART+DET		IV1S	-
	Stem	NOUN	IV	FUT_PART	NEG_PART	NOUN		IV	FUT_PART
	Suffix	POSS_PRON_3MS	IVSUFF_SUBJ:1S	-	-	NSUFF_FEM_SG		IVSUFF_SUBJ:1S	-
IR.BG	**Raw**	له	روح		وما	الرسالة	هاي	كتب	رح
	CODA	له	اروح		وما	الرسالة	هاي	اكتب	رح
	Lemma	li	rAH		mA	risAlap	hAy	katab	raH
	Morph	l +h	A+ rwH +φ		w+ mA	Al+ rsAlp	hAy	A+ ktb +φ	rH
	Prefix	-	IV1S		CONJ	DET	-	IV1S	-
	Stem	PREP	IV		NEG_PART	NOUN	DEM_PRON_FS	IV	FUT_PART
	Suffix	PRON_3MS	IVSUFF_SUBJ:1S		-	NSUFF_FEM_SG	-	IVSUFF_SUBJ:1S	-
MA.RB	**Raw**	ليه	نمشي	غاديش	وما	الرسالة	هاد	نكتب	غادي
	CODA	ليه	نمشي	غاديش	وما	الرسالة	هاد	نكتب	غادي
	Lemma	li	m$aY	gAdy	mA	risAlap	hAd	ktab	gAdy
	Morph	l +h	n+ m$y +φ	gAdy +$	w+ mA	Al+ rsAlp	hAd	n+ ktb +φ	gAdy
	Prefix	-	IV1S	-	CONJ	DET	-	IV1S	-
	Stem	PREP	IV	FUT_PART	NEG_PART	NOUN	DEM_PRON_FS	IV	FUT_PART
	Suffix	PRON_3MS	IVSUFF_SUBJ:1S	NEG_PART	-	NSUFF_FEM_SG	-	IVSUFF_SUBJ:1S	-

Table 2: An annotation example from DIWAN for Modern Standard Arabic, Taizi, Sanaani, Najdi, Jordanian, Syrian, Iraqi and Moroccan Arabic dialects. All the sentences have the same meaning: 'I will write this letter and not go to him'. The table is presented in a right-to-left direction. **Raw** represents a spontaneous word spelling. **CODA** represents the conventional orthography we use. **Lemma** shows the diacritized lemma form; this is the only line where we show diacritics. **Morph** represent the sequence of prefixes, the stem, and the sequence of suffixes. **Prefix**, **Stem**, and **Suffix** show the part of speech tags for the components of the word shown in the **Morph** line.

Error Type	Dialects	Word	gloss	Error	Correction
Null Subject	SA.NJ	أمر |mr	order	+|mr/CV+	+|mr/CV+(null)/CVSUFF_SUBJ:2MS
	YE.TZ	أصابحك >SAbHk	fight	>/IV1S+SAbH/IV+k/IVSUFF_DO:2MS	>/IV1S+SAbH/IV +(null)/IVSUFF_SUBJ:1S +k/IVSUFF_DO:2MS
Ta-Marbuta	SY.DM	جعبتي jEbty	pouch	+jEb/NOUN+p/NSUFF_FEM_SG +y/POSS_PRON_1S	+jEb/NOUN+t/NSUFF_FEM_SG +y/POSS_PRON_1S
Case	SY.DM	بالسقف bAlsqf	roof	b/PREP+Al/DET+sqf/NOUN +(null)/CASE_DEF_GEN	b/PREP+Al/DET+sqf/NOUN+

Table 3: Examples of annotation errors found during error analysis: null morphemes should be added; ta-marbuta is a common source of errors; case should never be annotated for the dialects

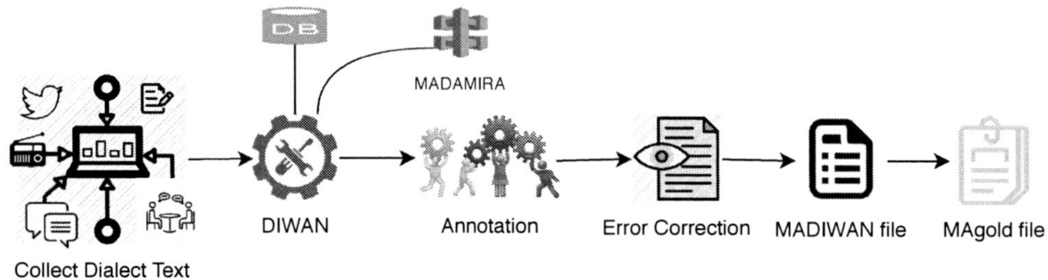

Figure 1: Steps to creating a new annotated corpus for a dialect

3. annotators.

The dialect leads verify the annotators' work, and the project manager organizes and monitors the flow of the progress of everyone using the tool in the project.

Annotation Steps First, the dialect leads collect the corpus text from different resources like social media, forms, websites, etc. The next step is to develop dialect-specific annotation guidelines, including the CODA specification for normalized orthography. The dialect leads then train the annotators before annotation starts. The leads follow the annotator's work. The annotations are not approved until the dialect leads check them. Wrong annotations are sent back to the annotator for correction. After the first round of annotation is done, we perform a second round of error checking, using both manual inspection and scripts that check for coherent annotations. The result is a DIWAN file which includes the correct annotation for the entire corpus. In the last step, we automatically reformat the annotations into a format which is best suited for computational purposes; we perform a third round of error checking for format errors, which we fix automatically. Figure 1 shows these steps.

Morphological Features Annotated The DIWAN interface assists human annotators in annotating each token with morphological and semantic information, including the following fields:

- The CODA spelling of the raw token.

- The lemma, or the citation form, of the token.

- The morphemes of the word (prefixes, stem, suffixes) and their part-of-speech (POS). The stem is marked by the symbol # on either side.

- The English gloss of the word.

- Features indicating proclitics and enclitics.

- Features indicating word POS, functional number and gender (Alkuhlani and Habash, 2011), and aspect.

The annotation for one sentence in different dialects is shown in Table 2. This is not actually a sentence from our corpora, of course; we have chosen it to illustrate the annotation.

Error Correction Linguistic annotation is carried out manually. In order to guarantee high levels of accuracy and precision, we performed extensive error checking and correction. After annotating the seven different corpora, the annotated words were compiled in the form of linguistic codes in either one file or separate files to be checked and corrected by a second reviewer. This form of error checking cannot of course identify annotation errors in context (for example, a noun is misidentified as a verb); instead, this approach is efficient at finding impossible annotations. Examining the data demonstrated that the most challenging part for the annotators was the suffixes part, especially when there are long and complicated words. Some examples indicating the errors are listed below in Table 3.

Distribution of Resources All created resources will be freely available for research purposes from Columbia (`http://innovation.columbia.edu`).

6 Conclusion and Future Work

We presented a collection of morphologically annotated corpora for seven Arabic dialects, collectively covering over 200,000 words. All corpora were manually annotated in a common set of standards for orthography, diacritized lemmas, tokenization, morphological units and English glosses. These corpora will be publicly available to serve as benchmarks for training and evaluating systems for Arabic dialect morphological analysis and disambiguation.

In future work, we will use these resources to train morphological taggers as described in (Eskander et al., 2016). We also plan to extend the collection of dialect to include additional less studied varieties following the lead of efforts such as Bouamor et al. (2018). We also plan to expand towards different historical and literature based varieties of Arabic.

7 Acknowledgments

This work is supported by the Air Force Research Laboratory (AFRL) under a grant administered by Ball Aerospace. Alkhereyf is supported by the KACST Graduate Studies program. The views expressed here are those of the authors and do not reflect the official policy or position of the U.S. Department of Defense or the U.S. Government We also would like to thank all the anonymous reviewers for their insightful and valuable comments and suggestions.

References

Abd Al-Salam Al-Amri, editor. 2000. *Texts in Sanani Arabic. O*. Harrassowitz, Wiesbaden, Germany.

Nora Al-Twairesh, Rawan Al-Matham, Nora Madi, Nada Almugren, Al-Hanouf Al-Aljmi, Shahad Alshalan, Raghad Alshalan, Nafla Alrumayyan, Shams Al-Manea, Sumayah Bawazeer, et al. 2018. Suar: Towards building a corpus for the Saudi dialect. *Procedia computer science*, 142:72–82.

Sarah Alkuhlani and Nizar Habash. 2011. A Corpus for Modeling Morpho-Syntactic Agreement in Arabic: Gender, Number and Rationality. In *Proceedings of the Conference of the Association for Computational Linguistics (ACL)*, Portland, Oregon, USA.

Faisal AlShargi, Aidan Kaplan, Ramy Eskander, Nizar Habash, and Owen Rambow:. 2016. Morphologically annotated corpora and morphological analyzers for Moroccan and Sanaani Yemeni Arabic. In *Proceedings of the Tenth International Conference on Language Resources and Evaluation (LREC 2016)*.

Faisal Alshargi and Owen Rambow. 2015. Diwan:a dialectal word annotation tool for Arabic. In *In: Proceedings of WANLP 2015 - ACL-IJCNLP, 2015*.

Raslan Bani-Yasin and Jonathan Owens. 1987. The phonology of a northern jordanian arabic dialect. *Zeitschrift der Deutschen Morgenländischen Gesellschaft*, 137(2):297–331.

Houda Bouamor, Nizar Habash, and Kemal Oflazer. 2014. A multidialectal parallel corpus of Arabic. In *Proceedings of the Ninth International Conference on Language Resources and Evaluation (LREC-2014)*. European Language Resources Association (ELRA).

Houda Bouamor, Nizar Habash, Mohammad Salameh, Wajdi Zaghouani, Owen Rambow, Dana Abdulrahim, Ossama Obeid, Salam Khalifa, Fadhl Eryani, Alexander Erdmann, and Kemal Oflazer. 2018. The MADAR Arabic dialect corpus and lexicon. In *Proceedings of the Language Resources and Evaluation Conference (LREC)*, Miyazaki, Japan.

Rahma Boujelbane, Mariem Ellouze Khemekhem, and Lamia Hadrich Belguith. 2013. Mapping rules for building a Tunisian dialect lexicon and generating corpora. In *Proceedings of the Sixth International Joint Conference on Natural Language Processing*, pages 419–428.

Kristen Brustad. 2000. *The Syntax of Spoken Arabic: A Comparative Study of Moroccan, Egyptian, Syrian, and Kuwaiti Dialects*. Georgetown University Press.

David Chiang, Mona Diab, Nizar Habash, Owen Rambow, and Safiullah Shareef. 2006. Parsing Arabic dialects. In *11th Conference of the European Chapter of the Association for Computational Linguistics*.

Mark Cowell. 1964. *A Reference Grammar of Syrian Arabic*. Georgetown University Press, Washington, D.C.

Mona Diab, Mohamed Al-Badrashiny, Maryam Aminian, Mohammed Attia, Heba Elfardy, Nizar Habash, Abdelati Hawwari, Wael Salloum, Pradeep Dasigi, and Ramy Eskander. 2014. Tharwa: A Large Scale Dialectal Arabic-Standard Arabic-English Lexicon. In *Proceedings of the Language Resources and Evaluation Conference (LREC)*, pages 3782–3789, Reykjavik, Iceland.

Wallace Erwin. 1963. *A Short Reference Grammar of Iraqi Arabic*. Georgetown University Press, Washington, D.C.

Ramy Eskander, Nizar Habash, and Owen Rambow. 2013. Automatic extraction of morphological lexicons from morphologically annotated corpora. In *Proceedings of the 2013 Conference on Empirical Methods in Natural Language Processing*, pages 1032–1043, Seattle, Washington, USA. Association for Computational Linguistics.

Ramy Eskander, Nizar Habash, Owen Rambow, and Arfath Pasha. 2016. Creating resources for dialectal Arabic from a single annotation: A case study on Egyptian and Levantine. In *Proceedings of COLING 2016, the 26th International Conference on Computational Linguistics: Technical Papers*, pages 3455–3465, Osaka, Japan. The COLING 2016 Organizing Committee.

Nizar Habash, Mona T. Diab, and Owen Rambow. 2012a. Conventional orthography for dialectal Arabic. In *LREC*.

Nizar Habash, Fadhl Eryani, Salam Khalifa, Owen Rambow, Dana Abdulrahim, Alexander Erdmann, Reem Faraj, Wajdi Zaghouani, Houda Bouamor, Nasser Zalmout, Sara Hassan, Faisal Al shargi, Sakhar Alkhereyf, Basma Abdulkareem, Ramy Eskander, Mohammad Salameh, and Hind Saddiki. 2018. Unified guidelines and resources for Arabic dialect orthography. In *Proceedings of the Language Resources and Evaluation Conference (LREC)*, Miyazaki, Japan.

Nizar Habash, Ramy Eskander, and Abdelati Hawwari. 2012b. A morphological analyzer for Egyptian Arabic. In *Proceedings of the twelfth meeting of the special interest group on computational morphology and phonology*, pages 1–9. Association for Computational Linguistics.

Nizar Habash, Ryan Roth, Owen Rambow, Ramy Eskander, and Nadi Tomeh. 2013. Morphological analysis and disambiguation for dialectal Arabic. In *Proceedings of the 2013 Conference of the North American Chapter of the Association for Computational Linguistics: Human Language Technologies*, pages 426–432.

Nizar Habash, Abdelhadi Soudi, and Tim Buckwalter. 2007. On Arabic Transliteration. In A. van den Bosch and A. Soudi, editors, *Arabic Computational Morphology: Knowledge-based and Empirical Methods*, pages 15–22. Springer, Netherlands.

Salima Harrat, Karima Meftouh, Mourad Abbas, and Kamel Smaili. 2014. Building resources for Algerian Arabic dialects. In *15th Annual Conference of the International Communication Association Interspeech*.

Richard Harrell. 1962. *A Short Reference Grammar of Moroccan Arabic: With Audio CD*. Georgetown classics in Arabic language and linguistics. Georgetown University Press.

Clive Holes. 1990. *Gulf Arabic*. Croom Helm Descriptive Grammars. Routledge, London / New York.

Clive Holes. 2004. *Modern Arabic: Structures, Functions, and Varieties*. Georgetown Classics in Arabic Language and Linguistics. Georgetown University Press.

Bruce Ingham. 1994. *Najdi Arabic*. John Benjamins.

Mustafa Jarrar, Nizar Habash, Diyam Akra, and Nasser Zalmout. 2014. Building a corpus for Palestinian Arabic: a preliminary study. In *Proceedings of the EMNLP 2014 Workshop on Arabic Natural Language Processing (ANLP)*, pages 18–27, Doha, Qatar. Association for Computational Linguistics.

Salam Khalifa, Nizar Habash, Dana Abdulrahim, and Sara Hassan. 2016. A large scale corpus of Gulf Arabic. *CoRR*, abs/1609.02960.

Salam Khalifa, Nizar Habash, Fadhl Eryani, Ossama Obeid, Dana Abdulrahim, and Meera Al Kaabi. 2018. A morphologically annotated corpus of Emirati Arabic. In *Proceedings of the Language Resources and Evaluation Conference (LREC)*, Miyazaki, Japan.

Hanaa Kilany, Hassan Gadalla, Howaida Arram, Ashraf Yacoub, Alaa El-Habashi, and Cynthia McLemore. 2002. Egyptian Colloquial Arabic Lexicon. LDC catalog number LDC99L22.

Mohamed Maamouri, Ann Bies, Tim Buckwalter, Mona Diab, Nizar Habash, Owen Rambow, and Dalila Tabessi. 2006. Developing and using a pilot dialectal Arabic treebank. In *Proceedings of the Fifth International Conference on Language Resources and Evaluation (LREC'06)*, Genoa, Italy. European Language Resources Association (ELRA).

Mohamed Maamouri, Ann Bies, Seth Kulick, Michael Ciul, Nizar Habash, and Ramy Eskander. 2014. Developing an Egyptian Arabic treebank: Impact of dialectal morphology on annotation and tool development. In *LREC*, pages 2348–2354.

Arfath Pasha, Mohamed Al-Badrashiny, Mona T Diab, Ahmed El Kholy, Ramy Eskander, Nizar Habash, Manoj Pooleery, Owen Rambow, and Ryan Roth. 2014. Madamira: A fast, comprehensive tool for morphological analysis and disambiguation of Arabic. In *LREC*, volume 14, pages 1094–1101.

Wael Salloum and Nizar Habash. 2014. Adam: Analyzer for dialectal Arabic morphology. *Journal of King Saud University-Computer and Information Sciences*, 26(4):372–378.

Clare Voss, Stephen Tratz, Jamal Laoudi, and Douglas Briesch. 2014. Finding romanized Arabic dialect in code-mixed tweets. In *Proceedings of the Ninth International Conference on Language Resources and Evaluation (LREC'14)*, pages 2249–2253, Reykjavik, Iceland. European Language Resources Association (ELRA). ACL Anthology Identifier: L14-1086.

Janet Watson, editor. 1993. *A syntax of Sanani Arabic*. O.Harrassowitz, Wiesbaden, Germany.

Janet Watson. 2002. *The Phonology and Morphology of Arabic*. Oxford University Press.

Inès Zribi, Rahma Boujelbane, Abir Masmoudi, Mariem Ellouze, Lamia Hadrich Belguith, and Nizar Habash. 2014. A conventional orthography for Tunisian Arabic. In *LREC*, pages 2355–2361.

Construction and Annotation of the Jordan Comprehensive Contemporary Arabic Corpus (JCCA)

Majdi Sawalha,[†] **Faisal Alshargi,**[*] **Abdallah Alshdaifat,**[†]
Sane Yagi,[‡] **and Mohammad A. Qudah**[†]
[†]University of Jordan, Jordan   [*]Universität Leipzig, Germany
[‡]University of Sharjah, UAE

`sawalha.majdi@ju.edu.jo, alshargi@informatik.uni-leipzig.de,`
`a.shdaifat@ju.edu.jo, saneyagi@yahoo.com, m.qudah@ju.edu.jo`

Abstract

To compile a modern dictionary that catalogues the words in currency, and to study linguistic patterns in the contemporary language, it is necessary to have a corpus of authentic texts that reflect current usage of the language. Although there are numerous Arabic corpora, none claims to be representative of the language in terms of the combination of geographical region, genre, subject matter, mode, and medium. This paper describes a 100-million-word corpus that takes the British National Corpus (BNC) as a model. The aim of the corpus is to be balanced, annotated, comprehensive, and representative of contemporary Arabic as written and spoken in Arab countries today. It will be different from most others in not being heavily-dominated by the news or in mixing the classical with the modern. In this paper is an outline of the methodology adopted for the design, construction, and annotation of this corpus. DIWAN (Al-Shargi and Rambow, 2015) was used to annotate a one-million-word snapshot of the corpus. DIWAN is a dialectal word annotation tool, but we upgraded it by adding a new tag-set that is based on traditional Arabic grammar and by adding the roots and morphological patterns of nouns and verbs. Moreover, the corpus we constructed covers the major spoken varieties of Arabic.

1 Introduction

A collection of texts in machine-readable format is called a corpus. The creation of a corpus is often motivated by interest in linguistic phenomena. Therefore, the design and creation of a corpus is always linked to purpose of usage. Thousands of corpora have been created and many are freely available. These corpora vary in size, type, format, usage, and purpose of creation. They are usually annotated with morphological, syntactic, semantic, discoursal, or prosodic information. Individual texts in a corpus often have meta-data in the header that give information about such attributes as genre of the text, author, source, date and country of publication, etc. (Baker et al., 2006).

Building a balanced and representative corpus remains an ideal goal for corpus creators. A balanced corpus includes a wide range of texts from the different genres and domains that the corpus claims to depict. Sometimes, this type of corpus is referred to as a reference, general, or core corpus. Similarly, a corpus is claimed to be representative if it contains the major linguistic variation in the concerned language. Although it is not an easy task to achieve balanceness and representiveness in a corpus, it can be done with a level of approximation and scalability (McEnery and Hardie, 2012; Baker et al., 2006).

The web provides a massive collection of texts which is growing rapidly. Constructing corpora by harvesting web pages is usually referred to as web-crawling. The web is an excellent information source with large amounts of data which one can select, organize, and compile into corpora of all types (McEnery and Hardie, 2012). Since the late 1980s, Arabic corpora have been constructed. However, not many of them are freely available as open-source. Most are for written Modern Standard Arabic (MSA). Morphosyntactically annotated Arabic corpora are very rare and not freely available to researchers.

This paper reports on the construction and annotation of a comprehensive 100-million-word corpus of contemporary Arabic. The purpose is to provide an open-source corpus of contemporary Arabic which is balanced, representative of the language, and comparable to the internationally recognized British National Corpus. The text of the corpus was selected from a wide range of genres, domains, and types. It consists of 83% written language and 17% spoken language. The texts of the corpus were collected primarily from text materials available online but also from the

Proceedings of the Fourth Arabic Natural Language Processing Workshop, pages 148–157
Florence, Italy, August 1, 2019. ©2019 Association for Computational Linguistics

transcripts of purpose-made recordings (see Section 3). The corpus was automatically annotated both morphologically and syntactically. A sample of one million words was manually and semi-manually verified; it was additionally annotated for sentiment and glossed in English. To accomplish this annotation, we used DIWAN (Al-Shargi and Rambow, 2015) but had to specifically develop for it morphological and syntactic annotation schemes on the basis of the long-established Arabic linguistic tradition (see Section 5). We also added new features to the DIWAN annotation tool to facilitate our semi-manual annotation process (see Section 6).

2   Literature Review

Arabic corpora vary in size, type, purpose, design, text type, etc. (Al-Sulaiti and Atwell, 2006). Zaghouani, 2017 surveyed freely available Arabic corpora and classified 66 of them into six main categories, namely (i) raw text corpora, (ii) annotated corpora, (iii) lexicons, (iv) speech corpora, (v) handwriting recognition corpora and (vi) miscellaneous corpora.

The Corpus of Contemporary Arabic (Al-Sulaiti and Atwell, 2006) was the first freely available Arabic corpus. Around one million words were collected from newspapers and magazines. Since then, most monolingual Arabic corpora have been constructed by collecting texts from news sources (i.e. newspaper articles). Examples of such corpora are: the Open Source Arabic Corpora (OSAC) which contain around 18 million words of written MSA and Classical Arabic (CA) texts (Saad and Ashour, 2010); Akhbar Al Khaleej 2004 Corpus consists of 3 million words of newspaper texts (Abbas and Smaïli, 2005); Al-Watan 2004 Corpus contains 10 million words of newspaper texts as well (Abbas et al., 2011); KACST Arabic Corpus includes more than 700 million words collected from 10 text source types such as newspapers, magazines, books, old manuscripts, university theses, refereed periodicals, websites, curricula, news agencies, and official prints (Al-Thubaity, 2015). There is also the International Corpus of Arabic (ICA) which was constructed by Bibliotheca Alexandrina and it contains 100 million words that were collected from the press, net articles, books, and academic text sources (Alansary and Nagi, 2014). The ArabiCorpus at Brigham Young University is one of the most pop-

ular web-based corpora. It consists of around 174 million words, 77% of which is from newspapers. It does, however, include around 9 million words of premodern literature, 1 million words of modern literature, 28 million words of non-fiction, and a token of colloquial Egyptian (0.164 million words).

The King Saud University Corpus of Classical Arabic (KSUCCA) consists of around 50 million words (Alrabia et al., 2014). The corpus includes texts of six genres, namely religion, linguistics, literature, science, sociology, and biography. The arTenTen corpus used web crawlers to automatically harvest 5.8 billion words from Arabic websites (Belinkov et al., 2013). Its purpose was linguistic and lexicographic in nature. It was automatically annotated using MADAMIRA and it is available on Sketch Engine.

The Historical Arabic Corpus (HAC) has 45 million words that were organized into primary and secondary resources, seven genres, and 100-year eras in the Gregorian calendar. Its intended purpose is historical semantics and etymological lexicography (Ismail et al., 2014).

Two specialized Arabic corpora use the Quran as a source of their textual content; hence, each consists of the same number of words in the Quran, 77430 words. The Quranic Arabic Corpus is morphologically and syntactically annotated. Its annotation was done automatically and verified collaboratively by the wider community (Dukes et al., 2013). The second corpus is the Boundary Annotated Quran Corpus. It is annotated with prosodic information and phrase boundaries (Brierley et al., 2012; Sawalha et al., 2012). It took advantage of boundary markups that flag starts and stops in the Quran (Sawalha et al., 2014; Brierley et al., 2016). Interest in dialectal Arabic corpora has recently surged. An example of such corpora is the Curras Palestinian Arabic corpus, a corpus of more than 56K tokens, which are annotated with morphological and lexical features (Jarrar et al., 2017). There are Arabic corpora that are only available for a fee, such as the Linguistic Data Consortium's[1] *The Penn Arabic Treebank*[2] and the European Language Resources Association's[3] *An-Nahar Newspaper Text Corpus*[4].

---

[1] https://www.ldc.upenn.edu/
[2] https://catalog.ldc.upenn.edu/LDC2016T02
[3] http://catalogue.elra.info/en-us/
[4] catalogue.elra.info/en-us/repository/browse/ELRA-W0027/

This brief review, which is based on a more extensive survey of the literature, points to the absence of resources that make the claim that they represent **in a comprehensive manner** the Arabic of today **as written and spoken** by contemporary native speakers. There is a great need for a corpus of modern Arabic as used by present-day native speakers of the language. The corpus must be truly representative of the language that the current inhabitants of the Arab World use, regardless of whether it is of the high or low variety. It must also be balanced in its representation of the written and spoken language, and of the various discourse genres. It must truly depict the language of the curricula and academia.

3 Methodology

To ensure that this corpus of modern Arabic is representative, balanced, comprehensive, and for general purposes, we followed the model of the British National Corpus (BNC)[5]. That is why this corpus contains slightly more than 100-million words of the same text types, domains, and genres. The corpus contains 87% of texts from written sources and 13% of transcribed spoken language. The written part includes texts from Applied Sciences, Arts, Belief and Thought, Commerce and Finance, Imaginative works, Leisure, Natural and Pure Sciences, Social Sciences, and World Affairs. The spoken subcorpus includes transcripts of Spontaneous Conversations (4.2%) and Context-Governed Spoken Language (6.2%) from the categories of Educational/Informative, Business, Public/Institutional, and Leisure. Tables 1 and 2 show the text categories of the corpus of the written and spoken subcorpora respectively.

Twenty million words of the category of World Affairs were selected from newspapers published in 20 Arab countries where around one million words were collected for each country from one or two newspapers published in that country. The different genres of newspaper articles include Politics; Arts and Culture; Economics; Local News; Opinions; Regional and International News; Sports; and Others (e.g., Weather Forecasts, News about Technology, Health, Tourism, etc.). The subcategory of Social Sciences includes around 14 million words of texts from books and online sources. It contains texts of the genres: Languages and Linguistics; Modern Arabic Dic-

tionaries; Philosophy; Islamic Studies and Quran Interpretation; History; Geography; Anthropology and Sociology; Law; Education; Food and Nutrition; Travel; Lectures; Sports; etc. The subcategory of Belief and Thought consists of about three million words of texts of sacred books such as: the *Quran*; Quran Interpretation; the Hadith including *Hadith Qudsi*; the *Old Testament*; the *New Testament*; *Dictionary of the Bible*; and Interpretations of the Testaments, etc.

More than seven million words were collected from online sources to fill the subcategory of Commerce and Finance. These articles belong to a variety of topics within the commerce and finance genre. They include Accounting; Taxes; Investment; Finance; Financial Legal Issues; Inventory; Currency, etc. The subcategory of Imaginative Language consists of 16 million words. The texts were collected from written sources that include; stories; novels; poetry; plays; translations of international stories and novels. The subcategory of Leisure consists of 12 million words which include articles on topics such as Animals; Cars; Technology; Health; Women; Tourism; Cooking Recipes; How to; Arabian Cities; Jordanian Stories and Traditions; and Fitness. The subcategory of Arts was collected from web sources and comprises around seven million words. The texts of this category contain articles on Arts; Digital Photography; Film and Video Production; Printing; Area Planning and Landscaping; Sculpture; Ceramics and Metals; Computer Graphic Arts; Entertainment and Performance; Cinema and Theater; Photography; Music; Architecture; Fine Arts; Decorative Arts; International Arts; Arabic Calligraphy, etc. Around seven million words were collected from books and web resources for the category of Applied Sciences. The topics included in this category are Medicine; Engineering; Information Technology; Energy, etc. Finally, the Natural and Pure Sciences subcorpus consists of around four million words that come from Mathematics, Physics, Chemistry, Biology, etc.

The corpus is designed to have detailed metadata about each article. This is valuable knowledge that can be used to guide the search within the corpus. It can also be used in text classification and text data mining. Moreover, the corpus and its metadata constitute an excellent dataset for training machine learning algorithms on such tasks as genre identification. The metadata include infor-

---

[5]http://www.natcorp.ox.ac.uk/

Written Subcategory	Words(million)	Percentage
Applied Sciences	7	8%
Arts	7	7.50%
Belief and Thought	3	4%
Commerce and Finance	7.2	8.30%
Imaginative	16	18.50%
Leisure	12	14%
Natural and Pure Sciences	3.8	4%
Social Sciences	14	16%
World Affairs	20	20%
Total	**90**	**100 %**

Table 1: Text categories of the written subcorpus

Context-Governed Subcategory	Words(million)	Percentage
Educational / Informative	1.6	26 %
Business	1.3	21 %
Public/ Institutional	1.7	27 %
Leisure	1.6	26 %
Total	**6.2**	**100 %**

Table 2: Categories of the Context-Governed Spoken Language subcorpus.

mation such as article ID, category, subcategory, country, author, date, source, and URL. Moreover, the title and the text of each article are stored in a traditional relational database and in XML format. Figure 1 shows a sample article in XML with the text, title and metadata clearly specified.

A corpus-representative snapshot of one million words are designated as the corpus gold standard. This is a sample of words semi-manually annotated and verified. Each word is morphologically decomposed into its prefixes, stem, suffixes, proclitics, and enclitics. Then, each morpheme is annotated with a morphological tag or possibly tags. The stem is labeled by one morphological tag, and its root and morphological pattern are specified. Other morphological attributes, such as the number and gender of a noun, are indicated as well. The tag set we used here was informed by traditional Arabic grammar (see Section 6). Moreover, each word was annotated for sentiment designation (i.e., positive, negative, or neutral sentiment). The annotation process was done using a specialized program, DIWAN (Al-Shargi and Rambow, 2015). Twenty annotators with expertise in Arabic linguistics were trained on the tag set and on the annotation tool and they were supervised by three linguists who ensured the accuracy of annotation and verification.

```
<Article Article_ID="11966" Category="World Affairs" SubCategory="محليات"
Date="2017-12-27 18:58:00" Author= "عمان- الرأي" source = "Alri جريدة الرأي"
URL ="http://alrai.com/article/10418936" Country="Jordan" >
<Title>"تكريم المشاركين في مسابقة الخطابة العربية في " الأردنية</Title>
<Text>
كرمت الجامعة الأردنية الداعمين والمشاركين في فعاليات مسابقة الخطابة العربية للطلبة الناطقين بغير
العربية.ونظمت المسابقة لجنة الوافدين في كلية الأداب بدعم من مكتب شؤون الوافدين في الجامعة وأقيمت الشهر
الحالي تستهدف النهوض باللغة العربية لدى الطلبة الوافدين من جنسيات متعددةوعرضت منسقة لجنة الوافدين
الطالبة نورماس القدومي أهداف ونشاطات اللجنة والدور الذي تقوم به في مساعدة طلبة من جنسيات عالمية لتعلم
العربية بهدف إكسابهم المهارات اللغوية لتكون عونا لهم في التواصل الاجتماعي مع طلبة الجامعة وتسهيل
دراستهم الجامعية وإقامتهم داخل المملكة الأردنية الهاشمية<Text>
</Article>
```

Figure 1: A stored article with XML markup.

4 Copyrights

The texts of the written subcorpus were primarily selected from sources available online. To get around copyrights, we followed Eckart's example by 'scrambling' the texts such that the original structure of a document would be destroyed. "This inhibits the reconstruction of the original documents. With respect to German copyright legislation this approach is considered safe" (Eckart et al., 2014). We assume this is satisfactory to copyright laws in most countries around the world.

5 Annotation

To create and annotate the comprehensive corpus of contemporary Arabic, we followed the principles presented in (AlShargi et al., 2016). This approach consists of several main steps. We started out by deciding on the categories, subcategories, and sizes in millions of words of the components of the corpus. To ensure balance, we simply followed the BNC proportions. Then we collected the target textual material from sources similar to those of the BNC, as well. We added texts from the social media, forums, and websites according to the various topical categories (cf. Tables 1, 2. Then, we modified the DIWAN annotation tool (Al-Shargi and Rambow, 2015) by adding new annotation tags such as root, pattern, and sentiment, by creating an elaborate CODA, and by developing a user interface that reflects these modifications. (See Tables 4, 5, 6 where the new tags we added appear in bold). After the primary annotation of the entire corpus was run automatically, we conducted an error detection round to find and correct annotation errors. (Figure 2 shows the workflow).

DIWAN assists human annotators in tagging each token with the relevant morphological, syntactic, and semantic information. DIWAN has the following annotation fields: 1) **Diac**: where the word to be annotated is shown with diacritics. 2) **Lex**: Here the lemma in its citation form appears. For example, the lemma of واحبابها *wAHbAbhA* 'and her lovers' will have the lex حبيب *Hbyb* 'lover' 3) ***BWhash***: In this field, the Buckwalter rendition of the lemma is split into prefix, stem, and suffix. The stem is marked by the symbol # on both sides, 4) ***Gloss***: the English translation of the lemma appears in this field.

There are features in DIWAN that indicate the proclitics and enclitics of words. The clitics are assigned slots: prc3, prc2, prc1, and prc0 for proclitics, and enc0; enc1, and enc2 for enclitics. A lower index indicates closer proximity to the stem. Additionally, there are features that mark the part of speech (POS), functional number and gender of nouns, and aspect of verbs. Functional number and gender refer to the function of a word, rather than its form. For example قادة *qAdp* 'leaders' is functionally masculine and plural, even though it ends in ة, which is the marker of feminine singular nouns.

We added three new features to DIWAN, (i) **root** which is a base form, for example لمس *lms* to touch is the root of these two words سيلمسونها *sylmswnhA* they will touch it and يلمس *ylms* 'he touches', (ii) **sentiment** which shows the attitude towards a word as to whether it is negative, positive, or neutral; for example, the sentiment annotation of the word 'sabba' in سب العدو *sb AlEdw* 'he cursed the enemy' is negative while that of the word 'ahabba' in أحب المرأة *>Hb Almr>p* 'he loved the woman' is positive and that of عمان *EmAn* 'Amman' is neutral. And (iii) **pattern** the morphological mold that the root is formed by; e.g., the word كاسِر *kAsir* breaker is derived by the mold فاعِل *fAEil* doer and the root كَسَر *kasara* he broke . To show the details of the annotation, we present table 3.

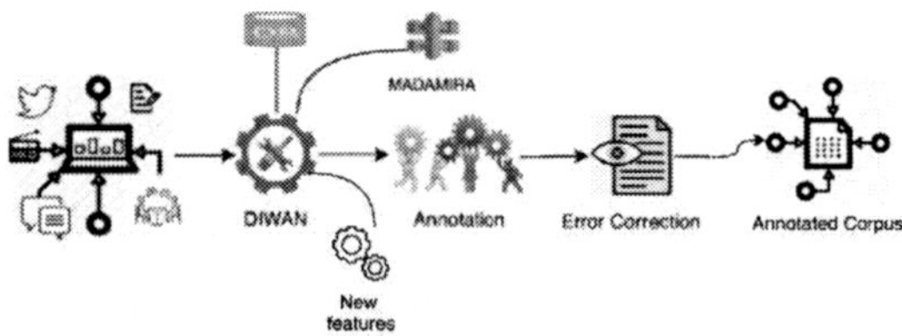

Figure 2: Steps to Creating a Comprehensive Corpus for Contemporary Arabic

6 Morphology

Morphological annotation of the whole corpus was automatically performed using MADAMIRA

(Pasha et al., 2014). We isolated a one-million word snapshot of the corpus for manual verification. Twenty-five B.A. students of Arabic at the University of Jordan carried out the manual verification and two professors of linguistics supervised their work and vetted their annotation. The annotators used DIWAN (Al-Shargi and Rambow, 2015) to review and verify MADAMIRA's analysis. The morphological annotation required (1) Development of a new tag-set with detailed morphological description. Fourteen new noun-tags were added to Madamira. These new tags fall into three groups: i) derived nouns: Active participle, Passive participle, Exaggeration, Qualificative adjective, Noun of time/place, Noun of Instrument, and Elative noun; ii) underived nouns: Concrete noun and Abstract noun; and iii) gerunds: Original gerund, Gerund with initial miim, Gerund of instance, Gerund of state, and Gerund of profession. (2) Providing the roots of the nouns and verbs, since such a root conveys the core lexical meaning of a word. It normally consists of three consonants, and less frequently of two or four consonants. The majority of Arabic words (nouns and verbs) are derived from triliteral roots, uncommonly from biliteral or quadriliteral roots. For instance, the consonantal root د ر س *d.r.s* has the basic lexical meaning of studying, from which these words are derived: دَرْس *darosN* 'lesson', مُدَرِّس *mudar~is* 'teacher', دِرَاسَة *diraAsap* 'sutdying', مَدْرَسَة *madorasap* 'school', دَارِس *daAris* 'student'. In all these derived words, the consonants d-r-s constitute their root (McCarthy, John, 1981; Prunet et al., 2000; Davis and Zawaydeh, 2001). (3) Providing the morphological pattern of each noun and verb. This pattern constitutes a canonical template that consists of a series of discontinuous consonants including those of the root, a series of discontinuous vowels, and a templatic pattern. It carries a schematic meaning and grammatical information together including the word's part of speech. For instance, the morphological pattern C1VVC2VC3 together with the vowel melody - a - i - represents the active participle of Form I verbs (Bat-El, 1994, 2001; Ratcliffe, Robert , 1998; Ussishkin, Adam, 1999, 2005).

7 Spoken vs Written Language

Languages often have a low variety that is used in everyday communication and a high variety that is used in formal settings. The spoken language

Analyze	Sentence					
Sentence	الدولي	بالقانون	الاستهتار	في	الشركة	أمعنت
BW	Aldwly	bAlqAnwn	AlAsthtAr	fy	Al$rkp	<mEnt
gloss	international	law	negligence	in	company	insisted
lex:	dawoliy_1	qAnuwn_1	AisotihotAr_1			<imoEn_1
pfx:	Al/DET	b/PREP+Al/DET	Al/DET		Al/DET	-
stm:	dwl/NOUN_RELATIVE	qAnwn/NOUN_ABSTRACT	AsthtAr/NOUN	fy/PREP	$rk/NOUN	>mEn/PV
sfx:	(null)/CASE_DEF_GEN	-			p/NSUFF_FEM_SG	t/PVSUFF_SUBJ:2FS
gen:, num:	m,s	m,s	m,s		f,s	f,s
root	دول	قنن	هتر	none	none	معن
sntmnt	neutral	positive	negative	neutral	neutral	neutral
ptrn	فَعْلي	فَاعُول	استِفعَال	none	فَعلَة	أُفعَل
Sentence		فرجت	حلقاتها	استحكمت	فلما	ضاقت
BW		frjt	HlqAthA	>stHkmt	flmA	DAqt
gloss		opened	rings	completed	when	intensified
lex:		far~aj_1	Haloqap_1	AstHkm_1	lam~A_1	dAq_1
pfx:		-		-	f/SUB_CONJ	-
stm:		frj/PV	Hlq/NOUN_ABSTRACT	AstHkm/PV	lmA/ADV	DAq/PV
sfx:		t/PVSUFF_SUBJ:3FS	At/NSUFF_FEM_PL+ (null)/CASE_DEF_GEN+ hA/POSS_PRON_3FS	t/PVSUFF_SUBJ:2FS	none , none	t/PVSUFF_SUBJ:3FS
gen:, num:		f,s	f,p	f,s	none, none	f,s
root		فرج	حلق	حكم	none	ضيق
sntmnt		positive	neutral	negative	neutral	negative
ptrn		فَعَل	فَعلَة	استَفعَل	none	فَعَل
Sentence		العلم	السميع	وهو	الله	فسيكفيكهم
BW		AlElym	AlsmyE	whw	AllAh	fsykfykhm
gloss		all-knowing	all-hearing	he	God	will suffice
lex:					All~'h_1	<imoEAn_1
pfx:		Al/DET	Al/DET	w/CONJ		f/CON+s/FUT_PART+ y/IV3MS
stm:		Elym/ADJ_INTENS	smyE/ADJ_INTENS	hw/PRON_3MS	Allh/NOUN_PROP	kfy/IV
sfx:		-	222	-	-	k/IVSUFF_DO:2MS+ hm/IVSUFF_DO:3MP
gen:, num:		m,s	m,s	m,s	m,s	m,s
root		علم	سمع	none	أله	كفي
sntmnt		positive	positive	neutral	positive	positive
ptrn		فَعِيل	فَعِيل	none	عَال	يَفعِل
Sentence	دقيقة	دراسة	المرصودة	الظاهرة	الباحثون	درس
BW	dqyqp	drAsp	AlmrSwdp	AlDAhrp	AlbAHvwn	drs
gloss	closely	studying	observed	phenomenon	researchers	studied
lex:	daqiyq_1	dirAsap_1	maroSuwd_1	ZAhir_1	bAHiv_1	darasa_1
pfx:	-	-	Al/DET	Al/DET	Al/DET	-
stm:	dqyq/ADJ_QUALIT	drAs/GERUND	mrSwd/NOUN_PASSIVE_PART	ZAhr/NOUN_ACTIVE_PART	bAHv/NOUN_ACTIVE_PART	drs/PV
sfx:	p/NSUFF_FEM_SG	p/NSUFF_FEM_SG	p/NSUFF_FEM_SG	-	p/NSUFF_FEM_SG -	-
gen:, num:	f,s	f,s	f,s	f,s	m,p	m,s
root	دقق	درس	رصد	ظهر	بحث	درس
sntmnt	positive	positive	neutral	neutral	positive	positive
ptrn	فَعِيلَة	فِعَالَة	مَفعُولَة	فَاعِلَة	فَاعِل	فَعَل
Sentence	الشارع	نبض	مع	يتماهى	الرسميّ	الموقف
BW	Al$ArE	nbD	mE	ytmAhY	Alrsmy~	Almwqf
gloss	public	pulse	with	identify	official	position
lex:	$AriE_1	naboD_1	maE_1	tamahY_1	rasomiy~_1	mawoqif_1
pfx:	Al/DET	-	-	y/IV3MS	Al/DET	Al/DET
stm:	$ArE/NOUN_CONCRETE	nbD/GERUND	mE/ADV	tmAhY/IV	rsmy/NOUN_RELATIVE	mwqf/GERUND_MEEM
sfx:	-	-	-	-	-	-
gen:, num:	m,s	m,s	none,none	m,s	m,s	m,s
root	شرع	نبض	none	مهي	رسم	وقف
sntmnt	neutral	positive	neutral	positive	neutral	neutral
ptrn	فَاعِل	فَعْل	none	يَتَفَاعَل	فَعْليّ	مَفعِل
Sentence		المأخوذ	يحيب	عخواله	القاروط	ودّيت
BW		AlmAxw*	yjyb	ExwAlh	AlqArwT	wd~yt
gloss		the thingy	to get	to his uncles	the kid	i sent
msa		المأخوذ	يجيء ب	على أخواله	القاروط	وأدّيتُ
lex:		maAxuw*_1	jaAb_1	xaAl_1	qaArwT_1	wd~Y_1
pfx:		AL/DET	y/IV3MS	EIY/PREP	AL/DET	-
stm:		mAxw*/NOUN_CONCRETE	jyb/IV	AxwAl/NOUN_CONCRETE	qArwT/NOUN_CONCRETE	wd~Y/PV
sfx:			-	h/POSS_PRON_3MS	-	t/PVSUFF_SUBJ:1S
gen:, num:		m,s	m,s	m,p	m,s	m,s
root		أخذ	جيء	خول	قرط	أدي
sntmnt		neutral	neutral	positive	negative	neutral
ptrn		مَفعُول	يَفعِل	فَعَال	فَاعُول	فَعَّل

Table 3: Annotated sentences of JCCA Corpus. In this table, the abbreviation *BW* represents Buckwalter transliteration, *gloss* the English meaning, *lex* the lexical entry, *pfx* the prefix, *stm* the stem, *sfx* the suffix, *gen* the gender, *root* the consonantal roots, *sntmnt* the sentiment designation, and *ptrn* the morphological pattern.

tends to be more liberal and more prone to change, the written variety more coded and more conservative. Arabic has three major varieties, two written and one spoken: Classical Arabic, the language of scholarship until the end of the eighteenth century; Modern Standard Arabic, the language of ed-

Tag	Description	Arabic
DET	Definite Article	أداة تعريف
PREP	Prepositions	حرف جر
CONJ	Conjunction	حرف عطف
INTERROG	Interrogative particles	حرف استفهام
FUT_PART	Particles of futurity	حرف استقبال
PREFIX	Prefix	زيادة في أول الكلمة
CV_PREF	Imperative prefix	حرف أمر
IMPERF_PREF	Imperfect prefix	حرف مضارعة
INF_PART	Infinitive particle	حرف مصدري
INF_SUBJUNC_PART	Infinitive/Subjunctive particle	حرف مصدري ونصب
INF_ANNUL_PART	Infinitive/Annulling particle	حرف مصدري ناسخ
NON_GOVERN	Non-Governing particle	حرف غير عامل
NEG_PART	Negative particle	حرف نفي
OTHER	Non-Governing particle	سابقة أخرى

Table 4: Prefix Tags (Bold is new)

Tag	Description	Arabic
GERUND	Gerund	المصدر
GERUND_MEEM	Gerund with initial miim	المصدر الميمي
GERUND_INSTANT	Gerund of instance	مصدر المرة
GERUND_STATE	Gerund of state	مصدر الهيئة
GERUND_PROFESSION	Gerund profession	مصدر صناعي
NOUN_CONCRETE	Concrete noun	اسم ذات
NOUN_ABSTRACT	Abstract noun	اسم معنى
NOUN_ACTIVE_PART	Active participle	اسم فاعل
NOUN_PASSIVE_PART	Passive participle	اسم مفعول
ADJ_INTENS	Form of exaggeration	صيغة المبالغة
ADJ_QUALIT	Adjective	الصفة المشبهة
NOUN_TIME_PLACE	Noun of time/place	اسم الزمان والمكان
NOUN_INSTRUMENT	Instrumental noun	اسم الآلة
ADJ_COMP	Elative noun	اسم التفضيل
NOUN_RELATIVE	Relative noun	اسم منسوب
NOUN_PROP	Proper noun	اسم علم
NOUN_PROP_FOREIGN	Foreign proper noun	اسم علم أجنبي
ADV	Adverb	الظرف
PRON	Pronoun	الضمير المنفصل
DEM_PRON	Demonstrative pronoun	اسم الإشارة
REL_PRON	Relative pronoun	اسم موصول
INTERROG_PRON	Interrogative pronoun	اسم استفهام
REL_ADV	Conditional noun	اسم شرط
NOUN_VERB_LIKE	Verb-like noun	اسم الفعل
NOUN_FIVE	Five nouns	الأسماء الخمسة
NOUN_DIMINUTIVE	Diminutive	اسم تصغير
NOUN_BLEND	Blend noun	اسم منحوت
NOUN_NUM	Numeral	اسم عدد
EXCEPT_NOUN	Exceptive Noun	اسم استثناء
COMP_NOUN	compound noun	اسم مركب
FOREIGN	Foreign word	كلمة أجنبية
ABBREV	Abbreviation	اختصار
PV	Perfect verb	فعل ماض
PV_PASS	Passive Perfect v.	فعل ماض مجهول
IV	Imperfect v.	فعل مضارع
IV_PASS	Passive Imperfect v.	فعل مضارع مجهول
UNINFLECTED_VERB	Uninflected Verb	فعل جامد
CV	Imperative verb	فعل أمر
PREP	Preposition	حرف جر
NEG_PART	Preposition	حرف نفي
CONJ	Conjunction	حرف عطف
INTERROG_PART	Interrogative particle	حرف استفهام
SUBJUNC_PART	Subjunctive particle	حرف نصب
JUSSIVE_PART	Jussive particle	حرف جزم
ANNUL_PART	Annulling particle	حرف ناسخ
VOC_PART	Vocative particle	حرف نداء
EXCEPT_PART	Exceptive par.	حرف استثناء
FUTUR_PART	Par. of futurity	حرف استقبال
YES_NO_RESP_PART	Yes/No particle	حرف جواب
CONDITION_PART	conditional particle	حرف شرط
CERT_PART	Certain/Uncertain particle	حرف تحقيق
PART	other particles	حروف أخرى
PUNC	Punctuation mark	علامة ترقيم
NUMBER	Number	رقم
CURRENCY	Currency	عملة
DATE	Date	تاريخ
NON_ARABIC	Non-Arabic word	كلمة غير عربية
OTHER	OTHER	أخرى

Table 5: Stem Tags (Bold is new)

ucation and formal written communication from the Arab renaissance in the nineteenth century onward; and the dialects, the colloquial regional varieties that are spoken in everyday communication. Since the corpus constructed here is comprehensive and since it claims to be representative of contemporary Arabic, it has to exclude Classical Arabic, but include Modern Standard Arabic, and the regional dialects. We define Contemporary Arabic as the language both written and spoken by living native speakers of Arabic; therefore, the dialects need to be represented. We are not alone in this view, check out *A Frequency Dictionary of Arabic* (Buckwalter and Parkinson, 2011) and the *Oxford Arabic Dictionary* (Arts et al., 2014).

The major spoken varieties are, therefore, represented in the corpus: North Africa is represented by the Moroccan dialect; the Nile region by Egyptian; the Arabian Peninsula by Taizi, Sanaani, and Najdi; Greater Syria by Shami, Jordanian, and Palestinian. The data in the form of contextualized sentences were collected from (1) personal communication in Facebook and Whatsapp family groups; (2) jokes, songs, videoclips, movie scripts, and TV interviews in the local dialects; and (3) personal interviews of old speakers, especially those with minimal education. The data were collected by students who came from these regions. Like any other language, Arabic has differences between the dialects and the standard variety, between the spoken and written varieties. There is variation in the pronunciation of some consonants and vowels (e.g., q, D, Z, v, *, A); suppression of word final inflections; fixed word-order (i.e., subject-verb-object (SVO)); contracted forms (e.g., مظلش *maZal~i$* for ما ظل شيء *mA Zal~a $ay'N* 'nothing remains'); use of high frequency lexical items(e.g., قاعد *qAEid* rather than

جالس *jAlis* 'sitting'); use of some lexical items that are archaic in MSA (e.g., افلح *AifliH* 'Partake of food' in Jordanian Arabic in addition to the senses in Standard Arabic of Plough! and Succeed!); liberal incorporation of foreign words (e.g., مسّج *mas~aj* 'sent a message'); abandonment of the dual and the passive voice (e.g., إنكسَر *<inkasar* 'broke' rather than كُسِرَ *kusira* 'it got broken'); abandonement of the yes-no question

Tag	Type	Arabic	Tag	Type	Arabic
POSS_PRON	Proclitic	ضمير متصل بالاسم	SUBJ_PRON	Suffix	ضمير متصل بالفعل
OBJ_PRON	Proclitic	ضمير متصل بالفعل (مفعول به)	SUFF_FEM_TA	Proclitic	تاء التأنيث
NSUFF_FEM_SG	Proclitic	تاء مربوطة	RELATIVE_YA	Proclitic	ياء النسبة
CASE_INDEF_ACC_GEN	Suffix	التنوين	**SUFF**	Suffix	زيادة في آخر الكلمة
NSUFF_FEM_PL	Proclitic	حروف جمع المؤنث	NSUFF_MASC_PL_NOM	Proclitic	حروف جمع مذكر مرفوع
NSUFF_MASC_PL_ACC	Proclitic	حروف جمع مذكر منصوب	NSUFF_MASC_PL_GEN	Proclitic	حروف جمع مذكر مجرور
NSUFF_MASC_DU_NOM	Proclitic	حروف المثنى مذكر مرفوع	NSUFF_MASC_DU_ACC	Proclitic	حروف المثنى مذكر منصوب
NSUFF_MASC_DU_GEN	Proclitic	حروف مثنى مذكر مجرور	NSUFF_FEM_DU_NOM	Proclitic	حروف المثنى مؤنث مرفوع
NSUFF_FEM_DU_ACC	Proclitic	حروف مثنى مؤنث منصوب	NSUFF_FEM_DU_GEN	Proclitic	حروف مثنى مؤنث مجرور
EMPHATIC_NUN	Suffix	نون التوكيد	**PROTECT_NUN**	Suffix	نون الوقاية
REL_PRON	Relative Pronoun	اسم موصول	**ADV**	Adverb	ظرف
SINGLAR	Number/Singular	مفرد	DUAL	Number/Dual	مثنى
PLURAL	Number/Plural	جمع سالم	**BROKEN_PLR**	Number/Broken plural	جمع تكسير
COLCV_NOUN	Number/Collective noun	اسم الجمع			

Table 6: Tags for suffixes (Bold is new)

particles هل *hal* and أ *>*; use of the suffix ش $ at the end of a verb (e.g., ما قعدش *mA qaEadi$* rather than ما قَعَدَ *mA qaEada* he did not sit); loss of gender distinction, especially in the language of females (e.g., إجو البنات *>ijw AlbanAt* rather than جاءت البنات *jA'at AlbanAt* 'the girls came'). Arabic has a free word order because of grammatical inflections. When all words' grammatical functions are marked with appropriate inflections, it is not necessary to restrict the arrangement of words in a sentence; hence, Classical Arabic exhibits a totally free word order. Modern Standard Arabic shows preference for verb-subject-object even though inflections are amongst its distinctive features. The spoken varieties continue a historical tradition that we suspect had started as early as Islamic times, where case inflection had lost grounds to fixed word order. Preference in Classical Arabic for the default word order (i.e., verb-subject-object) in an otherwise free word order system was a portent of developments to come. As Islamic conquest brought Arabs in contact with foreigners who soon adopted the language, and as the diglossic gap widened, grammatical inflection lost favor in the low variety while it retained its glamour in the high variety, under the influence of the Quran. The spoken, the low, variety started to favor the subject-verb-object word order as a result of the loss of case inflections and to set apart the agent from the patient of the predicate. The written variety manifested in MSA, on the other hand, used the verb-subject-object order as the unmarked default and retained other combinations for special purposes. All modern regional varieties are descendants of old spoken varieties of Arabic in much the same way as Modern Standard Arabic is a successor of Classical Arabic, the written variety. Regional varieties of Arabic share

great many syntactic features. For example, they have two negation patterns: single negation and discontinuous negation (Alqassas, 2015). The first uses the negative particle ما *mA* followed by the verb phrase, whilst the second adds the negative marking suffix ش $ to the verb in addition to the negative particle that precedes it. Thus, I didnt say may be expressed as ماقلتِش *mA qult-i$* or ماقُلت *mA qult*. To negate the future, however, there are three options: (1) the negative particle followed by the imperfect verb as in ما أسافر *mA >asAfir* 'I will not travel'; (2) or followed by the imperfect inflicted with the negative marking suffix as in ما أسافِرش *mA >asAfr-i$* ; (3) or followed by the future particle رح *raH* and the imperfect verb as in ما رح أسافر *mA raH >asAfir*. JCCA consists in part of a spoken language component that is annotated morphologically and syntactically, glossed with MSA forms, and translated into English. This is especially useful with contractions, the hallmarks of spoken Arabic. The gloss is often the non-contracted equivalent in MSA as demonstrated in Table 7.

8 Conclusion and Future Work

This paper outlined the methodology for the design, construction, and annotation of the Jordan Comprehensive Contemporary Arabic Corpus (JCCA). The corpus is balanced, comprehensive, and representative of contemporary Arabic as written and spoken in Arab countries today. It consists of 100 million words that reflect current usage of the language. The corpus consists of 87% written and 13% spoken language. The text of the corpus was selected such that it would be representative of a wide range of geographical regions, genres, subject matters, modes, and media. DI-

Contracted	BW	Full Form	Gloss
شـلونك	$lwnk	أي شيء لونك	how are you?
أصطفل	ASTfl	أصطِف الذي تريد	whatever you want
إيش	<y$	أي شيء	pardon me?
ليش	ly$	لأي شيء	why?
شو	$w	أي شيء هو	what?
بيش	by$	بأي شيء	for how much?
قديش	qdy$	قدر أي شيء	how much?
معلش	mEly$	ما عليك شيء	it's OK!
مظلش	mZl$	ما ظل شيء	nothing left
إللي	<lly	الذي، التي	that/which

Table 7: Contracted words in colloquial Arabic, In this table, the abbreviation *Contracted* represents examples of spoken words (i.e. contractions), *BW* is Buckwalter transliteration, *Full Form* is the non-contracted equivalent in MSA, *gloss* the English meaning.

WAN was upgraded and used to annotate and manually verify the annotation of a one-million-word snapshot of the corpus, making it a gold standard of superior quality that can serve as a resource against which automatic annotation may be compared. JCCA construction made these additional contributions: (i) Development of a new and elaborate tag-set that is based on the morphology of traditional Arabic grammar; (ii) Addition of the roots and morphological patterns of nouns and verbs; (iii) Coverage of the major spoken varieties of Arabic: North Africa; the Nile; the Arabian Peninsula; and Levant. Future work is to make this corpus a monitor corpus where new texts are added proportionally every year. This will facilitate tracking language change and will render the corpus more amiable to lexicography.

9 Acknowledgment

The research reported here was supported by the Scientific Research Fund of the Ministry of Higher Education and Scientific Research, Jordan (Grant No. Soci/2/1/2016).

References

Mourad Abbas and Kamel Smaïli. 2005. Comparison of Topic Identification methods for Arabic Language. In *International Conference on Recent Advances in Natural Language Processing - RANLP 2005*, 14-17, Borovets, Bulgaria.

Mourad Abbas, Kamel Smaili, and Berkani. 2011. Evaluation of topic identification methods on Arabic corpora. *Journal of Digital Information Management*, 9(5):185–192.

Faisal Al-Shargi and Owen Rambow. 2015. DIWAN: A dialectal word annotation tool for Arabic. In *Proceedings of the Second Workshop on Arabic Natural Language Processing*, pages 49–58, Beijing, China. Association for Computational Linguistics.

Latifa Al-Sulaiti and Eric Steven Atwell. 2006. The design of a corpus of Contemporary Arabic. *International Journal of Corpus Linguistics*, 11(2):135–171.

Abdulmohsen Al-Thubaity. 2015. A 700m+ Arabic corpus: KACST Arabic corpus design and construction. *Language Resources and Evaluation*, 49(3):721–751.

Sameh Alansary and Magdy Nagi. 2014. The International Corpus of Arabic: Compilation, Analysis and Evaluation. In *Proceedings of the EMNLP 2014 Workshop on Arabic Natural Language Processing (ANLP)*, pages pages 8–17, Doha, Qatar.

Ahmad Alqassas. 2015. Negation, tense and npis in jordanian arabic. *Lingua*, 156:101–128.

Maha Sulaiman Alrabia, AbdulMalik Al-Salman, Eric Atwell, and Nawal Alhelewh. 2014. KSUCCA: A Key To Exploring Arabic Historical Linguistics. *International Journal of Computational Linguistics (IJCL)*, 5(2):27–36.

Faisal AlShargi, Aidan Kaplan, Ramy Eskander, Nizar Habash, and Owen Rambow. 2016. Morphologically annotated corpora and morphological analyzers for moroccan and sanaani yemeni arabic. In *Proceedings of the Tenth International Conference on Language Resources and Evaluation (LREC 2016)*.

Tressy Arts, Yonatan Belinkov, Nizar Habash, Adam Kilgarriff, and Vit Suchomel. 2014. artenten: Arabic corpus and word sketches. *Journal of King Saud University - Computer and Information Sciences*, 26(4):357 – 371. Special Issue on Arabic NLP.

Paul Baker, Andrew Hardie, and Tony McEnery. 2006. *A Glossary of Corpus Linguistics*. Edinburgh University Press.

Outi Bat-El. 1994. *Stem modification and cluster transfer in Mmodern Hebrew*. Natural Language Linguistic Theory, 12(4), 571-596.

Outi Bat-El. 2001. *In search for the roots of the C-root: The essence of Semitic morphology*. Workshop on Root and Template Morphology. Los Angeles: University of South California.

Yonatan Belinkov, Nizar Habash, Aadm Kilgarriff, Noam Ordan, Ryan Roth, and Vit Suchomel. 2013. arTenTen12: A new, vast corpus for Arabic. In *Second Workshop on Arabic Corpus Linguistics, WACL'S*, Lancaster University, UK.

Claire Brierley, Majdi Sawalha, and Eric Atwell. 2012. Open-Source Boundary-Annotated Corpus for Arabic Speech and Language Processing. In *LREC*, pages 1011–1016.

Claire Brierley, Majdi Sawalha, Barry Heselwood, and Eric Atwell. 2016. A Verified Arabic-IPA Mapping for Arabic Transcription Technology, Informed by Quranic Recitation, Traditional Arabic Linguistics, and Modern Phonetics. *Journal of Semitic Studies*, 61(1):157–186.

Tim Buckwalter and Dilworth Parkinson. 2011. *A frequency dictionary of Arabic: Core vocabulary for learners*. London: Routledge.

Stuart Davis and Bushra Zawaydeh. 2001. *Arabic hypocoristics and the status of the consonantal root*. Linguistic Inquiry, 32(3): 512-520.

Kais Dukes, Eric Atwell, and Nizar Habash. 2013. Supervised collaboration for syntactic annotation of quranic arabic. *Language Resources and Evaluation*, 47(1):33–62.

Thomas Eckart, Faisal Al-shargi, Uwe Quasthoff, and Dirk Goldhahn. 2014. Large arabic web corpora of high quality: The dimensions time and origin. In *Workshop on Free/Open-Source Arabic Corpora and Corpora Processing Tools, LREC*, Reykjavk.

Omaima Ismail, Sane Yagi, and Basam Hammo. 2014. Corpus Linguistic Tools for Historical Semantics in Arabic. *International Journal of Arabic-English Studies (IJAES)*, 15:135–152.

Mustafa Jarrar, Nizar Habash, Faeq Alrimawi, Diyam Akra, and Nasser Zalmout. 2017. Curras: an annotated corpus for the palestinian arabic dialect. *Language Resources and Evaluation*, 51(3):745–775.

McCarthy, John. 1981. *A prosodic theory of nonconcatenative morphology*. Linguistic Inquiry, 12, 373-418.

Tony McEnery and Andrew Hardie. 2012. *Corpus Linguistics: Method, Theory and Practice*. Cambridge Textbooks in Linguistics. Cambridge University Press.

Arfath Pasha, Mohamed Al-Badrashiny, Mona T Diab, Ahmed El Kholy, Ramy Eskander, Nizar Habash, Manoj Pooleery, Owen Rambow, and Ryan Roth. 2014. Madamira: A fast, comprehensive tool for morphological analysis and disambiguation of arabic. In *LREC*, volume 14, pages 1094–1101.

Jeam-Francois Prunet, Renee Bland, and Ali Idrissi. 2000. *The mental representation of Semitic words*. Linguistic Inquiry, 31(4). 609-648.

Ratcliffe, Robert . 1998. *The broken plural problem in Arabic and comparative Semitic: allomorphy and analogy in non-concatenative morphology*. Amsterdam/Philadelphia: John Benjamins.

Motaz Saad and Wesam Ashour. 2010. Osac: Open source arabic corpora. In *EEECS10 the 6th International Symposium on Electrical and Electronics Engineering and Computer Science*, pages 118–123.

Majdi Sawalha, Claire Brierley, and Eric Atwell. 2012. Prosody Prediction for Arabic via the Open-Source Boundary-Annotated Quran Corpus. *Journal of Speech Sciences*, 2(2):175–191.

Majdi Sawalha, Claire Brierley, and Eric Atwell. 2014. Automatically generated, phonemic Arabic-IPA pronunciation tiers for the Boundary Annotated Qur'an Dataset for Machine Learning (version 2.0). In *proceedings of LRE-Rel 2: 2nd Workshop on Language Resource and Evaluation for Religious Texts, LREC 2014 post-conference workshop 31st May 2014, Reykjavik, Iceland*, page 42. LRA.

Ussishkin, Adam. 1999. *The inadequacy of the consonantal root: Modern Hebrew denominal verbs and output-output correspondence*. Phonology, 16(3), 401-442.

Ussishkin, Adam. 2005. *A Fixed prosodic theory of nonconcatenative templatic morphology*. Natural Language Linguistic Theory, 23(1), 169-218.

Wajdi Zaghouani. 2017. Critical Survey of the Freely Available Arabic Corpora. *CoRR*, abs/1702.07835.

Translating Between Morphologically Rich Languages: An Arabic-to-Turkish Machine Translation System

İlknur Durgar El-Kahlout   Emre Bektaş   Naime Şeyma Erdem   Hamza Kaya

Tübitak-Bilgem, Kocaeli, Turkey

{ilknur.durgar,emre.bektas,seyma.erdem,
hamza.kaya}@tubitak.gov.tr

Abstract

This paper introduces the work on building a machine translation system for Arabic-to-Turkish in the news domain. Our work includes collecting parallel datasets in several ways for a new and low-resource language pair, building baseline systems with state-of-the-art architectures and developing language specific algorithms for better translation. Parallel datasets are mainly collected three different ways; i) translating Arabic texts into Turkish by professional translators, ii) exploiting the web for open-source Arabic-Turkish parallel texts, iii) using back-translation. We performed preliminary experiments for Arabic-to-Turkish machine translation with neural (Marian) machine translation tools with a novel morphologically motivated vocabulary reduction method.

1 Introduction

It is a well-known fact that to develop robust systems with data-driven methods, it is crucial to have large amounts of data. If the problem needs only raw monolingual data, the solution is straightforward; crawl the web and collect the data in the specific domain. In cases of annotating the data (e.g., treebanks) or parallel data (e.g., for machine translation) collecting the needed data is a bit harder.

Even though machine translation (MT) is one of the popular topics in natural language processing, most of the existing parallel texts include English as one of the languages (e.g., Europarl (Koehn, 2005), Multi-UN (Eisele and Chen, 2010)). For the rest of the languages, generating a new language pair from scratch is tough work that needs extensive human effort and substantial funding. One way of translating languages with no parallel data is pivoting, which means one should find corpora for two language pairs such as source-to-pivot and pivot-to-target with sufficient number of sentences in the same domain and then train and maintain two MT systems. Even though we can find such corpora in the expected domain for the given languages, the error propagation is the biggest problem of pivoting as the second system will try to translate erroneous output of the previous system.

In this work, our goal is building an Arabic-Turkish machine translation on the news domain. The task is very interesting for several reasons; primarily, both the source and the target languages are morphologically rich which proves to be a quite challenging task. Our attention on this language pair has both social and political grounds. Arabic is the official language in most of the Middle East countries that Turkey has relations with. Moreover, there is a need for quick and cheap translation solutions in communicating with the increasing number of refugees in Turkish spoken areas.

The news domain is selected as it has several benefits such as the fact that at least one side of the parallel texts can be found publicly on the web (e.g. several news portals) and Arabic is written in Modern Standard Arabic format for the news domain which is common for all Arabic speakers. To collect the data, both monolingual and bilingual data on the web is exploited. Selected portion of a monolingual data is translated into Turkish by professional translators, the publicly available but out-of-domain parallel data is cleaned and used directly and, lastly, rest of the monolingual Turkish data is back-translated to train our systems. Both unsupervised and supervised morphology reduction techniques are used to reduce the vocabulary size to a fixed number and let to fit our vocabulary into a given number of tokens while training the neural machine translation (NMT) systems .

This paper is organized as follows; Section 2 gives brief information about the source and tar-

Proceedings of the Fourth Arabic Natural Language Processing Workshop, pages 158–166
Florence, Italy, August 1, 2019. ©2019 Association for Computational Linguistics

get languages. Section 3 describes the data obtaining methods, and Section 4 introduces the segmentation methods for Turkish to alleviate the morphological differences and explains generation of surface word forms as post-processing. In section 5, we talk about our experimental setup including the data sizes and morphology abstraction/separation experiments with Marian (Junczys-Dowmunt et al., 2018) NMT tool. Finally, we conclude in Section 6.

2 Arabic and Turkish

2.1 Arabic

Arabic is a member of the Central Semitic language family. It is spoken by approximately 300 million people (ranked as sixth language) and accepted as official language in 27 countries (ranked as the third language after English and French). Arabic can be classified into three categories as; Classical Arabic (the language of the Qur'an), Modern Standard Arabic (is used in written texts and formal speeches, not a native language) and Arabic dialects (spoken by locals, mostly not written). Arabic is written from right to left with distinct 28 letters with various combinations of dots above or below these shapes. There are no capital letters. Roots are mostly composed of consonants and can have different meanings with the help of the vowels and diacritics. Arabic has a very complex and sometimes inconsistent orthography [1].

Arabic has a highly complex concatenative derivational and inflectional morphology. Words can take prefixes and suffixes at the same time for tense, number, person, gender information. For an example of the concatenation processes, the Arabic word, وسينهي (gloss; and he will finish) can be decomposed as ينهي (finished), ‎+س (he will), and ‎+و (and).

2.2 Turkish

Turkish is a member of the Ural-Altay language family and is the most commonly spoken Turkic language by more than 90 million people. It is the official language of Turkey and Northern Cyprus. There are lots of minority groups all over the world mainly in Europe (approximately 5M speakers).

From the machine translation point of view, Turkish has interesting and challenging properties when compared to the mostly studied languages in data-driven MT research such as English, German, French and Spanish. First of all Turkish is a highly agglutinative language where words are formed by concatenating morphemes (by suffixation) with very productive inflectional and derivational processes. Turkish morpheme surface realizations are generated by several morphophonemic processes such as vowel harmony, consonant assimilation, and elisions. The morphotactics of word forms could be quite complex when multiple derivations are involved. Indeed, Turkish is one of the languages that needs special attention because of its morphological richness. An example of the Turkish morphology can be shown with the Turkish word *partisindeydi* (gloss: s/he was at his/her party), this word can be decomposed into four morphemes as *parti* (party), *+si* (her/his), *+nde* (in) and *+ydi* (s/he was).

3 Obtaining Data

The backbone of the machine translation system is a "good" data like the most of the machine learning problems. In case of MT, a parallel corpora is required. The domain of the data, the quality and the quantity directly effect the translation output. On the other hand, obtaining such data for the machine translation purpose is not that easy. There have been efforts made to obtain parallel texts for machine translation by crawling web for parallel data (Uszkoreit et al., 2010), and by using MechanicalTurk (Ambati and Vogel, 2010; Zbib et al., 2012). Even though we spent some efforts to use MTurk, it is not yet available for requesters outside USA.

We specify three different ways to obtain the Arabic-Turkish parallel corpora; i) by translating Arabic texts into Turkish by professional translators, ii) by exploiting web for open-source Arabic-Turkish parallel texts and, iii) by back-translating monolingual Arabic data by using existing machine translation systems.

3.1 Obtaining In-domain Training Data

We selected approximately 170K Arabic sentences in the news domain from LDC datasets and had them translated to Turkish by professional translators in order to obtain gold-standard training data. Even though the translators are experts, quality assurance is an important issue. We aimed to avoid low-quality translations with a few steps.

---

[1] http://www.nizarhabash.com/tutorials/EMNLP-2014-Diab+Habash-Tutorial.pdf

Before the translation process, we labeled each sentence to keep the parallelism in translations. This labeling is done to prevent translators not to join any two sentences or split one sentence into pieces while translating. Then, we asked each translator to translate 50 sentences. We analyzed the outputs, detected common translation errors and prepared a translation procedure for machine translation purpose. The translation procedure had rules such as;

- Every information in the source sentence should be translated into Turkish. Neither addition nor deletion of a part of a sentence was allowed.

- Translations should not have any meaning disorder or fluency problems. Constituents can be arranged due to grammar rules without changing the meaning. Phrases should be chosen as precisely as possible.

- Each sentence should be translated independently, without considering the previous context.

- Sentences in two different lines should not be combined into a single sentence or vice versa.

After the translation was completed, we employed a bilingual consultant to randomly select 5% of the sentence pairs from each document and score them according to the quality of translation. If the quality is lower than given threshold, translators re-translated each problematic document once more. After this process, if the quality was still low, we rejected the translations for this document.

We separated 1,600 sentences for development and 1,357 sentences for testing and demanded four Turkish references to be translated by four different translators. Table 1 shows the time and cost spent to generate the gold-standard translations for training and development. As seen in the table, generating a parallel corpora by human translation from Turkish to Arabic is a time and money consuming task as the number of such translators are limited [2]. Moreover, after spending a huge budget and time, the size of the corpora is not still sufficient to train a NMT system. These facts forced us to search the web for publicly available data.

Corpus	# Sents	Cost ($)	Time
Training	160,764	202K	7 months
Development	11,828	12K	2 months

Table 1: Time and cost spent to generate gold-standard translations.

3.2 Searching Web for Publicly Available Data

We exploited the web in order to take advantage of already existing parallel Arabic-Turkish data. We obtained two subsets of parallel data with small effort but both were out-of-domain. The corpora are;

WIT: Web Inventory of Transcribed and Translated Talks (Cettolo et al., 2012) contains transcriptions of TED talks in more than hundred languages. We selected the IWSLT 2014[3] training data as it contains both Arabic-English and Turkish-English language pairs. Firstly, common talk titles are searched and then on these common talks, Arabic and Turkish sentences that have the same English translation for each talk are matched. As a result, 130K such Arabic-Turkish parallel sentences are obtained.

OpenSubtitles2018[4]: OpenSubtitles2018 (Lison and Tiedemann, 2016) is a large database of TV and movie subtitles for sixty languages. The database has Arabic-Turkish parallel texts that contains almost 28M sentences. Even though these subtitles are aligned based on time stamps, the word order differences between the languages make one-to-one sentence alignment harder. To solve this problem and obtain more reliable parallel data, the text was re-aligned by a bilingual sentence aligner (Moore, 2002). Using this method, 21M out of 28M sentences are selected.

Both WIT and OpenSubtitles2018 are out-of-domain (OOD) for the news domain MT task, and the ratio of this OOD corpora to the news domain is huge (20M to 130K). To increase the size of the news corpora, we used a well known technique, backtranslation.

3.3 Monolingual Turkish Data and Backtranslation

In recently published NMT systems, backtranslation (Sennrich et al., 2016a) is applied commonly to increase the parallel corpora if the training data

---

[2]As the Arabic part of the corpus is licensed by LDC, the generated corpora can not be shared with any third parties

[3]https://wit3.fbk.eu/mt.php?release=2014-01
[4]http://opus.nlpl.eu/OpenSubtitles2018.php

Corpus	In-Dom.?	# Sents
Baseline (BASE)	Yes	160K
Subtitles (OOD1)	No	21M
WIT (OOD2)	No	130K
Monolingual (MONO)	Yes	3M
Test	Yes	1357
Development	Yes	1600

Table 2: Type and size of the corpora used in the experiments.

is limited. For backtranslation, two freely available monolingual Turkish news corpora CNN-Turk[5] (2.14M sentences) and Aljazeera[6] (718K sentences) are used.

Collected monolingual Turkish corpora is preprocessed to separate each sentence to a line, to remove sentences only consisting of foreign words, symbols, numbers, and blank lines, and to replace carriage returns with line feed characters. Lastly, the corpus is sorted and the duplicate sentences are removed.

After backtranslation, as automatic systems can not produce gold-standard translations for all sentences, we need to filter the translated output to obtain a "better" subset of it. We remove translations if; i) output has only one word, ii) the ratio of input/output words is more than three and, iii) any word except the Turkish stop-words repeats more than three times. After all the collection efforts, the size and the domain of the parallel corpora is shown Table 2.

4 Incorporating Linguistically Segmented Subwords

4.1 Previous Work

Incorporating morphology when working with morphologically rich languages in SMT has been addressed by several researchers for many years. (Yang and Kirchhoff, 2006) decomposed the unknown source words at the test time into morphological subwords and translated these subwords that are unknown to the decoder by using phrase-based (PB) back-off models. For Arabic, (Zollmann et al., 2006; Sadat and Habash, 2006) exploited morphology by using morphologically-analyzed and/or tagged resources. (Popovic and Ney, 2004) presented different ways of improv-

ing translation quality for inflected languages Serbian, Catalan and Spanish by using stems, suffixes and part-of-speech information. (Goldwater and McClosky, 2005) replaced Czech words with lemmas and pseudo words to obtain improvements in Czech-to-English statistical machine translation. (Minkov et al., 2007) used morphological postprocessing on the target side by using structural information and information from the source side in order to improve translation quality for Russian and Arabic. (Luong et al., 2010) proposed a hybrid morpheme-word representation in the translation models of morphologically-rich languages.

The first effort for Turkish morphological segmentation, (Durgar El-Kahlout and Oflazer, 2010), used morphological analysis to separate some Turkish inflectional morphemes that have counterparts on the English side in English-to-Turkish statistical machine translation. (Bisazza and Federico, 2009) present a series of segmentation schemes to explore the optimal segmentation for statistical machine translation of Turkish. (Mermer and Akin, 2010) worked on unsupervised morphological segmentation from parallel data for the task of statistical machine translation.

With the rise of neural machine translation, fitting the whole corpora into a fixed number vocabulary has become a challenge. Despite its success over the previous SMT methods, NMT has the lack of using large vocabularies as the training/decoding complexity is directly proportional to the vocabulary size. One solution is to limit the vocabulary size to a fixed number but this is a challenging problem especially for morphologically rich languages.

A well-known and effective method to solve this problem is the Byte-pair encoding (Sennrich et al., 2016b) (BPE) which splits words into "reasonable" number of subwords to satisfy the fix vocabulary criteria. BPE is an unsupervised word segmentation method originally used as a word compression algorithm. It iteratively "merges" the most frequent character n-grams into subwords leaving no out-of-vocabulary words. BPE is totally statistical, likelihood-based word splitting method and involves no means of linguistic information. So, researchers exploit morphology once more to incorporate "linguistically" separated subword representation when translating from/to morphologically rich languages (Sánchez-Cartagena and Toral, 2016; Bradbury and Socher, 2016) with

---

[5]https://www.cnnturk.com/

[6]http://www.aljazeera.com.tr/

neural machine translation.

Recently, (Ataman et al., 2017) incorporate both supervised and unsupervised morphological segmentation methods for Turkish sub-word generation for Turkish-to-English NMT. They used morphological features for the suffixes in order to decrease the sparseness caused by suffix allomorphy.

4.2 Morphological Abstraction of Turkish

The productive morphology of Turkish potentially implies a very large vocabulary size: noun roots have about 100 inflected forms and verbs have much more. These numbers are much higher when derivations are allowed. For example, one can generate thousands of words from a single root even when at most two derivations are allowed. Turkish employs about 30,000 root words (about 10,000 of which are highly frequent) and about 150 distinct suffixes. As an example to the morphological variation, in our Turkish corpora, the root word *inisiyatif* (literally: initiative) occurs totally 258 times in 47 different forms where 25 of these forms are singletons. Using morphologically segmented subwords is straightforward and sufficient when Turkish is on the source side of the translation. In case of Turkish is on the target side, any process such as segmentation or abstraction must be done more carefully as in the final representation the surface word should be generated. As a result, the "best" representation have to be selected that covers the whole information for Turkish words to generate the correct surface form.

In this work, we present an abstraction method similar to our previous work (Durgar El-Kahlout and Oflazer, 2010). Our abstraction can generate back the surface form after translation easily which allows us to use this method even if Turkish is on the target side. Simply we abstracted all possible letters in the morpheme suffixes to alleviate the differences due to the morphophonemic processes such as vowel harmony, consonant assimilation, and elisions. First we apply a morphological analysis and detect the root and the morpheme of the word, and then on morpheme we replace i) vowels *a* and *e* to capital *A* (vowel harmony); ii) *i, ı, u and ü* to capital *H*; iii) *ğ* and *k* to *K* (consonant assimilation) and; iv) *t* and *d* to *D* (consonant assimilation). In order to combine the statistics and reduce the data sparseness problem, abstraction is a better choice for morpheme representation as most surface distinctions are manifes-

tations of word-internal phenomena such as vowel harmony and morphotactics. When surface morphemes are considered by themselves as the units in BPE, statistics are fragmented.

Table 3 shows examples of Turkish words in surface form, abstracted word and the gloss in English with highlights for the common parts. As seen in table, the first and the second columns share three morphemes +mAK+DA+DHr (Write Features) but differentiate on the surface form because of the morphophonemic processes. After the abstraction, the morphemes are same as in the English case.

On top of abstraction, we also kept *root +morphemes* separated versions of the both surface and abstracted Turkish words and experimented with each scenario to understand the effect of abstraction and separation (Table 4 number (5)). In each case we also employed BPE for the vocabulary fitting.

Table 4 shows a Turkish sentence with surface form, abstraction and separation and also BPE applied on each version. Root word *inisiyatif* (literally: initiative) separated by BPE into two or three segments depending on the length of the morphemes in the surface and abstracted representations. In representation (4), we observe that BPE tends to keep first (root) segment longer than the surface case because of the abstracted morphemes. By applying separation over surface or abstraction form, the effect of BPE is lost and only the unknown/singleton words are segmented by the algorithm as in the word *IGAD* in representation (6).

4.3 Word Generation

As stated above, making abstraction and/or segmentation processes on the target side always requires much more attention then the source side. Generating the correct surface form is crucial for the end user as they do not need to be aware of the inner representations. In order to generate the correct surface form, we employed an in-house morphological generation tool which transforms the given text with words in the format of root word and abstracted morphemes, to the correct single-word form. As a first step, this generation tool has been trained by a large Turkish corpus and works by simply creating a reverse-map through morphological segmentation of the corpus. This map contains root+morpheme sequences as keys and their corresponding surface word forms as values.

Word	Abstraction	Gloss
kahrolmaktadır	kahrol+**mAKDADHr**	**s/he is** depressed
şüphelenilmektedir	şüphe+lAnHl**mAkDADHr**	**s/he is** suspected
partisindeydi	parti+s**HnDAyDH**	**s/he was at his/her** party
sarayındaydı	saray+**HnDayDH**	**s/he was in her/his** palace

Table 3: Turkish abstraction examples

(1) TR: Bu ortak inisiyatif kapsamında Sudan sorununa kapsamlı bir çözüm yer alıyor , IGAD inisiyatifinde ise yalnızca güneyle sınırlı .

(2) 1+BPE: Bu ortak inisiya@ @ tif kapsamnda Sudan sorununa kapsamlı bir çözüm yer alyor , I@ @ G@ @ AD inisiya@ @ tifi@ @ nde ise yalnızca gün@ @ eyle sınırlı .

(3) 1+Abst.: Bu ortak inisiyatif kapsamHnDA Sudan sorunHnA kapsamlH bir çözüm yer alHyor , IGAD inisiyatifHnDA ise yalnzca güneylA snrlH .

(4) 3+BPE: Bu ortak inisiyat@ @ if kapsamHnDA Sudan sorunHnA kapsamlH bir çözüm yer alHyor , I@ @ GA@ @ D inisiyat@ @ ifH@ @ nDA ise yalnzca gün@ @ eylA snrlH .

(5) 3+Sep.: Bu ortak inisiyatif kapsam +HnDA Sudan sorun +HnA kapsam +lH bir çözüm yer al +Hyor , IGAD inisiyatif +HnDA ise yalnzca güney +lA snr +lH .

(6) 4+BPE: Bu ortak inisiyatif kapsam +HnDA Sudan sorun +HnA kapsam +lH bir çözüm yer al +Hyor , I@ @ G@ @ AD inisiyatif +HnDA ise yalnzca güney +lA snr +lH .

English: Within this joint initiative, there is a comprehensive solution to the Sudanese problem, while in the IGAD initiative it is limited to the south

Table 4: Turkish sentences after different segmentation schemes

While creating this map, disambiguation step of morphological segmentation is omitted to increase the coverage, as keeping multiple resolutions for a surface word form will increase the number of keys for the reverse-map. Then the reverse-map is sorted by the number of occurrences of segmentation in order to select the most common ones.

In our experiments, the reverse-map succeeds to recover the 92% of the abstracted words into surface forms successfully. For the rest of the words, we defined 23 hand-written rules to generate the words which works with 97% success. Defining the generation rules are not straightforward. For example the morphemes attached to the proper foreign words can be different depending on how the words are pronounced in Turkish.

5   Machine Translation Setup

All available data shown in Table 2 was tokenized, truecased (for Turkish) and the maximum sentence length were fixed to 90 for the translation model. As different segmentations of Arabic is out of our scope in this paper, we segmented Arabic prefixes and suffixes from with MADAMIRA (Pasha et al., 2014) with ATB parameter.

To produce the abstracted Turkish words, the first step is the segmentation of morphemes and then an accurate disambiguation of the morphemes within the sentence. Thus, we first pass each word through a morphological analyzer (Oflazer, 1994). The output of the analyzer contains the morphological features encoded for all possible analyses and interpretations of the word. Then we perform morphological disambiguation using morphological features (Sak et al., 2007). Once the contextually-salient morphological interpretation is selected, we process the abstraction algorithm. On top of the abstraction and segmentation processes, we also trained BPE models over the training sets, for each language disjointly.

For the neural machine translation experiments reported in this paper, comparatively new and better performing NMT architecture, Transformer (Vaswani et al., 2017) is used by Marian (Junczys-Dowmunt et al., 2018) toolkit. System is trained on a workstation housing 4 NVIDIA titan GPUs. The GPU memory parameters are set as follows; *mini-batch-fit* is checked, workspace reserved to 8000, and maxi-batch to 900. With this setup, 24k words/s training speed using all the GPUs in parallel is achieved. Transformer *-type* is employed for training. Depth of the network is set to 4, learning rate is set to 0.0001 with no warmup, and vocabulary size is set to 40k. *Mini-batch-fit* option is enabled. Usually it took 4-5 days to converge for the experiments.

Our early stopping criteria is 20 runs without a BLEU (Papineni et al., 2002) increase. Moreover, we use Marian-decoder's beam search decoding with size 16. We ensemble two different models which resulted in the highest two BLEU scores on the development set during validation runs. We then merge the subwords back together in the hypothesis as described in 4.3.

5.1 Results

First group of experiments are performed to evaluate the effect of the data collected from different sources. As seen in Table 5, our baseline experiment is trained on the union of in-domain human translated corpora (BASE) and out-of-domain corpora WIT (OOD1) with a ratio 1:1. We did not perform with only BASE corpora as it is quite small to make sense for NMT training. On top of this experiment, we augmented corpora with approximately 2M backtranslated corpora (MONO) with a ratio almost 1:7. Even though this ratio is above the suggested (Sennrich et al., 2016a), we observed an improvement of +6 BLEU points. We argue that if the backtranslated data is preprocessed to satisfy some quality criterion as we described in Section 3.3, one can extend training corpora with much more backtranslated data. As a last experiment, we combined the Subtitles18 data (OOD2) with 21M sentences with a ratio 1:10 to the experiment (2). As a result, despite adding a huge out-of-domain, we again obtained an improvement more than +2 BLEU points. The improvement on BLEU scores seems lower than predicted when compared to the size of the data but we should be aware of that the OOD2 corpora share very limited part with news domain.

For the second group of experiments, we investigate the effect of abstraction and segmentation of Turkish. In experiment (3), we applied three different segmentation/abstraction representations. In the first representation (exp. 4), we separated root words and morphemes into two (e.g. *kahrolmaktadır* as *kahrol +maktadır*), in second representation (exp. 5), we only employed abstraction (e.g. *kahrolmaktadır* as *kahrolmAK-DADHr*) and in the third representation (exp. 6), we applied both segmentation and abstraction to-

Corpora/System	Dev	Test
(1) BASE + OOD1	15.70	15.91
(2) 1 + MONO	21.91	21.78
(3) 2 + OOD2	22.76	24.09
(4) (3) + Separated	23.01	24.13
(5) (3) + Abstracted	23.98	**24.92**
(6) (3) + Abst.+ Sep.	24.11	24.83
Google	19.62	20.70
Yandex	10.91	11.82

Table 5: Arabic-to-Turkish MT BLEU scores due to the different traning corpora

gether (e.g. *kahrolmaktadır* as *kahrol +mAK-DADHr*). It is noticed that both segmentation and abstraction processes help to improve the translation. The improvement caused by segmentation is expected as supported with previous researches. The results achieved by this work show that our novel abstraction representation is a better alternative than segmentation to help BPE for Turkish. We observe almost no improvement with segmentation (some small positive change in development data) but an improvement of +0.8 BLEU with abstraction even with huge training data of 24M sentences. Similarly, combining both segmentation and abstraction in one representation does not help the system as much as abstraction does.

As this work is the first attempt for Arabic-to-Turkish MT to our best knowledge, in order to compare our systems, we also translated test data with Google[7] and Yandex [8] and listed the scores in last two rows. The unique word counts (vocabulary) after each representation are shown in Table 6. It is noticed that just separation root words and morphemes drops the vocabulary more than half but as the final vocabulary is fitted to 40K this reduction does not make a significant impact on the translation. The small count increases in the abstracted representations comes from the different morphological disambiguations of the same word.

In the following example, we show both ours and Google translations of an Arabic sentence. Even both of the translations are almost perfect, there is an important difference in handling the correct tense selection (present vs. past tense). Our translation selects the more suitable tense than Google translation which is also closer to the reference.

---

[7]translate.google.com
[8]ceviri.yandex.com.tr

Corpora Type	# Unique Tokens
Baseline	1026957
Separated	425216
Abstracted	1027991
Abst. + Sep.	426585

Table 6: Type and size of the corpora used in the experiments.

- **Source:** الصين تحقق منجزات باهرة فى تطوير العلوم والتكنولوجيا فى فترة ٢٠٠١-٢٠٠٥

- **Morp-NMT:** Çin , 2001-2005 yıllarında bilim ve teknolojinin gelişiminde büyük başarılar elde etti .

- **Google:** Çin 2001-2005 yıllarında bilim ve teknolojinin gelişmesinde önemli baarılar elde ediyor

- **Reference:** Çin 2001-2005 yıllarında bilim ve teknolojinin gelişmesinde önemli baarılar elde ediyor

- **English:** Between 2001 and 2005, China Recording Science and Technological Innovation

6   Conclusion

This paper focused on machine translation system for a new low-resourced language pair Arabic-Turkish in news domain which is the first effort for this language pair to the best of our knowledge. We obtained standard in-domain data by human translators. As this method is both time consuming and expensive, we exploited publicly available corpora such as TED talks and subtitle translations. Later, we backtranslated monolingual Turkish news corpora. Finally, we performed experiments with all of these corpora and reported +8 BLEU increase over the baseline setup for state-of-the-art neural machine translation system Marian. On top of these experiments, we also incorporate language specific processes such as the abstraction of morphemic processes caused by vowel harmony and consonant assimilation. We showed an improvement of +0.8 BLEU points with our abstraction representation. We also run a morphological generation tool after the translation process which covers 98% words correctly. Our future work includes applying the same abstraction algorithm to Turkish while translating from/to other European languages.

Acknowledgments

We thank the anonymous reviewers for their detailed and constructive comments. This work is supported by The Scientific and Technological Research Council of Turkey (project no: 110G125)

References

Vamshi Ambati and Stephan Vogel. 2010. Can crowds build parallel corpora for machine translation systems? In *Proceedings of the NAACL HLT 2010 Workshop on Creating Speech and Language Data with Amazon's Mechanical Turk*, CSLDAMT '10, pages 62–65.

Duygu Ataman, Matteo Negri, Marco Turchi, and Marcello Federico. 2017. Linguistically motivated vocabulary reduction for neural machine translation from turkish to english. *CoRR*, abs/1707.09879.

Arianna Bisazza and Marcello Federico. 2009. Morphological pre-processing for Turkish to English statistical machine translation. In *Proceedings of the International Workshop on Spoken Language Translation (IWSLT)*, pages 129–135.

James Bradbury and Richard Socher. 2016. Metamind neural machine translation system for wmt 2016. In *Proceedings of the First Conference on Machine Translation*, pages 264–267.

Mauro Cettolo, Christian Girardi, and Marcello Federico. 2012. Wit³: Web inventory of transcribed and translated talks. In *Proceedings of the 16th Conference of the European Association for Machine Translation (EAMT)*, pages 261–268, Trento, Italy.

İlknur Durgar El-Kahlout and Kemal Oflazer. 2010. Exploiting morphology and local word reordering in english-to-turkish phrase-based statistical machine translation. *Audio, Speech, and Language Processing, IEEE Transactions on*, 18(6):1313–1322.

Andreas Eisele and Yu Chen. 2010. MultiUN: A multilingual corpus from United Nation Documents. In *LREC*.

Sharon Goldwater and David McClosky. 2005. Improving statistical MT through morphological analysis. In *Proceedings of Human Language Technology Conference and Conference on Empirical Methods in Natural Language Processing*, pages 676–683, Vancouver, British Columbia, Canada.

Marcin Junczys-Dowmunt, Roman Grundkiewicz, Tomasz Dwojak, Hieu Hoang, Kenneth Heafield, Tom Neckermann, Frank Seide, Ulrich Germann, Alham Fikri Aji, Nikolay Bogoychev, Andr F. T.

Martins, and Alexandra Birch. 2018. Marian: Fast neural machine translation in c++. *arXiv preprint arXiv:1804.00344*.

Philipp Koehn. 2005. Europarl: A parallel corpus for statistical machine translation. In *MT Summit*.

Pierre Lison and Jörg Tiedemann. 2016. Opensubtitles2016: Extracting large parallel corpora from movie and tv subtitles. In *In Proceedings of the 10th International Conference on Language Resources and Evaluation (LREC)*.

Minh-Thang Luong, Preslav Nakov, and Min-Yen Kan. 2010. A hybrid morpheme-word representation for machine translation of morphologically rich languages. In *Proceedings of the 2010 Conference on Empirical Methods in Natural Language Processing*, pages 148–157, Cambridge, MA. Association for Computational Linguistics.

Coşkun Mermer and Ahmet Afşin Akin. 2010. Unsupervised search for the optimal segmentation for statistical machine translation. In *Proceedings of the ACL 2010 Student Research Workshop*, ACLstudent '10, pages 31–36, Stroudsburg, PA, USA. Association for Computational Linguistics.

Einat Minkov, Kristina Toutanova, and Hisami Suzuki. 2007. Generating complex morphology for machine translation. In *Proceedings of the 45th Annual Meeting of the Association of Computational Linguistics*, pages 128–135, Prague, Czech Republic. Association for Computational Linguistics.

Robert C. Moore. 2002. Fast and accurate sentence alignment of bilingual corpora. In *Machine Translation: From Research to Real Users*, pages 135–144, Berlin, Heidelberg. Springer Berlin Heidelberg.

Kemal Oflazer. 1994. Two-level description of turkish morphology. *Literary and Linguistic Computing*, 9:137–148.

Kishore Papineni, Salim Roukos, Todd Ward, and Wei-Jing Zhu. 2002. BLEU: A method for automatic evaluation of machine translation. In *Proceedings of the 41st Annual Meeting of the Association for Computational Linguistics (ACL)*, pages 311–318.

A Pasha, Mohamed Elbadrashiny, Mona Diab, A Elkholy, Rushdi Eskandar, Nizar Habash, M Pooleery, Owen Rambow, and Ryan Roth. 2014. Madamira: A fast, comprehensive tool for morphological analysis and disambiguation of arabic. In *Proceedings of the 9th International Conference on Language Resources and Evaluation*, pages 1094–1101.

Maja Popovic and Hermann Ney. 2004. Towards the use of word stems and suffixes for statistical machine translation. In *Proceedings of the 4th LREC*, pages 1585–1588.

F Sadat and Nizar Habash. 2006. Combination of arabic prerocessing schemes for statistical machine translation. In *Proceedings of the COLING/ACL, AMTA*.

Haşim Sak, Tunga Güngör, and Murat Saraçlar. 2007. Morphological disambiguation of turkish text with perception algorithm. In *Proceeding of CICLING, LNCS 4394*, pages 107–118.

Víctor M. Sánchez-Cartagena and Antonio Toral. 2016. Abu-matran at wmt 2016 translation task: Deep learning, morphological segmentation and tuning on character sequences. In *WMT*.

Rico Sennrich, Barry Haddow, and Alexandra Birch. 2016a. Improving neural machine translation models with monolingual data. In *Procceedings of the 54th Annual eeting of the Association for Computational Linguistics*.

Rico Sennrich, Barry Haddow, and Alexandra Birch. 2016b. Neural machine translation of rare words with subword units. *Procceedings of the 54th Annual eeting of the Association for Computational Linguistics*, 1715-1725.

Jakob Uszkoreit, Jay M. Ponte, Ashok C. Popat, and Moshe Dubiner. 2010. Large scale parallel document mining for machine translation. In *Proceedings of the 23rd International Conference on Computational Linguistics*, COLING '10, pages 1101–1109.

Ashish Vaswani, Noam Shazeer, Niki Parmar, Jakob Uszkoreit, Llion Jones, Aidan N. Gomez, Lukasz Kaiser, and Illia Polosukhin. 2017. Attention is all you need. *CoRR*, abs/1706.03762.

Mei Yang and Katrin Kirchhoff. 2006. Phrase-based backoff models for machine translation of highly inflected languages. In *Proceedings of EACL*, pages 41–48.

Rabih Zbib, Erika Malchiodi, Jacob Devlin, David Stallard, Spyros Matsoukas, Richard Schwartz, John Makhoul, Omar F. Zaidan, and Chris Callison-Burch. 2012. Machine translation of Arabic dialects. In *Proceedings of the 2012 Conference of the North American Chapter of the Association for Computational Linguistics: Human Language Technologies*, NAACL HLT '12, pages 49–59.

Andreas Zollmann, Ashish Venugopal, and Stephan Vogel. 2006. Bridging the inflection morphology gap for Arabic statistical machine translation. In *Proceedings of the Human Language Technology Conference of the NAACL, Companion Volume: Short Papers*, pages 201–204, New York City, USA.

Improved Generalization of Arabic Text Classifiers

Alaa Khaddaj   Hazem Hajj   Wassim El-Hajj
American University of Beirut
Beirut, Lebanon
{awk11, hh63, we07}@aub.edu.lb

Abstract

While transfer learning for text has been very active in the English language, progress in Arabic has been slow, including the use of Domain Adaptation (DA). Domain Adaptation is used to generalize the performance of any classifier by trying to balance the classifier's accuracy for a particular task among different text domains. In this paper, we propose and evaluate two variants of a domain adaptation technique: the first is a base model called Domain Adversarial Neural Network (DANN), while the second is a variation that incorporates representational learning. Similar to previous approaches, we propose the use of proxy A-distance as a metric to assess the success of generalization. We make use of ArSentD-LEV, a multi-topic dataset collected from the Levantine countries, to test the performance of the models. We show the superiority of the proposed method in accuracy and robustness when dealing with the Arabic language.

1 Introduction

Natural Language Processing (NLP) for Arabic is challenging due to the complexity of the language. Additionally, resources in Arabic are scarce making it difficult to achieve NLP progress at the pace of other resource-rich languages such as English (Badaro et al., 2019). As a result, there is a need for transfer learning methods that can overcome the resource limitations. In this paper, we propose the use of domain adaptation to address this challenge while considering the task of sentiment analysis (SA) also referred to as Opinion Mining (OM).

When training over a dataset with multiple domains, different domains have different data distributions. This has a negative impact when training on one domain and testing on another, since the model would not be able to generalize well.

Although domains within the same dataset have differences, they share some characteristics. For example, consider reviews of Amazon products: reviews of electronic products are different from book reviews, but these two domains share the general structure of reviews. We say there exists a shift in the data's distribution between the two domains. To solve this problem, many approaches were proposed within the field of Domain Adaptation (DA) (Ben-David et al., 2010). This field is receiving a lot of attention in English, a lot more than its Arabic counterpart.

Solving the data shift problem is of interest for many reasons. First, it is harder for machine learning to learn good internal representations on the Arabic text as opposed to English text. This is due to the sparsity of the Arabic language, and its morphological complexity compared to English. Another reason is the limited amount of available data, especially for dialects, which causes deep learning models to perform bad on any task. Lastly, we are not aware of domain adaptation techniques for the Arabic language, and thus much work needs to be done in this area to catch up with the research in English.

Traditionally, researchers focused their efforts on extracting features shared between the source and target domains (Blitzer et al., 2006, 2007; Pan et al., 2010). After the advancement of representational learning (Bengio et al., 2013), several algorithms were introduced. The most notable approaches are Stacked Denoising Autoencoder (SDA) (Vincent et al., 2010; Glorot et al., 2011). Later, a modified version was introduced by (Chen et al., 2012). This version, called marginalized Stacked Denoising Autoencoder (mSDA), introduced a speedup compared to the original SDA since the input/output relation was provided in closed form. After Generative Adversarial Nets (Goodfellow et al., 2014) were

Proceedings of the Fourth Arabic Natural Language Processing Workshop, pages 167–174
Florence, Italy, August 1, 2019. ©2019 Association for Computational Linguistics

introduced, the interest in adversarial training increased. Researchers developed new approaches that solve the DA problem through adversarial training, with emphasis on applications in computer vision and limited exploration for NLP. The most notable approaches are Domain Adversarial Neural Networks (DANN) (Ganin et al., 2016), Domain Separation Network (DSN) (Bousmalis et al., 2016), Adversarial Discriminative Domain Adaptation (ADDA) (Tzeng et al., 2017) and Conditional Adversarial Domain Adaptation (Long et al., 2018). Although limited in Arabic, some efforts have been spent to solve the domain shift problem (Jeblee et al., 2014; Monroe et al., 2014).

In this paper, we propose and evaluate some adversarial approaches for domain adaptation. The first is a regular DANN model while the second is a variant of DANN that incorporates representational learning. To assess the success of domain adaptation, we use the proxy A-distance as a matrix (Ben-David et al., 2007). The rest of the paper is organized as follows. Section 2 presents different approaches for DA. Section 3 introduces the algorithms to be evaluated, and describes the dataset. Section 4 presents the experiments and the results. We finally summarize our work and conclude the paper in Section 5.

2 Related Work

Domain Adaptation passed through several development stages. The first stage was based on feature engineering methods, while in the later stages, DA experienced a shift towards deep learning.

Initial approaches included finding words that behaved similarly in both the source and target domains. Blitzer et al. (2006) called such words *pivot features*, and proposed different approaches for extracting them. He first proposed using the most frequent common words as pivot features (Blitzer et al., 2006), and later on proposed using words with highest mutual information with the source labels (Blitzer et al., 2007). The extracted pivot features are then used by the algorithm to augment the initial dataset. This is done by learning a mapping to a vector space with dimensionality smaller than the dimensionality of the input data. Then, an optimization problem is solved in the new space, with the objective function being a similarity measure. Using the results of the optimization problem, new features are added to the original dataset. The resulting algo-

rithm is called Structural Correspondence Learning (SCL) (Blitzer et al., 2006, 2007). A similar approach was introduced by Gong et al. (2013) where they suggested finding words, which they called *landmarks*, that have similar distributions over the source and target domains. These landmarks were used to increase the confusion between source and target domains, through optimizing a series of auxiliary tasks. Another point of view was introduced by Pan et al. (2010) based on the Spectral Graph Theory. Their approach, called Spectral Feature Alignment (SFA), aligned features from source and target domains using bipartite graphs. Although these approaches improved accuracies in domain adaptation tasks, the improvements remained limited.

The hype of deep learning motivated finding deep learning algorithms that could solve this problem. An interesting approach by Glorot et al. (2011) was preparing the input of any classifier by passing the input through Stacked Denoising Autoencoders (SDA) (Vincent et al., 2010). The use of SDAs helps find a new representation of the data that is domain invariant. This is achieved by reconstructing the input from stochastically disrupted data (via noise injection). Once the data is transformed, a linear SVM is trained on the new representation. This approach was more accurate than the previous approaches in predicting target domain labels. However, training SDAs is very time consuming. That is why Chen et al. (2012) forced the reconstruction mapping to be linear. This restriction yielded a closed form output solution. The new model, called marginalized Stacked Denoising Autoencoder (mSDA), was able to perform as good as the original SDA, and took much less time for training.

After the publication of GANs (Goodfellow et al., 2014), many researchers took interest in adversarial training. Ganin et al. (2016) proposed an adversarial network for domain adaptation. By introducing a Gradient Reversal Layer (GRL) that inverts the gradient's sign during backpropagation, the Domain Adversarial Neural Network (DANN) was forced to find a saddle point between 2 errors: a label prediction error (that is to be minimized) and a domain classification error (to be maximized). This approach led to the emergence of domain invariant features. DANN achieved state-of-the-art performance in domain adaptation tasks for two specific applications, namely: senti-

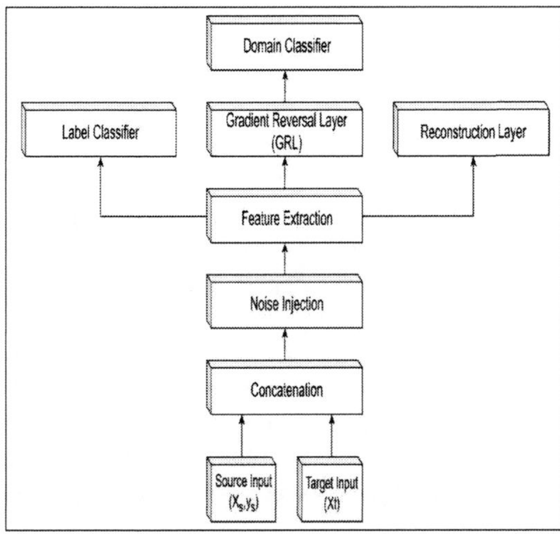

Figure 1: Proposed Model Architecture

ment analysis and computer vision.

For the Arabic language, the domain adaptation research area is still very limited. Joty et al. investigated the problem of cross-language adaptation for question-question similarity, and proposed a Cross-Language Adversarial Neural Network (CLANN) (Joty et al., 2017). Monroe et al. used *feature space augmentation* presented by (Daume III, 2007) for word segmentation (Monroe et al., 2014). Both approaches were successful.

3   Proposed Method

A Domain Adaptation task is, in general, a prediction problem where given label data from a source domain S, we are to predict the labels of a target domain T with unlabeled data (Ben-David et al., 2010). In this paper, we focus on domain adaptation for sentiment analysis: Given data with sentiment labels from one domain, the model should be able to predict the sentiment of data coming from another domain.

Let $(X_s, Y_s) = \{(x_i, y_i)\}_{i=1}^{N_s}$ represent the source domain input data of N_s observations x_i, where x_i could be any textual data (*e.g.* Bag-Of-Words, Sequence, etc...), and y_i the corresponding label. The domain input data $X_t = \{x_i\}_{i=1}^{N_t}$ consists of N_t unlabeled observations. The source and target observations are concatenated to form the input data X of $N_s + N_t$ observations to the model. The architecture of DANN adopted is similar to the one in (Ganin et al., 2016). The variant, shown in Figure 1, is composed of 5 main parts:

- Feature Extractor

- Label Predictor
- Reconstruction Layer
- Domain Predictor
- Gradient Reversal Layer

The above model uses denoising reconstruction (Vincent et al., 2010; Chen et al., 2012) and adversarial training (Ganin et al., 2016), in order to learn features that are discriminative towards the tasks at hand, while at the same time being able to generalize from one domain to another.

Three loss functions are associated with the network: 1) a loss function related to the classification task at hand, denoted as $\mathcal{L}_{task}$, 2) a loss function associated with the domain classifier, which could be the binary cross-entropy function (or log loss, etc...) and denoted as $\mathcal{L}_{domain}$, and 3) a loss function associated with the reconstruction of the input data, denoted as $\mathcal{L}_{recon}$, and could be the mean-squared error (or hinge loss, etc...). The model tries to minimize the sum of the 3 loss functions, *i.e.* it wants to find the parameters θ^* such that:

$$\theta^* = \arg\min_{\theta} \; \mathcal{L}_{task} + \lambda \cdot \mathcal{L}_{domain} + \mu \cdot \mathcal{L}_{recon} \quad (1)$$

where λ and μ are real numbers in the range $[0, 1]$. Since the reconstruction error tends to be larger than the other 2 losses by orders of magnitude, its corresponding scalar μ tends to be small.

3.1   Label Predictor

Using the label predictor, the model predicts the labels of the input data. During training, since only the source domain data has labels, the input is sliced in a way that the N_s observations associated with the source domain are passed into the label predictor. The loss function $\mathcal{L}_{task}$ depends on the task at hand (Janocha and Czarnecki, 2017). For example, one could use the mean squared error for regression, or the binary cross entropy for classification. For our purpose, we use the binary cross entropy.

3.2   Domain Classifier

The model above should be robust towards shift in data distribution. Said differently, the model should be able to predict accurately the label of a given observation even when it comes from the target domain instead of the source domain. Mathematically, this is equivalent to minimizing the error on label prediction and maximizing the error on domain classification. Ganin et al. (2016) showed that this can be done using a special layer they called Gradient Reversal Layer (GRL). The GRL does not affect the network during forward propagation, but it flips the sign of the gradients in backpropagation. The domain loss $\mathcal{L}_{domain}$ adopted by (Ganin et al., 2016) is the log-loss between the true domain and the predicted domain. Other binary loss functions are possible (Janocha and Czarnecki, 2017). In our approach, we use the binary cross entropy. The error of the domain classifier is scaled by λ.

3.3 Denoising Autoencoder

The noised version of X, denoted $\tilde{X}$, is obtained from X by using a masking noise, *i.e.* some elements of X are set to 0 with probability p (Glorot et al., 2011). Then, $\tilde{X}$ is propagated through an encoder network $h(\cdot)$ (Baldi, 2012) to get $h(\tilde{X})$. The decoder network $r(\cdot)$ reconstructs the input data X from the encoder's output $h(\tilde{X})$. A possible loss function is the mean squared error

$$\mathcal{L}_{recon} = \left\| r\left(h(\tilde{X}) \right) - X \right\|^2 \qquad (2)$$

The error of the autoencoder is scaled by μ.

3.4 Proxy A-distance as a Generalization Metric

Ben-David et al. (2007) developed a distance metric called proxy A-distance. The lower the distance, the more similar the domains are. Intuitively, this would mean the source and target domains share more common features. Hence, machine learning models won't lose too much accuracy when trained over source domain and tested over the target domain.

Let $\mathcal{D}$ and $\mathcal{D}'$ be 2 probability distributions defined over a domain χ, and a hypothesis class $\mathcal{A}$. The A-distance of $\mathcal{D}$ and $\mathcal{D}'$ is defined as

$$d_\mathcal{A}(\mathcal{D}', \mathcal{D}) = 2 \sup_{A \in \mathcal{A}} \left| \Pr_\mathcal{D}[A] - \Pr_{\mathcal{D}'}[A] \right| \qquad (3)$$

Intuitively, this is equivalent to finding the maximum $L1$ distance between the 2 probability distributions $\mathcal{D}$ and $\mathcal{D}'$. Since computing this metric is intractable, Ben-David et al. (2007) proposed a way to approximate it from finite samples as follows: a linear SVM is trained to discriminate between the 2 domains, then the error ϵ, called generalization error, is used to compute a proxy of the A-distance $\hat{d}_\mathcal{A} = 2(1 - 2\epsilon)$. This proxy A-distance (PAD) can then be used to represent the distance between the 2 domains.

4 Experiments and Results

To test the effectiveness of the proposed approach, we conduct a 5-point sentiment classification on ArSentD-LEV[1] (Baly et al., 2018), once using the country of origin of the tweet as domain, and once the category to which the tweet belongs. We then show the effect of the data size on the performance of the adaptation algorithms. We start by describing the available dataset, then we describe each experiment alongside its results and we include some insights.

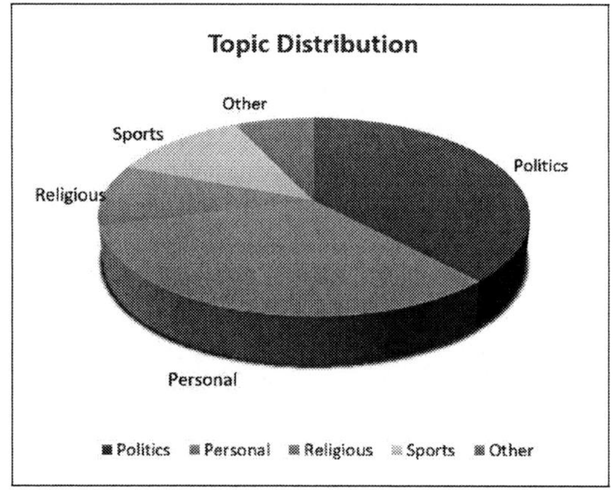

Figure 2: Topic Distribution of Tweets in ArSentD-LEV

4.1 Dataset Description and Experiment Setup

ArSentD-LEV is a multi-domain dataset containing almost 4,000 tweets collected equally from the 4 Levantine countries: Jordan, Lebanon, Palestine and Syria. For each tweet, the following labels are available: the country of origin, the sentiment conveyed by the tweet on 5-point scale (from very negative to very positive), the way of expressing the sentiment (explicit vs implicit) and the category to which the tweet belongs. The tweets were divided into 5 categories: politics, personal, sports, religious and other. The distribution of the tweets amongst these categories is shown in figure 2.

---

[1]The dataset is publicly available at `http://oma-project.azurewebsites.net/ArSenL/ArSenTD_Lev_Intro`

Following the approach used by (Chen et al., 2012; Ganin et al., 2016), we extract from the dataset the 5,000 most frequent unigrams and bigrams, as was adopted in (Ganin et al., 2016) for English. We then form, using these unigrams and bigrams, a bag-of-words matrix that will be used as input data for the learned models. Although many models represent text better (e.g. sequence models, tree models, etc...) we limit ourselves to a simpler model to show the improvement by the domain adaptation technique rather than by the text model.

The different experiments evaluated the performance of four models. A Linear SVM was used as a baseline and representative of feature based models. For the deep learning models, we consider a fully-connected neural network (Rumelhart et al., 1988) consisting of a hidden layer of 100 neurons and a label predictor of size 2. The setup of DANN is similar to that in (Ganin et al., 2016). The hidden layer is composed of 100 neurons, and the label predictor is of size 2. The domain classifier of DANN (of size 2) is preceded by a GRL. The proposed model is identical to the description in section 3. All neural networks were trained using ADAM optimizer (Kingma and Ba, 2014) using a learning rate of 10^{-3}.

Source	Target	SVM	NN	DANN	Prop
	Lebanon	**30**	27.5	29	**30**
Jordan	**Palestine**	33.5	33	34.5	**35**
	Syria	30.5	31.5	32	**33**
	Jordan	**32**	28	29	**32**
Lebanon	**Palestine**	**35**	25.5	31	**35**
	Syria	30.5	33	37	**37.5**
	Jordan	29.5	31	32	**32.5**
Palestine	**Lebanon**	**32**	29.5	31	31
	Syria	**37.5**	21.5	28.5	27.5
	Jordan	**32.5**	32	30.5	32
Syria	**Lebanon**	35	31.5	35	**35.5**
	Palestine	37	28	31.5	**37.5**

Table 1: Accuracies of linear SVM, NN, DANN and the proposed approach for Cross-Country adaptation on ArSentD-LEV. We can see that the proposed variant outperforms other models in almost all DA tasks.

4.2 Evaluation for Cross Country Adaptation

For this experiment, we evaluate the adaptation task between tweets from different countries. This means the source domain will consist of tweets from one of the 4 Levantine countries, and the target domain will consist of tweets coming from other countries. We thus have a total of 12 adaptation tasks. Baly et al. showed that Twitter is used for different purposes in different countries (Baly et al., 2017), which presents an additional challenge.

The result of the domain adaptation tasks are shown in Table 1. The proposed method outperformed all other models in most of the adaptation tasks. Although many real-life applications showed that traditional machine learning models are usually better when the available data is little (Cortes and Vapnik, 1995; Goodfellow et al., 2016), the proposed model was able to outperform the linear SVM in most of the tasks in our experiment. This means it was able to extract useful representation from the data. The model was also able to outperform DANN, which shows that the representational learning provides intrinsic representation of the data.

4.3 Evaluation for Cross Topic Adaptation

In this second experiment, we consider the task of adapting tweets from different topics. ArSentD-LEV (Baly et al., 2018) contains 5 classes for topic: politics, personal, religious, sports and other. This means we have a total of 20 tasks. The models evaluated are the linear SVM, DANN and the proposed model. The models' structure is identical to the one defined in section 4.2.

The results of the experiment are shown in Table 2. The behavior of the algorithms is significantly different in these categories. This is caused by the unbalanced data distribution amongst the different topics, as can be seen in Figure 2. We can see that whenever the data is very limited, the linear SVM outperforms the deep learning models. This is expected since neural networks cannot learn well the underlying representation when the data is scarce.

Looking at the radar plot in Figure 3, we can find the following interesting property. The higher the PAD distance between the source and target domains, the better the performance of the proposed model. This can be related to the fact that the proposed model tries to find a hidden representation that combines features from both source and target domains, *i.e.* decrease the distance between the 2 domains. Whenever the distance is low, the proposed model can not thus decrease it much further.

Source	Target	SVM	DANN	Prop
Politics	**Personal**	29.5	28.7	**33.3**
	Religious	20.5	20.3	**25.3**
	Sports	26.8	**35.1**	**35.1**
	Other	16.1	22.5	**24.2**
Personal	**Politics**	37.5	**41.7**	36.8
	Religious	19	22.8	**23.4**
	Sports	**34**	26.8	25.8
	Other	**40.3**	33.8	35.4
Religious	**Politics**	**16.8**	15.5	15.5
	Personal	**26.4**	24.1	26.1
	Sports	**28.8**	25.8	26.8
	Other	**48.4**	30.6	27.4
Sports	**Politics**	**41.4**	36.4	30.7
	Personal	**28.4**	25.3	24.5
	Religious	16.5	**20**	19
	Other	33.8	**35.5**	**35.5**
Other	**Politics**	20.5	**23.2**	**23.2**
	Personal	28.4	**30.3**	24.9
	Religious	**53.2**	41.8	43
	Sports	26.8	23.7	**27.8**

Table 2: Accuracies of linear SVM, DANN and the proposed approach for Cross-Topic on ArSentD-LEV. We can see that the SVM and the proposed variant are performing better than DANN, with SVM performing better when available data is little.

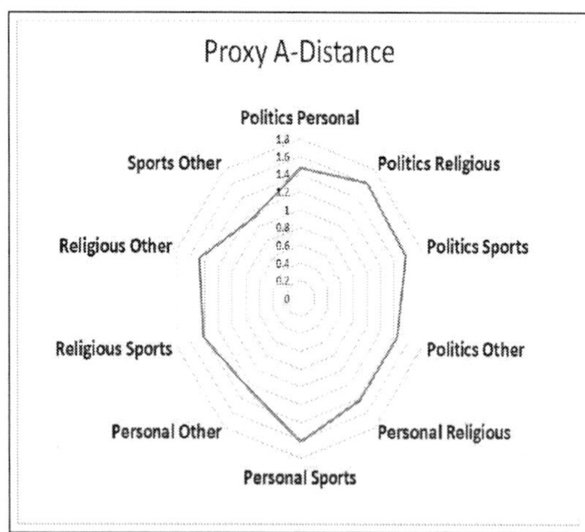

Figure 3: Proxy A-distance Between Different Domains. This radar plot shows the proxy A-distances between the different domains. The closer the vertex of a combination to the center, the closer the 2 domains.

4.4 Performance with Limited Data Size

To test the limitation of the proposed approach with data size, we consider the task where the source domain is "Politics" and the target domain is "Personal", since the available data is larger than the data available for other tasks. We then start by gradually increasing the size, and test the performance of the model with each dataset size. Looking at Figure 4, we can see that the performance of the proposed method is better than that of DANN at all sizes. This confirms our assumption that DANN with SDA learns a better representation through the incorporation of autoencoder. In contrast, DANN focuses on the discriminative task at hand, and thus fails to generalize. We also have a generally increasing trend which comes from the fact that more data is available, hence the models are able to learn better features.

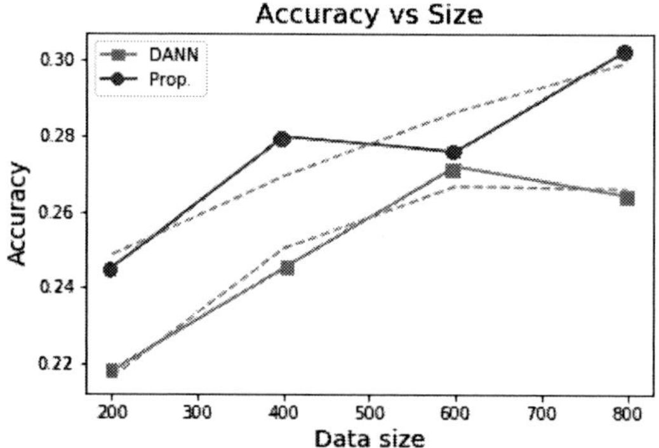

Figure 4: DANN and Proposed Method Performance vs Data size. We can see that the proposed variant outperforms DANN at all data sizes, and learns more with the increase in data size.

5 Conclusion

In this paper, we presented the first application of domain adaptation to the Arabic language. Although there exists work in English for domain adaptation, no work exists for Arabic. We considered in this paper the Domain Adversarial Neural Network (DANN) (Ganin et al., 2016) and proposed a variant that incorporates into DANN a stacked denoising autoencoder (SDA). The experiments and results provided several insights. We observed that integrating a reconstruction loss into DANN helped the model learn a better latent representation. This proved useful in all experiments, especially when the available data is little. These observations are consistent with what has been observed in English. The success of domain adaptation suggests the possibility of usage of DA to bridge the gap between different dialects of the Arabic language. Future work includes testing DA techniques to more Arabic dialects, trying other domain adaptation algorithms in Arabic, developing new domain adaptation techniques, evaluating the DA tasks using better text representation (*e.g.* sequence models...) and integrating transfer learning techniques in the models (Ng et al., 2015).

References

Gilbert Badaro, Ramy Baly, Hazem Hajj, Wassim El-Hajj, Khaled Shaban, Nizar Habash, Ahmad Sallab, and Ali Hamdi. 2019. A survey of opinion mining in arabic: A comprehensive system perspective covering challenges and advances in tools, resources, models, applications and visualizations. *ACM Transactions on Asian Language Information Processing*, 18.

Pierre Baldi. 2012. Autoencoders, unsupervised learning, and deep architectures. In *Proceedings of ICML Workshop on Unsupervised and Transfer Learning*, volume 27 of *Proceedings of Machine Learning Research*, pages 37–49, Bellevue, Washington, USA. PMLR.

Ramy Baly, Gilbert Badaro, Georges El-Khoury, Rawan Moukalled, Rita Aoun, Hazem Hajj, Wassim El-Hajj, Nizar Habash, and Khaled Shaban. 2017. A characterization study of Arabic twitter data with a benchmarking for state-of-the-art opinion mining models. In *Proceedings of the Third Arabic Natural Language Processing Workshop*, pages 110–118, Valencia, Spain. Association for Computational Linguistics.

Ramy Baly, Alaa Khaddaj, Hazem Hajj, Wassim El-Hajj, and Khaled Shaban. 2018. Arsentd-lev: A multi-topic corpus for target-based sentiment analysis in arabic levantine tweets. In *Proceedings of the Eleventh International Conference on Language Resources and Evaluation (LREC 2018)*, Paris, France. European Language Resources Association (ELRA).

Shai Ben-David, John Blitzer, Koby Crammer, Alex Kulesza, Fernando Pereira, and Jennifer Wortman Vaughan. 2010. A theory of learning from different domains. *Machine Learning*, 79(1):151–175.

Shai Ben-David, John Blitzer, Koby Crammer, and Fernando Pereira. 2007. Analysis of representations for domain adaptation. In B. Schölkopf, J. C. Platt, and T. Hoffman, editors, *Advances in Neural Information Processing Systems 19*, pages 137–144. MIT Press.

Yoshua Bengio, Aaron Courville, and Pascal Vincent. 2013. Representation learning: A review and new perspectives. *IEEE Transactions on Pattern Analysis and Machine Intelligence*, 35(8):1798–1828.

John Blitzer, Mark Dredze, and Fernando Pereira. 2007. Biographies, bollywood, boom-boxes and blenders: Domain adaptation for sentiment classification. In *Proceedings of the 45th Annual Meeting of the Association of Computational Linguistics*, pages 440–447. Association for Computational Linguistics.

John Blitzer, Ryan McDonald, and Fernando Pereira. 2006. Domain adaptation with structural correspondence learning. In *Proceedings of the 2006 Conference on Empirical Methods in Natural Language Processing*, pages 120–128. Association for Computational Linguistics.

Konstantinos Bousmalis, George Trigeorgis, Nathan Silberman, Dilip Krishnan, and Dumitru Erhan. 2016. Domain separation networks. In D. D. Lee, M. Sugiyama, U. V. Luxburg, I. Guyon, and R. Garnett, editors, *Advances in Neural Information Processing Systems 29*, pages 343–351. Curran Associates, Inc.

Minmin Chen, Zhixiang Xu, Kilian Q. Weinberger, and Fei Sha. 2012. Marginalized denoising autoencoders for domain adaptation. In *Proceedings of the 29th International Coference on International Conference on Machine Learning*, ICML'12, pages 1627–1634, USA. Omnipress.

Corinna Cortes and Vladimir Vapnik. 1995. Support-vector networks. In *Machine Learning*, pages 273–297.

Hal Daume III. 2007. Frustratingly easy domain adaptation. In *Proceedings of the 45th Annual Meeting of the Association of Computational Linguistics*, pages 256–263, Prague, Czech Republic. Association for Computational Linguistics.

Yaroslav Ganin, Evgeniya Ustinova, Hana Ajakan, Pascal Germain, Hugo Larochelle, François Laviolette, Mario Marchand, and Victor Lempitsky. 2016. Domain-adversarial training of neural networks. *J. Mach. Learn. Res.*, 17(1):2096–2030.

Xavier Glorot, Antoine Bordes, and Yoshua Bengio. 2011. Domain adaptation for large-scale sentiment classification: A deep learning approach. In *Proceedings of the 28th International Conference on International Conference on Machine Learning*, ICML'11, pages 513–520, USA. Omnipress.

Boqing Gong, Kristen Grauman, and Fei Sha. 2013. Connecting the dots with landmarks: Discriminatively learning domain-invariant features for unsupervised domain adaptation. In *Proceedings of the 30th International Conference on Machine Learning*, volume 28 of *Proceedings of Machine Learning Research*, pages 222–230, Atlanta, Georgia, USA. PMLR.

Ian Goodfellow, Yoshua Bengio, and Aaron Courville. 2016. *Deep Learning*. MIT Press. http://www.deeplearningbook.org.

Ian J. Goodfellow, Jean Pouget-Abadie, Mehdi Mirza, Bing Xu, David Warde-Farley, Sherjil Ozair, Aaron Courville, and Yoshua Bengio. 2014. Generative adversarial nets. In *Proceedings of the 27th International Conference on Neural Information Processing Systems - Volume 2*, NIPS'14, pages 2672–2680, Cambridge, MA, USA. MIT Press.

Katarzyna Janocha and Wojciech Czarnecki. 2017. On loss functions for deep neural networks in classification. 25.

Serena Jeblee, Weston Feely, Houda Bouamor, Alon Lavie, Nizar Habash, and Kemal Oflazer. 2014. Domain and dialect adaptation for machine translation into egyptian arabic. In *ANLP@EMNLP*.

Shafiq Joty, Preslav Nakov, Llus Mrquez, and Israa Jaradat. 2017. Cross-language learning with adversarial neural networks. pages 226–237.

Diederik Kingma and Jimmy Ba. 2014. Adam: A method for stochastic optimization.

Mingsheng Long, Zhangjie Cao, Jianmin Wang, and Michael I Jordan. 2018. Conditional adversarial domain adaptation. In S. Bengio, H. Wallach, H. Larochelle, K. Grauman, N. Cesa-Bianchi, and R. Garnett, editors, *Advances in Neural Information Processing Systems 31*, pages 1640–1650. Curran Associates, Inc.

Will Monroe, Spence Green, and Christopher D. Manning. 2014. Word segmentation of informal arabic with domain adaptation. In *Proceedings of the 52nd Annual Meeting of the Association for Computational Linguistics (Volume 2: Short Papers)*, pages 206–211. Association for Computational Linguistics.

Hong-Wei Ng, Viet Dung Nguyen, Vassilios Vonikakis, and Stefan Winkler. 2015. Deep learning for emotion recognition on small datasets using transfer learning. In *Proceedings of the 2015 ACM on International Conference on Multimodal Interaction*, ICMI '15, pages 443–449, New York, NY, USA. ACM.

Sinno Jialin Pan, Xiaochuan Ni, Jian-Tao Sun, Qiang Yang, and Zheng Chen. 2010. Cross-domain sentiment classification via spectral feature alignment. In *Proceedings of the 19th International Conference on World Wide Web*, WWW '10, pages 751–760, New York, NY, USA. ACM.

David E. Rumelhart, Geoffrey E. Hinton, and Ronald J. Williams. 1988. Neurocomputing: Foundations of research. chapter Learning Representations by Back-propagating Errors, pages 696–699. MIT Press, Cambridge, MA, USA.

Eric Tzeng, Judy Hoffman, Kate Saenko, and Trevor Darrell. 2017. Adversarial discriminative domain adaptation. In *The IEEE Conference on Computer Vision and Pattern Recognition (CVPR)*.

Pascal Vincent, Hugo Larochelle, Isabelle Lajoie, Yoshua Bengio, and Pierre-Antoine Manzagol. 2010. Stacked denoising autoencoders: Learning useful representations in a deep network with a local denoising criterion. *J. Mach. Learn. Res.*, 11:3371–3408.

OSIAN: Open Source International Arabic News Corpus - Preparation and Integration into the CLARIN-infrastructure

Imad Zeroual[*], Dirk Goldhahn[†], Thomas Eckart[†], Abdelhak Lakhouaja[*]

[*]Computer Sciences Laboratory, Mohamed First University, Morocco
{mr.imadine, abdel.lakh}@gmail.com

[†]Natural Language Processing Group, University of Leipzig, German
{dgoldhahn, teckart}@informatik.uni-leipzig.de

Abstract

The World Wide Web has become a fundamental resource for building large text corpora. Broadcasting platforms such as news websites are rich sources of data regarding diverse topics and form a valuable foundation for research. The Arabic language is extensively utilized on the Web. Still, Arabic is relatively an under-resourced language in terms of availability of freely annotated corpora. This paper presents the first version of the Open Source International Arabic News (OSIAN) corpus. The corpus data was collected from international Arabic news websites, all being freely available on the Web. The corpus consists of about 3.5 million articles comprising more than 37 million sentences and roughly 1 billion tokens. It is encoded in XML; each article is annotated with metadata information. Moreover, each word is annotated with lemma and part-of-speech. The described corpus is processed, archived and published into the CLARIN infrastructure. This publication includes descriptive metadata via OAI-PMH, direct access to the plain text material (available under Creative Commons Attribution-Non-Commercial 4.0 International License - CC BY-NC 4.0), and integration into the WebLicht annotation platform and CLARIN's Federated Content Search FCS.

1 Introduction

The Arabic language is spoken by 422 million people, making it the fourth most used language on the Web[1]. Its presence on the Web had the highest growth of the ten most frequent online languages in the last 18 years. However, a few years ago, Arabic was considered relatively an under-resourced language that lacks the basic resources and corpora for computational linguistics, not a single modern standard Arabic tagged corpus was freely or publicly available. Since then, major progress has been made in building Arabic linguistic resources, primarily corpora (Zeroual and Lakhouaja, 2018a); still, building valuable annotated corpora with a considerable size is expensive, time-consuming, and requires appropriate tools. Therefore, many Arabic corpora builders produce their corpora in a raw format.

For building the Open Source International Arabic News (OSIAN) corpus, the typical procedures of the Leipzig Corpora Collection were utilized. Furthermore, a language-independent Part-of-Speech (PoS) tagger, Treetagger, is adapted to annotate the OSIAN corpus with lemma and part-of-speech tags.

The prime motivation for building OSIAN corpus is the lack of open-source Arabic corpora that can cope with the perspectives of Arabic Natural Language Processing (ANLP) and Arabic Information Retrieval (AIR), among other research areas. Hence, we expect that the OSIAN corpus can be used to answer relevant research questions in corpus linguistics, especially investigating variation and distinction between international and national news broadcasting platforms with a diachronic and geographical perspective.

After this introduction, the remainder of the paper is structured as follows: In section 2, we highlight the state-of-the-art of web-crawled

---

[1] http://www.internetworldstats.com/stats7.htm

Proceedings of the Fourth Arabic Natural Language Processing Workshop, pages 175–182
Florence, Italy, August 1, 2019. ©2019 Association for Computational Linguistics

corpora of the Arabic language. Further, the methodology and tools used to build the OSIAN corpus are presented in Section 3. In Section 4, the OSIAN corpus is described in more detail, yet, some data analyses are performed and discussed. Finally, Section 5 contains some concluding remarks and future work.

2 Literature review

The World Wide Web is an important source for researchers interested in the compilation of very large corpora. A recent survey (Zeroual and Lakhouaja, 2018b) reports that 51% of corpora are constructed based, totally or partially, on Web content. Web corpora continue to gain relevance within the computational and theoretical linguistics. Given their size and the variety of domains covered, using Web-derived corpora is another way to overcome typical problems faced by statistical corpus-based studies such as data-sparseness and the lack of variation.

The web corpora continue to gain relevance within the computational and theoretical linguistics. Given their size and the variety of domains covered, using web-derived corpora is another way to overcome typical problems faced by statistical corpus-based studies such as data-sparseness and the lack of variation. Besides, they can be used to evaluate different approaches for the classification of web documents and content by text genre and topic area (e.g., (Chouigui et al., 2017)). Furthermore, web corpora have become a prime and well-established source for lexicographers to create many large and various dictionaries using specialised tools such as the corpus query and corpus management tool Sketch-Engine (Kovář et al., 2016). Moreover, some completely new areas of research, for which they deal exclusively with web corpora, have emerged. Indeed, the aim was to build, investigate, and analyse corpora based on online social networks posts, short messages, and online forum discussions.

Publicly available Arabic web corpora are quite limited, which greatly impacts research and development of Arabic NLP and IR. However, some research groups (Zaghouani, 2017) have shown potentials in building web-derived corpora in recent years. Among them are:

- Open Source Arabic Corpora[2] (OSAC) (Saad and Ashour, 2010): It is a collection of large and free accessible raw corpora. The OSAC corpus consists of web documents extracted from over 25 Arabic websites using the open source offline explorer, *HTTrack*. The compilation procedure involves converting HTML/XML files into UTF-8 encoding using "Text Encoding Converter" as well as removing the HTML/XML tags. The final version of the corpus comprises roughly 113 million tokens. Besides, it covers several topics namely Economy, History, Education, Religion, Sport, Health, Astronomy, Law, Stories, and Cooking Recipes.

- arTenTen (Arts et al., 2014): It is a member of the TenTen Corpus Family (Jakubíček et al., 2013). The arTenTen is a web-derived corpus of Arabic crawled using Spiderling (Suchomel et al., 2012) in 2012. The arTenTen corpus is partially tagged. i.e., one sample of the corpus, comprises roughly 30 million, is tagged using the Stanford Arabic part-of-speech tagger. While, another sample, contains over 115 million words, is tokenised, lemmatised, and part-of-speech tagged using MADA system. All in all, the arTenTen comprises 5.8 billion words but it can only be explored by paying a fee via the Sketch Engine website[3].

- ArabicWeb16: Since 2009, the ClueWeb09 web crawl (Callan et al., 2009), that includes 29.2 million of Arabic pages, was considered the only and largest Arabic web crawl available. However, in 2016, a new and larger crawl of today's Arabic web is publicly available. This web crawl is called ArabicWeb16 (Swuaileh et al., 2016) and comprises over 150M web pages crawled over the month of January 2016. In addition to addressing the limitation of the ClueWeb09, ArabicWeb16 covers both dialectal and Modern Standard Arabic. Finally, the total size of the compressed dataset of ArabicWeb16 is about 2TB and it is available for download after filling a request form[4].

- The GDELT Project[5] is a free open platform for research and analysis of the global

[2] https://sites.google.com/site/motazsite/corpora/osac
[3] https://www.sketchengine.co.uk/
[4] https://sites.google.com/view/arabicweb16
[5] https://www.gdeltproject.org/

database. All the datasets released are free, open, and available for unlimited and unrestricted use for any academic, commercial, or governmental use. Also, it is possible to download the raw datafiles, visualize it, or analyse it at limitless scale. Recently, the GDELT Project is starting to create linguistic resources. In fact, 9.5 billion words of worldwide Arabic news has been monitored over 14 months (February 2015 to June 2016) to make a trigram dataset for the Arabic language. Consequently, an Arabic trigram table of the 6,444,208 trigrams that appeared more than 75 times is produced[6].

It is worth mentioning that larger corpora in the region of billions of words are usually created by downloading texts from the web unselectively with respect to their text type or content. Therefore, the content of such corpora cannot be determined before their construction, thus, it is necessary to filter, clean, and evaluate it afterwards.

3   Methodology and tools

In this section, we describe the crawling, processing and annotation tasks alongside with the tools used.

3.1   Data acquisition

In a first step the data needs to be crawled from the World Wide Web. Since the crawled data are often duplicated or in other ways problematic, they need to be cleaned and filtered. Therefore, the following processing steps were executed.

3.1.1 Leipzig Corpora Collection

The Leipzig Corpora Collection (LCC) (Goldhahn et al., 2012; Quasthoff et al., 2014) started as "Projekt Deutscher Wortschatz[7]" in the Nineties as a resource provider for digital texts in the German language mostly based on newspaper articles and royalty-free text material.

Today, the LCC offers corpus-based monolingual full form dictionaries in more than 200 languages mainly based on online accessible text material, divided under several aspects like the year of acquisition, text genre, country of origin and more. Since June 2006, LCC can be accessed at http://corpora.uni-leipzig.de. In addition to direct access via a Web interface, LCC data is also offered for free download.

For each word the dictionaries contain:

- Word frequency information.

- Sample sentences.

- Statistically significant word co-occurrences (based on left or right neighbours or whole sentences).

- A semantic map visualizing the strongest word co-occurrences.

- Part of speech information (partially).

- Similar words and other semantic information (partially).

3.1.2 Crawling and processing of data

For corpus creation, an adapted version of the CURL-portal (Crawling Under-Resourced Languages[8]) (Goldhahn et al., 2016) of the LCC was utilized. CURL allows creating Web-accessible and downloadable corpora by simply entering URLs into the portal. In order to build a balanced corpus of international Arabic news, the data have been drawn from a wide range of reliable sources around the world. Six million webpages were downloaded, three and a half million pages which contain Arabic text were extracted and sub-corpora for several Arabic speaking countries were created.

The crawling was conducted in March 2018 using Heritrix, the crawler of the Internet Archive. Further processing was carried out according to the language independent processing chain described in (Goldhahn et al., 2012) and involved steps as extracting raw text from the Web ARChive file format, sentence separation and removal of non-sentences using regular expressions. Finally, texts were extracted based on Web domain and assigned to the respective country. Furthermore, since the crawler writes the data in one large file, we developed a tool for extracting the texts based on the Web domain. For each Web domain, the tool extracts and saves each article/page in a single file. Finally, these articles are assigned to the respective country. A list of the crawled Web domains, the number of articles extracted, and the countries covered are provided in the Appendix "A".

---

[6] https://goo.gl/MZZkDJ
[7] http://wortschatz.uni-leipzig.de
[8] http://curl.corpora.uni-leipzig.de/

The number of articles extracted from the crawled data is varying from one website to another. Some domains were only restricted by the short duration of the crawling, whereas others ran out of crawlable URLs early due to a low amount of crawlable resources, robots.txt-restrictions or external links to other domains which were not followed.

3.2 Corpus annotation

Among the widely used and relevant types of corpus annotations are e.g. lemma and part of speech. Lemmatization is a basic morphological analysis to deal with derivation paradigms, whereas part-of-speech tagging is part of a further syntactic analyses (i.e., parsing) to determine the sentence's syntactic structure. Both annotation forms affect the performance of subsequent text analysis in NLP and IR.

For both part of speech tagging and lemmatization tasks, we used a previously adapted and well-established version of Treetagger for the Arabic language (Imad and Abdelhak, 2016). Further, we improved this model and retrained it using new linguistic resources namely the Frequency Dictionary of Arabic (Buckwalter and Parkinson 2014). This frequency dictionary contains the top 5,000 words that were derived from a collection of representative corpora that include 30 million words of both written texts and

4 The OSIAN Corpus

Instead of using unselected data from the Web, the aim of the OSIAN corpus is to build a balanced corpus in which the data must be drawn from a wide range of reliable and open sources. Therefore, this corpus is compiled based on 31 different international Arabic news broadcasting platforms, all being freely available on the Web.

We extracted six million webpages. After cleaning and filtering, we were left with about three and half million articles comprising more than 37 million sentences and roughly 1 billion tokens.

4.1 Word length distribution

The average length of words varies from 7 to 12 letters in many languages[9]. According to Mustafa (2012), the average length of Arabic words in a normal text is five letters. When analyzing the OSIAN corpus the length of 36% of the words is above six letters, this percentage is increased to 75% if duplicate words are considered. This makes the corpus a good soil to evaluate techniques that aim to reduce a word to its base form.

It is worth mentioning that tokens with length superior to 10 letters are not considered since news articles contain phrases written without space characters between words as well as non-derived and concatenated words, such as "الأورومتوسطي"/Euro-Mediterranean,

Word length	Occurrence (Unique)	Percentage	Occurrence (Duplicated)	Percentage
2	4,180	0,03%	113,129,168	12,22%
3	45,723	0,28%	148,295,530	16,03%
4	412,528	2,52%	154,159,209	16,66%
5	1,550,485	9,48%	175,925,523	19,01%
6	2,877,426	17,59%	133,290,941	14,40%
7	3,353,777	20,50%	107,877,916	11,66%
8	2,864,584	17,51%	54,007,298	5,84%
9	1,919,115	11,73%	20,526,042	2,22%
10	1,196,370	7,31%	9,072,780	0,98%
>10	2,137,492	13,06%	9,050,623	0,98%
Total	16,361,680	100%	925,335,030	100%

Table 1: Word length statistics

transcribed speech.

A sample of 10,000 words of the corpus has been manually checked to evaluate the performance of Treetagger and the achieved accuracy rate is 95.02%.

"الكهرومغناطيسية"/Electromagnetism, etc. This explains why we found more than two million unique tokens that consist of over 11 letters which is an irrational result for the Arabic language.

---

[9] http://www.ravi.io/language-word-lengths

Table 1 displays the percentage of words covered in the OSIAN corpus with respect to their lengths, including unique and duplicate words.

4.2 Word frequency list

Calculating word frequencies enables us to indicate the distribution of words across the text categories. Besides, it is feasible to produce word frequency lists using the tokens' PoS tags instead of their orthographic status.

Obviously, function words will be at the top of the frequency wordlist. Nevertheless, the words thematically organized in Table 2 are also among the most frequent words.

In the context of IR and corpus linguistics, many of the top frequently words have no value or effect on further analyses since they are typical in news articles; examples include "العالم" (World: F=1,182,181; R=37), "الحكومة" (Government: F=667,862; R=73), and "مفاوضات" (Negotiations: F=524,035; R=101). However, the words listed in Table 2 are a result of the circumstances of the Middle East in recent years, FIFA World Cup, and the Brexit, which make these words occur frequently in various world news. Using LancsBox to analyze the corpus data, it was possible to calculate frequencies of words that are obvious collocates such as "كأس العالم" (World Cup), "الاتحاد الأوربي" (European Union), and "البيت الأبيض" (White House). Moreover, it is also possible to

4.3 Corpus format

The XML-format is used to facilitate the use of the corpus. This is the first version of the OSIAN corpus which consists of separate directories for each country. Furthermore, each directory includes the articles in XML format, where the sentences are lemmatized and PoS tagged. Moreover, the XML files contain metadata to provide information about domain names, webpage location, and the date of extraction. For more illustration, Figure 1 presents a sample of the XML files.

Note that some Web domains include in their URLs the topic of the published articles like the sample provided in Figure 1 where the word "Science and tech" appeared in the article's URL. This is another feature that can be used to classify the articles based on their topics, one among other techniques, to prepare them for classification and topic detection. Unfortunately, not all the URLs include such information; therefore, the topic label remains "unknown" till a solution is found (using topic detection and tracking methods).

4.4 CLARIN Integration

CLARIN[10] (Common Language Resources and Technology Infrastructure) is a European Research Infrastructure established in 2012 and took up the mission to create an online environment to provide access to language

Theme	Word	Frequency (F)	Rank (R)
Persons	ترامب (Trump, President of USA)	608,176	81
	سلمان (Salman, King of Saudi)	380,086	164
	السيسي (El-Sisi, President of Egypt)	114,586	687
Countries	سوريا (Syria)	960,732	51
	بريطانيا (United Kingdom)	862,156	57
	قطر (Qatar)	704,457	70
Topics	الانتخابات (Election)	482,688	117
	بريكست (Brexit)	434,376	134
	كأس العالم (World Cup)	349,873	188
Organizations	الناتو (NATO)	387,174	161
	الاتحاد الأوربي (European Union)	177,383	448
	البيت الأبيض (White House)	124,762	648

Table 2: Relevant words from the frequency wordlist

calculate statistical information about the association, the strength of collocation, and the comparative frequencies of word forms in the overall data of the OSIAN corpus or in country-separated data.

resources (in written, spoken, or multimodal form)

```xml
<?xml version="1.0" encoding="UTF-8"?>
<Article num="1">
<Source name="BCC">
  <Date>2018-03-19</date>
  <Location>http://www.bbc.com/arabic/scienceandtech/2014/08/140829_smart_watches_samsung_lg
  </Location>
  <Topic> Science and Tech</Topic>
  <Language>ara</Language>
</Source>
<Text>
أعلنت شركتا سامسونغ وإلى جي الكوريتين الجنوبيتين طرح المزيد من الساعات الذكية...
</Text>
<Annotation>
  <Sentence id="1">
    <Word Surfaceform="أعلنت" PoS="VERB" Lemma="أَعْلَنَ" />
    <Word Surfaceform="شركتا" PoS="NOUN" Lemma="شَرِكَة" />
    <Word Surfaceform="سامسونغ" PoS="PN" Lemma="سَامْسُونْغ" />
    <Word Surfaceform="وإلى" PoS="PRT" Lemma="إِلى" />
    <Word Surfaceform="جي" PoS="ABR" Lemma="جى" />
    <Word Surfaceform="الكوريتين" PoS="ADJ" Lemma="كُورِيّ" />
    <Word Surfaceform="الجنوبيتين" PoS="ADJ" Lemma="جَنُوبِيّ" />
    <Word Surfaceform="طرح" PoS="NOUN" Lemma="طَرْح" />
    <Word Surfaceform="المزيد" PoS="NOUN" Lemma="مَزِيد" />
    <Word Surfaceform="من" PoS="PRT" Lemma="مِنْ" />
    <Word Surfaceform="الساعات" PoS="NOUN" Lemma="سَاعَة" />
    <Word Surfaceform="الذكية" PoS="ADJ" Lemma="ذَكِيّ" />
    ...
  </Sentence>
  ...
</Annotation>
</Article>
```

Figure 1: A sample of OSIAN corpus encoded in XML format

for the support of scholars in the humanities and social sciences, and beyond (de Jong et al., 2018). Currently, CLARIN also offers advanced tools to discover, explore, exploit, annotate, analyse, and combine such data sets wherever they are located.

Unsurprisingly, a strong focus of CLARIN has been laid so far on resources for European languages. The integration of more data for non-European languages will broaden and extend possible research questions that users of the infrastructure can approach. Among others, the CLARIN centre at the University of Leipzig is working on expanding available resources for a variety of languages with a dedicated focus on lesser-resourced ones.

Based on standard procedures and workflows that have been proven effective for "in-house" resources, the OSIAN corpus is processed, archived and published into the CLARIN infrastructure. This publication includes descriptive metadata via OAI-PMH[11], direct access to the plain text material (available under Creative Commons Attribution-NonCommercial 4.0 International License - CC BY-NC 4.0), and integration into the WebLicht annotation platform and CLARIN's Federated Content Search FCS. In the future, the corpus will be made available via the KonText advanced corpus query interface for the Manatee-open corpus search engine (as used in the NoSketchEngine). This will enable compatibility with the FCS-QL specification v2.0 and will allow querying text and annotation layers such as part of speech and lemmas.

5   Conclusion and future work

In this paper we presented a new open source corpus based on well-known and reliable international broadcasting platforms. After cleaning and filtering processes, the datasets are automatically annotated with lemma and PoS tags.

---

[11] See for example http://hdl.handle.net/11022/0000-0007-C65C-3

At the moment, this corpus comprises roughly 1 billion tokens that have been stored in a uniform XML format. The XML format of the OSIAN corpus will be publicly available for download and use in research. In addition, the current version and any updates of the OSIAN corpus can be found through the CLARIN research infrastructure, connecting them to central services such as VLO and FCS for metadata and content search.

In the future, we will extend the OSIAN corpus to cover more international Arabic news with a diachronic and geographical perspective to make the corpus an ideal choice to explore language change and variation. Additionally, we will aim to improve the accuracy of the used tools as well as to adopt new and meaningful forms of annotation. Regarding CLARIN-integration, FCS 2.0 and the querying of annotation layers is planned to be supported. Furthermore, we will explore the usage of the OSIAN corpus in corpus linguistics, ANLP, and AIR.

References

Tressy Arts, Yonatan Belinkov, Nizar Habash, Adam Kilgarriff, and Vit Suchomel. 2014. arTenTen: Arabic Corpus and Word Sketches. *Journal of King Saud University - Computer and Information Sciences*, 26(4):357–371.

Tim Buckwalter and Dilworth Parkinson. 2014. A frequency dictionary of Arabic: Core vocabulary for learners. *Routledge*.

Jamie Callan, Mark Hoy, Changkuk Yoo, and Le Zhao. 2009. *Clueweb09 data set*. Available at http://lemurproject.org/clueweb09/.

Amina Chouigui, Oussama Ben Khiroun, and Bilel Elayeb. 2017. ANT Corpus: An Arabic News Text Collection for Textual Classification. In *proceedings of the 14th ACS/IEEE International Conference on Computer Systems and Applications (AICCSA 2017)*, pages 135–142, Hammamet, Tunisia.

Franciska de Jong, Bente Maegaard, Koenraad De Smedt, Darja Fišer, and Dieter Van Uytvanck. 2018. CLARIN: Towards FAIR and Responsible Data Science Using Language Resources. In *Proceedings of the Eleventh International Conference on Language Resources and Evaluation (LREC 2018)*, pages 3259–3264.

Dirk Goldhahn, Thomas Eckart, and Uwe Quasthoff. 2012. Building Large Monolingual Dictionaries at the Leipzig Corpora Collection: From 100 to 200 Languages. In *LREC*, pages 759–765.

Dirk Goldhahn, Maciej Sumalvico, and Uwe Quasthoff. 2016. Corpus Collection for Under-Resourced Languages with More than One Million Speakers. In *Collaboration and Computing for Under-Resourced Languages (CCURL)*, pages 67–73, Portorož.

Zeroual Imad and Lakhouaja Abdelhak. 2016. Adapting a decision tree based tagger for Arabic. In *proceedings of the International Conference on Information Technology for Organizations Development (IT4OD)*, pages 1–6. IEEE.

Miloš Jakubíček, Adam Kilgarriff, Vojtěch Kovář, Pavel Rychlý, and Vít Suchomel. 2013. The tenten corpus family. In *proceedings of the 7th International Corpus Linguistics Conference CL*, pages 125–127.

Vojtěch Kovář, Vít Baisa, and Miloš Jakubíček. 2016. Sketch Engine for bilingual lexicography. *International Journal of Lexicography*, 29(3):339–352.

Suleiman H. Mustafa. 2012. Word stemming for Arabic information retrieval: The case for simple light stemming. *Abhath Al-Yarmouk: Science & Engineering Series*, 21(1):2012.

Uwe Quasthoff, Dirk Goldhahn, and Thomas Eckart. 2014. Building large resources for text mining: The Leipzig Corpora Collection. In *Text Mining*, pages 3–24. Springer.

Motaz K. Saad and Wesam Ashour. 2010. Osac: Open source arabic corpora. In *proceeding of the 6th International Conference on Electrical and Computer Systems (EECS'10)*, volume 10.

Vít Suchomel and Jan Pomikálek. 2012. Efficient web crawling for large text corpora. In *proceedings of the seventh Web as Corpus Workshop (WAC7)*, pages 39–43.

Reem Swuaileh, Mucahid Kutlu, Nihal Fathima, Tamer Elsayed, and Matthew Lease. 2016. ArabicWeb16: A New Crawl for Today's Arabic Web. In *proceedings of the 39th International ACM SIGIR conference on Research and Development in Information Retrieval*, pages 673–676. ACM.

Wajdi Zaghouani. 2017. Critical survey of the freely available Arabic corpora. arXiv preprint arXiv:1702.07835.

Imad Zeroual and Abdelhak Lakhouaja. 2018a. Arabic Corpus Linguistics: Major Progress, but Still a Long Way to Go. In *Intelligent Natural Language Processing: Trends and Applications, Studies in Computational Intelligence*, pages 613–636. Springer, Cham.

Imad Zeroual and Abdelhak Lakhouaja. 2018b. Data science in light of natural language processing: An overview. *Procedia Computer Science*, 127:82–91.

A Appendices

Region or country	Web-domain	Nb. of articles
International	news.un.org arabic.euronews.com ara.reuters.com namnewsnetwork.org arabic.sputniknews.com	693,629
Middle-east	aljazeera.net alarabiya.net	366,211
Algeria	djazairess.com	588,514
Australia	eltelegraph.com	4,614
Canada	arabnews24.ca halacanada.ca	30,135
China	arabic.cctv.com	1,365
Egypt	alwatanalarabi.com	85,351
France	france24.com	74,718
Iran	alalam.ir	344,011
Iraq	iraqakhbar.com	28,248
Germany	dw.com	117,261
Jordon	sarayanews.com	49,461
Morocco	www.marocpress.com	188,045
Palestine	al-ayyam.ps	81,495
Qatar	raya.com	8,986
Russia	arabic.rt.com	57,238
Saudi Arabia	alwatan.com.sa	1,512
Sweden	alkompis.se	33,790
Syria	syria.news	36542
Tunisia	www.turess.com	495,674
Turkey	turkey-post.net aa.com.tr	76,638
UAE	emaratalyoum.com	25,081
UK	bbc.com	10,686
USA	arabic.cnn.com	113,557

Table 1: List of crawled web-domains

Arabic Tweet-Act: Speech Act Recognition for Arabic Asynchronous Conversations

Bushra Algotiml
Department of Computer Science
Umm Al-Qura University
Mecca, Saudi Arabia
bagotiml@uqu.edu.sa

AbdelRahim Elmadany
College of Computer and Information
Jazan University
Jazan, Saudi Arabia
aelmadany@jazanu.edu.sa

Walid Magdy
School of Informatics
University of Edinburgh
Edinburgh, UK
wmagdy@inf.ed.ac.uk

Abstract

Speech acts are the actions that a speaker intends when performing an utterance within conversations. In this paper, we proposed speech act classification for asynchronous conversations on Twitter using multiple machine learning methods including SVM and deep neural networks. We applied the proposed methods on the ArSAS tweets dataset. The obtained results show that superiority of deep learning methods compared to SVMs, where Bi-LSTM managed to achieve an accuracy of 87.5% and a macro-averaged F1 score 61.5%. We believe that our results are the first to be reported on the task of speech-act recognition for asynchronous conversations on Arabic Twitter.

1 Introduction

Speech act in linguistics is defined as the action that a speaker intends when performing an utterance such as asking question, recommending something, greeting or thanking, expressing a thought or making suggestion. Knowing speakers intention within a conversation is considered the one of the recent active research in Natural Language Understanding (NLU); which is called speech act recognition/classification. Speech act classification has been utilized in different Natural Language Processing (NLP) applications, such as summarization (Zhang et al., 2013; Bhatia et al., 2014), rumors verification (Vosoughi, 2015; Vosoughi and Roy, 2016a), hate speech or cyberbullying detection (Gambäck and Sikdar, 2017; Saravanaraj et al., 2016), and in the educational forum (Bayat et al., 2016).

Speech act classification task is usually treated as a multi-class classification problem. Most of researchers tend to use machine learning (ML) paradigm for the task in order to analyze and utilize the massive amount of data that found in online conversations. They usually apply their experiments to two type of conversations: 1) synchronous conversations, where the conversation is one-to-one, such as dialogues, chatting, meetings and transcribed phone conversations; and 2) asynchronous conversations, where the conversation is one-to-many such as emails, discussion forums and social media. Existing work on speech act classification mostly focuses on English language, with some focus on other languages such as German, French and Korean. Moreover, these studies have been conducted for both synchronous and asynchronous conversations. Limited studies have tackled this task for Arabic, and all focusing on synchronous conversations. To the best of our knowledge, there is no work so far for Arabic speech act classification for asynchronous conversations, such as that on social media. Twitter has become a communication medium containing a massive amount of data suitable for social and behavioural studies. Communication between users in Twitter can be considered as asynchronous conversations, within which people post questions, express feelings, recommend, request, report, or claim; all of which can be considered speech acts. Classifying the speech act of tweets can aid in understanding the intentions behind users posts, analyzing Twitter content, and understanding how users interact on social media (Vosoughi and Roy, 2016b).

Proceedings of the Fourth Arabic Natural Language Processing Workshop, pages 183–191
Florence, Italy, August 1, 2019. ©2019 Association for Computational Linguistics

Recently, an Arabic speech-act and sentiment corpus (ArSAS) of tweets corpus was released (Elmadany et al., 2018). It contains more than 21K tweets, annotated with six speech acts. In this paper, this corpus is used to evaluate the effectiveness of different supervised ML approaches for speech act classification for Arabic tweets. In our work, we proposed two approaches based on SVM and multiple deep learning models to classify Arabic tweets into speech act labels. Our results show that Bi-LSTM models achieves the highest performance overall and over each of the individual speech-act classes, where it achieves an accuracy of 87.5% and a macro-F1 of 0.615.

2   Problem Definition

Linguistically, speech act theory studies the ways in which the words can be used to carry out actions rather than transmitting information. The speech act can be defined as the actions that may be performed by speakers to carry out their intentions when performing utterances. According to Searle (Searle, 1975), which is based on Austins work (Austin, 1975), speech acts can be classified by their intent of usage and he categorized it into five categories: Assertive, Directive, Commissive, Expressive, and Declaration.

The concept of a speech act in Arabic can be defined in the same manner as in English. However, a speech act is more profound in the Arabic rhetoric discipline, which is concerned with the semantics of stylistic. Rhetoric in Arabic lies between syntax and semantics and aims to enable the Arabic speaker to relay his or her intended communicative meaning to the listener through the application of rhetorical means and eloquent criteria. The speech act as part of Arabic rhetoric is concerned with the ways of delivering some relevant information with utterance in order to attract the listeners attention (Abdul-Raof, 2006). Interestingly, researchers (Al-Hindawi et al., 2014) have shown the existence of speech acts in Arabic prior to the work of Austin and Searle on English speech acts. They refer to the speech act that is mentioned in the holy Quran and pointed out that Arab scholars have seeded the Arabic Speech act theory even before Austin theory. All the aforementioned examples are written using classical Arabic; however, our work targets the speech act in Arabic dialects. For that, we use a domain-specific taxonomy of six speech act categories

that are commonly seen on Twitter (Vosoughi and Roy, 2016b), including assertion, recommendation, expression, question, request, and miscellaneous. These categories are all derived from Searles taxonomy but modified to make it suitable for speech acts in Twitter.

3   Literature Review

Extensive research has been conducted on speech acts classification in different languages using various techniques. The vast majority of literature in this field uses either supervised ML techniques with a variety of lexical, syntactic, contextual, and semantics features, or adopts deep learning techniques to automatically identify the speech act.

3.1   Trends in Speech Act Recognition

(Cohen et al., 2004) classified English email according to the intent of the sender using SVM classifiers with the use of bi-gram and Part-of-Speech (POS) tags as features. (OShea et al., 2010) proposed a novel technique based on function words (e.g. articles, prepositions, determiners etc.) that appear in the utterances using decision tree classifiers. Their results strongly demonstrate the ability of function words to discriminate between speech act classes. Bhatia et al. (Bhatia et al., 2014) used speech act classification to aid in the summarization of online forum discussion threads using Nave Bayes and they demonstrated the effectiveness of speech act labels in summarizing discussion threads. Additionally, (Tavafi et al., 2013) aimed to determine a domain-independent classifier that could achieve good results across all types of conversations (synchronous and asynchronous). They used different ML techniques such as SVM, Conditional Random Fields (CRF) and Hidden Markov Model (HMM) with a set of domain-independent features, including lexical features and the length of utterances as another feature. They demonstrated that HMM classifiers achieved the best performance for speech act classification on different synchronous and asynchronous English conversations.

Similar techniques was applied for speech-act recgonition for other languages. For example, (Kim et al., 2011) used a Decision Tree (DT), SVM and the Maximum Entropy Model (MEM) with a set of lexical, grammatical and contextual features for speech act classification tasks using a Korean dialogue corpus in a schedule management domain. They showed that SVM outperformed other classifiers by achieving accuracy equal to 93%. Similarly, (Ko, 2015) used Korean corpus to conduct an experiment using SVM and k-NN classifiers with POS and lexical words as features. Ko also pointed out the inadequacy of the tf.idf feature weighting scheme for the task due to the short length of utterances in comparison to the documents length. He proposed a new weighting scheme and showed the effectively of SVM with the new weighting scheme in speech act classification using Korean corpus. Additionally, Bayat et al. (Bayat et al., 2016) used SVM and a set of lexical, contextual, and syntactic features to classify German messages posted on an online forum. They showed the effect of adding features to SVM classifiers in order to increase the performance for the task.

Recently, many researchers have recently applied deep learning techniques using word embeddings to capture speech act of the utterance in synchronous conversations. This is because deep learning techniques afford a significant advantage in capturing the semantics of lexical features (Yoo et al., 2017). The effectiveness of deep learning techniques for speech act recognition is evident in the work of (Cerisara et al., 2018), who proposed a novel deep neural network model based on Long Short Term Memory (LSTM) Recurrent Neural Networks (RNN) and validated this model in three different languages using synchronous conversation corpora. They demonstrated that the performance of this approach is consistent across these three languages (with an accuracy of 72%, 98% and 92% for English, Czech and French, respectively). Similarly, (Khanpour et al., 2016) used LSTM to classify dialogue acts in open-domain conversations. They reported that the word embedding parameters, dropout regularization, decay rate and number of layers have a significant impact on the final systems accuracy. (Yoo et al., 2017) applied a CNN to capture speech acts on Korean dialogues corpus. Their model has obtained a high accuracy (89%) in the speech act recognition task. (Kim and Kim, 2018) proposed an integrated neural network model based on CNN for identifying speech acts, predictors, and sentiments of dialogue utterances. They concluded that the integrated model can help in increasing the performance of intention identification. (Lee and Dernoncourt, 2016) applied both RNN and

CNN on three different synchronous conversations datasets. They stated that the CNN model outperformed the LSTM model for all datasets by a very small margin.

Recently, more attention was directed to speech act classification for tweets as a kind of asynchronous conversations. (Zhang et al., 2011) proposed a set of word-based and character-based features to recognise the speech acts of tweets in order to analyze tweeters behavior collectively or individually. They suggested word-based features composed of a set of N-grams, abbreviations, acronyms, vulgar and opinion words, emoticon, and Twitter-specific features. SVM was used for this task, and showed a weighted-average F1 value of nearly 0.70. Another work by (Vosoughi and Roy, 2016b) explored speech act recognition on Twitter by training SVM, Naive Bayes, decision tree and logistic regression classifiers with a set of semantic and syntactic features. Their approach in features engineering is similar to (Zhang et al., 2011), though they added the dependency subtrees and POS tags to their syntactic features set. They achieved a performance with a weighted-average F1 score equal to 0.70, which is similar to the results of (Zhang et al., 2011). Furthermore, they also applied their speech act classifier to detect rumors on Twitter based on assertion speech act detection in tweets (Vosoughi, 2015). Another work by (Joty and Hoque, 2016) applied deep learning techniques by proposing a model that used LSTM and RNNs for speech acts modeling showed the effectiveness on asynchronous conversations, such as emails and forums.

3.2 Arabic Speech Act Recognition

Much less attention was directed to speech act classification for Arabic. Only limited amount of work exist in literature, but only for classifying speech act in Arabic synchronous conversations. One of the earliest works in this area is (Graja et al., 2013) who used CRF to perform a semantic labelling task for spontaneous speech in Tunisian dialects by using the TuDiCol corpus. Another work, (Elmadany, 2016; Elmadany et al., 2016) utilized the JANA corpus to solve the issue of automatic dialogue act classification for Egyptian Arabic dialect using SVM. Also, (Sherkawi et al., 2018) applied different machine learning techniques on a small Arabic corpus. Their corpus is relatively small and written in MSA.

Recently, a new corpus of Arabic tweets (Ar-SAS) annotated speech-act was released (El-madany et al., 2018), which is the first to model speech-act in asynchronous conversations for Arabic. Nonetheless, no work has been published on this data yet. In this paper, we utilise the Ar-SAS dataset for speech-act classification of Arabic tweets. We believe we are the first exploring speech act classification for Arabic asynchronous conversations.

4 Methodology

We propose two different approaches for classifying Arabic tweets into pre-defined speech act categories: 1) SVM with a set of syntactic and semantic features, and 2) Deep learning with word embedding using different neural network architectures.

4.1 Support Vector Machine Model

SVM has demonstrated significant performance in most of the related work for speech act classification (Cohen et al., 2004; Elmadany, 2016; Hemphill and Roback, 2014; Kim et al., 2011; Ravi and Kim, 2007; Zhang et al., 2013; Tavafi et al., 2013; Zhang et al., 2011; Vosoughi, 2015; Ko, 2015). In preliminary experimentation using simple bag-of-words as features, we found SVM to be superior to other basic ML methods including Naive Bayes, k-NN, RF and DT. Thus, it was chosen for further experiments with additional set of features.

4.1.1 Features Selection

Based on literature, we extracted multiple set of features from tweets to model speech act. We grouped the features into three groups: lexical, syntactic, and structural features.

Lexical features: This is simply the words n-grams in the tweet text. We used uni-gram, bi-gram and tri-gram phrases. These features were extracted after applying preprocessing to the text, including character normalisation to the different forms of the Arabic letters {ﺍ، ﺓ، ﺀ، ﻯ} and diacritics removal (Darwish and Magdy, 2014).

Syntactic features: These features represent the syntactic style of the text of the tweet, and it include four sets of features: punctuation marks, Twitter special characters, Emojis, and Links. Binary features representing specific punctuation such as question and exclamation marks are set to

one when appear, since they can be indicative to specific speech act classes such as expressions, requests or question. In addition, the rest of punctuation marks are combined and added as additional binary features to indicate the appearance of any other punctuation marks in the tweet. Twitter special characters such as presence of hashtags (#) and mentions (@) were also used as binary features. Hashtags might be an indicative feature of some speech act classes such as assertion, where user might use hashtags to announce something. In addition, emojis are usually used in tweets to communicate specific feelings thus it was added as an additional feature. Finally a binary feature indicating the presence of links in the tweets was also used.

Structural features: These set of features represent the structural form of the sentence, and it includes: (1) The length of the tweet in characters and words, which was shown previously to be a useful feature for speech act recognition (Zhang et al., 2013; Tavafi et al., 2013; Elmadany, 2016). (2) POS tags of the words in the tweets, which has been shown to be an effective features in speech act recognition for English (Zhang et al., 2013; Vosoughi and Roy, 2016b). We used FARASA POS tagger [1] for extracting the POS tags. We modified the tagger to include hashtags, URLs and emojis as tags within the sequence. Then, we added uni-gram, bi-gram and tri-gram PoS sequences to the features vector for each tweet.

4.2 Deep Learning Approach

In this paper, we implemented different variants of deep learning neural network in order to determine the most effective type of neural network for the task of Arabic speech act recognition. Two variants of deep learning approaches were considered in this task using different architectures: RNN in particular LSTM and BiLSTM; and CNN. In addition, several combinations of neural networks variants have been applied for this task such as CNN on top of LSTM, CNN on top of BiLSTM, LSTM on top of CNN, and BiLSTM on top of CNN.

A skip-gram word2vec embedding have been used to represent the words in each tweet before inputting them to any neural network. An Arabic pretrained word embedding has been utilized for this work called "AraVec" (Soliman et al., 2017). AraVec is a skip-gram model trained on 70M Ara-

---

[1] http://qatsdemo.cloudapp.net/farasa/

Speech Acts	Examples
Assertion	‏#الشروق: السسي: كلي فخر واعتزاز بالنخبة المتميزة المشاركة في شباب العالم
	#Sunrise: El-Sisi: I am proud of all the elite who are contributed in the world cup forum
Expression	‏أشعر أن الربيع العربي إشعاع من الحرية
	I feel that Arab revolutions are radiation of freedom
Recommendation	‏الكرة الايطالة تحتاج لتركي ال الشيخ
	Italian football needs Tukey Al-Shaikh
Request	‏بعد منتدي شباب العالم أطالب بعمل منتدي للفساد لإظهار الحقائق
	After the world cup forum, I request to do a forum to reveal truths
Miscellaneous	‏ولد سلمان ممكن يلعب مكان محمد صلاح وممكن يلعب مكان عبد الشافي
	Walid Suliman can play instead of Muhammad Salah or possibly instead of Abdul-Shafy

Table 1: Example tweets of different speech acts categories in the ArSAS dataset

bic tweets containing 204K unique words and 300 dimensions.

5 Experimental Setup

5.1 Dataset

We utilized the recently published tweets corpus "Arabic Speech Act and Sentiment" (ArSAS) for our experimentation (Elmadany et al., 2018). ArSAS contains a large set of 21,081 Arabic tweets in different Arabic dialects and annotated by six speech act classes: Assertion, Recommendation, Expression, Question, Request, and Miscellaneous. The tweets in the corpus covers 20 topics including long-standing topics, events and entities (celebrities or organization). Table 1 shows few examples of tweets in the corpus with their corresponding speech act label.

The size of samples in each speech acts class varies a lot in ArSAS corpus, ranging between 60 samples to 11.7K samples per class. The smallest two classes are miscellaneous and recommendation classes that have only 60 and 109 tweets respectively. Therefore, we decided to merge these two classes into one and called it miscellaneous. The final distribution of the five classes in the corpus is: expression (11734), assertion (8233), question (752), request (183), and miscellaneous (169).

5.2 Classifiers Implementation and Setup

For the SVM classifier, SVM LinearSVC implemented in the SKlearn[2] was utilised for our experiments. We examined "One-vs-All" and "One-vs-One" strategies for SVM, and noticed better performance for the "One-vs-All" implementation, and thus it was conducted for our experiments.

Hyper-parameters	Choice
Output layer activation function	softmax
Cost Function	Cross-entropy
Optimizer	ADAM
Learning Rate	0.0001
Batch size	50
Epoch size	30
Dropout rate	0.5
LSTM Units	100
CNN filters	2 and 3
CNN features map	32
Pool size	2
LSTM hidden layers	2
B-LSTM hidden layers	2
CNN hidden layers	4

Table 2: Neural network hyper-parameters

For the neural network classifiers, we used Keras 2.1.3[3] implementations of the multiple models we examined. For the training process of our deep learning models, Table 2 describes the hyper-parameters we used after multiple iterations for reaching the optimal performance.

5.3 Evaluation

For measuring the performance of our approaches, we split the data into five folds and applied 5-fold cross validation for training and testing. Data are split into folds over the class level, where we insure that 20% of the samples of each class exists in each fold. This was essential step to ensure the presence of samples from the small classes in each fold.

For evaluation, three scores are applied: accuracy, micro F-score, and macro F-score. Accuracy and micro-F1 should demonstrate the overall performance of the approaches, while macro-F1 would indicate the average performance of the approaches over each class individually.

[2]https://scikit-learn.org/

[3]https://github.com/keras-team/keras

	Macro-F1	Micro-F1	Accuracy
Lexical	0.510	0.840	0.840
Lexical+Syntactic	0.520	0.850	0.850
Lexical+Structural	0.520	0.850	0.860
All features	**0.532**	**0.862**	**0.865**

Table 3: The performance of SVM for Arabic speech act classification using different sets of features

	Macro-F1	Micro-F1	Accuracy
CNN	0.540	0.841	0.850
LSTM	0.570	0.850	0.860
BiLSTM	**0.615**	**0.86**	**0.875**
CNN on top of LSTM	0.535	0.850	0.865
CNN on top of BiLSTM	0.558	0.850	0.860
LSTM on top of CNN	0.585	0.860	0.870
BiLSTM on top of CNN	0.600	0.860	0.870

Table 4: Comparison between different deep learning architectures for Arabic speech act classification in term of macro-averaged F1, micro-F1 and accuracy

6 Results

6.1 SVM Results

Table 3 reports the results obtained when applying SVM classifier for our task using different sets of features on the ArSAS dataset with 5-fold cross-validation. As shown, the performance of different set of features is almost similar, and the performance when applying all the set of features achieves the best results of accuracy 86.5%, micro-F1 of 0.862, and macro-F1 of 0.532. While the overall performance is relatively high, the performance for some of the classes is considerably low. This could be explained as a reason to the high imbalance of our classes, where some of the classes (such as 'miscellaneous', 'requests', and 'questions') are tiny compared to the two major classes 'expression' and 'assertion'. Actually, nearly 90% of the samples in the classes miscellaneous and request were incorrectly classified.

These results are comparable to the state-of-the-art in other languages such as English. Comparing our work to the work by (Vosoughi and Roy, 2016b) and (Zhang et al., 2011) for speech act classification for English tweets, they report in term of micro F1 (0.69 and 0.70) respectively, and they also explain this due to the high imbalance of classes. Our achieved micro-F1 is even higher 0.86. This might indicate the suitability of using the same techniques —used for English speech act classification— for the Arabic task.

6.2 Deep Learning Results

Table 4 reports the results obtained when applying seven different architectures of RNN and CNN for Arabic speech act classification on the ArSAS dataset with 5-fold cross-validation. As shown, the performance of most of the models is close to those obtained by the SVM models in terms of accuracy, but consistently higher when measured using macro-F1. The BiLSTM and the BiLSTM on top of CNN architectures achieved significantly higher results in terms of macro-F1 compared to all the other models, which indicates better performance on the class level. The best performing model was the BiLSTM model with an accuracy of 87.5%, micro-F1 of 0.86, and macro-F1 of 0.615. This confirms the effectiveness of using the bidirectional LSTM to capture the context in the tweet, which the miscellaneous class actually need. Additionally, BiLSTM succeeded in recognizing both question and request classes better than any other model.

Table 5 shows the performance on the best performing model using BiLSTM on each of the classes individually. As shown, the performance over the two large classes 'assertion' and 'expression' is high (0.9 and 0.87 F1 respectively) compared to the other classes. The 'request' class achieved the lowest performance (0.2 F1). This shows the challenge of recognising the speech act in asynchronous conversations for some of the in-

Class	F1 Score
Assertion	0.90
Expression	0.87
Miscellaneous	0.53
Question	0.57
Request	0.20

Table 5: The performance of best performing BiLSTM model on each class

	Macro-F1	Micro-F1	Accuracy
SVM	0.532	**0.862**	0.865
Bi-LSTM	**0.615**	0.860	**0.875**

Table 6: The best performing SVM model and neural network architecture on the ArSAS dataset

frequent classes.

While our performance is comparable to performance in other languages, we believe there is still large room for improving the performance. We hope that our work would be considered as a baseline for future work on speech act classification for Arabic.

6.3 Discussion

We explored speech act classification in Twitter using SVM classifier with sets of lexical, syntactic, and structural features, and using several neural network architectures with pretrained word embedding for word representation. The best SVM model with all the extracted features has achieved 53.2% in the term of macro-averaged F1 using 5-folds cross validation on the ArSAS dataset. After applying deep learning for the task using variants of neural network architectures, our experiments showed that all the suggested architectures have outperformed the best SVM model with the sets of features. This highlights the superiority of deep learning models especially for a highly inflected language such as Arabic, and in particular Arabic dialect as present in our tweets dataset. BiLSTM has achieved 61.5% in the term of macro-averaged F1, which is 8.3% higher than the best SVM model as shown in Table 6. This confirms the fact that deep learning usually performing better even without any feature engineering.

Potentially, the performance of BiLSTM might improve if these extracted features get fed as an input to the network, especially the PoS tags. PoS features might give some structural characteristics to the neural network.

Moreover, the overall performance was highly affected by the imbalance distribution for the classes amongst the corpus. During our experimentation, we examined some solutions for this issue, such as data over sampling, but it did not lead to improved performance. We believe it might be useful if there are more new examples for the small classes, which would potentially enhance the performance of neural networks as well.

Furthermore, ArSAS corpus contains labels for the type of the topic for each tweet such as long-standing, entity, and event. We suggest considering this attribute in implementation by training different classifier for each type of topics separately. It might be better for the classifier to classify tweets in the same type than classifying tweets from mixed types.

7   Conclusion

In this paper, we have presented two ML approaches for speech act classification in Twitter platform using dialectical Arabic tweets. An SVM classifier with different sets of lexical, syntactic, and structural features was proposed. In addition, a set of different neural network architectures was examined for the task. For both approaches, we exploited the recent published Arabic corpus called "ArSAS" which has more than 21K tweets that annotated by six different speech acts, that we decided to squash to only five classes after merging the smallest two classes into one. Our results showed that deep learning is a more effective approach for speech act classification of Arabic tweets compared to SVM. In particular, the BiLSTM implementation achieved the highest performance especially with the macro-F1 score that was 61.5% compared to only 53.2% for SVM. The best achieved overall accuracy for BiLSTM and SVM were comparable with values of 87.5% and 86.5% respectively.

As a general observation, all the used techniques have showed an acceptable performance, especially when compared to the current state-of-the-art for English speech act classification for asynchronous conversations. Nevertheless, as we discussed, there is the potential of multiple directions for improvements that could be explored in future work.

References

Hussein Abdul-Raof. 2006. *Arabic rhetoric: A pragmatic analysis*. Routledge.

Fareed Hameed Al-Hindawi, Hameed Hasoon Al-Masudi, and Ramia Fuad Mirza. 2014. The speech act theory in english and arabic. *Open Journal of Modern Linguistics*, 4(01):27.

John Langshaw Austin. 1975. *How to do things with words*. Oxford university press.

Berken Bayat, Christopher Krauss, Agathe Merceron, and Stefan Arbanowski. 2016. Supervised speech act classification of messages in german online discussions. In *The Twenty-Ninth International Flairs Conference*.

Sumit Bhatia, Prakhar Biyani, and Prasenjit Mitra. 2014. Summarizing online forum discussions–can dialog acts of individual messages help? In *Proceedings of the 2014 conference on empirical methods in natural language processing (EMNLP)*, pages 2127–2131.

Christophe Cerisara, Pavel Kral, and Ladislav Lenc. 2018. On the effects of using word2vec representations in neural networks for dialogue act recognition. *Computer Speech & Language*, 47:175–193.

William W. Cohen, Vitor R. Carvalho, and Tom M. Mitchell. 2004. Learning to classify email into speech acts. In *Proceedings of the 2004 Conference on Empirical Methods in Natural Language Processing*, pages 309–316.

Kareem Darwish and Walid Magdy. 2014. Arabic information retrieval. *Foundations and Trends® in Information Retrieval*, 7(4):239–342.

AbdelRahim Elmadany. 2016. *Automatic Act Classification for Arabic Dialogue Context*. Ph.D. thesis, Thesis.

AbdelRahim Elmadany, Sherif M. Abdou, and Mervat Gheith. 2016. Jana: A human-human dialogues corpus for egyptian dialect ldc2016t24.

AbdelRahim Elmadany, Hamdy Mubarak, and Walid Magdy. 2018. Arsas: An arabic speech-act and sentiment corpus of tweets. In *OSACT 3: The 3rd Workshop on Open-Source Arabic Corpora and Processing Tools*, page 20.

Björn Gambäck and Utpal Kumar Sikdar. 2017. Using convolutional neural networks to classify hate-speech. In *Proceedings of the first workshop on abusive language online*, pages 85–90.

Marwa Graja, Maher Jaoua, and Lamia Hadrich Belguith. 2013. Discriminative framework for spoken tunisian dialect understanding. In *International Conference on Statistical Language and Speech Processing*, pages 102–110. Springer.

Libby Hemphill and Andrew J Roback. 2014. Tweet acts: how constituents lobby congress via twitter. In *Proceedings of the 17th ACM conference on Computer supported cooperative work & social computing*, pages 1200–1210. ACM.

Shafiq Joty and Enamul Hoque. 2016. Speech act modeling of written asynchronous conversations with task-specific embeddings and conditional structured models. In *Proceedings of the 54th Annual Meeting of the Association for Computational Linguistics (Volume 1: Long Papers)*, volume 1, pages 1746–1756.

Hamed Khanpour, Nishitha Guntakandla, and Rodney Nielsen. 2016. Dialogue act classification in domain-independent conversations using a deep recurrent neural network. In *Proceedings of COLING 2016, the 26th International Conference on Computational Linguistics: Technical Papers*, pages 2012–2021.

Hark-Soo Kim, Choong-Nyoung Seon, and Jung-Yun Seo. 2011. Review of korean speech act classification: machine learning methods. *Journal of Computing Science and Engineering*, 5(4):288–293.

Minkyoung Kim and Harksoo Kim. 2018. Integrated neural network model for identifying speech acts, predicators, and sentiments of dialogue utterances. *Pattern Recognition Letters*, 101:1–5.

Youngjoong Ko. 2015. New feature weighting approaches for speech-act classification. *Pattern Recognition Letters*, 51:107–111.

Ji Young Lee and Franck Dernoncourt. 2016. Sequential short-text classification with recurrent and convolutional neural networks. In *Proceedings of the 2016 Conference of the North American Chapter of the Association for Computational Linguistics: Human Language Technologies*, pages 515–520, San Diego, California. Association for Computational Linguistics.

James OShea, Zuhair Bandar, and Keeley Crockett. 2010. A machine learning approach to speech act classification using function words. In *KES International Symposium on Agent and Multi-Agent Systems: Technologies and Applications*, pages 82–91. Springer.

Sujith Ravi and Jihie Kim. 2007. Profiling student interactions in threaded discussions with speech act classifiers. *Frontiers in Artificial Intelligence and Applications*, 158:357.

A Saravanaraj, JI Sheeba, and S Pradeep Devaneyan. 2016. Automatic detection of cyberbullying from twitter. *International Journal of Computer Science and Information Technology & Security (IJCSITS), ISSN*, pages 2249–9555.

John R. Searle. 1975. A taxonomy of illocutionary acts.

Lina Sherkawi, Nada Ghneim, and Oumayma Al Dakkak. 2018. Arabic speech act recognition techniques. *ACM Transactions on Asian and Low-Resource Language Information Processing (TALLIP)*, 17(3):18.

Abu Bakr Soliman, Kareem Eissa, and Samhaa R. El-Beltagy. 2017. Aravec: A set of arabic word embedding models for use in arabic nlp. *Procedia Computer Science*, 117:256–265.

Maryam Tavafi, Yashar Mehdad, Shafiq Joty, Giuseppe Carenini, and Raymond Ng. 2013. Dialogue act recognition in synchronous and asynchronous conversations. In *Proceedings of the SIGDIAL 2013 Conference*, pages 117–121.

Soroush Vosoughi. 2015. *Automatic detection and verification of rumors on Twitter*. Ph.D. thesis, Massachusetts Institute of Technology.

Soroush Vosoughi and Deb Roy. 2016a. A semi-automatic method for efficient detection of stories on social media. In *Tenth International AAAI Conference on Web and Social Media*.

Soroush Vosoughi and Deb Roy. 2016b. Tweet acts: A speech act classifier for twitter. In *Tenth International AAAI Conference on Web and Social Media*.

Donghyun Yoo, Youngjoong Ko, and Jungyun Seo. 2017. Speech-act classification using a convolutional neural network based on pos tag and dependency-relation bigram embedding. *IEICE Transactions on Information and Systems*, 100(12):3081–3084.

Renxian Zhang, Dehong Gao, and Wenjie Li. 2011. What are tweeters doing: Recognizing speech acts in twitter. In *Workshops at the Twenty-Fifth AAAI Conference on Artificial Intelligence*.

Renxian Zhang, Wenjie Li, Dehong Gao, and You Ouyang. 2013. Automatic twitter topic summarization with speech acts. *IEEE transactions on audio, speech, and language processing*, 21(3):649–658.

Mazajak: An Online Arabic Sentiment Analyser

Ibrahim Abu Farha
School of Informatics
University of Edinburgh
Edinburgh, UK
aibrahim@ed.ac.uk

Walid Magdy
School of Informatics
University of Edinburgh
Edinburgh, UK
wmagdy@inf.ed.ac.uk

Abstract

Sentiment analysis (SA) is one of the most useful natural language processing applications. Literature is flooding with many papers and systems addressing this task, but most of the work is focused on English. In this paper, we present "Mazajak", an online system for Arabic SA. The system is based on a deep learning model, which achieves state-of-the-art results on many Arabic dialect datasets including SemEval 2017 and ASTD. The availability of such system should assist various applications and research that rely on sentiment analysis as a tool.

1 Introduction

Sentiment analysis (SA) can be defined as the process of extracting and analysing the sentiment and polarity in a given piece of text (Liu, 2012). It is one of the tasks in the larger natural language processing (NLP) field. The rapid and wide increase in the use of social media platforms, and the reliance on online shopping and marketing resulted in a flood of information. Many researchers started analysing and mining data for the task of public opinion mining. Sentiment analysis is one of the vital approaches to extract public opinion from large corpora of text. Companies can benefit from understanding the feedback of their costumers and their opinions. Governments as well can use it to understand the reaction of people to their policies and actions.

Work on SA started in early 2000s, particularly with the work of (Pang et al., 2002), where they studied the sentiment of movies' reviews. The work has developed since then and it spanned different topics and fields such as social media. SA gained a lot of interest from researchers who recognised its importance and benefits. However, most of the work is focused on English whereas

Arabic did not receive much attention until recently, but it still lacks behind due to the many challenges of the Arabic language; including the large variety in dialects (Habash, 2010; Darwish et al., 2014) and the complex morphology of the language (Abdul-Mageed et al., 2011).

Recently, the world witnessed a strong revolution in deep learning which was the driving force for many improvements in many fields. The work on English NLP started utilising deep learning models from an early stage, then followed by Arabic NLP. The utilisation of deep learning for Arabic SA started to receive more attention recently showing significant improvement in performance (Dahou et al., 2016; Al-Sallab et al., 2015; Alayba et al., 2018; Al-Smadi et al., 2018).

While there is a considerable amount of work that studies Arabic SA (Al-Ayyoub et al., 2019), to the best of our knowledge, there is no existing open-source tool for Arabic SA that could be used directly. The only work that we are aware of is SentiStrength[1] (Thelwall et al., 2010), which is mainly developed for English, but supports other languages including Arabic. However, it uses a basic dictionary-based approach that works with Arabic MSA and terribly fails with dialects which is the main language used in social media.

In this paper, we present Mazajak[2], an Online Arabic sentiment analysis system that utilises deep learning and massive Arabic word embeddings. The system is available as an online API that can be used by other researchers.

2 Related work

The literature of Arabic SA has many attempts to tackle the problem, however most of the work

---

[1] http://sentistrength.wlv.ac.uk/#Non-English

[2] http://mazajak.inf.ed.ac.uk:8000/

Proceedings of the Fourth Arabic Natural Language Processing Workshop, pages 192–198
Florence, Italy, August 1, 2019. ©2019 Association for Computational Linguistics

is based on conventional machine learning algorithms with few attempts to use deep learning. A recent publication (Al-Ayyoub et al., 2019) presents a comprehensive survey on Arabic SA.

In (Al-Smadi et al., 2017a), the authors proposed an aspect-based SA system for Arabic hotel reviews, in which they used SVM and recurrent neural networks (RNNs). In another work (Shoeb and Ahmed, 2017), the authors applied SA on tweets using Naive Bayes (NB) and KNN, they achieved relatively good results. Al-Ayyoub et al. (2015) also created a large lexicon of Arabic terms extracted from news articles. Based on their lexicon, they built an SA system and tested it on data collected from Twitter. In (Elmasry et al., 2014), the authors aimed to tackle the problem of dialects. They built a slang sentimental words and idioms lexicon (SSWIL) and conducted some experiments using SVM and the new lexicon.

In the realm of social media analysis, the work in (Abdulla et al., 2013) introduced a dataset of 2000 tweets, which the authors used to conduct an experiment with lexicon-based and ML-based systems. They found that combining both approaches would achieve better results. Abdul-Mageed et al. (2014) proposed an SA system for social media. In their work, they experimented and studied a large variety of features. They also studied the effect of the dialects and morphological richness of Arabic. Moreover, In (Abdul-Mageed, 2017a,b), the authors studied the different ways to handle the Arabic morphological richness for SA. They studied the effect of segmentation in representing the lexical input, also they tried to study the weight and importance of these segments for SA.

In SemEval 2017, a sentiment analysis task was presented that included Arabic (Rosenthal et al., 2017). El-Beltagy et al. (2017) were ranked first in SemEval 2017 task for Arabic SA. They used a set of hand-engineered and lexicon-based features, the classifier of choice was a complement NB classifier. The second rank in the same task was for the work of Jabreel and Moreno (2017), who introduced a rich set of features that are mostly based on bag of words (BoW) model in addition to some features extracted from word embeddings. They used SVM as their classification algorithm.

Dahou et al. (2016) proposed a set of word embeddings to be used for Arabic SA, which was built using a corpus of 3.4 billion words. They used a convolutional neural network (CNN) based

system to evaluate their embeddings and the results were promising. Another use of word embeddings was in (Aziz Altowayan and Tao, 2016), where the authors created their own word embeddings and used them as the only features to be fed to the classifier without any engineered features, the results were comparable and slightly better than those of other systems.

In (Alayba et al., 2017), the authors presented their own SA dataset of opinions on health services. They built an SA system and it was tested on the new dataset. Their experiments included the use of many ML algorithms including CNNs. Al-Sallab et al. (2015) experimented with different deep learning models such as recursive auto-encoder (RAE), deep belief networks (DBN) and deep auto-encoder (DAE). They relied on the ArSenL lexicon (Badaro et al., 2014) to build the feature vectors. In (Al-Smadi et al., 2017b), the authors addressed the aspect-based sentiment analysis (ABSA). In their experiments, they used RNNs and SVM as classifiers, the results showed that SVM was superior. Alayba et al. (2018) built an SA system that is based on a combination of CNNs and LSTMs. They tested their model on two datasets, Ar-Twitter and Arabic Health Services datasets, where they achieved accuracies of 88.1% and 94.3% respectively. In (Al-Smadi et al., 2018), the authors proposed an aspect-based sentiment analysis system, their model is based on a Bi-LSTM and conditional random field (CRF). They tested their model on Arabic hotels' reviews dataset, they achieved an F-score of 70%. Elshakankery and Ahmed (2019) proposed a hybrid system for Arabic SA, that utilises lexicon-based and machine learning based approaches. In their work, they experimented with multiple dataset such as ASTD and ArTwitter. They used different classifiers for the task, which varied from using conventional machine learning, to deep learning models.

Among the previous mentioned work, we are not aware of any released open-source tool for Arabic SA, which is considered one of the largest limitations in Arabic NLP. While there are many Arabic NLP tools for various tasks, including segmentation, POS tagging, and diacritization (Pasha et al., 2014; Abdelali et al., 2016), the Arabic NLP research community still lack a tool for sentiment analysis. In this work, we offer the first open-source SA tool for Arabic social media .

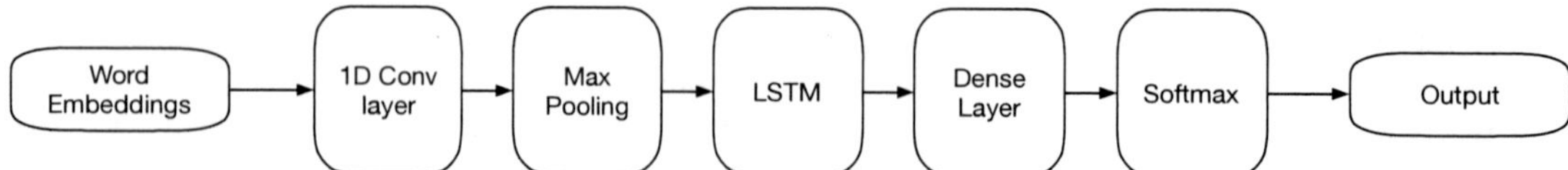

Figure 1: Model architecture.

3   Methodology

This section describes the different components and steps that are used by our system, Mazajak.

3.1   Data Preprocessing

In general, this step is an initial step that aims to reduce the inconsistencies and normalise the data into a coherent form so that it can be handled easily. The steps are mainly based on the work in (El-Beltagy et al., 2017). In our implementation, we used the following steps:

- Letter normalisation: unifying the letters that appear in different forms. We replace {إ أ آ ء} with {ا}, {ة} with {ه} and {ى} with {ي} (Darwish et al., 2014).
- Elongation removal: removing the repeated letters which might appear specially in social media data (Darwish et al., 2012).
- Cleaning: removing unknown characters, diacritics, punctuation, URLs, etc.

3.2   Text representation

Sentences are represented as two dimensional matrix where each row represents a word, and each word is represented by its corresponding embedding. We set the size of the embedding D to 300. In our work, short sentences are padded to match the longest sentence in the training set.

Word embeddings were created using the word2vec (Mikolov et al., 2013), the skip-gram architecture was used. The embeddings were built using a corpus of 250M unique Arabic tweets; this makes it the largest Arabic word embeddings set when compared to the available AraVec (Soliman et al., 2017), which is currently the largest set, built using a corpus of 67M tweets. The tweets were collected over different time periods between 2013 and 2016 to ensure the coverage of different topics. The large and diverse corpus ensures that many dialects are covered which would help in reducing the effect of dialectal variation. When creating the embeddings, the same preprocessing steps utilised in the SA system were used.

Parameter	Value
#LSTM cells	128
Recurrent dropout	20%
Output dropout	20%
#Filters	300
Filter size	3
Pooling size	2
Optimizer	Adam
Learning rate	0.0001
Activation	ReLU

Table 1: CNN-LSTM model hyper-parameters.

3.3   Model Architecture

The model is built on a CNN followed by an LSTM. The CNN works as a feature extractor, where it learns the local patterns inside the sentence and provides representative features. The LSTM works on the extracted features where the context and word ordering would be taken into consideration. The model has been designed after extensive comparison to existing models in literature, and has been shown to be the most effective one among the state-of-the-art models, as demonstrated in next section. Figure 1 shows the architecture, the embeddings are fed into the CNN, after that they are fed to a max-pooling layer, the reason behind using max pooling is to have the most important features which conforms with the fact that sentiment is usually expressed in specific words. The extracted features are fed into an LSTM which is followed by a softmax layer that would give a probability distribution over the output classes. The hyper-parameters used in our architecture is shown in Table 1.

4   Model Performance

4.1   Experimental Setup

To examine the effectiveness of our model before offering it online for public use, we tested the model on three different datasets. The first is SemEval 2017 task 4-A benchmark dataset (Rosenthal et al., 2017), which consists of 6,100 testing tweets and 3,555 training ones. All tweets are labelled to one of three classes: positive, negative or neutral. The second dataset is ASTD benchmark dataset (Nabil et al., 2015), which con-

Dataset	System	AvgRec	$\mathbf{F}^{PN}$	Acc
SemEval	(El-Beltagy et al., 2017)	0.58	0.61	0.58
	Mazajak	**0.61**	**0.63**	**0.62**
ASTD	(Heikal et al., 2018)	0.61	0.71	0.65
	Mazajak	**0.62**	**0.72**	**0.66**
ArSAS	Mazajak	**0.90**	**0.90**	**0.92**

Table 2: Mazajak performance in sentiment analysis in comparison to the state-of-the-art systems over three benchmark datasets

sists of 10,006 tweets, 6,691 of them are objective which means that they are not useful for SA. The rest are divided over three sentiment classes. The third dataset is ArSAS (Elmadany et al., 2018), the largest available dataset for Arabic SA which consists over 21K tweets labelled over four sentiment classes: positive, negative, neutral, and mixed. The mixed class has the smallest number of samples, thus we decided to ignore it. In addition, ArSAS has a confidence value for each label. We decided to keep only the tweets with confidence level over 50% and ignore the rest. After this step, we end up with 17,784 tweets in the ArSAS dataset labelled with three sentiment labels. Both ASTD and ArSAS datasets have no specific splitting of the data to test and train; thus, we applied random sampling to split both datasets to 80/20% for train/test respectively.

4.2 Baselines and Evaluation

To ensure having Mazajak achieving state-of-the-art performance, we compared its effectiveness to the existing best reported performance on each of the three datasets. For evaluation, we followed the same methodology adopted by SemEval 2017 task which uses average recall, F^{PN} and accuracy. F^{PN} is the macro-average F-score over the positive and negative classes only while neglecting the neutral class (Rosenthal et al., 2017). The best performing system in the SemEval 2017 task is the one described in (El-Beltagy et al., 2017) which achieved an F^{PN} of 0.61. For the ASTD, the best reported results are by (Heikal et al., 2018) who used an ensemble system combining output of CNN and Bi-LSTM architectures, which achieved an F^{PN} of 0.71. These two systems are used as our baselines. For the ArSAS dataset, we are not aware of any reported results on it yet.

4.3 Classification Performance

Table 2 reports the classification results of our system Mazajak and compares it to the state-of-the-

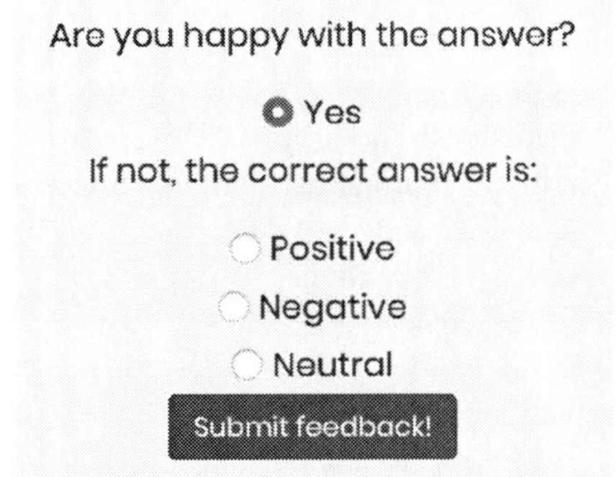

Figure 2: Sentiment feedback form on Mazajak.

art systems for the three benchmark datasets. As shown in the table, Mazajak model outperformed the current state-of-the-art models on the SemEval and ASTD datasets. In addition, it achieved a high performance on the ArSAS dataset. Our reported scores are higher than current top systems for all the evaluation scores, including average recall, F^{PN}, and accuracy. These results confirm that our model choice for our tool represents the current state-of-the-art for Arabic SA.

5 Mazajak Online API

Our Arabic SA model is deployed as an online system, **Mazajak**[3], and can be accessed online at "`Mazajak.inf.ed.ac.uk:8000`".

The final model hosted online is trained on the SemEval and ASTD dataset combined[4].

Our online tool provides four modes of operation as follows:

- **Text Input:** where the user can input any piece of text into a text-box, and the system will display the polarity of the sentiment in the text. This mode allows the user to give

---

[3] the word "Mazajak" (مزاجك), is an Arabic word which means "your mood".

[4] this is different from the experimentation above when we were comparing the system to state-of-the-art.

Tweet	Sentiment
يعني لولا ما هالدكتور بدو يفصلني كان هسا انا بالبيت. اوفت.	negative
يعني خلاص الشتا خلص و هندخل في الحر و التلزيق و مش هلبس اللبس اللي مرمي في الدولاب وملبستوش ده	negative
مش كل اللي بيقرب منك عايز يخدعك في قلوب طيبة بدور علي اللي زيها	positive
وشلون اضيق بحضورك وانت كل الدروب اللي ليآ ضآق صدري سقت رجلي لها	positive
خروج ايطاليا من تصفيات كاس العالم اليوم علي يد السويد بالتعادل بعد ستين عام بدون انقطاع عن المونديال	neutral
غوغل تتحدى أبل وسامسونغ: أعلنت جوجل يوم الثلاثاء عن هاتف بيكسل جديد بكاميرا مميزة.	neutral

Table 3: Examples of some tweets classified using Mazajak.

feedback on the output sentiment using the form shown in Figure 2. This, in turn, would help to continuously collect more training data. The collected data is used periodically to update our model to improve the system performance.

- **Batch Mode:** where the user provides a file with multiple lines of text, and the system returns back an output file with the corresponding sentiment to each line in the input file.

- **Timeline mode:** where the user provides a Twitter account name, and the system will analyse the sentiment of the tweets in the account's timeline. The output is a graph showing the number of the tweets of each of the classes over time and an overall ratio of the percentages of the tweets corresponding to each class as shown in Figure 3.

- **Online API:** where an API could be downloaded to help other research that utilises sentiment analysis. The API provides two functions, either getting the sentiment of a sentence or a list of sentences. The API functions are provided in Python, but with a few lines of coding it can be accessed using other programming languages.

Table 3 shows some examples of classified tweets using the tool, these examples show that the model can handle the dialectal variations.

Our online system would be updated periodically with new training data and potentially better preforming models. We aim that Mazajak would serve the research community in analysing sentiment in Arabic text in a simple way, which, as we hope, would further promote the research in Arabic language.

6 Conclusion

In this paper, we presented Mazajak, the first online Arabic sentiment analysis tool. The system

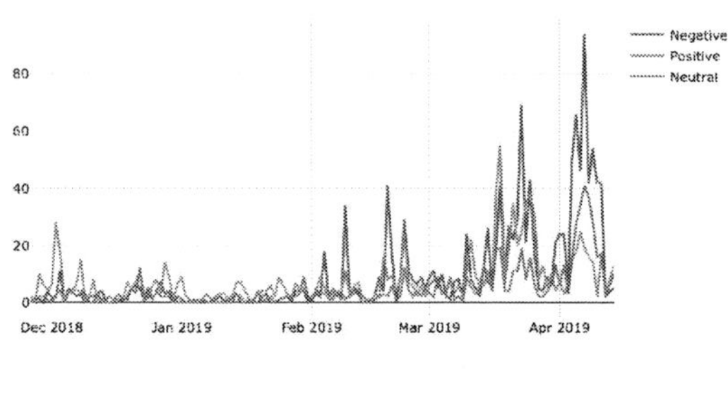
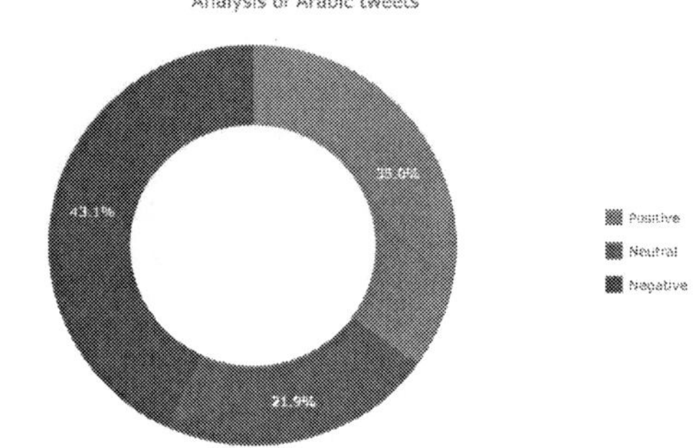

Figure 3: Twitter timeline analysis sample output.

utilises the advancements in the NLP and deep learning fields. The model, on which the system relies, achieves state-of-the-art results on three of the benchmark datasets for Arabic SA including SemEval 2017 task, ASTD and ArSAS. The system is available as an online API that can be accessed easily, which would help and ease the work of other researchers in applications that make use of sentiment information.

Mazajak is offered for free use for research purposes. For commercial usage, please contact the authors.

In the future, we hope to improve the model so it would achieve better results. Also, we look forward to add more features such as the ability to handle Arabizi –Arabic written in English alphabet– and emojis.

References

Ahmed Abdelali, Kareem Darwish, Nadir Durrani, and Hamdy Mubarak. 2016. Farasa: A fast and furious segmenter for arabic. In *Proceedings of the 2016 Conference of the North American Chapter of the Association for Computational Linguistics: Demonstrations*, pages 11–16.

Muhammad Abdul-Mageed. 2017a. Modeling arabic subjectivity and sentiment in lexical space. *Information Processing & Management*.

Muhammad Abdul-Mageed. 2017b. Not all segments are created equal: Syntactically motivated sentiment analysis in lexical space. In *Proceedings of the third Arabic natural language processing workshop*, pages 147–156.

Muhammad Abdul-Mageed, Mona Diab, and Sandra Kübler. 2014. Samar: Subjectivity and sentiment analysis for arabic social media. *Computer Speech & Language*, 28(1):20–37.

Muhammad Abdul-Mageed, Mona T. Diab, and Mohammed Korayem. 2011. Subjectivity and sentiment analysis of modern standard arabic. In *Proceedings of the 49th Annual Meeting of the Association for Computational Linguistics: Human Language Technologies: Short Papers - Volume 2*, HLT '11, pages 587–591, Stroudsburg, PA, USA. Association for Computational Linguistics.

Nawaf A. Abdulla, Nizar A. Ahmed, Mohammed A. Shehab, and Mahmoud Al-Ayyoub. 2013. Arabic sentiment analysis: Lexicon-based and corpus-based. In *Applied Electrical Engineering and Computing Technologies (AEECT), 2013 IEEE Jordan Conference on*, pages 1–6. IEEE.

Mahmoud Al-Ayyoub, Safa Bani Essa, and Izzat Alsmadi. 2015. Lexicon-based sentiment analysis of arabic tweets. *International Journal of Social Network Mining*, 2(2):101–114.

Mahmoud Al-Ayyoub, Abed Allah Khamaiseh, Yaser Jararweh, and Mohammed N. Al-Kabi. 2019. A comprehensive survey of arabic sentiment analysis. *Information Processing & Management*, 56(2):320–342.

Ahmad Al-Sallab, Hazem Hajj, Gilbert Badaro, Ramy Baly, Wassim El-Hajj, and Khaled Bashir Shaban. 2015. Deep learning models for sentiment analysis in arabic. In *Proceedings of the Second Workshop on Arabic Natural Language Processing*, pages 9–17.

Mohammad Al-Smadi, Omar Qawasmeh, Mahmoud Al-Ayyoub, Yaser Jararweh, and Brij Gupta. 2017a. Deep recurrent neural network vs. support vector machine for aspect-based sentiment analysis of arabic hotels' reviews. *Journal of Computational Science*.

Mohammad Al-Smadi, Omar Qawasmeh, Mahmoud Al-Ayyoub, Yaser Jararweh, and Brij Gupta. 2017b. Deep recurrent neural network vs. support vector machine for aspect-based sentiment analysis of arabic hotels' reviews. *Journal of Computational Science*.

Mohammad Al-Smadi, Bashar Talafha, Mahmoud Al-Ayyoub, and Yaser Jararweh. 2018. Using long short-term memory deep neural networks for aspect-based sentiment analysis of arabic reviews. *International Journal of Machine Learning and Cybernetics*, pages 1–13.

Abdulaziz M. Alayba, Vasile Palade, Matthew England, and Rahat Iqbal. 2017. Arabic language sentiment analysis on health services. *CoRR*, abs/1702.03197.

Abdulaziz M. Alayba, Vasile Palade, Matthew England, and Rahat Iqbal. 2018. A combined cnn and lstm model for arabic sentiment analysis. *arXiv preprint arXiv:1807.02911*.

A. Aziz Altowayan and Lixin Tao. 2016. Word embeddings for arabic sentiment analysis. In *2016 IEEE International Conference on Big Data (Big Data)*, pages 3820–3825.

Gilbert Badaro, Ramy Baly, Hazem Hajj, Nizar Habash, and Wassim El-Hajj. 2014. A large scale arabic sentiment lexicon for arabic opinion mining. In *Proceedings of the EMNLP 2014 Workshop on Arabic Natural Language Processing (ANLP)*, pages 165–173.

Abdelghani Dahou, Shengwu Xiong, Junwei Zhou, Mohamed Houcine Haddoud, and Pengfei Duan. 2016. Word embeddings and convolutional neural network for arabic sentiment classification. In *Proceedings of COLING 2016, the 26th International Conference on Computational Linguistics: Technical Papers*, pages 2418–2427.

Kareem Darwish, Walid Magdy, and Ahmed Mourad. 2012. Language processing for arabic microblog retrieval. In *Proceedings of the 21st ACM international conference on Information and knowledge management*, pages 2427–2430. ACM.

Kareem Darwish, Walid Magdy, et al. 2014. Arabic information retrieval. *Foundations and Trends® in Information Retrieval*, 7(4):239–342.

Samhaa R. El-Beltagy, Mona El Kalamawy, and Abu Bakr Soliman. 2017. Niletmrg at semeval-2017 task 4: Arabic sentiment analysis. *arXiv preprint arXiv:1710.08458*.

AbdelRahim Elmadany, Hamdy Mubarak, and Walid Magdy. 2018. Arsas: An arabic speech-act and sentiment corpus of tweets.

Mostafa Elmasry, Taysir Soliman, and Abdel-Rahman Hedar. 2014. Sentiment analysis of arabic slang comments on facebook. *International Journal of Computers & Technology*, 12(5):3470–3478.

Kariman Elshakankery and Mona F. Ahmed. 2019. Hilatsa: A hybrid incremental learning approach for arabic tweets sentiment analysis. *Egyptian Informatics Journal*.

Nizar Y. Habash. 2010. Introduction to arabic natural language processing. *Synthesis Lectures on Human Language Technologies*, 3(1):1–187.

Maha Heikal, Marwan Torki, and Nagwa El-Makky. 2018. Sentiment analysis of arabic tweets using deep learning. *Procedia Computer Science*, 142:114–122.

Mohammed Jabreel and Antonio Moreno. 2017. Sitaka at semeval-2017 task 4: Sentiment analysis in twitter based on a rich set of features. In *Proceedings of the 11th International Workshop on Semantic Evaluation (SemEval-2017)*, pages 694–699.

Bing Liu. 2012. Sentiment Analysis and Opinion Mining. *Synthesis Lectures on Human Language Technologies*, 5(1):1–167.

Tomas Mikolov, Kai Chen, Greg Corrado, and Jeffrey Dean. 2013. Efficient estimation of word representations in vector space. *arXiv preprint arXiv:1301.3781*.

Mahmoud Nabil, Mohamed Aly, and Amir Atiya. 2015. Astd: Arabic sentiment tweets dataset. In *Proceedings of the 2015 Conference on Empirical Methods in Natural Language Processing*, pages 2515–2519.

Bo Pang, Lillian Lee, and Shivakumar Vaithyanathan. 2002. Thumbs up?: sentiment classification using machine learning techniques. In *Proceedings of the ACL-02 conference on Empirical methods in natural language processing-Volume 10*, pages 79–86. Association for Computational Linguistics.

Arfath Pasha, Mohamed Al-Badrashiny, Mona T. Diab, Ahmed El-Kholy, Ramy Eskander, Nizar Habash, Manoj Pooleery, Owen Rambow, and Ryan Roth. 2014. Madamira: A fast, comprehensive tool for morphological analysis and disambiguation of arabic. In *LREC*, volume 14, pages 1094–1101.

Sara Rosenthal, Noura Farra, and Preslav Nakov. 2017. Semeval-2017 task 4: Sentiment analysis in twitter. In *Proceedings of the 11th International Workshop on Semantic Evaluation (SemEval-2017)*, pages 502–518.

Md Shoeb and Jawed Ahmed. 2017. Sentiment analysis and classification of tweets using data mining. *International Research Journal of Engineering and Technology*, 4(12).

Abu Bakr Soliman, Kareem Eissa, and Samhaa R. El-Beltagy. 2017. Aravec: A set of arabic word embedding models for use in arabic nlp. *Procedia Computer Science*, 117:256 – 265. Arabic Computational Linguistics.

Mike Thelwall, Kevan Buckley, Georgios Paltoglou, Di Cai, and Arvid Kappas. 2010. Sentiment strength detection in short informal text. *Journal of the American Society for Information Science and Technology*, 61(12):2544–2558.

The MADAR Shared Task
on Arabic Fine-Grained Dialect Identification

Houda Bouamor, Sabit Hassan, Nizar Habash[†]
Carnegie Mellon University in Qatar, Qatar
[†]New York University Abu Dhabi, UAE
{hbouamor,sabith}@qatar.cmu.edu
nizar.habash@nyu.edu

Abstract

In this paper, we present the results and findings of the MADAR Shared Task on Arabic Fine-Grained Dialect Identification. This shared task was organized as part of The Fourth Arabic Natural Language Processing Workshop, collocated with ACL 2019. The shared task includes two subtasks: the MADAR Travel Domain Dialect Identification subtask (Subtask 1) and the MADAR Twitter User Dialect Identification subtask (Subtask 2). This shared task is the first to target a large set of dialect labels at the city and country levels. The data for the shared task was created or collected under the Multi-Arabic Dialect Applications and Resources (MADAR) project. A total of 21 teams from 15 countries participated in the shared task.

1 Introduction

Arabic has a number of diverse dialects from across different regions of the Arab World. Although primarily spoken, written dialectal Arabic has been increasingly used on social media. Automatic dialect identification is helpful for tasks such as sentiment analysis (Al-Twairesh et al., 2016), author profiling (Sadat et al., 2014), and machine translation (Salloum et al., 2014). Most previous work, shared tasks, and evaluation campaigns on Arabic dialect identification were limited in terms of dialectal variety targeting coarse-grained regional dialect classes (around five) plus Modern Standard Arabic (MSA) (Zaidan and Callison-Burch, 2013; Elfardy and Diab, 2013; Darwish et al., 2014; Malmasi et al., 2016; Zampieri et al., 2017; El-Haj et al., 2018). There are of course some recent noteworthy exceptions (Bouamor et al., 2018; Zaghouani and Charfi, 2018; Abdul-Mageed et al., 2018).

In this paper, we present the results and findings of the MADAR Shared Task on Arabic Fine-Grained Dialect Identification. The shared task was organized as part of the Fourth Arabic Natural Language Processing Workshop (WANLP), collocated with ACL 2019.[1] This shared task is the first to target a large set of dialect labels at the city and country levels. The data for the shared task was created under the Multi-Arabic Dialect Applications and Resources (MADAR) project.[2]

The shared task featured two subtasks. First is the MADAR Travel Domain Dialect Identification subtask (Subtask 1), which targeted 25 specific cities in the Arab World. And second is the MADAR Twitter User Dialect Identification (Subtask 2), which targeted 21 Arab countries. All of the datasets created for this shared task will be made publicly available to support further research on Arabic dialect modeling.[3]

A total of 21 teams from 15 countries in four continents submitted runs across the two subtasks and contributed 17 system description papers. All system description papers are included in the WANLP workshop proceedings and cited in this report. The large number of teams and submitted systems suggests that such shared tasks on Arabic NLP can indeed generate significant interest in the research community within and outside of the Arab World.

Next, Section 2 describes the shared task subtasks. Section 3 provides a description of the datasets used in the shared task, including the newly created MADAR Twitter Corpus. Section 4 presents the teams that participated in each subtask with a high-level description of the approaches they adopted. Section 5 discusses the results of the competition. Finally, Section 6 concludes this report and discusses some future directions.

---

[1]http://wanlp2019.arabic-nlp.net
[2]https://camel.abudhabi.nyu.edu/madar/
[3]http://resources.camel-lab.com.

Proceedings of the Fourth Arabic Natural Language Processing Workshop, pages 199–207
Florence, Italy, August 1, 2019. ©2019 Association for Computational Linguistics

2 Task Description

The MADAR Shared Task included two subtasks:
the MADAR Travel Domain Dialect Identification
subtask, and the MADAR Twitter User Dialect
Identification subtask.

2.1 Subtask 1: MADAR Travel Domain Dialect Identification

The goal of this subtask is to classify written Arabic sentences into one of 26 labels representing the
specific city dialect of the sentences, or MSA. The
participants were provided with a dataset from the
MADAR corpus (Bouamor et al., 2018), a large-
scale collection of parallel sentences in the travel
domain covering the dialects of 25 cities from the
Arab World in addition to MSA (Table 1 shows
the list of cities). This fine-grained dialect identification task was first explored in Salameh et al.
(2018), where the authors introduced a system that
can identify the exact city with an averaged macro
F1 score of 67.9%. The participants in this subtask received the same training, development and
test sets used in (Salameh et al., 2018). More details about this dataset are given in Section 3.

2.2 Subtask-2: MADAR Twitter User Dialect Identification

The goal of this subtask is to classify Twitter user
profiles into one of 21 labels representing 21 Arab
countries, using only the Twitter user tweets. The
Twitter user profiles as well as the tweets are part
of the MADAR Twitter Corpus, which was created specifically for this shared task. More details
about this dataset are given in Section 3.

2.3 Restrictions and Evaluation Metrics

We provided the participants with a set of restrictions for building their systems to ensure a common experimental setup.

Subtask 1 Restrictions Participants were asked
not to use any external manually labeled datasets.
However, the use of publicly available unlabelled
data was allowed. Participants were not allowed
to use the development set for training.

Subtask 2 Restrictions First, participants were
asked to only use the text of the tweets and the specific information about the tweets provided in the
shared task (see Section 3.2). Additional tweets,
external manually labelled data sets, or any meta
information about the Twitter user or the tweets

Region	Country	City
Gulf of Aden	Yemen	Sana'a
	Djibouti	
	Somalia	
Gulf	Oman	Muscat
	UAE	
	Qatar	Doha
	Bahrain	
	Kuwait	
	KSA	Riyadh, Jeddah
	Iraq	Baghdad, Mosul, Basra
Levant	Syria	Damascus, Aleppo
	Lebanon	Beirut
	Jordan	Amman, Salt
	Palestine	Jerusalem
Nile Basin	Egypt	Cairo, Alexandria, Aswan
	Sudan	Khartoum
Maghreb	Libya	Tripoli, Benghazi
	Tunisia	Tunis, Sfax
	Algeria	Algiers
	Morocco	Rabat, Fes
	Mauritania	
		MSA

Table 1: The list of the regions, countries, and cities
covered in Subtask 1 (City column) and Subtask 2
(Country column).

(e.g., geo-location data) were not allowed. Second, participants were instructed not to include the
MADAR Twitter Corpus development set in training. However, any publicly available unlabelled
data could be used.

Evaluation Metrics Participating systems are
ranked based on the macro-averaged F1 scores obtained on blind test sets (official metric). We also
report performance in terms of macro-averaged
precision, macro-averaged recall and accuracy
at different levels: region (Acc_{region}), country
($\text{Acc}_{country}$) and city (Acc_{city}). Accuracy at
coarser levels (i.e., country and region in Sub-
task 1; and region in Subtask 2) is computed by
comparing the reference and prediction labels after mapping them to the coarser level. We follow
the mapping shown in Table 1. Each participating
team was allowed to submit up to three runs for
each subtask. Only the highest scoring run was
selected to represent the team.

3   Shared Task Data

Next, we discuss the corpora used for the subtasks.

3.1   The MADAR Travel Domain Corpus

In Subtask 1, we use a large-scale collection of parallel sentences covering the dialects of 25 Arab cities (Table 1), in addition to English, French and MSA (Bouamor et al., 2018). This resource was a commissioned translation of the Basic Traveling Expression Corpus (BTEC) (Takezawa et al., 2007) sentences from English and French to the different dialects. It includes two corpora. The first consists of 2,000 sentences translated into 25 Arab city dialects in parallel. We refer to it as Corpus 26 (25 cities plus MSA). The second corpus has 10,000 additional sentences (non-overlapping with the 2,000 sentences) from the BTEC corpus translated to the dialects of only five selected cities: Beirut, Cairo, Doha, Tunis and Rabat. We refer to it as Corpus 6 (5 cities plus MSA). An example of a 27-way parallel sentence (25 cities plus MSA and English) extracted from Corpus 26 is given in Table 2. The train-dev-test splits of the corpora are shown in Table 3. Corpus 6 test set was not included in the shared task.[4]

3.2   The MADAR Twitter Corpus

For Subtask 2, we created a new dataset, the MADAR Twitter Corpus, containing 2,980 Twitter user profiles from 21 different countries.

Corpus collection Inspired by the work of Mubarak and Darwish (2014) we collected a set of Twitter user profiles that reflects the way users from different regions in the Arab World tweet. Unlike previous work (Zaghouani and Charfi, 2018), we do not search Twitter based on specific dialectal keywords. Rather, we search for tweets that contain a set of 25 seed hashtags corresponding to the 22 states of the Arab League (e.g., #Algeria, #Egypt, #Kuwait, etc.), in addition to the hashtags: "#ArabWorld", "#ArabLeague" and "#Arab". We collected an equal number of profiles (175 * 25 = 4,375) from the search results of each of the hashtags. The profiles were all manually labeled by a team of three annotators. For each labeled user profile, only the first 100 available tweets at collection time are kept.

Dialect	Sentence
Aleppo	بدي كنزة اطفال.
Alexandria	عاوز بلوفر أطفال.
Algiers	راني حاب تريكو تع أطفال.
Amman	بدي بلوفر أطفال.
Aswan	كنت عايز بلوفر اطفال.
Baghdad	اريد سترة مال أطفال.
Basra	اريد سترة جهال.
Beirut	بدي كنزة للولاد.
Benghazi	نبي مالية بتاع أطفال.
Cairo	عايز بلوفر أطفال.
Damascus	بدي كنزة أطفال.
Doha	بغيت فانلة يهال.
Fes	بغيت لبيسة ديال الدراري الصغار.
Jeddah	أبا سترة اطفال.
Jerusalem	بدي جرزة أطفال.
Khartoum	داير بلوفر أطفال.
Mosul	اغيد سترة اطفال.
Muscat	أبغا سترة للأطفال.
Rabat	بغيت تريكو ديال الدراري الصغار.
Riyadh	ابغى سترة للأطفال.
Salt	بدي بلوفر للأطفال .
Sana'a	أشتي سترة أطفالي.
Sfax	نحب مريول للأولاد.
Tripoli	نبي ماليه متاع صغار.
Tunis	نحب مريول متاع صغار.
MSA	أريد جاكيت للأطفال.

Table 2: An example from Corpus 26 for the English sentence 'I'd like a children's sweater.'

	Sentences * Variant	Total
Corpus 6 train	9,000 * 6	54,000
Corpus 6 dev	1,000 * 6	6,000
Corpus 26 train	1,600 * 26	41,600
Corpus 26 dev	200 * 26	5,200
Corpus 26 test	200 * 26	5,200

Table 3: Distribution of the train, dev and test sets provided for Subtask 1.

Corpus annotation Three annotators, all native speakers of Arabic were hired to complete this task. They were provided with a list of Twitter user profiles and their corresponding URLs. They were asked to inspect each profile by checking if the user indicated his/her location, checking his/her tweets, and label it with its corresponding country when possible. In the context of dialect identification, the country label here refers to the Twitter

DrBehbehaniAM	Kuwait	وتقولون ليش الأطباء داشين تويتر
DrBehbehaniAM	Kuwait	لا القافلة وقفت ، ولا الكلاب تعبت .
DrBehbehaniAM	Kuwait	مسالنور على قوم التويتر مساء ما يليق الا بالطيبين مساء الابتسامة من القلب
HederAshraf	Egypt	الى عايز يجيب جون فى الأهلى يجيب زى ما هو عايز بس الهدف يتحسب أو لا دى بتاعتنا
HederAshraf	Egypt	يعنى هى جت عالجون دة بس الدورى مليان بلاوى
HederAshraf	Egypt	هههههههه مش عارف انت مكبر الموضوع كدة ليه انا حاسيت اننا هنحرر فلسطين
samykhalildz	Algeria	اعطيلهم فكرة علاش راك غير تنتقد ..
samykhalildz	Algeria	صلاة المغرب رسميا سيصبح اسمها صلاة الجزائر في السعودية
samykhalildz	Algeria	تسريبات : نائب افلاني من بليدة قد يكون متهما في قضية كوكايين العاصمة.

Table 4: Three examples from the MADAR Twitter Corpus.

user geopolitical identity with the assumption that such identity could be expressed either explicitly through the location indicated in the Twitter bio section, or implicitly through dialectal and MSA usage in the tweets. Annotators were instructed not to rely only on the location provided by the user, and were invited to use all the extra-linguistic information available in the profile such as images, proclamations of loyalty and pride, etc. They were also allowed to check other sources such as corresponding Facebook profiles, if available, to confirm the user's country. Profiles may be marked as *Non Person*, *Non Arab* or *too hard to guess*. To measure inter-annotator agreement, a common set of 150 profiles were labeled by all annotators. They obtained an average Cohen Kappa score of 80.16%, which shows substantial agreement.

We discarded all profiles that became unavailable after the collection step, as well as profiles marked as *Non Person*, *Non Arab* or *too hard to guess*. Our final data set contained 2,980 country-labeled profiles. Three examples from the MADAR Twitter Corpus are shown in Table 4.

The distribution of the Twitter profiles by country is given in Table 5. The majority of the users obtained were from Saudi Arabia, representing 35.91% of the total profiles. Since there were zero Twitter user profiles from the Comoros in our dataset, we exclude it from the shared subtask.

Dataset splits and additional features We split the Twitter corpus into train, dev and test sets. The split distribution is given in Table 6. Participants were provided with the pointers to the tweets together with automatically detected language by Twitter, as well as the 26 confidence scores of the Salameh et al. (2018) system for the 26-way classification task applied per tweet.

Country	Count	Percentage
Saudi Arabia	1,070	35.91
Kuwait	213	7.15
Egypt	173	5.81
UAE	152	5.10
Oman	138	4.63
Yemen	136	4.56
Qatar	126	4.22
Bahrain	113	3.79
Jordan	107	3.59
Sudan	100	3.36
Iraq	99	3.32
Algeria	92	3.09
Libya	78	2.62
Palestine	74	2.48
Lebanon	66	2.21
Somalia	60	2.01
Tunisia	51	1.71
Syria	48	1.61
Morocco	45	1.51
Mauritania	37	1.24
Djibouti	2	0.07
Comoros	0	0
Total Annotated	**2,980**	**100**

Table 5: Distribution of the tweet Profiles by country label in the MADAR Twitter Corpus.

	Users	Tweets
Twitter Corpus train	2,180	217,592
Twitter Corpus dev	300	29,869
Twitter Corpus test	500	49,962

Table 6: Distribution of the train, dev and test sets provided for Subtask 2.

Team	Affiliation	Tasks
A3-108 (Mishra and Mujadia, 2019)	International Institute of Information Technology (IIIT), Hyderabad, India	1,2
ADAPT-Epita (De Francony et al., 2019)	Cork Institute of Technology, Ireland; and EPITA, France	1
ArbDialectID (Qwaider and Saad, 2019)	Göteborg Universitet, Sweden; and The Islamic University of Gaza, Palestine	1
CURAISA (Elaraby and Zahran, 2019)	Raisa Energy; and Cairo University, Egypt	2
DNLP	Dalhousie University, Canada	1
JHU (Lippincott et al., 2019)	Johns Hopkins University, USA	1,2
JUST (Talafha et al., 2019a)	Jordan University of Science and Technology, Jordan	1
khalifaaa	Cairo University, Egypt	1
LIU_MIR (Kchaou et al., 2019)	Laboratoire d'Informatique de l'Universitè du Mans (LIUM), France; and Multimedia, InfoRmation Systems, and Advanced Computing Laboratory (MIRACL), Tunisia	1
Mawdoo3 _AI_Team (Ragab et al., 2019; Talafha et al., 2019b)	Mawdoo3, Jordan, Egypt and Italy	1,2
MICHAEL (Ghoul and Lejeune, 2019)	Sorbonne University, France	1
Eldesouki	Qatar Computing Research Institute (QCRI), Qatar	1
OscarGaribo	Universitat Politècnica de València and Autoritas Consulting, Spain	1
QC-GO (Samih et al., 2019)	Qatar Computing Research Institute (QCRI), Qatar; and Google Inc, USA	1,2
QUT (Eltanbouly et al., 2019)	Qatar University, Qatar	1
Safina	Cairo University, Egypt	1
SMarT (Meftouh et al., 2019)	Badji Mokhtar University, Algeria; Lorraine University, France; and École Normale Supérieure de Bouzaréah, Algeria	1
Speech Translation (Abbas et al., 2019)	Le Centre de Recherche Scientifique et Technique pour le Développement de la Langue Arabe (CRSTDLA), Algeria and University of Trento, Italy	1,2
Trends (Fares et al., 2019)	Alexandria University, Egypt	1,2
UBC-NLP (Zhang and Abdul-Mageed, 2019)	The University of British Columbia, Canada	2
ZCU-NLP (Přibáň and Taylor, 2019)	Západočeská Univerzita v Plzni, Czech Republic	1,2

Table 7: List of the 21 teams that participated in Subtasks 1 and 2 of the MADAR Shared Task.

4 Participants and Systems

A total of 21 teams from 15 countries in four continents participated in the shared task. Table 7 presents the names of participating teams and their affiliations. 19 teams participated in Subtask 1; and 9 in Subtask 2. The submitted systems included a diverse set of approaches that incorporated machine learning, ensemble learning and deep learning frameworks, and exploited a various range of features. Table 8 summarizes the approaches adopted by each team for the two subtasks. In the table, ML refers to any non-neural machine learning technique such as multinomial naive Bayes (MNB) and support vector machines (SVM). Neural refers to any neural network based model such as bidirectional long short-term memory (BiLSTM), or convolutional neural network (CNN). In terms of features, word and character ngram features (in Table 8 as WC), sometimes weighted with TFIDF, were among the most commonly used features. Language-model based features (in Table 8 as LM) were also used a lot. A few participants used pre-trained embeddings. All details about the different systems submitted could be found in the papers cited in Table 7.

5 Results and Discussion

5.1 Subtask 1 Results

Table 9 presents the results for Subtask 1. The last two rows are for the state-of-the-art system by Salameh et al. (2018), and the character 5-gram LM based baseline system from Zaidan and Callison-Burch (2013). The best result in terms of macro-averaged F1-score is achieved by the winning team ArbDialectID (67.32%), very closely followed by SMART and Mawdoo3_AI_Team with F1 scores of 67.31% and 67.20%, respectively. The top five systems all used non-neural ML models and word and character features. Two of the top three systems used ensemble methods (See Table 8). Generally, the neural methods did not do well. This is consistent with what Salameh et al. (2018) reported, and is likely the result of limited training data. It is noteworthy that none

Team	F1	ML	Neural	Ensemble	WC	LM	Embeddings
		Techniques			Features		
Subtask 1							
ArbDialectID	67.32	X		X	X		
SMarT	67.31	X			X		
Mawdoo3 LTD	67.20	X		X	X	X	
Safina	66.31	X			X	X	
A3-108	66.28	X			X	X	
ZCU-NLP	65.82	X		X	X	X	
Trends	65.66	X	X		X		X
QUT	64.45	X			X		
DNLP	64.20	X					
ADAPT-Epita	63.02	X					X
Eldesouki	63.02	X	X		X		
Speech Translation	62.12						
JHU	61.83			X		X	X
QC-GO	58.72		X				X
OscarGaribo	58.44		X				
LIU_MIR	56.66	X				X	
khalifaaa	53.21	X	X				
MICHAEL	52.96	X	X				
JUST*	66.33	X			X	X	
Subtask 2							
UBC-NLP	71.70		X				X
Mawdoo3 LTD	69.86	X			X		
QC-GO	66.68		X				X
CURAISA	61.54		X		X	X	
A3-108	57.90	X			X	X	
JHU	50.43		X	X			X
ZCU-NLP	47.51	X				X	
Speech Translation	3.82	X			X		
Trends	3.32	X	X		X		X

Table 8: Approaches (techniques and features) adopted by the participating teams in Subtasks 1 and 2. ML refers to any non-neural machine learning technique such as MNB, SVM, etc. Neural refers to any neural network based model such as BILSTM, CNN, GRUs, etc. LM refers to language-model based features. WC corresponds to word and character features.

of the competing systems overcame the previously published Salameh et al. (2018) result.

5.2 Subtask 2 Results

Table 10 presents the results for Subtask 2. The last three rows are for three baselines. First is a maximum likelihood estimate (MLE) baseline, which was to always select Saudi Arabia (the majority class). Second is the state-of-the-art system setup of Salameh et al. (2018) trained on the MADAR Twitter Corpus data. And third is the baseline system from Zaidan and Callison-Burch (2013) using character 5-gram LM models. The winning system is UBC-NLP beating the next system by almost 2% points. The best performer in

this subtask used a neural model (See Table 8).

Unavailable Tweets One of the concerns with any Twitter-based evaluation is that some of the tweets and Twitter users included in the manually annotated training, development and test data sets become unavailable at the time of the shared task. In our shared task, the percentage of missing tweets from train and development immediately after the conclusion of the shared task was 12.7%, which is basically the upper limit on unavailability. The corresponding number for unavailable Twitter users was 7.6%. The range of percentages of unavailable tweets as reported by some of the participating teams is between 6.0% and 11.3%. However, there seems to be no significant effect on the systems performance, as the correlation between the percentage of unavailable tweets and performance rank is -62%. The range in percentages of unavailable tweets for the test set is much smaller (11.5% to 12.1%) since all the teams received the test set at the same time and much later after the training and development data release.

6   Conclusion and Outlook

In this paper, we described the framework and the results of the MADAR Shared Task on Arabic Fine-Grained Dialect Identification. In addition to making a previously collected city-level dataset publicly available, we also introduced a new country-level dataset built specifically for this shared task. The unexpected large number of participants is an indication that there is a lot of interest in working on Arabic and Arabic dialects. We plan to run similar shared tasks in the near future, possibly with more naturally occurring (as opposed to commissioned) datasets. We also plan to coordinate with the VarDial Arabic Dialect Identification organizers to explore ways of leveraging the resources created in both competitions.

Acknowledgments

We would like to thank our dedicated annotators who contributed to the building the MADAR Twitter Corpus: Anissa Jrad, Sameh Lakhal, and Syrine Guediche. This publication was made possible by grant NPRP 7-290-1-047 from the Qatar National Research Fund (a member of the Qatar Foundation). The statements made herein are solely the responsibility of the authors.

Team	F1		Precision		Recall		Acc$_{city}$		Acc$_{country}$		Acc$_{region}$	
ArbDialectID	**67.32**	**(1)**	67.60	(2)	67.29	(2)	67.29	(2)	75.23	(2)	84.42	(5)
SMarT	67.31	(2)	**67.73**	**(1)**	**67.33**	**(1)**	**67.33**	**(1)**	**75.69**	**(1)**	**85.13**	**(1)**
Mawdoo3 LTD	67.20	(3)	67.53	(3)	67.08	(3)	67.08	(3)	75.19	(3)	84.75	(2)
Safina	66.31	(4)	66.68	(4)	66.48	(4)	66.48	(4)	75.02	(5)	84.48	(4)
A3-108	66.28	(5)	66.56	(5)	66.31	(5)	66.31	(5)	75.15	(4)	84.62	(3)
ZCU-NLP	65.82	(6)	66.45	(6)	65.85	(6)	65.85	(6)	74.27	(6)	84.10	(6)
Trends	65.66	(7)	65.79	(7)	65.75	(7)	65.75	(7)	74.08	(7)	83.46	(7)
QUT	64.45	(8)	64.99	(8)	64.58	(8)	64.58	(8)	73.29	(8)	83.02	(8)
DNLP	64.20	(9)	64.72	(9)	63.98	(9)	63.98	(9)	72.27	(9)	82.52	(10)
ADAPT-Epita	63.02	(10)	63.43	(11)	63.08	(10)	63.08	(10)	72.15	(10)	82.56	(9)
Eldesouki	63.02	(11)	63.53	(10)	63.06	(11)	63.06	(11)	71.96	(11)	82.23	(11)
Speech Translation	62.12	(12)	63.13	(13)	62.17	(12)	62.17	(12)	71.23	(12)	81.71	(13)
JHU	61.83	(13)	62.06	(14)	61.90	(13)	61.90	(13)	71.06	(13)	81.88	(12)
QC-GO	58.72	(14)	59.77	(15)	59.12	(14)	59.12	(14)	69.29	(14)	81.29	(14)
OscarGaribo	58.44	(15)	58.58	(16)	58.52	(15)	58.52	(15)	67.67	(15)	79.31	(15)
LIU_MIR	56.66	(16)	57.06	(17)	56.52	(16)	56.52	(16)	67.62	(16)	78.77	(16)
khalifaaa	53.21	(17)	63.14	(12)	53.37	(17)	53.37	(17)	64.71	(17)	78.19	(17)
MICHAEL	52.96	(18)	53.38	(18)	53.25	(18)	53.25	(18)	62.29	(18)	73.90	(18)
JUST*	66.33	(19)	66.56	(19)	66.42	(19)	66.42	(19)	74.71	(19)	84.54	(19)
Salameh et al (2018)	67.89		68.41		67.75		67.75		76.44		85.96	
Character 5-gram LM	64.74		65.01		64.75		64.75		73.65		83.40	

Table 9: Results for Subtask 1. Numbers in parentheses are the ranks. The table is sorted on the macro F1 score, the official metric,. The JUST system result was updated after the shared task as their official submission was corrupted. The last two rows are for baselines ((Salameh et al., 2018) and (Zaidan and Callison-Burch, 2013)).

Team	F1		Precision		Recall		Acc$_{country}$		Acc$_{region}$	
UBC-NLP	**71.70**	**(1)**	82.59	(3)	**65.63**	**(1)**	**77.40**	**(1)**	**88.40**	**(1)**
Mawdoo3 LTD	69.86	(2)	78.51	(4)	65.20	(2)	76.20	(2)	87.60	(2)
QC-GO	66.68	(3)	82.91	(2)	59.36	(4)	70.60	(4)	80.60	(5)
CURAISA	61.54	(4)	67.27	(7)	60.32	(3)	72.60	(3)	83.40	(3)
A3-108	57.90	(5)	**83.37**	**(1)**	47.73	(5)	67.20	(5)	81.60	(4)
JHU	50.43	(6)	70.45	(6)	43.18	(6)	62.20	(6)	77.80	(6)
ZCU-NLP	47.51	(7)	74.16	(5)	38.88	(7)	59.00	(7)	72.80	(7)
Speech Translation	3.82	(8)	5.22	(9)	5.37	(8)	5.00	(9)	31.80	(9)
Trends	3.32	(9)	6.82	(8)	4.97	(9)	33.00	(8)	61.40	(8)
MLE - KSA	2.64		1.79		5.00		35.80		64.20	
Salameh et al (2018)	13.08		41.91		11.15		42.20		66.80	
Character 5gram LM model	50.31		66.15		43.90		65.80		79.20	

Table 10: Results for Subtask 2. Numbers in parentheses are the ranks. The table is sorted on the macro F1 score, the official metric. The last three rows are for baselines.

References

Mourad Abbas, Mohamed Lichouri, and Abded Alhakim Freihat. 2019. ST MADAR 2019 Shared Task: Arabic Fine-Grained Dialect Identification. In *Proceedings of the Fourth Arabic Natural Language Processing Workshop (WANLP 2019)*, Florence, Italy.

Muhammad Abdul-Mageed, Hassan Alhuzali, and Mohamed Elaraby. 2018. You tweet what you speak: A city-level dataset of Arabic dialects. In *Proceedings of the 11th Language Resources and Evaluation Conference*, Miyazaki, Japan. European Language Resource Association.

Nora Al-Twairesh, Hend Al-Khalifa, and Abdulmalik AlSalman. 2016. AraSenTi: Large-Scale Twitter-Specific Arabic Sentiment Lexicons. In *Proceedings of the Conference of the Association for Computational Linguistics (ACL)*, Berlin, Germany.

Houda Bouamor, Nizar Habash, Mohammad Salameh, Wajdi Zaghouani, Owen Rambow, Dana Abdulrahim, Ossama Obeid, Salam Khalifa, Fadhl Eryani, Alexander Erdmann, and Kemal Oflazer. 2018. The MADAR Arabic Dialect Corpus and Lexicon. In

Proceedings of the Language Resources and Evaluation Conference (LREC), Miyazaki, Japan.

Kareem Darwish, Hassan Sajjad, and Hamdy Mubarak. 2014. Verifiably Effective Arabic Dialect Identification. In *Proceedings of the Conference on Empirical Methods in Natural Language Processing (EMNLP)*, Doha, Qatar.

Gaël De Francony, Victor Guichard, Praveen Joshi, Haithem Afli, and Abdessalam Bouchekif. 2019. Hierarchical Deep Learning for Arabic Dialect Identification. In *Proceedings of the Fourth Arabic Natural Language Processing Workshop (WANLP 2019)*, Florence, Italy.

Mahmoud El-Haj, Paul Rayson, and Mariam Aboelezz. 2018. Arabic Dialect Identification in the Context of Bivalency and Code-Switching. In *Proceedings of the Language Resources and Evaluation Conference (LREC)*, Miyazaki, Japan.

Mohamed Elaraby and Ahmed Zahran. 2019. A Character Level Convolutional Bilstm for Arabic Dialect Identification. In *Proceedings of the Fourth Arabic Natural Language Processing Workshop (WANLP 2019)*, Florence, Italy.

Heba Elfardy and Mona Diab. 2013. Sentence Level Dialect Identification in Arabic. In *Proceedings of the Conference of the Association for Computational Linguistics (ACL)*, Sofia, Bulgaria.

Sohaila Eltanbouly, May Bashendy, and Tamer El-sayed. 2019. Simple but not Naïve: Fine-Grained Arabic Dialect Identification using only N-Grams. In *Proceedings of the Fourth Arabic Natural Language Processing Workshop (WANLP 2019)*, Florence, Italy.

Youssef Fares, Zeyad El-Zanaty, Kareem Abdel-Salam, Muhammed Ezzeldin, Aliaa Mohamed, Karim El-Awaad, and Marwan Torki. 2019. Arabic Dialect Identification with Deep learning and Hybrid Frequency Based Features. In *Proceedings of the Fourth Arabic Natural Language Processing Workshop (WANLP 2019)*, Florence, Italy.

Dhaou Ghoul and Gaël Lejeune. 2019. MICHAEL: Mining Character-level Patterns for Arabic Dialect Identification (MADAR Challenge). In *Proceedings of the Fourth Arabic Natural Language Processing Workshop (WANLP 2019)*, Florence, Italy.

Saméh Kchaou, Fethi Bougares, and Lamia Hadrich-Belguith. 2019. LIUM-MIRACL Participation in the MADAR Arabic Dialect Identification Shared Task. In *Proceedings of the Fourth Arabic Natural Language Processing Workshop (WANLP 2019)*, Florence, Italy.

Tom Lippincott, Pamela Shapiro, Kevin Duh, and Paul McNamee. 2019. JHU System Description for the MADAR Arabic Dialect Identification Shared Task. In *Proceedings of the Fourth Arabic Natural Language Processing Workshop (WANLP 2019)*, Florence, Italy.

Shervin Malmasi, Marcos Zampieri, Nikola Ljubešić, Preslav Nakov, Ahmed Ali, and Jörg Tiedemann. 2016. Discriminating between Similar Languages and Arabic Dialect Identification: A Report on the Third DSL Shared Task. In *Proceedings of the Workshop on NLP for Similar Languages, Varieties and Dialects (VarDial)*, Osaka, Japan.

Karima Meftouh, Karima Abidi, Salima Harrat, and Kamel Smaili. 2019. The SMarT Classifier for Arabic Fine-Grained Dialect Identification. In *Proceedings of the Fourth Arabic Natural Language Processing Workshop (WANLP 2019)*, Florence, Italy.

Pruthwik Mishra and Vandan Mujadia. 2019. Arabic Dialect Identification for Travel and Twitter Text. In *Proceedings of the Fourth Arabic Natural Language Processing Workshop (WANLP 2019)*, Florence, Italy.

Hamdy Mubarak and Kareem Darwish. 2014. Using Twitter to collect a multi-dialectal corpus of Arabic. In *Proceedings of the Workshop for Arabic Natural Language Processing (WANLP)*, Doha, Qatar.

Pavel Přibáň and Stephen Taylor. 2019. ZCU-NLP at MADAR 2019: Recognizing Arabic Dialects. In *Proceedings of the Fourth Arabic Natural Language Processing Workshop (WANLP 2019)*, Florence, Italy.

Chatrine Qwaider and Motaz Saad. 2019. ArbDialectID at MADAR Shared Task 1: Language Modelling and Ensemble Learning for Fine Grained Arabic Dialect Identification. In *Proceedings of the Fourth Arabic Natural Language Processing Workshop (WANLP 2019)*, Florence, Italy.

Ahmad Ragab, Haitham Seelawi, Mostafa Samir, Abdelrahman Mattar, Hesham Al-Bataineh, Mohammad Zaghloul, Ahmad Mustafa, Bashar Talafha, Abed Alhakim Freihat, and Hussein T. Al-Natsheh. 2019. Mawdoo3 AI at MADAR Shared Task: Arabic Fine-Grained Dialect Identification with Ensemble Learning. In *Proceedings of the Fourth Arabic Natural Language Processing Workshop (WANLP 2019)*, Florence, Italy.

Fatiha Sadat, Farnazeh Kazemi, and Atefeh Farzindar. 2014. Automatic Identification of Arabic Dialects in Social Media. In *Proceedings of the Workshop on Natural Language Processing for Social Media (SocialNLP)*, pages 22–27, Dublin, Ireland.

Mohammad Salameh, Houda Bouamor, and Nizar Habash. 2018. Fine-grained Arabic dialect identification. In *Proceedings of the International Conference on Computational Linguistics (COLING)*, pages 1332–1344, Santa Fe, New Mexico, USA.

Wael Salloum, Heba Elfardy, Linda Alamir-Salloum, Nizar Habash, and Mona Diab. 2014. Sentence Level Dialect Identification for Machine Translation System Selection. In *Proceedings of the Conference of the Association for Computational Linguistics (ACL)*, Baltimore, Maryland, USA.

Younes Samih, Hamdy Mubarak, Ahmed Abdelali, Mohammed Attia, Mohamed Eldesouki, and Kareem Darwish. 2019. QC-GO Submission for MADAR Shared Task: Arabic Fine-Grained Dialect Identification . In *Proceedings of the Fourth Arabic Natural Language Processing Workshop (WANLP 2019)*, Florence, Italy.

Toshiyuki Takezawa, Genichiro Kikui, Masahide Mizushima, and Eiichiro Sumita. 2007. Multilingual Spoken Language Corpus Development for Communication Research. *Computational Linguistics and Chinese Language Processing*, 12(3):303–324.

Bashar Talafha, Ali Fadel, Mahmoud Al-Ayyoub, Yaser Jaraweh, Mohammad Al-Smadi, and Patrick Juola. 2019a. Team JUST at the MADAR Shared Task on Arabic Fine-Grained Dialect Identification . In *Proceedings of the Fourth Arabic Natural Language Processing Workshop (WANLP 2019)*, Florence, Italy.

Bashar Talafha, Wael Farhan, Ahmed Altakrouri, and Al-Natsheh Hussein. 2019b. Mawdoo3 AI at MADAR Shared Task: Arabic Tweet Dialect Identification. In *Proceedings of the Fourth Arabic Natural Language Processing Workshop (WANLP 2019)*, Florence, Italy.

Wajdi Zaghouani and Anis Charfi. 2018. ArapTweet: A Large Multi-Dialect Twitter Corpus for Gender, Age and Language Variety Identification. In *Proceedings of the Language Resources and Evaluation Conference (LREC)*, Miyazaki, Japan.

Omar Zaidan and Chris Callison-Burch. 2013. Arabic dialect identification. *Computational Linguistics*.

Marcos Zampieri, Shervin Malmasi, Nikola Ljubešić, Preslav Nakov, Ahmed Ali, Jörg Tiedemann, Yves Scherrer, and Noëmi Aepli. 2017. Findings of the VarDial Evaluation Campaign 2017. In *Proceedings of the Workshop on NLP for Similar Languages, Varieties and Dialects (VarDial)*, Valencia, Spain.

Chiyu Zhang and Muhammad Abdul-Mageed. 2019. No Army, No Navy: BERT Semi-Supervised Learning of Arabic Dialects. In *Proceedings of the Fourth Arabic Natural Language Processing Workshop (WANLP 2019)*, Florence, Italy.

ZCU-NLP at MADAR 2019: Recognizing Arabic Dialects

Pavel Přibáň　　**Stephen Taylor**

pribanp@kiv.zcu.cz　　stepheneugenetaylor@gmail.com

Department of Computer Science and Engineering,
Faculty of Applied Sciences, University of West Bohemia,
Pilsen, Czech Republic

http://nlp.kiv.zcu.cz

Abstract

In this paper, we present our systems for the *MADAR Shared Task: Arabic Fine-Grained Dialect Identification.* The shared task consists of two subtasks. The goal of Subtask–1 (S-1) is to detect an Arabic city dialect in a given text and the goal of Subtask–2 (S-2) is to predict the country of origin of a Twitter user by using tweets posted by the user.

In S-1, our proposed systems are based on language modelling. We use language models to extract features that are later used as an input for other machine learning algorithms. We also experiment with recurrent neural networks (RNN), but these experiments showed that simpler machine learning algorithms are more successful. Our system achieves 0.658 macro F_1-score and our rank is 6th out of 19 teams in S-1 and 7th in S-2 with 0.475 macro F_1-score.

1 Introduction

The Madar shared tasks (Bouamor et al., 2019) are a follow-up to Salameh's (Salameh et al., 2018) work with the synthetic corpus of Bouamor (Bouamor et al., 2014) and Salameh's work with tweets based on the corpus. Two corpora are provided, a six-city corpus of travel sentences rendered into the dialects of five cities and MSA[1], and a 25-city + MSA corpus using a smaller number of sentences. In the first task, test data is classified as one of the 25 cities or MSA. For the second task, the organizers chose training, development and test tweet-sets for download from Twitter. The tweets are from 21 Arabic countries, and the goal is to determine, for each tweet author, the country of origin.

For S-1 we did not use any external data, only data provided by the shared task organizers.

The organizers provided training and development data[2] consisting of sentences in different dialects with a label denoting the corresponding dialect. The training data contain 41K sentences and development data contain 5.2K sentences. Organizers also provided additional data with Arabic sentences in seven dialects.

S-2 uses a corpus of tweets. Twitter does not permit the organizers to distribute tweets, only the user ids and tweet ids. Every participant must arrange with Twitter to download the tweets themselves, and because tweets are subject to deletion over time, it is possible that each participant's version of the corpus and test is unique.

2 Related Work

The Arabic dialects have a common written form and unified literary tradition, so it seems most logical to distinguish dialects on the basis of acoustics, and there is a fair amount of work there, including Hanani et al. (2013, 2015); Ali et al. (2016).

Biadsy et al. (2009) distinguish four Arabic dialects and MSA based on (audio) phone sequences; the phones were obtained by phone recognizers for English, German, Japanese, Hindi, Mandarin, Spanish, and three different MSA phone-recognizer implementations. The dialects were distinguished by phoneme sequences, and the results of classifications based on each phone-recognizer were combined using a logistic regression classifier. They train on 150 hours per dialect of telephone recordings. They report 61% accuracy on 5-second segments, and 84% accuracy on 120 second segments.

Zaidan and Callison-Burch (2011) describe building a text corpus, based on reader commen-

---

[1] Modern Standard Arabic

[2] The participants were not allowed to use these data for any training purposes.

Proceedings of the Fourth Arabic Natural Language Processing Workshop, pages 208–213
Florence, Italy, August 1, 2019. ©2019 Association for Computational Linguistics

tary on newspaper websites, with significant dialect content; the goal is to provide a corpus to improve machine translation for Arabic dialects. They used Amazon Mechanical Turk to provide annotation for a portion of the corpus. Zaidan and Callison-Burch (2014) describe the same work in greater detail, including dialect classifiers they built using the Mechanical Turk data for classes and origin metadata as additional features. They say these classifiers are 'approaching human quality.'

ElFardy and Diab (2013) classify EGY[3] and MSA sentences from the Zaidan and Callison-Burch (2011) corpus, that is, from text. Not only is this a binary task, but orthographic hints, including repeated long vowels, emojis and multiple punctuations, give strong clues of the register, and hence whether MSA is being employed. They do a number of experiments comparing various pre-processing schemes and different training sizes, ranging from 2-28 million tokens. They achieve 80% – 86% accuracy for all of their attempts.

Malmasi et al. (2015) do Arabic dialect identification from text corpora, including the Multi-Dialect Parallel Corpus of Arabic (Bouamor et al., 2014) and the Arabic Online Commentary database (Zaidan and Callison-Burch, 2011).

Hanani et al. (2015) perform recognition of several Palestinian regional accents, evaluating four different acoustic models, achieving 81.5% accuracy for their best system, an I-vector framework with 64 Gaussian components.

Ali et al. (2016) developed the corpus on which the DSL Arabic shared task is based. Their own dialect detection efforts depended largely on acoustical cues.

Arabic dialect recognition appeared in the 2016 edition of the VarDial workshop's shared task (Malmasi et al., 2016). The shared task data was text-only.

The best classifiers (Malmasi et al., 2016; Ionescu and Popescu, 2016) for the shared task performed far below the best results reported by some of the preceding researchers, in particular Ali et al. (2016) which used some of the same data.

Part of the reason must be that the amount of training data for the workshop is much smaller than that used by some of the other researchers; the workshop data also did not include the audio recordings on which the transcripts are based.

---

[3]Egyptian dialect

The absence of audio was remedied for the 2017 and 2018 VarDial workshops, (Zampieri et al., 2017, 2018)

However, the five dialects plus MSA targeted by the VarDial shared task comprise a small fraction of Arabic's dialectical variation. Salameh et al. (Salameh et al., 2018) use a corpus (Bouamor et al., 2018) which differentiates between twenty-five different cities and MSA. This still doesn't address urban rural divides, but it begins to reflect more realistic diversity.

3   Overview

3.1   Language Modelling

In `S-1`, both of our systems used for the official submission take as an input language model features. In our case the objective of a language model in its simplest form is to predict probability $p(S)$ of sentence S which is composed from strings (words or character n-grams) $s_1, s_2 \ldots s_N$, where N is a number of strings in the sentence. The probability estimation of $p(S)$ can be computed as a product of conditional probabilities $p(s_i|h_i)$ of its strings $s_1, s_2 \ldots s_N$, where h_i is a history of a string s_i. The probability of string s_i is conditioned by history h_i i.e. $n - 1$ preceding strings $s_{i-n+1}, s_{i-n+2}, \ldots s_{i-1}$ which can be rewritten as s_{i-n+1}^{i-1}. The resulting formula for the $p(S)$ estimation looks as follows:

$$p(S) = \prod_{i=1}^{N} p(s_i|h_i) = \prod_{i=1}^{N} p(s_i|s_{i-n+1}^{i-1}) \quad (1)$$

The conditioned probability $p(s_i|h_i)$ can be estimated with *Maximum Likelihood Estimate (MLE)* which is defined as:

$$p^{MLE}(s_i|h_i) = \frac{c(s_{i-n+1}, s_{i-n+2} \ldots s_i)}{c(s_{i-n+1}, s_{i-n+2} \ldots s_{i-1})} \quad (2)$$

where $c(s_{i-n+1}, s_{i-n+2} \ldots s_i)$ is a number of occurrences of string s_i with history h_i and $c(s_{i-n+1}, s_{i-n+2} \ldots s_{i-1})$ is a number of occurrences of history h_i. These counts are taken from a training corpus.

We followed Salameh (Salameh et al., 2018) in using the `kenlm` language modelling tool (Heafield et al., 2013). `kenlm` doesn't have an option to use character n-grams instead of words, so in order to get character-based language models, we prepared input files with characters separated by spaces. Instead of encoding space as a special word, we surrounded words with a <w></w>pair. This enables noticing strings which occur at the beginning or end of a word (as would a special sequence for space) but reduces the possible amount of inter-word information which the language model can keep for a given order, the parameter which indicates to `kenlm` the largest n-gram to index. We used order 5 for all our `kenlm` language models. We prebuilt models for each dialect. We prepared six directories, each containing word or character models for each dialect in one of the three corpora.

We wrote a `LangModel` class which quacks like a `sklearn` classifier, that is, it supports `fit()`, `predict()`, and `predict_proba()`, but its choices are based on a directory of language models. `predict()` returns the dialect name whose model gives the highest score. `predict_proba()` provides a list of language-model-score features, adjusted to probabilities.

4 Subtask–1 System Description

In this section we describe our models[4]. We submitted results for the S−1 from two systems – *Tortuous Classifier* and *Neural Network Classifier*.

4.1 Tortuous Classifier

This submission uses a jumble of features and classifiers, most from the sklearn module (Buitinck et al., 2013). The final classifier is a hard voting classifier with three input streams:

1. Soft voting classifier on:

    (a) Multinomial naive Bayes classifier on word 1-2grams,

    (b) Multinomial naive Bayes classifier on char 3-5grams,

    (c) Language model scores adjusted to probabilities, for word-based language models of the corpus 26 dialects

    (d) Language model scores adjusted to probabilities, for char-based language models of the corpus 26 dialects

    (e) Multinomial naive Bayes classifier on language-model-scores for character and language models on the

corpus-6 language models and character language models for the corpus-26 language models.

2. Support vector machine, `svm.SVC( gamma='scale', kernel = 'poly', degree = 2)` with the same features as item 1e.

3. Multinomial naive Bayes classifier using word and char language model features for corpus-6 and corpus-26 features, tfid vectorized word 1-2grams, and tfid vectorized char 3-5grams.

The classifier did better on the development data, suggesting that it is over-fitted, but the language model features, which are the most predictive, also did better on the development data.

4.2 Neural Network Classifier

We experimented with several neural networks. Our model for the S−1 submission uses as input 26 features which correspond to one of our 26 pretrained dialect language models. Each feature represents the probability of a given sentence for one language model. The probability scores measure how close each sentence is to the dialect.

We train Multilayer Perceptron (MLP) with one hidden (dense) layer with 400 units. The output of the hidden layer is passed to a final fully-connected softmax layer. The output of the softmax layer is a probability distribution over all 26 classes. The class with the highest probability is predicted as a final output of our model. As an activation function in the hidden layer of the MLP a Rectified Linear Unit (ReLu) is employed.

We also tried to combine character n-gram features with the language model features. The input is a sequence of first 200 character n-grams of a given text. Each sequence of character n-grams is used as a separate input followed by a randomly initialized embedding layer and then two layers of Bidirectional LSTM (BiLSTM)(Graves and Schmidhuber, 2005) with 64 units are employed (see Figure 1).

The output vector of the BiLSTM layers is concatenated with the language model features and this concatenated vector is passed to the MLP layer with 400 units (the same as described above). All models were implemented by using Keras (Chollet et al., 2015) with TensorFlow backend (Abadi et al., 2015)

---

[4]The source code is available at `https://github.com/StephenETaylor/Madar-2019`

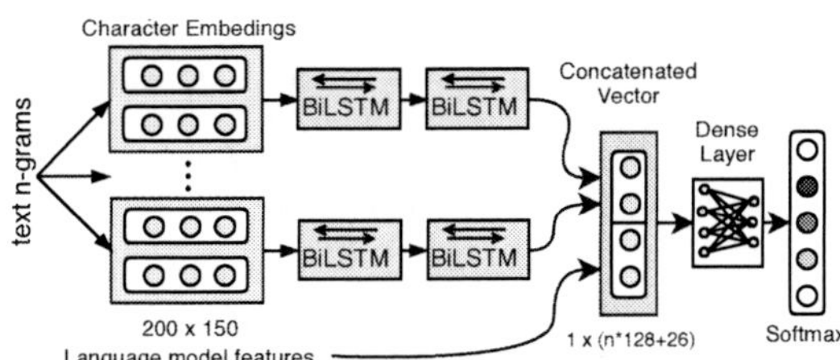

Figure 1: Neural network model architecture

4.3 Neural Netwok Model Training

We tune all hyperparameters on the development data. We train our model with Adam (Kingma and Ba, 2014) optimizer with learning rate 0.01 and without any dropout. The number of epochs is 800 and we do not use mini-batches or dropout regularization technique. The model with these hyperparameters achieves the best result (0.661 macro F_1-score) on the development data and was used for the final submission.

We also experimented with the n-gram inputs. We tried a different number of character n-grams and we achieve the best result (0.555 macro F_1-score) on the development data using three inputs - character unigrams, bigrams and trigrams, with learning rate 0.005, mini-batches of size 256 for 11 epochs and with the Adam optimizer.

5 Subtask–2 System Description

Our tortuous classifier did less well on the tweet data, so we used a simpler classifier.

The features are the kenlm language model scores for the 21 countries, computed for each of the training tweets, then exponentiated and normalized to sum to 1. The tweets are classified using

```
y_test = KNeighborsClassifier
        (n_neighbors=31)
        .fit(X_train,y_train)
        .predict(X_test)
```

The users are predicted based on the plurality prediction for all of their tweets, that is, the country to which the largest number of their tweets were assigned.

There were a significant number of tweets unavailable, about 10% in the training and development sets, and 12% in the test set. After the submissions had closed we experimented with eliminating the unavailable and non-Arabic tweets from

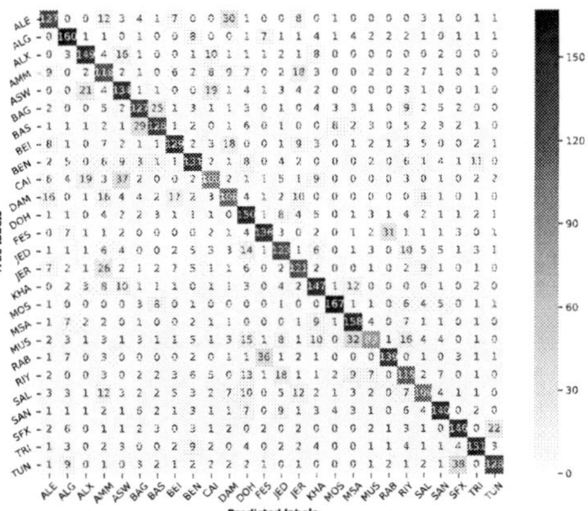

Figure 2: Tortuous Classifier confusion matrix

training and testing and choosing *Saudi_Arabia* (which is the origin for the plurality of tweets at 36%) for users with no remaining tweets. This improved tweet classification accuracy by about 5%, but actually decreased user classification accuracy on the development set.

6 Results

For the Subtask–1 we achieved 0.658 macro F_1-score on the test data, sixth among nineteen submissions with the *Tortuous Classifier*. The *Neural Network Classifier* achieved a macro F_1-score of 0.648 on the test data. For the Subtask–2 we submitted a single entry. It ranked 7th among 9 submissions with 0.475 macro F_1-score.

Figure 2 shows that many of the errors are geographically plausible. For example, ASWan ALXandria and CAIro are all in Egypt, and each has a sizeable chunk of mistaken identity for the others. Similarly, DAMascus, ALEppo, AMMan, BEIrut, JERusalem which are all 'Levantine' and only a few hundred miles apart.

7 Conclusion

This paper presents an automatic approach for Arabic dialect detection in the *MADAR Shared Task*. Our proposed systems for the Subtask-1 use language model features. Our experiments showed that simpler machine learning algorithms outperform RNN using language model features. Subtask–2 turned out to be more challenging because Tweets, which are real-world wild data, are more difficult to process than systematically prepared texts.

Acknowledgments

This work has been partly supported by Grant No. SGS-2019-018 Processing of heterogeneous data and its specialized applications, and was partly supported from ERDF "Research and Development of Intelligent Components of Advanced Technologies for the Pilsen Metropolitan Area (InteCom)". Access to computing and storage facilities owned by parties and projects contributing to the National Grid Infrastructure MetaCentrum provided under the programme "Projects of Large Research, Development, and Innovations Infrastructures" (CESNET LM2015042), is greatly appreciated.

References

Martín Abadi, Ashish Agarwal, Paul Barham, Eugene Brevdo, Zhifeng Chen, Craig Citro, Greg S. Corrado, Andy Davis, Jeffrey Dean, Matthieu Devin, Sanjay Ghemawat, Ian Goodfellow, Andrew Harp, Geoffrey Irving, Michael Isard, Yangqing Jia, Rafal Jozefowicz, Lukasz Kaiser, Manjunath Kudlur, Josh Levenberg, Dandelion Mané, Rajat Monga, Sherry Moore, Derek Murray, Chris Olah, Mike Schuster, Jonathon Shlens, Benoit Steiner, Ilya Sutskever, Kunal Talwar, Paul Tucker, Vincent Vanhoucke, Vijay Vasudevan, Fernanda Viégas, Oriol Vinyals, Pete Warden, Martin Wattenberg, Martin Wicke, Yuan Yu, and Xiaoqiang Zheng. 2015. TensorFlow: Large-scale machine learning on heterogeneous systems. Software available from tensorflow.org.

Ahmed Ali, Najim Dehak, Patrick Cardinal, Sameer Khurana, Sree Harsha Yella, James Glass, Peter Bell, and Steve Renals. 2016. Automatic dialect detection in Arabic broadcast speech. In *Proceedings of Interspeech 2016*, pages 2934–2938.

Fadi Biadsy, Julia Hirschberg, and Nizar Habash. 2009. Spoken arabic dialect identification using phonotactic modeling. In *Proceedings of the EACL Workshop on Computational Approaches to Semitic Languages*, pages 53–61.

Houda Bouamor, Nizar Habash, and Kemal Oflazer. 2014. A multidialectal parallel corpus of Arabic. In *Proceedings of the Ninth International Conference on Language Resources and Evaluation (LREC14)*. European Language Resources Association (ELRA).

Houda Bouamor, Nizar Habash, Mohammad Salameh, Wajdi Zaghouani, Owen Rambow, Dana Abdulrahim, Ossama Obeid, Salam Khalifa, Fadhl Eryani, Alexander Erdmann, and Kemal Oflazer. 2018. The madar arabic dialect corpus and lexicon. In *Proceedings of the 11th International Conference on Language Resources and Evaluation*.

Houda Bouamor, Sabit Hassan, and Nizar Habash. 2019. The MADAR Shared Task on Arabic Fine-Grained Dialect Identification. In *Proceedings of the Fourth Arabic Natural Language Processing Workshop (WANLP19)*, Florence, Italy.

Lars Buitinck, Gilles Louppe, Mathieu Blondel, Fabian Pedregosa, Andreas Mueller, Olivier Grisel, Vlad Niculae, Peter Prettenhofer, Alexandre Gramfort, Jaques Grobler, Robert Layton, Jake VanderPlas, Arnaud Joly, Brian Holt, and Gaël Varoquaux. 2013. API design for machine learning software: experiences from the scikit-learn project. In *ECML PKDD Workshop: Languages for Data Mining and Machine Learning*, pages 108–122.

François Chollet et al. 2015. Keras. `https://keras.io`.

Heba ElFardy and Mona Diab. 2013. Sentence level dialect identification in Arabic. In *Proceedings of the 51st Annual Meeting of the Association for Computational Linguistics (ACL)*, pages 456–461.

Alex Graves and Jürgen Schmidhuber. 2005. Framewise phoneme classification with bidirectional lstm and other neural network architectures. *Neural Networks*, 18(5-6):602–610.

Abualsoud Hanani, Hanna Basha, Yasmeen Sharaf, and Stephen Taylor. 2015. Palestinian Arabic regional accent recognition. In *The 8th International Conference on Speech Technology and Human-Computer Dialogue*.

Abualsoud Hanani, Martin J. Russell, and Michael J. Carey. 2013. Human and computer recognition of regional accents and ethnic groups from British english speech. *Computer Speech and Language*, 27(1):5974.

Kenneth Heafield, Ivan Pouzyrevsky, Jonathan H. Clark, , and Philipp Koehn. 2013. Scalable modified kneser-ney language model estimation. In *ACL*.

Radu Tudor Ionescu and Marius Popescu. 2016. UnibucKernel: An Approach for Arabic Dialect Identification Based on Multiple String Kernels. In *Proceedings of the Third Workshop on NLP for Similar Languages, Varieties and Dialects (VarDial3)*, pages 135–144, Osaka, Japan.

Diederik P. Kingma and Jimmy Lei Ba. 2014. Adam: A method for stochastic optimization. *arXiv:1412.6980v9*.

Shervin Malmasi, Eshrag Refaee, and Mark Dras. 2015. Arabic dialect identification using a parallel multidialectal corpus. In *Proceedings of the 14th Conference of the Pacific Association for Computational Linguistics (PACLING 2015)*, pages 209–217, Bali, Indonesia.

Shervin Malmasi, Marcos Zampieri, Nikola Ljubei, Preslav Nakov, Ahmed Ali, and Jrg Tiedemann. 2016. Discriminating between similar languages and arabic dialect identification: A report on the third dsl shared task. In *Proceedings of the Third Workshop on NLP for Similar Languages, Varieties and Dialects (VarDial 2016)*.

Mohammad Salameh, Houda Bouamor, and Nizar Habash. 2018. Fine-grained arabic dialect identification. In *Proceedings of the International Conference on Computational Linguistics (COLING)*, pages 1332–1344, Santa Fe, New Mexico, USA.

Omar F. Zaidan and Chris Callison-Burch. 2011. The Arabic Online Commentary dataset: An annotated dataset of informal Arabic with high dialectal content. In *Proceedings of ACL*, pages 37–41.

Omar F. Zaidan and Chris Callison-Burch. 2014. Arabic dialect identification. *Computational Linguistics*, 40(1):171–202.

Marcos Zampieri, Shervin Malmasi, Nikola Ljubei, Preslav Nakov, Ahmed Ali, Jrg Tiedemann, Yves Scherrer, and Nomi Aepli. 2017. Findings of the vardial evaluation campaign 2017. In *Proceedings of the Fourth Workshop on NLP for Similar Languages, Varieties and Dialects (VarDial 2017*.

Marcos Zampieri, Shervin Malmasi, Preslav Nakov, Ahmed Ali, Suwon Shon, James Glass, Yves Scherrer, Tanja Samardžić, Nikola Ljubešić, Jörg Tiedemann, Chris van der Lee, Stefan Grondelaers, Nelleke Oostdijk, Dirk Speelman, Antal van den Bosch, Ritesh Kumar, Bornini Lahiri, and Mayank Jain. 2018. Language identification and morphosyntactic tagging: The second VarDial evaluation campaign. In *Proceedings of the Fifth Workshop on NLP for Similar Languages, Varieties and Dialects (VarDial 2018)*, pages 1–17, Santa Fe, New Mexico, USA. Association for Computational Linguistics.

Simple but *not* Naïve:
Fine-Grained Arabic Dialect Identification using only N-Grams

Sohaila Eltanbouly, May Bashendy, and Tamer Elsayed
Qatar University
Doha, Qatar
{se1403101, ma1403845, telsayed}@qu.edu.qa

Abstract

This paper presents the participation of Qatar University team in MADAR shared task, which addresses the problem of sentence-level fine-grained Arabic Dialect Identification over 25 different Arabic dialects in addition to the Modern Standard Arabic. Arabic Dialect Identification is not a trivial task since different dialects share some features, e.g., utilizing the same character set and some vocabularies. We opted to adopt a very simple approach in terms of extracted features and classification models; we only utilize word and character n-grams as features, and Naïve Bayes models as classifiers. Surprisingly, the *simple* approach achieved *non-naïve* performance. The official results, reported on a held-out testing set, show that the dialect of a given sentence can be identified at an accuracy of 64.58% by our best submitted run.

1 Introduction

The Arabic Language is one of the oldest languages in the world, which made Arabic dialects emerge over the years. Although Modern Standard Arabic (MSA) is the only standardized form of the Arabic language that has a predefined set of grammatical rules, it is only used in education, some media channels, and official written documents. This owes to the fact that people tend to use dialects more in their daily life. Those dialects deviate from the classical MSA in terms of morphology, phonology, lexicon, and syntax (Janet, 2007). For example, a morphological difference could be seen in the affixes that are appended to the verb to indicate its tense, like the prefix عَـ which indicate the present tense in Jordanian dialect. The existence of many varieties of the Arabic dialects gave rise to the task of automatic identification of written Arabic dialects, since a prior identification of those dialects is essential to many

applications, such as sentiment analysis, opinion mining, author profiling, and machine translation. Despite the significant differences between the dialects, they still share some similarities such as having common character/vocabulary sets and basic language rules which make dialect identification an interesting but challenging problem. Moreover, the closeness between some dialects that are within the same country makes it even more challenging to distinguish between them.

Unlike most of the previous work which targeted coarse-grained Arabic dialect identification, this work presents the participation of Qatar University team in the Multi Arabic Dialect Applications and Resources (MADAR) shared task (Bouamor et al., 2019) that addresses a fine-grained classification of 25 dialects of different Arabic cities in addition to MSA. We propose a *simple* classification approach that only utilizes word and character n-grams using Naïve Bayes learning model. While our approach is so simple (depending only on two categories of lexical features), it proved *not* to be *naïve*; the official testing results show that our best submitted run achieved reasonably-good F_1 scores across the different dialects, ranging from 0.52 to 0.84.

The rest of the paper is organized as follows. Section 2 outlines the data used in building/training our models. Section 3 details our proposed approach. Section 4 presents our runs and official testing results. Section 5 discusses and analyzes the performance of our best run. Finally, Section 6 concludes our work with some directions of future work.

2 Data

In this work, we used MADAR dataset (Bouamor et al., 2018) for training our models. The dataset consists of 2 corpora, namely corpus-

Proceedings of the Fourth Arabic Natural Language Processing Workshop, pages 214–218
Florence, Italy, August 1, 2019. ©2019 Association for Computational Linguistics

26 and corpus-6, that include sentences translated from the Basic Traveling Expression Corpus (BTEC) (Takezawa, 2007) into different Arabic dialects and MSA, however, we only used the first corpus for developing our models. Corpus-26 contains 2,000 sentences translated into 25 parallel dialects plus MSA. This corpus is divided into training, development, and testing sets of 1600, 200, and 200 sentences per dialect respectively.

Several tools were used to build our system and process our data. Two main Python libraries were used for Arabic processing: pyarabic[1] for tokenization and diacritics removal, and the natural language toolkit (NLTK) for stop-words removal. For classification, we used both Scikit-learn and sklearn Python libraries.

3 System

The aim of this work is to design a system that can identify 25 different Arabic dialects (classes) in addition to MSA. We have adopted a similar approach to the one proposed by Salameh et al. (2018). They trained a Multinomial Naïve Bayes classifier over a feature combination of word n-grams, character n-grams, language models per dialect, and sentence probabilities given by the language models, achieving an accuracy of 67.9%. In this section, the main blocks of our proposed system are presented.

3.1 Data Pre-processing

Arora et al. (2012) introduced the phrase "Garbage In, Garbage Out" to indicate that the data quality greatly affects the classification task. In our system, the data was pre-processed by tokenizing over white spaces, removing Arabic stop words, and removing punctuation.

3.2 Feature Extraction

Extracting a set of discriminative features from the data helps in differentiating between the different classes. In our proposed models, only two categories of features were considered: word n-grams and character n-grams.

- **Word n-grams**: The word unigrams and bigrams are extracted and used as features. This category helps in distinguishing between the different dialects since some words

---

Classifier	Accuracy
Multinomial Naïve Bayes	**63.21%**
Bernoulli Naïve Bayes	**63.37%**
Stochastic Gradient Descent	52.79%
Gaussian Naïve Bayes	49.37%
Perceptron (one versus all)	46.92%
Perceptron (one versus one)	46.79%

Table 1: Performance of different classifiers on the development set using word unigrams features only.

are uniquely found in specific dialects, capturing their lexical variations at the *word* level.

- **Character n-grams**: The character n-grams, ranging from 2-grams to 5-grams, are extracted and used as features. This category captures the morphological characteristics of the dialects by capturing prefixes and suffixes that distinguish some dialects at the *character* level.

3.3 Feature Selection

Feature selection is an optimization technique that narrows down the feature space by selecting a subset of the most important features from the original set. In this work, we used Random Forest algorithm to select the top features. It is an ensemble learning algorithm that is based on combining a number of de-correlated decision trees in which the tree-based structure is naturally used to *rank* the features.

3.4 Training Classifiers

We have experimented with a number of classifiers: Multinomial Naïve Bayes, Bernoulli Naïve Bayes, Stochastic Gradient Descent, Gaussian Naïve Bayes, and Perceptron.

To choose the best classifiers for this task, we initially trained all classifiers only on word unigrams features. Table 1 shows that Multinomial Naïve Bayes classifier (MNB) and Bernoulli Naïve Bayes classifier (BNB) had, by far, the highest (approximately equal) performance on the development set. Therefore, we only use those two in the rest of the experiments. Some previous studies also used Naïve Bayes classifiers for dialect identification, e.g., (Sadat et al., 2015).

Next, we focus on the performance of MNB and BNB classifiers with different combinations of features. We used word unigrams and bigrams,

Features		Accuracy	
word	character	MNB	BNB
1	-	63.21%	63.37%
1	2	57.40%	57.21%
1	3	62.52%	62.21%
1	4	65.67%	65.65%
1	5	65.85%	65.23%
1+2	-	63.50%	62.56%
1+2	2	58.56%	59.15%
1+2	3	62.85%	62.71%
1+2	4	66.00%	65.86%
1+2	5	65.75%	64.85%
1	2 + 3	59.42%	58.77%
1	3 + 4	64.37%	64.90%
1	3 + 5	65.35%	65.27%
1	4 + 5	**66.25%**	**65.90%**
1	3 + 4 + 5	65.33%	65.52%
1	2 + 3 + 4 + 5	64.98%	64.42%

Table 2: Performance of MNB and BNB classifiers on the development set using different combinations of features.

Classifier	#Features	Time	Accuracy
MNB	228,585	1:42h	64.71%
MNB-FS	203,200	1:31h	64.13%

Table 3: Training time and accuracy for MNB (trained over all character n-grams) and MNB-FS classifiers on the development set.

and character 2-grams to 5-grams. Table 2 shows the performance of different combinations of those features for both classifiers. The combination of the word unigrams with the character 4-grams and 5-grams achieved the highest accuracy.

Based on the performance of different classifiers and different combinations of features (shown in Tables 1 and 2), we chose the following models to represent our runs in the shared task:

1. **MNB**: In this run, a MNB classifier is trained with features that are obtained from combining word unigrams, character 4-grams and character 5-grams. No feature selection is performed here.

2. **Voting**: In this run, two Naïve Bayes classifiers are trained, the first one is MNB and the second is BNB. The classifiers are trained using the word unigrams and character 4 and 5 grams. The classification is done by voting between the two classifiers based on the

Run	Prec.	Recall	F_1	Acc.
MNB	0.6458	0.6440	0.6418	64.40%
Voting	**0.6499**	**0.6458**	**0.6445**	**64.58%**
MNB-FS	0.6292	0.6262	0.6232	62.62%

Table 4: Official performance of the 3 runs on test set.

higher probability. No feature selection is performed here.

3. **MNB-FS**: In this run, a MNB classifier is trained with character n-grams features ranging from 2-grams to 5-grams after feature selection. The main motivation behind this run is to improve the efficiency by reducing the feature space while maintaining good performance. The top 200 features of character bigrams, 3,000 of character 3-grams, and 200,000 of character 4-grams and character 5-grams were selected. As shown in Table 3, feature selection reduced the size of the feature space by about 11% which yields a drop in training time by about 10%. However, the performance is maintained across both models, where the difference in accuracy is only about 0.6%.

3.5 Official Performance

Table 4 shows the overall performance on the test set for our three submitted runs. The results show that MNB run exhibited better performance than MNB-FS run. However, the Voting run, which exploits the predictions proposed by both MNB and BNB classifiers, got the best performance. This indicates that the two basic classifiers had some different predictions with different confidence (represented by the classification probabilities) that were better leveraged by the voting scheme.

4 Discussion

Figure 1 illustrates the F_1 score per dialect for the best run, where dialects of the same country are colored the same. We notice that F_1 scores range from 0.52 to 0.84. We also notice that performance on different countries within the same geographical regions is relatively consistent. For example, performance on Maghrebi group (Algeria, Morocco, and Tunisia) is relatively good, while on Levantine group (Syria, Jordan, and Lebanon) is relatively bad, and on Gulf group (Oman, KSA, and Qatar) is probably the worst. Performance

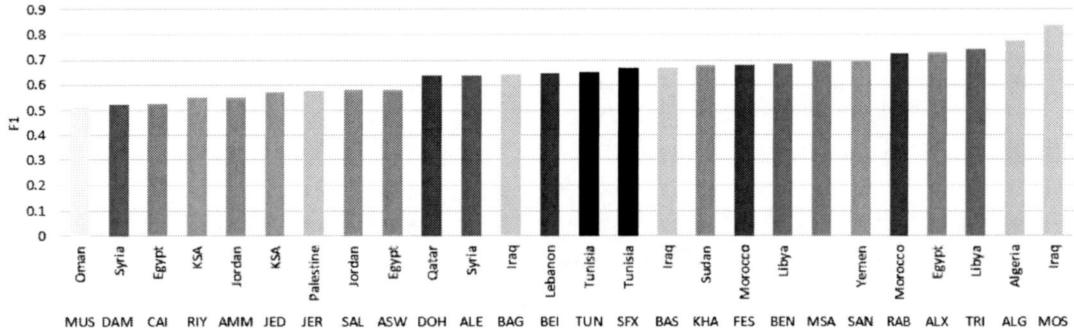

Figure 1: F_1 scores for the 25 dialects and the MSA for the best run. Same color indicates same country.

on Iraq and Libya is considered among the best. Moreover, Egypt has a noticeable but different observation; its 3 representative cities/dialects (almost) span the entire spectrum, with performance on Cairo and Alexandria (almost) make the extremes. Finally, performance on MSA is among the top third, which is expected.

To shed more light on and gain more insights about the different performance on different dialects, we illustrate the confusion matrix in Figure 2. From the matrix, it is clear that some dialects were confused with other dialects on the same country or other countries that are relatively close to it. The highest confusion is between Tunis (TUN) and Sfax (SFX) where 49 examples of TUN examples are misclassified as SFX and 29 vice versa. For example, misclassification of the TUN sentence "شنوة الفيلم الي تنصح بيه؟" as SFX can be due to the fact that the word "شنوة" appeared 41 times in SFX examples and only 14 times in TUN examples in the training data. Also, for Egypt, we can see from the confusion matrix that many examples are misclassified between these three dialects: Alexandria (ALX), Aswan (ASW), and Cairo (CAI), most notably in CAI which achieved a low F_1 score of 0.53 because 35 examples misclassified as ASW and 20 as ALX. Similarly, there is a recognizable confusion between the countries in the same geographic area. For example, for the gulf area, 13 examples of Doha (DOH) were classified as Jeddah (JED) and 14 examples of Muscat (MUS) were classified as Riyad (RIY).

5 Conclusion & Future Work

In this work, we adopted a *simple* approach to classify the Arabic sentences into one of 25 di-

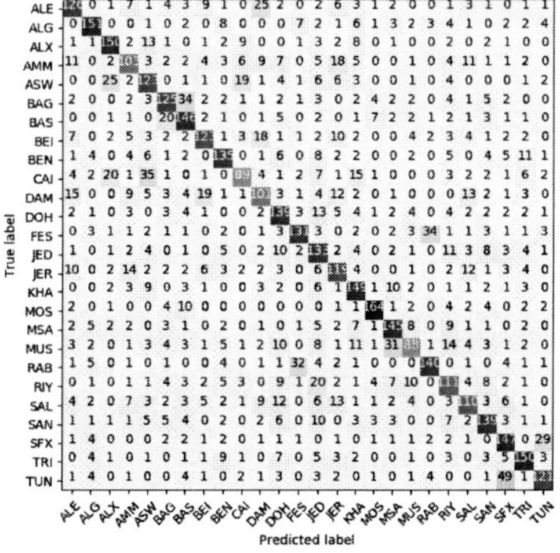

Figure 2: Confusion Matrix for the best run.

alects of different cities all over the Arab world, in addition to MSA, utilizing only the word and character n-grams features. Our best submitted run to MADAR shared task, that represents a voting scheme over two simple (both based on Naïve Bayes) classifiers, achieved an overall accuracy of 66.34% on the development set and 64.58% on the testing set.

That was indeed just the start. There are several directions that can potentially improve the performance of the system and address the limitations. First, extensive failure analysis has to be conducted to identify the major missclassification problems. For feature extraction, better term representation techniques, such as word and character embeddings, can be used to improve the quality of the features. For classification models, more traditional learning models (e.g., SVM) can be tried, in addition to the recently-hot deep learning models whenever applicable.

References

Alka Arora, P K Malhotra, Sudeep Marwah, Anshu Bhardwaj, and Shashi Dahiya. 2012. Data preprocessing techniques in data mining.

Houda Bouamor, Nizar Habash, Mohammad Salameh, Wajdi Zaghouani, Owen Rambow, Dana Abdulrahim, Ossama Obeid, Salam Khalifa, Fadhl Eryani, Alexander Erdmann, and Kemal Oflazer. 2018. The MADAR Arabic Dialect Corpus and Lexicon. *Lrec*, pages 3387–3396.

Houda Bouamor, Sabit Hassan, and Nizar Habash. 2019. The MADAR Shared Task on Arabic Fine-Grained Dialect Identification. In *Proceedings of the Fourth Arabic Natural Language Processing Workshop (WANLP19)*, Florence, Italy.

Watson Janet. 2007. *The Phonology and Morphology of Arabic*. Oxford University Press.

Fatiha Sadat, Farzindar Kazemi, and Atefeh Farzindar. 2015. Automatic Identification of Arabic Language Varieties and Dialects in Social Media. *Proceedings of the Second Workshop on Natural Language Processing for Social Media (SocialNLP) Dublin, Ireland*, pages 22–27.

Mohammad Salameh, Houda Bouamor, and Nizar Habash. 2018. Fine-Grained Arabic Dialect Identification. *Processdings of the 27th International Conference on Computational Linguistics Santa Fe, New Mexico, USA*, pages 1332–1344.

Toshiyuki Takezawa. 2007. Multilingual spoken language corpus development for communication research. In *Lecture Notes in Computer Science (including subseries Lecture Notes in Artificial Intelligence and Lecture Notes in Bioinformatics)*, pages 303–324. The Association for Computational Linguistics and Chinese Language Processing.

LIUM-MIRACL Participation in the MADAR Arabic Dialect Identification Shared Task

Saméh Kchaou
University of Sfax, Tunisia
samehkchaou4@gmail.com

Fethi Bougares
University of Le Mans, France
fethi.bougares@univ-lemans.fr

Lamia Hadrich Belguith
University of Sfax, Tunisia
lamia.belguith@gmail.com

Abstract

This paper describes the joint participation of the LIUM and MIRACL Laboratories at the Arabic dialect identification challenge of the MADAR Shared Task (Bouamor et al., 2019) conducted during the Fourth Arabic Natural Language Processing Workshop (WANLP 2019). We participated to the Travel Domain Dialect Identification subtask. We built several systems and explored different techniques including conventional machine learning methods and deep learning algorithms. Deep learning approaches did not perform well on this task. We experimented several classification systems and we were able to identify the dialect of an input sentence with an F1-score of **65.41%** on the official test set using only the training data supplied by the shared task organizers.

1 Introduction

Dialect can be defined as the language characteristics of a specific community (Etman and Beex, 2015). For all their daily communications, Arabic speakers use their local dialect. Dialects are commonly known as spoken or colloquial Arabic, acquired naturally as their mother tongue.

Being able to identify the dialect of a given sentence is a fundamental step for various applications such as machine translation, speech recognition and multiple Natural Language Processing (NLP) related services. Therefore, the dialect identification task has been the subject of several earlier research and exploration activities. For instance, Arabic dialect identification in speech transcripts was introduced as a subtask of the Discriminating between Similar Languages (DSL) Shared Task of the Third, Fourth and the Fifth Workshop on NLP for Similar Languages, Varieties and Dialects (VarDial) (Malmasi et al., 2016; Zampieri et al., 2017, 2018).

In practice, the number of existing dialects are as many as there are cities in the Arab world. Going to the city-level of granularity for dialect identification is a complex and expensive task. It is for this reason that earlier work in dialect identification generally study the problem at a region or country level (Zaidan and Callison-Burch, 2014). In this respect, dialects are generally classified into five main groups: *Maghrebi, Egyptian, Levantine, Gulf,* and *Iraqi* (El Haj et al., 2018; Elaraby and Abdul-Mageed, 2018).

Quite recently, and in contrast with the overall previous work, (Bouamor et al., 2018) presented the MADAR corpus which is now the existing resource with the greatest dialectal coverage. Indeed, the MADAR corpus includes 25 Arabic different dialects from east to west. The MADAR shared task is organized to make the most efficient use of this corpus. Dialect Identification (DID) is already a hard task, even when taking into account only 5 groups. This task became more perplexing when taking into consideration 25 groups of MADAR shared task. Indeed, taking into consideration additional dialects will reduce the overall classes dissimilarity and thus make the discrimination process harder. In the following sections of this paper, we will describe our participation to the MADAR Shared task. We investigate different classification techniques based on conventional machine learning algorithms with different kinds of features and various deep learning sequence2sequence architectures.

The paper is structured as follows: Section 2 describes the MADAR shared task and presents brief description of the training data. Section 3 presents a detailed overview of our systems and a discussion of our results. Finally, section 4 will draw a brief conclusion.

Proceedings of the Fourth Arabic Natural Language Processing Workshop, pages 219–223
Florence, Italy, August 1, 2019. ©2019 Association for Computational Linguistics

2 MADAR Shared Task

Arabic Dialect processing is a challenging task since dialects are mainly *spoken* and do not have an explicit written set of grammar rules. In this context, the MADAR corpus (Bouamor et al., 2018) is a valuable resource to push forward the field Arabic Dialect processing. The MADAR Dialect Identification shared task is partially based on this corpus. MADAR Shared task is the first DID shared task to target a large set of dialects. The challenge offered two subtasks: subtask 1 focuses on Travel Domain Dialect Identification, whereas subtask 2 is centred around Twitter User Dialect Identification. We will describe only the subtask 1 in which we have participated.

Subtask 1 Dataset: The provided data-sets are presented in table 1. The organizers provided a training and development sets from two sources created by translating the Basic Traveling Expression Corpus (BTEC) (Takezawa, 2006): *(i)* corpus-6, a large-scale additional sentences of the BTEC corpus of 5 regional representative dialects and MSA, *(ii)* corpus-26, a smaller-scale parallel corpus of 25 dialects in addition to MSA.

Corpus	#lines	#token
Corpus-26-train	41.6k	343.7k
Corpus-26-Dev	5.2k	43.7k
Corpus-6-train	54k	452.3k
Corpus-6-Dev	6k	49.6k
Corpus-26-Test	5.2k	43.1k

Table 1: Statistics of MADAR Subtask 1 Data Sets.

The shared task allowed participants to exploit all the data presented in Table 1 for the development of their DID systems[1]. Submission must be constrained in the sense that external manually annotated data sets are prohibited. Submissions are evaluated automatically on the test set *Corpus-26-Test*, using F1 score. Both Corpus-26-dev and Corpus-26-Test consist of 5.2k dialectal sentences, uniformly distributed over the 26 addressed dialects (200 sentences for each dialect). We note that we only use *corpus-26* train and dev to develop our DID systems.

3 LIU-MIR Submission

3.1 Data pre-processing

All Arabic dialects came from the same source, use the same character set, and share a large number of common words seen throughout their substantial vocabulary overlap. None of the existing Arabic dialects, at least until now, has an official status and none is regulated and taught in schools. As there is at present no dialect-specific computationally motivated pre-processing methods, our pre-processing is limited to a few steps of cleaning up applied to all the data without distinction. This includes the normalization of few arabic characters (أ, آ, إ, ى, ئ, ؤ[2]), the deletion of short vowels and tatweel[3] and the deletion of punctuation numbers and non arabic words.

3.2 Dialect Identification systems

In this section we present our experiments for MADAR Travel Domain Dialect Identification task. All our systems are constrained as we only used the supplied data from table 1.

3.3 Baseline systems

As a baseline for our DID system, we tried to reproduce the results presented in (Salameh et al., 2018). Just like them, we trained a Multinomial Naive Bayes (MNB) classifier using Word and character n-gram features. We also used Term Frequency-Inverse Document Frequency (Tf-Idf) scores learned on extracted character n-grams ranging from 1-grams to 5-grams.

	N-Gram Features		F1 score	
	Word	Char	Dev-26	Test-26
1.	1	-	59.64	57.42
2.	-	1	10.96	9.99
3.	-	1→5	56.44	54.34
4.	1	1	59.14	57.15
5.	1	1→3	60.07	58.51
6.	1	1→5	**60.97**	**59.21**

Table 2: MNB system using pre-processed training and evaluation data..

Table 2 reports the results of our baseline systems accuracy on the development set of CORPUS-26 (Dev-26). We performed several experiments using TF-IDF features of word and char

---

220

level n-grams. The best identification accuracy is obtained using uni-gram word level 1→5-gram character level.

We have tested also to evaluate the above systems without any pre-processing or normalization of the training data. The results are presented in the following table.

N-Gram Features		F1 score	
Word	Char	Dev-26	Test-26
1	-	64.42	63.33
-	1	16.84	15.51
-	1→5	62.16	60.63
1	1	64.45	63.52
1	1→3	65.29	64.52
1	1→5	**66.41**	**65.41**

Table 3: MNB system using raw training and evaluation data.

As shown in the table above, the dialect identification results are better when the systems are trained using the raw data. Knowing that data were created by translating sentences from English and French, we suspect that the translation was performed by one single person per dialect. If this is true, This could explain this result since the system learns as a side effect, to distinguish between the style of the translators (*i.e* spelling, punctuation, lexical choices, with or without vowels ...).

3.4 LM-based Systems

In addition to the baseline system presented in the previous section, we evaluated the identification performance using only n-gram word and character level Language Models(LM) trained using only corpus 26 training data. This has been done by directly comparing LM perplexity for each input sentence: Given an input sentence S to classify into one of k dialects $d_1, d_2, ..., d_k$ we select the dialect d^* of the model that gives the lowest perplexity on this sentence (*i.e* equation 1).

$$d^* = \arg\min_{k} PP(S) \tag{1}$$

For this experiment, we considered forward and backward word (LMWF, LMWB) and character-level (LMCF, LMCB) LMs, trained using sequences of words and characters in the reverse order. All LMs are 5-gram order, trained using KenLM toolkit with default parameters and Kneser–Ney smoothing (Heafield, 2011).

Table 4 presents the results of the DID systems with only LMs. While the character level LMs is

	Word LMs		Char LMs	
	LMWF	LMWB	LMCF	LMCB
dev-26	60.34	60.34	61.07	**61.36**
test-26	60.07	60.15	60.21	**60.63**

Table 4: F1-scores of DID system using LM Scores

lightly better than word-level LMs, both shows a lower accuracy compared to the MNB with word n-gram features (line 1 in table 3). The best LM based DID system is obtained using Backward character level LM with F1-score of **60.63** on the test-26 set.

3.5 LM Scores as Features

In this section we present our attempt to integrate LMs scores as extra feature to the MNB classifier. Each sentence is evaluated using the 26 trained LMs presented in section 3.4 and their scores are used as input features to the MNB.

N-Gram Feat.		LM Feat.		F1 score
Word	Char	Char	Word	Dev-26
1	1→5	-	-	**66.41 (65.41)**
1	1→5	F	-	65.97 (64.60)
1	1→5	B	-	66.03 (64.58)
1	1→5	FB	-	65.74 (63.73)
1	1→5	-	F	45.19 (61.51)
1	1→5	-	B	45.19 (61.78)
1	1→5	-	FB	44.76 (61.49)
1	1→5	F	F	46.09 (61.51)

Table 5: MNB system with N-Gram and LMs features.

As shown in table 5, adding LMs scores as features to MNB results in a decrease of F1-score on both dev-26 and test-26 sets. We tried both word and character level LMs trained in either Forward or Backward fashion. However, none of them and not even their combination had a positive effect on the system's accuracy.

3.6 Analysis and Discussion

In this section, we present an analysis of the classification results of our DID system. Table 6 presents the details of the F1-score per dialect. Overall, we can see that the system has a good prediction (high F1 score) for several dialects wheres the identification of other dialects are more challenging. This result is in accordance with the rate of token dissimilarity presented in Figure 2 of (Salameh et al., 2018). For example, ALG, SAN and MOS dialects have high pairwise token dissimilarity rate and they are also the easier to identify compared to CAI and RIY for instance.

Dialect	F1-score	Dialect	F1-score
ALE	0.64	JED	0.62
ALG	**0.78**	JER	0.57
ALX	0.74	KHA	0.69
AMM	0.56	MOS	**0.84**
ASW	0.60	MSA	0.69
BAG	0.65	MUS	0.54
BAS	0.68	RAB	0.70
BEI	0.67	RIY	0.56
BEN	0.67	SAL	0.56
CAI	0.53	SAN	0.71
DAM	0.56	SFX	0.72
DOH	0.63	TRI	0.75
FES	0.68	TUN	0.70

Table 6: F1-score per dialect of the best system on the test-26 set

After analyzing the full confusion matrix, we figured out that identification confusion tends to be bigger for geographical close cities. This is expected since sentences from close cities has a big vocabulary overlap and thus harder to discriminate. In order to investigate further this, we conducted a deeper analysis of two dialects belonging to the same geographical area. The primary objective of this study is to measure the upper bound of the classification accuracy for these dialects (*i.e.* the best possible prediction accuracy).

We conducted this analysis for the Top-2 most confused dialects: TUN (TUNIS) and SFX (SFAX). These dialects belongs to the same country, Tunisia, and present a high level of lexical similarity. In addition, there are the only ones for which we have native speakers. Table 7, presents the TUN *vs.* SFX dialects confusion matrix.

		Predicted	
		SFX	TUN
Actual	SFX	153	18
	TUN	41	123

Table 7: TUN - SFX dialects Confusion matrix.

As shown in Table 7, TUN and SFX dialects are source of confusion for the system. For instance, from among all the 200 SFX test sentences, 153 were well predicted and 18 predicted TUN. Similarly, 123 from the 200 TUN test sentences are well identified whereas 41 are predicted SFX.

In order to understand this substantial SFX-TUN confusion, we conducted a manual evaluation of the "*18 + 41*" sentences. This evaluation was performed as following: each of the incorrectly predicted 18 SFX sentences was presented to a TUN native speaker who decide whether the sentence seems to be a natural in his view, or whether he will formulate it differently. Table 8 presents examples of sentences from the test-26 and their transliteration.

Sentences	Label
فما حانوت قريب من هوني؟ fmA .hAnwt qryb mn hwny?	TUN
نحب مايو قياس أس، يعيشك n.hb mAyw qyAs As, y' y^sk	TUN
نحب تفاح يعيشك n.hb tfA.h y'y^sk	TUN
وقتاش تسكر البوسته؟ wqtAy^s tskr Albwsth?	SFX
باهي، وتيل الشيراتون قريب من هوني؟ bAhy, wtyl Aly^syrAtwn qryb mn hwny?	SFX
دجاج، يعيشك djAj, y'yy^sk	SFX

Table 8: Examples of TUN and SFX mis-classified sentences from test-26 with their ground truth label.

The evaluation has shown that, almost all the "*18 + 41*" studied examples may belongs to both dialect and hardly distinguishable even for native speakers. This exemplifies the increasing complexity the dialect identification task when we consider close dialects of a large lexical overlap.

4 Conclusion

In this paper we described our participation to the MADAR dialect identification task. We participated to the the Travel Domain Dialect Identification subtask where the goal is to design a system able to predict the correct dialect among 26 considered classes. We performed several experiments showing that the DID is a very challenging task. We were able to reach a F1-score of **65.41** on the official corpus-26-test set. We also conducted a manual assessment of the Top-2 most confused classes (SFX and TUN). We have found that almost all the confused SFX-TUN sentences are cases for which even a native speaker cannot decide. This shows that dialect identification is reaching its effective limit when considered dialects have many commonalities.

References

Houda Bouamor, Nizar Habash, Mohammad Salameh, Wajdi Zaghouani, Owen Rambow, Dana Abdulrahim, Ossama Obeid, Salam Khalifa, Fadhl Eryani, Alexander Erdmann, and Kemal Oflazer. 2018. The MADAR Arabic dialect corpus and lexicon. In *Proceedings of the 11th Language Resources and Evaluation Conference*, Miyazaki, Japan. European Language Resource Association.

Houda Bouamor, Sabit Hassan, and Nizar Habash. 2019. The MADAR Shared Task on Arabic Fine-Grained Dialect Identification. In *Proceedings of the Fourth Arabic Natural Language Processing Workshop (WANLP19)*, Florence, Italy.

Mahmoud El Haj, Paul Edward Rayson, and Mariam Aboelezz. 2018. Arabic dialect identification in the context of bivalency and code-switching. In *LREC 2018, Eleventh International Conference on Language Resources and Evaluation*, pages 3622–3627.

Mohamed Elaraby and Muhammad Abdul-Mageed. 2018. Deep models for Arabic dialect identification on benchmarked data. In *Proceedings of the Fifth Workshop on NLP for Similar Languages, Varieties and Dialects (VarDial 2018)*, pages 263–274, Santa Fe, New Mexico, USA. Association for Computational Linguistics.

A. Etman and A. A. L. Beex. 2015. Language and dialect identification: A survey. pages 220–231.

Kenneth Heafield. 2011. Kenlm: Faster and smaller language model queries. In *Proceedings of the Sixth Workshop on Statistical Machine Translation*, WMT '11, pages 187–197, Stroudsburg, PA, USA. Association for Computational Linguistics.

Shervin Malmasi, Marcos Zampieri, Nikola Ljubešić, Preslav Nakov, Ahmed Ali, and Jörg Tiedemann. 2016. Discriminating between similar languages and arabic dialect identification: A report on the third dsl shared task. In *Proceedings of the Third Workshop on NLP for Similar Languages, Varieties and Dialects (VarDial3)*, pages 1–14, Osaka, Japan.

Mohammad Salameh, Houda Bouamor, and Nizar Habash. 2018. Fine-grained arabic dialect identification. In *Proceedings of the International Conference on Computational Linguistics (COLING)*, pages 1332–1344, Santa Fe, New Mexico, USA.

Toshiyuki Takezawa. 2006. Multilingual spoken language corpus development for communication research. In *Chinese Spoken Language Processing*, pages 781–791, Berlin, Heidelberg. Springer Berlin Heidelberg.

Omar F. Zaidan and Chris Callison-Burch. 2014. Arabic dialect identification. *Comput. Linguist.*, 40(1).

Marcos Zampieri, Shervin Malmasi, Nikola Ljubešić, Preslav Nakov, Ahmed Ali, Jörg Tiedemann, Yves Scherrer, and Noëmi Aepli. 2017. Findings of the vardial evaluation campaign 2017. In *Proceedings of the Fourth Workshop on NLP for Similar Languages, Varieties and Dialects (VarDial)*, pages 1–15, Valencia, Spain. Association for Computational Linguistics.

Marcos Zampieri, Shervin Malmasi, Preslav Nakov, Ahmed Ali, Suwon Shon, James Glass, Yves Scherrer, Tanja Samardžić, Nikola Ljubešić, Jörg Tiedemann, Chris van der Lee, Stefan Grondelaers, Nelleke Oostdijk, Antal van den Bosch, Ritesh Kumar, Bornini Lahiri, and Mayank Jain. 2018. Language identification and morphosyntactic tagging: The second VarDial evaluation campaign. In *Proceedings of the Fifth Workshop on NLP for Similar Languages, Varieties and Dialects (VarDial)*, Santa Fe, USA.

Arabic Dialect Identification
with Deep Learning and Hybrid Frequency Based Features

Youssef Fares Zeyad El-Zanaty Kareem Abdel-Salam Muhammed Ezzeldin
Aliaa Mohamed Karim El-Awaad Marwan Torki

Faculty of Engineering, Alexandria University
{youssefe.fares, zeyadzanaty, karimamd95}@gmail.com,
{not.muhammedezz, aliaamohamedali284, kelawaad}@gmail.com
mtorki@alexu.edu.eg

Abstract

Studies on Dialectical Arabic are growing more important by the day as it becomes the primary written and spoken form of Arabic online in informal settings. Among the important problems that should be explored is that of dialect identification. This paper reports different techniques that can be applied towards such goal and reports their performance on the Multi Arabic Dialect Applications and Resources (MADAR) Arabic Dialect Corpora. Our results show that improving on traditional systems using frequency based features and non deep learning classifiers is a challenging task. We propose different models based on different word and document representations. Our top model is able to achieve an F1 macro averaged score of 65.66 on MADAR's small-scale parallel corpus of 25 dialects and Modern Standard Arabic (MSA).

1 Introduction

Dialect identification is the task of identifying the dialect of a particular segment of speech or text of any size (i.e., word, sentence, or document) automatically. The task of Arabic Dialect identification has attracted more attention recently. However, most efforts focus on a smaller and more distinct number of dialects, dialects by country rather than by city for example. Fine grained or city-based Arabic dialect identification is the more challenging task of not only classifying dialect by country but also by city. As such, the similarity between classes grows higher and the task grows more challenging.

Other efforts that did tackle such fine grained dialects and a larger number of classes have not explored the use of state of the art embedding models, language models and the use of deep learning in general.

The task remains challenging primarily because of the similarity between documents labeled with cities that are within the same country. The number of samples available for each class is 1,600 for each of the 26 cities given in Table 1 from (Salameh and Bouamor, 2018).

We report different data augmentation techniques used to expand the training set used. We also report the data analysis done on class similarity and model confusion from which we draw conclusions for suggested future work.

2 Data

The data used in all of the proposed system is one of the two parallel corpora made available by the Multi Arabic Dialect Applications and Resources (Bouamor et al., 2019) (MADAR) project: a 2,000-sentence parallel corpus with 25 parallel translations plus Modern Standard Arabic (MSA) which we will refer to as CORPUS-26 and the second corpus which has another 10,000 additional sentences translated to five selected dialects, which we will refer to as CORPUS-6.

The metrics reported for each model on CORPUS-6 or CORPUS-26 are trained on the same corpus for which the accuracy is reported. No more additional data is used except augmentations of the corpus used.

Data Preprocessing We apply a generic transformation that removes punctuation, diacritization and vowel elongation.

Data Augmentation Although there is no class imbalance, the number of samples per class and the fine grained classes were motivation to experiment with different data augmentation techniques. We used the following methods inspired by (Ibrahim et al., 2018)'s work to augment already existing documents:

- Unique Words Augmentation: for each document that contains a word repeated more than once, we remove duplicate words from it

Proceedings of the Fourth Arabic Natural Language Processing Workshop, pages 224–228
Florence, Italy, August 1, 2019. ©2019 Association for Computational Linguistics

Region	Maghreb				Nile Basin	Levant		Gulf		Yemen
Sub-region	Moroco	Algeria	Tunisia	Libya	Egypt/Sudan	South Levant	North Levant	Iraq	Gulf	Yemen
Cities	Rabat (RAB) Fes (FES)	Algeris (ALG)	Tunis (TUN) Sfax (SFX)	Tripoli (TRI) Benghazi (BEN)	Cairo (CAI) Alexandria (ALX) Aswan (ASW) Khartoum (KHA)	Jerusalem (JER) Amman (AMM) Salt (SAL)	Beirut (BEI) Damascus (DAM) Aleppo (ALE)	Mosul (MOS) Baghdad (BAG) Basra (BAS)	Doha (DOH) Muscat (MUS) Riyadh (RIY) Jeddah (JED)	Sanaa (SAN)

Table 1: Different region, sub-region, and city dialects in the MADAR dataset.

and create a new comment with only unique words.

- Random Mask Augmentation: for each document, we create a different new document by randomly removing up to 20% of the original document words.

- Random Swap Augmentation: for each document, we create a different new document by randomly swapping up to 20% of the original document words.

- Random Concatenation Augmentation: we choose two documents with few number of words at random and append them forming a new one with longer length.

We report that using data augmentation prevented over-fitting when using deep learning as we chose between applying different techniques or using the original document at random for each sample in each epoch.

For non deep learning models, we used such augmentation to increase the size of the data used to around quadruple the original number of documents, which resulted in a slight increase (close to 1%) in the baseline model accuracy.

3 Methodology

For such a complicated task we tried multiple approaches using different techniques to achieve the best results. We started by tuning the baseline given in (Salameh and Bouamor, 2018) which is a Multinomial Naive Bayes (MNB) using TF-IDF character + word features (without the KenLM language model). Experiments concluded with n-gram ranges of one to five for character features and one-gram for word features. A grid-search using (Pedregosa et al., 2011) was applied to the MNB which delivered an F1-score of **64.94%** on the dev-set.

We then took to deep neural networks, the models submitted are given in Table 2 and experiments that lead to those submission are given in Table 3. We did not observe much improvement over the baseline (MNB) until our first submission model.

3.1 LSTM + CharCNN, FastText embeddings + LSTM and Baseline Ensemble

It is an ensemble of three models, the first being an adaptation of the character-level model proposed in (Ali, 2018), which takes one-hot-encoded character features to multiple (five in our case) convolution layers with filter size of 256 -which is the same as the max length set for a sentence-preceded by a Gated Recurrent Unit (GRU) for context capturing of these features then a softmax layer for calculating log probabilities.

After multiple experiments and tuning we replaced the GRU with an LSTM. The second model we ensemble is another shallow network consisting of an embedding layer of fastText word embeddings(Mikolov et al., 2018) through a spatial dropout layer to avoid over-fitting, then through an LSTM, again for context capturing, but in this case for word features, then finally a softmax layer. The outputs of both softmax layers are averaged to give the final probabilities. We chose this approach to combine both character features and word features, this gave us the best result we could achieve on the dev-set with **63%** F1-score. After ensembling it with our MNB baseline (the third and final model) with weighted averaging, we surpassed the baseline achieving **66.1%** F1-score on the dev-set and ranked second among all of our submissions with an F1-score of **65.35%** on the test-set. All neural network models were built using Keras (Chollet et al., 2015). The full architecture can be seen in Figure 1.

Model	F1-Macro	Precision-Macro	Recall-Macro	Accuracy
ArbDialectID (Winning Team)	**67.32%**	**67.60%**	**67.29%**	**67.29%**
LSTM +CharCNN, fastText embeddings + LSTM, Baseline (1st submission)	65.36%	**66.07%**	65.38%	65.38%
Char TFIDF + WordTFIDF + NN, Baseline (2nd submission)	**65.66%**	65.79%	**65.75%**	**65.75%**
Bert + Document Pooling (3rd submission)	35.14%	42.61%	36.25%	36.25%

Table 2: Models submitted and their corresponding scores on the test-set.

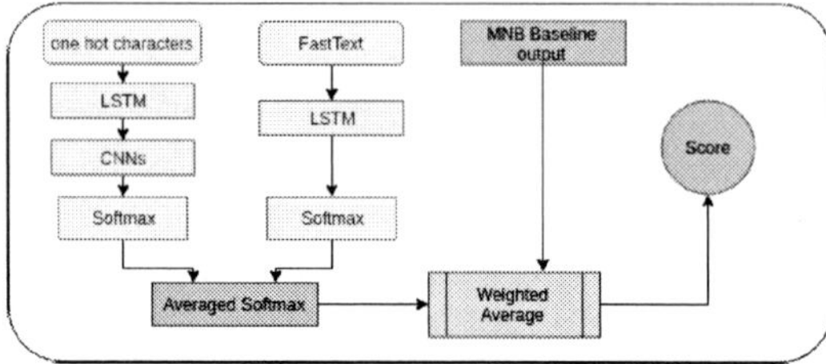

Figure 1: 1st Submission Architecture

Figure 2: 2nd Submission Architecture

3.2 CharTFIDF + WordTFIDF + NN and Baseline Ensemble

It is an ensemble of the MNB baseline and a deep learning model applied to baseline features. The deep learning model takes as input the frequency based features for which the MNB achieved 64.94% dev-set F1-score and improves it to **65.57%**.

The model architecture in Figure 2 consists of two hidden fully connected layers followed by an output layer. The two hidden layers are followed by ReLU activations and dropout layers with 20% probability. The number of inputted features to the neural network is equal to the number of dimensions of the frequency based vectors (char-based and word-based). Adam optimizer (Kingma and Ba, 2014) is used for training with 3e-6 learning rate and the cross entropy loss as criterion.

The ensemble of the model produced with the baseline using log probability averaging produces **66.78%** dev-set F1-score and **65.66%** test-set F1-score which is less than 2% below the winning team results and was ranked the seventh out of 19 submissions in the shared task competition.

3.3 Language-Model Based Models

We propose a number of other systems that produced sub-optimal results on corpus-26 data, but are experiments worth mentioning towards other future ensembles and systems.

i. A character level forward and backward language model trained using multi-layer RNNs whose features are combined with fastText and bytepair (Heinzerling and Strube, 2017) subword embeddings produced 58% devset F1-score.

ii. A model using multi-lingual BERT (Devlin et al., 2018) and a multi-layer RNN for document representation also followed by a single layer linear classifier reaches 55% dev-set F1-score.

iii. A model using Aravec (Mohammad et al., 2017) word embeddings and a shallow LSTM for document representation (feeding word embedding sequence to LSTM and using hidden layers as features) produces 50% dev-set F1-score when using a one layer linear classifier.

4 Discussion

Multiple observations and experiments show that the fine-grained nature of classes is the most challenging aspect of the task. Differentiating between Cairo and Alex or Beirut and Damascus is a much harder problem than differentiating between Levant and Gulf for example. We report some results towards such conclusions when classifying by city within a single regions' data as shown in Figure 3 and Figure 4.

Bench-marking all of the fore-mentioned models on corpus-26 data with regions and MSA as classes instead of cities produces results comparable to that of corpus-6 data (80% at worst on the dev-set). So the higher scores reported on corpus-6 data are not only owing to the larger number of samples but also owing to the affinity between sub region classes in corpus-26.

Another conclusion we can draw from how

Model	Dev-set F1-score
Char TFIDF + WordTFIDF + NN, Baseline	66.6%
LSTM + CharCNN, fastText embeddings LSTM, Baseline	66.1%
Character-level bi-directional LM (RNNs) + fastText + BytePair, Linear Classifier	58%
Bert + RNN Document Representation + Linear Classifier	55%
AraVec Word Embeddings + Shallow LSTM with dropout	50%

Table 3: Top scoring models on the dev-set

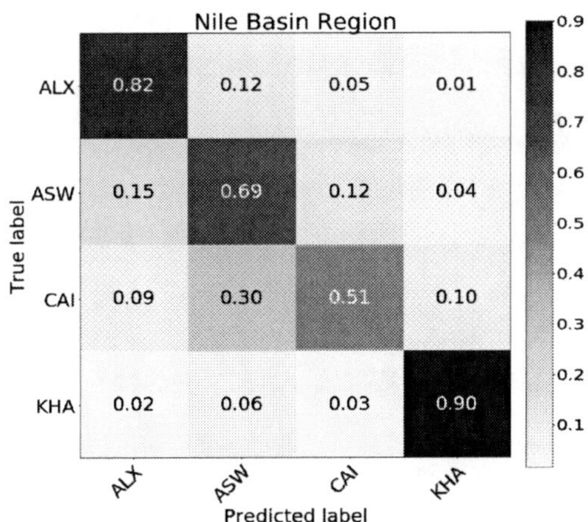

Figure 3: Confusion matrix for MNB classifier on Nile Basin region data and classes only

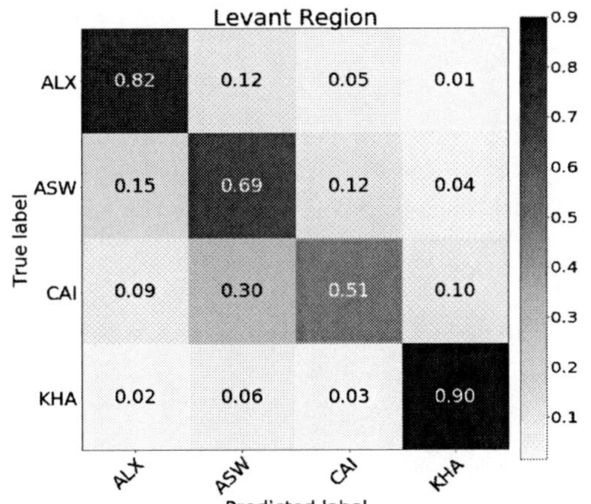

Figure 4: Confusion matrix for MNB classifier on Levant region data and classes only

closely all of the deep learning based models plateau, is that coming up with a better system for this task may require the use of other external labelled or unlabelled data. With the internet rich with blogs that are country specific or city specific. We can use unlabelled data from specific sources (e.g. tweets on Alexandria, Facebook posts from a public group based in Khartoum, and so on and so forth).

That can enable the training of embeddings from scratch on large data, and it can also be used on language model training improving the performance of models based on such techniques. The training of embeddings on such data specifically makes sense because of the percentage of out of vocab words and how they are handled in the embedding techniques we used. Because the embeddings were for the most part trained themselves on MSA data. The out of vocab (OOV) words which were usually 10-20% of the words in the corpus-26 data, were handled by averaging the rest of the embeddings of all words in the document or by being given a zero vector. Inconveniently, the OOV words are clearly the words we are most interested in because they are most likely to be the dialect specific words that differentiate between the classes. Therefore, if we are able to reduce the number of OOV words, the scores are expected to significantly improve. That can be achieved by the fore-mentioned training of embeddings on corpora that are not MSA only, or at least using smarter techniques to handle OOV words, such as character-based representation (Bojanowski et al., 2016).

5 Conclusion

We introduce multiple neural network based models built on word and document representations. We are able to produce results comparable to the MNB baseline on n-gram frequency based features despite of the small size of the dataset, which maybe an indication of even better results on larger data. We ensemble the neural network based models with the baseline to produce better results than the baseline.

Future work will explore further ensembles of

the language model based classifiers and ensembling using other techniques than probability averaging (e.g. stacking). We will also explore the training of embeddings on data that is comprised of diverse dialectical data, not only MSA, and better handling of OOV words when using embeddings.

References

Mohamed Ali. 2018. Character level convolutional neural network for Arabic dialect identification. In *Proceedings of the Fifth Workshop on NLP for Similar Languages, Varieties and Dialects (VarDial 2018)*, pages 122–127, Santa Fe, New Mexico, USA. Association for Computational Linguistics.

Piotr Bojanowski, Edouard Grave, Armand Joulin, and Tomas Mikolov. 2016. Enriching Word Vectors with Subword Information. *arXiv e-prints*, page arXiv:1607.04606.

Houda Bouamor, Sabit Hassan, and Nizar Habash. 2019. The MADAR Shared Task on Arabic Fine-Grained Dialect Identification. In *Proceedings of the Fourth Arabic Natural Language Processing Workshop (WANLP19)*, Florence, Italy.

François Chollet et al. 2015. Keras. `https://keras.io`.

Jacob Devlin, Ming-Wei Chang, Kenton Lee, and Kristina Toutanova. 2018. BERT: Pre-training of Deep Bidirectional Transformers for Language Understanding. *arXiv e-prints*, page arXiv:1810.04805.

Benjamin Heinzerling and Michael Strube. 2017. BPEmb: Tokenization-free Pre-trained Subword Embeddings in 275 Languages. *arXiv e-prints*, page arXiv:1710.02187.

Mai Ibrahim, Marwan Torki, and Nagwa El-Makky. 2018. Imbalanced toxic comments classification using data augmentation and deep learning. In *2018 17th IEEE International Conference on Machine Learning and Applications (ICMLA)*, pages 875–878.

Diederik P. Kingma and Jimmy Ba. 2014. Adam: A Method for Stochastic Optimization. *arXiv e-prints*, page arXiv:1412.6980.

Tomas Mikolov, Edouard Grave, Piotr Bojanowski, Christian Puhrsch, and Armand Joulin. 2018. Advances in pre-training distributed word representations. In *Proceedings of the International Conference on Language Resources and Evaluation (LREC 2018)*.

Abu Bakr Mohammad, Kareem Eissa, and Samhaa El-Beltagy. 2017. Aravec: A set of arabic word embedding models for use in arabic nlp. *Procedia Computer Science*, 117:256–265.

Fabian Pedregosa, Gaël Varoquaux, Alexandre Gramfort, Vincent Michel, Bertrand Thirion, Olivier Grisel, Mathieu Blondel, Peter Prettenhofer, Ron Weiss, Vincent Dubourg, Jake Vanderplas, Alexandre Passos, David Cournapeau, Matthieu Brucher, Matthieu Perrot, and Édouard Duchesnay. 2011. Scikit-learn: Machine learning in python. *J. Mach. Learn. Res.*, 12:2825–2830.

Mohammad Salameh and Houda Bouamor. 2018. Fine-grained Arabic dialect identification. In *Proceedings of the 27th International Conference on Computational Linguistics*, pages 1332–1344, Santa Fe, New Mexico, USA. Association for Computational Linguistics.

MICHAEL: Mining Character-level Patterns for Arabic Dialect Identification (MADAR Challenge)

Dhaou Ghoul
STIH Lab, Sorbonne University
dhaou.ghoul@sorbonne-universite.fr

Gaël Lejeune
STIH Lab, Sorbonne University
gael.lejeune@sorbonne-universite.fr

Abstract

We present MICHAEL, a lightweight method developed for the MADAR shared task on travel domain Dialect Identification (DID). It uses character-level features and perform classification without any pre-processing. Character N-grams extracted from the original sentences are used to train a Multinomial Naive Bayes classifier. MICHAEL achieved an official score (accuracy) of 53.25% with $1 \leq N \leq 3$ but showed a much better result with character 4-grams (62.17%).

1 Introduction

The Arabic language is one of the most widely spoken language in the world, currently considered as the fifth language (Chung, 2008) with more than 330 million Arabic speakers. It is the official language of more than 22 countries. In its written form, commonly referred as Literary Arabic, it is divided into two categories: Classical Arabic and Modern Standard Arabic (MSA). However, Arabic speakers mostly use dialects which are a linguistic variant of classical Arabic with their own features, varying with respect to the country or the region. If MSA is used only for written and official communication, dialects are used for oral communication as well as for many device mediated communication forms: email, sms, chat or blogs. Therefore, Arabic dialects identification (DID) has become a very important pre-processing step that attracts many attention from NLP research. Indeed, the knowledge about the dialect of an input text is useful in several NLP tasks such as sentiment analysis (Al-Twairesh et al., 2016).

We propose a simple, light-weight, character-based method to classify Arabic sentences into 26 classes (25 dialects + MSA) based on the MADAR corpus provided for this competition (Bouamor et al., 2019). This paper is organized as follows: in Section 2, we present some related word for DID. In section 3, we describe some aspects of the Arabic dialects and in section 4 we present the MADAR dataset and we introduce MICHAEL, the system we designed to tackle the DID task. Finally, we show our results in Section 5 and give some future directions in section 6

2 Previous Work

Arabic Dialect Identification is a very difficult task because of several factors like the lack of NLP tools that deal with Arabic variants. So far, the researchers have tried to address this task using different methods.

Salameh *et al.* (Salameh et al., 2018), presented a MNB (Multinomial Naive Bayes) classifier trained to identify a tweet among 26 classes (MSA+25 dialects) using a large-scale of parallel sentences (Bouamor et al., 2018). Their models reach 67.9% accuracy for sentences with an average length of 7 word and reached more than 90% with 16 words.

Elfardy and Diab (Elfardy and Diab, 2013) proposed a supervised method for identifying whether a given sentence in prevalently MSA or Egyptian using the Arabic online commentary dataset(AOC) (Zaidan and Callison-Burch, 2011). Their system achieves an accuracy of 85.5% on an Arabic online-commentary dataset.

Najafian *et al.* (Najafian et al., 2018), presented different approaches for Dialect Identification (DID) in Arabic broadcast speech using use Support Vector Machines (SVM), and Convolutional Neural Networks (CNN) as backend classifiers. The final system merges these results and obtains 24.7% and 19.0% relative error rate reduction compared to conventional phonotactic DID, and i-vectors with bottleneck features. Rabee *et al.* (Naser and Hanani, 2018), describes an Automatic Dialect Recognition (ADI) system for the VarDial 2018 challenge, with the goal of distinguishing four major Arabic dialects, as well as Modern Standard Arabic (MSA) using four sys-

Proceedings of the Fourth Arabic Natural Language Processing Workshop, pages 229–233
Florence, Italy, August 1, 2019. ©2019 Association for Computational Linguistics

tems. The first system uses word transcriptions and tries to recognize the speaker's dialect by modeling the word sequence of each dialect. The second one aims to recognize the dialect by modeling the telephonesequences produced by non-Arabic telephone recognition devices. The other two systems use GMM trained in acoustic functions to recognize the dialect. This system reached 68.77% in micro F1. Elaraby *et al.* (Elaraby and Abdul-Mageed, 2018), presented a deep learning models for DID taking advantage of the performance of several conventional machine learning models under different conditions. Their model showed a 87.65% score in accuracy for the binary task (MSA vs. dialects), 87.4% for the 3 class task (Egyptian, Gulf and Levantine).

3 The Dialectal Varieties of Arabic

Arabic language is a rather generic term that refers in fact to many variants and dialects. Nowadays, one can consider that Arabic language is divided into three major categories: classical Arabic, standard Arabic (MSA) and dialectal Arabic. The 2019 MADAR competition focused on the latter.

Dialectal Arabic is a proper form of the Arabic language used in everyday communication, usually called "darija". It varies from one country to another and even from one region to another within the same country. All Arab countries have their own dialects that are more or less close to each other. The differences the dialects exhibit depend mainly on the history of each country and its geographical location. For example, the Tunisian dialect (TUN) integrates several borrowings from French language as it has been colonized by France. Words like "*stylo*" (pen/pencil) or "*cartable*" (schoolbag) are examples of borrowings completely integrated into TUN. According to Zaidan and Callison-Burch (2014), arabic dialects can be classified into five major classes (these classes can have several subclasses):

- **Egyptian:** The most widely understood dialect, due to a thriving Egyptian television and movie industry (Haeri, 2003).

- **Levantine:** A set of dialects that differ somewhat in pronunciation and intonation, but are largely equivalent in written form. They are closely related to Aramaic (Amara, 2010).

- **Gulf:** Probably the closest to MSA, perhaps because the current form of MSA evolved from an Arabic variety originating in the Gulf region. There are differences between Gulf and MSA but Gulf kept more of MSA's verb conjugation than other dialects (Versteegh, 2001).

- **Iraqi:** Despite its similarity to Gulf dialects it exhibits some very distinctive features in terms of prepositioning, verb conjugation and pronunciation (Mitchell, 1993).

- **Maghrebi:** These dialects were influenced by both French and Berber languages. The Western-most varieties could be unintelligible for speakers from other regions in the Middle East, especially in spoken form. Maghreb is a large region with more variation than regions like the Levant or the Gulf. It makes it probably easier to distinguish its local variants : Tunisia, Algeria, Morocco, Libya. . . (Tilmatine, 1999).

Arabic dialect differ from one another and from MSA on several levels of linguistic representation such as phonology, morphology, lexicon and syntax. Table 1 exhibits examples of differences between some dialects. For instances, the phonem "qaf" (first column) will not have the same pronounciation in all the dialects. In the second column one can see that the future tense is not marked by the same morpheme in each variant. The syntax of negation (third column) is not the same in Maghrebian dialects and in othe dialects. Regarding lexicon (fourth column) the concept "car" in ALG and MAR dialects reflects a borowing from the French term "automobile".

	Phon.	Morph.	Synt.	Lex.
MSA	qaf	s or swf	mA	sayyaara
ALG	qaf and /g/	ghadi or rH	mA	tomobile
EGY	hamza	h	muw	3arabiyya
GUL	/g/	ba	lA	sayyaara
LEV	hamza	H or rH	muw	sayyaara
MAR	qaf	ghadi	mA	tomobile
TUN	qaf and /g/	bAsh	mA	krhba

Table 1: Examples of differences between MSA and ALG (Algeria), EGY (Egyptian), GUL (Gulf), LEV (levantine), MOR (Moroccan) and TUN (Tunisian) regarding phonetics, morphology, syntax and lexicon.

4 Arabic Dialect Identification: Methods for classification

4.1 Some Difficulties of Arabic DID

Despite the differences between the different dialects, their automatic identification remains a very difficult task, even impossible in some cases. This difficulty is due to several factors:

- Shared lexicon: dialects have a common vocabulary and a dialectal sentence can contain several dialects as well as MSA.

- Grammatical Ambiguity: some identical words are used with different functions. For example, the word "Tyb" can be an adjective in some dialects and an interjection in others.

- Homonyms: mostly due to the omission of short vowels, a dialectal word can have the same spelling as an MSA word but an entirely different meaning. This includes strongly dialectal words such as *dwl*: it is either the Egyptian (EGY) word for "these" (pronounced dowl) or the MSA word for "countries" (pronounced duwal) (Zaidan and Callison-Burch, 2014).

4.2 Data: The MADAR corpus

The purpose of the shared task is to give each short sentence a label among 26 avialable labels. We took advantage of the MADAR corpus supplied for the competition in order to train various classifiers. We did not use anay external resource. The MADAR corpus has been created by translating sentences from the Basic Traveling Expression Corpus (BTEC) from English and French to the different dialects. This corpus has been splitted into Train, Validation and Test sets, they are priefly presented in Table 2.

Datasets	Train	Dev	Test
# sentences	41,600	5,200	5,200
# words	336,342	42,586	36,811
# characters	1,301,599	166,898	162,185

Table 2: Size of the Train, Dev and Test sets

4.3 Method: Character N-grams

MICHAEL has been built on the assumption that the features most prone to discriminate languages are found at character-level. With this idea in mind

Trained on Tested on	Train Set Dev Set	Train Set Test Set	Train+Dev Test Set
$N = 1$	19.08	18.46	18.48
$1 \leq N \leq 2$	40.04	37.29	37.44
$N = 2$	42.62	39.90	40.38
$1 \leq N \leq 3$	55.00	**53.25**	53.54
$2 \leq N \leq 3$	56.17	54.31	54.40
$N = 3$	58.25	57.50	57.92
$1 \leq N \leq 4$	60.73	59.62	59.88
$2 \leq N \leq 4$	61.21	60.04	60.25
$3 \leq N \leq 4$	62.44	60.88	61.42
$N = 4$	62.96	**61.94**	**62.17**
$1 \leq N \leq 5$	62.65	60.98	61.71
$2 \leq N \leq 5$	63.17	61.02	61.77
$3 \leq N \leq 5$	**63.48**	61.65	62.12
$5 \leq N \leq 5$	62.62	61.71	61.88
$N = 5$	60.71	59.77	60.48

Table 3: Results for the Multinomial Naive Bayes Classifier, character N-grams with various range of N from $N_{min} = 1$ to $N_{max} = 5$ with different training and testing configurations (blue score is our official score)

we tried different classifiers but quickly found that, under the technical constraints we were facing, Naive Bayes algorithms were the most appropriate for such a multi-class problem. The One VS Rest implementation of SVM we tested were unable to reach a result and we did not want to train 26 different classifiers separately. We used the SCI-KIT LEARN implementation of MNB and it proves quickly that among the NB implementations of this library, the Multinomial Naive Bayes (MNB) was the most efficient. We will show in the next section different learning configurations and various size of n-grams for feature engineering.

5 Results and Error Analysis

5.1 Results

The results obtained by MICHAEL are shown on Table 3. One can see that character $1 - grams$ ($N_{min} = N_{max} = 1$) alone can achieve more than 18% in accuracy which is an interesting result for a 26-class task. Increasing the maximum size of the N-grams increases the accuracy quickly: +19 percentage points (pp) with $N_{max} = 2$ and another 16 points with $N_{max} = 3$. The gain with $N_{max} = 4$ is lower but it is still a 6 pp gain.

Working on the minimal size of the n-grams is also a good way to improve the score. In our particular learning setting, removing short n-grams helps to improve the results. For instance with $N_{max} = 3$, setting $N_{min} = 3$ instead of $N_{min} = 1$ improves the accuracy by 4 percentage points. Finally, the best results were obtained with 4-grams.

	Maghreb							Egyptian				S. Levant			N. Levant			Iraqi			Gulf					MSA
	ALG	BEN	FES	RAB	SFX	TRI	TUN	ALX	ASW	CAI	KHA	AMM	JER	SAL	ALE	BEI	DAM	BAG	BAS	MOS	DOH	JED	MUS	RIY	SAN	MSA
ALG	153	3	5	6	4	3	5	1	0	3	2	0	0	2	0	1	0	0	0	0	0	0	5	1	0	1
BEN	7	127	2	3	2	8	0	2	0	0	0	4	6	3	1	3	3	3	3	2	3	5	5	9	4	0
FES	8	1	135	36	1	0	1	1	2	1	2	2	3	1	2	5	2	1	2	0	2	2	2	1	2	0
RAB	7	2	34	138	3	2	6	1	2	2	1	1	1	3	1	1	0	0	1	0	1	0	0	0	1	0
SFX	3	5	5	4	149	3	47	0	0	1	1	1	1	2	0	1	1	2	1	0	2	4	1	1	2	2
TRI	2	11	0	4	3	145	3	0	3	1	3	1	1	1	1	1	1	1	2	6	5	3	0	2	4	0
TUN	1	1	1	1	22	3	119	0	1	2	0	0	1	0	1	3	1	0	0	0	1	0	1	0	0	0
ALX	2	0	1	1	0	0	1	143	27	20	3	4	3	2	0	2	2	0	1	2	2	3	2	1	0	2
ASW	0	7	1	0	0	3	0	14	116	36	11	4	2	4	1	3	3	3	1	0	1	6	3	0	2	0
CAI	1	1	2	0	0	2	1	12	22	88	2	4	2	3	0	4	2	1	1	0	0	2	2	4	3	1
KHA	3	3	1	0	0	5	0	8	3	14	139	3	2	2	2	4	2	1	2	1	4	7	10	2	5	9
AMM	0	4	0	0	1	2	1	5	3	6	1	108	21	10	8	5	13	2	1	0	2	4	1	3	2	0
JER	2	3	0	3	2	3	1	2	4	3	2	18	112	15	8	7	9	0	0	0	4	1	0	3	1	0
SAL	0	0	1	0	1	3	3	0	1	2	1	6	12	106	4	6	10	1	2	2	4	5	3	3	3	2
ALE	0	1	0	1	1	2	0	0	0	7	0	6	7	3	122	9	16	2	0	2	3	0	2	1	0	2
BEI	1	1	0	0	0	2	0	1	0	2	1	5	7	4	6	113	15	2	1	0	1	2	1	1	0	0
DAM	1	1	0	0	1	0	1	0	2	0	3	9	5	6	25	18	100	1	1	1	3	5	3	0	2	2
BAG	0	1	1	0	2	1	1	1	0	1	0	1	0	2	3	1	7	123	26	1	3	1	5	3	5	4
BAS	2	1	0	0	0	0	3	0	1	0	2	0	3	3	2	2	2	31	128	8	3	0	3	3	2	1
MOS	1	0	1	0	2	0	1	1	0	1	2	1	0	3	3	1	0	7	12	165	4	2	1	6	3	0
DOH	0	3	2	1	1	4	2	0	3	1	4	6	3	4	0	2	2	2	3	0	119	9	12	5	5	1
JED	2	7	0	1	0	2	3	4	5	4	3	5	3	4	5	1	4	1	2	1	13	115	4	21	6	3
MUS	1	3	3	0	1	1	1	0	1	0	6	4	2	5	2	3	0	0	2	3	9	0	94	13	2	23
RIY	2	10	2	0	2	2	0	1	3	1	1	5	2	6	0	3	1	7	3	3	7	13	12	102	7	5
SAN	0	4	3	1	0	4	0	1	1	3	1	2	1	4	1	1	2	5	4	3	3	8	5	10	130	2
MSA	4	1	3	0	0	2	0	4	1	0	8	2	1	2	2	0	0	2	1	1	0	2	12	3	0	137

Table 4: Confusion matrix for our best system (MNB with character 4-grams) with dialects grouped with respect to regions, with true positives in blue, and in blod dialect pairs with more than ten false positives.

It appears that the results obtained on the Test Set were worse than those obtained on the Dev Set (third column of Table 3), with an average loss of 1.6 percentage points. Merging the Train and the Dev Set resulted in a gain that in most cases was marginal (+0.26 pp). With $N_{max} > 4$ we did not find much improvement in results, except on the dev set but this can be a bias. This threshold may be related to the fact that character N-grams with $N > 4$ tend to represent the lexicon more than general properties of the dialect itself.

5.2 Error Analysis

Table 4 shows the confusion matrix of our best configuration. The 25 dialects are grouped by regions and MSA appears as the last class. We can see that MUS and SAN are the closest dialects to MSA with respectively 35 and 17 errors involving the MUS-MSA and the SAN-MSA pairs. CAI, MUS and DAM dialects were the most difficult to detect with respectively 112, 106 and 100 False Negatives (FN). Regarding False Positives (FP), the most problematic cases were ASW (106) , RIY (105) and JED (103). Interestingly, the most difficult dialect pairs to discriminate were from Maghreb: FES–RAB (36 and 34 FP) and SFX–TUN (47 and 22). Most of FPs occured between dialects of the same regions with two exceptions : (I) a minor one because North Levant dialects are hard to distinguish from South Levant dialects and (II) a more strange situation with BEN-RIY and KHA-MUS being rather difficult pairs to distinguish despite their apparent distance.

6 Conclusion and Future Work

In this paper, we explored the problem of Arabic dialect classification into 26 classes (covering 25 cities from the Arab World in addition to Modern Standard Arabic(MSA)). We presented MICHAEL a simple, pre-processing free, system design for this DID task. MICHAEL uses character N-Grams features to train a Multinomial Naive Bayes classifier. Beside its simplicity, MICHAEL does not need a huge amount of training data to achieve good results. This system achieved an official score (accuracy) of 53.25% with $1 \leq N \leq 3$ but showed a much better result with only character 4-grams (62.17% accuracy). Using N-grams with $N > 4$ did not seem to improve the results. However, an accurate feature selection technique, like mutual information, may help to get advantage of these longer n-grams that capture more lexical information than shorter N-grams.

Using other types of character features like closed motifs (Buscaldi et al., 2018) would be a first way to assess the influence of the classifier and the features. We plan to explore if adding pre-processing steps like tokenization into words or normalization may improve the results. Another interesting perspective would be to test a Bilstm RNN architecture since this has proven to be adapted to sequential data and Bilstm can exploit both character-level and word-level features. In another perspective it would be very interesting to perform a deeper analysis of classification errors.

References

Nora Al-Twairesh, Hend Al-Khalifa, and Abdulmalik AlSalman. 2016. AraSenTi: Large-scale twitter-specific Arabic sentiment lexicons. In *Proceedings of the 54th Annual Meeting of the Association for Computational Linguistics (Volume 1: Long Papers)*, pages 697–705, Berlin, Germany. Association for Computational Linguistics.

Muhammad Amara. 2010. Reem bassiouney: Arabic sociolinguistics. *Language Policy*, 9:379–381.

Houda Bouamor, Nizar Habash, Mohammad Salameh, Wajdi Zaghouani, Owen Rambow, Dana Abdulrahim, Ossama Obeid, Salam Khalifa, Fadhl Eryani, Alexander Erdmann, and Kemal Oflazer. 2018. The madar arabic dialect corpus and lexicon. In *Proceedings of LREC 2018*.

Houda Bouamor, Sabit Hassan, and Nizar Habash. 2019. The MADAR Shared Task on Arabic Fine-Grained Dialect Identification. In *Proceedings of the Fourth Arabic Natural Language Processing Workshop (WANLP19)*, Florence, Italy.

Davide Buscaldi, Joseph Le Roux, and Gaël Lejeune. 2018. Character-level models for polarity detection in tweets. In *Atelier DEFT 2018*, Rennes, France.

Wingyan Chung. 2008. Web searching in a multilingual world. *Commun. ACM*, 51(5):32–40.

Mohamed Elaraby and Muhammad Abdul-Mageed. 2018. Deep models for arabic dialect identification on benchmarked data. In *VarDial@COLING 2018*.

Heba Elfardy and Mona Diab. 2013. Sentence level dialect identification in Arabic. In *Proceedings of the 51st Annual Meeting of the Association for Computational Linguistics (Volume 2: Short Papers)*, pages 456–461, Sofia, Bulgaria. Association for Computational Linguistics.

Niloofar Haeri. 2003. *Sacred Language, Ordinary People: Dilemmas of Culture and Politics in Egypt*. Sacred Language, Ordinary People: Dilemmas of Culture and Politics in Egypt. Palgrave Macmillan.

Terence Frederic Mitchell. 1993. *Pronouncing Arabic*. vol. 2. Clarendon Press.

Maryam Najafian, Sameer Khurana, Suwon Shon, Ahmed Ali, and James Glass. 2018. Exploiting convolutional neural networks for phonotactic based dialect identification. In *ICASSP*, pages 5174–5178. IEEE.

Rabee Naser and Abualsoud Hanani. 2018. Birzeit arabic dialect identification system for the 2018 vardial challenge. In *VarDial@COLING 2018*.

Mohammad Salameh, Houda Bouamor, and Nizar Habash. 2018. Fine-grained arabic dialect identification. In *Proceedings of the International Conference on Computational Linguistics (COLING)*, pages 1332–1344, Santa Fe, New Mexico, USA.

Mohand Tilmatine. 1999. Substrat et convergences: le berbre et l'arabe nord-africain. *Estudios de dialectolog'ia norteafricana y andalus'i, EDNA*, pages 99–120.

Cornelis Henricus Maria Versteegh. 2001. *The Arabic Language*. Edinburgh University Press Series. Edinburgh University Press.

Omar Zaidan and Chris Callison-Burch. 2011. Crowdsourcing translation: Professional quality from non-professionals. In *Proceedings of the 49th Annual Meeting of the Association for Computational Linguistics: Human Language Technologies*, pages 1220–1229, Portland, Oregon, USA. Association for Computational Linguistics.

Omar Zaidan and Chris Callison-Burch. 2014. Arabic dialect identification. *Computational Linguistics*, 40(1):171–202.

Arabic Dialect Identification for Travel and Twitter Text

Pruthwik Mishra and **Vandan Mujadia**
IIIT, Hyderabad
{pruthwik.mishra,vandan.mu}@research.iiit.ac.in

Abstract

This paper presents the results of the experiments done as a part of MADAR Shared Task in WANLP 2019 on Arabic Fine-Grained Dialect Identification. Dialect Identification is one of the prominent tasks in the field of Natural language processing where the subsequent language modules can be improved based on it. We explored the use of different features like char, word n-gram, language model probabilities, etc on different classifiers. Results show that these features help to improve dialect classification accuracy. Results also show that traditional machine learning classifier tends to perform better when compared to neural network models on this task in a low resource setting.

1   Introduction

In general, Arabic (language), refers to a wide spectrum of native languages used in Middle East and North Africa. As mentioned in Zaidan and Callison-Burch (2014), native languages of Arabic speakers differ with each other and with Modern Standard Arabic (MSA). These native languages or dialects can be categorized based on their common linguistic features and geographical locations (Elaraby and Abdul-Mageed, 2018). This categorization is described in detail in Bouamor et al. (2019). In the technological expansion of communication era, automatic identification of these dialects becomes an essential task for major natural language applications. These applications can be Machine Translation (Ling et al., 2013), Speech Recognition (Bouamor et al., 2018), Tourist Guide (Alshutayri and Atwell, 2017), Real-time Disaster Management (Elaraby and Abdul-Mageed, 2018; Alkhatib et al., 2019) and in health care. The task at hand was to identify a natural language dialect given a sequence of text for Arabic (Salameh and Bouamor, 2018). As per the shared tasks, these texts were either tourist help guide (subtask1) or the social media text (subtask2).

2   Related Work

Dialect identification is well known task in the Natural Language processing community. We can find work on different languages like English, German, Chinese, etc (Jauhiainen et al., 2018) for natural language dialect processing. Mostly it can be categorized into spoken and text level tasks. These categorization also includes work on resource creation for dialects (Zaidan and Callison-Burch, 2014; Zampieri et al., 2018) as well as the building a robust system for Dialect Identification. In Arabic, it is prerequisite for most NLP tasks, where many subsequent tasks depend on it. We can find spoken dialect identification work in Biadsy et al. (2009); Najafian et al. (2018); Shon et al. (2017), etc. For text, one can find recent work in Elaraby and Abdul-Mageed (2018); Salameh and Bouamor (2018); Abdul-Mageed et al. (2018); Butnaru and Ionescu (2018); Guellil et al. (2019).

MADAR shared task (Bouamor et al., 2019) consists of two sub-tasks which are

- MADAR Travel Domain Dialect Identification - this subtask requires identification of the dialect of a sentence, the dialect can be of any one of the pre-defined 26 arabic dialects as described in Bouamor et al. (2019)

- MADAR Twitter User Dialect Identification - this subtask requires the origin country of a tweet for a given user. We consider this classification task as a pipeline of 2 tasks. First we classify each tweet according to its country. Each user can tweet several times. The user to country mapping is decided based on frequency of the previous classification task. Each user is mapped to the most likely country predicted by the tweets s/he posts.

Proceedings of the Fourth Arabic Natural Language Processing Workshop, pages 234–238
Florence, Italy, August 1, 2019. ©2019 Association for Computational Linguistics

We utilized features and model described in Salameh and Bouamor (2018) as baselines for Arabic dialect identification on Corpus-26 (Bouamor et al., 2018). We wanted to replicate their model which used multinomial naive bayes classifier (Pedregosa et al., 2011) on character and word n-gram with language model score as features to get state of the art accuracy.

3 Data

The details of the datasets used for training, development and test, in different subtasks are given in the tables 1 and 2. In table 1, the training data was distributed into 26 classes named as MADAR-Corpus-26 where each class had 1600 samples. Each class had a representation of 200 samples in the dev data.

Type	#Sentences
train	41600
dev	5200
test	5200

Table 1: Corpus Details for subtask1

Type	#Users	#Tweets
train	2180	217592
dev	300	29869
test	500	49962

Table 2: Corpus Details for subtask2

4 Experimental Setup

4.1 Prepossessing

Preprocessing is a necessary step while handing textual data. The preprocessing steps involved in the subtasks are detailed below:-

- **Tokenization and Normalization :** We did not use any off-the-shelf tokenizer for the tweets. We used the standard technique of tokenizing the text on white spaces for both the tasks.

- **Text cleaning (Tweets) :** Unlike standard texts, tweets can contain different spelling variations of words, special characters, twitter handles, urls due to limited space. We tried different experiments to observe the impact of removal of the twitter handles and urls

on the overall classification accuracy. We observed that removal of these terms adversely affects the classification score. So we chose to keep the tweets as they were.

4.2 Feature Engineering

The features used for subtask1 were similar to those used in Salameh and Bouamor (2018). 3 different machine learning models were explored. All the below mentioned models were implemented using scikit-learn (Pedregosa et al., 2011) machine learning library.

- Linear SVM

- Multinomial Naive Bayes

- Logistic Regression

The individual features used in different subtasks are explained in detail here.

- **Subtask1**

  - **TF-IDF:** We used different combinations of word and character level n-grams for the tasks. We observed that combining word and character level n-gram TF-IDF vectors performed significantly better than individual word or character TF-IDF vectors. For our final submissions, combinations of word unigrams and character level n-grams were considered where n lies in $\{2, 3, 4, 5\}$.

  - **Language Modeling:** We trained different language models (LM) for the two types of corpora available to us. We trained the language model on sentences specific to a particular class for both MADAR-Corpus-6 (6 LMs) and MADAR-Corpus-26 (26 LMs). 2 features were included for these language models while developing machine learning models for subtask1. The coarse probabilities mentioned in table 3 came from the scores of the language model trained on MADAR-6 corpus. The final language model score was arrived at by adding the scores of the word and character 5-gram LMs for both the corpora.

- **Subtask2** For the first classification task in subtask2, we used the same word, character TF-IDF features and the same classifiers as

Model	N-gram Features		Other Features	P	R	F1	Acc
	Word	Char					
Baseline			Word 5-gram + Char 5-gram LM	67.7	67.4	67.4	67.4
mNB	1	1+2+3		64.9	63.9	63.7	63.9
mNB	1	2+3+4+5		66.3	65.0	64.9	65.0
mNB	1	1+2+3	Word&Char-5gram LM+Corpus 6 probs	**67.7**	**67.5**	**67.5**	**67.5**
mNB	1	2+3+4+5	Word&Char-5gram LM+Corpus 6 probs	**67.7**	**67.5**	67.4	**67.5**
SVM	1	1+2+3		64.3	63.9	63.9	63.9
SVM	1	2+3+4+5		64.8	64.4	64.4	64.4
SVM	1	1+2+3	Word&Char-5gram LM+Corpus 6 probs	67.7	67.4	67.4	67.4
SVM	1	2+3+4+5	Word&Char-5gram LM+Corpus 6 probs	67.7	67.4	67.4	67.4
logreg	1	1+2+3		64.4	64.0	63.9	64.0
logreg	1	2+3+4+5		65.3	65.0	65.0	65.0
logreg	1	1+2+3	Word&Char-5gram LM+Corpus 6 probs	67.7	67.4	67.4	67.4
logreg	1	2+3+4+5	Word&Char-5gram LM+Corpus 6 probs	67.7	67.4	67.4	67.4
MLP	1+2	1+2+3+4+5	50 neurons	65.12	64.17	64.37	64.17
MLP	1+2	1+2+3+4+5	100 neurons	66.68	65.9	66.0	65.9
MLP	1+2	1+2+3+4+5	200 neurons	67.39	66.63	66.78	66.63
MLP	1+2	1+2+3+4+5	50 neurons + Char LM	67.05	66.85	66.82	66.85
MLP	1+2	1+2+3+4+5	100 neurons + Char LM	66.83	66.67	66.62	66.67
MLP	1+2	1+2+3+4+5	200 neurons + Char LM	67.76	66.60	66.55	66.60

Table 3: Results On Dev Set for subtask1

mentioned in subtask1. We used the dialect probabilities as an additional feature which were present in the column 4 in the provided data. These dialect probabilities were obtained by the best model in Salameh and Bouamor (2018). We followed an ensemble approach for the classification task. Some of the tweets were unavailable in the training set. Some tweets consisted of only english tokens, so the arabic dialect probabilities were missing for those tweets. So we used two separate classifiers with the following features to handle data of different types

- Word Unigram, Character 2-5 gram TF-IDF vectors, dialect probabilities for the tweets which contained arabic text

- Word Unigram, Character 2-5 gram TF-IDF vectors for the tweets which contained no arabic text or contained only urls or twitter handles

During testing, different classifiers were used for inferencing with appropriate feature. We marked 'Saudi_Arabia' as the country of origin for a tweet which was unavailable because most of the tweets in the training set were from the users of Saudi Arab.

4.3 Deep Models

For subtask1, We have also tried out deep learning based classifier, where we used character and word level TF-IDF features as described above as input to the multi-layer perception (MLP). Here we used

Model	N-gram Features		Other Features	P	R	F1	Acc
	Word	Char					
SVM	1	1+2+3		87.8	49.8	60.0	66.3
SVM	1	2+3+4+5		88.0	50.0	60.07	66.7
SVM	1	2+3+4+5	Dialect Probabilities	87.9	49.6	59.8	66.3

Table 4: Results on Dev Set for subtask2

Subtask-Model	N-gram Features		Other Features	P	R	F1	Acc
	Word	Char					
subtask1-mNB	1	1+2+3	Word&Char-5gram LM+Corpus 6 probs	66.56	66.31	66.21	66.31
subtask2-SVM	1	1+2+3	Dialect Probabilities	83.37	47.73	57.90	67.20

Table 5: Results On Test Set for subtask1 and subtask2

sequential pipeline of keras[1] which contains one dense layer (with ReLU (Li and Yuan, 2017) activation) and output layer with softmax activation with categorical_crossentropy as loss function and Adam as optimizer. We trained this classifier for 30 epochs with early stopping criteria on GeForce GTX 1060 GPU. In result section, we show and discuss results in detail.

5 Observations

We could observe that all the classifiers performed similarly when all the features were used. Combination of character and word level TF-IDF vectors performed better than character or word level TF-IDF vectors in isolation. We could see that the language models trained at word and character level were the biggest contributor to the system's performance for subtask1. TF-IDF features and coarse probabilities did not add much to the overall accuracy. Logistic Regression and multinomial naive bayes techniques performed significantly poor for subtask2, so we did not report the results in this paper. Machine learning approaches performed marginally better than the multi-layer perceptrons. This could be due to the higher number of parameters that deep learning approaches try to learn compared to traditional approaches. One of the main reasons for lower classification accuracy in subtask2 is our assumption to assign country of origin for unavailable tweets as 'Saudi_Arabia'.

There were 5992 unavailable tweets in the test corpus.

6 Conclusion and Future Work

We presented our experiments on supervised dialect identification task (MADAR) in Arabic. Our experiments demonstrate that for relatively low resource task such as MADAR, traditional machine learning algorithms with feature engineering show their potentials compared to the deep learning approaches. Unlabelled Arabic corpora can be used to learn character and word embeddings in Arabic. It would be an interesting area to explore how recurrent neural networks perform on this task.

References

Muhammad Abdul-Mageed, Hassan Alhuzali, and Mohamed Elaraby. 2018. You tweet what you speak: A city-level dataset of arabic dialects. In *Proceedings of the Eleventh International Conference on Language Resources and Evaluation (LREC-2018)*.

Manar Alkhatib, May El Barachi, and Khaled Shaalan. 2019. An arabic social media based framework for incidents and events monitoring in smart cities. *Journal of Cleaner Production*, 220:771–785.

Areej Alshutayri and Eric Atwell. 2017. Exploring twitter as a source of an arabic dialect corpus. *International Journal of Computational Linguistics (IJCL)*, 8(2):37–44.

Fadi Biadsy, Julia Hirschberg, and Nizar Habash. 2009. Spoken arabic dialect identification using phonotactic modeling. In *Proceedings of the eacl 2009*

---
[1] https://keras.io

workshop on computational approaches to semitic languages, pages 53–61. Association for Computational Linguistics.

Houda Bouamor, Nizar Habash, Mohammad Salameh, Wajdi Zaghouani, Owen Rambow, Dana Abdulrahim, Ossama Obeid, Salam Khalifa, Fadhl Eryani, Alexander Erdmann, et al. 2018. The madar arabic dialect corpus and lexicon. In *Proceedings of the Eleventh International Conference on Language Resources and Evaluation (LREC-2018)*.

Houda Bouamor, Sabit Hassan, and Nizar Habash. 2019. The MADAR Shared Task on Arabic Fine-Grained Dialect Identification. In *Proceedings of the Fourth Arabic Natural Language Processing Workshop (WANLP19)*, Florence, Italy.

Andrei M Butnaru and Radu Tudor Ionescu. 2018. Unibuckernel reloaded: First place in arabic dialect identification for the second year in a row. *arXiv preprint arXiv:1805.04876*.

Mohamed Elaraby and Muhammad Abdul-Mageed. 2018. Deep models for arabic dialect identification on benchmarked data. In *Proceedings of the Fifth Workshop on NLP for Similar Languages, Varieties and Dialects (VarDial 2018)*, pages 263–274.

Imane Guellil, Houda Saâdane, Faical Azouaou, Billel Gueni, and Damien Nouvel. 2019. Arabic natural language processing: An overview. *Journal of King Saud University-Computer and Information Sciences*.

Tommi Jauhiainen, Marco Lui, Marcos Zampieri, Timothy Baldwin, and Krister Lindén. 2018. Automatic language identification in texts: A survey. *arXiv preprint arXiv:1804.08186*.

Yuanzhi Li and Yang Yuan. 2017. Convergence analysis of two-layer neural networks with relu activation. In *Advances in Neural Information Processing Systems*, pages 597–607.

Wang Ling, Guang Xiang, Chris Dyer, Alan Black, and Isabel Trancoso. 2013. Microblogs as parallel corpora. In *Proceedings of the 51st Annual Meeting of the Association for Computational Linguistics (Volume 1: Long Papers)*, volume 1, pages 176–186.

Maryam Najafian, Sameer Khurana, Suwon Shan, Ahmed Ali, and James Glass. 2018. Exploiting convolutional neural networks for phonotactic based dialect identification. In *2018 IEEE International Conference on Acoustics, Speech and Signal Processing (ICASSP)*, pages 5174–5178. IEEE.

Fabian Pedregosa, Gael Varoquaux, Alexandre Gramfort, Vincent Michel, Bertrand Thirion, Olivier Grisel, Mathieu Blondel, Peter Prettenhofer, Ron Weiss, Vincent Dubourg, Jake Vanderplas, Alexandre Passos, David Cournapeau, Matthieu Brucher, Matthieu Perrot, and Edouard Duchesnay. 2011. Scikit-learn: Machine learning in Python. *Journal of Machine Learning Research*, 12:2825–2830.

Mohammad Salameh and Houda Bouamor. 2018. Fine-grained arabic dialect identification. In *Proceedings of the 27th International Conference on Computational Linguistics*, pages 1332–1344.

Suwon Shon, Ahmed Ali, and James Glass. 2017. Mitqcri arabic dialect identification system for the 2017 multi-genre broadcast challenge. In *2017 IEEE Automatic Speech Recognition and Understanding Workshop (ASRU)*, pages 374–380. IEEE.

Omar F Zaidan and Chris Callison-Burch. 2014. Arabic dialect identification. *Computational Linguistics*, 40(1):171–202.

Marcos Zampieri, Shervin Malmasi, Preslav Nakov, Ahmed Ali, Suwon Shon, James Glass, Yves Scherrer, Tanja Samardžić, Nikola Ljubešić, Jörg Tiedemann, et al. 2018. Language identification and morphosyntactic tagging: The second vardial evaluation campaign. In *Proceedings of the Fifth Workshop on NLP for Similar Languages, Varieties and Dialects*. Association for Computational Linguistics.

Mawdoo3 AI at MADAR Shared Task:
Arabic Tweet Dialect Identification

Bashar Talafha   **Wael Farhan**   **Ahmed Altakrouri**   **Hussein T. Al-Natsheh**
Mawdoo3 Ltd, Amman, Jordan
{bashar.talafha, wael.farhan, ahmed.altakrouri, h.natsheh}@mawdoo3.com

Abstract

Arabic dialect identification is an inherently complex problem, as Arabic dialect taxonomy is convoluted and aims to dissect a continuous space rather than a discrete one. In this work, we present machine and deep learning approaches to predict 21 fine-grained dialects form a set of given tweets per user. We adopted numerous feature extraction methods most of which showed improvement in the final model, such as word embedding, Tf-idf, and other tweet features. Our results show that a simple LinearSVC can outperform any complex deep learning model given a set of curated features. With a relatively complex user voting mechanism, we were able to achieve a Macro-Averaged F1-score of 71.84% on MADAR shared subtask-2. Our best submitted model ranked second out of all participating teams.

1 Introduction

In recent years, an extensive increase in social media platforms usages, such as Facebook and Twitter, led to an exponential growth in the user-base generated content. The nature of this data is diverse. It comprises different expressions, languages, and dialects which attracted researchers to understand and harness language semantics such as sentiment, emotion, dialect identification, and many other Natural Language Processing (NLP) tasks. Arabic is one of the most spoken languages in the world, being used by many nations and spread across multiple geographical locations led to the generation of language variations (i.e., dialects) (Zaidan and Callison-Burch, 2014).

In this paper, we tackle the problem of predicting the user dialect from a set of his given tweets. We describe our work on exploring different machine and deep learning methods in our attempt to build a classifier for user dialect identification as part of MADAR (Multi-Arabic Dialect Applications and Resources) shared subtask-2 (Bouamor et al., 2018) (Bouamor et al., 2019). The task of user dialect identification can be seen as a text classification problem, where we predict the probability of a dialect given a sequence of words and other features provided by the task organizers. Besides reporting the results from different models, we show how the provided dataset for the task is not straightforward and requires additional analysis, feature engineering, and post-processing techniques.

In the next sections, we describe the methods followed to achieve our best model. Section 2 lists previous work done, Section 3 analyses the dataset, while Section 4 describes models and different approaches. Section 5 compares and discusses empirical results and finally conclude in Section 6.

2 Related Work

Recent work in the Arabic language tackles the task of dialect identification. Fine-grained dialect identification models proposed by Salameh et al. (2018) to classify 26 specific Arabic dialects with an emphasis on feature extraction. They trained multiple models using Multinomial Naive Bayes (MNB) to achieve a Macro-Averaged F1-score of 67.9% for their best model.

In addition to traditional models, deep learning methods tackle the same problem. The research proposed by Elaraby and Abdul-Mageed (2018), shows an enhancement in accuracy when compared to machine learning methods. In Huang (2015), they used weakly supervised data or distance supervision techniques. They crawled data from Facebook posts combined with a labeled dataset to increase the accuracy of dialect identification by 0.5%.

In this paper, we build on top of methods from Salameh et al. (2018) and Elaraby and Abdul-

Proceedings of the Fourth Arabic Natural Language Processing Workshop, pages 239–243
Florence, Italy, August 1, 2019. ©2019 Association for Computational Linguistics

	Train	**Dev**	**Test**
Available	195227	26750	43918
Unavailable	22365	3119	6044
Total	217592	29869	49962
Retweet	135388	17612	29868

Table 1: Distribution of the Train, Dev and Test sets used in our experiments.

Mageed (2018), by exploring machine and deep learning models to tackle the problem of fine-grained Arabic dialect identification.

3 Dataset

The dataset used in this work represents information about tweets posted from the Arabic region, where each tweet is associated with its dialect label (Bouamor et al., 2018) (Bouamor et al., 2019). This dataset is collected from 21 countries which are Algeria, Bahrain, Djibouti, Egypt, Iraq, Jordan, Kuwait, Lebanon, Libya, Mauritania, Morocco, Oman, Palestine, Qatar, Saudi_Arabia, Somalia, Sudan, Syria, Tunisia, United_Arab_Emirates, Yemen.

As shown in Figure 1, the distribution of tweets among countries is unbalanced. Around 35% of the tweets belong to Saudi Arabia, where only 0.08% belong to Djibouti.

The dataset contains 6 features for each user; username of the Twitter user, tweet ID, the language of the tweet as automatically detected by Twitter, a probability scores of 25 city dialects and MSA (Modern Standard Arabic) for each tweet obtained by running the best model described in (Salameh et al., 2018) and most importantly the tweet text.

Each user has at most 100 tweets, labeled with the same dialect, and exists in one set. For example, if a user is listed in the training set then that user will not exist in development nor test set. Moreover, the maximum length of each tweet is 280 characters including spaces, URLs, hashtags, and mentions which makes it challenging to identify the dialects automatically (Twitter).

Another challenge of the dataset is that around 61% of the tweets are retweets, as shown in Table 1. This means that the majority of the tweets are a re-post of other Twitter users. For example, the

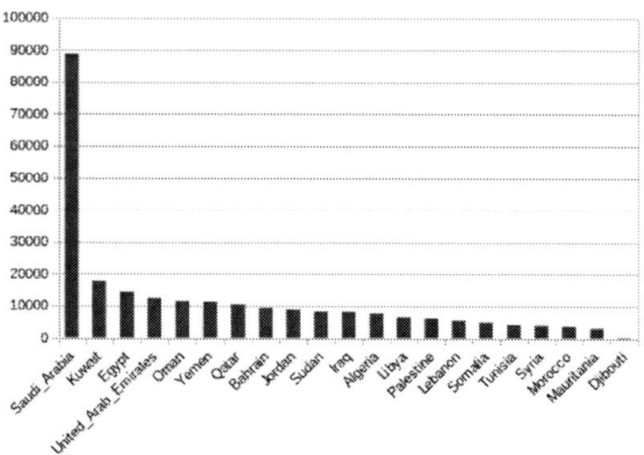

Figure 1: The distribution of 21 Arabic dialects in MADAR Twitter corpus

tweet "RT @Bedoon120: المخــرج عــاوز كـدا https://t.co/sIKqXCUSAn for the user @abushoooq8 is an Egyptian tweet but it has a label of Kuwait because the user who retweeted is Kuwaiti (i.e. @abushoooq8), where the original author is Egyptian (i.e. @Bedoon120).

Table 1 shows the distribution of available and unavailable data across different sets. It is also worth mentioning that around 10% of the data is missing; some tweets are not accessible because they were deleted by the author or owner account was deactivated.

4 Models

In this section, we explain our feature extraction methodology then we go over the various experimented approaches.

4.1 Feature Extraction

As a preprocessing step, normalization of Arabic letters is common when it comes to deal with Arabic text. We adopted the same preprocessing methodology used in (Soliman et al., 2017).

Aravec: A pre-trained word embedding models proposed by (Soliman et al., 2017) for the Arabic language using three different datasets: Twitter tweets, World Wide Web pages, and Wikipedia Arabic articles. Those models were trained using Word2Vec skip-gram and CBOW (Mikolov et al., 2013). In our experiments, we used the 300-dimensional Twitter Skip-gram AraVec model.

fastText: An extension to Word2Vec model proposed by (Bojanowski et al., 2017). The model feeds an input based on sub-words rather than passing the entire words. In our experiments, a model with 300 dimension was trained on a combination of 5 different datasets: AutoTweet (Almerekhi and Elsayed, 2015), ArapTweet (Zaghouani and Charfi, 2018), DART (Alsarsour et al., 2018), PADIC (Parallel Arabic DIalectal Corpus) (Harrat et al., 2014), MADAR shared tasks (Bouamor et al., 2018) (Bouamor et al., 2019).

Tf-idf: It has been proven that Tf-idf is efficient to encode textual information into real-valued vectors that represent the importance of a word to a document (Salameh et al., 2018). One of the drawbacks of Tf-idf vectorized representation of the text is that it looses the information of the word order (i.e., syntactical information). Considering n-grams, for both levels word and characters, reduces the effect of that drawback. Accordingly, unigram and bigram word level Tf-idf vectors were extracted in addition to a character level Tf-idf vectors with n-gram values ranging from 1 to 5.

Features specific to tweets: There are features that are unique to Twitter such as user mentions, (e.g., @abushooooq8) and emojis. It has been found that using username as a feature can help the model understand the user dialect, for instance, it can easily find that the users @7abeeb_ksa, @a_ksa2030 @alanzisaudi have a Saudi_Arabia dialect. Character level unigram Tf-idf has been extracted from each of the mentioned features.

4.2 Classification Methods

We used a range of classification methods starting from traditional machine learning methods into more complicated deep learning techniques.

4.2.1 Machine Learning Approaches

Traditional models include linear and probabilistic classifiers with various feature engineering techniques. We used SVM classifier that implements LinearSVC from the Scikit-learn library (Pedregosa et al., 2011). We used the LinearSVC model to predict the dialect given the tweet text represented as Tf-idf, username features and language model probabilities as formulated in Equation 1:

$$\hat{y} = \underset{d \in \mathcal{D}}{\operatorname{argmax}} P(d|tfidf, tweet\_feat, lm) \quad (1)$$

where $\hat{y}$ is the predicted dialect, D is probability space of all dialects, *tfidf* is the Tf-idf features extracted from a given tweet, *tweet_feat* is the tweet features and *lm* is the language model probabilities.

4.2.2 Deep Learning Approaches

fastText Classification: The word embedding of the words in an input sentence that is fed into a weighting average layer. Then, it is fed to a linear classifier with softmax output layer (Joulin et al., 2017).

SepCNN: Stands for Separable Convolutional Neural Networks (Denk, 2017), and is composed of two consecutive convolutional layers. The first is operating on the spatial dimension and performed on channels separately, while the second layer convolutes over the channel dimension only. Word embedding of the sentences is looked up from AraVec(Soliman et al., 2017). Then, the embedding of each word in the sentence (i.e., the tweet) are passed into a number of SepCNN blocks followed by a max pooling layer.

Word-level LSTM: A traditional deep learning classification method. The word sequence is passed into an AraVec layer to look up word embedding and then fed into a number of LSTM layers. The final word sequence is used as an input to a softmax layer to predict the dialect (Liu et al., 2016).

Char-Level CNN: In this architecture, the input is represented as characters that are converted into 128 character embedding. Those embedding vectors are then passed into a number of one-dimensional convolutional layers. Each convolutional layer is followed by a batch normalization layer to optimize training and to add a regularization factor. The final output is then passed into one hidden layer and followed by a softmax output layer (Zhang et al., 2015).

Char-Level CNN and Word-level LSTM: A combination of the previous two methods. The output of word-level LSTM is concatenated with character-Level CNN before passing both of them into a hidden layer followed by a softmax output layer.

Char-Level CNN and Word-level CNN: In this network words are transformed into word embedding using AraVec, then concatenated with the output of character level CNN. The concatenated result is fed into the LSTM layer, which computes the final output. Then, passed into a hidden layer and a softmax output layer to make the final prediction (Zhang et al., 2017).

Model	Hyperparameters	Dev		Test	
		Acc	F1	Acc	F1
LinearSVC	C=1.0, penalty=L2, loss=hinge, tolerance=0.0001	54.26	38.95	-	-
fastText Classifier	emb_size = 100	48.5	31.12	-	-
SepCNN	filters=128, dense_units=256, emb_size=300, kernel=4, blocks=3	45.46	26.30	-	-
Word LSTM	embed_size=300, dense_units=256, lstm_size=512	44.91	26.89	-	-
Word Bi-LSTM	embed_size=300, dense_units=256, lstm_size=512	45.08	26.36	-	-
Word LSTM with fastText	embed_size=300, dense_units=256, lstm_size=512	50.59	34.65	-	-
Char CNN	dense_units=256, char_embed=128, filters=64, kernel_sizes= [3, 3, 4]	41.55	20.25	-	-
Char CNN and Word LSTM	Combining hyperparameters of Char CNN and Word LSTM models	47.12	30.32	-	-
Char CNN and Word CNN	embed_size=300, char_embed_size=128, char_filters=[6,5,4,3,2]	43.96	29.0	-	-
LinearSVC Combined	C=1.0, penalty=L2, loss=hinge, tolerance=0.0001	77.33	70.43	75.40	65.54
LinearSVC with User Voting	ranges=5, retweet_weight=8, unavailable_weight=1, saudi_weight=1	**81.67**	**71.60**	**76.20**	**69.86**
LinearSVC with Threshold	C=1.0, penalty=L2, loss=hinge, tolerance=0.0001, threshold=75%	80.02	70.72	78.00	67.75

Table 2: Final results on the development set for MADAR shared subtask-2

5 Results and Discussion

Two types of experiments were conducted to evaluate our models. At first, each tweet was treated independently with its corresponding label in the training and testing stages without grouping tweets for each user. All our experiments on MADAR shared subtask-2 were evaluated using the Macro-Averaged F1-score. Table 2 shows the accuracy and Macro-Averaged F1-score of the LinearSVC model. LinearSVC outperformed other traditional machine learning models hence we discarded reporting their results. On the other hand, deep learning models are known to generalize better on a large dataset, but unexpectedly it under-performed machine learning models.

The second type of experiments were done by grouping predictions per user. The unifying approach was done by either combining all tweets together in one document per user or by applying voting per tweet. In the former, we applied LinearSVC on the combined data with averaging the language model scores for all the tweets per user. This model achieved results of 77.33% accuracy and 70.43% Macro-Averaged F1-score. In the latter, we took the output of the first model (Uncombined LinearSVC) and applied two voting techniques.

The first technique was user voting based on dialect weighting. This approach aims to give more emphasis on less frequent dialects by multiplying each predicted label with a weight associated for each dialect d_weight. Which is calculated as follows:

$$step = \frac{\sqrt[3]{max\_count} - \sqrt[3]{min\_count}}{5}$$

$$d\_weight = 6 - ceil\left(\frac{\sqrt[3]{d\_count} - \sqrt[3]{min\_count}}{step}\right)$$

Where max_count is the number of tweets for the largest dialect (i.e., Saudi_Arabia), min_count is the number of tweets for the smallest dialect (i.e., Djibouti), $step$ is a range defined as inverse cubic difference between maximum and minimum dialect counts divided by 5. $dialect\_weight$ is an integer between 1 and 6 that defines dialect weight. Moreover, we found that increasing the weight of a retweet to 6 enhanced the accuracy of the model, and decreasing the weight of <UNAVAILABLE> tweets to 1 had a similar effect. The final user voting model achieved 81.67% accuracy and 71.60% F1-score which is the best model as shown in Table 2

Secondly, the other voting technique is based on majority voting with a penalty on the largest dialect. In this approach, we took the most frequent label from user tweets as the final label for that user. We impose selecting Saudi_Arabia only if 75% of the predictions were Saudi_Arabia for a given user. This approach achieved 80.02% accuracy and 71.84% Macro-Averaged F1-score.

6 Conclusion

This paper describes various methods applied on MADAR shared subtask-2 to predict an Arabic dialect from a set of given tweets, username, and other features. Experimental results show that LinearSVC was the most powerful prediction model, achieving the best Macro-Averaged F1-score than other machine learning models and deep learning ones. Despite the fact that there was a substantial amount of unavailable tweets in our dataset, yet we were able to achieve a relatively high F1-score of 71.60% on the development set and 69.86% on the test set, ranking second in the competition.

References

Hind Almerekhi and Tamer Elsayed. 2015. Detecting automatically-generated arabic tweets. In *AIRS*, pages 123–134. Springer.

Israa Alsarsour, Esraa Mohamed, Reem Suwaileh, and Tamer Elsayed. 2018. Dart: A large dataset of dialectal arabic tweets. In *Proceedings of the Eleventh International Conference on Language Resources and Evaluation (LREC-2018)*.

Piotr Bojanowski, Edouard Grave, Armand Joulin, and Tomas Mikolov. 2017. Enriching word vectors with subword information. *Transactions of the Association for Computational Linguistics*, 5:135–146.

Houda Bouamor, Nizar Habash, Mohammad Salameh, Wajdi Zaghouani, Owen Rambow, Dana Abdulrahim, Ossama Obeid, Salam Khalifa, Fadhl Eryani, Alexander Erdmann, and Kemal Oflazer. 2018. The MADAR Arabic Dialect Corpus and Lexicon. In *Proceedings of the Language Resources and Evaluation Conference (LREC)*, Miyazaki, Japan.

Houda Bouamor, Sabit Hassan, and Nizar Habash. 2019. The MADAR Shared Task on Arabic Fine-Grained Dialect Identification. In *Proceedings of the Fourth Arabic Natural Language Processing Workshop (WANLP19)*, Florence, Italy.

Timo I. Denk. 2017. Text classification with separable convolutional neural networks.

Mohamed Elaraby and Muhammad Abdul-Mageed. 2018. Deep models for arabic dialect identification on benchmarked data. In *Proceedings of the Fifth Workshop on NLP for Similar Languages, Varieties and Dialects (VarDial 2018)*, pages 263–274.

Salima Harrat, Karima Meftouh, Mourad Abbas, and Kamel Smaili. 2014. Building resources for algerian arabic dialects. In *15th Annual Conference of the International Communication Association Interspeech*.

Fei Huang. 2015. Improved arabic dialect classification with social media data. In *Proceedings of the 2015 Conference on Empirical Methods in Natural Language Processing*, pages 2118–2126.

Armand Joulin, Edouard Grave, Piotr Bojanowski, and Tomas Mikolov. 2017. Bag of tricks for efficient text classification. In *Proceedings of the 15th Conference of the European Chapter of the Association for Computational Linguistics: Volume 2, Short Papers*, pages 427–431. Association for Computational Linguistics.

Pengfei Liu, Xipeng Qiu, and Xuanjing Huang. 2016. Recurrent neural network for text classification with multi-task learning. *arXiv preprint arXiv:1605.05101*.

Tomas Mikolov, Ilya Sutskever, Kai Chen, Greg S Corrado, and Jeff Dean. 2013. Distributed representations of words and phrases and their compositionality. In *Advances in neural information processing systems*, pages 3111–3119.

Fabian Pedregosa, Gaël Varoquaux, Alexandre Gramfort, Vincent Michel, Bertrand Thirion, Olivier Grisel, Mathieu Blondel, Peter Prettenhofer, Ron Weiss, Vincent Dubourg, et al. 2011. Scikit-learn: Machine learning in python. *Journal of machine learning research*, 12(Oct):2825–2830.

Mohammad Salameh, Houda Bouamor, and Nizar Habash. 2018. Fine-grained Arabic dialect identification. In *Proceedings of the International Conference on Computational Linguistics (COLING)*, pages 1332–1344, Santa Fe, New Mexico, USA.

Abu Bakr Soliman, Kareem Eissa, and Samhaa R El-Beltagy. 2017. Aravec: A set of arabic word embedding models for use in arabic nlp. *Procedia Computer Science*, 117:256–265.

Twitter. Api reference index twitter developers.

Wajdi Zaghouani and Anis Charfi. 2018. Arap-tweet: A large multi-dialect twitter corpus for gender, age and language variety identification. *arXiv preprint arXiv:1808.07674*.

Omar F Zaidan and Chris Callison-Burch. 2014. Arabic dialect identification. *Computational Linguistics*, 40(1):171–202.

Shiwei Zhang, Xiuzhen Zhang, and Jeffrey Chan. 2017. A word-character convolutional neural network for language-agnostic twitter sentiment analysis. In *Proceedings of the 22nd Australasian Document Computing Symposium*, page 12. ACM.

Xiang Zhang, Junbo Zhao, and Yann LeCun. 2015. Character-level convolutional networks for text classification. In *Advances in neural information processing systems*, pages 649–657.

Mawdoo3 AI at MADAR Shared Task:
Arabic Fine-Grained Dialect Identification with Ensemble Learning

Ahmed Ragab[*]   **Haitham Seelawi**[*]   **Mostafa Samir**[*]   **Abdelrahman Mattar**
Hesham Al-Bataineh   **Mohammad Zaghloul**   **Ahmad Mustafa**
Bashar Talafha   **Abed Alhakim Freihat**   **Hussein T. Al-Natsheh**
Mawdoo3 Ltd, Amman, Jordan
ai@mawdoo3.com

Abstract

In this paper we discuss several models we used to classify 25 city-level Arabic dialects in addition to Modern Standard Arabic (MSA) as part of MADAR shared task (sub-task 1). We propose an ensemble model of a group of experimentally designed best performing classifiers on a various set of features. Our system achieves an accuracy of 69.3% macro F1-score with an improvement of 1.4% accuracy from the baseline model on the DEV dataset. Our best run submitted model ranked as third out of 19 participating teams on the TEST dataset with only 0.12% macro F1-score behind the top ranked system.

1   Introduction

The term Arabic language is better thought of as an umbrella term for a gamut of the language varieties, spanning the far and apart geographies constituting the Arab world, some of which are not even mutually intelligible (Palmer, 2007). Until recently, the standard variety referred to as Modern Standard Arabic (MSA), was the only socially acceptable form of written communication. However, with the advent and ever-increasing adoption of web 2.0 technologies in the day to day life of Arab societies, dialectical variants of Arabic came to dominate written Arabic online, even though they usually don't have a formalized orthography or grammar (Zaidan and Callison-Burch, 2014). As a consequence, the detection of such dialects is having an increasingly larger number of use-cases of service and communication personalization for services providers targeting Arabic speaking customers over the internet.

The paper describes our submitted system to the MADAR shared task (sub-task 1) (Bouamor et al.,

2019). The task problem is to predict the Arabic dialect out of 26 class which include 25 city-level dialect in addition to MSA. The number of the participating team who submitted the prediction of their proposed system on the TEST dataset were 19 teams. Our proposed system was ranked 3rd in the shared task leader board with F1-macro score of 67.20%, and a difference of 0.12% from the winning system.

Our approach to the problem involves using TF–IDF features, both at the level of tokens and characters, augmented with class probabilities of a number of linear classifiers, and language model probabilities; all together as our set of potential features. For the classification system we developed for the sub-task, we used a standalone logistic regression model, and an ensemble of different types of classifiers, taking into a hard vote the prediction of each (i.e. we use the most probable class of each model instead of the full classes probabilities, to decide on the final prediction of the total ensemble). The choice of an ensemble system stems from the empirical evidence that on the whole, they perform significantly better than a single model (Dietterich, 2000).

In Section 2, we briefly present a previous work that was proposed to solve the same task and the same DEV dataset which is described in Section 3. The description of our proposed models is then discussed in detail in Section 4. Finally, the results of our models on the share task DEV and TEST datasets are discussed in Section 5 in comparison with both the baseline and the best performing model of the task.

2   Related Work

The closest work to our approach is presented in Salameh et al. (2018). The authors of that work proposed several classification methods and ex-

---

[*] These authors contributed equally to the work and ordered alphabetically on the first-name.

Proceedings of the Fourth Arabic Natural Language Processing Workshop, pages 244–248
Florence, Italy, August 1, 2019. ©2019 Association for Computational Linguistics

plore a large space of features to identify the exact city of a speaker. The task covers 25 cities from across the Arab World (from Rabat to Muscat), in addition to Modern Standard Arabic. The authors extract word n-grams ranging from unigrams to 5-grams and use them as features, in addition to character n-grams ranging from 1-grams to 5-grams. They computed TF–IDF scores. To boost up the accuracy they used language model to measure how close each sentence is to the dialect. For classification, they trained Multinomial Naive Bayes. The authors reported accuracy score of 67.9%.

3 Dataset

The dataset used for this shared task is the one provided by the Multi-Arabic Dialect Applications and Resources (MADAR). The task name is *MADAR travel domain dialect identification task.* This task is one of two sub-tasks presented and run in the Fourth Arabic Natural Language Processing Workshop (WANLP 2019)[1].The dataset is divided into two separate corpora; the first one is referred to as CORPUS-26 which consists of 25 city-level Arabic dialect in addition to MSA forming 26 dialect classes, with each of the 26 classes consists of 1,600 examples as training data and 200 examples per class as the DEV set. The second corpus, referred to as CORPUS-6, consists of 9,000 examples in 6 classes (5 cities plus MSA) as the training data and 1,000 for each of the 6 classes as the DEV set (Bouamor et al., 2018). Both corpora are annotated with the a code for the respective city dialect it represents.
Tokenizing on spaces, CORPUS-26, has a total of 294,718 words with 85,249 of them are unique, while CORPUS-6, has a total of 388,041 words with 63,860 of them are unique.

In Figure 1, we show the percentage of unique words, i.e. words that exclusively appear in the respective dialect class in the CORPUS-26 dataset. The figure also shows that most of the words in each class, appear in more than 4 of the other dialect classes, which in turn, help us choosing the set of features to build our model.

4 Models

The three models corresponding with the three submissions we made were mainly built upon:

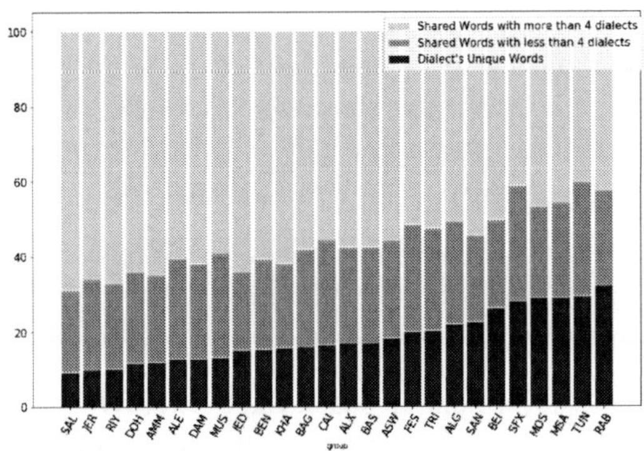

Figure 1: Words distribution among the 25 dialects and MSA sorted by the percentage of exclusive words.

i. TF–IDF vectorization of sentences

ii. Multinomial Naive Bayes classifier (MNB) similar to what is used in Salameh et al. (2018)

iii. The voting ensemble of multiple classifiers.

4.1 TF–IDF Features

We first preprocessed the data from CORPUS-26 by removing emojis and special characters. Then we extracted two sets of TF–IDF vectroized features: one on the words level, and the other on the character level.

Word n-grams: Word n-grams is one of the basic features used in dialect detection tasks and text classification tasks in general. We extracted word n-grams and vectorized the extractions in a feature vector using TF–IDF scores. Our experiments show that the feature vectors consisting of both word uni-grams and bi-grams result in more superior models than using any of them alone.

Character n-grams: While word n-grams are powerful features, they can suffer from a high out-of-vocabulary words (OOVs) rate when the testing set has a lot of varieties. This usually happens with Arabic text due to its morphological variance. Character n-grams on the other hand are able to mitigate this problem by capturing different parts of the word and hence reduces the effect of morphological segmentation on word similarities. We follow (Salameh et al., 2018) and use a TF–IDF vectorized feature set of character n-grams that range from 1-grams to 5-grams.

---

[1]https://sites.google.com/view/wanlp-2019

Moreover, we make sure that the extracted character n-grams respect the word boundaries; this has shown to perform better in our experiments in contrast to character n-grams that cross over the word boundaries.

We concatenate this feature vector into a bigger one that amounts to 236K features. This big vector is the main feature vector for our models.

4.2 Multinomial Naive Bayes (MNB)

In our base approach, we trained a multinomial naive Bayes classifier with additive smoothing to reduce the penalty of missing features in testing examples. While the smoothing parameter α is usually set to 1, our experiments showed that the best value for α was 0.1, which consists a Lidstone smoothing.

This setting achieved 68.3% accuracy on CORPUS-26 DEV set, which is 0.6% less than the best model in Salameh et al. (2018) although their model uses more features from dialectical language models. This MNB model was only used as a base for the other models that were submitted and it was not submitted itself.

4.3 Logistic Regression (LR)

Our second approach consisted of appending the class probabilities from the MNB model to the big features vector we constructed from word/character n-grams. This new feature vector is then fed into a logistic regression model with L2-regularization.

This 2-layered model improved about 0.04% over the MNB's accuracy. This suggests that more classifiers trained on the same feature vector can yield a bigger improvement by accumulating their smaller improvements, and this was the motivation behind our highest accuracy model.

4.4 Ensemble Model

Instead of training just an MNB model on TF–IDF features vector, we also trained a logistic regression model and weak dummy classifier used on prior probabilities of each dialect. The class probabilities from these three models were concatenated with the TF–IDF feature vector and the concatenation is then used for the second layer of the model.

In the second layer, instead of training just a logistic regression model, we included other classifiers to be trained on the TF–IDF plus probability features. In addition to the logistic regression, we trained:

i. Another MNB with one-vs-rest approach

ii. Support vector machine

iii. Bernoulli Naive Bayes classifier

iv. k-nearest-neighbours classifier with one-vs-rest approach and with samples weighted by distance

v. A weak dummy classifier based on prior probabilities of each dialect.

These classifiers were ensembled together by hard voting where we pick the dialect that was detected most by all the classifiers to be the final predicted dialect. This ensemble managed to score 69.3% in accuracy on CORPUS-26 DEV set.

4.5 Enemble with Language Model Scores as Features

We trained several language models (LMs) on character and word level using KenLM (Heafield, 2011) from Moses using default parameters. Twenty six character level language models were trained on CORPUS-26. We preprocessed the data to replace the spaces between words with special character and inserted spaces between characters so that each character is considered as a single token. Character based language models capture fine specifics of each dialect such as using the letter Meem (م) as a prefix of a verb and the letter Sheyn (ش) as a suffix negates the verb in the Egyptian dialect. Moreover, Character level LMs complement word based LMs by reducing the number of out-of-vocabulary words (OOVs). In addition to the 64 language models suggested by (Salameh et al., 2018) (i.e., twenty six 5-gram character-level LMs trained on CORPUS-26, twenty six 5-gram word-level LMs trained on CORPUS-26, six 5-gram char level LMs and six 5-gram word-level LMs trained on CORPUS-6), we added 26 bi-gram word level LMs trained on CORPUS-26 and 6 bi-gram word level LMs trained on CORPUS-6. Each sentence in training, DEV, and TEST data was scored by these 96 language models and we scaled the scores to 0-1 scale to lie within the same range of the other features, mainly TF-IDF. We used the scaled scores as input features to the classifiers.

Model	DEV		TEST	
	F1	Acc	F1	Acc
Baseline MNB	68.28	68.23	-	-
Run1: Ensemble	**69.33**	**69.28**	67.17	67.06
Run2: LR	68.32	68.27	66.37	66.37
Run3: Ensemble+LMs	69.16	69.11	67.20	67.08
MNB	-	68.90	**69.00**	**67.90**
ArbDialectID	-	-	67.32	67.29

Table 1: Results in terms of macro F1-score (F1) and accuracy (Acc) of our experimental baseline, our three models (i.e., runs) which are *Ensemble*, *LR* and *Ensemble + LMs* respectively, the best model of (Salameh et al., 2018) (MNB), and the top ranked system in MADAR shared task (ArbDialectID).

5 Results and Discussion

In Table 1, we report the results of our models and Salameh et al. (2018) best model on the DEV and TEST sets using the macro F1-score and accuracy metrics. First, it is shown that our baseline MNB model have outperformed Salameh et al. (2018) exact counterpart model with the same set of features on the DEV set. We deem this as a result of the Lidstone smoothing of an α equal to 0.1 instead of 1, which we hypothesize that it reduced the noise to signal ratio in the 236k element feature vector by reducing the pseudo-count for the missing features which constitute the majority of the feature vector in comparison to the actual features present in the input text. It is also shown that the Ensemble model described in section 4.4 is the best scorer on the DEV set, although it was out performed by Salameh et al. (2018) MNB on the TEST set. Also on the contrary of Salameh et al. (2018) findings that the word uni-gram and the character n-grams ranging from 1-grams to 3-grams resulted in the best performing model on the DEV set, we have found that the word uni-grams and bi-grams combined, alongside character n-grams ranging from 1-gram to 5-grams are the best performing features for our models.

It can be deduced from Figure 2 that the bulk of the error originates from the confusion between dialects within the same country or those that are very close geographically (e.g Cairo, Alexandria and Aswan dialects), the only exception to this would be the confusion between Mosul's dialect and MSA. This is demonstrated further by the best scoring Ensemble model on DEV which we hy-

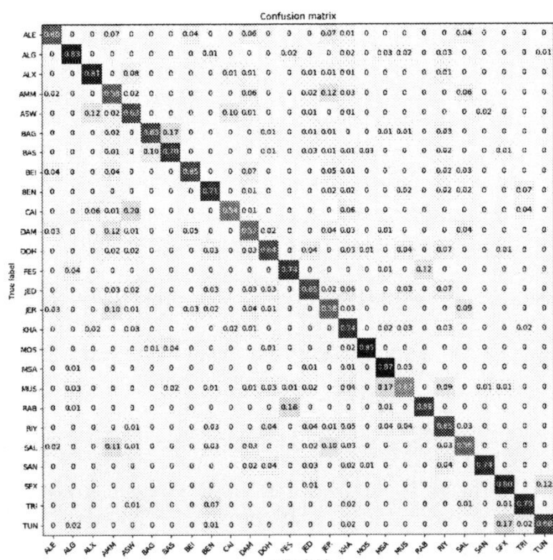

Figure 2: Normalized confusion matrix of our baseline MNB model on the DEV dataset.

pothesize that its second layer managed to learn from the non-orthographic probability features of the first layer by detecting its biases and error distribution, thus enhancing upon it. We believe that a human benchmark might be useful for this fine-grained dialect detection problem, for which it would set a reasonable upper-bound that shows the significance of the orthographic features in determining the writer's dialect through the analysis of the human error.

6 Conclusion

We proposed a system for classifying 26 dialects of Arabic. Our system uses ensembles at the level of features and classifiers. At the feature level, we augment textual features extracted directly from text with class probabilities of a few linear classifiers. For the model level, we use an ensemble of a number of different discriminators. Our system achieved a macro F-1 score of 69.33% and 66.7% on the development and test sets of the MADAR Arabic Dialect Corpus, respectively. In the future, we plan on using word embedding as an extra set features to experiment with. This will focus on context aware word embedding such as ELMo (Peters et al., 2018), and BERT (Devlin et al., 2018).

References

Houda Bouamor, Nizar Habash, Mohammad Salameh, Wajdi Zaghouani, Owen Rambow, Dana Abdulrahim, Ossama Obeid, Salam Khalifa, Fadhl Eryani, Alexander Erdmann, and Kemal Oflazer. 2018. The MADAR Arabic Dialect Corpus and Lexicon. In *Proceedings of the Language Resources and Evaluation Conference (LREC)*, Miyazaki, Japan.

Houda Bouamor, Sabit Hassan, and Nizar Habash. 2019. The MADAR Shared Task on Arabic Fine-Grained Dialect Identification. In *Proceedings of the Fourth Arabic Natural Language Processing Workshop (WANLP19)*, Florence, Italy.

Jacob Devlin, Ming-Wei Chang, Kenton Lee, and Kristina Toutanova. 2018. BERT: pre-training of deep bidirectional transformers for language understanding. *CoRR*, abs/1810.04805.

Thomas G. Dietterich. 2000. Ensemble methods in machine learning. In *Multiple Classifier Systems, First International Workshop, MCS 2000, Cagliari, Italy, June 21-23, 2000, Proceedings*, volume 1857 of *Lecture Notes in Computer Science*, pages 1–15. Springer.

Kenneth Heafield. 2011. Kenlm: Faster and smaller language model queries. In *Proceedings of the Sixth Workshop on Statistical Machine Translation, WMT@EMNLP 2011, Edinburgh, Scotland, UK, July 30-31, 2011*, pages 187–197. Association for Computational Linguistics.

Jeremy Palmer. 2007. Arabic diglossia: Teaching only the standard variety is a disservice to students. *The Arizona Working Papers in Second Language Acquisition and Teaching*, 14:111–122.

Matthew E. Peters, Mark Neumann, Mohit Iyyer, Matt Gardner, Christopher Clark, Kenton Lee, and Luke Zettlemoyer. 2018. Deep contextualized word representations. In *Proceedings of the 2018 Conference of the North American Chapter of the Association for Computational Linguistics: Human Language Technologies, NAACL-HLT 2018, New Orleans, Louisiana, USA, June 1-6, 2018, Volume 1 (Long Papers)*, pages 2227–2237. Association for Computational Linguistics (ACL).

Mohammad Salameh, Houda Bouamor, and Nizar Habash. 2018. Fine-grained Arabic dialect identification. In *Proceedings of the International Conference on Computational Linguistics (COLING)*, pages 1332–1344, Santa Fe, New Mexico, USA.

Omar Zaidan and Chris Callison-Burch. 2014. Arabic dialect identification. *Computational Linguistics*, 40(1):171–202.

Hierarchical Deep Learning for Arabic Dialect Identification

Gaël de Francony
LSE, EPITA, France
gael.de-francony@epita.fr

Victor Guichard
LSE, EPITA, France
victor.guichard@epita.fr

Praveen Joshi
CIT, Ireland
praveen.joshi@mycit.ie

Haithem Afli
ADAPT Centre, CIT, Ireland
haithem.afli@adaptcentre.ie

Abdessalam Bouchekif
LSE, EPITA, France
abdessalam.bouchekif@epita.fr

Abstract

In this paper, we present two approaches for Arabic Fine-Grained Dialect Identification. The first approach is based on Recurrent Neural Networks (BLSTM, BGRU) using hierarchical classification. The main idea is to separate the classification process for a sentence from a given text in two stages. We start with a higher level of classification (8 classes) and then the finer-grained classification (26 classes). The second approach is given by a voting system based on Naive Bayes and Random Forest. Our system achieves an $F1$ score of 63.02% on the subtask evaluation dataset.

1 Introduction

Online platforms such as Social Media have become the default channel for people to actively participate in the generation of online content in different languages and dialects. Arabic is one of the fastest growing languages used on these platforms. There are many differences between Dialectal Arabic and Modern Standard Arabic which cause many challenges for Arabic language processing. Therefore, identifying the dialect in which posts are written is very important for understanding what has been written over these online platforms.

Shoufan and Alameri (2015) presents a wide literature review of natural language processing for dialectical Arabic. The authors highlighted the huge lack of freely available dialectal corpora which was mentioned in (Zaghouani, 2014).

Although Arabic dialects are related but there are some lexical, phonological and morphological differences between them (Habash et al., 2013; Azab et al., 2013; Attia et al., 2012). Most recently, (Bouamor et al., 2018; Salameh et al., 2018; AL-Walaie and Khan, 2017) started to investigate the problem of the Arabic Dialect Identification with different classification methods.

In this paper, we are describing our work in the same research direction using the MADAR shared task corpus described in (Bouamor et al., 2019). The goal of this task is to classify a given text into one of 26 classes, corresponding to various dialects of Arabic language.

The remainder of this paper is organized as follows. In section 2, we describe the different techniques used in this work. In Section 3, we present our experimental setup and discuss the models and features used as well as our results. Finally, in Section 4 we conclude and give our future directions.

2 System Description

In the next few paragraphs, we will describe the two main methods we used in the MADAR shared task. The first one is based on deep learning with a hierarchical classification of dialects. The second one is based on the combination of Naive Bayes and Random Forest.

2.1 Hierarchical Deep Learning

We address the fine-grained identification of 25 dialects and the Modern Standard Arabic (MSA). Given the number of different dialects and the small size of the data set provided, deep learning algorithms didn't perform well. Our proposed method will aim to handle this problem by decreasing the number of classes the models need to predict. This is achieved using a hierarchical classification similar to the work described in Kowsari et al. (2017).

The classes are separated geographically and represent the dialects of 25 Arabic cities. Some of these dialects are remarkably similar, in particular for cities of the same country/region (Salameh et al., 2018).Some dialects can be clustered to form a larger group. These groups are determined by the geographical distribution of the cities and the similarities between each dialect. This distribution is shown in table 1.

Proceedings of the Fourth Arabic Natural Language Processing Workshop, pages 249–253
Florence, Italy, August 1, 2019. ©2019 Association for Computational Linguistics

Group 1	Group 2	Group 3	Group 4	Group 5	Group 6	Group 7	Group 8
Tunis Sfax	Rabat Fes Algiers	Tripoli Benghazi	Cairo Alexandria Aswan Khartoum	Doha Muscat Riyadh Jeddah Sana'a	Mosul Baghdad Basra	Jerusalem Amman Salt Beirut Damascus Aleppo	MSA

Table 1: Dialect distribution in groups.

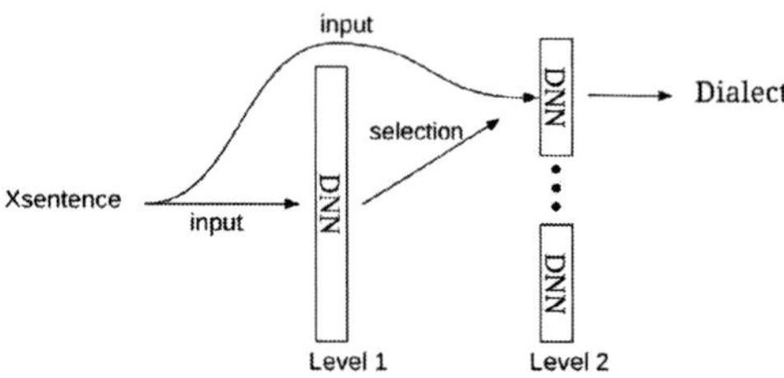

Figure 1: Hierarchical deep learning architecture.

A deep neural network (DNN) is trained to predict a group given a sentence. This model serves as the base for our system. Then for each dialect, a different model is trained. These models make predictions on their respective subset of dialects. Following this technique, two levels of DNNs are defined. First a base whose predictions are used to choose from a set of DNNs. The chosen one is then used to identify the dialect. The system architecture is presented in figure 1.

2.2 Vote Based Probabilistic Classifier

The low size of our data set made statistical models perform much better than the deep learning methods. Our proposed method will take into account the large number of classes by creating two different pipelines. The first one uses a Multinomial Naive Bayes. The second model uses a Random Forest Classifier. These models were implemented using the package scikit-learn (Pedregosa et al., 2011). The pipelines are pre-trained before they are given to the voting classifier. Then, the whole system is trained again to maximize the model performance for the dialects classification task. The data is first given into a count vectorizer then into a TF-IDF tranformer to extract meaningful information on word level. The voting classifier uses a hard voting method to select the model with the correct prediction.

3 Experiments and Results

3.1 Data

We used the data set provided by the MADAR Shared Task. The corpus covers the dialects of 25 Arab cities and the MSA. It is the same data set described in Bouamor et al. (2019) and Salameh et al. (2018). This corpus is composed of 2000 sentences translated to each dialect, with a total of 52000 sentences. We refer to this set as the MADAR corpus. We split this data set evenly between dialects in three parts: 80% constitutes the Train set, 10% the Dev and the last 10% the Test set. In our experiment, we limit the length of the sequences to 40 words and pad the sequences with zeros. For preprocessing we remove all non Arabic characters with the exception of Arabic numbers. To maximize the precision of the hierarchical deep learning system the input of the models is produced by a word2vec. The word2vec we used was trained separately using a database of over 32 million tweets. This data was downloaded using keywords extracted from the MADAR corpus. We used the score of a TF-IDF to find the most relevant words from each dialect. Tweets containing one of these words were downloaded and added to this data set. This way we could ensure a dialectal weight on the word embeddings.

3.2 Hierarchical Deep Learning

In our models, we used Bidirectional Long Short-Term Memory networks (B-LSTM) (Schuster and Paliwal, 1997). It consists of two LSTM networks running in parallel in different directions. Each LSTM generates a hidden representation: the first is generated by reading the input sequence from left to right and the second form right to left. This representations are then combined to compute the output sequence.

The architecture of the hierarchical system is composed of two levels (see the figure 1). The level one is a DNN with three layers: A B-LSTM

Dialect	Precision	Recall	F1-sore
ALE	0.58	0.68	0.63
ALG	0.82	0.75	0.78
ALX	0.78	0.73	0.75
AMM	0.53	0.49	0.51
ASW	0.59	0.55	0.57
BAG	0.58	0.75	0.66
BAS	0.68	0.68	0.68
BEI	0.60	0.69	0.64
BEN	0.70	0.67	0.68
CAI	0.47	0.66	0.55
DAM	0.54	0.56	0.55
DOH	0.64	0.60	0.62
FES	0.70	0.63	0.66
JED	0.61	0.57	0.59
JER	0.61	0.45	0.52
KHA	0.69	0.53	0.60
MOS	0.78	**0.83**	**0.80**
MSA	**0.84**	0.61	0.71
MUS	0.42	0.60	0.49
RAB	0.55	0.75	0.63
RIY	0.61	0.53	0.57
SAL	0.49	0.59	0.53
SAN	0.70	0.81	0.75
SFX	0.77	0.68	0.72
TRI	0.76	0.76	0.76
TUN	0.64	0.77	0.70
ALL	0.64	0.65	0.64

Table 2: Macro average of precision, recall and F1-score for vote based approach (Higher is better).

Model	F1
Deep learning	0.56
Hierarchical Deep Learning	0.58
Voting Classifier	**0.64**

Table 3: F1-score summary (higher is better).

Model	Precision	Recall	F1-score
G1	0.78	0.88	0.83
G2	0.82	0.89	0.85
G3	0.69	0.80	0.74
G4	0.82	0.79	0.81
G5	0.66	0.74	0.70
G6	0.84	0.80	0.82
G7	0.89	0.77	0.83
MSA	0.76	0.71	0.73
Avg.	0.79	0.80	0.78

Table 4: Hierarchical system level 1 precision.

of 128 neurons followed by a fully-connected layer of size 64 and a fully-connected layer of size 8 with softmax activation for the output. The level two is a set of 7 DNNs. For each of this models the size of the layers and the type of Recurrent Neural Network (RNN) units used is different. This is done in order to adapt each model to the number of classes it has to handle as well as to have a proportional number of parameters with the size of the groups data set. The models utilize the following pattern: They are composed of three layers. The first is a RNN layer, either B-LSTM or a B-GRU with a size ranging between 32 and 64 units. Then a fully-connected layer of size ranging between 32 and 64. Finally a fully-connected layer with softmax activation for the output.

All models were trained using the following parameters: batch size = 100, learning rate = 0.001, $\beta1 = 0.9$, $\beta2 = 0.999$, decay = 0. The cost function used was the cross entropy. Two gradient descent optimizers where used for training: the RMSProp and the Adamax. To metric the possible improvement of this system we compare the results with a baseline. This baseline is a deep neural network with a similar architecture as the ones found in the hierarchical system.

3.3 Vote Based Probabilistic Classifier

The statistical method performed much better than the Deep learning method. In this section we describe the pipeline using different parameters. To define the accuracy we used the F-1 macro average score. By changing parameters of each pipeline, our results change drastically. We found that for the Naive Bayes the *alpha* at 0.3 was giving the best performance. For the Random Forest Classifier (RFC), random states set to 2 was also giving the best results. Using 250 estimators and a 200 depth, the RFC was performing the best, leading up to a 4% increase in F1-score.

3.4 Results

The table 5 shows the result of each DNN in the hierarchical system. We notice good performance for some groups such as G3 and G2. However, the improvement in accuracy is not as substantial in most of the groups. Notably the performance of the seventh group only reaching a score of 0.55. This translates to a poor performance on the overall system. We see in table 3 that the hierarchical separation of dialects outperforms the simpler DNN by only 1.4%. Both models can have trou-

Model	Class	Precision	Recall	F1-score	Model	Class	Precision	Recall	F1-score
G1	TUN	.65	.76	.70	G5	DOH	.74	.68	.71
	SFX	.80	.69	.74		MUS	.69	.73	.71
	Avg.	.72	.73	.72		RIY	.61	.60	.61
G2	RAB	.69	.70	.70		JED	.69	.73	.70
	FES	.65	.68	.66		SAN	.77	.75	76
	ALG	.89	.83	.86		Avg.	.70	.70	.70
	Avg.	.74	.74	.74	G6	MOS	.84	.85	.85
G3	TRI	.89	.86	.87		BAG	.73	.65	.69
	BEN	.86	.88	.87		BAS	.60	.66	.63
	Avg.	.87	.87	.87		Avg.	.72	.72	.72
G4	CAI	.58	.64	.61	G7	JER	.55	.47	.51
	ALX	.79	.71	.75		AMM	.53	.49	.51
	ASW	.60	.63	.61		SAL	.58	.61	.59
	KHA	.86	.84	.85		BEI	.58	.70	.63
	Avg.	.71	.70	.71		DAM	.50	.46	.48
						ALE	.58	.64	.61
						Avg.	.56	.55	.55

Table 5: Hierarchical system level 2 precision.

Sentence	Prediction	Label
نحب كاس ماء باش نشرب الدواء ، يعيشك I want a glass of water to take my medicine, please.	SFX	TUN
نحب كاس ماء باش ناخذ الدواء ، يعيشك I want a glass of water to drink my medicine, please.	SFX	SFX

Table 6: Voting classifier predictions on close sentence of similar dialects.

ble on similar dialects. For example, the first two sentences of table 6, are very similar. The first one is from *Tunis* whereas the second one is from *Sfax* which both belong to the same group. Because of this similarity, the models cannot make a correct distinction and often miss predict the correct label. Nonetheless, the statistical method provides good result when dialects are very close. Tunis and *Sfax* have both a good F1-score, even with some confusion due to similar sentences. However it struggles to identify dialects such as *Mosul* (MOS), *Cairo* (CAI) and *Salt* (SAL) which have a very low precision (table 2). The results can be explained by the fact that the amount of data available was very low which can lead to an overfitting of the deep learning model. The voting classifier perform 9% better (table 3).

4 Conclusion and Future Work

In this paper, we propose to use two different methods for Arabic dialect identification: the Hierarchical Deep Neural Network and the Hard Voting Classifier. The hierarchical model uses two levels of DNNs where the first one predicts the group of a dialect, and the second one predicts the dialect according to the previous prediction. The method based on a statistical model is composed of a Multinomial Naive Bayes and a Random Forest Classifier connected by a Hard Voting Classifier. This model outperformed the F1-score results of the Hierarchical Deep Neural Network.

In the future, we plan to work on the combination of two neural networks. The output of the first model will be a vector composed of probabilities for each group. The second one, will take as input the sentence as well as the output of the previous model as a new feature.

Acknowledgments

This research is partially supported by EPITA Systems Laboratory (www.lse.epita.fr) and Science Foundation Ireland through ADAPT Centre (Grant 13/RC/2106) (www.adaptcentre.ie) at Cork Institute of Technology.

References

Mona Abdullah AL-Walaie and Muhammad Badruddin Khan. 2017. Arabic dialects classification using text mining techniques . In *Proceedings of the International Conference on Computer and Applications (ICCA)*, pages 325–329, Dubai, United Arab Emirates.

Mohammed Attia, Pavel Pecina, Younes Samih, Khaled Shaalan, and Josef van Genabith. 2012. Improved spelling error detection and correction for arabic. In *Proceedings of COLING 2012*, pages 103–112.

Mahmoud Azab, Houda Bouamor, Behrang Mohit, and Kemal Oflazer. 2013. Dudley north visits north london: Learning when to transliterate to arabic. In *Proceedings of NAACL-HLT 2013*, pages 439–444.

Houda Bouamor, Nizar Habash, Mohammad Salameh, Wajdi Zaghouani, Owen Rambow, Dana Abdulrahim, Ossama Obeid, Salam Khalifa, Fadhl Eryani, Alexander Erdmann, and Kemal Oflazer. 2018. The MADAR Arabic Dialect Corpus and Lexicon. In *Proceedings of the Eleventh International Conference on Language Resources and Evaluation (LREC 2018)*, Miyazaki, Japan.

Houda Bouamor, Sabit Hassan, and Nizar Habash. 2019. The MADAR Shared Task on Arabic Fine-Grained Dialect Identification. In *Proceedings of the Fourth Arabic Natural Language Processing Workshop (WANLP19)*, Florence, Italy.

Nizar Habash, Ryan Roth, Owen Rambow, Ramy Eskander, and Nadi Tomeh. 2013. Morphological analysis and disambiguation for dialectal arabic. In *Proceedings of NAACL-HLT 2013*, pages 426–432.

Kamran Kowsari, Donald E. Brown, Mojtaba Heidarysafa, Kiana Jafari Meimandi, Matthew S. Gerber, and Laura E. Barnes. 2017. Hdltex: Hierarchical deep learning for text classification. In *16th IEEE International Conference on Machine Learning and Applications, ICMLA 2017, Cancun, Mexico, December 18-21, 2017*, pages 364–371.

Fabian Pedregosa, Gael Varoquaux, Alexandre Gramfort, Vincent Michel, Bertrand Thirion, Olivier Grisel, Mathieu Blondel, Peter Prettenhofer, Ron Weiss, Vincent Dubourg, Jake Vanderplas, Alexandre Passos, David Cournapeau, Matthieu Brucher, Matthieu Perrot, and Edouard Duchesnay. 2011. Scikit-learn: Machine learning in Python. *Journal of Machine Learning Research*.

Mohammad Salameh, Houda Bouamor, and Nizar Habash. 2018. Fine-Grained Arabic Dialect Identification. In *Proceedings of the 27th International Conference on Computational Linguistic*, page 13321344, Santa Fe, New Mexico, USA.

Mike Schuster and Kuldip K. Paliwal. 1997. Bidirectional recurrent neural networks. *IEEE Transactions on Signal Processing*.

Abdulhadi Shoufan and Sumaya Alameri. 2015. Natural language processing for dialectical arabic: A survey. In *ANLP@ACL*.

Wajdi Zaghouani. 2014. Critical survey of the freely available arabic corpora. In *International Conference on Language Resources and Evaluation (LREC'2014), OSACT Workshop*.

ArbDialectID at MADAR Shared Task 1:
Language Modelling and Ensemble Learning
for Fine Grained Arabic Dialect Identification

Kathrein Abu Kwaik
Gothenburg University
Sweden
kathrein.abu.kwaik@gu.se

Motaz Saad
The Islamic University of Gaza
Palestine
motaz.saad@gmail.com

Abstract

In this paper, we present a Dialect Identification system (ArbDialectID) that competed at Task 1 of the MADAR shared task, MADAR Travel Domain Dialect Identification. We build a coarse and a fine grained identification model to predict the label (corresponding to a dialect of Arabic) of a given text. We build two language models by extracting features at two levels (words and characters). We firstly build a coarse identification model to classify each sentence into one out of six dialects, then use this label as a feature for the fine grained model that classifies the sentence among 26 dialects from different Arab cities, after that we apply ensemble voting classifier on both subsystems. Our system ranked 1st that achieving an f-score of 67.32%. Both the models and our feature engineering tools are made available to the research community.

1 Introduction

Arabic Language is one of the most spoken languages in the world. Furthermore, Arabic presents us with a special case of Diglossia (Ferguson, 1959), where the spoken language is different than the formal language. Speakers of Arabic use Modern Standard Arabic (MSA) as the official language in very formal situations like education, religion, media, and politics, while they use an Arabic Dialect (AD) for everyday conversation (Shah, 2008; Versteegh, 2014).

With the emergence of social media, speakers of Arabic use their dialects to tweet, post, socialize and express themselves. The Arabic Dialects (AD) do not have a standardized writing and/or orthography, and they do not have a formal grammar. These characteristics make the task of identifying dialects more challenging.

The task of Arabic Dialect Identification (ADI) has recently attracted research attention, building identification systems able to differentiate among the dialects have been attempted. Even though dialects share similar features in term of lexical, syntax, morphology and semantics, they still have many differences which, of course, complicates the identification task.

Many works addressed the problem of dialect identification. They have reported different dialectal divisions, according to the geo-location, the country or, in some cases, on the level of cities. Most of those works used Machine learning classifiers and language modelling and achieved a good accuracy depending on the level of identification and either they explored the coarse grained identification, where the differences between the individual dialects are clear or a fine grained identification, where the differences become hard to detect in text as the dialects look very similar to each others (Zbib et al., 2012; Cotterell and Callison-Burch, 2014; Zaidan and Callison-Burch, 2014; Qwaider et al., 2018; Elfardy and Diab, 2013).

Other approaches investigated the use of Deep Learning (DL) methods to identify dialects. As such, they tried different DL architectures like LSTMs, CNNs and attention networks, and have employed different word embedding models. Elaraby and Abdul-Mageed (2018) benchmarked the Arabic Online Commentary (AOC) (Zaidan and Callison-Burch, 2011) and tested six different deep learning methods on the ADI task, comparing performance to several classical machine learning models under different conditions (both binary and multi-way classification). Their models reached 87.65% accuracy on the binary task (MSA vs. dialects), 87.4% accuracy on the three-way dialect task (Egyptian, Gulf, Levantine), and 82.45% accuracy on the four-way classification task (MSA, Egyptian, Gulf, Levantine). Similarly, Lulu and Elnagar (2018) explored the DL methods with different networks structure using AOC

Proceedings of the Fourth Arabic Natural Language Processing Workshop, pages 254–258
Florence, Italy, August 1, 2019. ©2019 Association for Computational Linguistics

on a three-way classification, with LSTM they achieved 71.4% accuracy

This paper presents our participation in MADAR shared task (Bouamor et al., 2019). We participate in Task 1: MADAR travel domain dialect identification, and we ranked 1st in the task with accuracy of 67.3%. We present our proposed model (ArbDialectID) in details and the code is available at GitHub[1].

The rest of this paper is organized as follow: Section 3 discusses the used data and presents our proposed model, we discusses the results in Section 4 and conclude in Section 5.

2 ArbDialectID: Arabic Dialect Identification System

This section introduces our proposed model which is applied on MADAR corpus for dialect identification shared task. MADAR corpus (Bouamor et al., 2018) is a parallel corpus in travel domain, it contains 25 dialects from different Arab cities in addition to the MSA. This corpus has been used for AID task in (Salameh et al., 2018), where the authors applied language modeling with various combinations of word and character levels and trained the model by MNB classifier. They got 67.9% accuracy for 26 classification task.

Our model consists of two sub models and exploiting two different data set as shown in Figure 1. The first model tries to predict the dialect among six different Arab dialects and known as coarse grained level, followed by the second model which goes much deeper and is known as a fine grained level to classify 26 Arabic dialects.

In both of our sub models we use MADAR data set to build and evaluate the models. Table 1 shows the number of sentences/samples per dialects and the total sentences for each data set. All of the experiments are implemented by Python and with the help of `scikit learn` library (Pedregosa et al., 2011).

MADAR	Split	sentences	Total
Corpus-6	train	9,000	41,600
	dev	1,000	6,000
Corpus-26	train	1,600	41,600
	dev	200	5,200
	test	200	5,200

Table 1: Statistics for MADAR data sets

[1]https://github.com/motazsaad/ArbDialectID

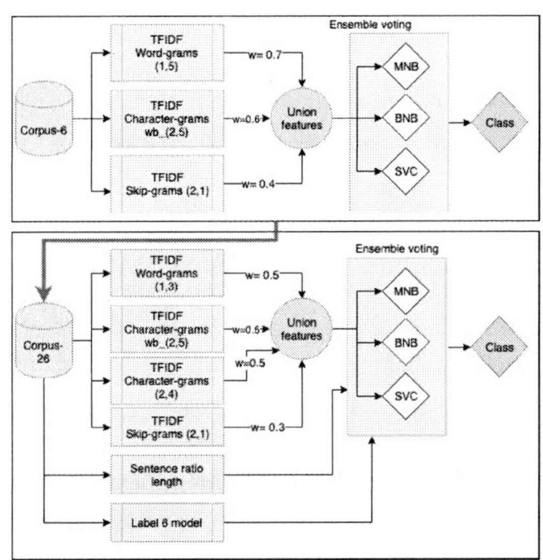

Figure 1: ArbDialectID proposed model

2.1 Coarse Grained Dialect Identification

This is the first model where we classify among five different Arab dialects from five Arabic countries, which are covered by MADAR corpus, they are: Beirut (BEI), Cairo (CAI), Doha (DOH), Rabat (RAB), Tunisia (TUN), In addition to (MSA).

We build a model that depends on the language modelling and exploring different combinations of n-grams in the word level and the character level. We use *FeatureUnion* in *sklearn*, which is an estimator that concatenates results of multiple transformer objects. To build and train the model we extract the following features:

- TF-IDF vectors from the word grams ranged from the unigram to 5-grams. We apply 0.7 weight for vector transformation
- TF-IDF vectors from the character n-grams with word boundary consideration ranged from bigrams to 5-grams and the transformation weight is 0.6
- Apply skip grams , then we extract the unigram words with one word skipping. We give it the lowest transformation weight of 0.4

The transformation weight is a weight used in *FeatureUnion* to give a weight for the feature. We choose these weights empirically after many experiments that investigate various weights with many features combinations.

After features extraction process, we build an ensemble voting classifier with hard voting, where it uses predicted class labels for majority rule voting. The ensemble classifiers consists of the following best standalone Machine Learning algorithms:

- MultinomialNB (MNB) , we set alpha to 0.01
- Linear SVC with l2 penalty and the learning rate sets to 0.0001
- BernoulliNB (BNB), set alpha = 0.01

We trained the model using "MADAR corpus-6" train set, and evaluate it by MADAR corpus-6 development set. We reach an accuracy of 92.7% and macro F-score of 93%. Finally, we combine the train and the dev-set together and rebuild the model again. We call it (MADAR model-6). We will use this model later in the second sub model.

2.2 Fine Grained Dialect Identification

This model is the core of the shared task, where it is going to predict the label for a given sentence and classify it to one of 26 dialects. MADAR corpus covers 25 cities in the Arab countries in addition to the MSA, they are : Aleppo (ALE), Algeria (ALG), Alexandria (ALX), Amman (AMM), Aswan (ASW), Baghdad (BAG), Basra (BAS), Beirut (BEI), Benghazi (BEN), Cairo (CAI), Damascus (DAM), Doha (DOH), Fes (FES), Jeddah (JED), Jerusalem (JER), Khartoum (KHA), Mosul (MOS), Muscat (MUS), Rabat (RAB), Riyadh (RIY), Salt (SAL),Sana'a (SAN), Sfax (SFX), Tripoli (TRI), Tunisia (TUN) and MSA.

In the same manner we build the second model by extracting some features as follow:

- TF-IDF vectors from the word grams with uni-gram, bi-gram and tri-gram words. we apply 0.5 weight for vector transformation
- TF-IDF vectors from the character n-grams with word boundary consideration ranged from bi-grams to 5-grams and the transformation weight is 0.5
- Extract another character n-grams but this time without word boundary consideration from bi-grams to 4 grams and the transformation weight is 0.5
- Again apply skip gram, then we extract the uni-gram words with one work skipping. We assign it 0.3 transformation weight

In addition to theses feature we add another two numerical features, the first is the sentence length ratio for every sentence in the data (train, dev, test) which in turn divides the total number of words appearing in the sentence by the total number of words appearing in the longest sentence. The second features depends on the previous MADAR-model-6. We exploit this model to predict the label for MADAR Corpus-26, so every sentence is combined with a predicted class number with one value from 1 to 6, for example 1 means CAI, 2 is for BEI and so on. So in total we have the TF-IDF vectors features in addition to the two numerical features (the coarse-grained label and the sentence length).

To build the model, we employ ensemble hard voting classifier with the previously mentioned three algorithms (Linear SVC, MNB and BNB). The system is trained on MADAR corpus-26 train set, evaluated by MADAR corpus-26 dev set and finally tested by MADAR corpus-26 test set. Table 1 reports the results for the dev set and test set and Figure 2 shows the classification report which is produced from the test set .

	Accuracy	macro F-score
Dev	68.7	69.00
Test	67.29	67.32

Table 2: Results for 26 dialects Identification system

```
classification report:
                  precision       recall   f1-score

          ALE       0.62         0.68       0.65
          ALG       0.77         0.81       0.79
          ALX       0.76         0.76       0.76
          AMM       0.54         0.53       0.54
          ASW       0.57         0.65       0.60
          BAG       0.65         0.68       0.66
          BAS       0.70         0.70       0.70
          BEI       0.73         0.64       0.68
          BEN       0.71         0.69       0.70
          CAI       0.54         0.54       0.54
          DAM       0.54         0.61       0.57
          DOH       0.65         0.67       0.66
          FES       0.77         0.70       0.73
          JED       0.57         0.61       0.59
          JER       0.58         0.60       0.59
          KHA       0.74         0.74       0.74
          MOS       0.89         0.82       0.85
          MSA       0.68         0.79       0.73
          MUS       0.56         0.46       0.50
          RAB       0.76         0.76       0.76
          RIY       0.58         0.60       0.59
          SAL       0.62         0.56       0.59
          SAN       0.75         0.73       0.74
          SFX       0.74         0.73       0.74
          TRI       0.78         0.80       0.79
          TUN       0.78         0.68       0.73

    micro avg       0.67         0.67       0.67
    macro avg       0.68         0.67       0.67
 weighted avg       0.68         0.67       0.67
```

Figure 2: Fine Grained Dialect Identification classification report for MADAR corpus-26 test set

3 Discussion

Building a language model for a language or a text is an informative way to describe and represent the language. In this work, we·try to extract as many discriminated features as possible that can be employed efficiently to distinguish among the desired 6 and 26 dialects. In the coarse grained dialect identification with MADAR Corpus-6 the task was more flexible, the dialects have a reasonable differences as they represent a large groups of dialects, for example DOH represents dialects from the Arab Gulf, BEI represents the Levantine dialects and so on. Due to the differences on the lexical level between thees dialects we emphasise the word n-grams by using greater weight transformation, and assign a smaller weight value for the character levels n-grams.

For the task of fine grained dialect identification, the task was more tough and we need more extra features and emphasise some of them more. Hence, we increase the number of n-grams and emphasise the character n-grams and pay attention to the words boundaries. We employ the first model as another feature to enhance the f-score for the second models. Given that, the corpus contains many short sentence that appears in more one dialects, it makes the models to some extent confused, then we add the length of the sentence as an extract helpful feature where some dialects need more words to express an idea, and the other use more suffixes. It is also impossible for Arabic speakers to detect the dialect from a very short sentence with 100% especially if it does not contain any clue words. In some cases the dialects become very similar to each others when they are spoken by neighbourhood, for instance the Jerusalem dialect and the dialect from Amman where they are considered in some researches in Arabic history as the same dialect (Owens, 2015; Bishop, 1998). From the classification report in Figure 2, it is very clear that some dialects were easier to detect than other, for example, the North Africa dialects gain high f-scores compare to others such as the following dialects: TRI (0.79), SFX(0.74), BEN(0.70), ALG(0.79) and TUN(0.73). The confusion matrix in Figure 3 shows the numbers of actual and predicate labels for each dialect. There are some similar pairs of dialects where the system confused like (BAG and BAS), (AMM and JER), (CAI and ASW), (ALE and DAM) and (SFX and TUN).

We investigate the word grams model as well as the character grams model. The best result is obtained when we combine both of these models, given that the differences may occur in terms of

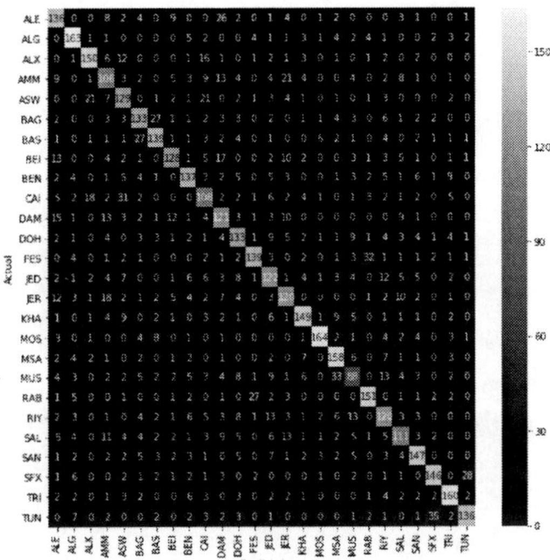

Figure 3: Fine Grained Dialect Identification confusion matrix for MADAR corpus-26 test set

lexical words, however there are many differences that occurred on character levels like different clitics, prefixes and suffixes. We try to exploit the best classifier that has been used for ADI and finally end up by ensemble learning that combines the Linear SVC , MNB and BNB with hard voting where the max probability is chosen as the correct class.

4 Conclusion

We participate in MADAR shared task, Task 1: "MADAR Travel Domain Dialect Identification". We build an ADI system consists of two subsystems. The first is a six dialects classification system, followed by a 26 classification system that classify 26 dialects from 25 cities in the Arab world in addition to MSA. We use different combinations of n-gram models (words, Characters) and skip gram models. In addition to these language modelling features, we compute the ratio length of each input sentence and use the predicted label from the first model. We achieve the best score in the competition with 67.32% f-score and an accuracy of 67.29%.

Acknowledgements

Kathrein Abu Kwaik is supported by grant 2014-39 from the Swedish Research Council, which funds the Centre for Linguistic Theory and Studies in Probability (CLASP) in the Department of Philosophy, Linguistics, and Theory of Science at the University of Gothenburg.

References

Brian Bishop. 1998. A history of the Arabic language. *Department of Linguistics, Brigham Young University.*

Houda Bouamor, Nizar Habash, Mohammad Salameh, Wajdi Zaghouani, Owen Rambow, Dana Abdulrahim, Ossama Obeid, Salam Khalifa, Fadhl Eryani, Alexander Erdmann, et al. 2018. The MADAR Arabic dialect corpus and lexicon. In *Proceedings of the Eleventh International Conference on Language Resources and Evaluation (LREC-2018).*

Houda Bouamor, Sabit Hassan, and Nizar Habash. 2019. The MADAR Shared Task on Arabic Fine-Grained Dialect Identification. In *Proceedings of the Fourth Arabic Natural Language Processing Workshop (WANLP19)*, Florence, Italy.

Ryan Cotterell and Chris Callison-Burch. 2014. A Multi-Dialect, Multi-Genre Corpus of Informal Written Arabic. In *LREC*, pages 241–245.

Mohamed Elaraby and Muhammad Abdul-Mageed. 2018. Deep Models for Arabic Dialect Identification on Benchmarked Data. In *Proceedings of the Fifth Workshop on NLP for Similar Languages, Varieties and Dialects (VarDial 2018)*, pages 263–274.

Heba Elfardy and Mona Diab. 2013. Sentence Level Dialect Identification in Arabic. In *Proceedings of the Conference of the Association for Computational Linguistics (ACL)*, Sofia, Bulgaria.

Charles A. Ferguson. 1959. Diglossia. *word*, 15(2):325–340.

Leena Lulu and Ashraf Elnagar. 2018. Automatic Arabic Dialect Classification Using Deep Learning Models. *Procedia computer science*, 142:262–269.

Jonathan Owens. 2015. Arabic language history and the comparative method. *International Journal of Arabic Linguistics*, 1(1):1–27.

Fabian Pedregosa, Gaël Varoquaux, Alexandre Gramfort, Vincent Michel, Bertrand Thirion, Olivier Grisel, Mathieu Blondel, Peter Prettenhofer, Ron Weiss, Vincent Dubourg, et al. 2011. Scikit-learn: Machine learning in Python. *Journal of machine learning research*, 12(Oct):2825–2830.

Chatrine Qwaider, Motaz Saad, Stergios Chatzikyriakidis, and Simon Dobnik. 2018. Shami: A Corpus of Levantine Arabic Dialects. In *Proceedings of the Eleventh International Conference on Language Resources and Evaluation (LREC-2018).*

Mohammad Salameh, Houda Bouamor, and Nizar Habash. 2018. Fine-Grained Arabic Dialect Identification. In *Proceedings of the International Conference on Computational Linguistics (COLING)*, pages 1332–1344, Santa Fe, New Mexico, USA.

Mustafa Shah. 2008. *The Arabic language.* Routledge.

Kees Versteegh. 2014. *The Arabic language.* Edinburgh University Press.

Omar F. Zaidan and Chris Callison-Burch. 2011. The Arabic online commentary dataset: an annotated dataset of informal Arabic with high dialectal content. In *Proceedings of the 49th Annual Meeting of the Association for Computational Linguistics: Human Language Technologies: short papers-Volume 2*, pages 37–41. Association for Computational Linguistics.

Omar F. Zaidan and Chris Callison-Burch. 2014. Arabic Dialect Identification. *Computational Linguistics*, 40(1):171–202.

Rabih Zbib, Erika Malchiodi, Jacob Devlin, David Stallard, Spyros Matsoukas, Richard Schwartz, John Makhoul, Omar F. Zaidan, and Chris Callison-Burch. 2012. Machine translation of Arabic dialects. In *Proceedings of the 2012 conference of the north american chapter of the association for computational linguistics: Human language technologies*, pages 49–59. Association for Computational Linguistics.

The SMarT Classifier for Arabic Fine-Grained Dialect Identification

Karima Meftouh
Badji Mokhtar University
Annaba - Algeria
karima.meftouh@univ-annaba.dz

Karima Abidi
Loria - Univ. Lorraine
Nancy - France
karima.abidi@loria.fr

Salima Harrat
École Normale Supérieure de Bouzaréah
Algiers - Algeria
slmhrrt@gmail.com

Kamel Smaïli
Loria - Univ. Lorraine
Nancy - France
kamel.smaili@loria.fr

Abstract

This paper describes the approach adopted by the SMarT research group to build a dialect identification system in the framework of the Madar shared task on Arabic fine-grained dialect identification. We experimented several approaches, but we finally decided to use a Multinomial Naïve Bayes classifier based on word and character ngrams in addition to the language model probabilities. We achieved a score of 67.73% in terms of Macro accuracy and a macro-averaged F1-score of 67.31%.

1 Introduction

Arabic is a complex language which presents significant challenges for natural language processing and its applications. Arabic is characterized by its plurality. It consists of a wide variety of languages, which includes the Modern Standard Arabic (MSA), and a set of various dialects differing according to regions and countries.

Language identification is the task of identifying the language of a given text. It is an important preprocessing step for many Natural Language Processing (NLP) tasks such as machine translation (Meftouh et al., 2018; Harrat et al., 2017), sentiment analysis (Rana et al., 2016; Abdul-Mageed et al., 2014; Saad et al., 2013), etc. In general, language identification is not a high challenging issue since this research has been supported for a long time and several machine learning techniques have been tested in this area that yielded to more or less good results. Nonetheless, in cases such as identifying languages from very little data, from mixed input or when the languages are extremely close to each other, the task becomes very challenging (Goutte et al., 2014).

This paper describes the submission of Loria (SMarT research group) to the Madar shared task on Arabic fine-grained dialect identification covering 25 specific cities from across the Arab World, in addition to Modern Standard Arabic (Bouamor et al., 2019). This shared task is the first to target a large set of dialect labels at the city and country levels. It has two subtasks.

Subtask 1: MADAR Travel Domain Dialect Identification.

Subtask 2: MADAR Twitter User Dialect Identification.

Our submission to this campaign is dealing with the first subtask.

The remainder of this paper is organized as follows: in the next section, we discuss related work pertaining to Arabic dialect identification. Section 3 reviews the modeling choices we made for the shared task, and Section 4 describes results in detail.

2 Related Work

Several research works addressed the problem of Arabic dialect identification. The authors of Habash et al. (2008) presented standard annotation guidelines to identify the switching between the MSA and at least one dialect. These guidelines can be used to annotate large collections of data used for training and testing NLP tools. In Zaidan and Callison-Burch (2012), a large annotated dataset, created by harvesting an important number of reader commentaries on online newspapers content, is used to train and evaluate automatic classifiers for dialect detection and identification. The authors crowdsourced an annotation task to obtain sentence-level labels indicating what proportion of the sentence is dialectal, and which dialect the sentence is written in. The approach used in dialect identification relies on training language models for the different varieties of Arabic. Another work presents a supervised approach for performing sentence level dialect identification

Proceedings of the Fourth Arabic Natural Language Processing Workshop, pages 259–263
Florence, Italy, August 1, 2019. ©2019 Association for Computational Linguistics

between Modern Standard Arabic and Egyptian Dialectal Arabic (Elfardy and Diab, 2013). The authors use token level labels to derive sentence-level features. These features are then used with other core and meta features to train a generative classifier that predicts the correct label for each sentence in the given input text. In addition to a multi-dialect, multi-genre, human annotated corpus, the authors in Cotterell and Callison-Bursh (2014) present the results of a language identification task extended to include 5 dialects. They considered Naïve Bayes and Support Vector Machines. The approach used by Darwish et al. (2014) for the identification of the Egyptian dialect was based on lexical, morphological and phonological information. They show that accounting for such information can improve dialect detection accuracy by nearly 10%. Using a set of surface features based on characters and words Malmasi et al. (2015) conduct three experiments with a linear SVM classifier and a meta-classifier using stacked generalization on the Multidialectal Parallel Corpus of Arabic (MPCA) compiled by Bouamor et al. (2014). They first conduct a 6-way multi-dialect classification task then investigate pairwise binary dialect classification and finally conduct cross-corpus evaluation on the Arabic Online Commentary (AOC) dataset. In Al-Badrashiny et al. (2015), the authors present a hybrid approach for performing token and sentence levels Arabic Dialect Identification. The token level component relies on a Conditional Random Field (CRF) classifier that take decisions based on several underlying components such as language models, a named entity recognizer and a morphological analyzer to label each word in the sentence. The sentence level component uses an ensemble of classifiers that models different aspects of the language. In another work, Al-Badrashiny and Diab (2016) present a system that detects points of code-switching in sentences between the MSA and dialectal Arabic. In Sadat et al. (2014), the authors present a bi-gram character-level model to identify the dialect of sentences, in the social media context, among dialects of 18 Arab countries. Bougrine et al. (2015) addressed the problem of spoken Algerian dialect identification by using prosodic speech information (intonation and rhythm). They performed an experiment on six dialects from different Algerian regions. In Salameh et al. (2018), the authors present the first system

dealing with fine-grained dialect classification task and covering 25 specific cities from across the Arab World, in addition to Standard Arabic. For this purpose, they build several classification systems using a Multinomial Naïve Bayes classifier and exploring a large space of features.

3 The Modeling Choices

3.1 Data

For the experiments reported in this paper, we only use the training and the development data available in the subtask 1 of the shared task. The dataset of this subtask is the same as the one reported on Bouamor et al. (2018) and Salameh et al. (2018). It is composed of two corpora. The first (Corpus-26) is a collection of parallel sentences, built to cover the dialects of 25 cities from the Arab World, in addition to MSA. The training part consists of 1600 labeled instances per class, while the development part has 200 labeled instances per class. The second (Corpus-6) contains $10,000$ additional sentences translated to the dialects of only five cities: Beirut, Cairo, Doha, Tunis and Rabat, in addition to MSA. They are splitted on two categories: $9,000$ instances per language for the training and $1,000$ instances per language for the development.

3.2 Method

In order to develop a language identification system that can distinguish between several Arabic dialects, we tested three methods namely simple neural networks (LSTM) (Sak et al., 2015), a method based on word embedding (Word2vec) (Mikolov et al., 2013) and Naïve Bayes classifiers. Given the limited size of the provided corpora, the first two methods have proven ineffective. We give in Table ?? the results we obtain using Corpus 26 in terms of Macro averaged F1-score, precision and recall.

Method	Corpus 26		
	Precision	Recall	F1-score
Word2vec	50.11	49.90	49.74
LSTM	58.04	61.54	58.33

Table 1: Macro averaged F1-score, Precison and Recall for Word2vec and LSTM method.

We used a Naïve Bayes method because in the past, we did a comparative study of methods for Topic identification. This method for French leads to the best results (Bigi et al., 2001). In this work we consider a Multinomial Naïve Bayes classifier, in fact a study proposed in McCallum and Nigam (1998) showed that the multinomial model is found to be almost better than the multivariate Bernoulli model and the experimental results yielded to better results. So, we consider a Multinomial Naïve Bayes classifier for this task. In this case, the term Multinomial Naïve Bayes lets us know that each $p(f_i|c)$ (where f_i is a feature and c the category or the class) is a multinomial distribution, rather than some other distribution such as a Bernoulli distribution.

To develop our system, we used Python, relying on Scikit-Learn module (Pedregosa et al., 2011).

3.3 Features

A Naïve Bayes model classifier identifies a category by calculating the distributions of the features within a category. It also assumes that each of the features it uses are conditionally independent of one another given a category. Identifying features is a critical step when applying Naïve Bayes classifiers. That is why we did several experiments to select some adequate features. After several experiments, we selected for each sentence, the following 38 features as follows:

- A unigram of words.

- A bigram of words

- Character n-grams: from 1 to 5

- Character n-grams: from 1 to 5, by taking into account the spaces between words; in other words ngrams at the edges of words are padded with space. All the symbols of punctuation have been removed from the training, development and test data.

- 26 likelihoods estimated by the 26 unigram language models

For all the features, we use a special character to mark the start of the sentences. We utilize Term Frequency-Inverse Document Frequency (Tf-Idf) scores (Spärck Jones, 1972) as it has been shown to outperform count weights in several NLP applications.

4 Results and Discussion

For the purpose of this campaign, we built several systems using the model described in section

3. We did several experiments to determine the smoothing adding value, necessary for the Naive Bayes method, and we set it to 0.093 for all the systems. In Table 2, we report the results of all the experiments concerning the Multinomial Naive Bayes method. For the evaluation purpose, we use the Macro averaged F1-score which is retained as the official metric by the organizers of Madar shared task.

Ngrams features			F1-score	
Word	Char_wo	Char_wi	Dev	Test
1	-	-	63.03	62.31
1-2	-	-	63.27	62.32
1-3	-	-	63.04	61.96
-	1-3	-	59.28	57.25
-	1-4	-	64.50	63.99
-	1-5	-	66.27	65.33
-	-	1-3	59.66	57.62
-	-	1-4	64.45	63.21
-	-	1-5	66.50	64.40
-	1-5	1-5	66.92	65.56
1-2	1-5	1-5	69.06	67.34
1-2	1-5	1-5 +LMs Prob	69.09	67.31

Table 2: Macro averaged F1-score on Development and Test sets for Corpus-26.

First, we train the multinomial NB on word ngrams. The best results are achieved with the use of unigrams and bigrams. For higher order of n-grams, the performance of the model degrades due to the data sparsity. Then, we tested the effect of character ngrams features with (wi) and without (wo) taking into account the space at the end of the words. We experimented using the features of each option alone and combined. In Table 2 the symbol x-y means that all the n-grams features from x to y of the corresponding column are taken into account in the classification.

In all the experiments, the best model is obtained for n ranging from 1 to 5. We remark that a classifier based on character ngrams features (1-5) outperforms the classifier based on word ngrams features by at least 3 points. Finally, the best classifier is the one using word unigrams and bigrams, and character ngrams ranging from 1 to 5 with and without space. The introduction of the language model features improved the result on the development corpus and reduced it on the test corpus. We decided finally to participate to the campaign with the classifier including the language model parameters.

5 Conclusion

In this paper, we described the experiments we conducted as part of the MADAR shared task on Arabic fine-grained dialect identification. This task is the first covering the dialects of 25 specific cities from across the Arab World, in addition to MSA. Thus, we tested several systems exploring a large set of features. A blind run on the test set was then performed and submitted as part of the shared task. The Macro accuracy is 67.73% (macro-averaged F1-score 67.31%), placing our classifier first among 19 participants. This result shows that our approach despite its simplicity performs very well and even if it is ranked first, we need to make more efforts to make it powerful so that it can become an effective tool for the community.

References

Muhammad Abdul-Mageed, Mona Diab, and Sandra Kbler. 2014. SAMAR: Subjectivity and sentiment analysis for Arabic social media. *Computer Speech & Language*, 28:2037.

Mohamed Al-Badrashiny and Mona Diab. 2016. Lili: A Simple Language Independent Approach for Language Identification. In *Proceedings of COLING 2016, the 26th International Conference on Computational Linguistics: Technical Papers*, pages 1211–1219.

Mohamed Al-Badrashiny, Heba Elfardy, and Mona Diab. 2015. Aida2: A hybrid approach for token and sentence level dialect identification in arabic. In *Proceedings of the Nineteenth Conference on Computational Natural Language Learning*, pages 42–51.

Brigitte Bigi, Armelle Brun, Jean-Paul Haton, Kamel Smaïli, and Imed Zitouni. 2001. A comparative study of Topic Identification on Newspaper and E-mail. In *Proceedings of the 8th International Symposium on String Processing and Information Retrieval - SPIRE'01*, pages 238–241, Laguna de San Rafael, Chili.

Houda Bouamor, Nizar Habash, and Kemal Oflazer. 2014. A Multidialectal Parallel Corpus of Arabic. In *Proceedings of the Language Resources and Evaluation Conference, LREC-2014*, pages 1240–1245.

Houda Bouamor, Nizar Habash, Mohammad Salameh, Wajdi Zaghouani, Owen Rambow, Dana Abdulrahim, Ossama Obeid, Salam Khalifa, Fadhl Eryani, Alexander Erdmann, and Kemal Oflazer. 2018. The MADAR Arabic Dialect Corpus and Lexicon. In *Proceedings of the 11th International Conference on Language Resources and Evaluation*, pages 3387–3396.

Houda Bouamor, Sabit Hassan, and Nizar Habash. 2019. The MADAR Shared Task on Arabic Fine-Grained Dialect Identification. In *Proceedings of the Fourth Arabic Natural Language Processing Workshop (WANLP19)*, Florence, Italy.

Soumia Bougrine, Hadda Cherroun, and Djelloul Ziadi. 2015. Prosody-based spoken Algerian Arabic dialect identification. In *International Conference on Natural Language and Speech Processing, ICNLSP'2015*.

Ryan Cotterell and Chris Callison-Bursh. 2014. A multidialect, multi-genre corpus of informal written Arabic. In *Proceedings of the Language Resources and Evaluation Conference, LREC-2014*, pages 241–245.

Kareem Darwish, Hassan Sajjad, and Hamdy Mubarak. 2014. Verifiably effective Arabic dialect identification. In *Proceedings of the EMNLP 2014 Workshop on Arabic Natural Language Processing (ANLP*, pages 1465–1468, Doha, Qatar. Association for Computational Linguistic.

Heba Elfardy and Mona Diab. 2013. Sentence Level Dialect Identification in Arabic. In *ACL (2)*, pages 456–461.

Cyril Goutte, Serge LÉger, and Marine Carpuat. 2014. The nrc system for Discriminating Similar Languages. In *Proceedings of the First Workshop on Applying NLP Tools to Similar Languages, Varieties and Dialects*, pages 139–145.

Nizar Habash, Owen Rambow, Mona Diab, and Reem Kanjawi-Faraj. 2008. Guidelines for annotation of Arabic dialectness. In *Proceedings of the Lrec workshop on hlt and nlp whthln the Arabic world*, pages 49–53.

Salima Harrat, Karima Meftouh, and Kamel Smaïli. 2017. Machine translation for Arabic dialects (survey). *Information Processing and Management*.

Shervin Malmasi, Eshrag. Refaee, and Mark. Dras. 2015. Arabic dialect identification using a parallel multidialectal corpus. In *In International Conference of the Pacific Association for Computational Linguistics*, pages 35–53. Springer.

Andrew McCallum and Kamal Nigam. 1998. A comparison of event models for naive bayes text classification. In *IN AAAI-98 WORKSHOP ON LEARNING FOR TEXT CATEGORIZATION*, pages 41–48. AAAI Press.

Karima Meftouh, Salima Harrat, and Kamel Smaïli. 2018. PADIC: extension and new experiments. In *7th International Conference on Advanced Technologies ICAT*, Antalya, Turkey.

Tomas Mikolov, Kai Chen, Greg Corrado, and Jeffrey Dean. 2013. Efficient estimation of word representations in vector space. In *ICLR (Workshop)*.

Fabian. Pedregosa, Gaël Varoquaux, Alexandre Gramfort, Vincent. Michel, Bertrand Thirion, Olivier Grisel, Mathieu Blondel, Peter Prettenhofer, Ron Weiss, Vincent Dubourg, Jake Vanderplas, Alexandre Passos, David Cournapeau, Matthieu Brucher, Matthieu Perrot, and Edouard Duchesnay. 2011. Scikit-learn: Machine learning in Python. *Journal of Machine Learning Research*, 12:2825–2830.

Toqir Rana, Yu-N Cheah, and Sukumar Letchmunan. 2016. Topic modeling in sentiment analysis: A systematic review. *Journal of ICT Research and Applications*, 10:76–93.

Motaz Saad, David Langlois, and Kamel Smaïli. 2013. Comparing Multilingual Comparable Articles Based On Opinions. In *Proceedings of the 6th Workshop on Building and Using Comparable Corpora*, pages 105–111, Sofia, Bulgaria. Association for Computational Linguistics ACL.

Fatiha Sadat, Farzindar Kazemi, and Atef Farzindar. 2014. Automatic identification of arabic dialects in social media. In *In Proceedings of the first international workshop on Social media retrieval and analysis*, page 3540. ACM.

Hasim Sak, Andrew Senior, and Franoise Beaufays. 2015. Long short-term memory recurrent neural network architectures for large scale acoustic modeling. In *Google, USA*.

Mohamed Salameh, Houda Bouamor, and Nizar Habash. 2018. Fine-grained Arabic Dialect Identification. In *Proceedings of the 27th International Conference on Computational Linguistics*, pages 1332–1344. Association for Computational Linguistics.

Karen Spärck Jones. 1972. A Statistical Interpretation of Term Specificity and Its Application in Retrieval. *Journal of Documentation*, 28:11–21.

Omar Zaidan and Chris Callison-Burch. 2012. Arabic Dialect Identification. *Association for Computational Linguistics, Volume 1*, pages 1–35.

JHU System Description
for the MADAR Arabic Dialect Identification Shared Task

Tom Lippincott
tom@cs.jhu.edu

Pamela Shapiro
pshapiro@jhu.edu

Kevin Duh
kevinduh@cs.jhu.edu

Paul McNamee
mcnamee@jhu.edu

Department of Computer Science
Johns Hopkins University
Baltimore, MD 21218

Abstract

Our submission to the MADAR shared task on Arabic dialect identification (Bouamor et al., 2019) employed a language modeling technique called Prediction by Partial Matching, an ensemble of neural architectures, and sources of additional data for training word embeddings and auxiliary language models.[1] We found several of these techniques provided small boosts in performance, though a simple character-level language model was a strong baseline, and a lower-order LM achieved best performance on Subtask 2. Interestingly, word embeddings provided no consistent benefit, and ensembling struggled to outperform the best component submodel. This suggests the variety of architectures are learning redundant information, and future work may focus on encouraging decorrelated learning.

1 Introduction

While Modern Standard Arabic (MSA) is used across many countries for formal written communication, regional Arabic dialects vary substantially. Dialect identification has traditionally been performed at the level of broad families of dialects—for instance grouping many dialects across the Arabian Peninsula together. However, even within a single country there is often noticeable variation from one city to another. The MADAR dataset and corresponding shared task aim to perform dialect identification at a finergrained level. Subtask 1 aims to distinguish travel phrases produced between Arabic dialect speakers from 25 different cities, as well as MSA. Sub-

task 2 aims to distinguish Twitter users from different Arabic-speaking countries. Along with the inherent difficulty of classifying short documents, highly-correlated modalities like topic and proper names can lead to overfitting, particularly for userdirected content like Twitter. Our method attempts to address the former by using a language modeling technique that has empirically been found to perform well on extremely short documents. For the latter, we employ ensembles of heterogeneous neural architectures and aggressive dropout, with the goal of finding a broad range of features that support the task without overfitting.

2 Data

In addition to the data provided by the MADAR subtasks, we used the following data sets to train embeddings or auxiliary language models.

1. Preexisting collections of the Arabic Dialect Corpus (ADC) of 150k comments from three Arabic-language newspaper sites focused on Saudi Arabia, Jordan, and Egypt (Zaidan and Callison-Burch, 2011)

2. The Twitter LID corpus of 70k Tweets in 70 languages [2].

3. Crawled posts from Reddit and the Twitter 1% sample either tagged as Arabic, or having a majority of Arabic characters, amounting to 11k and 100m posts, respectively, are used.

The ADC and Twitter LID corpora were also used to train additional PPM language models,

---

[1]Code available at https://bit.ly/2Kouo5X

[2]https://bit.ly/2KlITre

Proceedings of the Fourth Arabic Natural Language Processing Workshop, pages 264–268
Florence, Italy, August 1, 2019. ©2019 Association for Computational Linguistics

though these proved to be ineffective in our ensembles (see Section 5)

Split	Missing
Train	13076 (6%)
Dev	1607 (5%)
Test	5763 (12%)

Table 1: Missing tweets from the Subtask 2 data splits, absolute number and percent of total.

Table 1 shows how many tweets were still available when we initialized Subtask 2.

3 System

3.1 PPM Language Models

Prediction by Partial Matching (PPM) was first introduced as a sequence compression algorithm (Cleary and Witten, 1984) but has been found to be particularly effective as a character language model for classifying short documents (Frank et al., 2000; McNamee, 2016), using the probabilities directly rather than as input to a numeric encoding.

PPM is based on a variable-order Markov model that contains a parameter N known as the *maximal order*. When compressing data files or training a classification model, observations from previously seen data are used to estimate the likelihood of observing a symbol following a given context of up to N characters. Longer contexts are used when available, starting with the maximal order N. However, PPM automatically backs off to use shorter contexts when a symbol has never been observed in a longer context. A context-dependent penalty, also known as an escape probability, is applied when backing off is required.

As an example, in English, an 'n' is the most likely character observed after the sequence "t i o". Other letters are observed less frequently, such as 'l', 'm', and 'p'. However, a 'z' is not observed. To account for a 'z' after "t i o" it is necessary to back off using the estimates from shorter contexts such as "i o". If a 'z' has never been observed after "i o" then the process continues, with an additional penalty and further recursive backoff for 'z' using the context of the single symbol ('i').

To use PPM for classification rather than compression, models $M_1, M_2, ..., M_n$ are trained for each discrete class. Then for a given textual sample t, choose the model that encodes t in the least number of bits. In reality the text is not compressed and the probabilities from the model are used to choose the model which best fits the text.

N	Subtask 1	Subtask 2
2	0.430	0.431
3	0.576	0.543
4	0.591	0.402
5	0.586	0.287

Table 2: Performance of PPM models on the subtask dev sets using different values of N.

For each labeled corpus, we trained PPM language models for distinguishing among the labels. This included each of the two subtasks, as well as the ADC and Twitter LID corpora that have a way to divide the instances into categories.

These models can either be used directly for their "native" task, or produce probabilities that may contain useful signal for a downstream task. Table 2 shows how the native models for each MADAR subtask perform with different values of maximal order N on dev data. $N = 4$ was best for Subtask 1, and $N = 3$ was best for Subtask 2.

3.2 Word Embeddings

For the word-based neural models, we use 300-dimensional word embeddings trained on different amounts of data as input representations. First, we use randomly initialized embeddings. Then, we train fastText continuous bag of words (cbow) models with default parameters on the MADAR data (Bojanowski et al., 2017).[3] Finally, we utilize additional data, training on MADAR in addition to the datasets mentioned above (MADAR+). We provide final results (Macro-Average F1) from the ensemble model using each of these variants in Table 3. We see that utilizing additional data provided marginal performance gains, helping more in Subtask 2 where much of our additional data was also Twitter data, making it in-domain.

Embedding	Subtask 1	Subtask 2
Random	0.632	0.399
MADAR	0.626	0.397
MADAR+	0.634	0.411

Table 3: Effect of different word embeddings, Macro-Average F1 for final ensemble models on dev data.

---

[3] https://fasttext.cc/

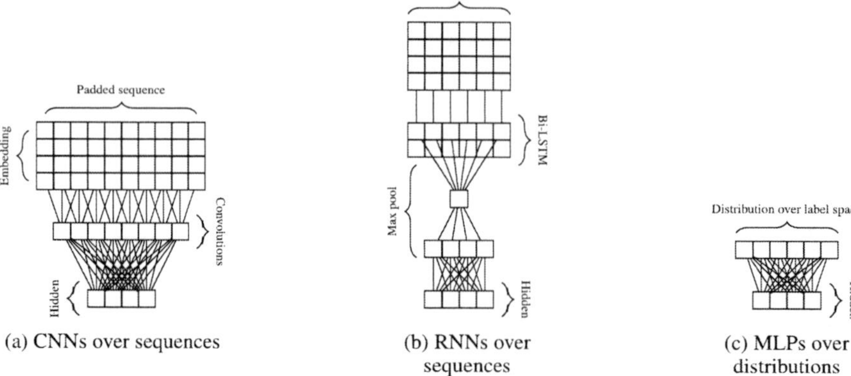

(a) CNNs over sequences (b) RNNs over sequences (c) MLPs over distributions

Figure 1: The three basic types of submodels combined into the final ensemble, where the top layer is the input representation. They all produce the same-sized final hidden representation that can either be mapped directly to the target value with a final linear layer (for individual training) or concatenated into an ensemble.

3.3 Ensemble Models

In what follows, all layers other than the final fully-connected input to softmax employ ReLU non-linearity.

We experimented with an ensemble model that combines submodels to extract signal from different features or incorporate information from non-neural methods. Figure 1 shows the three types of submodels: CNNs and RNNs over character and word sequences, and MLPs over probability distributions from language models and metadata. We integrate the metadata provided with Subtask 2 as additional distributions: the probabilities from the organizers' 26-class model are incorporated the same way as LM scores, while the Twitter label is treated as a one-hot distribution and also incorporated alongside the LM scores.

Each submodel, regardless of architecture, eventually produces a same-sized hidden representation, which are initially mapped to the target output via cross-entropy to train as an individual model. Once the submodels have converged, their parameters are frozen, their hidden layers are detached from the target output, and instead concatenated into a single representation. This representation is then the input to the shared ensemble architecture, as shown in Figure 2. Note that the "Step-down FCs" layer is actually composed of several fully-connected layers, each dividing the representation size in half until it is one factor larger than the output label space.

Other specific choices for the models in this paper are: 100-dim char embeddings, char/word CNN filter sizes 1,2,3,4,5, bidirectional 2-layer LSTMs with 32-dim states, and SGD with LR=0.1, momentum=0.9, patience of 10 for LR decay, early stop patience of 20, and minibatch size of 512.

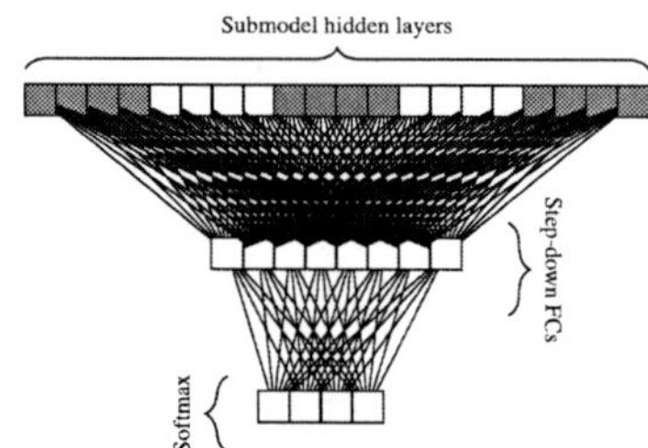

Figure 2: The ensemble model concatenates the hidden representations produced by the submodels and stacks one or more dense, non-linear layers, stepping down in size to a final softmax output over the label space.

Due to a misreading of the task description, our models were designed to classify tweets individually: this was handled at the submission deadline by taking a majority vote over each user's tweets.

4 Results

Table 4 reports the final precision, recall, and F1 scores for the best-performing model on each subtask.

The ensemble for Subtask 1 incorporates the best-performing (PPM-4) language model (see Table 2). The PPM-3 model for Subtask 2 performed text normalization to only include Arabic characters, followed by prepending the user name.

Subtask	Model	Prec	Rec	F1
Subtask 1	Ensemble	63.7	63.4	63.4
Subtask 2	PPM-3	74.9	46.5	54.3

Table 4: Precision, recall, and f-score of the best model for each subtask.

5 Discussion

Table 5 shows the final performance (Macro-Average F1) of the *submodels* of the ensemble on Subtask 1, before they were frozen, and the performance of the final ensemble model (which used the submodels). The modest 4-point improvement of the ensemble over the PPM submodel, and the fact that the Subtask 2 ensemble under-performed the PPM-3 model, suggests poor coordination of the representational power of the constituents. Distributions from language models trained on our other data sets unfortunately provided no benefit under the ensemble, and were not included.

Submodel	F1 Score
CNN	0.545
RNN	0.554
MLP-PPM	0.591
Ensemble	0.634

Table 5: F1 Scores of the submodels of the best ensemble for Subtask 1.

Figures 3 and 4 show the confusion matrices of the best models on Subtask 1 and 2, respectively. Our Task 1 misclassifications closely track those reported in (Salameh and Bouamor, 2018), e.g. TUN/SFX and BAS/BAG.

For Task 2, the preponderance of Saudi Arabian documents dominates the misclassifications, but also striking is how asymmetric the heatmap is compared to Subtask 1. This may largely be due to the small number of instances (half of the classes have counts in the single digits), but even better-represented pairs like Oman (14) and Iraq (10) are largely unidirectional, with Iraq much likelier to be misclassified as Oman than the reverse.

6 Conclusion

We experimented with a non-standard character language model (PPM) designed for classifying short text sequences, and an ensemble model that combined several neural architectures and input

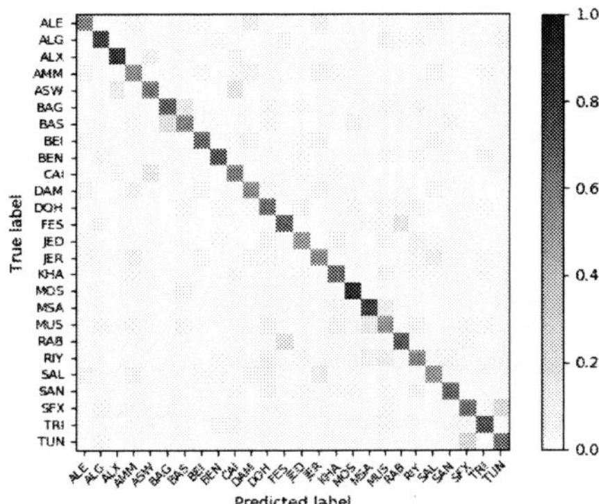

Figure 3: Confusion matrix for the Subtask 1 dev set using an ensemble model with word embeddings and language model scores constructed from the full suite of MADAR and external data sets

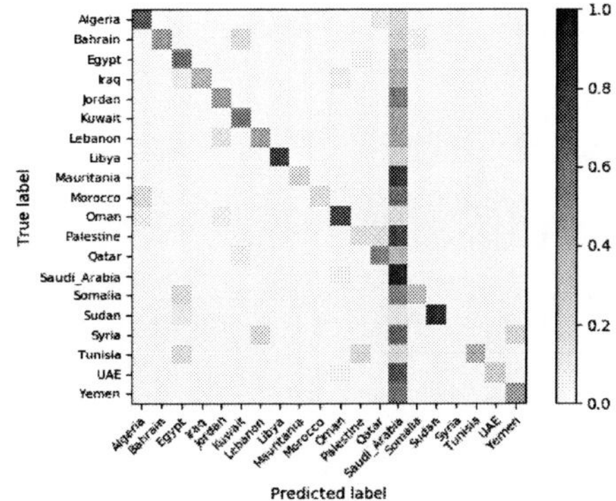

Figure 4: Confusion matrix for Subtask 2 dev set using a 3-gram PPM model constructed from the train set

features. The language model proved difficult to beat, even by ensembles that include the LM itself: this under-performance indicates the ensembling is not optimally leveraging its inputs. Future work might focus on techniques for encouraging uncorrelated training, perhaps by sequential submodel training that modifies the data as a function of previous submodel predictions.

References

Piotr Bojanowski, Edouard Grave, Armand Joulin, and Tomas Mikolov. 2017. Enriching word vectors with subword information. *Transactions of the Association for Computational Linguistics*, 5:135–146.

Houda Bouamor, Sabit Hassan, and Nizar Habash. 2019. The MADAR Shared Task on Arabic Fine-Grained Dialect Identification. In *Proceedings of the*

Fourth Arabic Natural Language Processing Workshop (WANLP19), Florence, Italy.

John Cleary and Ian Witten. 1984. Data compression using adaptive coding and partial string matching. *Transactions on Communications*, 32:396–402.

Eibe Frank, Chang Chui, and Ian Witten. 2000. Text categorization using compression models. In *Proceedings of the IEEE Data Compression Conference*, pages 200–209.

Paul McNamee. 2016. Language and Dialect Discrimination Using Compression-Inspired Language Models. *Proceedings of the Third Workshop on NLP for Similar Languages, Varieties and Dialects*.

Mohammad Salameh and Houda Bouamor. 2018. Fine-grained arabic dialect identification. In *Proceedings of the 27th International Conference on Computational Linguistics*, pages 1332–1344.

Omar Zaidan and Chris Callison-Burch. 2011. The arabic online commentary dataset: an annotated dataset of informal arabic with high dialectal content. In *Proceedings of the Association for Computational Linguistics*, pages 37–41.

ST MADAR 2019 Shared Task:
Arabic Fine-Grained Dialect Identification

Mourad Abbas, Mohamed Lichouri
Computational Linguistics Department-CRSTDLA
Algeria

Abed Alhakim Freihat
Trento University
Italy

{m.abbas, m.lichouri}@crstdla.dz abed.freihat@unitn.it

Abstract

This paper describes the solution that we propose on MADAR 2019 Arabic Fine-Grained Dialect Identification task. The proposed solution utilized a set of classifiers that we trained on character and word features. These classifiers are: Support Vector Machines (SVM), Bernoulli Naive Bayes (BNB), Multinomial Naive Bayes (MNB), Logistic Regression (LR), Stochastic Gradient Descent (SGD), Passive Aggressive(PA) and Perceptron (PC). The system achieved competitive results, with a performance of 62.87% and 62.12% for both development and test sets.

1 Introduction

Dialect identification (Zaidan and Callison-Burch, 2014) is a sub field of language identification which can be coarse-grained or fine-grained. Coarse-grained dialect identification or simply dialect identification (Meftouh et al., 2015) refers to the process of dividing a language into the main dialects that belong to that language. On the other hand, fine-grained dialect identification (Salameh et al., 2018) considers the differences between the sub dialects inside a dialect of some language.

In this paper, we describe a fine grained dialect identification systems that participated in MADAR 2019 Arabic Fine-Grained Dialect Identification task (Bouamor et al., 2019) In this task, our system was trained on a data-set of short sentences in the travel domain. A sentence in this data set belongs to one or more Arabic fine-grained dialects. These dialects are -Aleppo (ALE), Algiers (ALG), Alexandria (ALX), Amman (AMM), Aswan (ASW), Baghdad (BAG), Basra (BAS), Beirut (BEI), Benghazi (BEN), Cairo (CAI), Damascus (DAM), Doha (DOH), Fes (FES), Jeddah (JED), Jerusalem (JER), Khartoum (KHA), Mosul (MOS), Muscat (MUS), Rabat (RAB), Riyadh (RIY), Salt (SAL), Sana'a (SAN), Sfax (SFX), Tripoli (TRI), Tunis (TUN) and Modern Standards Arabic (MSA) (Bouamor et al., 2018). The task of our system is to identify the dialect of a given sentence that belong to these 26 dialects.

The multi-way classification system that we propose uses word n-grams and char n-grams as features, and MNB, BNB and SVM as classifiers.

The rest of the paper is organized as follows. In Section 2, we describe the data-set. In Section 3.1, we address the task as a multiway text-classification task; where we describe the proposed system in 3. We report our experiments and results in 4 and conclude with suggestions for future research and conclusion in 5 and 6.

2 Dataset

In this work, we used the MADAR Travel Domain dataset built by translating the Basic Traveling Expression Corpus (BTEC) (Takezawa et al., 2007). The whole sentences have been translated manually from English and French to the different Arabic dialects by speakers of 25 dialects (Salameh et al., 2018; Bouamor et al., 2019). The training data is composed of 1600 sentences for each of the 25 dialects in addition to MSA. The size of the development and test sets is 200 sentences per dialect. The sentences are short, ranging from 4 to 15 words each. Each sentence is annotated with the speaker dialect. In table 1, we provide some statistics on the used corpora.

Arabic dialects can be considered as variants of Modern Standard Arabic. However, the absence of a standard orthography (Habash et al., 2018) (Habash et al., 2012) for dialects generates many different shapes of the same word. Despite this, there are still similarities between these dialects which make their identification difficult under textual format. In figure 3, we present respectively the number of words and sentences, shared be-

Proceedings of the Fourth Arabic Natural Language Processing Workshop, pages 269–273
Florence, Italy, August 1, 2019. ©2019 Association for Computational Linguistics

	Train	Dev	Test	Total
# sentences	41,600	5,200	5,200	52,000
# distinct sentences	38,506	4,873	4,870	48,249
# words	294,718	37,383	36,810	368,911
# distinct Words	27,501	6,136	6,062	39,699

Table 1: Madar Task 1 Dataset statistics

tween n dialects where n varies from 2 to 26.

3 System

The presentation of our proposed approach is shown in figure 2.

3.1 Feature extraction

We applied a light preprocessing step where a simple blank tokenization and punctuation filtering have been achieved. It is worthy to say, that we deployed in our preliminary experiments Low level NLP processing such as POS-tagging (Freihat et al., 2018b) features and lemmatization (Freihat et al., 2018a) but without a significant enhancement of the achieved results. Besides the word and character n-grams features used in previous work such as (Salameh et al., 2018; Lichouri et al., 2018), we added the character-word_boundary (char_wb). In the following, we present a description of the three adopted features.

- **Word n-grams**: We extract word n-grams, with n ranging from 1 to 3.

- **Char n-grams**: The character first to third grams are used as features.

- **Char_wb n-grams**: This feature creates character n-grams only from text inside word boundaries; n-grams at the edges of words are padded with space.

The count matrix obtained using these features are transformed to a tfidf representation.

3.2 Classification Models

Our model is based on a set of classifiers using the scikit-learn library (Pedregosa et al., 2011), namely: Support Vector Machines (SVM), Bernoulli Naive Bayes (BNB), Multinomial Naive Bayes (MNB), Logistic Regression (LR), Stochastic Gradient Descent (SGD), Passive Aggressive (PA) and Perceptron (PC). In the following, we present the selected parameters for each classifier.

- **SVM_r:** C:1.0, kernel:"rbf", degree:3, decision-function-shape:"One-vs-Rest".

- **SVM_l:** C:10, kernel:"linear", degree:3, decision-function-shape:"One-vs-Rest".

- **BNB:** alpha:1.0, fit-prior:True.

- **MNB:** alpha:1.0, fit-prior:True.

- **LR:** penalty:"l2", C:1.0, solver:"sag", max-iter:100.

- **SGD:** loss:"hinge", penalty:"l2", alpha:0.0001, l1-ratio:0.15, max-iter:1000, shuffle:True, epsilon:0.1, learning-rate:"optimal".

- **PA:** C:1.0, max-iter:1000, shuffle:True, loss:"epsilon-insensitive", epsilon:0.1.

- **PC:** alpha:0.0001, max-iter:1000, shuffle:True, eta0:1.0.

4 Results

Using the aforementioned classifiers, the best achieved performance (F1-Macro) for coarse-grained and fine-grained dialect identification was 90.55% (table 4) and 62.87% (table 3) respectively. The best results are obtained using the three classifiers: **SVM_l**, BNB and MNB with F1-Macro of 61.94%, 62.72% and 62.87% respectively (table 3). Based on these findings, we adopted the three models for test phase. The results are presented in table 2.

Model	Precision	Recall	F1	Accuracy
MNB	63.13	62.17	62.12	62.17
BNB	62.85	62.13	62.07	62.13
SVM_l	60.41	60.48	60.26	60.48

Table 2: Three first best results achieved by **MNB**, **BNB** and **SVM_l** (Test Phase). The F1, Precision and Recall Metrics are in Macro Mode.

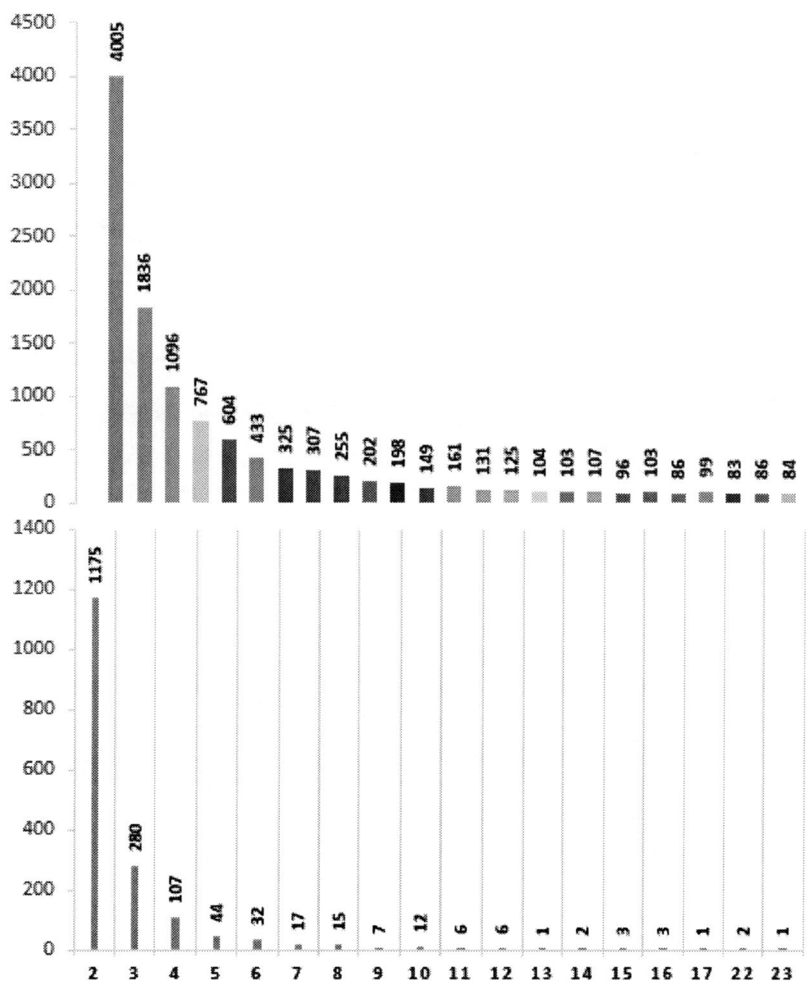

Figure 1: Number of tokens (**above**) and sentences (**below**) shared between the different dialects.

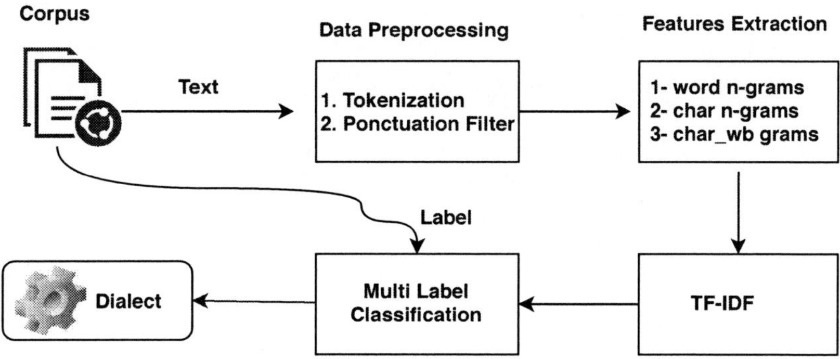

Figure 2: Dialect identification system

	SVM_r	SVM_l	BNB	MNB	LR	PA	SGD	PC
word n-grams	n=2	-	n=1	n=1	n=1	n=2	n=2	n=2
char_wb n-grams	-	n=3	-	-	-	-	-	-
Precision-Macro	60.09	62.29	64.09	64.28	59.67	60.55	58.40	56.97
Recall-Macro	59.19	62.19	62.73	62.87	59.33	60.10	57.88	55.90
F1-Macro	59.17	**61.94**	**62.72**	**62.87**	59.08	60.06	57.30	55.89
Accuracy	59.19	**62.19**	**62.73**	**62.87**	59.33	60.10	57.88	55.90

Table 3: Best results on the development dataset (**Corpus-26**) using the word n-grams and char_wb n-grams.

	SVM_r	SVM_r	BNB	MNB	LR	PA	SGD	PC
word n-grams	n=3	n=3	n=1 n=2	n=1 n=2	n=1 n=2	n=3	n=1 n=2	n=3
Precision-Macro	88.78	89.81	90.47	90.63	88.41	89.48	87.68	87.37
Recall-Macro	88.53	89.65	90.2	90.53	88.28	89.33	87.5	87.22
F1-Macro	88.59	**89.68**	**90.26**	**90.55**	88.32	89.36	87.53	87.24
Accuracy	88.53	**89.65**	**90.2**	**90.53**	88.28	89.33	87.5	87.22

Table 4: Best results on the development dataset (**Corpus-6**) using the word n-grams.

5 Discussion

We experimented different classifiers and a set of features to solve fine-grained dialect identification, i.e. a 26-way classification problem. The results show that fine grained dialect identification is more difficult given the similarity between dialects on one side, and on the other side, the non-standardization of writing dialectal texts that generates unpredictable texts. In addition, we noted the presence of MSA texts in several dialectal tweets which distorts the results. By using the test data-set, we calculated the accuracy achieved by our best model and presented in table 2. In addition, we dress in table 5 our best results compared to the baseline.

	Precision	Recall	F1	Accuracy
Baseline	69.00	68.00	69.00	67.90
ST Team	63.13	62.17	62.12	62.17

Table 5: Speech Translation team results compared to the baseline system -evaluated on test dataset-

In table 6, we note that the best results using both dev and test datasets were obtained for the MOS dialect with an accuracy of 80% and 78%. Whereas the (ALG and TRI) dialects have achieved, for both datasets, an F1-score of more than 70%. For Tunisian dialects (SFX, TUN), more than 69%. For Morrocan ones (FES, RAB), the best result was around 64%. The last results for both (AMM and MUS) showed an accuracy below 49%.

Dialect	Precision		Recall		F1	
	Test	Dev	Test	Dev	Test	Dev
ALE	55	62	62	57	58	60
ALG	71	73	76	80	73	76
ALX	72	70	76	78	74	74
AMM	49	43	54	54	51	48
ASW	53	47	66	60	58	53
BAG	65	74	61	58	63	65
BAS	70	68	62	64	66	66
BEI	75	77	56	56	64	65
BEN	62	65	68	70	65	68
CAI	64	65	41	41	50	50
DAM	56	65	54	49	55	56
DOH	64	57	61	61	63	59
FES	65	63	62	69	64	66
JED	53	63	56	61	55	62
JER	50	45	60	58	55	51
KHA	55	49	72	68	62	57
MOS	78	82	78	78	78	80
MSA	62	60	71	82	66	69
MUS	60	60	44	41	51	49
RAB	68	74	59	56	63	64
RIY	54	52	57	61	56	56
SAL	51	55	50	47	51	51
SAN	66	82	67	69	66	75
SFX	63	68	72	77	67	72
TRI	74	73	70	73	72	73
TUN	78	79	61	63	69	70
macro avg	63	64	62	63	62	63

Table 6: Best Results for the Test and Dev datasets, in terms of Precision, Recall and F1.

In figure 3, we show the average accuracy of the 5-regions and MSA, as described in (Salameh et al., 2018), for both development and test set. We notice that the best results were achieved for Yemen region with an accuracy of 75%, and an average accuracy of over 67% for the Maghreb Region.

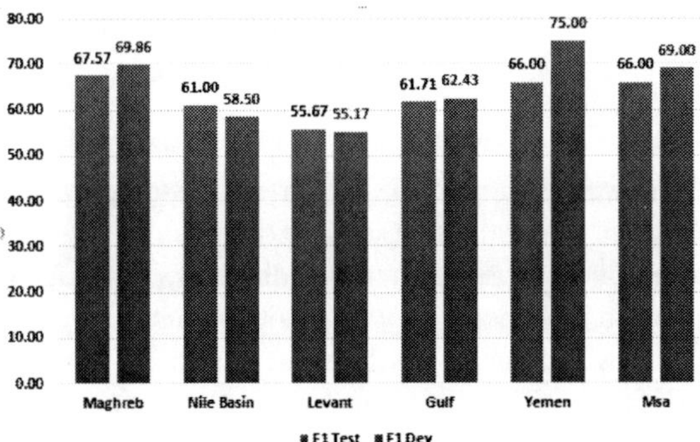

Figure 3: Average accuracy per region

6 Conclusion

In this paper, we proposed an Arabic fine-grained dialect identification system. Our best run on the test data yielded an F1-Macro score of 62% using Naive Bayes classifier and word n-gram features. Despite the simplicity of these features, the results were promising. In order to improve performance, we intend to investigate alternative methods as deep learning architectures and rule-based techniques in future work.

References

Houda Bouamor, Nizar Habash, Mohammad Salameh, Wajdi Zaghouani, Owen Rambow, Dana Abdulrahim, Ossama Obeid, Salam Khalifa, Fadhl Eryani, Alexander Erdmann, and Kemal Oflazer. 2018. The MADAR Arabic Dialect Corpus and Lexicon. In *Proceedings of the Language Resources and Evaluation Conference (LREC)*, Miyazaki, Japan.

Houda Bouamor, Sabit Hassan, and Nizar Habash. 2019. The MADAR Shared Task on Arabic Fine-Grained Dialect Identification. In *Proceedings of the Fourth Arabic Natural Language Processing Workshop (WANLP19)*, Florence, Italy.

Abed Alhakim Freihat, Mourad Abbas, Gábor Bella, and Fausto Giunchiglia. 2018a. Towards an optimal solution to lemmatization in arabic. *Procedia computer science*, 142:132–140.

Abed Alhakim Freihat, Gabor Bella, Hamdy Mubarak, and Fausto Giunchiglia. 2018b. A single-model approach for arabic segmentation, pos tagging, and named entity recognition. In *2018 2nd International Conference on Natural Language and Speech Processing (ICNLSP)*, pages 1–8. IEEE.

Nizar Habash, Mona Diab, and Owen Rambow. 2012. Conventional orthography for dialectal Arabic. In *Proceedings of the Eighth International Conference on Language Resources and Evaluation (LREC-2012)*, pages 711–718, Istanbul, Turkey. European Language Resources Association (ELRA).

Nizar Habash, Fadhl Eryani, Salam Khalifa, Owen Rambow, Dana Abdulrahim, Alexander Erdmann, Reem Faraj, Wajdi Zaghouani, Houda Bouamor, Nasser Zalmout, Sara Hassan, Faisal Al-Shargi, Sakhar Alkhereyf, Basma Abdulkareem, Ramy Eskander, Mohammad Salameh, and Hind Saddiki. 2018. Unified guidelines and resources for Arabic dialect orthography. In *Proceedings of the 11th Language Resources and Evaluation Conference*, Miyazaki, Japan. European Language Resource Association.

Mohamed Lichouri, Mourad Abbas, Abed Alhakim Freihat, and Dhiya El Hak Megtouf. 2018. Word-level vs sentence-level language identification: Application to algerian and arabic dialects. In *Proceedins of the 4th International Conference on Arabic Computational Linguistics (ACLing 2018)*.

Karima Meftouh, Salima Harrat, Salma Jamoussi, Mourad Abbas, and Kamel Smaïli. 2015. Machine translation experiments on PADIC: A parallel arabic dialect corpus. In *Proceedings of the 29th Pacific Asia Conference on Language, Information and Computation, PACLIC 29, Shanghai, China, October 30 - November 1, 2015*.

Fabian Pedregosa, Gaël Varoquaux, Alexandre Gramfort, Vincent Michel, Bertrand Thirion, Olivier Grisel, Mathieu Blondel, Peter Prettenhofer, Ron Weiss, Vincent Dubourg, et al. 2011. Scikit-learn: Machine learning in python. *Journal of machine learning research*, 12(Oct):2825–2830.

Mohammad Salameh, Houda Bouamor, and Nizar Habash. 2018. Fine-grained Arabic dialect identification. In *Proceedings of the International Conference on Computational Linguistics (COLING)*, pages 1332–1344, Santa Fe, New Mexico, USA.

Toshiyuki Takezawa, Genichiro Kikui, Masahide Mizushima, and Eiichiro Sumita. 2007. Multilingual spoken language corpus development for communication research. *International Journal of Computational Linguistics & Chinese Language Processing, Volume 12, Number 3, September 2007: Special Issue on Invited Papers from ISCSLP 2006*, 12(3):303–324.

Omar F Zaidan and Chris Callison-Burch. 2014. Arabic dialect identification. *Computational Linguistics*, 40(1):171–202.

A Character Level Convolutional BiLSTM
for Arabic Dialect Identification

Mohamed Elaraby
Raisa Energy
msalem@raisaenergy.com

Ahmed Ismail Zahran
Cairo University
zahran@ieee.org

Abstract

In this paper, we describe the contribution of CU-RAISA team to the 2019 Madar shared task 2 [1], which focused on Twitter User fine-grained dialect identification. Among participating teams, our system ranked the *4th (with 61.54%) F1-Macro measure.* Our system is trained using a character level convolutional bidirectional long-short-term memory (BiLSTM) network trained on approximately 2k users' data. We show that training on concatenated user tweets as input is further superior to training on user tweets separately and assign user's label on the mode of user's tweets' predictions.

1 Introduction

Dialect identification is a sub-domain of language identification, a task that aims to differentiate between different languages given a sample of spoken or written text. Language and dialect identification are active research areas due to their usefulness as preliminary steps for other applications, such as automatic speech recognition and machine translation. The task of dialect identification poses harder challenges due to the higher inter-class similarity, which becomes harder to learn with hidden text solely due to the absence of pronunciation information that exists in audio data. (Sibun and Reynar, 1996) made the first effort to distinguish between languages with high similarity. Their dataset contained some languages with similar content, such as Serbian and Croatian, among others.

Arabic dialect identification (ADI) aims to differentiate between dialects of the Arab world, spoken by citizens of the Middle East and North Africa. Multiple forms of categorization can exist when it comes to Arabic dialect identification.

The first form is based on the geographic location, where the text is categorized with respect to the home origin of the individual. The second form is concerned with major dialects, grouping the variations from different countries into larger classes. The most common categorization of the second form for Arabic dialects is the one described by (Habash et al., 2012), which details five major dialects (Egyptian, Gulf, Iraqi, Levantine, and Maghrebi). In this paper, we will be exploring the first form of categorization. This form poses more challenges due to the increased granularity it adds to the classification task.

2 Related Work

Deep learning models have gained attention in the tasks of text-based ADI, spoken language-based ADI and hybrid (text+spoken language) ADI with the introduction of context-dependent architectures such as Long short-term memory (LSTM) and Convolutional neural networks (CNN's). Research in the past few years has explored both character-level and word-level models, along with combining these models with acoustic features from the audio recordings. (Sayadi et al., 2017) achieved a classification accuracy of 92.2% on a two-way classification task between Modern Standard Arabic (MSA) and Tunisian using a character-level LSTM model. The experiments were performed on the Tunisian Election Twitter dataset (Sayadi et al., 2016). For a fine-grained six-class classification task (MSA, Egyptian, Syrian, Jordanian, Palestinian and Tunisian) on the Multidialectal Parallel Corpus of Arabic dataset (Bouamor et al., 2014), the authors reached a classification accuracy of 63.4%. Elaraby and Abdul-Mageed (2018) experimented with attention-based bidirectional LSTM (BiLSTM) models on a two-way classification task (MSA vs. other dialects), a

---

[1]https://competitions.codalab.org/competitions/22475

Proceedings of the Fourth Arabic Natural Language Processing Workshop, pages 274–278
Florence, Italy, August 1, 2019. ©2019 Association for Computational Linguistics

three-way classification task (Egyptian, Gulf, and Levantine), and a four-way classification task that adds the MSA dialect to the previous three-way task. The dataset used in this study is the Arabic Online Commentary (AOC) dataset. (Zaidan and Callison-Burch, 2011). The system achieved an accuracy of 87.65%, 87.4% and 82.45% on the three aforementioned tasks, respectively using pretrained word embeddings trained on a large dialectly rich corpus described in (Abdul-Mageed et al., 2018). (Ali, 2018) used a character-level convolution neural network with a GRU layer for a five-way classification task (MSA, Egyptian, Gulf, Levantine, and North African). This architecture achieved 92.64% cross-validation accuracy on the training set, and a 57.59% F1 (macro) score on the test set. (Lulu and Elnagar, 2018) isolated the three most frequent dialects in AOC (Gulf, Egyptian, and Levantine). Using a word-based LSTM to differentiate between the three dialects, the authors obtained an accuracy of 71.4%, exceeding the performance of CNN, BLSTM and CLSTM models.

Along with exploring the performance of deep learning models on ADI, research has also continued to explore more classical models, such as kernel-based models and linear models, in addition to classical representations such as tf-idf. In a geographic location-based ADI task, Salameh et al. (2018) researched the effectiveness of combining multiple features with a Multinomial Naive Bias (MNB) classifier. The system combined multiple word-based and character-based n-grams with language models scoring probabilities as features. The authors used a translated version of the Basic Traveling Expression Corpus (BTEC) (Takezawa et al., 2007). For sentences with an average length of seven words, the system obtained a classification accuracy of 67.9%. As the average length of the sentence increases to 16 words, the performance of the system increased to more than 90%. This finding gives an intuition about the positive effect of sentence length on the performance of the classifier. In addition to the classification task, the authors analyzed the amount of pairwise dialect similarity between the dialects. To perform the analysis, the authors used hierarchical agglomerative clustering on the similarity matrix obtained from the percentage of shared tokens between dialects. The resulting analysis shows the amount of similarity between dialects in a certain

area, as well as the proximity of some dialects to others (e.g.: Egyptian and Levantine). MSA falls closest to Muscat and Khartoum. (Butnaru and Ionescu, 2018) used multiple kernel learning on character n-grams from text and phonetic transcriptions, along with dialectal embeddings from the audio recordings. Their model obtained an accuracy of 58.65%. (El Haj et al., 2018) researched the subjects of code-switching and bivalent words (words that occur in multiple languages or dialects with similar semantic content) in dialect identification. They developed a method called Subtractive Bivalency Profiling to build a system that can handle both of these issues. Using support vector machines (SVM) for a task to distinguish between four dialects (MSA, Egyptian, Levant, and Gulf), they achieved 76% accuracy. (Lichouri et al., 2018) researched word-based and sentence-based methods on tf-idf vectors, in addition to applying majority and minority voting techniques. The authors experimented with Bernoulli Naive Bayes (BNB) and MNB, along with Linear SVM's (LSVM). Two datasets were used for this research. The first dataset, PADIC (Meftouh et al., 2015; Harrat et al., 2014), consists of multiple dialects (MSA, Tunisian, Moroccan, Algerian, Palestenian and Syrian). For this dataset, a sentence-level BNB achieved the highest accuracy (73.15%). The second dataset consisted of eight Algerian dialects (Tenes, Constantine, Djelfa, Ain-Defla, Tizi-Ouzou, Batna, Annaba, and Algiers), for which an LSVM model achieved the highest accuracy (41.05%).

3 Data

3.1 Dataset Description

We used the Arabic twitter dataset released by the organizers of the "User Dialect Identification task". The dataset is portioned into 217,593 tweets representing 2180 users for training, 29,870 for development representing 300 users, and 49,962 for testing representing 500 users. Full detailed description of the data can be found in task description paper Bouamor et al. (2019).

3.2 Accessibility of tweets

One challenging part of this task was the accessibility of tweets as some users' tweets weren't accessible at the time we crawled their timelines from twitter. Training data portion were reduced from 2180 users to 2032 users. The total number of training tweets were reduced to 192,389. Development data were reduced from 300 to 281 users, while the number of development tweets was reduced to 26,528. The number of test users was reduced from 500 to 463.

4 Methods

4.1 Pre-processing

We adopt basic preprocessing techniques to our training, development, and test sets. This involves filtering out URLs and user mentions. For the vocabulary V, we train using character-based vocabulary. We filter out least frequent characters occurring < 20 times, which leaves $|V| = 2377$ of unique characters.

4.2 Data Preparation:

We conduct two sets of experiments; (1): train on tweet level annotated by the country of the user. In that case, the maximum input sequence length is 140. (2) : train on user's concatenated tweets together. Maximum sequence length grown to 12000 characters. In the results section, we show that training on concatenated user tweets improves performance compared to training on individual tweets. On the hidden units layer to prevent the network from over-fitting on training set.

4.3 Models

4.3.1 Traditional Models

Traditional models refer to models based on feature engineering methods with linear and probabilistic classifiers. In our experiments, we use (1) logistic regression, and (2) multinomial Naive Bayes as baselines. We use character ngrams, word ngrams, and a combination of both as feature set.

4.3.2 Deep Learning Models

We develop models based on deep neural networks based on variations of (1) convolution neural networks (CNNs) and (2) recurrent neural networks (RNNs) which have proved useful for several NLP tasks. Both RNNs, and CNNs s are able to capture sequential dependencies especially in time series data, of which language can be seen as an example.

Our Model: We use a combination of convolution neural network and bidirectional long short term memory (BiLSTM). The following part describes how we apply CNN to extract higher-level sequences of word features and BiLSTM to capture long-term dependencies over window feature sequences respectively.

- *Input layer:* an input layer to map word sequence w into a sequence vector x where x_w is a real-valued vector ($X_w \epsilon \mathbb{R}^{d_{emb}}$ where $d_{emb} = 50$). Character embedding are randomly initialized and not learnt externally.

- *Convolution layer:* Multiple convolution operations are applied in parallel to the input layer to map input sequence **x** into a hidden sequence **h**

  A filter $k \epsilon \mathbb{R}^{w d_{emb}}$ is applied to a window of concatenated word embedding of size w to produce a new feature c_i . Where $c_i \epsilon \mathbb{R}, c_i = k \cdot x_{i:i+w-1+b}$ b is the inductive bias term $b \epsilon \mathbb{R}$, and $x_{i:i+w-1}$ is a concatenation of $x_i, x_{i+1}, .., x_{i+w-1}$

  The filter sizes used are ranging from 1-13 and the number of filters used is ranging from 10-150. Finally, different convolution outputs are concatenated into a sequence $c \epsilon \mathbb{R}^{n-h+1}$ and passed into a time distributed layer to convert it into suitable output for the BiLSTM layer.

- *BiLSTM Layer:* We use a Bidirectional LSTM architecture consisting of 256 dimensions hidden units. The BiLSTM is designed to capture long-term dependencies via augmenting a standard RNN with two memory states, forward and backward. The forward direction state $\overrightarrow{C}_t$, with $\overrightarrow{C}_t \in \mathbb{R}$ at time step t. The forward LSTM takes in a previous state $\overrightarrow{h}_{t-1}$ and input x_t, to calculate the hidden state $\overrightarrow{h}_t$ as follows:

$$\overrightarrow{i}_t = \sigma(W_{\overrightarrow{i}}[\overrightarrow{h}_{t-1}, x_t] + b_{\overrightarrow{i}})$$
$$\overrightarrow{f}_t = \sigma(W_{\overrightarrow{f}} \cdot [\overrightarrow{h}_{t-1}, x_t] + b_{\overrightarrow{f}})$$
$$\overrightarrow{C}_t = tanh(W_{\overrightarrow{C}} \cdot [\overrightarrow{h}_{t-1}, x_t] + b_{\overrightarrow{C}})$$
$$\overrightarrow{C}_t = \overrightarrow{f}_t \odot \overrightarrow{C}_{t-1} + i_t \odot \overrightarrow{C}$$
$$\overrightarrow{o}_t = \sigma(W_o[\overrightarrow{h}_{t-1}, x_t] + b_{\overrightarrow{o}})$$
$$\overrightarrow{h}_t = o_t \odot tanh(\overrightarrow{C}_t)$$

where σ is the sigmoid, $tanh$ is the hyperpolic tangent function, and $\odot$ is the dot product between two vectors. The $\overrightarrow{i}_t, \overrightarrow{f}_t, \overrightarrow{o}_t$

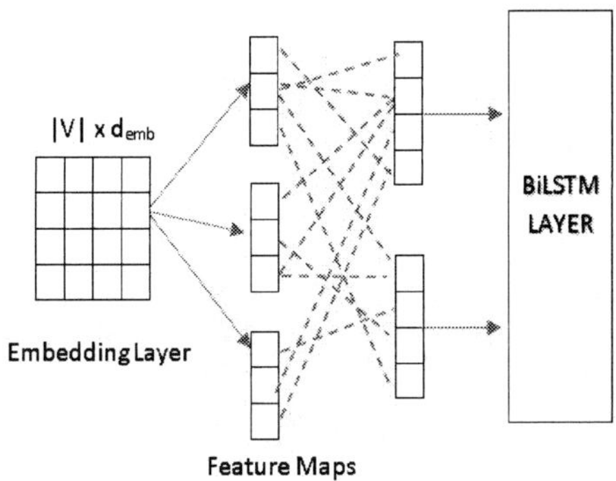

Figure 1: Our char level Convolution -BiLSTM

are the *input, forget,* and *output* gates, and the $\overrightarrow{C}_t$ is a new memory cell vector with candidates that could be added to the state in the forward direction. The same operation is done for the backward direction. We apply L2 regularization to avoid network overfitting.

- *Softmax Layer:* Finally, the combined hidden units (forward and backward) is converted into a probability distribution over l via softmax function, where l is the number of classes in our case (21 classes).

Figure 1 shows a block diagram of our network architecture.

Training and Optimization

We try a small set of hyper-parameters, identifying best settings on our validation set using grid search. We train the network for 40 epochs each. For optimization, we use Adam (Kingma and Ba, 2014), The models weights W are initialized from a normal distribution $W \sim N$ with a small standard deviation of $= 0.05$ We apply two sources of regularization: dropout: we apply a dropout rate of 0.2 on the input embeddings to prevent co-adaptation of hidden units activation, and $L2$ norm: we also apply an L2-norm regularization with a small value (0.002)

5 Results

We evaluated most of the experiments on the development set using an accuracy metric. Table 1 concluded our experimentation results on development set which consists of 281 users in total after excluding tweets of non-accessible users.

For the test which set consists of 500 users, we were able to access 463 users which we predicted

Models	Accuracy	F1-Macro
Individual tweets		
Logistic Regression (1-11 ngrams)	36.5	-
Multinomial Naive Bayes (1-11 ngrams)	36.75	-
Char-Level CNN	50.12	-
Char-Level C-BiLSTM	**51.7**	42.3
Concatenated tweets		
Logistic Regression (1-11 ngrams)	45.5	-
Multinomial Naive Bayes (1-11 ngrams)	46.7	-
Char-Level CNN	68.8	-
Char-Level C-BiLSTM	**71.92**	62.21

Table 1: Experimental results on development set

using our C-BiLSTM network. For the left 37 users we assign the most common class to it which is *"Saudi_Arabia"* . The final result reported by organizers on the test set was very close in terms of both accuracy and F1 macro measure achieving an accuracy of 72.6% and 61.5%.

6 Conclusion

In this paper, we described our system submitted to MADAR shared task, focused on country level dialect identification from Twitter data. We explored the utility of tuning different word- and character-level based models. A char based convolutional BiLSTM achieved the best performance in terms of both accuracy and F1-macro measure. Given our limited resources at that time we weren't able to experiment transfer learning techniques as pre-trained embeddings or language models which proved to be beneficial in various Natural Language Processing tasks. In future work, we plan to exploit a number of those techniques in the fine-grained dialect identification task.

References

Muhammad Abdul-Mageed, Hassan Alhuzali, and Mohamed Elaraby. 2018. You tweet what you speak: A city-level dataset of arabic dialects. In *Proceedings of the Eleventh International Conference on Language Resources and Evaluation (LREC-2018)*.

Mohamed Ali. 2018. Character level convolutional neural network for arabic dialect identification. In *Proceedings of the Fifth Workshop on NLP for Similar Languages, Varieties and Dialects (VarDial 2018)*, pages 122–127.

Houda Bouamor, Nizar Habash, and Kemal Oflazer. 2014. A multidialectal parallel corpus of arabic. In *LREC*, pages 1240–1245.

Houda Bouamor, Sabit Hassan, and Nizar Habash. 2019. The MADAR Shared Task on Arabic Fine-

Grained Dialect Identification. In *Proceedings of the Fourth Arabic Natural Language Processing Workshop (WANLP19)*, Florence, Italy.

Andrei M Butnaru and Radu Tudor Ionescu. 2018. Unibuckernel reloaded: First place in arabic dialect identification for the second year in a row. *arXiv preprint arXiv:1805.04876*.

Mahmoud El Haj, Paul Edward Rayson, and Mariam Aboelezz. 2018. Arabic dialect identification in the context of bivalency and code-switching.

Mohamed Elaraby and Muhammad Abdul-Mageed. 2018. Deep models for arabic dialect identification on benchmarked data. In *Proceedings of the Fifth Workshop on NLP for Similar Languages, Varieties and Dialects (VarDial 2018)*, pages 263–274.

Nizar Habash, Mona T Diab, and Owen Rambow. 2012. Conventional orthography for dialectal arabic. In *LREC*, pages 711–718.

Salima Harrat, Karima Meftouh, Mourad Abbas, and Kamel Smaili. 2014. Building resources for algerian arabic dialects. In *15th Annual Conference of the International Communication Association Interspeech*.

Diederik P Kingma and Jimmy Ba. 2014. Adam: A method for stochastic optimization. *arXiv preprint arXiv:1412.6980*.

Mohamed Lichouri, Mourad Abbas, Abed Alhakim Freihat, and Dhiya El Hak Megtouf. 2018. Word-level vs sentence-level language identification: Application to algerian and arabic dialects. *Procedia Computer Science*, 142:246–253.

Leena Lulu and Ashraf Elnagar. 2018. Automatic arabic dialect classification using deep learning models. *Procedia computer science*, 142:262–269.

Karima Meftouh, Salima Harrat, Salma Jamoussi, Mourad Abbas, and Kamel Smaili. 2015. Machine translation experiments on padic: A parallel arabic dialect corpus. In *The 29th Pacific Asia conference on language, information and computation*.

Mohammad Salameh, Houda Bouamor, and Nizar Habash. 2018. Fine-grained Arabic dialect identification. In *Proceedings of the International Conference on Computational Linguistics (COLING)*, pages 1332–1344, Santa Fe, New Mexico, USA.

Karim Sayadi, Mansour Hamidi, Marc Bui, Marcus Liwicki, and Andreas Fischer. 2017. Character-level dialect identification in arabic using long short-term memory. In *International Conference on Computational Linguistics and Intelligent Text Processing*, pages 324–337. Springer.

Karim Sayadi, Marcus Liwicki, Rolf Ingold, and Marc Bui. 2016. Tunisian dialect and modern standard arabic dataset for sentiment analysis: Tunisian election context. In *Second International Conference on Arabic Computational Linguistics, ACLING*, pages 35–53.

Penelope Sibun and Jeffrey C Reynar. 1996. Language identification: Examining the issues.

Toshiyuki Takezawa, Genichiro Kikui, Masahide Mizushima, and Eiichiro Sumita. 2007. Multilingual spoken language corpus development for communication research. *International Journal of Computational Linguistics & Chinese Language Processing, Volume 12, Number 3, September 2007: Special Issue on Invited Papers from ISCSLP 2006*, 12(3):303–324.

Omar F. Zaidan and Chris Callison-Burch. 2011. The arabic online commentary dataset: an annotated dataset of informal arabic with high dialectal content. In *Proceedings of the 49th Annual Meeting of the Association for Computational Linguistics: Human Language Technologies: short papers-Volume 2*, pages 37–41. Association for Computational Linguistics.

No Army, No Navy: BERT Semi-Supervised Learning of Arabic Dialects [*]

Chiyu Zhang   **Muhammad Abdul-Mageed**
Natural Language Processing Lab
The University of British Columbia
chiyu94@alumni.ubc.ca, muhammad.mageeed@ubc.ca

Abstract

We present our deep leaning system submitted to MADAR shared task 2 focused on twitter user dialect identification. We develop tweet-level identification models based on GRUs and BERT in supervised and semi-supervised settings. We then introduce a simple, yet effective, method of porting tweet-level labels at the level of users. Our system ranks top 1 in the competition, with 71.70% macro F_1 score and 77.40% accuracy.

1 Introduction

Language identification (LID) is an important NLP task that usually acts as an enabling technology in a pipeline involving another downstream task such as machine translation (Salloum et al., 2014) or sentiment analysis (Abdul-Mageed, 2017b,a). Although several works have focused on detecting languages in global settings (see Jauhiainen et al. (2018) for a survey), there has not been extensive research on teasing apart similar languages or language varieties (Zampieri et al., 2018). This is the case for Arabic, the term used to collectively refer to a large number of varieties with a vast population of native speakers ($\sim$ 300 million). For this reason, we focus on detecting fine-grained Arabic dialect as part of our contribution to the MADAR shared task 2, twitter user dialect identification (Bouamor et al., 2019).

Previous works on Arabic (e.g., Zaidan and Callison-Burch (2011, 2014); Elfardy and Diab (2013); Cotterell and Callison-Burch (2014)) have primarily targeted cross-country regional varieties such as Egyptian, Gulf, and Levantine, in addition to Modern Standard Arabic (MSA). These

works exploited social data from blogs (Diab et al., 2010; Elfardy and Diab, 2012; Al-Sabbagh and Girju, 2012; Sadat et al., 2014), the general Web (Al-Sabbagh and Girju, 2012), online news sites comments sections (Zaidan and Callison-Burch, 2011), and Twitter (Abdul-Mageed and Diab, 2012; Abdul-Mageed et al., 2014; Mubarak and Darwish, 2014; Qwaider et al., 2018). Other works have used translated data (e.g., Bouamor et al. (2018)), or speech transcripts (e.g., Malmasi and Zampieri (2016). More recently, other works reporting larger-scale datasets at the country-level were undertaken. These include data spanning 10-to-17 different countries (Zaghouani and Charfi, 2018; Abdul-Mageed et al., 2018).

To solve Arabic dialect identification, many researchers developed models based on computational linguistics and machine learning (Elfardy and Diab, 2013; Salloum et al., 2014; Cotterell and Callison-Burch, 2014), and deep learning (Elaraby and Abdul-Mageed, 2018). In this paper, we focus on using state-of-the-arts deep learning architectures to identify Arabic dialects of Twitter users at the country level. We use the MADAR twitter corpus (Bouamor et al., 2019), comprising 21 country-level dialect labels. Namely, we employ unidirectional Gated Recurrent Unit (GRU) (Cho et al., 2014) as our baseline and pre-trained Multilingual Bidirectional Encoder Representations from Transformers (BERT) (Devlin et al., 2018) to identify dialect classes for individual tweets (which we then port at user level). We also apply semi-supervised learning to augment our training data, with a goal to improve model performance. Our system ranks top 1 in the shared task. The rest of the paper is organized as follows: data are described in Section 2. Section 3 introduces our methods, follow by experiments in Section 4. We conclude in Section 5.

---

[*] The title is word play on the Yiddish linguist Max Weinreich much quoted metaphor (in Yiddish) "A language is a dialect with an army and navy". See: https://en.wikipedia.org/wiki/A_language_is_a_dialect_with_an_army_and_navy.

Proceedings of the Fourth Arabic Natural Language Processing Workshop, pages 279–284
Florence, Italy, August 1, 2019. ©2019 Association for Computational Linguistics

2 Data

Twitter user dialect identification is the second sub-task of 2019 MADAR shared task (Bouamor et al., 2019). This task is set up as fine-grained multi-class classification where corpus released by organizers are labeled with the tagset {*Algeria, Bahrain, Djibouti, Egypt, Iraq, Jordan, Kuwait, Lebanon, Libya, Mauritania, Morocco, Oman, Palestine, Qatar, Saudi_Arabia, Somalia, Sudan, Syria, Tunisia, United_Arab_Emirates, Yemen*}. The corpus is divided into train, dev and test (with the test set shared without labels). For each tweet, organizers released a user id and tweet id and participants needed to crawl the actual tweets. We were not able to crawl part of the data because of unavailability on the Twitter platform. The distribution of the data in our splits after crawling is as follows: 2,036 (TRAIN-A), 281 (DEV) and 466 (TEST). For our experiments, we also make use of the task 1 corpus (95,000 sentences (Bouamor et al., 2018)). More specifically, we concatenate the task 1 data to the training data of task 2, to create TRAIN-B. Note that both DEV and TEST across our experiments are exclusively the data released in task 2, as described above. TEST labels were only released to participants after the official task evaluation. Table 1 shows statistics of the data.

	# of tweets		
	TRAIN	**DEV**	**TEST**
TRAIN-A	193,086	26,588	43,909
TRAIN-B	288,086	–	–

Table 1: Distribution of classes within the MADAR twitter corpus.

3 Methods

3.1 Pre-processing & Architectures

With tweet ids at hand, we crawl users tweets via the Twitter API. We remove all usernames, URLs, and diacritics in the data. For evaluation, we use accuracy and macro $F_1 - score$. For modeling, we use two main deep learning architectures, Gated Recurrent Unit (GRU) and Bidirectional Encoder Representations from Transformers (BERT). For GRU, we tokenize tweets into word sequences by white-space. For BERT input, we apply Word-Piece tokenization. We set the maximal sequence length to 50 words/WordPieces. A GRU (Cho et al., 2014; Chung et al., 2014) is a simplification of long-short term memory networks (LSTM), which in turn are a version of recurrent neural networks.

For BERT (Devlin et al., 2018), it was introduced to dispense with recurrence and convolution. Its model architecture is a multi-layer bidirectional Transformer encoder (Vaswani et al., 2017). It uses masked language models to enable pre-trained deep bidirectional representations, in addition to a binary *next sentence prediction* task. The pre-trained BERT can be easily fine-tuned on large suite of sentence-level and token-level tasks.We also use semi-supervised learning in our modeling, as we explain next.

3.2 Semi-supervise Learning

Supervised deep learning requires a large number of labeled data points. For this reason, we investigate augmenting our training data with automatically-predicted tweets using semi-supervised learning (SSL). More specifically, we use self-training. Self-training is a wrapper method for SSL (Triguero et al., 2015; Pavlinek and Podgorelec, 2017) where a classifier is initially trained on a small set of labeled samples D^l. Then, the learned classifier is used to classify the unlabeled sample set D^u. Based on the predication output, the most confident samples with their predicted labels are added to the labeled set. The classifier can then be re-trained on the new 'labeled' set. This process can be repeated until all the samples from D^u are added to D^l or a given stopping criteria is reached. We now introduce our experiments.

4 Experiments

We illustrate our four main sets of experiment. We present (i) our baseline model, GRU (Section 4.1), (ii) fine-tuning on BERT-Base, Multilingual Cased model for dialect identification (Section 4.2), (iii) semi-supervised learning with unlabeled data 4.3, (iv) user-level dialect identification (DID) 4.4.

4.1 GRU

We train a baseline GRU network with TRIAN-A. This network has one layer unidirectional GRU with 500 unites and a linear, output layer. The input word tokens are embedded by the trainable word vectors which are initialized with a standard normal distribution, with $\mu = 0$, and $\sigma = 1$, i.e., $W \sim N(0, 1)$. We apply Adam (Kingma and Ba, 2014) with a fixed learning rate of $1e - 3$ for optimization. For regularization, we use dropout (Srivastava et al., 2014) rate of 0.5 on the hidden layer. We set the maximal length of sequence in our GRU model to 50, and choose an arbitrary vocabulary size of 10,000 words. We employ batch training with a batch size of 8 on this model. We run the network for 10 epochs and save the model at the end of each epoch, choosing the model that performs highest on DEV as our best model. We report our best result on dev in Table 2. Our best result is acquired with 3 epochs. As Table 2 shows, the baseline obtains $accuracy = 46.81\%$ and $F_1 = 28.84$.

4.2 BERT

As mentioned earlier, we use the BERT-Base Multilingual Cased model released by the authors [1]. The model is trained on 104 languages (including Arabic) with 12 layer, 768 hidden units each, 12 attention heads, and has 110M parameters in entire model. The model has 119,547 shared Word-Pieces vocabulary, and was pre-trained on the entire Wikipedia for each language. For fine-tuning, we use a maximum sequence size of 50 tokens and a batch size of 32. We set the learning rate to $2e-5$ and train for 10 epochs. We use the same hyper-parameters in all of our BERT models. We fine-tune BERT on TRAIN-A and TRAIN-B sets, and call these BERT-A and BERT-B respectively. As Table 2 shows, both BERT models acquire better performance than the GRU models. On accuracy, BERT-A is 1.69% better than the baseline, and BERT-B is 1.95% better than baseline. BERT-B obtains 34.87 F_1 which is 5.03 better than the baseline and 0.94 better than BERT-A. Our best model of above two sets of experiment is BERT-B which obtains the best accuracy and F_1. Hence, we use BERT-B in our following semi-supervised learning experiments.

4.3 Semi-supervised Learning

As we mentioned earlier, we apply self-training in order to augment training set. For this purpose, we use an in-house unlabeled, Arabic dataset of 9,981,965 tweets. We refer to this unlabeled dataset as `unlabeled-10M`. We pre-process unlabeled-10M using the same method as the rest of our data. We use the best model from Section 4.2 (i.e. BERT-B, which is trained on TRAIN-

Model	Acc.	F1
Baseline (GRU)	46.81	29.84
BERT-A	48.50	33.93
BERT-B	**48.76**	**34.87**

Table 2: Model performance. Baseline is a unidirectional 500-unit, one-layered GRU. Baseline and BERT-A are trained on TRAIN-A. BERT-B is trained on TRAIN-B.

	# of tweets	
	New	**Total**
5%_SEMI	499,102	787,188
10%_SEMI	998,196	1,286,282
25%_SEMI	2,495,491	2,783,577
5%_Class_SEMI	499,087	787,173
10%_Class_SEMI	998,186	1,286,272
25%_Class_SEMI	2,495,486	2,783,572

Table 3: Data splits for our emi-supervised learning experiments. *New:* The new dataset confidently predicted with semi-supervised learning that are added to TRAIN-B.

B) to predict dialect labels for unlabeled-10M. To obtain the best performance, we investigate various settings to select the most reliable samples before adding such samples to our training data. These settings are based on the per-class value in the softmax/output layer, as follows: **(i) Top-N%:** We select samples which obtain top $n\%$ softmax values and add them with their predicted labels to TRAIN-B. We refer to the new training set as N_SEMI. **(ii) Top-N%_Class:** We also extract the samples which obtain top $n\%$ softmax value within each county class and add them to our training data, referring to the new train set as N_Class_SEMI. In our experiments, we choose n from the set $\{5\%, 10\%, 25\%\}$. Then, we fine-tune the BERT-Base, Multilingual Cased model on the resulting six new training sets (e.g., 5%_SEMI, 5%_Class_SEMI, 10%_SEMI) with the same hyper-parameters as Section 4.2. We evaluate on DEV. For reference, BERT-N denotes the model which is trained on N_SEMI, and BERT-NClass_SEMI denotes the model which is trained on N_Class_SEMI. We present the description of these six train sets in Table 3. As Table 4 shows, most semi-supervised models outperform BERT-B. For accuracy, the best model is

Model	Acc.	F1
Baseline (GRU)	46.810	29.840
BERT-B	48.755	34.868
BERT-5%	<u>48.958</u>	**35.931**
BERT-10%	**49.394**	<u>35.440</u>
BERT-25%	48.751	<u>35.305</u>
BERT-5%_Class_SEMI	48.706	34.774
BERT-10%_Class_SEMI	<u>48.842</u>	33.835
BERT-25%_Class_SEMI	<u>49.097</u>	<u>35.813</u>

Table 4: Semi-supervised learning. All models are evaluated on DEV, with TRAIN-B as training data. Results higher than BERT-B are <u>underlined</u>. Best result is in **bold**.

BERT_10% ($acc = 49.34\%$) with 4 epochs. It is 0.639% higher than BERT-B. For F_1, the best model is BERT_5% ($F_1 = 35.931$) with 3 epochs. We use these two model in the following user-level DID. Since the official metric of the shared task is *macro F_1 score*, we also consider BERT-25%_Class_SEMI as a candidate model for user-level DID since it acquires better F_1 than BERT-10% as Table 4 shows.

4.4 User-level DID

Our aforementioned models identify dialect on the tweet-level, rather than directly detect the dialect of a user. Hence, we use tweet-level predicted labels (and associated softmax values) as a proxy for user-level labels. For each predicted label, we use the softmax value as a threshold for including only highest confidently predicted tweets. Since in some cases softmax values can be low, we try all values between 0.00 and 0.99 to take a softmax-based majority class as the user-level predicted label, fine-tuning on our DEV set. Figure 1 provides performance of the `BERT-25%_Class_SEMI` model on DEV using different softmax threshold values. Note that the shared task requires a maximum of three models submitted. For these, we chose the top 3 models in Table 4 (i.e., BERT-5%, BERT-10%, and BERT-25%_Class_SEMI). As a precauion, we also use the BERT-B when we fine-tune on the user-level on DEV. We then use only the 3 models that perform best on DEV as our official task submission. As Table 5 shows, the best three systems on DEV are BERT-B, BERT-5% and BERT-25%_Class_SEMI. For the 34 unavailable users,

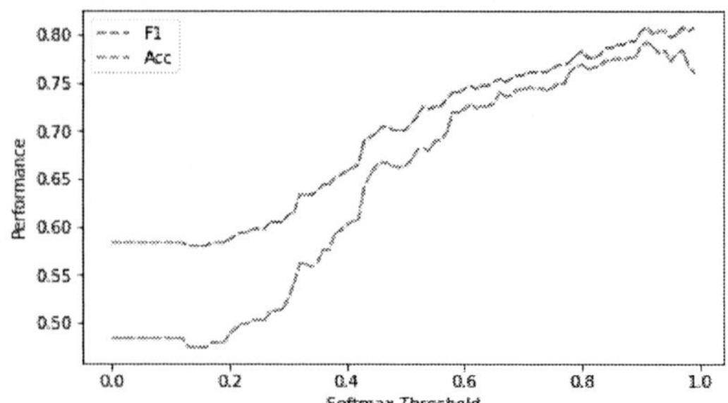

Figure 1: User-level Performance on DEV using different softmax value thresholds.

we assigned the majority class in TRAIN-A (i.e., '*Saudi_Arabia*'). According to 5, our best system on TEST set is BERT-5% with 77.04% accuracy and 71.70 F_1. It rank *top 1* in the shared task.

Model	Thresh	DEV		TEST	
		Acc.	F1	Acc.	F1
BERT-B	0.91	79.36	75.19	76.40	68.47
BERT-5%	0.89	79.36	76.05	**77.40**	**71.70**
BERT-10%	0.92	77.94	74.47	-	-
B-25%CS	0.91	**80.78**	**79.25**	75.80	69.17

Table 5: User-level results. TEST results come from the official leaderboard of the shared task. ***B-25%CS=*** `BERT-25%_Class_SEMI`.

5 Conclusion

In this paper, we described our submission to the MADAR shared task 2, focused on user-level Arabic dialect identification. We show how we acquire effective models using various supervised and semi-supervised methods, porting tweet-level labels to the user level. Our semi-supervised model with BERT achieves best results in the official task evaluation. In the future, we will investigate more extensive semi-supervised methods to improve performance.

6 Acknowledgement

We acknowledge the support of the Natural Sciences and Engineering Research Council of Canada (NSERC), the Social Sciences Research Council of Canada (SSHRC), and Compute Canada (`www.computecanada.ca`).

References

Muhammad Abdul-Mageed. 2017a. Modeling arabic subjectivity and sentiment in lexical space. *Information Processing & Management*.

Muhammad Abdul-Mageed. 2017b. Not all segments are created equal: Syntactically motivated sentiment analysis in lexical space. In *Proceedings of the third Arabic natural language processing workshop*, pages 147–156.

Muhammad Abdul-Mageed, Hassan Alhuzali, and Mohamed Elaraby. 2018. You tweet what you speak: A city-level dataset of arabic dialects. In *LREC*, pages 3653–3659.

Muhammad Abdul-Mageed, Mona Diab, and Sandra Kübler. 2014. Samar: Subjectivity and sentiment analysis for arabic social media. *Computer Speech & Language*, 28(1):20–37.

Muhammad Abdul-Mageed and Mona T Diab. 2012. Awatif: A multi-genre corpus for modern standard arabic subjectivity and sentiment analysis. In *LREC*, pages 3907–3914.

Rania Al-Sabbagh and Roxana Girju. 2012. Yadac: Yet another dialectal arabic corpus. In *LREC*, pages 2882–2889.

Houda Bouamor, Nizar Habash, Mohammad Salameh, Wajdi Zaghouani, Owen Rambow, Dana Abdulrahim, Ossama Obeid, Salam Khalifa, Fadhl Eryani, Alexander Erdmann, et al. 2018. The madar arabic dialect corpus and lexicon. In *Proceedings of the Eleventh International Conference on Language Resources and Evaluation (LREC-2018)*.

Houda Bouamor, Sabit Hassan, and Nizar Habash. 2019. The MADAR Shared Task on Arabic Fine-Grained Dialect Identification. In *Proceedings of the Fourth Arabic Natural Language Processing Workshop (WANLP19)*, Florence, Italy.

Kyunghyun Cho, Bart Van Merriënboer, Caglar Gulcehre, Dzmitry Bahdanau, Fethi Bougares, Holger Schwenk, and Yoshua Bengio. 2014. Learning phrase representations using rnn encoder-decoder for statistical machine translation. *arXiv preprint arXiv:1406.1078*.

Junyoung Chung, Caglar Gulcehre, KyungHyun Cho, and Yoshua Bengio. 2014. Empirical evaluation of gated recurrent neural networks on sequence modeling. *arXiv preprint arXiv:1412.3555*.

Ryan Cotterell and Chris Callison-Burch. 2014. A multi-dialect, multi-genre corpus of informal written arabic. In *LREC*, pages 241–245.

Jacob Devlin, Ming-Wei Chang, Kenton Lee, and Kristina Toutanova. 2018. Bert: Pre-training of deep bidirectional transformers for language understanding. *arXiv preprint arXiv:1810.04805*.

Mona Diab, Nizar Habash, Owen Rambow, Mohamed Altantawy, and Yassine Benajiba. 2010. Colaba: Arabic dialect annotation and processing. In *Lrec workshop on semitic language processing*, pages 66–74.

Mohamed Elaraby and Muhammad Abdul-Mageed. 2018. Deep models for Arabic dialect identification on benchmarked data. In *Proceedings of the Fifth Workshop on NLP for Similar Languages, Varieties and Dialects (VarDial 2018)*, pages 263–274, Santa Fe, New Mexico, USA. Association for Computational Linguistics.

Heba Elfardy and Mona T Diab. 2012. Simplified guidelines for the creation of large scale dialectal arabic annotations. In *LREC*, pages 371–378.

Heba Elfardy and Mona T Diab. 2013. Sentence level dialect identification in arabic. In *ACL (2)*, pages 456–461.

Tommi Jauhiainen, Marco Lui, Marcos Zampieri, Timothy Baldwin, and Krister Lindén. 2018. Automatic language identification in texts: A survey. *arXiv preprint arXiv:1804.08186*.

Diederik Kingma and Jimmy Ba. 2014. Adam: A method for stochastic optimization. *arXiv preprint arXiv:1412.6980*.

Shervin Malmasi and Marcos Zampieri. 2016. Arabic dialect identification in speech transcripts. *VarDial 3*, page 106.

Hamdy Mubarak and Kareem Darwish. 2014. Using twitter to collect a multi-dialectal corpus of arabic. In *Proceedings of the EMNLP 2014 Workshop on Arabic Natural Language Processing (ANLP)*, pages 1–7.

Miha Pavlinek and Vili Podgorelec. 2017. Text classification method based on self-training and lda topic models. *Expert Systems with Applications*, 80:83–93.

Chatrine Qwaider, Motaz Saad, Stergios Chatzikyriakidis, and Simon Dobnik. 2018. Shami: A corpus of levantine arabic dialects. In *Proceedings of the Eleventh International Conference on Language Resources and Evaluation (LREC-2018)*.

Fatiha Sadat, Farnazeh Kazemi, and Atefeh Farzindar. 2014. Automatic identification of arabic language varieties and dialects in social media. *Proceedings of SocialNLP*, page 22.

Wael Salloum, Heba Elfardy, Linda Alamir-Salloum, Nizar Habash, and Mona Diab. 2014. Sentence level dialect identification for machine translation system selection. In *Proceedings of the 52nd Annual Meeting of the Association for Computational Linguistics (Volume 2: Short Papers)*, volume 2, pages 772–778.

Nitish Srivastava, Geoffrey Hinton, Alex Krizhevsky, Ilya Sutskever, and Ruslan Salakhutdinov. 2014. Dropout: a simple way to prevent neural networks from overfitting. *The Journal of Machine Learning Research*, 15(1):1929–1958.

Isaac Triguero, Salvador García, and Francisco Herrera. 2015. Self-labeled techniques for semi-supervised learning: taxonomy, software and empirical study. *Knowledge and Information Systems*, 42(2):245–284.

Ashish Vaswani, Noam Shazeer, Niki Parmar, Jakob Uszkoreit, Llion Jones, Aidan N Gomez, ukasz Kaiser, and Illia Polosukhin. 2017. Attention is all you need. In *Advances in neural information processing systems*, pages 5998–6008.

Wajdi Zaghouani and Anis Charfi. 2018. Arap-tweet: A large multi-dialect twitter corpus for gender, age and language variety identification. In *Proceedings of the Eleventh International Conference on Language Resources and Evaluation (LREC-2018)*.

Omar F Zaidan and Chris Callison-Burch. 2011. The arabic online commentary dataset: an annotated dataset of informal arabic with high dialectal content. In *Proceedings of the 49th Annual Meeting of the Association for Computational Linguistics: Human Language Technologies: short papers-Volume 2*, pages 37–41. Association for Computational Linguistics.

Omar F Zaidan and Chris Callison-Burch. 2014. Arabic dialect identification. *Computational Linguistics*, 40(1):171–202.

Marcos Zampieri, Shervin Malmasi, Preslav Nakov, Ahmed Ali, Suwon Shon, James Glass, Yves Scherrer, Tanja Samardžić, Nikola Ljubešić, Jörg Tiedemann, et al. 2018. Language identification and morphosyntactic tagging: The second vardial evaluation campaign. In *Proceedings of the Fifth Workshop on NLP for Similar Languages, Varieties and Dialects*. Association for Computational Linguistics.

Team JUST at the MADAR Shared Task
on Arabic Fine-Grained Dialect Identification

Bashar Talafha
Jordan University of Science
and Technology, Jordan
`talafha@live.com`

Ali Fadel
Jordan University of Science
and Technology, Jordan
`aliosm1997@gmail.com`

Mahmoud Al-Ayyoub
Jordan University of Science
and Technology, Jordan
`malayyoub@gmail.com`

Yaser Jararweh
Duquesne University, USA
`jararwehy@duq.edu`

Mohammad AL-Smadi
Jordan University of Science
and Technology, Jordan
`maalsmadi9@just.edu.jo`

Patrick Juola
Duquesne University, USA
`juola@mathcs.duq.edu`

Abstract

In this paper, we describe our team's effort on the MADAR Shared Task on Arabic Fine-Grained Dialect Identification. The task requires building a system capable of differentiating between 25 different Arabic dialects in addition to MSA. Our approach is simple. After preprocessing the data, we use Data Augmentation (DA) to enlarge the training data six times. We then build a language model and extract n-gram word-level and character-level TF-IDF features and feed them into an MNB classifier. Despite its simplicity, the resulting model performs really well producing the 4th highest F-measure and region-level accuracy and the 5th highest precision, recall, city-level accuracy and country-level accuracy among the participating teams.

1 Introduction

Give a piece of text, the Dialect Identification (DI) is concerned with automatically determining the dialect in which it is written. This is a very important problem in many languages including Arabic. Unlike previous works on Arabic DI (ADI), which take a coarse-grained approach by considering regional-level (Zaidan and Callison-Burch, 2014; Elfardy and Diab, 2013; Zampieri et al., 2018) or country-level (Sadat et al., 2014) dialects, a new task has been proposed for the fine-grained ADI focusing on a large number of city-/country-level dialects (Bouamor et al., 2019).

This task is quite challenging as it covers 25 different dialects in addition to Modern Standard Arabic (MSA). Some of these dialects are very close to each other as we observe in our analysis of the training data (see Section 2). Also, due to the relatively small size of the dataset, cutting-edge techniques for document/sentence classification, which are based on word embeddings and deep learning models, perform poorly on it. In fact, according to (Bouamor et al., 2019), the top performing systems for this task as well as the previously published baseline (Salameh et al., 2018) all use traditional (non-neural) machine learning approaches. This is very surprising if one takes into account that the use of Deep Learning in Arabic NLP is still at its early stages (Al-Ayyoub et al., 2018).

In this paper, we describe our team's effort to tackle this task. After preprocessing the data, we use Data Augmentation (DA) to enlarge the training data six times. We then build a language model and extract n-gram word-level and character-level TF-IDF features and feed them into a Multinomial Naive Bayes (MNB) classifier. Despite its simplicity, the resulting model performs really well producing the 4th highest Macro-F1 measure (66.33%) and Region-level Accuracy (84.54%) and the 5th highest Macro-Precision (66.56%), Macro-Recall (66.42%), City-level Accuracy (66.42%) and Country-level Accuracy (74.71%) among the participating teams. Unfortunately, due to a problem with our submission file, the official results for our system were extremely poor, which placed our team at the bottom of the official ranking.

The rest of this paper is organized as follows. In Section 2, we discuss the task at hand while analyzing the provided data. In Section 3, we describe our system and its details while, in Section 4, we present and analyze its results and performance. Finally, the paper is concluded in Section 5.

Proceedings of the Fourth Arabic Natural Language Processing Workshop, pages 285–289
Florence, Italy, August 1, 2019. ©2019 Association for Computational Linguistics

2 MADAR Task, Dataset and Metrics

The shared task at hand comprises of two subtasks. The first one is the Travel Domain ADI, whose data are taken from Multi-Arabic Dialect Applications and Resources (MADAR) project (Bouamor et al., 2018). Our team only focused on this subtask. The second subtask is the Twitter User ADI and it is outside the scope of this work.

For the subtask at hand, the organizers provide three sets: train (stored in a file called `MADAR-Corpus-26-train` and we refer to it as Corpus-26), development (dev) and test. The train, dev and test sets consist of 41,600, 5,200 and 5,200 parallel sentences, respectively, written in MSA as well as the local dialect of 25 cities: Rabat (RAB), Fes (FES), Algiers (ALG), Tunis (TUN), Sfax (SFX), Tripoli (TRI), Benghazi (BEN), Cairo (CAI), Alexandria (ALX), Aswan (ASW), Khartoum (KHA), Jerusalem (JER), Amman (AMM), Salt (SAL), Beirut (BEI), Damascus (DAM), Aleppo (ALE), Mosul (MOS), Baghdad (BAG), Basra (BAS), Doha (DOH), Muscat (MUS), Riyadh (RIY), Jeddah (JED) and Sana'a (SAN).

To aid in the training and model building processes, the organizers also provide additional train & dev data sets consisting of 54,000 and 6,000 parallel sentences covering only six dialects: BEI, CAI, DOH, MSA, RAB and TUN. The additional train set is stored in a file called `MADAR-Corpus-6-train` and we refer to it as Corpus-6.

Before we go into the details of our system, we present a simple analysis of the provided data. Figure 1 shows that the sentences of the dialects do not differ much in terms of average word/sentence lengths per dialect (Figures 1(a) and 1(b)) or the number of unique words per dialect (Figures 1(c)). Our analysis shows that while there are 27,501 unique words in all dialects, there is a small number of words (specifically, 84 words) common in all dialects. Examples of such words include: ‏اليابانية، الشارع، المجرم، جوليا، فرانسيسكو،‏
‏شهر، جولة، البريد، مفتاح، بعيد.‏

Now, the most interesting part in our analysis is the varying similarity between the different dialects pairs under consideration. Overall, there are 7,280 common sentences between dialects pairs and the average number of common sentences between dialects pairs, on average the-

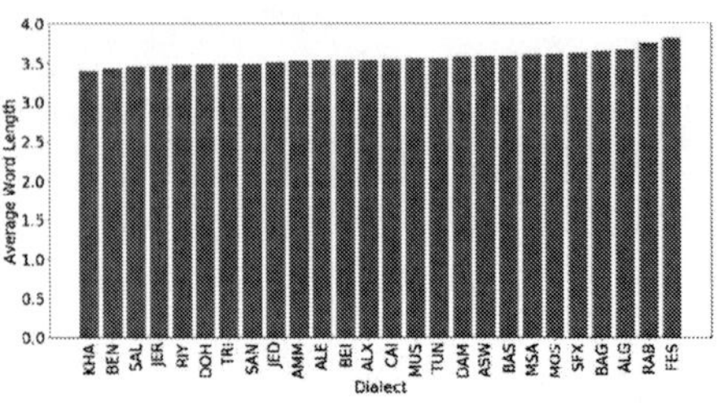

(a) Average word length per dialect

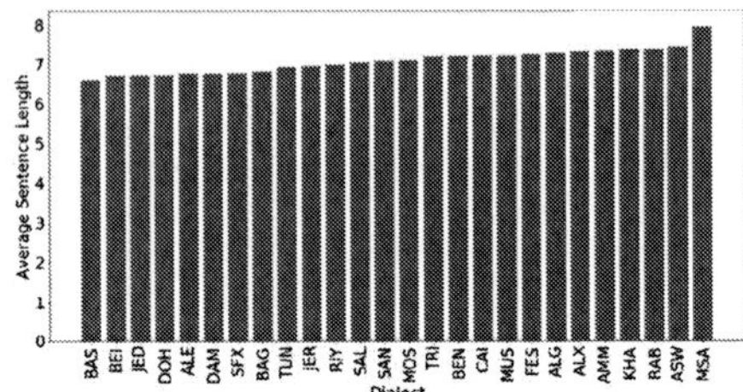

(b) Average sentence length per dialect

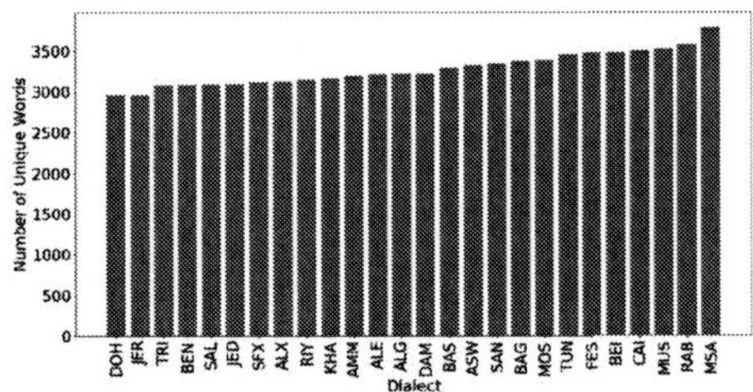

(c) Number of unique words per dialect

Figure 1: Corpus-26 statistics.

re is 22.4 common sentences between any dialects pairs. Another relevant observation is the repetition of sentences across different dialects pairs, which is not limited to the dialects from the same country or region. For example, the dialect pairs with 100 or more common sentences are: AMM-JER, DAM-ALE, JER-SAL, AMM-SAL, DAM-JER & AMM-DAM, whereas, the pairs with less than 5 common sentences are: BEI-FES, MSA-BEI, MSA-MOS, MSA-SFX, MSA-TRI, MSA-TUN, RAB-ASW, RAB-KHA, RAB-RIY, RAB-SAN, RAB-BAS & RAB-MOS. Below, we list all dialects under consideration grouped per country and per region. We also list in the parentheses the average number of common sentences within each country (with more than one dialect) and each region.

1. Maghreb (18.29): Morroco: RAB & FES (50); Algeria: ALG; Tunisia: TUN & SFX (52); Libya: TRI & BEN (66).

2. Nile Basin (42.67): Egypt: CAI, ALX & ASW (67); Sudan: KHA.

3. Levant (88.4): Palestine: JER; Jordan: AMM & SAL (101); Lebanon: BEI; Syria: DAM & ALE (129).

4. Gulf (42.52): Iraq: MOS, BAG & BAS (54.33); Qatar: DOH; Oman: MUS; Saudi: RIY & JED (72.0);

5. Gulf of Aden: Yemen: SAN.

6. MSA.

This list shows that Levant dialects are the most similar while the Maghrib ones are the least similar.

Finally, to evaluate the participating systems, the subtask organizers use Accuracy (on the city, country and region levels denoted here by Acc_{cty}, Acc_{cntr} and Acc_{rgn}, respectively) in addition to Macro-averaged Precision, Recall and F1 measure (denoted here by Pre, Rec and F1, respectively).

3 System

In this section. we describe the system that produces the highest accuracy on the dev set starting from the preprocessing stage all the way up to the final classification stage.

Preprocessing and Data Augmentation (DA). Our system starts with a couple of preprocessing steps. The first one is a very simple one in which quotation marks, Arabic quotation marks, commas, Arabic commas, question marks, Arabic question marks and emoticons are replaced with spaces.

Another preprocessing step the system performs is DA. While DA has been shown to be very effective for image processing tasks (Chatfield et al., 2014; He et al., 2016; Chollet, 2016; Ebrahim et al., 2018), it use in text processing tasks is still limited (Fadaee et al., 2017; Kafle et al., 2017). Since the training data is small, a data augmentation step is performed on Corpus-26 by applying random shuffling on Corpus. In Corpus-26, there are 1,600 sentences for each dialect, while, in Corpus-6, there are 9,000 sentences for each of the six dialects in this corpus: BEI, CAI, DOH, MSA, RAB and TUN. The system takes 8,000 sentences

(instead of 9,000) for each dialects in order to balance them with the other dialects (shuffled). Therefore, overall, we have 8,000 sentences (from Corpus-6) + 1,600 sentences (from Corpus-26) = 9,600 sentences for each of these six dialects. For the remaining dialects, and since the order of words is not necessary to identify the dialect, we apply a random shuffling to generate five new sentences from each sentence by using different random seed for each generated sentence. So, for each of these 20 dialects, we have $1,600 \times 6 = 9,600$ sentences. To sum up, the training data has a total of 249,600 sentences; 9,600 sentences for each of the 26 dialects under consideration.

Features Extraction. For each dialect, a language model is extracted using Kenlm[1] with its default parameters using the training data (Corpus-26). For each sentence, we extract a vector of size 26 that represents a language model probability for each dialect. We also extract a word-level Term Frequency-Inverse Document Frequency (TF-IDF) features ranging from unigram to 6-gram in addition to character-level n-grams TF-IDF features where n ranges from 1-gram to 5-grams.

Classifier. An MNB classifier with $\alpha = 0.5$ is applied using the One-vs-the-rest strategy. It is worth mentioning that we experiment with several deep learning-based classifiers such as Convolutional Neural Networks (CNN) (Kim, 2014), Recurrent Neural Networks (RNN) with Long Short-Term Memory (LSTM) cells,[2] Separable Convolutional Network (sepCNN) (Chollet, 2017), Doc2Vec-FFNN,[3] Transformer (Vaswani et al., 2017) and Bidirectional Encoder Representations from Transformers (BERT) (Devlin et al., 2018). However, none of them performed well on the validation set. So, we did not submit their results.

4 Results and Discussion

In this section, we present and analyze the results and performance of our best model. Nothing is mentioned about the other models with which we experimented. The results of the model on the test set are presented in Table 1. The table shows that,

---

[1] https://github.com/kpu/kenlm

[2] https://bit.ly/2K3lNFM

[3] We train a Doc2Vec model (Le and Mikolov, 2014) and extract the feature vectors from it for each sentence. We then feed these vectors into a feed-forward neural network (FF-NN) to classify the sentence as one of 26 classes.

	Ours	Top System	Base-line	Overall Comparison
F1	66.33	67.32	67.89	4th highest
Pre	66.56	67.73	68.41	5th highest (tied)
Rec	66.42	67.33	67.75	5th highest
Acc_{cty}	66.42	67.33	67.75	5th highest
Acc_{cntr}	74.71	75.69	76.44	5th highest
Acc_{rgn}	84.54	85.13	85.96	4th highest

Table 1: The results of our model on the test set compared with the other models.

	F1	Pre	Rec	Acc_{cty}
w/ DA	67.51	69.28	67.29	67.29
w/o DA	66.83	68.69	66.6	66.6

Table 2: Effect of DA

In order to show the effect of DA, we perform an ablation study using the dev set. Table 2 shows the results of this experiment. The results show that DA had a slight effect on improving the performance of the proposed model. Perhaps, this is due to the generative nature of the MNB classifier and its assumption of independence between the features. In the future, we plan on focusing more on DA techniques and their application with neural models, where the intuition is that such models make better use of any additional data in order to learn new things.

5 Conclusion

In this paper, we presented a simple model for the fine-grained ADI subtask. The model's performance was good producing results competitive with the top system for the task. In the future, we plan on exploring approaches based on better DA techniques in addition to the concepts of transfer learning and semi-supervised learning (Talafha and Al-Ayyoub, 2019) in order to obtained better results.

Acknowledgment

We gratefully acknowledge the support of NVIDIA Corporation with the donation of the Titan Xp GPU used for this research.

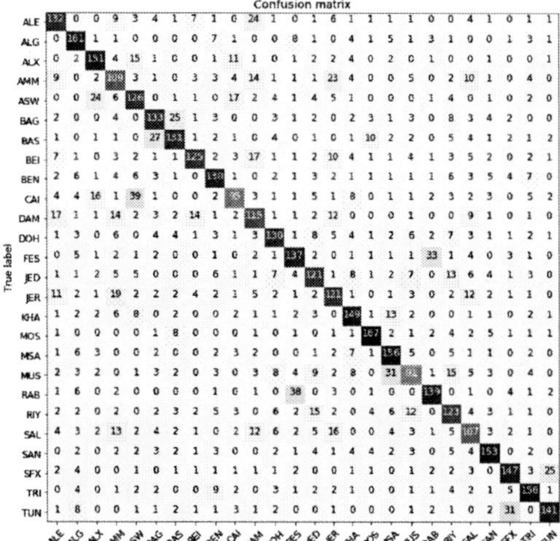

Figure 2: Our model's confusion matrix for the test set.

despite our models' simplicity, its results (which range between 4th highest and 5th highest numbers) are surprisingly good. It differs only by a small number from the top system.

To understand the strengths and weaknesses of our model, we analyze the confusion matrix for the test set (shown in Figure 2). The figure shows that the model suffers while trying to differentiate between similar dialects. For example, 39 test samples from CAI are labeled as ASW and 38 from RAB are labeled as FES. Moreover, among the hardest to classify is CAI, perhaps, due to its high similarity with many dialects. After all, CAI is among the most well-known Arabic and Egyptian dialects due to the cultural influence of Cairo and Egypt on the Arab world, which means that other dialects (especially Egyptian ones) might have been influenced by it. On the other hand, ALG and MOS are among the easiest to classify due to their low similarity with the dialects under consideration.

References

Mahmoud Al-Ayyoub, Aya Nuseir, Kholoud Alsmearat, Yaser Jararweh, and Brij Gupta. 2018. Deep learning for arabic nlp: A survey. *Journal of computational science*, 26:522–531.

Houda Bouamor, Nizar Habash, Mohammad Salameh, Wajdi Zaghouani, Owen Rambow, Dana Abdulrahim, Ossama Obeid, Salam Khalifa, Fadhl Eryani, Alexander Erdmann, et al. 2018. The madar arabic dialect corpus and lexicon. In *Proceedings of the Eleventh International Conference on Language Resources and Evaluation (LREC-2018)*.

Houda Bouamor, Sabit Hassan, and Nizar Habash. 2019. The MADAR Shared Task on Arabic Fine-Grained Dialect Identification. In *Proceedings of the Fourth Arabic Natural Language Processing Workshop (WANLP19)*, Florence, Italy.

Ken Chatfield, Karen Simonyan, Andrea Vedaldi, and Andrew Zisserman. 2014. Return of the devil in the details: Delving deep into convolutional nets. *arXiv preprint arXiv:1405.3531*.

Francois Chollet. 2016. Building powerful image classification models using very little data. The Keras Blog. Https://blog.keras.io/building-powerful-image-classification-models-using-very-little-data.html.

François Chollet. 2017. Xception: Deep learning with depthwise separable convolutions. In *Proceedings of the IEEE conference on computer vision and pattern recognition*, pages 1251–1258.

Jacob Devlin, Ming-Wei Chang, Kenton Lee, and Kristina Toutanova. 2018. Bert: Pre-training of deep bidirectional transformers for language understanding. *arXiv preprint arXiv:1810.04805*.

Maad Ebrahim, Mohammad Alsmirat, and Mahmoud Al-Ayyoub. 2018. Performance study of augmentation techniques for hep2 cnn classification. In *2018 9th International Conference on Information and Communication Systems (ICICS)*, pages 163–168. IEEE.

Heba Elfardy and Mona Diab. 2013. Sentence level dialect identification in arabic. In *Proceedings of the 51st Annual Meeting of the Association for Computational Linguistics (Volume 2: Short Papers)*, volume 2, pages 456–461.

Marzieh Fadaee, Arianna Bisazza, and Christof Monz. 2017. Data augmentation for low-resource neural machine translation. *arXiv preprint arXiv:1705.00440*.

Kaiming He, Xiangyu Zhang, Shaoqing Ren, and Jian Sun. 2016. Deep residual learning for image recognition. In *Proceedings of the IEEE conference on computer vision and pattern recognition*, pages 770–778.

Kushal Kafle, Mohammed Yousefhussien, and Christopher Kanan. 2017. Data augmentation for visual question answering. In *Proceedings of the 10th International Conference on Natural Language Generation*, pages 198–202.

Yoon Kim. 2014. Convolutional neural networks for sentence classification. *arXiv preprint arXiv:1408.5882*.

Quoc Le and Tomas Mikolov. 2014. Distributed representations of sentences and documents. In *International conference on machine learning*, pages 1188–1196.

Fatiha Sadat, Farnazeh Kazemi, and Atefeh Farzindar. 2014. Automatic identification of arabic dialects in social media. In *Proceedings of the first international workshop on Social media retrieval and analysis*, pages 35–40. ACM.

Mohammad Salameh, Houda Bouamor, and Nizar Habash. 2018. Fine-grained Arabic dialect identification. In *Proceedings of the International Conference on Computational Linguistics (COLING)*, pages 1332–1344, Santa Fe, New Mexico, USA.

Bashar Talafha and Mahmoud Al-Ayyoub. 2019. Iohrcnn: Pursue the ingredients of happiness using recurrent convolutional neural networks. In *Proceedings of the 2nd Workshop on Affective Content Analysis (AffCon 2019) co-located with Thirty-Third AAAI Conference on Artificial Intelligence (AAAI 2019), Honolulu, USA, January 27, 2019.*, pages 191–197.

Ashish Vaswani, Noam Shazeer, Niki Parmar, Jakob Uszkoreit, Llion Jones, Aidan N Gomez, Łukasz Kaiser, and Illia Polosukhin. 2017. Attention is all you need. In *Advances in neural information processing systems*, pages 5998–6008.

Omar F. Zaidan and Chris Callison-Burch. 2014. Arabic dialect identification. *Computational Linguistics*, 40(1):171–202.

Marcos Zampieri, Shervin Malmasi, Preslav Nakov, Ahmed Ali, Suwon Shon, James Glass, Yves Scherrer, Tanja Samardžić, Nikola Ljubešić, Jörg Tiedemann, et al. 2018. Language identification and morphosyntactic tagging: The second vardial evaluation campaign. In *Proceedings of the Fifth Workshop on NLP for Similar Languages, Varieties and Dialects*. Association for Computational Linguistics.

QC-GO Submission for MADAR Shared Task:
Arabic Fine-Grained Dialect Identification

Younes Samih[1]   **Hamdy Mubarak**[1]   **Ahmed Abdelali**[1]   **Mohammed Attia**[2]

Mohamed Eldesouki[1]   **Kareem Darwish**[1]

[1]{ysamih,hmubarak,aabdelali,mohamohamed,kdarwish}@hbku.edu.qa

[2]{attia}@google.com

[1]Qatar Computing Research Institute, HBKU Research Complex, Doha, Qatar

[2]Google LLC, New York City, USA

Abstract

This paper describes the QC-GO team submission to the MADAR Shared Task Subtask 1 (travel domain dialect identification) and Subtask 2 (Twitter user location identification). In our participation in both subtasks, we explored a number of approaches and system combinations to obtain the best performance for both tasks. These include deep neural nets and heuristics. Since individual approaches suffer from various shortcomings, the combination of different approaches was able to fill some of these gaps. Our system achieves F1-Scores of 66.1% and 67.0% on the development sets for Subtasks 1 and 2 respectively.

1 Introduction

Arabic, similar to other languages have a number of dialectal varieties. With the emergence of social media, many of these varieties of Arabic started having wide representation in the written form. Twitter, Facebook, and YouTube are among the leading sources of such data (Zaidan and Callison-Burch, 2011; Mubarak and Darwish, 2014; Samih et al., 2017; Samih and Maier, 2016). The wide spread of dialectal use has increased the richness and diversity of the language, requiring greater complexity in dealing with it. Non-standard orthography, increased borrowing and coinage of new terms, and code switching are just a few among a long list of new challenges researchers have to deal with.

Studying language varieties in particular is associated with important applications such as Dialect Identification (DID), Machine Translation (MT), and other text mining tasks. Performing DID can be achieved using a variety of features, such as character n-grams (Darwish, 2014; Zaidan and Callison-Burch, 2014; Malmasi et al., 2015), and a myriad of techniques, such as

string kernels (Ionescu and Popescu, 2016) and DNN (Elaraby and Abdul-Mageed, 2018).

In this paper, two resources created under the Multi-Arabic Dialect Applications and Resources (MADAR) project were used as the main resources for the task of Fine-Grained Dialect Identification (Salameh et al., 2018; Bouamor et al., 2018). The MADAR Shared Task (Bouamor et al., 2019) aims to identify dialects at the city/country level for two datasets . Subtask 1 uses a travel domain collection of 110k sentences that contain both Modern Standard Arabic (MSA) sentences and their translations into 25 dialects representing major cities in the Arab world. Subtask 2 aims to classify tweeps (Twitter users) per their location using 100 of their tweets or less. In this paper, we describe the approaches that we utilized for dialect identification, which include the use of deep neural networks and heuristics.

2 System descriptions

For both SubTask 1 and SubTask 2, we employed a hybrid system that incorporates different classifiers and components such DNNs and heuristics to perform sentence level dialectal Arabic identification. The classification strategy is built as a cascaded voting system that tags each sequence based on the decisions from two other underlying classifiers.

DNNs: This model uses both Bidirectional Long Short Term Memory (Bi-LSTM) and Convolutional Neural Network (CNN) architectures to jointly learn both word-level and character-level representations, and project them to a softmax output layer for dialectal Arabic identification. At the word level, we use pre-trained word embeddings for Dialectal Arabic to initialize our look-up table. Words with no pre-trained embeddings are randomly initialized with uniformly sampled em-

Proceedings of the Fourth Arabic Natural Language Processing Workshop, pages 290–294

Florence, Italy, August 1, 2019. ©2019 Association for Computational Linguistics

beddings. To use these embeddings in our model, we simply replace one hot encoding word representations with corresponding 300-dimensional vectors. Note that in this settings, we trained our embeddings on the provided training set. We used two approaches for preparing the embeddings, namely gensim word2vec (Řehůřek and Sojka, 2010) and fastText (Joulin et al., 2016), which will be referred later as DNN-wv and DNN-ft respectively.

At the character level, to capture word morphology and reduce out-of-vocabulary, we used convolutions to learn local n-gram features. This approach has also been especially useful for handling languages with rich morphology and large character sets (Kim et al., 2016). The first layer projects each character into its corresponding character embeddings, as with a look-up table, and stacks them to form a matrix C^k. Convolution operations with the same padding are applied between C^k and multiple filter matrices. A max-over-time pooling operation is then executed to infer a fixed-dimensional representation of the words. This representation is then concatenated with word embeddings and fed to a highway network (Srivastava et al., 2015). The highway network's output is applied to a multi-layer Bi-LSTM. At the output layer, a softmax is applied over the hidden representation of the two LSTMs to obtain the probability distribution over all labels. Training is performed using stochastic gradient descent with momentum, optimizing the cross-entropy objective function.

FastText: FastText is a deep learning based library for efficient learning of word representations and text classification. It represents words as the sum of their character n-grams vectors. It has been shown to be effective for text classification for different tasks (Joulin et al., 2017).

Arabic is a rich Semitic language with complex morphology where a large number of prefixes and suffixes can be attached to words. Additionally, in Arabic dialects, words can be written in many different ways, because there is no conventional orthography. The aforementioned reasons suggest that using words alone as features for classification is less optimal. We opted to compliment that with variable length character n-grams to capture sub-word information and local contextual information. For Subtask 1 and Subtask 2, we tuned different settings on the development set, and the

System	Dev. F-1 Score	Test F-1 Score
DNN-ft	59.78%	57.25%
DNN-wv	58.11%	58.72%
FastText	63.09%	60.42%
QC-GO1	64.53%	58.72%
QC-GO2	63.49%	58.45%
QC-GO3	63.29%	57.26%

Table 1: SubTask 1 Results for the submissions for Development and Test sets.

best results were obtained when using character n-grams varying from 3 to 6 characters, dimensions of vectors of 100, a learning rate of 0.1, and 50 training epochs.

Heuristics: For sub-task 2, we constructed a list of all Arabic speaking countries (e.g. مصر (Egypt)) along with major cities in these countries (e.g. القاهرة (Cairo)). Given our list, we counted the number of times a tweep mentions the names of countries or any of the cities therein in his/her tweets. Then, we labeled a tweep with the county that is mentioned most in the tweets.

Ensemble model: For both sub-tasks, our final system combines the output from the different systems using a simple majority vote to perform dialectal Arabic predictions. The ensemble model can either assign varying weights to different systems depending on their overall performance on the dev set or it takes the average by setting equal weights for all systems.

3 Results

In this section we present the results of our system output for Subtask 1 and Subtask 2 on both the validation and the test sets.

3.1 SubTask 1

The results, shown in Table 1, contain a combination of the systems described above with variable weighting. Since the results of individual systems varied greatly, their combination proved to be more effective. Combining DNN-ft with DNN-wv with a weight of 0.66, 0.33 respectively improved the predictions from 57.25% to 58.45%. Adding fastText to the mix achieved 60.85%: a boost of more than 6.2%.

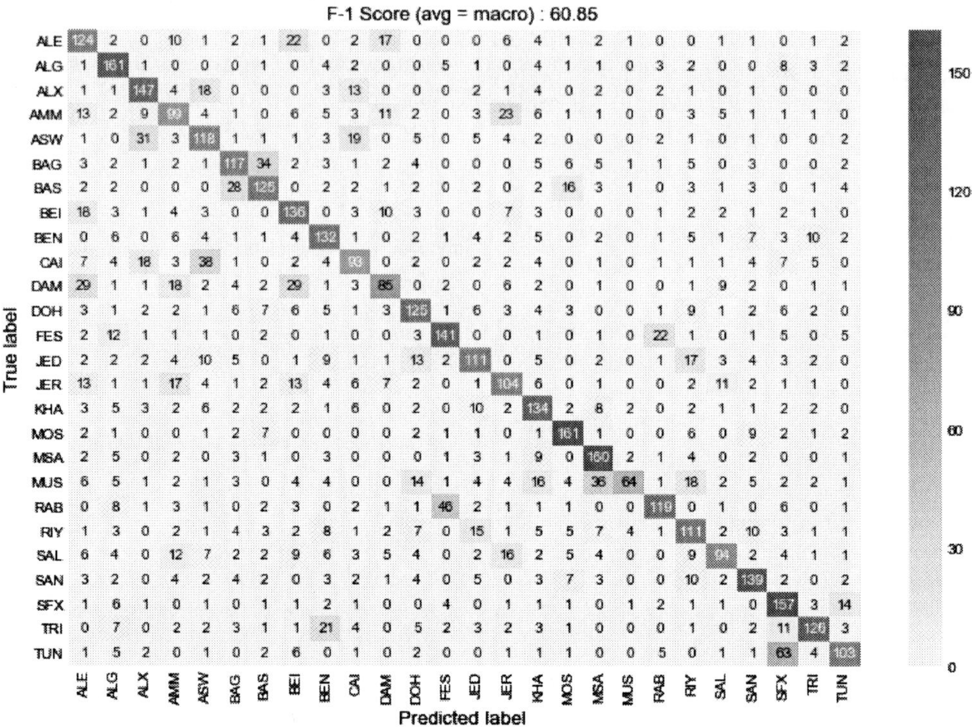

Figure 1: Confusion matrix for results of SubTask 1 system combination

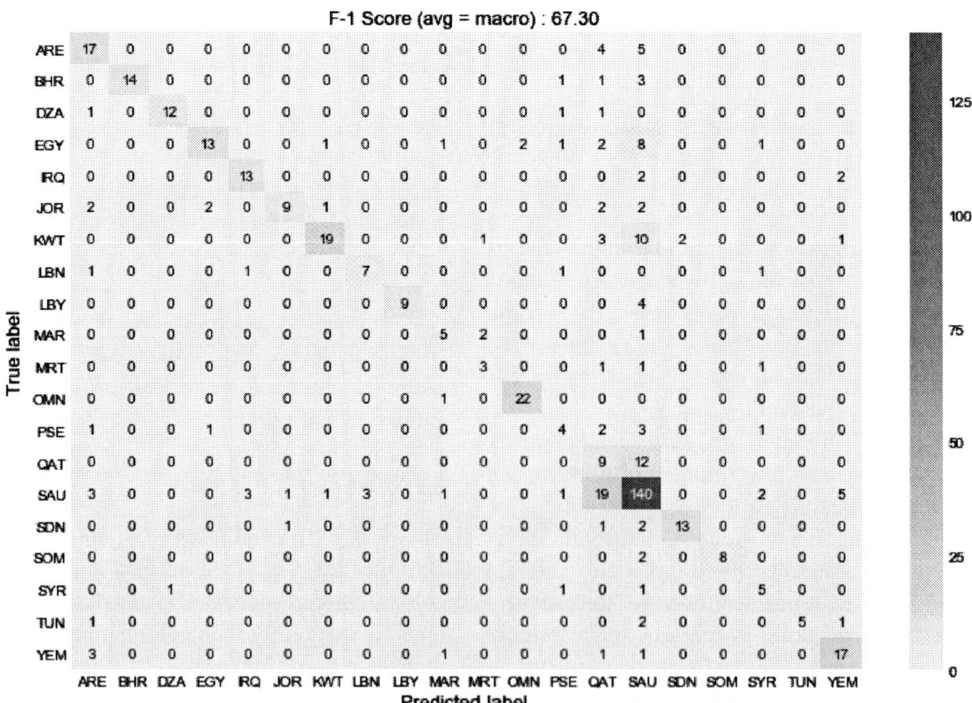

Figure 2: Confusion matrix for results of SubTask 2 FastText

Submission	Dev. F-1 Score	Test F-1 Score
DNN-ft	44.54%	54.50%
DNN-wv	47.04%	43.23%
FastText	57.41%	57.23%
Hueristics	65.22%	67.30%
QC-GO1	63.77%	66.68%
QC-GO3	63.77%	66.34%
QC-GO2	66.60%	63.92%

Table 2: SubTask 2 results for the submissions for Development and Test sets.

3.2 SubTask 2

As for SubTask 2, the combination of DNN-ft with DNN-wv was not as effective as either alone. A decrease of 1.2% was observed. On the other hand using fastText by itself achieved an F-1 score of 57.23%, which is higher than both DNN-ft and DNN-wv. Using the heuristics approach yielded the best performance with 64.09%. Adding a back-off to use a majority vote per user, when a tweep did not mention any country or any city therein, to get the most frequent predicted country improved result to 67.30%. This system ranked third among all submitted systems for SubTask 2.

4 Discussion and conclusions

Our analysis of the system output on the validation set for Subtask 1 shows that the highest accuracy obtained at the dialect level was for MSA, SFX, ALX, and MOS, (Figure 1) while the lowest accuracy was for MUS, DAM, and AMM. Local dialects within the same country caused the vast majority of confusion. For example, the most confusion for SFX came from TUN, for BAS came from BAG, and for JED came from RIY. We also observed a heightened confusion between cities from neighboring countries, such as ALG and FES, BEI and ALE, and JER and AMM. This observation emphasizes the perception that there is a level of homogeneity between dialects with physical proximity whether at the national and regional levels. As for the Subtask 2, the challenging ambiguity between gulf dialects is still a major issue that caused the accuracy drop; See (Figure 2). Expanding the data for these subdialects would enhance their respective accuracy.

References

Houda Bouamor, Nizar Habash, Mohammad Salameh, Wajdi Zaghouani, Owen Rambow, Dana Abdulrahim, Ossama Obeid, Salam Khalifa, Fadhl Eryani, Alexander Erdmann, and Kemal Oflazer. 2018. The MADAR Arabic Dialect Corpus and Lexicon. In *Proceedings of the Language Resources and Evaluation Conference (LREC)*, Miyazaki, Japan.

Houda Bouamor, Sabit Hassan, and Nizar Habash. 2019. The MADAR Shared Task on Arabic Fine-Grained Dialect Identification. In *Proceedings of the Fourth Arabic Natural Language Processing Workshop (WANLP19)*, Florence, Italy.

Kareem Darwish. 2014. Arabizi detection and conversion to arabic. *Proceedings of the EMNLP 2014 Workshop on Arabic Natural Language Processing (ANLP)*, pages 217–224.

Mohamed Elaraby and Muhammad Abdul-Mageed. 2018. Deep models for Arabic dialect identification on benchmarked data. In *Proceedings of the Fifth Workshop on NLP for Similar Languages, Varieties and Dialects (VarDial 2018)*.

Radu Tudor Ionescu and Marius Popescu. 2016. Unibuckernel: An approach for arabic dialect identification based on multiple string kernels. In *Proceedings of the Third Workshop on NLP for Similar Languages, Varieties and Dialects (VarDial3)*, pages 135–144.

Armand Joulin, Edouard Grave, Piotr Bojanowski, Matthijs Douze, Hérve Jégou, and Tomas Mikolov. 2016. Fasttext.zip: Compressing text classification models. *arXiv preprint arXiv:1612.03651*.

Armand Joulin, Edouard Grave, Piotr Bojanowski, and Tomas Mikolov. 2017. Bag of tricks for efficient text classification. In *Proceedings of the 15th Conference of the European Chapter of the Association for Computational Linguistics: Volume 2, Short Papers*, pages 427–431. Association for Computational Linguistics.

Yoon Kim, Yacine Jernite, David Sontag, and Alexander M Rush. 2016. Character-aware neural language models. In *Thirtieth AAAI Conference on Artificial Intelligence*.

Shervin Malmasi, Eshrag Refaee, and Mark Dras. 2015. Arabic dialect identification using a parallel multidialectal corpus. In *Conference of the Pacific Association for Computational Linguistics*, pages 35–53. Springer.

Hamdy Mubarak and Kareem Darwish. 2014. Using twitter to collect a multi-dialectal corpus of arabic. In *Proceedings of the EMNLP 2014 Workshop on Arabic Natural Language Processing (ANLP)*, pages 1–7.

Radim Řehůřek and Petr Sojka. 2010. Software Framework for Topic Modelling with Large Corpora. In

Proceedings of the LREC 2010 Workshop on New Challenges for NLP Frameworks, pages 45–50, Valletta, Malta. ELRA.

Mohammad Salameh, Houda Bouamor, and Nizar Habash. 2018. Fine-grained Arabic dialect identification. In *Proceedings of the International Conference on Computational Linguistics (COLING)*, pages 1332–1344, Santa Fe, New Mexico, USA.

Younes Samih, Mohamed Eldesouki, Mohammed Attia, Kareem Darwish, Ahmed Abdelali, Hamdy Mubarak, and Laura Kallmeyer. 2017. Learning from relatives: Unified dialectal Arabic segmentation. In *(CoNLL 2017)*, pages 432–441, Vancouver, Canada. Association for Computational Linguistics.

Younes Samih and Wolfgang Maier. 2016. An Arabic-Moroccan Darija code-switched corpus. In *Proceedings of the Tenth International Conference on Language Resources and Evaluation (LREC 2016)*, pages 4170–4175, Portorož, Slovenia. European Language Resources Association (ELRA).

Rupesh K. Srivastava, Klaus Greff, and Jürgen Schmidhuber. 2015. Training very deep networks. In *Advances in neural information processing systems*, pages 2377–2385.

Omar F. Zaidan and Chris Callison-Burch. 2011. The arabic online commentary dataset: an annotated dataset of informal arabic with high dialectal content. In *Proceedings of the 49th Annual Meeting of the ACL-HLT: short papers-Volume 2*, pages 37–41.

Omar F. Zaidan and Chris Callison-Burch. 2014. Arabic dialect identification. *Computational Linguistics*, 40(1):171–202.

Author Index

Association for Computational Linguistics
209 N. Eighth Street
Stroudsburg, Pennsylvania 18360

ISBN 978-1-5108-9112-8